JUDICIAL REVIEW IN THE COMMONWEALTH CARIBBEAN

The establishment of the Caribbean Court of Justice sees the countries of the Commonwealth Caribbean at an important and exciting judicial crossroads. Debate, often acrimonious, continues over the abolishment of ties to the Judicial Committee of the Privy Council and increasingly those influencing the debate are a more educated and articulate Caribbean people, insisting on proper governance of the area's public bodies. This new book analyses judicial review, a mechanism for achieving public justice, through emerging case law in the hope that it will cast light on the jurisprudential evolution of Caribbean society in the twenty-first century.

Bringing together cases and materials on judicial review in the Caribbean for the first time, the book examines what judicial review is before going on to discuss the grounds, obstacles and conduct within the judicial review process. It concludes by examining the future of judicial review and justice more generally in the Caribbean.

Legal professionals in the Caribbean will find *Judicial Review in the Commonwealth Caribbean* a useful and comprehensive reference tool.

Rajendra Ramlogan obtained his BA in English Literature from the University of the West Indies, Trinidad. He graduated with an LLB from the University of the West Indies, Barbados, and an LLM (International Legal Studies) from New York University School of Law. Dr Ramlogan received his PhD in International Environmental Law from the University of Cambridge and is currently a Law Lecturer in the Department of Management Studies at the University of the West Indies, Trinidad.

Commonwealth Caribbean Law Series

The Commonwealth Caribbean Law Series is the only series of law books that covers the jurisdiction of the English speaking Caribbean nations. The titles in the series were first published in 1995 to acclaim from academics, practitioners and the judiciary in the region. Several editions followed, and they have now become essential reading for those learning and practising Caribbean law.

This must-have series is required holdings for any law library specializing in Caribbean legal information.

Titles in this series include:

Commonwealth Caribbean Public Law 2/e, Albert Fiadjoe
Commonwealth Caribbean Law of Trusts 2/e, Gilbert Kodilinye
Commonwealth Caribbean Tort Law, Gilbert Kodilinye
Commonwealth Caribbean Business Law, Rajendra Ramlogan and Natalie Persadie
Commonwealth Caribbean Civil Procedure 2/e,
Gilbert Kodilinye and Vanessa Kodilinye
Commonwealth Caribbean Property Law 2/e, Gilbert Kodilinye
Commonwealth Caribbean Law and Legal Systems, Rose-Marie Belle Antoine
Commonwealth Caribbean Criminal Practice and Procedure 2/e, Dana S. Seetahal

Forthcoming:

Commonwealth Caribbean Land Law, Sampson Owusu
Commonwealth Caribbean Public Law 3/e, Albert Fiadjoe
Commonwealth Caribbean Law and Legal Systems 2/e, Rose-Marie Belle Antoine

JUDICIAL REVIEW IN THE COMMONWEALTH CARIBBEAN

Rajendra Ramlogan

Routledge
Taylor & Francis Group
LONDON AND NEW YORK

First published 2007 by Routledge-Cavendish

This edition published 2013 by Routledge
2 Park Square, Milton Park, Abingdon, Oxfordshire OX14 4RN
Simultaneously published in the USA and Canada by Routledge
711 Third Avenue, New York, NY 10017

First issued in hardback 2016

Routledge is an imprint of the Taylor & Francis Group, an informa business

Typeset in Palatino by
RefineCatch Limited, Bungay, Suffolk

British Library Cataloguing in Publication Data
A catalogue record for this book is available from the British Library

Library of Congress Cataloging in Publication Data
A catalog record for this book has been requested

ISBN 13: 978-1-138-14164-3 (hbk)
ISBN 13: 978-1-84568-042-8 (pbk)

To

My Village that sustained me, Mr Ralph Cape, Ms Annie Cape, Pa Roy Richardson and many others

My Ancestors who made the journey, Kowlessar, Moonia, Goodal, Raimoon and Mahatoo

My Grandparents, Madan, Mamin, Sukeran and Phooljarya

ACKNOWLEDGEMENTS

I wish to acknowledge those who contributed tremendously to the completion of this book. My research assistants, Camille Neil (Jamaica), Dale Kingston (Guyana), Phedessa Wallace (Barbados) and, in particular Dwight Dacres (Jamaica), provided much assistance in locating cases. I wish to thank my typists, Pavitra Moonsammy from the Department of Management Studies and Verneshia Jugmohan. My gratitude goes out to Natalie Persadie who assisted in the text. Finally, I wish to thank my family, Joy, Rhea, Rohan and Rishon who had to share my time during the research phase, even to the extent of having the family holiday scheduled to facilitate my field work in St. Lucia on the cases from the Eastern Caribbean States.

CONTENTS

LIST OF ABBREVIATIONS

Antigua and Barbuda	AG
Bahamas	BS
Barbados	BB
Belize	BZ
Bermuda	BM
British Virgin Islands	BVI
Dominica	DM
Guyana	GY
Jamaica	JM
St. Kitts and Nevis	KN
St. Lucia	LC
St. Vincent & the Grenadines	VC
Trinidad and Tobago	TT
People's National Movement	PNM
United National Congress	UNC
National Alliance for Reconstruction	NAR

TABLE OF CASES

TABLE OF LEGISLATION

1

JUDICIAL REVIEW: AN INTRODUCTION

1.1 WHAT IS JUDICIAL REVIEW?

Commonwealth Caribbean countries are now at an exciting judicial crossroad with the establishment of the Caribbean Court of Justice and the continuing, and sometimes acrimonious, debate on the abolishment of ties to the Judicial Committee of the Privy Council. Influencing this debate is an increasingly educated and articulate Caribbean people more prepared to insist on proper governance by its public bodies. An examination of the development of judicial review, as a mechanism for achieving public justice through emerging case law, can cast light on the jurisprudential evolution of Caribbean society in the twenty-first century.

Judicial review is concerned, not with the decision, but with the decision-making process. According to Lord Brightman, unless that restriction on the power of the court is observed, 'the Court will, in my view, under the guise of preventing the abuse of power, be itself guilty of usurping power . . . Judicial review, as the words imply, is not an appeal from a decision, but a review of the manner in which the decision was made'.[1] The corollary of such a definition is that once a decision is made in accordance with the principles of legality, fairness and rationality, and is therefore legally sound, an application for judicial review cannot be made to the High Court to determine the issue of correctness. As Morris P affirmed 'the function of the High Court on an application for judicial review is limited to determining whether or not the impugned decision was legal, not whether or not it was correct. The freedom to exercise a discretion necessarily entails the freedom to get it wrong; this does not make the decision unlawful'.[2]

In the Application of Dennis Graham – **HCA No S-156 of 2005 (TT)**
Pemberton J

[PP3–4] The Courts in Judicial Review actions seek to pronounce **not on the decision** arrived at by the decision maker **but the process** by which that decision was arrived at. It is immaterial whether a judge may have arrived at another decision but it is material whether the means used to arrive at that decision by the decision maker are beyond question. The purpose of Judicial Review therefore is not to solve relational issues or personality issues unless those are manifested in a decision maker employing a process of decision making that can be characterized as:

- Unreasonable
- Illegal or
- Tainted by *mala fides*.

In the Application of Chandresh Sharma – **HCA No S-109 of 2005 (TT)**
Pemberton J

[P2] Judicial review is not an appellate process, but a review of the manner in which a decision is made by a public officer exercising administrative or other powers conferred by statute. In other words, the Court does not and cannot pronounce on the correctness or veracity of the substance of the decision *per se* but rather puts the decision maker to

1 Per Lord Brightman in *Chief Constable of The North Wales Police v Evans* [1982] 3 All ER 141 at 154.
2 Per Morris P in *Bailey v Flood Tribunal*, High Court, 6 March 2000 (unreported).

the test as to the methodology or process that was employed to arrive at that decision. It seeks to ensure the proper use of the decision making process. The action must be predicated upon facts and circumstances existing and which the decision maker knew or ought to have known at the time that the decision to be impugned was made. Subsequent events cannot be taken into account . . . [PP17–18] 37. . . . I do think that not only is the DPP entitled to take public interest matters into account in exercising any of his functions, prosecutorial or consenting to prosecute but also he would be open to severe criticism if, as the holder of a public office designated by the Constitution, these issues formed no part of his deliberations. It is expected that holders of public office must import into their deliberations matters of public interest. It goes with the territory. 38. Thus, in the absence of any statutory provisions, the DPP is entitled to take into consideration whichever factors he deems appropriate in assisting him in arriving at his decision provided those factors are relevant and reasonable, offend no law and do not produce a result so perverse that no reasonable DPP standing in his shoes would not have so acted. For these reasons, I cannot interfere with the DPP's decision.

***In the Application of Chandresh Sharma* – Civil Appeal No 115 of 2003 (TT)**
Nelson JA

[P10] It is trite law that judicial review is a discretionary jurisdiction. Indeed a Court may in its discretion refuse to grant a remedy, even if the Applicant can prove unlawful administration . . . [P11] An appeal against the exercise of a discretion will only be granted if it can be shown that the Judge exercised his discretion under a mistake of law or otherwise misapprehended the facts. An appellate Court must defer to the Judge's exercise of his or her discretion and must not interfere with it merely upon the ground that the appellate Court would have exercised the discretion differently . . . It is only where the decision is plainly wrong that an appellate Court should interfere.

***In the Application of Florence Bobb and Girlie Moses* – Civil Appeal No 97 of 2002 (TT)**
Nelson JA

[P8] Counsel for the Respondent reminded the Court of the words of Lord Diplock in *Hadmor Productions v Hamilton* [1982] 2 WLR 322, at p 325: '[An appellate Court] must not interfere with it merely upon the ground that the members of the appellate Court would have exercised the discretion differently. The function of the appellate Court is initially one of review only.' Counsel also referred to the dictum of Asquith LJ approved by Lord Fraser of Tullybelton in *G v G* [1985] 1 WLR 647, 651: 'It is only where the decision exceeds the generous ambit within which reasonable disagreement is possible, and is, in fact, plainly wrong, that an appellate body is entitled to interfere.' See also *Jones v Solomon* (1989) 41 WIR 299, 336B–337H *per* Sharma JA (as he then was). I would respectfully adopt these statements of the law in deciding whether to reverse the exercise of the Judge's discretion against granting leave.

***In the Application of Felix Augustus Durity* – HCA No S-283 of 1993/Civil Appeal No 49 of 1993 (TT)**
Sharma JA

[P9] If by construing 'decision' in this way it would undoubtedly confer a right of appeal whether as of right or with leave, then there is absolutely no reason to reject this generous approach, to vest that right. In my view, as I have already said that although it is not *stricto sensu*, a fundamental right, yet it is undisputable that a right of appeal does impact in the most crucial way, and is unarguably an important part of the 'due process' clause and the fundamental right to the protection of the law, which are rights guaranteed under the Constitution . . . [P10] Further the fact that the Court of Appeal is exercising an original jurisdiction in an area of law, which goes to the heart of any civilized system of justice is not to be ignored. Matters touching the livelihood, reputation of citizens, their rights to be heard, especially against the mighty executive, make it more compelling to conclude that a right of appeal cannot lightly be construed away . . .

[PP10–11] In the result, therefore I am respectfully of the view that refusal of a renewed application for judicial review is a decision which is appealable to the Privy Council, provided other conditions are satisfied.

In the Application of Jules Bernard – Civil Appeal No 13 of 1993 (TT)
Ibrahim JA

[P9] The remedy of judicial review is concerned with reviewing not the merits of the decision in respect of which the application for judicial review is made but the decision process itself. 'It is important to remember that in every case that the purpose [of the remedy of judicial review] is to ensure that the individual is given fair treatment by the authority to which it has been subjected and that it is no part of that purpose to substitute the opinion of the judiciary or of individual Judges for that of the authority constituted by law to decide the matter in question.' (*Chief Constable of North Wales Police v Evans* [1982] 1 WLR 1155 at p 1160).

In the Application of Gladstone Solomon – Civil Appeal No 85 of 1986 (TT)
Sharma JA

[P25] The authorities are clear on the function of the Court of Appeal in respect of a judge exercising a discretion . . . [PP26–27] In *Ward v James* [1965] 1 All ER 563 at p 570 Lord Denning said: 'REVIEWING DISCRETION. This brings me to the question: in what circumstances will the Court of Appeal interfere with the discretion of the Judge? At one time it was said that it would interfere only if he had gone wrong in principle; but since *Evans v Bartlam*, that idea has been exploded. The true proposition was stated by Lord Wright in *Charles Osenton & Co. v Johnston*. This Court can, and will, interfere if it is satisfied that the Judge was wrong. Thus it will interfere if it can see that the Judge has given no weight (or no sufficient weight) to those considerations which ought to have weighed with him. A good example is *Charles Osenton & Co. v Johnston* itself, where Tucker J., in his discretion ordered trial by an official referee, and the House of Lords reversed the order because he had not given due weight to the fact that the professional reputation of surveyors was at stake. Conversely it will interfere if it can see that he has been influenced by other considerations which ought not to have weighed with him, or not weighed so much with him, as in *Hennell v Ranaboldo*. It sometimes happens that the Judge has given reasons which enable this Court to know the considerations which have weighed with him; but even if he has given no reasons, the Court may infer from the way he has decided, that the Judge must have gone wrong in one respect or the other, and will thereupon reverse his decision; see *Grimshaw v Dunbar*'. It is now settled, that the Court of Appeal will apply the same principles in the review of all matters in which the exercise of a judge's discretion is called into question. In other words, the principles will not vary according to the type of case nor because it belongs to a particular category.

R v Resident Magistrate for St. Andrew ex Parte Ervin Walker (1981) 18 JLR 6 (JM)
Parnell J

[P8] Now, where a statute gives a person power to do something coupled with a discretion a very strong case would have to be made out to say that Mandamus should go to that person to do his duty, if that person has exercised the discretion given judiciously. In other words, where there was no application of a wrong principle; or there was no consideration of any irrelevant matter what has been done cannot be controverted. And, even if the Court were to take the view that it would not have exercised its discretion in the way it was done, if that is the only thing, then mandamus cannot go because there could be no question of compelling a person to do what he honestly thinks, by the exercise of his discretion, should not be done at all. It seems that that is what happened in this case.

***In the Application of Aubrey Roberts* – Civil Appeal No 53 of 1998 (GY)**
Chang JA

> [P4] It is instructive to note that, generally, Certiorari does not lie to determine whether an inferior tribunal acted rightly or wrongly in a matter but rather whether it acted lawfully or unlawfully . . . [P5] Lord Brightman captured the point when he succinctly stated in *Chief Constable of North Wales Police v Evans* [1982] 3 All ER 141 at 154: 'Judicial review is concerned not with the decision but with the decision making process. Unless restriction on that power of the Court is observed, the Court will, in my view, under the guise of preventing an abuse of power, be itself guilty of usurping power.' . . . [P6] Every tribunal has the jurisdiction to determine the extent of its own jurisdiction. The law has not given the tribunal the right to make a wrong determination on this question of jurisdiction. Therefore, the determination of such a jurisdictional question must necessarily be reviewable by the Court as a matter of law. The determination of this jurisdictional question of law may depend on a preliminary or collateral issue of law. Both issues of law are reviewable by the Court . . . [P8] It should be noted, *per curiam*, that judicial review does lie against a wrong finding of jurisdictional fact. [PP8–9] It is essential that where the exercise of administrative power depends on the prior establishment of an objective fact, the Court will be the final arbiter as to whether that requirement has been satisfied. Otherwise, the Court will be surrendering the rule of law to the rule of administrative discretion. In my view, whether a collateral jurisdictional question of fact or law or of mixed fact and law arises and is determined by an administrative tribunal whether positively or negatively either in conferment of jurisdiction or in denial of it, the Court has the power to quash the preliminary ruling as to jurisdiction if such a question has been wrongly decided by the administrative tribunal.

Acts, decisions, determinations, orders and omissions of individuals and bodies performing public law functions can be judicially reviewed.[3] Judicial review is an integral feature of public law or administrative law. 'Judicial' here does not mean strictly the acts of a judge or a legal tribunal sitting for the determination of matters of law, but rather a [judicial] act done by a competent authority which has been conferred the right of a lawful exercise of power.[4] Competent authority can refer to either a person or body (such as a statutory body, tribunal or inferior court) carrying out public law functions with the ability to impose liability or affect the right of others.[5] It was realised as early as the thirteenth century that in order to stem possible abuses, a system was required to provide checks and balances on the behaviour of public bodies. According to Fordham, the judiciary assumes the constitutional responsibility of curbing abuses of executive power which promotes the public interest by ensuring that public bodies are not above the law and thereby protecting the rights and interests of those so affected.[6] This system reflects somewhat the Gallic concepts of *légalité* and *détournement de pouvoir* which seek to ensure that power given to such bodies is not abused.

1.2 PREROGATIVE ORDERS

Judicial review has its roots in the historical development of legal remedies such as the ancient writs[7] of *certiorari* (now quashing order), mandamus (now mandatory order)

3 See Stanley de Smith, Lord Woolf and Jeffrey Jowell, *Judicial Review of Administrative Action* (London: Sweet and Maxwell, 1995), p 3.
4 Per O'Byrne J, *The State (Crowley) v The Irish Land Commission* [1951] IR 250 at 256.
5 See s 5(1) of the Judicial Review Act, No 60 of 2000 (Trinidad and Tobago), hereinafter referred to as 'the JR Act'.
6 Michael Fordham, *Judicial Review Handbook* (Portland, Oregon: Hart Publishing, 2001), p 21.
7 Renamed prerogative orders in 1938 by the now named Supreme Court Act of England.

and prohibition (now prohibiting order), and contemporarily in the public law context, in conjunction with declaratory orders and injunctions.[8] The order of mandamus lies to secure the performance of a public duty; prohibition forbids a public body from acting contrary to law or in excess of its jurisdiction; and *certiorari* orders a decision of a public body to be brought before the High Court for judicial review and, if contrary to law, quashes it.[9]

These orders came into existence during the time of medieval England and were originally associated exclusively with the King but later on, selectively, with the King's subjects.[10] The writ of *certiorari* was developed by the Court of the King's Bench in the thirteenth century to regulate the activities of the Justices of the Peace who held a great deal of statutory powers. The writ of prohibition forbade the commencement or continuance of proceedings in absence or excess of jurisdiction and was initially directed toward limiting the jurisdiction of the ecclesiastical courts. The writ of mandamus was issued to compel performance of a public duty and evolved in the early 1600s to restore persons to public offices of which they had been unlawfully deprived. *James Bagg's Case*[11] defined the role of mandamus where the court ordered the reinstatement of a dispossessed chief to his office as he was removed from his office without notice or hearing, both of which oppose the rules of natural justice. Incidentally, this case was a landmark decision in the evolutionary development of the *audi alteram partem* rule which gives the aggrieved the right to be heard.

***In the Application of Aldric Tudor* – HCA No 5461 of 1984 (TT)**
Permanand J

[PP5–6] The Order of certiorari (like the order of prohibition) will lie to bodies and persons other than Courts *stricto sensu*. Any body of persons having legal authority to determine questions affecting the rights of subjects and having the duty to act judicially is subject to the controlling jurisdiction of the High Court of Justice exercised by means of the order of certiorari (and prohibition). It is not necessary that it should be a Court; an administrative body in ascertaining facts or law may be under a duty to act judicially. This is an ancient jurisdiction which the High Court exercises in supervising inferior Courts, commanding Magistrates and other persons to do what their duty requires. This ancient jurisdiction stemmed from the Common law which regarded the King as the source or fountain of justice and the ancient remedial processes known as prerogative writs were from the earliest times issued from the Court of Queen's Bench as the Sovereign was always present in contemplation of law. The prerogative writs were issued only upon cause shown as distinguished from the original or judicial writs which commence suits between party and party and which issue as of course. The Queen's Bench Division retained the jurisdiction of the *Curia Regis* which included the granting of prerogative writs and which by the Supreme Court of Judicature Consolidation Act 1925 (15 and 16 George 5 C.49) is vested in the High Court of Justice and is exercised by the Queen's Bench Division in accordance with rules of Court: *Halsbury's Laws of England* 3rd Ed. Vol. II p 23 paras 37–39 and footnote 't': p 27 note 'h'. Section 9 of the Supreme Court of Judicature Act Chap 4:01 preserves this jurisdiction which originally vested in and is exercisable by the High Court of Justice, England.

8 Gavin Drewry, 'Judicial Review: The Historical Background' in Michael Supperstone and James Goudie (eds), *Judicial Review* (London: Butterworths, 1997), p 1.1.
9 de Smith, Woolf and Jowell, *Judicial Review of Administrative Action*, p 693.
10 Unless otherwise stated, this section on the historical development of prerogative orders is derived mainly from Drewry, 'Judicial Review', pp 1.5–1.7.
11 (1615) 11 Co Rep 93b.

With the emergence of a new system of local government in the United Kingdom in the 1830s, the prerogative writs assumed a new importance in the regulation of local government authorities and ad hoc bodies with extensive powers over individuals and property. The application of the writs was no longer restricted only to courts but now extended to individuals and bodies conferred the right to exercise statutory powers. According to Drewry, the 1860s marked the entry of judicial review into a modern era and the expansion of the role of the courts 'with the translation of the Victorian night-watchman state into the modern era of large-scale and interventionist government'.[12]

In addition to compelling performance of a public duty, mandamus will lie to compel a body to give (adequate) reasons for its acts or decisions; to properly exercise its discretion (it must not improperly sub-delegate its powers, illegally fetter its discretion, or assume an unfettered discretion); and to hear and determine a matter according to law where there was an abuse of statutory discretion.[13] Mandamus will not, however, lie against the government nor to a public servant to order the performance of a duty owed only to the government, but to a Minister or body to perform a public duty for which a member of the public or group of individuals has sufficient personal interest.

Certiorari and prohibition will issue to quash and prevent, respectively, an order or decision on any of the following grounds:

- Excess or absence of jurisdiction
- Breach of the rules of natural justice or of the duty to act fairly
- Error of law on the face of the record
- Fraud, perjury or duress in procuring a decision.[14]

These two orders are meant to examine the decision-making process and determine whether the body deciding any question which affects the rights, legitimate interests or expectations of an individual or group of individuals is required to act fairly towards the affected. If the decision was unfairly issued, then *certiorari* will issue to quash that decision.

Injunctions may be prohibitory (to restrain the commission or continuance of unlawful conduct) or mandatory (to compel the performance of a duty); prohibitory injunctions are used more much more frequently as mandatory injunctions are deemed to be of little practical importance.[15] At the court's discretion, an interim or interlocutory injunction may be awarded as a matter of urgency *ex parte* (on the strength of the applicant's representation alone) to temporarily halt the commission or repetition of an allegedly illegal act (or an act committed on the basis of an illegally made decision) which is likely to cause serious harm, pending a full hearing of the case.[16] Although the injunction is fundamentally a private law remedy, it is available against public authorities and officials, including the government and public servants acting on the govern-

12 Drewry, 'Judicial Review', p 1.7.
13 Stanley de Smith and Rodney Brazier, *Constitutional and Administrative Law* (London: Penguin Books, 1998), p. 560. See the leading case in this area: *Padfield v Minister of Agriculture* [1968] AC 997.
14 de Smith and Brazier, *Constitutional and Administrative Law*, p 562.
15 Ibid., p 565.
16 See the JR Act, s 10.

ment's behalf not only for actionable wrongs (such as trespasses or nuisances) but also to prevent acts or decisions that are ultra vires.[17]

A declaratory order is relatively new to judicial review and can be awarded in nearly every situation where an injunction will lie and extends to instances where an injunction would be inappropriate.[18] As a discretionary remedy, the courts may refuse a declaration where its award would serve no useful purpose or where there are more appropriate alternative remedies.[19] De Smith and Brazier hold, however, that the limitations on the use of declarations are few in public law. Declarations can be obtained that invalidate administrative notices or orders; invalidate conditions attached to a grant of planning permission; declare the decision of a public authority invalid for excess or absence of jurisdiction or breach of natural justice or ultra vires.[20] Declarations need not be only to declare invalidity as an individual may obtain a declaration as to his nationality or marital status.[21]

1.3 COUNTRY PERSPECTIVES ON JUDICIAL REVIEW

1.3.1 Trinidad and Tobago

Trinidad and Tobago had a major revolution in judicial review with the passage of the Judicial Review Act No 60 of 2000 ('JR Act'). Section 5(3) of the JR Act summarises the instances in which someone may file an application for judicial review:

> The grounds upon which the Court may grant relief to a person who filed an application for judicial review includes the following:
>
> (a) that the decision was in any way unauthorised or contrary to law;
>
> (b) excess of jurisdiction;
>
> (c) failure to satisfy or observe conditions or procedures required by law;
>
> (d) breach of the principles of natural justice;
>
> (e) unreasonable, irregular or improper exercise of discretion;
>
> (f) abuse of power;
>
> (g) fraud, bad faith, improper purpose or irrelevant consideration;
>
> (h) acting on instructions from an unauthorised person;
>
> (i) conflict with the policy of an Act;
>
> (j) error of law, whether or not apparent on the face of the record;
>
> (k) absence of evidence on which a finding or assumption of fact could reasonably be based;
>
> (l) breach of or omission to perform a duty;
>
> (m) deprivation of a legitimate expectation;

---

17 The doctrine of *ultra vires* permits the Courts to strike down decisions made by public bodies exercising public functions which they have no power to make. de Smith, Woolf and Jowell, *Judicial Review of Administrative Action*, p 229. See for example the Trinidad and Tobago case: *Fishermen and Friends of the Sea v The Environmental Management Authority*, CA No 106 of 2002 and HCA No 1715 of 2002.

18 de Smith and Brazier, *Constitutional and Administrative Law*, p 567.

19 Ibid., p 568.

20 Ibid., p 568.

21 Ibid., p 569.

(n) a defect in form or a technical irregularity resulting in a substantial wrong or miscarriage of justice; or

(o) an exercise of a power in a manner that is so unreasonable that no reasonable person could have so exercised the power.

This summary covers all the issues mentioned in section 1.2 above but is not an exhaustive list. It adds to it the test of Wednesbury unreasonableness where the decision-maker with broad discretionary powers exercises said discretion in bad faith or improperly and comes to a conclusion 'so unreasonable that no reasonable authority could ever have come to it'.[22] Wednesbury unreasonableness deals with misdirection in law concerning (1) disregard of relevancies; (2) consideration of irrelevancies; and (3) patent unreasonableness[23] in coming to a decision.

The remedies clause, s 8 of the JR Act, states that the court may grant as relief to the applicant:

(1) (a) an order of mandamus, prohibition or certiorari;

(b) a declaration or injunction;

(c) an injunction under Section 19; or

(d) such other orders, directions or writs as it considers just and as the circumstances warrant.

(2) A declaration may be made or an injunction granted.

Anyone seeking any of these prerogative orders must be able to show:

(1) a sufficient interest in the matter to which the application relates, and

(2) that a justiciable determination, decision, act or omission has been made by a public authority.[24]

He must therefore demonstrate that there is an arguable case that a ground for seeking judicial review exists and that he has sufficient interest in the matter.[25] Section 6(2) of the JR Act states that 'The Court shall not grant such leave unless it considers that the applicant has a sufficient interest in the matter to which the application relates'. Section 7(1) provides, however, that once the 'Court is satisfied that an application for judicial review is justifiable in the public interest, it may . . . grant leave to apply for judicial review of a decision to an applicant whether or not he has a sufficient interest in the matter to which the decision relates'.

Sufficient interest may be determined by the court. Section 5(2) of the JR Act defines who may have sufficient interest, notwithstanding s 7(1):

(2) The Court may, on an application for judicial review, grant relief in accordance with this Act—

(a) to a person whose interests are adversely affected by a decision; or

(b) to a person or a group of persons if the Court is satisfied that the application is justifiable in the public interest in the circumstances of the case.

Section 5(6) states further that:

22 Per Lord Greene MR in *Associated Provincial Picture Houses Ltd v Wednesbury Corporation* [1948] 1 KB 223 at 229–230.
23 Fordham, *Judicial Review Handbook*, p 691.
24 de Smith, Woolf and Jowell, *Judicial Review of Administrative Action*, p 695.
25 Clive Lewis, *Judicial Remedies in Public Law* (London: Sweet & Maxwell, 2000), pp 263–264.

(6) Where a person or group of persons aggrieved or injured by reason of any ground referred to in paragraphs (a) to (o) of subsection (3), is unable to file an application for judicial review under this Act on account of poverty, disability, or socially or economically disadvantaged position, any other person or group of persons acting *bona fide* can move the Court under this section for relief under this Act,

where the court makes a determination as to whether such person or group is in fact *bona fide*.

Leave to apply for judicial review will be refused where applications are:

- frivolous, vexatious or hopeless;
- made by busybodies with misguided or trivial complaints of administrative error;
- misconceived;
- unarguable or groundless; or
- where there is a more appropriate alternative remedy[26];
- where there has been unreasonable delay and where as a result of said delay granting relief would cause substantial hardship or substantial prejudice to the rights of the Respondent or would be detrimental to good administration.[27]

With respect to the last ground, s 11(1) of the JR Act provides that 'An application for judicial review shall be made promptly and in any event within three months' from the date of the act, decision, determination, order or omission of the public authority. The use of the word 'promptly' indicates that the applicant shall not take the full three months to file for leave to apply for judicial review if, for example, he is made aware of the decision within one week of its having been made. The court can decide that filing two months after knowledge of the decision constitutes undue delay even though it was filed before the three month period. In accordance with s 11(2) of the JR Act, where the application is filed outside of the three month period, the court can exercise its discretion to extend the time within which the application may be made if it finds that there is good reason for extending time. This notwithstanding, the court may still refuse to grant relief where such a grant would result in substantial hardship or substantial prejudice to the respondent or would be detrimental to good administration.

1.3.2 Barbados

Like Trinidad and Tobago, Barbados has utilised the legislative route to develop judicial review. The Administrative Justice Act 1980 and the Judicial Review (Applications) Rules 1983 provide the statutory basis for judicial review in Barbados.

***Narsham Insurance (Barbados) Ltd v Supervisor of Insurance and Another* (1999) 56 WIR 101 (BB)**
Sir Williams CJ

[PP111–112] The Administrative Justice Act enables an application for judicial review to be made to the High Court for relief against an administrative act or omission, which expression is defined to include an act or omission of a public official or other authority of the Government of Barbados exercising or purporting to exercise any power or duty conferred or imposed by any enactment (ss 2 and 3). Section 5(1) sets out the remedies which the Court may grant by way of relief, and these include certiorari for quashing

26 de Smith, Woolf and Jowell, *Judicial Review of Administrative Action*, p 663.
27 Lewis, *Judicial Remedies in Public Law*, pp 276 and 278.

unlawful acts. The Court may also, having regard to the scope of the remedies mentioned in s 5(1), grant in addition or alternatively a declaratory judgment, an injunction, and restitution or damages in money or an order for the return of property real or personal (s 5(2)). By virtue of s 5(3), any of the remedies mentioned in s 5(1) and (2) may be applied for together or in the alternative and the Court may grant one or more of them as law and justice may require. Section 4 prescribes the grounds upon which the Court may grant relief and they include at s 4(d) 'breach of the principles of natural justice'. Section 6 enables relief to be granted to a person whose interests are adversely affected by an administrative act or omission or to any other person if the Court is satisfied that that person's application is justifiable in the public interest in the circumstances of the case. Section 7(1) enables an interlocutory application to be made in any application for judicial review and provides that the Court or judge may make any interlocutory order and grant any interim relief as it or he might think fit. Section 7(2) enables the Court or judge at any stage to direct that the proceedings to which the application relates be stayed until further order. Section 8 enables the Court to refuse relief—'if it considers that there has been undue delay in making the application for judicial review, and that the grant of the relief sought would cause substantial hardship to, and would substantially prejudice the rights of any person, or would be detrimental to good administration.' Section 16 enacts: '(1) The law relating to natural justice applies (a) to any person or body refusing, modifying or revoking any licence, permission, qualification or authority or imposing any penalty under powers conferred by any enactment; (b) to any person or body listed in the Second Schedule and making a decision of the kind there specified. (2) This Section does not restrict the application of the law relating to natural justice in any other case.' The Second Schedule lists the Judicial and Legal Service Commission, the Public Service Commission, the Police Service Commission and the Statutory Boards Service Commission in respect of a decision against a member of the service in question in a disciplinary matter; and the Minister responsible for Town and Country Planning in respect of a decision to approve a development plan under s 9 of the Town and Country Planning Act and a decision given upon a review under s 19 of that Act ... [PP114–115] With great respect we do not think that the non-inclusion of a reference to the Supervisor of Insurance in the Second Schedule to the Administrative Justice Act affords a good ground for inferring that the acts or omissions of the Supervisor cannot be challenged under that Act. For one thing, the Second Schedule is linked to s 16(1)(b) and is concerned with particular kinds of decisions made by the person and bodies specified in the Schedule. Section 16(1)(a) is a provision that relates to other kinds of decisions made by persons and bodies generally and is completely separate from s 16(1)(b). The kind of decision challenged in these proceedings is clearly within the description 'modifying ... any licence, permission, qualification or authority ... under powers conferred by any enactment' in s 16(1)(a). An overwhelming argument against the interpretation placed by the trial Judge upon the Section lies in the terms of s 16(2) which make it manifestly clear that the law relating to natural justice applies in any case not caught by s 16(1): 'This section does not restrict the application of the law of natural justice in any other case.' So that s 16 does not rule out the application of the rules of natural justice in situations in which the common law would say that they are applicable. On this point it is relevant to refer to a passage from the judgment of Davies J in *Marine Hull & Liability Insurance Co Ltd v Hurford* [1986] 67 ALR 77 at 81 (the *'Marine Hull' case*): 'I accept that, in the giving of directions under s 62 of the Insurance Act 1973, the acting Treasurer was under a duty to act fairly, in the sense of according procedural fairness. The principles to be applied have recently been restated in *Kioa v Minister for Immigration and Ethnic Affairs* [1985] 62 ALR 321. At pp 345, 346 Mason J said: *It is a fundamental rule of the common-law doctrine of natural justice* expressed in traditional terms that, generally speaking, when an order is to be made which will deprive a person of some right or interest or the legitimate expectation of a benefit, he is entitled to know the case sought to be made against him and to be given an opportunity of replying to it ... The reference to "right and interest" in this formulation must be understood as relating to personal liberty, status, preservation of

> livelihood or reputation, as well as to proprietary rights and interests. The law has now developed to a point where it may be accepted that there is a common-law duty to act fairly, in the sense of according procedural fairness, in the making of administrative decisions which affect rights, interests and legitimate expectations, subject only to the clear manifestation of a contrary intention. It seems that, as early as 1911, Lord Loreburn LC understood that this was the law when he spoke of the obligation to "fairly listen to both sides" being "a duty lying upon every one who decides anything" (*Board of Education v Rice* [1911] AC 179 at 182)' [emphasis supplied]. 'Wilson, Brennan and Deane JJ expressed views to the same effect.' So that in our opinion the rules of natural justice do apply in respect of the acts or omissions of the Supervisor to the extent that they fall within the ambit of s 16(1)(a) of the Act and to the extent that they can be challenged at common law in any circumstances in which s 16(1)(a) does not apply.

Of major interest in the Administrative Justice Act 1980 is s 8 which deals with undue delay. Although there is no stipulated time for filing an action for judicial review, the law preserves the jurisdiction in the court to refuse to grant leave for judicial review where there is undue delay.

1.3.3 Guyana

The presence of judicial review in Guyana is distinct and separate from that which obtains in the rest of the Commonwealth Caribbean. In England the prerogative writs of mandamus, *certiorari* and prohibition were the means by which the King's Bench Division exercised supervisory power over inferior jurisdictions.[28] The procedure for the issue of such writs was governed by the Crown Office Rules 1906. The Supreme Court Ordinance 1893 established the Supreme Court of British Guiana which provided for its exercise of 'all the authorities, powers and functions belonging or incident to such a Court according to the Law of England.' The position adopted in Guyana is that the courts inherited the prerogative writs which were governed by the Crown Office Rules 1906 and that notwithstanding the abolishment of the prerogative writs in England in 1938, by the Administration of Justice (Miscellaneous Provisions) Act 1938, the said writs continued to be governed by the Crown Office Rules 1906 in Guyana.

In the Application of Carl Hanoman – HCSCJ No 23M of 1999 (GY)
Bernard CJ

> [PP6–7] Counsel for the Applicant referred the Court to 'Wade on *Administrative Law*', 7th Edition, which I have found most instructive. At page 623 the author states that unlike private law remedies, the prerogative remedies have never been dependent on the Applicant showing a specific personal right. Application for judicial review was introduced in the Courts of England in 1977 with new rules of procedure. Therefore the old procedure is more relevant to our practice, and in this regard I refer to an excerpt on page 702 of Wade with regard to standing under the prerogative writs of certiorari and prohibition: 'The prerogative remedies being of a "public" character . . . have always had more liberal rules about standing than the remedies of private law. Prerogative remedies are granted at the suit of the Crown, as the title of the cases shows; and the Crown always has standing to take action against public authorities, including its own Ministers, who act or threaten to act unlawfully . . . Consequently the Court is prepared to act at the instance of a mere stranger, though it retains discretion to refuse to do so if it considers that no good would be done to the public. Every citizen has standing to invite

28 See *In the Application of Claude Jardim*—Civil Appeal No 134 of 1998 (GY).

the Court to prevent some abuse of power, and in doing so he may claim to be regarded not as a meddlesome busybody but as a public benefactor'.

***In the Application of Claude Jardim* – Civil Appeal No 134 of 1998 (GY)**
Bernard C

[PP3–9] In deciding this preliminary procedural point one ought to begin by tracing the importation of the prerogative writs into the laws of Guyana. In England the prerogative writs of mandamus, certiorari and prohibition were the means by which the King's Bench Division exercised supervisory power over inferior jurisdictions. The procedure for the issue of such writs was governed by the Crown Office Rules, 1906. The Supreme Court Ordinance, 1893 established the Supreme Court of British Guiana which provided for its exercise of 'all the authorities, powers and functions belonging or incident to such a Court according to the Law of England.' Our Courts therefore inherited the prerogative writs which were governed by the Crown Office Rules 1906. However, in 1938 by the Administration of Justice (Miscellaneous Provisions) Act, 1938 the prerogative writs were abolished in England. This, notwithstanding the said writs continued to be governed by the Crown Office Rules, 1906 in our jurisdiction. This was held to be so by Stoby J, in the case of *Coghlan v Vieira* (*supra*) who at page 120 came to the conclusion that the English Act of 1938 did not abolish the writs in this country since the procedure provided by the English Order 59 Rule 3(1) was designed to meet a situation which arose by reason of the introduction of a new scheme of legislation. Cummings JA, in *Re Application by Gerriah Sarran* (*supra*) concurred with this conclusion. The prerogative writs not having been abolished in our jurisdiction are still governed by the Crown Office Rules 1906, and one has to decide where they stand in relation to the State Liability and Proceedings Act 1984 which was an Act 'to amend the law relating to the civil liabilities and rights of the State and for matters connected therewith.' Part II of the Act is intituled 'Substantive Law' which provides for liability of the State in tort including provisions as to industrial property, application of law as to indemnity and contribution between joint tortfeasors, salvage claims against the State, provisions relating to the armed forces, and saving clauses in respect of acts done under prerogative and statutory powers (prerogative here relates to the prerogative of the State conferred by any written law). Part III of the Act relates to jurisdiction and procedure providing a right to sue the State as of right without the fiat of a Minister, and also enforcement of claims by or against the State. It provides that 'claims against the State' includes a claim by way of set-off or counterclaim. It also provides for time for entering appearance, interpleader proceedings, judgment and proceedings thereon, discovery, injunction, specific performance and parate execution. The whole tenor of the Act relates to civil liability and the rights of the State in matters connected therewith. This leads to the next question—is the prerogative writ a civil action or proceeding? To assist in determining this one needs to look at the history of the prerogative writ. In early times the Court of King's Bench was a committee of the sovereign who sat in the Court himself. The jurisdiction of the Court was very high, and its purpose was to keep all inferior jurisdictions within the bounds of its authority. It superintended all civil corporations, and protected the liberty of the subject by speedy and summary interposition according to Short & Mellor, 2nd Edn. of *The Practice on the Crown Side of the King's Bench Division*. The jurisdiction in criminal causes was called the Crown Side, or Crown Office, which embraced both a strictly criminal jurisdiction as well as a general superintending jurisdiction. The Crown Office Rules 1906 were enacted to regulate the general practice on the Crown Side. The prerogative writ of mandamus is defined as a high prerogative writ which issued from the Crown Side of the King's Bench Division commanding the person to whom it is addressed to perform some public legal duty which he has refused to perform. According to Short & Mellor these writs were originally letters or mandates from the sovereign of England, and were in no sense judicial writs being merely commands. Over time the term mandamus which derived from these letters was confined in its application to the judicial writ issued by the King's Bench, and later developed into the writ of mandamus. The writ being a high prerogative writ cannot be demanded *ex debito justitiae*, but issues only in the discretion of the Court. Lord Chelmsford in the case of *R v The Church Wardens of All Saints, Wigan and Others* [1876] 1 AC 611 at page 620 expressed the view that a writ of mandamus is a prerogative writ, and not a writ of right, and is in the discretion of the Court whether to grant it or not. The prerogative writs of certiorari and prohibition also were writs issued out of the Kings Bench Division at the discretion of the Court. On the question of whether a prerogative writ was a proceeding or action I refer to a view expressed by Bankes LJ, in the Court of Appeal case of *R v Port of London Authority, Ex Parte Kynock Ltd.* [1918] 1 KB 176 where the effect of the Public Authorities Act, 1893 on a writ of mandamus was considered. At page 186 he had this to say: 'I express no confident opinion without further considering the dicta cited, but my present impression is that the language of that Act does not extend to proceedings of this class. The essence of the prerogative writ of mandamus is a command to a tribunal to do something which it has omitted or refused to do, <u>and an application for the writ is not an action, prosecution, or other proceeding</u> for any act done in pursuance or execution or intended execution, nor, as I think, for any neglect or default in the execution, of any Act of Parliament or public duty or authority. But apart from that, the Act seems to contemplate something which results, if successful, in the payment of damages or in the enforcing of some penalty, and the words "action, prosecution, or other proceeding" were not intended to include a prerogative writ calling upon a public authority to perform a public duty.' [emphasis mine]. Scrutton, LJ also expressed similar views when he said at p 188: 'As to the Public Authorities Protection Act, 1893, the writ of mandamus, like that of certiorari and prohibition, is a high prerogative writ, and a very valuable right in the Crown for keeping subordinate tribunals within their Jurisdiction. Clear words are necessary to impair such a right, and the words of this Act, "action, prosecution, or other proceeding against any person", are no such clear words as to have effect.' The Court of Appeal without deciding inclined to the view that the limitation to actions, prosecutions and proceedings prescribed by Section 1 of the Public Authorities Act, 1893 did not apply to the prerogative writ of mandamus. The dicta of these two illustrious Judges of the English Court of Appeal are relevant to the instant appeal only to the extent that they emphasize that the prerogative writ is not an action or proceeding. In the English case the relevant statute made reference to 'any action, prosecution, or other proceeding' commenced against any person. Our State Liability and Proceedings Act, 1984 also speaks of 'proceedings' against the State in Part II, in Section 3 under the Substantive Law as well as in Section 9 which relates to enforcement of claims by or against the State, and in Sections 12, 13, 14, 15, 16 and 17 under Part III 'Jurisdiction and Procedure'; Section 19 of Part IV—Miscellaneous—also makes mention of 'proceedings *in rem*.' The English Crown Proceedings Act, 1947 excepted the prerogative remedies from its definition of 'civil proceedings' which in any event do not lie against the Crown. 'The Crown' meaning the sovereign acting in a public or official capacity which hitherto could not be sued, is now since 1947 in the position of an ordinary employer or an ordinary litigant in private law. This was the main purpose of the Act, and the exclusion of the prerogative remedies from its definition of 'civil proceedings' is an indication that these remedies were never regarded as 'proceedings' in the realm of private liability. Counsel for the Respondent made reference to the case of *Minister of Foreign Affairs, Trade & Industry v Vehicles and Supplies Ltd and Another* (1989) 39 WIR 270, a decision of the Privy Council on appeal from the Court of Appeal of Jamaica which had ruled in a case involving application for a prerogative order that as the proceedings were not 'civil proceedings' within the meaning of the Jamaican Crown Proceedings Act, the Attorney General was not a necessary party to them. The Privy Council affirmed the decision of the Court of Appeal on this point. Rowe P, of the Jamaican Court of Appeal, in his judgment concluded that from the history of the development of the prerogative remedies of mandamus, prohibition and certiorari, it is clear that they were remedies to which the subject was not entitled as of right, but only at the discretion of the Court. He also made reference to dicta of Lord Denning MR, in *O'Reilly v Mackman* [1982] 3 All ER 680 to the same effect. The Crown

Proceedings Act 1959 in Jamaica had as its precedent the English Crown Proceedings Act, 1947, and the provisions are substantially similar. The Jamaican Act made the Crown in Jamaica liable in tort in the same way as an ordinary subject, as does our State Liability and Proceedings Act, 1984. However, unlike our Act, in both Crown Proceedings Acts the term 'civil proceedings' is defined to exclude 'Crown Side proceedings'. The reason for excluding Crown Side proceedings in both the English and Jamaican Crown Proceedings Acts is that in both countries the old prerogative writs have been replaced by prerogative orders although still referred to as Crown Side proceedings. To ensure that these proceedings retain their character of remedies which are granted at the discretion of the Court and because of their history as emanating from the Crown, it was necessary to exclude them from being regarded as ordinary civil proceedings. In Guyana as stated earlier in the judgment the old prerogative writs based on the Crown Office Rules 1906 are still in existence. I reiterate that they were never regarded as civil proceedings and were at all times Crown Side proceedings. This being so the drafters of the State Liability and Proceedings Act 1984 may have seen no need to define 'civil proceedings' as the long title of the Act is 'to amend the law relating to the **civil liabilities** and rights of the State and for matters connected therewith' [emphasis mine]. This refers solely to civil liability in tort and not to the prerogative writs. Counsel for the Appellant in his written submissions sought to replace the words 'Crown Side proceedings' with 'State Side proceedings'. I beg to differ. The words 'Crown Side proceedings' have a special meaning because of their history as emanating from the Crown, and there are no proceedings called 'State Side proceedings'. The words cannot be simplistically substituted. For all of the reasons stated in the judgment I find that the Attorney General is not a proper party to the appeal, and as such it cannot be launched in his name. The preliminary objection is accordingly upheld. As this is fundamental to the validity of the appeal there is no need to determine it on its merits.

***Re Application by Lennox Arthur and Calvin Hermanstyne* (1972) 19 WIR 20 (GY)**
Luckhoo J

[PP29–30] But the Constitution, conscious as it must have been of having expressly ousted the Court's jurisdiction in such instances, contrived to utilize from the vantage point of an interpretation article, viz art 125(8), a provision designated to allow for a limited intervention by the Courts. Without it, the argument for the Appellant in *Evelyn v Chichester* ((1970) 15 WIR 410)—that the Respondent after dismissal could claim no right to a judicial review 'as the Constitution provided none'—might well have found favour. With it, it could not. The Constitution was, with realism, carving out a 'special' jurisdiction for the Courts similar to that which the Courts at common law possessed and exercised for centuries, viz, the right to enquire into and quash errors of law appearing on the face of the record. Its language is identifiable with the basic feature of this common law supervisory jurisdiction. The motif behind the bestowal of this power is the same which inspired the common law to superintend and control the exercise of statutory powers to prevent certain kinds of misuse or abuse of power, and to control actions which were *ultra vires*. As, for example, where a person or authority had to decide 'rights', after hearing evidence and opposition, its decision was required to possess two essential characteristics: (i) it must be within that person or authority's jurisdiction, and (ii) there must be no error of law on the face of the record of what had taken place. In effect, the jurisdiction under art 125(8) is a jurisdiction to check on the exercise of other 'jurisdictions' not only for defects of jurisdiction, but for contravention of law. The origin of this controlling power was the writ of certiorari, a special remedy devised for this purpose to command that the record of what is being questioned should be sent 'forthwith to enable what of right and according to law' shall be 'fit to be done'. The issue of this writ was such an essential and integral part of this control that it is difficult to think of 'control' without 'certiorari'. To test the propriety of proceedings by the supervision of certiorari would be a test which (in the words of Lord Sumner) 'goes to two points; one is the area of the inferior jurisdiction and the qualifications and conditions of its exercise;

> the other is the observance of the law in the course of its exercise'. So great has been the urge of the common law to preserve the salutary effects of this jurisdiction that even when or where statute may provide that a particular determination 'of a certain function' 'shall not be called in question in any Court of law' (a sort of no certiorari clause), yet a Court will not be precluded from inquiring whether or not the 'determination' was or was not a nullity, as, for example, whether it was made in accordance with the permitted jurisdiction or not. For, as Lord Wilberforce said in *Anisminic v Foreign Compensation Commission* ([1969] 1 All ER 208, [1969] 2 AC 147, [1969] 2 WLR 163, 113 Sol Jo 55 HL, Digest Cont Vol C, 282, 2557b) ([1969] 2 WLR at p 204): 'The Courts, when they decide that a "decision" is a "nullity", are not disregarding the preclusive clause. For just as it is their duty to attribute autonomy of decision of action to the tribunal within the designated area, so, as the counterpart of this autonomy, they must ensure that the limits of that area which have been laid down are observed (see the formulation of Lord Sumner in *Rex v Nat Bell Liquors, Ltd* ([1922] 2 AC 128, 91 LJPC 146, 127 LT 437, 38 TLR 541, 27 Cox, CC 253, PC, 16 Digest (Repl) 469, 2897) [1922] 2 AC 128, 156). In each task they are carrying out the intention of the legislature, and it would be a misdescription to state it in terms of a struggle between the Courts and the executive. What would be the purpose of defining by statute the limit of a tribunal's powers if, by means of a clause inserted in the instrument of definition, those limits could safely be passed?' And Lord Reid in the same case made this authoritative pronouncement (ibid at p 170): 'there are many cases where, although the tribunal had jurisdiction to enter on the inquiry, it has done or failed to do something in the course of the inquiry which is of such a nature that its decision is a nullity. It may have given its decision in bad faith. It may have made a decision which it had no power to make. It may have failed in the course of the inquiry to comply with the requirements of natural justice. It may in perfect good faith have misconstrued the provisions giving it power to act so that it failed to deal with the question remitted to it and decided some question which was not remitted to it. It may have refused to take into account something which it was required to take into account. Or it may have based its decision on some matter which, under the provisions setting it up, it had no right to take into account. I do not intend this list to be exhaustive. But if it decides a question remitted to it for decision without committing any of these errors it is as much entitled to decide that question wrongly as it is to decide it rightly.' In like manner, in my view, art 125(8) has succeeded in preserving the salutary effect of this jurisdiction. It has within its stated limitation qualified the impress of finality elsewhere appearing.

The courts of Guyana are now making a plea for the introduction of statutory provisions to deal with judicial review in light of the uncertainties created by the use of the prerogative writs and the statutory developments taking place in other Caribbean countries.

In the Application of Guyana Telephone and Telegraph Company Ltd
– HCSCJ No 13-M of 1999 (GY)
Singh J

> [PP1–2] The parties in these proceedings have come full circle in relation to the practice and procedure associated with the prerogative writs. In High Court Suit No. 4491 of 1995, involving these very parties, the point was argued before me on behalf of the Respondent Public Utilities Commission (hereinafter referred to as the PUC) that Guyana had no rules or law touching judicial review. I rejected that contention and in the course of my judgement I said: 'I would say that what we do not have in Guyana, are statutory provisions relating to an application for judicial review, akin to the provisions of the Administrative Justice Act of Barbados 1980 or Order 53 of the English Rules of Court and I respectfully adopt the views of Cummings, J.A., in *Sarran's case,* that the High Court can, in a manner that is jurisdictionally correct, embark upon judicial review of the administrative act(s) of inferior tribunals.' [P10] Of course, I would not let this opportunity pass by without seizing upon it to make what I consider to be a timely call.

> With the ever increasing importance of judicial review in public law, the time is long past due for the introduction of a statutory framework regulating these proceedings and such considerations should be given priority in any revision of our Rules of Court. I hope this appeal is not made in vain. I believe we may be the only jurisdiction in the Commonwealth Caribbean without statutory provisions regulating judicial review proceedings.

1.3.4 Jamaica

While Jamaica does not have a specific judicial review act, Part 56 of the Supreme Court of Civil Procedure Rules 2002 makes provision for administrative law claims under which judicial review and constitutional claims fall. As with the JR Act of Trinidad and Tobago, anyone wishing to apply for judicial review must first apply for leave to apply for judicial review. It is expected that the application will be made promptly (with the same interpretation as obtains for the JR Act of Trinidad and Tobago); however, the Supreme Court of Civil Procedure Rules 2002 does not make any reference to when the applicant becomes aware of the decision but states simply that the application is to be made 'promptly and in any event within three months from the date when grounds for the application first arose' (r 56.6(1)). The application must be completed in accordance with r 56.3(3) which lists what information is to be included in the application for leave. Further, r 56.4(12) states that the grant of leave is conditional on the applicant making a claim for judicial review within 14 days of receipt of the order granting leave.

Remedies for judicial review under this Part include:

(a) *certiorari*, for quashing unlawful acts;

(b) prohibition, for prohibiting unlawful acts; and

(c) mandamus, for requiring performance of a public duty, including a duty to make a decision or determination or to hear and determine any case.

According to r 56.2, an application for judicial review may be made by any person, group or body which has sufficient interest in the subject matter of the application. This includes:

(a) any person who has been adversely affected by the decision which is the subject of the application;

(b) any body or group acting at the request of a person or persons who would be entitled to apply under paragraph (a);

(c) any body or group that represents the views of its members who may have been adversely affected by the decision which is the subject of the application;

(d) any statutory body where the subject matters fall within its statutory remit;

(e) any body or group that can show that the matter is of public interest and that the body or group possesses expertise in the subject matter of the application;

(f) any other person or body who has a right to be heard under the terms of any relevant enactment or the Constitution.

The application may be refused if not filed promptly. Like the JR Act of Trinidad and Tobago, where the application is filed outside of the three month period, the Court can exercise its discretion to extend the time within which the application may be made if it finds that there is good reason to do so (r 56.6(2)) but may still refuse to grant relief if doing so would cause substantial hardship to, or substantially prejudice the rights of, any person (not necessarily the respondent) or would be detrimental to good administration (r 56.6(5)).

***Regina v Board of the School of Physical Therapy ex parte Christopher Edwards* (1989) 26 JLR 400 (JM)**
Langrin J

[PP402–403] I now come back to the question whether the Board is the body of persons amenable to the supervisory jurisdiction of this Court. It is indeed true that the Board was not set up by statute, but the fact that it was set up by the Minister of Health does not render its acts any less lawful. Indeed the prerogative orders have issued not only to tribunals set up by statute but to tribunals whose authority is derived *inter alia* from the Executive. Moreover, the Board though set up under the executive powers of the Minister and not by Statute had in fact the recognition of Parliament in debate and Parliament as well as other public agencies provided the money to satisfy its needs . . . The absence of a statutory power should not in itself be a conclusive reason for a refusal by the Courts to entertain proceedings in which it was alleged that an essentially public authority had breached the rules of natural justice. To draw so sharp a distinction between the exercise of different governmental powers solely on the basis that if the discretion is not to be found in statute it must be found in contract is difficult to justify as a matter of principle. [P404] 'Today the controlling factor in determining whether the exercise of power is subject to judicial review is not its source but its subject matter' (*Per* Lords Scarman and Diplock). In the light of the affidavit evidence we find as a fact that the Board is a body of persons of a public as opposed to a purely private or domestic character, having power to determine matters affecting subject and has a duty to act judicially.

2

GROUNDS FOR JUDICIAL REVIEW

A classical analysis of judicial review establishes three main limbs under which courts will interevene to provide redress against a decision by a public authority. These three grounds are illegality, irrationality and procedural impropriety.

***In the Application of the Director of Public Prosecutions* – HCA No 3367 of 2001 (TT)**
Dean-Armorer J

[P8] The grounds on which decisions are reviewable in public law have been placed into three broad general categories of irrationality, illegality and procedural impropriety . . . A decision will be reviewable on the ground of irrationality if it is so outrageous in its defiance of logic or of accepted moral standards that no sensible person who had applied his mind to the question to be decided could have arrived at that decision . . . An error of law is identified as a ground for judicial review at s. 5(3)(j) of the Judicial Review Act 2000. The concept of errors of law going to the jurisdiction is now obsolete. All errors of law are now regarded as jurisdictional errors . . . [P11] It is now trite law that in Judicial Review proceedings, the reviewing Court does not exercise an appellate jurisdiction but is confined to examining the relevant decision-making process.

Regina v The Jamaica Racing Commission ex parte Harold Clemetson
(1994) 31 JLR 390 (JM)
Langrin J

[PP395–396] The Court is then entrusted with a supervisory jurisdiction bereft of an appellate role when it hears certiorari proceedings from any Domestic Tribunal. Lord Diplock in the House of Lords case of *Council of Civil Service Unions v Minister for the Civil Service* [1984] 3 All ER 935 at 950 classified under three heads the grounds on which administrative action is subjected to the control of Judicial Review. They are firstly, illegality, secondly irrationality and thirdly procedural impropriety. It is the view of the Court that the three heads are equally applicable to Domestic Tribunals, such as the one appointed by the Jamaica Racing Commission. A Domestic Tribunal in order to prevent the ground of illegality coming into play, must demonstrate not only a correct understanding of the Law that regulates its decision making power, but must give effect to it. In other words, the Domestic Tribunal appointed by Jamaica Racing Commission must understand and apply its rules correctly in any given direction. Whether or not this is done is a question of fact. Can it then be said that the Jamaica Racing Commission (JRC) tribunal acted within the 'illegality' concept so as to subject itself to judicial review by the Courts? In the opinion of the Court, the answer is no. The Tribunal as well as the Applicant understood the rules and based on the evidence presented there is no room for argument that elements of illegality as used in this context were present. The Tribunal presided over by distinguished counsel understood the rules and applied them correctly. Attention then must be focused on the ground of 'irrationality'. Irrationality hinges on Wednesbury unreasonableness as stated in *Associated Provincial House Limited v Wednesbury Company* [1947] (*supra*). The ground was succinctly stated by Lord Diplock in *Council of Civil Service Unions v Minister for the Civil Service* (*supra*): 'It applies to a decision which is so outrageous in its defiance of logic or of accepted moral standards that no sensible person who had applied his mind to the question to be decided could have arrived at it.' Whether a decision can be said to be unreasonable is a matter for the Court to determine. In all cases it is the Judge's discretion to determine whether there is ground to exercise the irrationality principle. The Courts have, for example, set aside decisions for irrationality where the Court has taken the view that the decision was without conceivable justification. See for example *R v Secretary of State for the Home Department, Ex*

Parte K. [1991] 1 QB 270. The question then to be asked is whether the Jamaican Racing Commission's Tribunal could have reasonably arrived at the decision it did. In other words was the decision so perverse that it lacks logic or violates the fundamental values of our society? The Court thinks not. Based on the facts and evidence, there is nothing to suggest that the Court could not have arrived at the conclusions it did and therefore the Applicant's case fails on the ground of irrationality. The third ground is procedural impropriety, a fairly broad heading which covers not only breaches of natural justice and procedural fairness, but also covers failure of the decision making body to observe procedural rules that are expressly laid down in the legislative instrument by which its jurisdiction is conferred. Traditionally the Courts have approached expressed statutory procedural rules by distinguishing between mandatory and directory procedural requirements. A directory procedural requirement is relatively unimportant. Whenever a directory requirement is broken the Court may well overlook the matter. For example, if the procedure has been substantially complied with or there is no injustice or hardship. A mandatory procedural requirement is essential and breach of this makes the decision invalid. It is the Court which essentially determines whether a procedural requirement is mandatory or mere directory. In its deliberations, the Court will be guided by statutory language and the particular presumptions which govern the right of the individual. The evidence presented before this Court indicated that the procedural requirement as authorized by the Jamaica Racing Commission Act has been complied with and, therefore, it is not necessary to determine the question as to whether the procedural aspect was directory or mandatory. On this limb therefore the Applicant's case fails. Procedural impropriety also includes fairness. Actually the law has developed at least in terminology from natural justice to fairness. See Council of *Civil Service Union v Minister for the Civil Service (supra)* [1984] 3 All ER 935 at 954. The concept of fairness is therefore much wider than natural justice. It is to be noted however that what is fair is still based upon an objective standard. And the Courts have consistently held that what is fair depends entirely on the circumstances of each case. See *Lloyd v McMahon* [1987] 1 All ER 1118. Fairness in effect is what is necessary to do justice in the particular circumstances and no more. It is true that fairness can include an advance notice of charges or accusations but this of course depends on the circumstances. In the instant case the Applicant, a trainer with over 44 years experience knew of the Rules surrounding the Jamaica Racing Commission investigating tribunal. The Applicant cannot therefore ignore the Rules of the Commission when it suits his purpose.

R v Commissioner of Customs and Excise ex parte A. & F. Farm Produce Company Ltd and Andre Chin (1993) 30 JLR 462 (JM)
Langrin J

[P466] The law relating to judicial review of administrative action has now developed to the stage at which it is necessary to establish one or more of three grounds in order to succeed on an application. See *CCSU v Minister for the Public Service* [1985] AC 374, 410. 1. **Illegality**: Where the decision maker has failed to understand correctly the law that regulates his decision making power, e.g. *ultra vires*. 2. **Irrationality**: The Wednesbury principle derived from *Associated Provincial Picture Houses Ltd. v Wednesbury Corporation* [1948] 1 KB 223. The decision must be so outrageously unreasonable that no sensible person who had applied his mind to the question to be decided could have arrived at that decision. 3. **Procedural Impropriety**: Failure to observe the basic rules of natural justice or failure to act with procedural fairness towards the person who will be affected by the decision. The Commissioner of Customs and Excise deponed in her affidavit at paragraph 5 that: 'Having reviewed the information from Robert Farr she believed that there were serious irregularities on the part of the Applicants in declaring the true value of the goods imported by them and so I directed that the consignment of margarine imported by the Applicant be seized and disposed of ... pursuant to Section 210/211 and 214 of the Customs Act respectively.'

Notwithstanding these three broad headings for judicial review, it is now apparent that there are several other headings by which a decision of a public authority may be attacked. It can be argued, although, that these other grounds ultimately make their way back to the three fundamental limbs of judicial review. The courts have recognised that new grounds of judicial review may arise in the future and there are no limits to the scope of judicial review.

***In the Application of Air Caribbean Ltd* – HCA No 707 of 1998 (TT)**
Hosein J

[PP11–12] The High Court has historically exercised a supervisory jurisdiction over the proceedings and decisions of inferior Courts, tribunals, public authorities and bodies that perform public duties and functions (all of whom are collectively referred to as 'the decision makers'). This jurisdiction is now exercisable under the public law remedy of judicial review. This remedy has become one of the principal methods by which the Courts now control the sometimes unfettered actions of decision makers. The source of the decision making power may be either statutory or common law. The remedy of judicial review is not directed at reviewing the merits of a decision but the decision making process itself. It is not within the competence of a Court to substitute its own opinion for that of the decision maker. A Court of law is not entrusted with the power to make the decision that is being reviewed and must guard against substituting its own concept of merit for that of the decision maker. It must confine its review to the decision making process that is being reviewed ... [P12] The grounds on which Courts have reviewed the decisions of decision makers have deliberately been kept open and flexible. From time to time the Courts have attempted to classify the grounds on which the actions of decision makers have been reviewed. Perhaps the most widely accepted attempt to do so was in the *Council of Civil Service Unions and Minister of the Civil Service* [1984] 3 All ER 935 where Lord Diplock stated at p 950 as follows: 'one can conveniently classify under three heads the grounds on which administrative action is subject to control by judicial review. The first ground I would call "illegality" the second "irrationality" and the third "procedural impropriety". That is not to say that further development on a case by case basis may not in course of time add further grounds.' [P14] The principle of legitimate expectation is an emergent doctrine, the boundaries of which have not been definitely determined ... [P18] In order to establish a legitimate expectation that amounts to a substantive right there must be a clear and unambiguous representation by a decision maker upon which it was reasonable for an Applicant to rely.

***In The Application of the Police Service Commission* – Civil Appeal No 143 of 1994 (TT)**
Sharma JA

[P2] Experience has shown that applications for Judicial Review and Constitutional reliefs are invariably made together. In my view, however, such an approach should not be encouraged for obvious reasons ... Judicial Review came into existence by virtue of Rules of Court, and there is no statutory underpinning to these rules (unlike England). The grounds on which judicial review can be sought are procedural impropriety, irrationality, illegality, proportionality and bad faith. No doubt other grounds may develop in the future, but one thing is clear, the grounds *per se* are far removed from the fundamental rights in the Constitution. There appears to be little kinship between them ... [P3] Rules and Regulations have been promulgated to ensure proper practice and procedure. Quite obviously, these rules of practice and procedure are also subject to the ouster clause in the Constitution. It has been made clear that the ouster clause would not apply, for example where there has been a breach of a fundamental right under the Constitution, or where a Commission has exercised a jurisdiction it does not have. There are no doubt others ... [P8] It inexorably follows then, that if one of the grounds, on which judicial review is sought, coincides with an alleged breach of a fundamental right, the Court will grant relief in judicial review proceedings and this would be so because the Ouster Clause in the Constitution would not apply. In the event there is a coincidence in one of the grounds for judicial review, and an alleged breach of a fundamental right then in those circumstances, it would be proper to proceed under the Constitution—where matters are viewed more broadly and in keeping with the supremacy of the Constitution.

In the Application of the Chief Immigration Officer – **Civil Appeal No 7 of 1994 (BVI)**
Floissac CJ

[P5] There is no doubt that the High Court has an inherent jurisdiction (either by way of judicial review or otherwise) to supervise and judicially control certain decisions and actions of public authorities constituted by law to make those decisions or to take those actions. Subject to the formalities prescribed by Rules of Court, the jurisdiction is exercisable whenever a public authority (purporting to exercise a constitutional, statutory or prerogative power) has made or taken or intends to make or take a justiciable judicial, quasi-judicial or administrative decision or action which affects or will affect a complainant who has *locus standi* by way of a relevant or sufficient interest in the decision or action and who alleges and proves that the decision or action is or will be illegal, irrational or procedurally improper. In such a case, the High Court may make such appropriate prerogative or other order as may be necessary to protect the complainant from the illegality, irrationality or procedural impropriety of the decision or action.

2.1 UNREASONABLENESS OF THE DECISION

One of the fundamental pillars of judicial review is that of the reasonableness of the decision-maker. This is often linked with the notion of irrationality.

In the Application of Gladys Gafoor – **HCA No 461 of 2003 (TT)**
Dean-Armorer J

[PP8–9] According to the evidence, Mr Anthony Ramjohn who replaced Mr Bahador notified the Registrar of his appointment on the 2nd of July, 2002. There could therefore be no doubt that the Registrar was fully aware that Mr Bahador had been replaced. Moreover, this was drawn to their attention by both the Applicant and her attorneys-at-law, who made repeated requests for her to be paid her allowance for the months in respect of which she had advanced payment to her chauffeur. In my view, the decision of the Registrar to withhold payment for these months and their obstinate refusal to make cheques to any one but Mr Bahador escapes my understanding and could only be described as ***Wednesbury*** unreasonable, such that no reasonable decision-maker could make.

In the Application of the Sawmillers Co-operative Society Ltd –
HCA No S426 of 2000 (TT)
Archie J

[P21] Whether it arises from an undertaking or from a contractual agreement, the breach of any such obligation by the Director of Forestry in the exercise of his statutory powers does not automatically render that exercise of his powers illegal ... Even if there had been such a breach, there is no evidence before the Court upon which it could conclude that the Director of Forestry has acted illegally.

In the Application of Societe Des Produits Nestle SA – **HCA No 436 of 1998 (TT)**
Archie J

[P18] There is, in the case of an application to extend the time for filing of evidence in opposition, no statutory right of appeal. If there is an unsuccessful appeal, the reason the tribunal or decision maker cannot reopen an inquiry would not be because there was no inherent power to do so, but because in the face of a decision by the appellate Court, it would amount to a collateral attack on a finding by which it was bound and by a Court against whose findings it had no jurisdiction to entertain an appeal . . . [PP22–23] As a matter of public policy, there is no reason why the primary tribunal should not be allowed in appropriate cases, such as when one side was not represented and had no opportunity to put its case, to reconsider an interlocutory decision where it is just to do so. As has been observed, it is a discretion which ought to be sparingly exercised but it nevertheless exists. The learned Deputy Registrar General has therefore mistakenly declined jurisdiction to entertain an application to rehear Nestle's application for extension of time. Due consideration of that application need not have extended to the requirement of an oral hearing. A refusal in the agreed circumstances would not necessarily have been unreasonable but it is the reason which she has given that cannot be supported.

***In the Application of Baldeo Goorie Singh* – HCA No Cv 3205 of 1992 (TT)**
Best J

[P6] So in the view of this Court, the Minister in exercising his discretion to add conditions to a grant of planning permission cannot impose conditions as he pleases. He can exercise his discretion and add conditions that are appropriate from a planning point of view as they reasonably relate to the permitted development . . . [P8] Further, I find that permission was granted by the Minister to develop lands subject to squatting but by the imposition of standard conditions as they relate to health, water, sewerage and safety standards in a market driven development in effect took away the substance of that permission. In the premises, I conclude that these conditions do not fairly and reasonably relate to a squatter regularization development and no reasonable Minister would have imposed such conditions on a developer, circumstanced as the Applicant.

***In the Application of Matthew Joseph, Asad Ali, Soogrim Bhaggan, Gunness Bhagewandeen, Rampersad Ragoo, Reeka Rampersad, Francis Gopaul, Clement Brizan, Radhay Kissoon, Jankinath Sookdeo, Ian Johnson, Seepersad Singh* – HCA No S–611 of 1988 (TT)**
Blackman J

[PP22–23] The only possible ground therefore, under the head of unreasonableness that could really be advanced by the Applicants for overturning the Minister's decision is that referred to by Lord Greene MR in *Associated Provincial Picture Houses Ltd v Wednesbury Corporation* [1948] 1 KB 223 at p 230 when he said: 'It is true to say that, if a decision on a competent matter is so unreasonable that no reasonable authority could ever have come to it, then the Courts can interfere. That, I think, is quite right, but to prove a case of that kind would require something overwhelming . . .' Lord Diplock in the *Council of Civil Service Unions and Others v Minister for the Civil Service* [1984] 3 All ER 935 at p 951 describes this ground in this way: 'By "irrationality" I mean what can now be succinctly referred to as *Wednesbury* unreasonableness (See *Associated Provincial Picture Houses Limited v Wednesbury Corporation* [1947] 2 All ER 880; [1940] 1 KB 223). It applies to a decision which is so outrageous in its defiance of logic or of accepted moral standards that no sensible person who had applied his mind to the question to be decided could have arrived at it' . . . [P24] Then it was submitted that the Minister in arriving at his decision in the case of the Applicants took irrelevant matters into account or failed to consider relevant matters. Now to establish this allegation, the Applicants must discharge the onus of showing what irrelevant matters were considered by the Minister, or what relevant matters he had failed to consider. In my view no such evidence was forthcoming. The Minister decided to remove the construction on the Highway put there by the Applicants either because they were structures thereon or because they were an impediment to the water course. My respectful view is that in so doing the Minister had properly interpreted the sections of the Act empowering him to do so.

***Belize Alliance of Conservation Non-Governmental Organizations* – Privy Council Appeal No 47 of 2003 (BZ) Lord Hoffman**

[PP18–19] The ground upon which the Appellants submit that they can satisfy this demanding requirement is that the DOE postponed consideration of matters which should have been contained in the EIA. But, as their Lordships have observed, that only raises the question of what should have been in the EIA. Both the Chief Justice and the Court of Appeal cited with approval the remarks of Cripps J in the Land and Environment Court of New South Wales in *Prineas v Forestry Commission of New South Wales* (1983) 49 LGRA 402, 417: 'I do not think the [statute] . . . imposes on a determining authority when preparing an environmental impact statement a standard of absolute perfection or a standard of compliance measured by no consideration other than whether it is possible in fact to carry out the investigation. I do not think the legislature directed determining authorities to ignore such matters as money, time, manpower etc. In my opinion, there must be imported into the statutory obligation a concept of reasonableness . . . [P]rovided an environmental impact statement is comprehensive in its treatment of the subject matter, objective in its approach and meets the requirement that it alerts the decision maker and members of the public . . . to the effect of the activity on the environment and the consequences to the community inherent in the carrying out or not carrying out of the activity, it meets the standards imposed by the Regulations. The fact that the environmental impact statement does not cover every topic and explore every avenue advocated by experts does not necessarily invalidate it or require a finding that it does not substantially comply with the statute and the Regulations.' Their Lordships also respectfully adopt these observations. It is not necessary that an EIA should pursue investigations to resolve every issue. This is not only common sense but contemplated by the terms of the Belize legislation itself. Thus Regulation 5(f) says that an EIA should include an indication of 'gaps in knowledge and uncertainty which may be encountered in computing the required information' and Regulation 19(b), prescribing the form of an EIA, says it should contain a summary which highlights the 'conclusions, areas of controversy and issues remaining to be resolved'.

While the courts will not ordinarily disturb findings of facts made by public bodies or by lower courts, this position is not without exceptions as the courts will intervene in specific circumstances to disturb findings of facts.

***In the Application of Oswald Wilson, Lance Murray, Raoul John and Mark Ramkerrysingh* – HCA No 2081 of 2002 (TT) Mendonca J**

[PP9–11] Many of the paragraphs were attacked by the Applicants on the basis of irrationality. Lord Diplock explains this ground in this way in *CCSU v Minister for the Civil Service* [1984] 3 All ER 935, 951: By 'irrationality' I mean what can now be succinctly referred to as 'Wednesbury unreasonableness' (see *Associated Provincial Picture Houses Ltd. v Wednesbury Corporation* [1947] 2 All ER 680, [1948] 1 KB 225). It applies to a decision which is so outrageous in its defiance of logic or accepted moral standards that no sensible person who has applied his mind to the question to be decided could have arrived at it. Whether a decision falls within this category is a question that Judges by their training and experience should be well equipped to answer . . . But the Court must always be careful not to substitute its own decision for that of the decision of the decision-maker if his decision is within the confines of reasonableness. In Wade on *Administrative Law* (8th edition) the authors there state (at page 365): But if the decision is within the confines of reasonableness, it is no part of the Court's function to look into its merits. 'With the question whether a particular policy is wise or foolish the Court is not concerned; it can only interfere if to pursue it is beyond the powers of the authority.' As Lord Hailsham LC has said, two reasonable persons can perfectly reasonably come to opposite conclusions on the same set of facts without forfeiting their title to be regarded as reasonable. The Court also does not act in judicial review proceedings as a Court of Appeal in reviewing factual conclusions of the body whose conclusions are being questioned. In *Mahon v Air New Zealand Ltd.* [1984] 3 WLR 884, 907 the Board stated: Throughout their consideration on this aspect of the inquiry into the Judge's findings . . . their Lordships have been at pains to remind themselves, as did the Court of Appeal, that in relation to findings of fact made by the Judge in his report they are not exercising the functions of an appellate Court in civil litigation where they would be entitled, while paying due deference to the advantages enjoyed by the trial Judge of seeing and hearing the witnesses give evidence in person, to make their own assessment of the weight of the evidence and to determine for themselves whether it is sufficient to justify the findings of fact that the trial Judge has made. As Courts whose functions in the instant case have been restricted to those of judicial review, both the Court of Appeal and this Board are disentitled to disturb findings of fact by the decision maker whose decision is the subject of review, unless (1) the procedure by which such findings were reached was unlawful (*in casu* by failure to observe the rule of *audi alteram partem*) or (2) primary facts were found that were not supported by any probative evidence or (3) the reasoning by which the decision-maker justified inferences of fact that he had drawn is self-contradictory or otherwise based upon an evident logical fallacy.

2.2 ERROR OF LAW

Error of law is one of the common grounds for judicial review. A public body may act outside of its jurisdiction due to a misapprehension of the legal basis of its action.

***In the Matter of Gulf Insurance Ltd* – Privy Council Appeal No 78 of 2002 (TT)**[1]
Lord Hoffmann

[P15] 47. In these circumstances, the Board did not hear submissions from Mr Brindle on whether the Court of Appeal were right in holding that the powers under section 44D were exercisable. The Board considers that even if they were, the transfer of the assets and undertaking of TCB was unlawful because the agreement did not provide for an independent valuation. Gulf is entitled to a declaration to that effect. It is not seeking a declaration that the transfer was null and void. It is now far too late to try to undo what happened that Sunday. But that does not make the original transfer lawful. Gulf are entitled to the declaration as a basis for such other remedies as they may be entitled to claim.

***In the Application of Sahadeo Maharaj* – HCA No S 50 of 2002 (TT)**
Mendonca J

[PP22–23] An authority cannot bind itself to act outside of its lawful functions. The duty on the part of the Ministry is to keep an accurate seniority list. The seniority of a teacher is important. A list with an incorrect date of appointment of a particular teacher may adversely affect not only that teacher but others on the list as well. That is so in this case. The date of appointment contended for by the Applicant will put him as senior to Mr

1 This decision of the Privy Council reversed a strong decision of the Court of Appeal of Trinidad and Tobago. *In the Application of Gulf Insurance Limited*—Civil Appeal No 32 of 2000 (TT), Nelson J: '[P28] In my judgment these submissions are based on a gross misreading of Section 44D(2) . . . [P38] I hold therefore that the transfer of the business of TCB to FCB was effected by the Manager under his powers pursuant to Section 44D(3)(c). The transfer of the business was *intra vires* the Act; it was not effected by the Central Bank pursuant to Section 44D(1)(vi). Consequentially the vesting order by the Minister at the request of the transferee, FCB, pursuant to Section 49 of the Financial Institutions Act 1993 was valid'.

Jones when it is clear on the evidence that that is not so. It can have repercussions throughout the teaching service. The duty to keep accurate seniority lists cannot be avoided or defeated by a mistake and if a mistake comes to light the authority is duty bound to correct it. Good public administration requires no less. If it were otherwise estoppel would operate to legitimize the keeping of inaccurate lists which would be in clear violation of the duty and adverse to the wider interest of the teaching service and the public.

Vinode Jhagroo – Privy Council Appeal No 35 of 2001 (TT)
Lord Walker of Gestingthorpe

[PP13–14] 34. Their Lordships consider that Mr Fitzgerald was right not to press the sham argument, and they derive little assistance from the Auckland case, which was concerned with the issue of unfair dismissal in a different statutory context. Their Lordships do see some force in the criticisms of the TSC's policy as described by Miss Roseman in her affidavit. But the policy is not clearly described and their Lordships are not willing to say that the policy must have involved an unlawful fettering of discretion. The rather sketchy evidential material is not a satisfactory foundation for a conclusion with such potentially far-reaching consequences and it is possible to dispose of this appeal on narrower grounds. 35. In his detailed review of the facts Mr Knox invited the Board to focus on the position at the end of 1994. During the latter part of 1994, he said, the Appellant did not have any letter of appointment and was not a member of the Teaching Service. Their Lordships agree that the most helpful approach is to look closely at the position at the end of the Appellant's time at Fyzabad ASS. But they cannot accept that the Appellant had by then ceased to be a member of the Teaching Service, or that his non-receipt of salary was evidence of anything other than administrative error. After 29th October 1994 the Appellant was on authorised sick leave, as Ms Duncan acknowledged in her affidavit. 36. The TSC's decision not to continue to employ the Appellant was taken, according to Ms Duncan, on 14th December 1994. The decision to issue a final standard-form letter of appointment (sent on 21st December 1994) must have been made on the same occasion, or as a consequential step. It was a flawed decision because although it was in form conferring on the Appellant the benefit of a fixed-term appointment, it was in substance part of a decision to terminate the Appellant's career in the Teaching Service. At the beginning of December 1994 the Appellant was a member of the Teaching Service, albeit absent on authorised sick leave. He was not holding an appointment for a fixed term. He was therefore holding office for an indeterminate period under Section 58 of the Act, as it was not open to the TSC, by a retrospective appointment letter, to deprive him of the protection of Section 62 of the Act.

***In the Application of D.S. Maharaj Furniture and Appliances Ltd* –**
HCA No S–1499 of 93 (TT)
Lucky J

[P8] It seems to me that the following grounds must be considered. Firstly, whether the Comptroller's decision was founded upon an erroneous proposition of law, and if so did he misconstrue the Regulations and misapply the relevant law—see *Anisminic Ltd. v Foreign Compensation Commission* [1969] 1 All ER 208. Secondly, did the Comptroller fail to comply with the rules of natural justice, was he fair to the Applicant? See *Ridge v Baldwin*. Thirdly, was the decision such, that no person or body properly directing itself on the relevant law, (the Customs Act and the Regulations made thereunder) and acting reasonably could have reached that decision (*Associated Provincial Picture Houses Limited v Wednesbury Corporation* [1947] 2 All ER 680)? The Court has to confine itself to the question of legality; which is whether the Comptroller, exceeded his power, committed an error of law, committed a breach of the rules of natural justice, reached a decision which no reasonable person or tribunal could have reached or abused his powers. Attorney for the Applicant, having referred to the Caricom Treaty, the Act, Regulations and case law argues that the Comptroller erred. Attorney for the Comptroller does not agree . . . [P11]

However, in the instant matter a Certificate of Origin has been produced. What therefore is the significance of the Certificate? I think the Certificate is subject to the Regulations which govern the actions of the Comptroller in arriving at his decision. Did he do anything wrong in arriving at his decision? I do not think so, he adhered to the law. He followed the principles applicable. He made an enquiry. He gave the Applicant an opportunity to explain. He communicated with the Exporter and the Comptroller in Grenada and then arrived at his decision. It seems to me that the principles enunciated in the *CCSU case* and *Anisminic* were followed and the *Wednesbury* principle was not violated.

***In the Application of Republic Bank Ltd* – HCA No 6921 of 1987 (TT)**
Deyalsingh J

[P11] The issue as I understand it could be put thus: is judicial review available where there is no error of law but only a possibility of one being made? Clearly review is available for error of law . . . [PP11–12] Prior to 1984, relief by way of judicial review was sought on a miscellany of grounds developed over the years. The remedy started with the prerogative writs but these as first designed, were very limited in scope. As Government expanded in scope and function, and as more and more power became vested in statutory tribunals and government officials, it became obvious that the prerogative writs were much too limited in scope to deal effectively with the wrongful use of governmental power. The Courts filled the need by gradually expanding the basis of review to include various grounds which had hitherto not been utilized because the occasion for their use had not yet arisen. The process of development was slow and sometimes confusing but shortly prior to 1984, with the tremendous increase in governmental activities into every sphere of life, the point was reached where the scope and extent of judicial review could be formulated very simply. This the House of Lords chose to do in *Council of Civil Service Unions v Minister of Civil Service* [1984] 3 All ER 935, a land-mark decision in the law of judicial review which made unnecessary the oftimes very difficult and artificial task of fitting a case into one of the several compartments that hitherto existed. The law is now that 'Administrative action is subject to judicial review under three heads: (1) illegality, where the decision making authority has been guilty of an error of law, e.g. by purporting to exercise a power it does not possess; (2) irrationality, where the decision making authority has acted so unreasonably that no reasonable authority would have made the decision; and (3) procedural impropriety, where the decision making authority has failed in its duty to act fairly.'

***In the Application of Sagram Bhagwandeen* – HCA No S–206 of 1996 (TT)**
Warner J

[P6] I conclude that on the evidence before me that the Magistrate did not properly direct himself on the law . . . [P7] I wish to emphasise however that I have found no bad faith, but the Applicant would be seriously prejudiced if the matter were to be allowed to continue.

***In the Application of the Institute of Jamaica* – Civil Appeal No 9 of 2002 (JM)**
Downer JA

[P30] The IDT was bound to follow the general law of the land together with the special provisions of the Act and the Code. It did not. It also behaved irrationally. It also did not grant the Institute a fair hearing before ordering reinstatement. The law on industrial relations is designed to strike a fair balance between the rights of the worker and the rights of the employer. The Institute's conduct in dismissing Mrs. Beecher was justifiable in law and practice.

***In the Application of Lorna Elaine Jackson, Merle O'Beron Palmer and Marva Elaine Phillips* – Civil Appeal Nos 52, 53 & 54 of 2001 (JM)**
Smith JA

[P13] It seems to me that on a true construction of these Regulations (54–59) the Board had no power to dismiss the teachers for the reason given. In issuing the letters to the teachers which purported to dismiss the teachers the Boards in my view were acting *ultra vires* ... [P16] In any event counsel on both sides are at one that in the circumstances of the purported termination of the Appellants' services the rules of natural justice must apply and the Appellants were entitled to a hearing before the determination ... [P19] In any event only the Board has the power to terminate the teachers' services and therefore the Board itself must give them the opportunity to be heard in compliance with the rules of natural justice. The unauthorized review process established by the Ministry cannot take the place of a 'hearing' conducted by the Board which made the decision. Indeed the Board cannot delegate its powers or duties to another body—*delegatus non potest delegare* ... It cannot therefore be seriously argued that by means of the review process the Appellants were afforded a 'hearing' by the Board in accordance with the principles of natural justice.

***In the Application of Health-Pro (Jamaica) Ltd* – Civil Appeal No 101 of 1998 (JM)**
Downer JA

[PP12–13] The Food and Drugs Act and the corresponding Regulations entrust the Ministry of Health with extensive regulatory powers to ensure that the public is protected against false or misleading advertisement for those items of food or drugs mentioned in the Act or Regulations. Further the Ministry has been provided with the necessary means to test the qualities of those drugs over which it has control. That it is empowered to censor advertisements is evidenced by the law previously cited in this judgment. The Ministry has restricted the advertisements in the interest of the health and welfare of the public. This is its legal duty. The Supreme Court has sanctioned restrictions on the advertisement of Pycnogenal and refused the issue of mandamus to compel the Ministry to permit the Appellant to advertise in its own discretion.

Langrin JA

[P20] The Minister in my judgment has correctly responded and notwithstanding the nomenclature which has been used in the licence granted to the Appellant it is in keeping with the application for the licence and consistent with the Statute. The licencee has the authority to import and sell the new drug Pycnogenol. I am in full agreement with the Full Court in a judgment written by Panton, J that the Minister has granted the Appellant a licence to import and to sell new drugs, but not to advertise and that the Minister acted in accordance with the provisions of the Statute and fulfilled his statutory duty.

***Regina v Commissioner of Police ex parte Leslie Harper* (1994) 31 JLR 34 (JM)**
Zacca CJ

[P38] Rule 4.3 does give the Commissioner of Police a discretion as to the time when an officer can be granted leave, but we are of the view that this discretion is limited to an application for leave by the officer or in consultation with the officer. This rule cannot therefore be invoked for the purpose for which the Commissioner of Police directed the Applicant to remain on leave. The rule is applicable only to the grant of vacation leave.

***Wesley Sampson v Air Jamaica Ltd* (1992) 29 JLR 225 (JM)**
Carey JA

[P226] Certiorari lies to quash error of law on the face of the record of inferior Courts and statutory tribunals, not quash awards of arbitrators. Error of law on the face of the award is referable rather to arbitration proceedings ... [P228] In my judgment the grounds filed constitute points of law or, to use the traditional language of certiorari, errors of law. In *Judicial Review of Administrative Action* by S.A. de Smith (3rd edition) at p 117 the learned writer pointed out: 'The concept of error of law includes the giving of reasons that are bad in law or (if there is a duty to give reasons) inconsistent, unintelligible or, it would seem, substantially inadequate. It includes also the application of a wrong legal test to the facts found, taking irrelevant considerations into account and failing to take relevant considerations into account.'

***R v Commissioner of Income Tax ex parte Donald Panton* (1990) 27 JLR 68 (JM)**
Panton J

[P74] In the instant situation it is common ground that the Applicant was not notified by the Commissioner of the need for him to make a return. As far as he is concerned he had already made a return and had paid his due. For there to have been a further assessment, the Commissioner would have firstly had to 'cause a notice to be served requiring him to make and deliver a return of his income.' So the Commissioner commenced the process of raising the additional assessments without serving the notice required by Section 70(1). She was thereby committing an error of law . . . However, I would observe that in committing these errors of law, the Commissioner has also proceeded in a manner which demonstrates procedural impropriety. She has not acted fairly in that she has raised additional assessments without giving the Applicant any notice, and has reopened matters which were final and conclusive.

***Regina v Racing Commission ex parte Clive Green* (1989) 26 JLR 83 (JM)**
Panton J

[PP89–90] In the instant case, there was therefore a clear error on the face of the record when the Tribunal said that there was an absolute duty on the trainer, from which duty and the subsequent penalty there is no means of escape.

Clarke J

[P92] As the Tribunal arrived at its findings on the basis that the Rule imposed an absolute obligation on the trainer there is an error of law appearing on the face of the record.

***R v The Industrial Disputes Tribunal ex parte Egbert A. Dawes* (1984) 21 JLR 49 (JM)**
Parnell J

[P58] It is my view that the award of the Tribunal cannot be upheld. In a well intentioned move to settle the dispute, the Tribunal erred in law with the result that a miscarriage of justice to a worker has occurred. For my part, I would order that certiorari should go and that Safety Supply Ltd. should pay the costs of the Applicant.

***R v Licensing Authority for the Western Area ex parte L.S. Panton, Ltd* (1970) 11 JLR 498 (JM)**
Parnell J

[P501] A discretion is given to the licensing authority after it has heard the merits of the application whether or not it should be granted having regard to any or all of the several matters which the licensing authority is required to consider. The authorities are all in agreement. If there is an error of law on the face of the record, or to put in another way, if there is a 'speaking order' which discloses an error of principle, there is good ground for an order of certiorari to bring up and quash the decision of the inferior tribunal. An inferior tribunal should be kept within its accredited authority. It cannot be allowed to disregard the law and Regulations under which it operates. If, as in this case, it is shown that the licensing authority has committed an error of law which error has deprived the Applicant of the hearing to which it is entitled, the Judges of the Supreme Court must intervene as we have done by granting an order to quash the decision based on the palpable error.

***In the Application of Cable and Wireless (Barbados) Ltd* – Supreme Court No 1970 of 2003 (BB)**
Kentish J

[PP23–24] First, however, I must consider another submission of Counsel for the Defendants relating to the interpretation of subsidiary legislation. In this regard Counsel contended that while subsidiary legislation must not be inconsistent with its enabling Act, such legislation need not be consistent with other statutes. Counsel argued that since the Procedural Rules have their origin in s 39 of the URA they cannot conflict with the provisions of the URA, but they may conflict with the provisions of the FTCA. In response to this submission and argument Counsel for the Applicant cited the case of *Reg v Secretary of State for Social Security, Ex Parte Joint Council for the Welfare of Immigrants* [1997] 1 WLR 275 at page 293 where Waite LJ stated: 'The principle is undisputed. Subsidiary legislation must not only be within the *vires* of the enabling statute but must also be so drawn as not to conflict with statutory rights already enacted by other primary legislation.' This submission of Counsel for the Defendants is therefore not correct in law ... [P36] The first principle is that as a subordinate legislative body the Commission cannot exceed its own statutory powers and limits. If it does so those powers may be held to be inconsistent with its enabling Act and invalid. On a proper construction of s 39(1)(a) of the URA it is purely a power given by Parliament to the Minister to make rules of procedure for the conduct of reviews, hearings of complaints and other proceedings before the Commission. It does not confer or impose any legal right or duty on the Commission to designate a sole Commissioner to preside over matters relating to utility Regulation. I am guided in this opinion by the distinction drawn by Sir Jack I.H. Jacobs QC between procedural law and substantive law in his well-known text *The Fabric of English Civil Justice* (1987) that there is:— 'a vital and essential dichotomy created between "substance" and "procedure" between substantive law, the function of which is to define, create, confer or impose legal rights and duties and procedural law, the function of which is to provide machinery, the manner or the means by which legal rights and duties may be enforced or recognized by the Courts of law or other recognized or properly constituted body.' ... [P37] Accordingly, to the extent that the Chairman purported to designate a member of the Commission to preside over the confidentiality hearing he acted outside the scope of the power given to it by s 39(1) of the URA ... [P46] The Commission, therefore, fell into error when it designated the second Defendant to preside over the confidentiality hearing as it ought properly to have been presided over by a panel of Commissioners.

***In the Application of McDonald Farms Ltd et al* – Civil Appeal No 1997 (BB)**
Williams CJ

[PP8–9] (2) Order 62 Rule 55, which was part of the rules of Court in accordance with which the jurisdiction was to be exercised and which gave to the Judge in Chambers a power to review the Registrar's taxations, was deliberately revoked. It is illogical to say that in spite of the deliberate revocation of the rule giving a Judge in Chambers the power to review, there is nevertheless an inherent power to do what the revoked rule had enabled to be done.

Failure to comply with the law will not always give rise to a successful action for judicial review. The courts will often examine the nature of the law in question and determine whether the requirements within that law are for absolute compliance or substantial compliance. A finding that substantial compliance is the requirement would often lead to an unsuccessful challenge of an administrative decision, even in the face of some established level of legislative non-compliance.

***In the Application of Reynold Makhan* – HCA No 562 of 2003 (TT)**
Narine J

[P19] The failure of the Magistrate to follow the procedure laid down in S. 23(2) of the Act is sufficient for the exercise of the Court's discretion to grant certiorari to quash the committal under S. 5(3)(c) of the Judicial Review Act No. 60 of 2000 . . . [P20] In the first place, the Respondent is not empowered or required at this stage to make any finding of fact at all. He is simply required to consider the whole of the evidence and decide whether a *prima facie* case has been made out. His function at this stage is Ministerial, not judicial. If he decides to commit the accused for trial, it is the jury which will make findings of fact in the case . . . [P28] In this case I have come to the conclusion that there has been a substantial error in the committal proceedings leading to manifest injustice and substantial adverse consequences for the Applicant. I therefore exercise my discretion to quash the committal made by the Respondent.

***In the Application of Corporal No 10089 Christopher Holder* –**
HCA No 2581 of 1993 (TT)
Bharath J

[P8] Where it is claimed in Judicial Review proceedings that failure to carry out procedural requirements vitiates the proceedings, it is necessary for the Court to consider (1) the scheme, object and the importance of any requirement; (2) whether it is strictly or substantially carried out; (3) the prejudice to the Applicant and whether it is such as to cause unfairness or breach of natural justice amounting to miscarriage of justice. If the Court finds that there was substantial compliance and the objectivity of the requirement was achieved and no or no substantial prejudice has occurred to the Applicant, then the Court would treat compliance as to purpose as mandatory and achieved and no strict compliance otherwise as directory or that the requirement is directory and non-compliance not fatal . . . [PP12–13] I have come to the conclusion that the giving of a warning notice was mandatory and that giving it under Regulation 84 achieved the same purpose as Regulation 81 as he was warned of the disorderly conduct in contemplation of disciplinary proceedings and consequently there is substantial compliance and no invalidity of the hearing and determination.

***In the Application of Vaughn Scott* – HCA No 6437 of 1986 (TT)**
Hamel-Smith J

[P5] There are some cases in which absolute compliance with Regulations is required, while in others 'substantial compliance' suffices. Here there has been substantial compliance with the Regulations. Those Regulations require the Commission to hear the Applicant before exercising its discretion to terminate his probation. It ensured that he was fully heard at all times. The Applicant could never say that he was ever given the impression that he was likely to be confirmed in the post or that, in the light of all the correspondence, he had been confirmed in the post, whether by inference or otherwise.

2.3 FAILURE TO COMPLY WITH MANDATORY DIRECTIONS

A controversial area of judicial review pertains to the meaning of words that *prima facie* appears mandatory but where the courts treat the interpretation of such words as directory. The mere mention of words such as 'shall' or 'must' is insufficient to clothe the affected provision with mandatory consequences giving rise to a successful judicial review application where the legislation was not accorded mandatory status.

In the Application of Dr Colin Furlonge – HCA No Cv 2098 of 2003 (TT)
Jamadar J

[P10] The Privy Council, in *Rajkumar v Lalla* PC Appeal No. 1 of 2001 (delivered on the 29th January, 2001), has stated unequivocally that the PSC Regulations 'set out a detailed code, for, amongst others, appointments in the prison service' (paragraph 10). The same is unquestionably true for all acting appointments (including those otherwise than as a prelude to a substantive appointment) governed by the Regulations under consideration . . . [P11] The PSC Regulations are thus intended to be in service of the aim of ensuring, with respect to acting appointments, that all such appointments are free from any political interference. In my opinion, this context creates a presumption that where these Regulations state that certain things 'shall' be done, the intention is for compliance. Moreover, an examination of the Regulations under consideration reveals that there is a carefully detailed scheme that has been prescribed by the legislature for the process of selection of officers for acting appointments. Such a scheme must be presumed to be purposeful. And, such a scheme was no doubt prescribed in order to (i) avoid both the mischief of political interference and arbitrariness; and (ii) ensure fairness and transparency/accountability in the selection process. To this extent these Regulations are mandatory, even if substantial compliance is sufficient . . . [P12] This 'focus on the consequences of non-compliance' (at page 236) resulted in Lord Woolf suggesting the following approach (at page 238): I suggest that the right approach is to regard the question of whether a requirement is directory or mandatory as only at most a first step. In the majority of cases there are other questions which have to be asked which are more likely to be of greater assistance than the application of the mandatory/directory test. The questions which are likely to arise are as follows. 1. Is the statutory requirement fulfilled if there has been substantial compliance with the requirement and, if so, has there been substantial compliance in the case in issue even though there has not been strict compliance? (The substantial compliance question.) 2. Is the non-compliance capable of being waived, and if so, has it, or can it and should it be waived in this particular case? (The discretionary question.) 3. If it is not capable of being waived or is not waived then what is the consequence of the non-compliance? (The consequences question.) Which questions arise will depend upon the facts of the case and the nature of the particular requirement. I agree with this approach of Lord Woolf and propose to apply it in this case . . . [P14] The consequences of Regulation 28 not being complied with (the consequence question) include: the likelihood of arbitrariness; an undermining of the appearance of independence and impartiality in appointments; the likelihood of irrational, discriminatory and extraneous considerations being determinative of the recommendations (including but not limited to political interference); a lack of transparency and accountability by the Respondent; and detriment and prejudice to officers passed over . . . [P15] In my opinion therefore, the provisions under consideration, which all operate together, are mandatory. Though substantial compliance with these Regulations may suffice, non-compliance with any one of them render the consequential recommendations by the Respondent and the appointments by the PSC, illegal and procedurally improper.

Matthews (Charles) v The State (2000) 60 WIR 390 (TT)
de la Bastide CJ

[P402] Turning to the argument based on the language of s 18, Courts no longer accept that it is possible, merely by looking at the language used by the legislature, to distinguish between mandatory (or imperative) provisions, the penalty for breach of which is nullification, and provisions that are merely directory, for breach of which the legislation is deemed to have intended a less drastic consequence. The fact of the matter is that most directions given by the legislature in statutes are in a form that is mandatory. It is now accepted that in order to determine what is the result of failure to comply with something prescribed by a statute, one has to look beyond the language and consider such matters as the consequences of the breach and the implications of nullification in the circumstances of the particular case. The modern approach is described in de Smith on *Judicial Review of Administrative Action* (4th Edn) p 142 in the following way: 'In assessing the importance of the provision, particular regard may be had to its significance as a protection of individual rights, the relative value that is normally attached to the rights that may be adversely affected by the decision and the importance of the procedural requirement in the overall administrative scheme established by the statute. Furthermore, much may depend upon the particular circumstances of the case in hand. Although "nullification is the natural and usual consequence of disobedience", breach of procedural or formal rules is likely to be treated as a mere irregularity if the departure from the terms of the Act is of a trivial nature, *or if no substantial prejudice has been suffered by those for whose benefit the requirements were introduced*, or if serious public inconvenience would be caused by holding them to be mandatory, or if the Court is for any reason disinclined to interfere with the act or decision that is impugned.' [emphasis supplied]. [P403] It is consistent with this approach that Courts should recognise, as the House of Lords did in *Neill* and Ibrahim J in *Latiff Ali*, that some breaches of the procedural rules for the conduct of preliminary inquiries are less grave than others. In our view, the degree of gravity may vary not only according to which rule is broken, but also according to the particular circumstances in which the breach occurs, so that different breaches of the same rule may produce different results, at least in the case of those rules which are not an essential part of due process. We consider that the requirement enshrined in s 18 is one of those, the consequences of a breach of which must be considered on a case-by-case basis.

***In the Application of Kenneth Lalla, Henley Wooding, Corinre Mohammed, Carlyle Walters, Sakal Seemungal (Members of the Public Service Commission)* – Civil Appeal No 128 of 1999 (TT)**
Sharma JA

[PP20–21] I have already indicated earlier in this judgment that it is not sufficient to chant the words 'mandatory', 'directory' or 'imperative' in order to determine the effect of a breach of a Regulation of one of the service commissions. In *Police Service Commission v Murray* (*supra*) I pointed out [at p 35 of the transcript] that one had to consider whether there was substantial compliance given the object of the Regulations.

***In the Application of the Public Service Commission Regulations Adopted by the Judicial and Legal Service Commission* – Civil Appeal No 76 of 1999 (TT)**
Warner JA

[PP8–9] In *Lewis Williams v Kenneth Lalla and Others* HCA 1713 of 1996 (unreported), the officer contended that a letter signed by the Director of Personnel Administration, informing him of misconduct came from an unauthorized source. The Court had regard to the importance of the provision that was disregarded, and held that it was not material. The Court of Appeal in *Lynette Maharaj v The Teaching Service Commission* CvA. 157 of 1994 (unreported) held that breach of a mandatory Regulation did not automatically mean that the decision arrived at was invalidated; that result would follow only if it resulted in a breach of natural justice. Recently, in CvA. 143 of 1994 *Police Service Commission v Rodwell Murray*, (unreported) Nelson J.A. in a detailed judgment reviewed the authorities and was of the view that it was more helpful to ask '***what was the provision designed to achieve,***' in that the Court may readily find reason for overlooking '***trivial or unimportant irregularities***'.

***In the Application of Charles Dougdeen* – HCA No 3063 of 1996 (TT)**
Persad Maharaj J

[P15] He submitted that the Magistrate, Mr Mohipp, was not served with the Notice of Motion and the other Judicial Review documents as filed by the Applicant. He said that the Applicant was duty bound so to do, as where certiorari is sought and the conduct of the Magistrate was challenged, then the rules must be obeyed. Paragraphs 18 and 19 appear to be objections to the conduct of Mr Mohipp. The rule stipulates that the motion 'must' be served. 'Shall' or 'may' are not used, so the decision in *St. Patrick County Council v Kubairsingh* 8 WIR at p 304, where the Rules of the Supreme Court Order 41 Rule 1 (TT) was held to be directory only, does not assist the Applicant. The word 'must' in the Oxford Dictionary carries the meaning—'be obliged to'. It appears to me that 'must' is used in Order 53 Rule 5(3) in its mandatory sense. I hold, therefore, that the Applicant was duty bound to serve the Magistrate with the Notice of Motion. As this was not done, the Applicant is not entitled to seek an order of certiorari.

In the Application of Cecil Singh – HCA No 1598 of 1993 (TT)
Bharath J

[PP5–6] The Respondent contends that Regulation 90(5) is directory or directory as to time, and consequently the late submissions of Ja[g]ram's report makes subsequent proceedings voidable and can only nullify them for prejudice shown. There is no dispute that Jagram's report was 4 months late but the question arises whether PSC Regulation 90(5) is mandatory or directory or directory as to time only. In deciding this question I have to examine the object and intent of the PSC Regulations . . . [PP6–7] I am of the view that Regulation 90(5) of the Public Service Commission Regulations was imperative and that the intention of the legislature was not to subject the working officer to delay and cause harm in having an adverse report hanging over his head. I am accordingly of the view that PSC Regulation 90(5) is mandatory and that non-compliance renders subsequent proceedings void . . . [PP7–8] As I have already decided PSC Regulation 90(5) is mandatory especially as to time and as said by Lord Penzance in the *Bodington Case* delay is harmful or prejudicial to the worker while a report is hanging over his head. I do not consider that the Regulation is for the benefit of the Commission but seeks to effect a timely investigation to avoid harm to the worker. I therefore conclude that the charges laid by the Public Service Commission and the subsequent hearing by the Tribunal are void and a nullity and I will quash the charge and the complaints made against the Applicant as well as the Tribunal's ruling made against the Applicant.

In The Application of Joseph Honore – HCA No 389 of 1992 (TT)
Jones J

[P5] By the Police Service Commission (Delegation of Powers) Order, the power to transfer police officers is vested in the Commissioner of Police. The valid exercise of this power requires a genuine application of the mind and a conscious choice by the proper authority, the Commissioner of Police. It follows in the circumstances that any document purporting to manifest the exercise of the power must on its face leave no doubt that the power was properly exercised. An examination of the document shows that it is headed 'Police Orders by Mr J. Bernard, Commissioner of Police'. It is signed by the Deputy Commissioner of Police on behalf of the Commissioner of Police . . . I find great difficulty therefore in accepting the submission of Attorney for the Applicant that on the face of Order No. 9 the transfer of the Applicant was effected by the Deputy Commissioner of Police . . . [P6] These are procedural matters and the Regulation in my view is directory only and not mandatory and the signature by the Deputy Commissioner of Police was at its highest an irregularity not affecting the validity of what had been properly done by the Commissioner of Police.

In the Application of the Mayor, Alderman and Burgesses of Point Fortin – HCA No 342 of 1988 (TT)
Hamel-Smith J

[PP34–35] I do not think that I could come to the conclusion that Mrs. Roseman pretended to exercise the Chairman's powers under the act. There would, therefore, be a presumption of regularity unless otherwise shown . . . [PP40–41] When Parliament prescribes the manner and form in which a duty is to be performed or a power exercised, it seldom lays down what will be the legal consequences of failure to observe its prescriptions. According to de Smith's *Judicial Review of Administrative Action* 4th Ed. 142, the Courts must formulate their own criteria for determining whether the procedural rules are to be regarded as mandatory, in which case disobedience will render void or voidable what has been done, or, as directory, in which case disobedience will be treated as an irregularity not affecting the validity of what has been done. This has never been an easy task and there are no exact rules for the assignment of a procedural provision to the appropriate category. The whole scope and purpose of the enactment must be considered, and one must assess 'the importance of the provision that has been disregarded, and the relation of that provision to the general object intended to be secured by the Act' (de Smith's). In doing so, particular regard may be had to its significance as a protection of individual rights, the relative value that is normally attached to the rights that may be adversely affected by the decision and the importance of the procedural requirement in the overall administrative scheme established by the statute. Much may depend on the particular circumstances of the case in hand. Although 'nullification' is the natural and usual consequence of disobedience, breach of procedural or formal rules is likely to be treated as a mere irregularity if the departure from the terms of the Act is of a trivial nature, or if no substantial prejudice has been suffered by those for whose benefit the requirements were introduced, or if serious public inconvenience would be caused by holding them to be mandatory, or if the Court is, for any reason, disinclined to interfere with the act or decision that is impugned. The practical effects of the exercise of a power upon the rights of individuals will often determine whether the relevant formal and procedural rules are to be classified interpretation as mandatory or directory. But in this area of statutory interpretation 'where guide-lines are so indistinct and the precedents often readily distinguishable, one's personal view of the merits of the case may well determine the method of approach' (de Smith's) . . . [P42] In coming to this conclusion I have had to ask—what prejudice did the Mayor or the Corporation for that matter, suffer as a result of the failure of the SASC to formally appoint Mr Ramdath or to issue an order of transfer in writing, and what was the importance of the procedural requirement the overall administrative scheme established by the statute? In answer to the first question, I find that no prejudice has been suffered.

***In the Application of Ronald Narine* – HCA No 1273 of 1984 (TT)**
Davis J

[P9] Now, in my view, a series of written complaints cannot be considered to be a full report; certainly not a full report as contemplated by Regulation 54. The term 'full report' is not defined in the Regulations. It must, therefore, be given its plain ordinary meaning, and that to my mind connotes a report in which, not only the officer's weaknesses are dealt with, but his strengths. In other words, his good and bad points must form the subject matter of such a report. Of course, if the officer has no good points the Permanent Secretary is entitled to say so . . . Is this breach fatal to the Commission's decision? I think so. The requirement that the Commission call for and consider a full report on the officer, seems to me to be a fundamental requirement of Regulation 54. The observations or recommendations contained in such a full report might well tip the balance one way or the other. This opportunity was denied the Applicant in this case.

***R v Office of Utilities Regulation ex parte World Telenet International Ltd* –**
Supreme Court No M81 of 2000 (JM)
Clarke J

[PP14–15] Undoubtedly, statutory words requiring things to be done as a condition of making a decision especially when the form of words requires that something 'shall' be done, raise an inference that the requirement is mandatory and therefore that failure to do the required act(s) renders the decision unlawful: see De Smith, Woolf and Howell, *Judicial Review of Administrative Action*, Fifth Edition at t–058 where the law is in my opinion correctly stated . . . [P15] Its purpose must be considered and an assessment made of the importance of the provisions in question, due regard being given to their significance as a protection of individual rights where applicable ... [P22] As has been demonstrated in this judgment the stance taken by the Applicants' legal representatives was untenable. They were wrong in law when they in effect advised the Applicants to withdraw from the meeting. The absence of a hearing was not due to any fault on the part of the Office. Rather, because of the fault of their legal representatives to whom they had entrusted the conduct of their case, the Applicants were deprived of the opportunity to be heard. They cannot now complain (unless their final arguments before me concerning bias and inadequate disclosure have merit) that they are the victims of procedural impropriety or that natural justice has been denied to them.

***In the Application of Veron Simpson* – Civil Appeal No 28 of 1999 (JM)**
Downer JA

[P11] To my mind, there was a derogation from the mandatory requirement stipulated in sec. 23(2) of the Act: more particularly, to state in the enforcement notice the period within which to take steps to demolish the extension of the building for which permission had not been granted.

***R v Resident Magistrate for St. James ex parte Michael Troupe, R v The Resident Magistrate for St. James ex parte Gladstone Jemmison* (1992) 29 JLR 29 (JM)**
Zacca CJ

[P31] The Recognizances and Sureties of the Peace Act sets out the specific procedure to be followed for the entering into recognizances and the manner in which they are enforceable in the event of default. We are of the view that these provisions which are penal in nature, should be strictly followed ... It is only in default of payment after the warrant has been issued and executed, that the resident Magistrate has the power to imprison the person making the default. It is to be noted that there is no provision for the sentence of imprisonment to be at hard labour ...

***R v Licensing Authority and Benchur Gordon & Anor ex parte Sun Enterprises Ltd* (1982) 19 JLR 206 (JM)**
Bingham J

[P209] When this section is examined it is beyond question that it is mandatory as to its terms. A failure to fulfill any of the requirements as laid down by the Act therefore renders any decision made by the Authority bad as to its validity. The Licensing Authority having owed its origin to an Act of Parliament can only act within the ambit of the powers given to it by Act.

***Re Charles Nathaniel Josephs* (1967) 10 JLR 180 (JM)**
Graham-Perkins J

[P185] The general principles to be applied in resolving the question whether the provisions of statute are to be regarded as mandatory or merely directory are rather conveniently stated at p 376 of Maxwell on the *Interpretation of Statutes* (10th edn.). 'It has been said that no rule can be laid down for determining whether the command is to be considered as a mere direction or instruction involving no invalidating consequence in its disregard, or as imperative, with an implied nullification for disobedience, beyond the fundamental one that it depends on the scope and object of the enactment ... A strong line of distinction may be drawn between cases where the prescriptions of the Act effect the performance of a duty and where they relate to a privilege or a power. Where powers, rights or immunities are granted with a direction that certain Regulations, formalities or conditions shall be complied with, it seems neither unjust nor inconvenient to exact a rigorous observance of them as essential to the acquisition of the right or authority conferred'. See also *Cullimore v Lyme Regis Corp* (6). The mandatory prescription contained in the closing paragraph of s. 55(2) by which the Licensing Authority is required to consider any representations which may be made by persons such as the Applicant could hardly be said to have any relevance or importance if it were possible to deny such persons the opportunity to make representations in protection of their quite obviously important interests by the device of notices eminently calculated to deceive. Such a device must inevitably operate to defeat the almost sacrosanct objects that s. 55(2) seeks to achieve.

In the Application of Errol E. Niles (2) – **Civil Appeal 2003 (BB)**
Simmons CJ

[P12] When a mandatory procedure is set out in an Act of Parliament, it must be followed and, even though the procedure may represent an elaborate code, it is still the function of the Courts to determine whether there has been compliance with the statutory procedure.

2.4 MAKING OF POLICIES

In making policies, it is important for a public body to ensure that the policies comply with all applicable laws.

In the Application of Chandresh Sharma – **HCA No S–1445 of 2004 (TT)**
Narine J

[PP13–14] It seems to me that the primary function of the Commission is to receive and examine declarations and statements regarding the financial affairs of persons in public life, and to take follow-up action where necessary, by way of enquiry or prosecution. This is the very raison d'etre of the Commission. To make a decision not to require persons to file declarations on the misapprehension that a new form was required, is unreasonable, and in direct contradiction of the very purpose for which the Commission was set up. The unreasonableness of the decision is patent when one considers the vital role the institution plays in the context of the politics of Trinidad and Tobago, where the issue of corruption occupies center stage. In such a context, the Commission must be seen to be politically neutral and independent. It must not appear to be making decisions which favour or are convenient to any particular party. In the case at hand, the income year for which the purported exemption was granted was a year in which there was a change of government and persons would have entered public life for the first time. It is important in these circumstances for the Commission to carry out the Constitutional functions for which it was created. The Commission in fact derives its existence from the Constitution itself. Section 138(1) of the Constitution creates the Commission. Section 138(2) charges the Commission with the duty of receiving declarations in writing of the financial affairs of persons in public life, the supervision of and monitoring of standards of ethical conduct prescribed by Parliament to be observed by such persons, and the monitoring and investigating of conduct, practices and procedures which are dishonest or corrupt. Section 139 of the Constitution expressly empowers Parliament to make provision for such matters as the procedure of the Commission, conferring powers on the Commission as are necessary to enable the Commission to carry out its functions effectively and generally to give effect to Section 138.

In the Application of Jusamco Pavers Ltd – **HCA No 1413 of 1999 (TT)**
Mendonca J

[P19] The price specification in stating that tenders containing a bid price below a certain sum will not be considered clearly expresses the position that the Respondent will not consider tenders of that nature. It falls into the category of cases referred to by Bankes LJ in the passage quoted above where the authority has passed a rule or adopted a policy that it will not hear applications at all . . . [P20] Such a policy is over-rigid with the result that the Respondent can fail to consider or to give its mind to tenders so as to give effect to its statutory obligation to accept the lowest price save for good reason ... The Respondent must be prepared to consider tenders even containing a bid price falling below what it considers to be a realistic price. That tenderer may be quite capable of achieving that price. Even if that is an exceptional case the policy must be sufficiently flexible to consider that case so as to give effect to the statutory policy to obtain the lowest price save for good reason. In my judgment the criteria dealing with the plant capacity is open to the same criticism. It also states that any plant with a capacity equal to or less than 1000 tonnes would not be considered. The application of [these] criteria can result in the Respondent failing to give effect to the statutory policy.

In the Application of Cecil Santana – HCA No S–1409 of 1991 (TT)
Brooks J

[P15] It follows therefore that any policy made, created or adopted by the Commissioner of Police or by the Commission with respect to the discipline of police officers must be in conformity with or must comply with Sections 123, 127 and 129 of the Constitution, and the Regulations made thereunder (i.e. under the Constitution). It must not be repugnant to the Constitution, or to the Regulations.

In the Application of Clyde Dipnarine – HCA No 3494 of 1991 (TT)
Wills J

[PP16–17] This case is a matter which is exclusively with the power of the Respondent to exercise its own decision within the context of the Regulations made pursuant to the statutory powers conferred upon the Respondent. And it is my opinion that when a Court is called upon to construe statutory powers which are expressed in language that [is] capable of more than one interpretations the Court is entitled to have recourse to common law presumptions of legislative intent. These presumptions include *inter alia* a presumption against the infliction of substantial detriment on individuals without giving notice and an opportunity to make representation ... Furthermore, in my view, it is not open to the Respondent by virtue of the powers conferred upon it to fetter itself by its own rules to unreasonably prejudice others to whom the rules apply. In *Halsbury's Laws of England* Volume 1, paragraph 33, 4th ed. under the rubric: 'Fettering discretion by own rules' the author states: 'A public body endowed with a statutory discretion may legitimately adopt general rules or principles of policy to guide itself as to the manner of exercising its own discretion in individual cases, provided that such rules or principles are legally relevant to the exercise of its powers consistent with the purpose of the enabling legislation and are not arbitrary or capricious. Nevertheless, it must not disable itself from exercising a genuine discretion in a particular case directly involving individual interests: hence *it must be prepared to consider making an exception to the general rule if the circumstances of the case warrant special treatment*.' Without more, this statement of law could be applied, in my opinion, to the present case. In this case there can be no doubt that there has been a failure to exercise properly its discretion by the Respondent. In this regard I would like to adopt the views of the author of de Smith's *Judicial Review of Administrative Action* Fourth Edition page 320, i.e.—'Partial or total failure to exercise a discretion may occur because the competent authority has failed to appreciate the amplitude of its discretion. In one case an authority had discretionary power to grant pension to its officers at amounts up to two-thirds of their retiring salaries; misconstruing the scope of its powers under the statute, it thought it had no discretion as to the amount, and for this reason it refused to award any pension at all to an officer who in its opinion did not deserve the full amount. Its error of law had caused it to refuse to exercise part of the discretion conferred upon it and the officer obtained mandamus to order the authority to consider and determine his claim (*R v St. Pancras Vestry* [1890] 24 QBD 371). And in another case (*R v Home Secretary, Ex Parte Mehta* [1975] 1 WLR 1087) a tribunal held that its discretion to entertain "in special circumstances" an appeal lodged out of time, extended only to circumstances that prevented the Appellant from instituting proceedings within the normal time limit. But the Court held that this was too narrow a view and that the Tribunal should have had regard to the merits of the Appellant's case and to the fact that the delay was caused by a misunderstanding on the part of her solicitor.' In the light of the above I also find that the Respondent has failed to appreciate the amplitude of its discretion. And it did not act reasonably nor did it, in my view, act in good faith when it refused to consider what can be regarded as a reasonable request of the Applicant.

***In the Application of Industrial Sawmilling and Pallet Manufacturing Ltd* – HCA No 4336 of 1987 (TT)**
Blackman J

[PP28–29] The steps taken by the Parliamentary Secretary, Forestry Division were not authorized by the Regulations. If the Forestry Division wishes to introduce the system proposed in KM 22, Regulations would have to be made amending the Rules. None were so made. I am not now questioning the motives of the Parliamentary Secretary. They are I am sure based upon his desire to act in the public interest. But in so doing he cannot override the law. If the Parliamentary Secretary or the Forestry Division acted in a manner for example in formulating a policy which is contrary to or does not fall within the Regulations made by the President under Section 4 of the Act, their acts would be null and void. Similarly if the policy given in KM 22 cuts into the area of management, administration or protection of State Lands, then it will have run foul of Section 4 and if the interests of the company have been prejudiced thereby it will be to that extent null and void because it is only the President who can do so by Regulations and the President has already been deemed to have made those Regulations under the Act. It would seem to me and I so hold that the instructions given by the Parliamentary Secretary that the company should be stopped from harvesting pine in the brickfield and Cap-de-ville coupes and the policy stated in KM 22, encroaches on the Rules and matters specified in Section 4 of the Act and is null and void for that reason. In my view the policy in KM 22 will have to be embodied in appropriate Regulations. Therefore the proper course would have been to amend the existing law to accommodate it. Neither the Parliamentary Secretary nor the Cabinet could change the law merely by proposing a policy. The Parliamentary Secretary does not under the State Lands Forest Rules have the power to freeze the sale of timber to anyone who has already been sold such timber by the C.F. or to whom the C.F. had granted a licence or concession to harvest timber. Rules were made by the President for the management, administration and protection of State Lands. The power to grant licences or concessions in respect of timber on State Lands is given to the C.F. Neither the Minister nor the Parliamentary Secretary could arrogate to themselves powers not given them under the Rules in these circumstances. I think it was wrong for the Ministry to deal with the matter in the way it did ... [P29] The next question is whether the company should be refused the reliefs it has claimed on the ground of delay in seeking redress.

***Regina v The Resident Magistrate and Coroner for the Parish of Clarendon ex parte Maung Maung* – SPJ No M–42 of 1997 (JM)**
Smith J

[P3] We are of the view that he was fortunate in the circumstances to have obtained leave at the time he did, to come to this Court bearing in mind the provisions of S. 564C of CPC. However, having come to the conclusion that the Inquisition is defective in substance, we would not wish to see the Applicant further burdened with the task of presenting the same arguments again before another Court of equal jurisdiction. Accordingly, we are of the view that the proper thing to do is to exercise our discretion and quash the Inquisition at this stage.

2.5 THE DECISION-MAKER MUST MAKE AN INDEPENDENT DECISION

A decision-maker must come to a decision that is independent and based on the facts before it.

In the Application of Jules Bernard – **Civil Appeal No 13 of 1993 (TT)**
Ibrahim JA

[P4] This Regulation clearly requires the Commission to make its own independent judgment on the facts before it and to come to its own conclusion as to whether the Applicant ought to be called upon to retire. If the Commission relied on the opinion and recommendations of the Permanent Secretary and did not itself evaluate the material then it has acted contrary to the provisions of the law.

Jamaica Association of Local Government Offices and National Workers Union v The Attorney-General **(1995) 32 JLR 49 (JM)**
Cooke J

[P53] The Tribunal is not a rubber stamp of the government . . . [P54] Now, if there is a stated policy by the Government—and I doubt it is so in this case—the Tribunal would be obliged to give any such policy due consideration being always mindful that 'the Cabinet shall be the principal instrument of policy and shall be charged with the general direction and control of the Government of Jamaica.' The Government submissions may be so well founded as to make the acceptance of them irresistible. However, the Tribunal can only come to that conclusion after consideration of the merits of the submissions made before it. When the Tribunal found that 'Cabinet's final approval constitutes a policy decision which . . . is not subject to modification by the Tribunal' it erred in law . . . The Tribunal abandoned its role as designated to it by law. If the Tribunal was so bound as it said, what was the purpose of the eight sittings that were held? What would be the purpose of the Tribunal? Accordingly, the award of the Tribunal cannot be regarded as 'final and conclusive' there being an error in law.

2.6 IMPROPER DELEGATION OF AUTHORITY

A decision-maker cannot delegate his authority to another but is not precluded from seeking the views of another party once there is no distinct relinquishment of authority or evidence that the decision-maker has allowed his discretion to be dictated by his advisor.

In the Application of Devant Maharaj – **HCA No 305 of 2004 (TT)**
Dean-Armorer J

[PP12–13] 6. The SASC is indeed empowered to regulate its own procedure and under the Statutory Authorities Regulations, the SASC is also empowered to consult anyone who appears to be proper or desirable. 7. In the event that the Honorable Prime Minister had been consulted pursuant to Regulation 8, fairness would have required that the Applicant be apprised of the reasons for his proposed rejection and be allowed to make representations against it. 8. This however was not the reason proffered by the Commission, which indicated that they wished to bring the statutory authorities in line with the other Commissions. Their deponent Ms. Renaud has referred to a procedural measure of consultation. In my view, however, mere consultation would have allowed the SASC the liberty to seek reasons, to disagree and arrive at a decision divergent from the advice given. 9. It is clear however from the facts of this case that the SASC, having received the objection of the Prime Minister felt constrained to depart from their original selection.

The so-called procedure was in reality an adoption by the SASC of a self-imposed fetter on their own jurisdiction by conferring on the Prime Minister an unsolicited power of veto. If this is to be achieved it must be accomplished by a statutory amendment. In the absence of clear statutory authority the rejection of an officer on the simple lack of approval by the Prime Minister would amount to the abdication of authority to an unauthorized person and therefore contrary to law . . . [P13] 11. The decision is also flawed under s 5(3)(i), in that it conflicts with the policy of the Statutory Authorities Act. By s 5(1), the Act invests the SASC with power to appoint, transfer, promote and remove and exercise disciplinary control over officers of statutory authorities. In so doing, the Act gives effect to the underlying policy adumbrated in *Thomas v AG* by Lord Diplock, that is to say to insulate the officers of the statutory authorities from the direct influence of the government of the day. A specific constitutional exception is made to this policy in respect of the Public Service Commission. No parallel statutory exception exists in respect of the SASC. Any adoption therefore of a procedure which will compromise the statutory insulation and expose the officer to the direct influence of the Government of the day would be contrary to the policy of the Act and therefore reviewable.

***In the Application of Sabita Jagessar, Hazra Ramjohn, Nirmala Lokhai* – HCA No S 2053 of 2002 (TT)**
Dean-Armorer J

[P47] In the instant case, the power of the Regional Corporation to maintain State buildings is regulated by a statutory provision namely s 232(h) of the Act. The power to maintain includes the power to provide security and to prevent invasions by trespassers. I therefore hold that the Minister of Labour was not invested with the requisite power to direct Mr Dabideen from acting as he did. It is therefore my judgment and I so hold that the Corporation and by extension, its Chairman had authority neither to evict the Applicants nor to permit other persons to enter into occupation.

***In the Application of Warnerville Grain Mills Ltd* – HCA No 772 of 1994 (TT)**
Sealey J

[P9] Attorney for the Applicant concedes that there is nothing wrong with the procedure whereby a person's recommendations are sought prior to the exercise of a statutory discretion. There is nothing *ultra vires* in the Minister of Trade seeking input from the Comptroller of Customs, who is someone in his own Ministry . . . [P11] It is clear that not all reference to another body is delegation in the true sense of the word. Delegation cannot be achieved other than by some distinct act: see Wade on *Administrative Law* 6th edition p 367. Additionally, one Minister cannot delegate his discretion to another.

2.7 ABDICATION OF FUNCTIONS

A public body entrusted with the responsibility to make a decision must so do and even where the decision on the surface is that of the decision maker, the court will review the decision to ensure that the decision maker was, in fact and law, the actual decision maker and arrived at its decision independently. This, however, is not to say that a decision maker cannot obtain advice from third parties.

***In the Application of Fishermen and Friends of the Sea* – HCA Cv 2148 of 2003 (TT)**
Stollmeyer J

[P45] It is well settled that a public body should 'own' its functions and decisions, and not surrender them by acting under dictation, improper delegation or by operating an inflexible policy (see Fordham, *Judicial Review Handbook*, 3rd Ed. page 741). This does not mean, however, that a public body cannot seek and act on expert advice from independent bodies. In the course of arriving at a reasoned and reasonable decision, public bodies have a right to obtain and give great weight to the advice of expert bodies on technical matters. This is not considered an abdication of duty so long as the decision is not treated as conclusively determined by the expert bodies (see *R v Tandridge District Council, Ex Parte Al Fayed* [1999] 1 PLR 104, 110 D–F).

***In the Application of Charles Vernon Frederick, Mookish Pulliah Shamshudeen Mohammed, Adrian Pascal, Wilbert Lovell and Kundan Nancoo* – HCA No S 111 of 2003 (TT)**
Dean-Armorer J

[PP9–10] It has been admitted on the evidence of the Respondent in this matter, that the Public Service Commission acted on the list which had been submitted by the Assistant Commissioner of Prisons rather than that which had been earlier submitted by the Commissioner of Prisons. This was clearly in contravention of the Regulation 168(2), which does not empower the Public Service Commission to act on the unsolicited recommendation of the Assistant Commissioner of Prisons. The Public Service Commission ought properly to have disregarded those later illicit recommendations and ought to have had recourse to the recommendations of the Commissioner of Prisons. Accordingly, this Court is drawn to the inescapable conclusion that the Public Service Commission acted illegally in its decision to make promotions on the basis of the list of the Assistant Commissioner of Prisons and that the Applicants are entitled to the declaration sought at paragraph (e).

***In the Application of Jusamco Pavers Ltd* – HCA No 1413 of 1999 (TT)**
Mendonca J

[P13] The result is that the Respondent in permitting a representative of the Ministry of Works and Transport to draw the Evaluation Specifications used in the evaluation of tenders did not give any consideration to the criteria to be used in making awards on the basis of the tenders received by it. It seems to me that the Respondent should have established the criteria with due regard to the provisions of the Ordinance as part of its functions to consider tenders. In my judgment the Respondent took an incorrect view of the law and in so doing abdicated its function.

***In the Application of the Chairman, Alderman, Councillors and Electors of the Region of Tunapuna/Piarco Regional Corp.* – HCA No 1066 of 1999 (TT)**
Bereaux J

[P32] An illegal direction by a Minister of Government can provide no legitimacy to the actions of a public officer who carries it into effect. In this case, there was a clear usurpation of the powers of the Council by both the Minister and the Respondent.

***In the Application of Jules Bernard* – Civil Appeal No 13 of 1993 (TT)**
Ibrahim JA

[P4] This Regulation clearly requires the Commission to make its own independent judgment on the facts before it and to come to its own conclusion as to whether the Applicant ought to be called upon to retire. If the Commission relied on the opinion and recommendations of the Permanent Secretary and did not itself evaluate the material then it has acted contrary to the provisions of the law.

***R v The Air Transport Licensing Board ex parte Tropical Airlines Ltd* (1996) 33 JLR 278 (JM)**
Langrin J

[P284] The next question which arises in this application concerns the question of whether the decision maker exercised its discretion under the dictation of another body or person. In answering this question it would be enough to show that a decision which ought to have been based on the exercise of independent judgment was dictated by those not entrusted with the power to decide . . . It is therefore wholly erroneous for the Applicant to submit that the Minister dictates to the Board the very decision which the Board made. Indeed there is not one scintilla of evidence to show that the Board acted as a result of any dictation of the Minister . . . [P285] The evidence before the Court clearly establishes that the Applicant was aware of the Heads of Agreement between the Government and Air Jamaica Express as indicated in the 'Notice of Objections' field before the Board. The Applicant had every opportunity to argue its objection before the Board but ironically was instrumental in having the objections removed from the Board's consideration. The Applicant must be taken to have waived his right to so argue the very question which gave rise to the objection.

***Noel Williams v The Attorney-General* (1995) 32 JLR 79 (JM)**
Malcolm JA

[P80] At the hearing of the action in the Resident Magistrate's Court, the Learned Resident Magistrate took the preliminary view that since an action was filed in the Supreme Court she would not hear the matter until the outcome of that action . . . [P81] There is adequate authority for the proposition that adjourning or postponing a matter before a public authority in the manner in which this was done by the Learned Resident Magistrate is tantamount to a refusal to decide the issue.

***In the Application of the Chief Immigration Officer* – Civil Appeal No 7 of 1994 (BVI)**
Liverpool JA

[PP17–18] It is an undoubted rule of Administrative Law that where a person or authority has been entrusted with a discretion, he or it must not in the purported exercise of that discretion act under the dictation of another body or person; and that in order to impeach the manner of the exercise of the discretion, it is enough to show that the decision which ought to have been based on the exercise of independent judgment was dictated by those not entrusted with the power to decide.

2.8 FETTERING DISCRETION

A public body or person may be endowed with a discretion to act but the courts will seldom interpret such a discretion as being unfettered and immune from judicial scrutiny.

***In the Application of the Sawmillers Co-operative Society Ltd* –**
HCA No S426 of 2000 (TT)
Archie J

[P7] It is that a public authority or person exercising a statutory power cannot by contract or undertaking improperly fetter its/his discretionary powers granted by the enabling statute. An alternative formulation of the principle is that the State or a Public Authority may lawfully depart from the terms of a valid contract or undertaking in order to exercise its overriding discretionary powers in the Public interest . . . [P12] That case illustrates the real issue, which is the balance that must be struck between two competing public policy considerations. The first is that parties who enter freely into a contract should not be allowed to resile from their obligations under a contract merely because it is convenient to do so. The second is that where a person or body is entrusted with a power to be exercised, not for their benefit, but for the benefit of the public as a whole then they must be free to do so and should be influenced only by considerations of what is for the public good . . . [PP14–15] It is apparent, therefore, that even if circumstances exist where as between private persons an aggrieved party would have enjoyed a remedy by way of damages or an injunction for breach of contract or breach of representation it does not automatically follow that a *public law* remedy will be granted. To the extent that the authorities reveal an underlying doctrine of general application to public authorities it may be summarized in the following propositions:

(i) A person or body exercising a statutory discretion in the public interest may validly contract or give an undertaking which has the effect of limiting the future exercise of its discretion;

(ii) Any such limitation whether expressed or implied can be lawful only to the extent that it is not incompatible with the statutory decision maker's public duty and will be construed as not restricting those actions genuinely and reasonably taken in pursuit of that public duty;

(iii) If the purported exercise of a statutory power breaches the terms of a valid contract then the Courts may grant relief by way of judicial review and declare such an exercise of power illegal if satisfied that it amounts to an abuse;

(iv) The exercise of a statutory power in breach of a valid contract or undertaking for an improper motive, or in the absence of an overriding public interest, or for considerations or objectives not contemplated by the statute will amount to an abuse;

(v) The illegality does not arise because the person or body acts outside the ambit of its statutory power for the *extent of the power* is not circumscribed by contract. The illegality arises from the *improper exercise of a discretion* within the limits of what the statute permits.

Da Costa v Minister of National Security and Others (1986) 38 WIR 1 (BS)
Adams J

[PP 4–6] It is clear that the Director of Immigration has the power to fix within her discretion a time limit for the plaintiff's departure. But such discretion is not unfettered. As Professor Wade says: 'Parliament constantly confers upon public authorities powers which on their face might seem absolute and arbitrary. But arbitrary power and unfettered discretion are what the Courts refuse to countenance. They have woven a network of restrictive principles which require statutory powers to be exercised reasonably and in good faith, for proper purposes only, and in accordance with the spirit as well as the letter of the empowering Act. They have also, as explained elsewhere, imposed stringent procedural requirements.' Professor Wade also points out that the Court assumes that Parliament cannot have intended to authorise unreasonable action, which is therefore *ultra vires* and void and it becomes the business of the Courts to see that the power is not exceeded or abused. However, it must be remembered that the power conferred on the Director of Immigration to be used in discretion is that of the director and is not that of the Courts. As long ago as 1598, in the *Rooke's case*, 5 Co Rep 99b, Coke had said: 'and notwithstanding the words of the Commission give authority to the Commissioners to do according to their discretions, yet their proceedings ought to be limited and bound with the rule of reason and law. For discretion is a science and understanding to discern between falsity and truth, between wrong and right, between shadows and substance, between equity and colourable glosses and pretences, and not to do according to their wills and private affections; for as one saith, *talis discretio discretionem confundit*'. In *Roberts v Hopwood* [1925] AC 578 at page 604, Lord Sumner said that the words 'as they think fit' contained a necessary implication both of honesty and reasonableness. Lord Wrenbury said (at page 613): 'A person in whom is vested a discretion must exercise his discretion upon reasonable grounds. A discretion does not empower a man to do what he likes merely because he is minded to do so—he must in the exercise of his discretion do not what he likes but what he ought. In other words, he must, by the use of his reason, ascertain and follow the course which reason directs. He must act reasonably.' As Professor Wade points out: 'the common theme of all the passages quoted is that the notion of absolute or unfettered discretion is rejected. Statutory power conferred for public purposes is conferred as it were upon trust, not absolutely; that is to say, it can validly be used only in the right and proper way which Parliament when conferring it is presumed to have intended.' Professor Wade concludes that unreviewable administrative action is just as much a contradiction in terms as is unfettered discretion in the case of statutory powers. The imposition of such legal limits applies even to Ministers of the Crown: *Padfield v Minister of Agriculture, Fisheries and Food* [1968] AC 997. In *Council of Civil Service Unions v Minister for the Civil Service* [1984] 3 All ER 935 at page 950, Lord Diplock conveniently classified under three heads the grounds on which administrative action was subject to control by judicial review, namely illegality, irrationality and procedural impropriety. By 'irrationality' he said that he meant what could be succinctly referred to as '*Wednesbury* unreasonableness', and it applied to a decision which was so outrageous in its defiance of logic or of accepted moral standards that no sensible person who had applied his mind to the question to be decided could have arrived at it. He added: 'whether a decision falls within this category is a question that Judges by their training and experience should be well equipped to answer or else there would be something badly wrong with our judicial system' . . . [P6] All the cases indicate that there has been judicial rejection of the proposition of unfettered discretion. Even if the discretions were described as unfettered, the Courts would reject such a proposition . . . [P7] There is judicial authority to say that the Court's control of administrative action cannot be evaded by the omission of the executive body to specify the grounds of decision . . . [P8] I have, therefore, come to the conclusion after due deliberation that the director's notification can be successfully reviewed on the ground of *Wednesbury* unreasonableness. It is not a decision that can be reconciled with all the material circumstances and cannot reasonably be supported by the evidence.

In the Application of Mossel Jamaica Ltd (T/A Digicel) –
Supreme Court No M. 074 of 2002 (JM)
Dukharan J

[P7] It is quite clear that a review Court cannot reverse the decision of a Minister unless he does not act or exercises his discretion within the ambit of the powers conferred on him . . . [P8] The Court is not in favour of a Minister or any public official having [an] unfettered discretion . . . [P10] It is quite clear from the authorities that the Courts guard against a Minister acting outside of the Statutory Provisions . . . [PP18–19] It would seem on the face of it that the Direction would prohibit and/or preclude the OUR's discharge of its statutory functions. Indeed, the OUR has the statutory power to make a determination of the terms and conditions of interconnection agreements and to set rates and price caps. Although it is quite clear that the Minister cannot legitimately issue a directive which would preclude the OUR from carrying out its functions under the Act, Section 6 of the Telecommunications Act gives the Minister the power to give directions as to policy matters. Once the direction is of a general nature and the Minister exercises that discretion reasonably then the OUR must comply. Section 6 of the Telecommunications Act refers to the OUR Act and its functions. Parliament must have intended (in Section 6) that the Minister is given the power to issue directions of a general nature as to policy. The section is quite clear and simple and needs no interpretation. The intention is quite clear. Whether the OUR disagrees or not with the Minister's direction they are bound in law to give effect to the Directions. They were not entitled to issue the Determination Notice until the Direction was challenged and set aside in a Review Court. Under the OUR Act there is no provision for any such Ministerial directions. However in relation to the service of telecommunication the OUR is governed by and answerable to the terms of the Telecommunications Act, an Act which was passed in the year 2000 and designed to meet the government's thrust and policy to promote economic development to Jamaica through competition in the telecommunications market. In conclusion, I am of the view that the reasons given by the Minister, taking into account the government's policy framework and the scope and objects of the Act; the direction was lawful. It was a direction of a general nature as to the policy to be followed by the OUR. There is no evidence of improper or irrelevant considerations on the part of the Minister. The Minister's Direction was issued validly. The Determination

Notice issued by the OUR contravenes the Direction and therefore cannot stand and ought not to have been issued.

***In the Application of Carl Hanoman* – HCSCJ No 23M of 1999 (GY)**
Bernard CJ

[P10] Where the discretion conferred is wide and unlimited there is always the unwritten caveat that it must not be abused and is not absolute. The Courts have invariably intervened over the years to check these abuses and fetter the discretion without eroding the fundamental power conferred on the public authority or functionary . . . Later decisions, however, indicate that the Courts guard very jealously and zealously their right to intervene and impose fetters on a discretion which is not exercised reasonably and fairly . . . [P11] The question of reasonableness is exemplified in *Associated Provincial Picture Houses Ltd. v Wednesbury Corporation* [1947] 1 All ER 498 which laid down what has come to be known as the *Wednesbury* principles breach of which gives rise to *Wednesbury* unreasonableness. Lord Greene, MR emphasized that the Courts can only interfere with an act of executive authority if it be shown that the authority has contravened the law which recognises certain principles on which a discretion must be exercised. Within the four corners of those principles the discretion is an absolute one and cannot be questioned in any Court of law. These principles mean that the discretion must be exercised reasonably, that is, the authority must not take into account matters which it ought not to take into account or conversely, must take into account matters which it ought to take into account.

2.9 BAD FAITH

A decision-maker must not be prompted by improper motives in arriving at his decision as his actions will be rejected by the court where he has acted in bad faith.

***In the Application of Matthew Joseph, Asad Ali, Soogrim Bhaggan, Gunness Bhagewandeen, Rampersad Ragoo, Reeka Rampersad, Francis Gopaul, Clement Brizan, Radhay Kissoon, Jankinath Sookdeo, Ian Johnson, Seepersad Singh* – HCA No S–611 of 1988 (TT)**
Blackman J

[PP24–25] Then again it was argued that the Minister acted in bad faith. Again, the onus of proving that such is the case lies on the Applicants. That onus in my view has not been discharged. There is just no basis for that charge.

The courts, at times, seem inclined to take a generous interpretation of the action of the decision maker and would appear to have set a high threshold for the determination of what constitutes bad faith.

***In the Application of Edward Cleghorn and 13 Others* –**
Civil Appeal No 112 of 1995 (TT)
Nelson JA

[P16] In any event, in the absence of any evidence of bad faith in the sense of fraudulent intent the presumption of due performance of their duties by public authorities must apply: *omnia praesumuntur rite esse acta* . . . [P19] The Appellants rely on certain dicta of Lord Reid and Lord Pearce. Both Lord Reid and Lord Pearce considered that if the effect of a refusal to give reasons for the exercise of an unfettered discretion was to frustrate the policy and objects of the Act the Court would infer that the Minister was not using the power given by Parliament to carry out its intentions and review its exercise . . . [P20] I therefore reject the Appellants' contention that failure to give reasons for the exercise of the power of summary dismissal on the facts of this case amounts to bad faith or gives rise to an inference of fraudulent intent.

***In the Application of No 6573 Sergeant Shaffiat Ali* – HCA No 3876 of 1991 (TT)**
Warner J

[P15] Bearing the above in mind, it is obvious and I am in agreement with Attorney for the State that on an examination of the provisions relating to transfer in the Public Service and the Teaching Service, express provisions are made for the Officer to make representations to the Commission for review, there is no such provision in the Police Service Regulations. In my view, I cannot construe the spirit and intent of the legislation as requiring the Court to attempt to 'interpolate any judicial type procedure' in relation to the Commissioner's power to transfer a Police Officer ... [P16] I accept the evidence of the Commissioner that he took into account the hardship advanced, that is to say that the Officer would have to travel 100 miles if he were placed in Matelot/Mayaro, that he was diabetic, had heart problems and was under medical supervision, and that he had to pay mortgages totaling $2,000.00 which left him with a take home salary of $400 ... [P18] In the absence of bad faith, fraud or misbehaviour of the like, I do not find it necessary to import into the legislation a general rule that an Officer who is transferred must be told the reasons for his transfer, or what the exigencies are. In this matter, there was no odium attached to the transfer, it was not imposed as a penalty, and the Applicant is entitled to make [an] application for a hardship allowance.

The Courts have recognised however that good administration requires public authorities to act in good faith as their actions may undermine public trust and confidence.

***In the Application of Krishna Rampersadsingh* – HCA No Cv S. 637 of 2004 (TT)**
Jamadar J

[P8] In my opinion, fundamental fairness demands that this Applicant be told, with sufficient particularity of the allegations against him, of the persons making them and of any investigations conducted. The failure to do so, in the circumstances of this case, especially where a written request for same was made since 1st March, 2004 amounts to a breach of the principles of fundamental fairness and natural justice; as also would any future actions against the Applicant related to appointments based on this letter of 31st October, 2003 ... [P9] This kind of conduct by a CMO and/or a Permanent Secretary is not conducive to good public administration. Such conduct can only undermine public trust and confidence in Public Administration, and demotivate and discourage public servants. Though true for all the Public Service, it is critically imperative that in the Health Care Sector, the highest standards of Public Administration are maintained—for here, what is at stake are the lives and limbs of the Nation's people.

2.10 FAILURE TO OBSERVE THE PRINCIPLE OF EQUALITY

An issue of particular sensitivity in Trinidad and Tobago is that of equality. With a population reflecting diverse races, the question of unequal treatment by public bodies is increasingly finding its way before the courts. The early attempts at introducing the equality argument focused on inequality as reflective of bad faith and, therefore, unreasonableness.

***In the Application of Matthew Joseph, Asad Ali, Soogrim Bhaggan, Gunness Bhagewandeen, Rampersad Ragoo, Reeka Rampersad, Francis Gopaul, Clement Brizan, Radhay Kissoon, Jankinath Sookdeo, Ian Johnson, Seepersad Singh* –**
HCA No S–611 of 1988 (TT)
Blackman J

[P25] Attorney for the Applicants also argued that there was inequality in the treatment of his clients in relation to others. He contended that this element was introduced in order to support his ground of unreasonableness on the part of the Minister. If the Applicants are right it would in my view show that the Minister did not act *bona fide* or that there may be some ulterior motive in his action. In this sense the Minister's act would have been unreasonable in the legal sense. But what are the facts? Mr Charles under cross-examination though admitting that there were other structures on the highway explained that it was the intention of the State to remove the others as well but that Government was awaiting the outcome of this action as it was advised to hold its hands until then. I accept Mr Charles' explanation and therefore I do not find that there has been any inequality of treatment. This ground of unreasonableness is therefore also rejected.

2.11 BREACH OF A LEGITIMATE EXPECTATION

Legitimate expectation is not only appropriate where there has been a settled practice or a promise held out by the relevant authority. The doctrine of legitimate expectation arises in situations where the very circumstances would entitle a person to expect to be treated in a particular way notwithstanding the absence of a promise or settled practice.

***In the Application of Ameena Ali* – HCA No S–1812 of 2003 (TT)**
Ventour J

[P25] It is generally accepted that employment by a public authority does not, *per se*, inject any element of public law into the contract of employment. If however, the contract of employment makes provision for special statutory restrictions on dismissal or other statutory underpinnings of the employee's contract, as is clearly manifested in the Applicant's case before this Court, then it seems to me that the presence of such statutory underpinnings would have the effect of injecting into the contract the element of public law . . . [PP26–27] I do not believe that there is any such difficulty by the Applicant on the facts of the instant case and therefore I hold that the decisions of the NWRHA which have affected the Applicant are subject to Judicial Review proceedings . . . [PP34–35] Nothing stated in the letter of termination suggests to this Court that the Applicant's legitimate expectations was factored into the deliberations of the Board. If it was, then the Authority is duty bound to demonstrate to the Court that there were overriding public interests to justify its decision. It has failed to do so and consequently, I am left with no alternative but to hold that the decision of the Board to terminate the services of the Applicant was, in all the circumstances, unjust, unfair, unreasonable and unlawful. Public officials have to be reminded that their source of power and authority comes from the people through their elected Representatives in Parliament. And in the exercise of that power they have a duty, nay an obligation, to be fair and be just to the people they have been empowered to serve. No matter how strong the temptation, they have to avoid acting out of spite, illwill or arbitrarily. These are general remarks and are not intended to suggest that the NWRHA has acted with spite or illwill against the Applicant. There is no evidence to support such a finding.

***In the Application of Vashti Sampson, Rajh Basdeo, Indar Samaroo, Grantley Prescott and James Chinapoo* – Civil Appeal No 96 of 2003 (TT)**
Nelson JA

[P21] I turn now to the issue of legitimate expectation. I respectfully agree with the Court of Appeal in England in *R (on the application of Bibi) v Newham LBC* [2002] 1 WLR 237 at para 19 that in all legitimate expectation cases, whether substantive or procedural, three practical questions arise:

(1) To what has the public authority committed itself?

(2) Whether the authority has acted or proposes to act unlawfully in relation to its commitment

(3) What the Court should do . . .

In the Application of Moonilal Ramhit and Company Ltd – **HCA No S 797 of 1999 (TT)**
Narine J

[P16] The essence of the case for the Applicant is that in the exercise of its public functions over the years, the Respondent caused him to have a legitimate expectation that he would be invited by the Respondent to tender for contracts. This in my view is clearly a matter of public law. The Applicant is not relying on any private rights. He is seeking to impugn the decision-making process of a public body in the exercise of its public functions. A legitimate expectation arises where a decision-maker induces in someone affected by his decision a reasonable expectation that he will receive or retain a benefit or that he will be granted a hearing before the decision is taken . . . [PP20–21] The basic principles upon which the doctrine is founded are summarized in pages 416–430 of de Smith, Woolfe and Jowell's *Judicial Review of Administrative Action* (5th ed.) See in particular page 421. 'The terms of the representation by the decision-maker (whether express or implied from past practice) must entitle the party to whom it is addressed to expect, legitimately, one of two things:

(1) that a hearing or other appropriate procedures will be afforded before the decision is made; or

(2) that a benefit of a substantive nature will be granted, or, if the person is already in receipt of the benefit, that it will be continued and not be substantially varied.'

In the second case, fairness dictates that the expectation of the benefit should not be summarily disappointed and that the recipient of the benefit should at least be permitted to argue for its fulfillment . . . [P23] It is clear on the evidence in this case that there has been an established and settled practice for the invitation to tenders, over a long period of time . . . [P24] Having carefully considered the facts of this case and the law, I hold that the established practice followed by the Respondent and its predecessors over a period of some 25 years for the invitation of tenders created in the Applicant a legitimate expectation that this practice would continue to be followed. It seems to me on the facts of this case that if the Respondent wished to change the practice (as it was entitled to do) by not inviting tenders from their list of approved contractors, at the very least procedural fairness required that the Applicant should have been informed of the change of practice, and should have been given an opportunity to make representations to the Respondent with respect to the change of practice and its adverse effect on the Applicant's interests.

In the Application of Peter Jaglal – **HCA No S–995 of 1998 (TT)**
Moosai J

[P10] It would therefore seem that in dealing with non-renewal of an existing licence and/or revocation of a licence, the traditional 'privilege' concept of a licence may not be appropriate, the reason being, *inter alia*, that it may result in economic loss, even serious pecuniary loss or deprivation of livelihood . . . [P13] In the instant case, the Applicant was entitled to have his application for the renewal of the sawmill licence heard and determined according to law, due consideration being given to the fact that he had been operating a sawmill business for the past 37 years. The Applicant would also have had a legitimate expectation, in the event that the authorities were not going to renew his licence, that he would have been given a hearing. As the sawmill was his source of livelihood, the Applicant would have suffered severe economic loss as a result of the non-renewal of the licence . . . [P14] The Applicant therefore, in order to succeed in the instant case, must establish that he has been deprived of his right to liberty, security of the person or enjoyment of property without due process . . . [P18] A legitimate claim of entitlement to a benefit is therefore a constitutionally protected property interest. Further I think that in the circumstances of the instant case, it cannot reasonably be argued that the Applicant had simply an abstract concern in the renewal of his licence . . . [P19] The Applicant in the instant case had a legitimate claim of entitlement to the renewal of the sawmill licence for the year 1998. That benefit is therefore a property interest protected by Section 4(a) of the Constitution. The deprivation of his right to liberty, and enjoyment of his property without due process of law amounts therefore to a breach of his constitutional right . . . I do not think that it can be disputed in the instant case that the Applicant had a legitimate claim of entitlement to the renewal of the sawmill licence. Moreover by its concession in the instant case, the State accepted that the refusal to grant a licence to the Applicant was illegal, null and void . . . [P20] In the instant case the Applicant would have had an objective expectancy of the continuance of the licence which had initially been conferred by the State, deprivation of which amounted to a deprivation of his right to the enjoyment of his property without due process of law . . . [PP25–26] I therefore came to the conclusion that the refusal to renew the sawmill licence in these circumstances amounted to a deprivation of the right to life, liberty, security of the person and the enjoyment of property without due process of law thereby entitling the Applicant to damages to be assessed.

***In the Application of Syed Mohamed Joseph Adrian Aziz* – HCA No 350 of 1994 (TT)**
Warner J

[P6] The doctrine of legitimate expectation has been relied on by Miss Jones . . . [P7] This doctrine has been used to ensure that public authorities act fairly, by conforming to past practices or to situations where an authority publishes a policy and which justifies that a person dealing with the authority ought reasonably to expect that he or she would be treated in a particular way.

***Re Gayman Jurisingh and Others* (1993) 48 WIR 301 (TT)**
Sharma JA

[PP313–315] Before dealing with the facts and submissions made on the doctrine of legitimate expectation, we think it appropriate to set out in some detail the origin and the development of this recent doctrine. In *Crane v Bernard* (unreported), Sharma JA dealt exhaustively with it, and quoted extensively from an article entitled 'Legitimate Expectations: Judicial Review of Administrative Policy Actions' by Raymond E Young (see *The Advocate* (a Canadian publication) Vol 44, Part 6, November 1986) and we only propose to repeat here what he said in *Crane*: 'The origin of this administrative form of estoppel rests on the introduction of the concept of "legitimate expectation" as a ground giving rise to the procedural protections characteristic of the duty of fairness'. Lord Denning MR appears to have coined the phrase in *Schmidt v Secretary of State for Home Affairs* [1969] 1 All ER 904 when, in summing-up the essential elements necessary for the application of natural justice/fairness, his lordship stated that it would depend on: '. . . whether he has some right or interest or I would add, some legitimate expectation of which it would not be fair to deprive him without hearing what he has to say'. In the circumstances of *Schmidt*, the idea was merely obiter; however, with knowledge of the predilection of the former Master of the Rolls for judiciously planting seeds for later cultivation, the seemingly passing reference to 'legitimate expectation' was obviously more than merely a casual comment. This became clear in *R v Liverpool Corporation, Ex Parte Liverpool Taxi Fleet Operators' Association* [1972] 2 All ER 589 a case in which a municipal council attempted to renege on a promise not to alter its policy as to the total number of licences to be issued without consulting a particular special interest group. The municipality argued that in respect of policy the Court could not require it to fetter its statutory discretion by any prior undertaking, no matter how clearly given. In response, Lord Denning MR, while agreeing that a public body could not enter into any contract or take any action incompatible with the discharge of its duties or the exercise of its power, stated (at page 594): 'But that principle does not mean that a corporation can give an undertaking and break it as they please. *So long as the performance of the undertaking is compatible with their public duty, they must honour it*, and *I should have thought that this undertaking was so compatible.* At any rate they ought not to depart from it except after the most serious consideration and hearing what the other party has to say: *and then only if they are satisfied that the overriding public interest requires it.* The public interest may be *better served by honouring their undertaking than by breaking it. This is just such a case*' [emphasis supplied]. Roskill LJ spoke in similar terms (at page 596): 'If I thought that the effect of granting to the Applicants the relief sought was to prevent the council validly using those powers which Parliament has conferred on it, I would refuse relief. But that is not the present case. It seems to me the relief claimed will in the end, as counsel for the corporation ultimately conceded, assist the council to perform rather than inhibit the performance of its statutory duties'. Subsequently, in *Attorney-General of Hong Kong v Ng Yuen Shiu* [1983] 2 All ER 346 the notion of legitimate expectation was recognised by the *Privy Council*. In *Ng* the facts were that the Colony of Hong Kong had had a long-standing practice of not deporting illegal aliens once they had reached the urban area. The policy was well known and popularly referred to as 'reaching base'. Ng was an illegal immigrant. The Government of the Colony decided to change the policy of not enforcing the existing law against those aliens who had 'reached base'. The change of policy was publicly announced in order to put all those interested on notice. The announcement was followed by public protests and mass rallies opposing the new policy. At one such demonstration, a senior official representing the Secretary of State for Security came out on the steps of Government House to address a crowd. He announced that no-one would be arbitrarily deported and all those arrested under the new policy would have their case reviewed before deportation. Ng was not in the crowd that day but saw a newsclip of the incident on the late night television news. Subsequently he was arrested and the Government sought summarily to deport him. Ng challenged the deportation on the basis of fairness, arguing that statements of the government official which he had seen on television raised in him a legitimate expectation to a fair hearing at which his case would be reviewed. The Privy Council issued *certiorari* to quash the order for removal without prejudice to any new order for removal being made after a fair inquiry. They did so not on the broader view *that persons subject to deportation under the statute were entitled to the protection of natural justice or fairness, but expressly only on the narrow issue that where representations have been made that induce a legitimate expectation* the doctrine of fairness applies. In describing the principles of legitimate expectation, Lord Fraser of Tullybelton giving the opinion of their lordships stated (at page 350): 'The expectation may be based upon a statement or undertaking by or on behalf of the public authority which has the duty of making the decision, if the authority has, through its officers, acted *in a way that would make it unfair or inconsistent with good administration for him to be denied such an inquiry*' [emphasis supplied]. 'The rationale for the application of the principles was explained in the following terms (at page 351): 'The justification for it is primarily that, when a public authority has promised to follow a certain procedure, it is in the interest of good administration that it should act fairly and should implement its promise, so long as implementation does not interfere with its statutory duty. The principle is also justified by the further consideration that, when the promise was made, the authority must have considered that it would be assisted in discharging its duty fairly by any representations from interested parties and as a general rule that is correct'. In *R v Jockey Club, Ex Parte RAM Racecourses Ltd* [1993] 2 All ER 225 Stuart-Smith LJ said: 'The doctrine has many similarities with the principles of estoppel in private law. In my judgment the matters that the Applicant has to prove in this case are these: (1) A *clear and unambiguous* representation; see *per* Bingham LJ in *Ex Parte M.F.K. Underwriting Agents Ltd* [1990] 1 All ER 91 at page 110 [emphasis supplied]. (2) That, since the Applicant was not a person to whom any representation was directly made, it was within the class of persons who are entitled to rely upon it; or at any rate that it was reasonable for the Applicants to rely upon it without more; see *Attorney-General of Hong Kong v Ng Yuen Shiu* [1983] 2 AC 629 at page 638. (3) That they did so rely on it. (4) That they did so to their detriment. While in some cases it is not altogether clear that this is a necessary ingredient, since a public body is entitled to change its policy if it is acting in good faith, but it is a necessary ingredient where, as here, an Applicant is saying "You cannot alter your policy now in my case; it is too late". (5) That there is no overriding interest arising from their duties and responsibilities for the proper conduct or due encouragement of horse-racing as required in their charter which entitled the Jockey Club to change their policy to the detriment of the Applicants'. 'The burden of proving the first four points is, in my judgment, upon the Applicants'. Having dealt with the principles of the doctrine we now turn to one of the matters upon which counsel has relied to which, in his submissions, he says that the doctrine is applicable . . . [PP321–322] We have strong reservations, however, whether the doctrine is applicable to all. In *Re Findlay* [1985] 1 AC 318, the Appellants alleged that they had a legitimate expectation that before the introduction of the Secretary of State's new policy as regards parole they would have been released from prison much earlier than became likely after its adoption. Lord Scarman (at page 338) in dealing with that submission, stated that while the doctrine of legitimate expectation had an important place in the developing law of judicial review, it was not necessary to explore the doctrine in that case but simply to note that a legitimate expectation can provide a sufficient interest to obtain leave to enable one who cannot point to the existence of a *substantive right* to obtain the leave of the Court for judicial review [emphasis supplied]. The Appellants there obtained leave, but their submissions went further. It was submitted that the refusal to except them from the new policy was an unlawful act on the part of the Secretary of State in that his decision frustrated their expectation. Lord Scarman then asked: 'but what was their legitimate expectation? Given the substance and purpose of the legislative provisions governing parole . . . the most that a convicted prison[er] can legitimately expect is that his case will be examined individually in the light of whatever policy the Secretary of State sees fit to adopt, provided always that the adopted policy is a lawful exercise of the discretion conferred on him by the statute. Any other view would entail the conclusion that the unfettered discretion conferred by the statute upon the Minister can in some cases be restricted so as to hamper, or even to prevent, changes of policy'. He concluded that: 'bearing in mind the complexity of the issues which the Secretary of State has to consider and the importance of the public interest in the administration of parole I cannot think that Parliament intended the discretion to be restricted in this way'. In this case the Appellants have sought redress by way of constitutional motion. No leave of the Court is required so to proceed. All the Appellants can do is point to a right to be heard before the Minister changes his policy. Fairness may demand such a right, but that right is not a substantive right. It simply affords the Appellants the opportunity to put their case to the Minister and, as in *Findlay*, the most they can legitimately expect is that their case will be examined individually in the light of whatever policy the Minister sees fit to adopt, provided always that the adopted policy is a lawful exercise of the discretion conferred on him by the statute. The Court, in such circumstances will not make a declaration (since no substantive right is in issue) but, if the facts are proved, will remit the matter for the particular authority to hear the Applicant before determining the issue, as was done in *Attorney-General of Hong Kong v Ng Yuen Shiu* [1983] 2 All ER 346. In that case Lord Fraser emphasised (at page 351): 'the Court order [in the *Liverpool Taxi case* [1972] 2 All ER 589] was limited to ensuring that the corporation followed a fair procedure by holding a fair inquiry before reaching a decision: provided such procedure was followed the decision was left with the corporation to whom it had been entrusted by Parliament'. We are of the view that perhaps, save in very exceptional circumstances, this doctrine should be kept within the narrow limits for which it was conceived. We have already dealt with the history of this doctrine, but it is well to remember that it comes within natural justice, 'fair play in action'. When applicable, it is premised on the right to be heard or the failure to consult in accordance with procedure and is an example of procedural impropriety in terms laid down by Lord Diplock in *Council of Civil Service Unions v Minister for the Civil Service*

[1985] 1 AC 374. We think that it would be an usurpation of the functions of the executive, and contrary to the doctrine of the separation of powers, if legitimate expectation were to be used as a device for reversing or hindering the executive from carrying out its functions. They are the representatives of the people and are the most appropriate body to deal with Government policy. It seems to us that so long as there is no unlawfulness in executive actions, the Court ought not to interfere. We wish to sound a cautionary note that, if this doctrine were to develop to a point where it could give rise to substantive rights, it could lead not only to serious conflict between the executive and the judiciary but it would be contrary to the democratic principles of government, which would lead to chaos and could have the effect of crippling the executive. Matters of policy and any changes thereof are always, we repeat, for the executive. So long as the executive or the appropriate Minister does not act *ultra vires* the Courts ought not to interfere.

***In the Application of Ashmeed Mohammed* – HCA No 3924 of 1992 (TT)**
Warner J

[P12] The concept of legitimate expectation has within the last two decades burgeoned and has now emerged to prevent a decision maker from making a decision which departs from a representation or undertaking as to the exercise of a discretionary power . . . [P14] I am of the view that the principle to be extracted from all the cases is this: if a public authority publishes a policy and then departs from it without adequately notifying persons affected of the change, then the exercise of discretion may be held to be unreasonable.

***In the Application of Andy Allan* – HCA No 1617 of 1990 (TT)**
Blackman J

[PP23–24] Legitimate Expectation: In the *CCSU case supra* at p 949, Lord Diplock in referring to this ground said, *inter alia*: 'To qualify as a subject for judicial review, the decision must have consequences which affect some person (or body or persons) other than the decision-maker, although it may affect him too. It must affect such other person either (a) by altering rights or obligations of that person which are enforceable by or against him in private law or (b) *by depriving him of some benefit or advantage which either (i) he has in the past been permitted by the decision-maker to enjoy and which he can legitimately expect to be permitted to continue to do until there has been communicated to him some rational ground for withdrawing it on which he has been given an opportunity to comment or (ii) he has received assurance from the decision-maker that it will not be withdrawn without giving him first an opportunity of advancing reasons for contending that they should not be withdrawn. I prefer to continue to call the kind of expectation that qualifies a decision for inclusion in class (b) a "legitimate expectation"* rather than a "reasonable expectation" '. Lord Fraser in the *CCSU case*, in stating the principle on which legitimate expectation is based, said at pp 943–944: 'But even where a person claiming some benefit or privilege has no legal right to it, as a matter of private law, he may have a legitimate expectation of receiving the benefit or privilege, and, if so, the Courts will protect his expectation by judicial review as a matter of public law. This subject has been fully explained by Lord Diplock in *O'Reilly v Mackman* [1982] 3 All ER 1124, [1983] 2 AC 237 and I need not repeat what he has so recently said. *Legitimate expectation* or reasonable expectation *may arise either from an express promise given on behalf of a public authority or from the existence of a regular practice which the claimant* can reasonably expect to continue.'

***In the Application of Harold Barcoo* – HCA No 1599 of 1990 (TT)**
Jones J

[P6] Several authorities which consider the doctrine of legitimate expectation deal with situations where there existed either a settled practice or a promise held out by the relevant authority. But is it true to say as contended by Attorney for the Respondent that it is only in such situations that the principle can be invoked? . . . [P7] Further examples of the application of the doctrine of legitimate or reasonable expectation can in my view be found in the licensing cases. Where there is a legitimate expectation of renewal of an existing licence there is implied a duty to be heard before a decision is taken not to renew ... [P8] I do not therefore subscribe to the view expressed by Attorney for the Respondent that 'the House of Lords' decision in the *Council of Civil Service Unions and others v Minister for Civil Service* [1984] 3 All ER 935 had confirmed that the doctrine of legitimate expectation can only arise where there had been a settled practice or a promise held out by the relevant authority ... [P9] Since the principle is closely connected with the right to be heard, it seems to me to arise in situations where the very circumstances would entitle a person to expect to be treated in a particular way notwithstanding the absence of a promise or settled practice, as the licensing cases clearly demonstrate ... [P11] I find as Ellicot J found in *Cunningham v Cole* (*supra*) that in the special circumstances of the case, the Applicant was entitled to expect in accordance with ordinary standards of fairness to be informed of the nature and extent of the material which was being considered against him so that he could make any representations he might wish. I am also of the view that the case falls into the category of case which Megarry VC in *McInnes v Orslow Fane* (*Supra*) describes as 'intermediate'—'the expectation cases', in which there is a legitimate expectation of an opportunity to be heard before any adverse decision is taken.

Chief Immigration Officer of the British Virgin Islands v Burnett (1995)
50 WIR 153 (BVI)
Sir Vincent Floissac CJ

[PP156–160] The grounds do not relate to the existence of the executive powers but to the manner of their exercise. The grounds involve principles of natural justice and other principles which transcend the questions of executive power and nationality. There is no doubt that the High Court has an inherent jurisdiction (either by way of judicial review or otherwise) to supervise and judicially control certain decisions and actions of public authorities constituted by law to make those decisions or to take those actions. Subject to the formalities prescribed by rules of Court, the jurisdiction is exercisable whenever a public authority (purporting to exercise a constitutional, statutory or prerogative power) has made or taken or intends to make or take a justiciable judicial, quasi-judicial or administrative decision or action which affects or will affect a complainant who has *locus standi* by way of a relevant or sufficient interest in the decision or action and who alleges and proves that the decision or action is or will be illegal, irrational or procedurally improper. In such a case, the High Court may make such appropriate prerogative or other order as may be necessary to protect the complainant from the illegality, irrationality or procedural impropriety of the decision or action. A complainant will be held to have *locus standi* by way of a relevant or sufficient interest in an actual or intended decision or action of a public authority (1) if the decision or action infringed or threatens to infringe any constitutional, statutory or common law right whatsoever vested in the complainant, or (2) if the decision or action infringed or threatens to infringe the complainant's specific constitutional, statutory or common-law right to the observance of the formalities required by the '*audi alteram partem*' rule of natural justice, or (3) if the decision or action disappointed or threatens to disappoint the complainant's legitimate expectation that certain benefits or privileges will be granted to him or that certain rules of natural justice or fairness would be observed in relation to him before the decision or action is made or taken. In *O'Reilly v Mackman* [1983] 2 AC 237 at page 275, Lord Diplock said: 'It is not, and it could not be, contended that the decision of the Board awarding him forfeiture of remission had infringed or threatened to infringe any right of the Appellant derived from private law, whether a common-law right or one created by a statute. Under the Prison Rules remission of sentence is not a matter of right but of indulgence. So far as private law is concerned all that each Appellant had was a legitimate expectation, based upon his knowledge of what is the general practice, that he would be granted the maximum remission, permitted by Rule 5(2) of the Prison Rules, of one-third of his sentence if by that time no disciplinary award of forfeiture of remission had been made against him. So the second thing to be noted is that none of the Appellants had any remedy in private law. 'In public law, as distinguished from private law, however, such legitimate expectation gave to each Appellant a sufficient interest to challenge the legality of the adverse disciplinary award made against him by the Board on the ground that in one way or another the Board in reaching its decision had acted outwith the powers conferred upon it by the legislation under which it was acting; and such grounds would include the Board's failure to observe the rules of natural justice: which means no more than to act fairly towards him in carrying out their decision-making process, and I prefer so to put it'. In *Attorney-General of Hong Kong v Ng Yuen Shiu* [1983] 2 AC 629 at page 634, Lord Fraser (delivering the opinion of the Privy Council) said: 'There is no doubt that the Director of Immigration had power under Section 19 (in the substituted form provided for in the Ordinance of 1980) to order removal of illegal immigrants. There is also no doubt that neither that section, nor any other statutory provision, expressly requires an inquiry to be held before such an order is made. The only question raised in the appeal is whether, at common law, the Applicant was entitled to have a fair inquiry held before a removal order was made against him'. Lord Fraser then answered the question in those words (at page 636): 'The narrower proposition for which the Applicant contended was that a person is entitled to a fair hearing before a decision adversely affecting his interests is made by a public official or body, if he has "a legitimate expectation" of being accorded such a hearing. The phrase "legitimate expectation" in this context originated in the judgment of Lord Denning MR in *Schmidt v Secretary of State for Home Affairs* [1969] 2 Ch 149 at page 170. It is in many ways an apt one to express the underlying principle, though it is somewhat lacking in precision. In *Salemi v MacKellar (No 2)* (1977) 137 CLR 396 at page 404, Barwick CJ construed the word "legitimate" in that phrase as expressing the concept of "entitlement or recognition by law". So understood, the expression (as Barwick CJ rightly observed) "adds little, if anything, to the concept of a right". With great respect to Barwick CJ, their lordships consider that the word "legitimate" in that expression falls to be read as meaning "reasonable". Accordingly "legitimate expectations" in this context are capable of including expectations which go beyond enforceable legal rights, provided they have some reasonable basis: see *R v Criminal Injuries Compensation Board, Ex Parte Lain* [1967] 1 QB 864. So it was held in *R v Board of Visitors of Hull Prison, Ex Parte St Germain (No 2)* [1979] 1 WLR 1041 that a prisoner is entitled to challenge, by judicial review, a decision by a prison board of visitors, awarding him loss of remission of sentence, although he has no legal right to remission, but only a reasonable expectation of receiving it'. In *Council of Civil Service Unions v Minister for the Civil Service* [1984] 3 All ER 935 at page 954, Lord Roskill said: 'The introduction of the phrase "reasonable expectation" into this branch of our administrative law appears to owe its origin to Lord Denning MR in *Schmidt v Secretary of State for Home Affairs* [1969] 1 All ER 904 at page 909 (when he used the phrase "legitimate expectation"). Its judicial evolution is traced in the opinion of the Judicial Committee delivered by Lord Fraser in *Attorney-General of Hong Kong v Ng Yuen Shiu* [1983] 2 All ER 346 at pages 350, 351. Though the two phrases can, I think, now safely be treated as synonymous for the reasons there given by [Lord Fraser], I prefer the use of the adjective "legitimate" in this context and use it in this speech even though in argument it was the adjective "reasonable" which was generally used. The principle may now be said to be firmly entrenched in this branch of the law. As the cases show, the principle is closely connected with "a right to be heard". Such an expectation may take many forms. One may be an expectation of prior consultation. Another may be an expectation of being allowed time to make representations, especially where the aggrieved party is seeking to persuade an authority to depart from a lawfully established policy adopted in connection with the exercise of a particular power because of some suggested exceptional reasons justifying such a departure'. In *Leech v Parkhurst Prison Deputy Governor* [1988] 1 All ER 485 at page 496, Lord Bridge of Harwich encapsulated the principle in one sentence which reads: 'The principle is now as well established as any principle can be in the developing field of public law that where any person or body exercises a power conferred by statute which affects the rights or legitimate expectations of citizens and is of a kind which the law requires to be exercised in accordance with the rules of natural justice, the Court has jurisdiction to review the exercise of that power' ... The rule invoked in this case is the *audi alteram partem* rule of natural justice and fairness. According to the *audi alteram partem* rule, where any authority (person or body of persons) intends to exercise a constitutional, statutory or prerogative power and thereby to make or take a judicial, quasi-judicial or administrative decision or action which will adversely affect the status, rights, interests or legitimate expectations of any other person (the complainant), the authority is under a common-law duty (and may also be under a constitutional or statutory duty) to observe certain formalities and the complainant has a correlative common-law right (and may also have a correlative constitutional or statutory right) to the observance of those formalities before such a decision or action is made or taken. Those formalities may include notice to the complainant of the specific allegations made against him and a fair and reasonable opportunity for the complainant to answer or rebut those allegations and to make representations in regard to the intended decision or action ... The Respondent must have legitimately expected a fair and reasonable opportunity to answer or rebut those grounds and to make representations in persuasion of the grant of permission for him to enter and remain in the Territory and in dissuasion of the refusal of such permission. In my judgment, the failure on the part of the Minister of Immigration and the Chief Immigration Office to give the said notice and opportunity to the Respondent was a breach of the *audi alteram partem* rule of natural justice and a procedural irregularity which nullified the refusal of permission for the Respondent to enter and remain in the Territory.

***Kent Garment Factory Ltd v Attorney-General and Another* (1991) 46 WIR 177 (GY)**
George CJ

[PP184–186] I shall, therefore, proceed to examine the fundamental right which counsel claims has been violated. It is contained in article 40(1) of the Constitution. That article reads as follows: 'Every person in Guyana is entitled to the basic right to a happy, creative, and productive life, free from hunger, disease, ignorance and want. That right includes the fundamental right and freedom of the individual, that is to say the right whatever his race, place of origin, political opinions, colour, creed or sex, but subject to respect for the rights and freedoms of others and for the public interest, to each and all of the following namely:—(a) life, liberty, security of the person, and *the protection of the law*; (b) freedom of conscience, of expression, and, of assembly and association; (c) protection of the privacy of his home and other property and from deprivation of property without compensation. The provisions of Title 1 of Part 2 shall have effect for the purpose of affording protection of the aforesaid fundamental rights and freedoms of the individual, subject to such limitations of that protection as are contained in those provisions, being limitations designed to ensure that the enjoyment of the said rights and freedoms by any individual does not prejudice the rights and freedoms of others or the public interest' [emphasis supplied]. Title 1 of Part 2 referred to above sets out in detail the fundamental rights and freedoms of the individual that are protected by the Constitution. It is counsel's contention that the right which has been violated is that of 'the protection of the law' in article 40(1)(a). His argument goes like this. Because of the practice of the competent authority to permit, in effect, an automatic extension of an importer's licence if the goods permitted to be imported had been paid for and shipped prior to its expiry date, the Appellants would have had a legitimate expectation that the same concession would have been accorded to them. Therefore by failing to accede to the Appellants' application the competent authority had deprived them of that expectation and thereby deprived them of the protection afforded by the law. I must now examine the validity of this argument. The concept of legitimate expectation seems to owe its origin to a statement by Lord Denning MR in his judgment in *Schmidt v Secretary of State for Home Affairs* [1969] 1 All ER 904. The Master of the Rolls was referring to the right to be heard before a decision is made by a public official which could affect a person's liberty or his property. He said (at page 908): 'I quite agree, of course that where a public officer has power to deprive a person of his liberty or his property the general principle is that it is not to be done without his being given an opportunity of being heard and of making representations on his own behalf'. And (at page 909) he said: 'The speeches in *Ridge v Baldwin* [1963] 2 All ER 66 show that the administrative body may, in a proper case, be bound to give a person who is affected by their decision an opportunity of making representations. It all depends on whether he has some right or interest or I would add some legitimate expectation of which it would not be fair to deprive him without hearing what he has to say'. Since then several decisions have emphasised the importance of this principle in the field of public law. In *Council of Civil Service Unions v Minister of Home Affairs* [1984] 3 All ER 935 at page 943 Lord Fraser said: 'But even where a person claiming some benefit or privilege has no legal right to it as a matter of private law, he may have a legitimate expectation of receiving the benefit or privilege and if so, the Courts will protect his expectation as a matter of public law. This subject has been fully explained by Lord Diplock in *O'Reilly v Mackman* [1982] 3 All ER 1124 ... Legitimate or reasonable expectation may arise either from an express promise given on behalf of a public authority or from the existence of a regular practice which the claimant can reasonably expect to continue'. And Lord Roskill said (at page 957): 'It was common ground before your lordships ... that there was no contractual relationship between the Crown and the staff at GCHQ. Counsel for the Respondent has accepted that the absence of a contractual relationship and thus a remedy in private law did not preclude the possibility of a remedy in public law if legitimate expectation of consultation were established. But he suggested that the absence of such a relationship in private law made it difficult to establish a legitimate expectation justifiable in the field of public law without eroding the basic principle that, at least in theory civil servants are dismissible by the Crown at will and thus have no remedy in private law ... My lords, if no question of national security were involved, I cannot doubt that the evidence and the whole history of the relationship between the management and staff since 1919 shows that there was a legitimate expectation of consultation before important alterations in the conditions of service of civil servants were made'. And in *O'Reilly v Mackman* [1983] 2 AC 237 referred to in the above decision, Lord Diplock had said (at page 275): 'In public law as distinguished from private law, however, such legitimate expectation gave each Appellant a sufficient interest to challenge the legality of the adverse disciplinary award made against him by the Board on the ground that in one way or another the Board in reaching its decision had acted out-with the powers conferred upon it by the legislation under which it was acting; and such grounds would include the Board's failure to observe the rules of natural justice'. It is a concept that is based on the desirability of, and indeed the necessity for, propriety and good faith on the part of a public official or authority towards a citizen, not to depart from a course of action which the latter has been led to believe or expect would be pursued or adopted and which departure would adversely affect his property or liberty, without due and adequate notice and, if appropriate, being permitted an opportunity to be heard. In the Nigerian case, *Stitch v Attorney-General of the Federation* [1987] LRC (Const) 948 at page 964, Aniagola JSC described the concept thus: 'The rationale which I gather from these decided cases is that a Government, in which the citizen is entitled to repose confidence and trust, is not expected to act in breach of the faith which it owes to the citizen and, if it does so act, the Courts will intervene'. According to the evidence, although the licence had expired, the practice of the competent authority has been to grant its automatic extension in order to facilitate the lawful importation of such items as had been purchased and/or shipped but had not arrived in port. It was such a well-known and accepted practice that it seems to have taken on the guise of an expressed concession. Indeed, it is a sensible practice. International shipping depends on so many vicissitudes, damage to the vessel due to mishaps at sea, delays at ports of call, and even the effects of belligerency. But, I dare say, that if it could be shown that the goods, the subject matter of the licence were only ordered at a point in time when it was impossible for them to arrive before the expiry date this would be a factor that may well influence a decision not to extend the licence. But there is no such evidence. Therefore, in my view, and subject to what I shall say later, the Appellants can be said to have had a legitimate expectation that the competent authority would have extended their licence, at least for a period which could have covered the arrival of those goods which had been paid for before its expiry date and shipped.

Elwin v Public Service Commission Commonwealth of Dominica and The Attorney General of The Commonwealth of Dominica –
High Court of Justice Civil Suit No 493 of 1998 (DM)
Cenac J

[Para19] On the issue of legitimate expectation, counsel refers to the well known textbook *Judicial Review of Administrative Action* 5th Edition by Professor de Smith at page 424 under the rubric 'The value of representation' where the learned author said—'An [expectation] will be derived from either (1) an express promise or representation; or (2) a representation implied from established practice based upon the past actions or the settled conduct of the decision maker'. [Para 20] It is on the second limb that the Applicant relies. Counsel submits that the established practice is based not simply on past actions or settled practice but on settled conduct which has been prescribed by Regulations 12 and 14; that the Applicant being a person suitably qualified for the post and having acted in that post for the frequency and duration that she did without any adverse report and having regard to the recommendation of the Permanent Secretary, was the leading contender for the appointment. In the circumstances she has and was entitled to have the legitimate expectation to be so appointed to the post . . . [Para46] I now deal with the issue of legitimate expectation. The authorities clearly show (and a plethora of cases was submitted by both the Applicant and the Respondents) that to succeed on the issue of legitimate expectation, such expectation must be derived either by (a) an express promise: *Attorney General of Hong Kong v Ng Yuen Shiu* [1983] 2 AC 629 (assurance of interview prior to deportation); *Reg. v Liverpool Corp, Ex Parte Liverpool Taxi Fleet Operators' Association* [1972] 2 QB 299; *R v Secretary of State for the Home Department, Ex Parte Asif Matmood Khan* (1984) 1 WIR 1337; or (b) a representation implied from established practice based upon the past actions or the settled conduct of the decision maker: *Council of Civil Service Unions v Minister for the Civil Service* [1984] 3 All ER 935; *Marks v Minister of Home Affairs* (1984) 35 WIR 106 (C.A. Bermuda); *R v Brent LBC, Ex Parte Gunning* [1985] 84 LGR 168. [Para47] In *Marks v Minister of Home Affairs* (1984), the Applicant, a consultant psychiatrist, had been born in England. He worked in Bermuda from 1971 to 1974. He left Bermuda in 1974. In 1976 he returned and from that year until 1982 his work permit was automatically renewed. During this time the Appellant built up a lucrative practice. In 1982 when he applied to renew his work permit the Chief Immigration Officer consulted the Bermuda Medical Council and the Bermuda Medical Society. As a result of representations made to him, the Chief Medical Officer renewed the Appellant's work permit for only six months; no further renewal was allowed. Under Section 61(6) of the Bermuda Immigration and Protection Act 1956 no reason for the decision had to be given, and none were. The Appellant suspected that the refusal to extend his work permit might have been influenced in part by professional jealousy; he also suspected that a conviction on a criminal charge (which had later been reversed on appeal) might have influenced the decision. The Appellant applied to the Court for orders of certiorari and mandamus. They were refused. On appeal it was held, allowing the appeal, that the Appellant had a legitimate expectation that his work permit would be renewed by reason of the previous virtually automatic renewals; accordingly he should have been advised of any factors which were likely to influence the decision not to renew his work permit and he should have been given an opportunity to make representations. Sir Alistair Blair-Kerr P who delivered the judgment of the Court had this to say: [PP109–110] 'This Court does not and cannot inquire into the merits of the Minister's decision. There is no appeal to this Court against the Minister's decision on its merits. The Court can only examine the legality of the process adopted to reach a decision. It can declare the decision a nullity if the decision has not been reached according to law.

An Applicant has no right to the renewal of his permission to engage in gainful occupation ... There can be no doubt that, having regard to the history of this case and the virtually automatic regular renewals of permission to engage in gainful occupation, the Appellant had a legitimate expectation of a further renewal. This case falls to be considered under that class of cases. The principles would not apply to first applications for the grant of permission or to any case in which legitimate expectation of renewal is absent.' [Para48] Having regard to the above and the circumstances of the present case, I am of the view that the conduct of the Commission established a legitimate expectation in the Applicant that she would be appointed to the post of Principal Nursing Tutor.

The courts will not use the doctrine of legitimate expectation to preserve an act that is illegal.

***In the Application of Sahadeo Maharaj* – Civil Appeal No 26 of 2003 (TT)**
Archie JA

[P2] This case is about the ability of a public body to reverse a decision taken in error when a person affected has relied upon and enjoyed the benefit of that decision. The Teaching Service Commission erroneously confirmed the Appellant's appointment to the office of Teacher II on an effective date earlier than his date of first appointment to that office. The effect of that was to give him a seniority date ahead of persons who had been originally appointed before him. It had no power to do so. The Appellant's claim of discrimination and inequality of treatment fails because the removal of a benefit to which he was not lawfully entitled cannot constitute discrimination or inequality of treatment ... [PP7–8] Neither reliance nor effluxion of time can alter the nature of an illegal act so as to confer a permanent substantive benefit or legitimate expectation. A public body cannot, by mistaking its own powers, enlarge them beyond what is conferred by statute. The Commission has an overriding duty to obey the statute. The doctrine of estoppel must give way to the principle of *ultra vires*. The fact that a decision of a public authority may remain effective until declared to be a nullity by the Court does not estop its authority from asserting lack of *vires* ... [P8] In fact, the interests of good administration may impose a duty on a public body to reconsider or correct a decision based on a mistake of fact when that mistake is discovered. That is especially so where failure to address the error would unfairly impact upon other persons in respect of whom similar powers are exercised.

It would seem that the dominant thinking of the courts is that legitimate expectation is grounded in procedural benefits which are in turn derived from the rules of natural justice.

***Barnwell v Attorney-General and Another* (1993) 49 WIR 88 (GY)**
Bishop CJ

[PP113–114] In those circumstances, it would not be unreasonable to suggest that right-minded citizens in our society, apprised of the allegations which required the Appellant's appearance before the JSC on two separate occasions, would have thought that he was put at risk in terms of disciplinary action being contemplated against him. The Appellant himself also would have apprehended this. Those two similar conceptions are relevant considerations, I think, in viewing the seriousness or otherwise of the complaints here. My analysis has shown that there was good reason for the Appellant, a judge, to have been aware of the removal procedure prescribed within article 197 and to assume that his being summoned to appear before the JSC was the first step in the process. He had twice appeared and repelled the allegations that could have put him at risk and now argues that when the third occasion (the present one) arose, he had every reason to believe that the same procedure would have been applied, particularly since senior Magistrate la Bennett's complaint had not only article 197(3) implications but raised concerns from the criminal law point of view. And so there is authority for the proposition that where a person or class previously enjoyed a benefit or advantage of procedure which, on reasonable grounds, seemed likely to be continued as a standard way or guide, with respect to the resolution or disposal of certain questions, a claim of legitimate expectation may arise; see *O'Reilly v Mackman* [1982] 3 All ER 1124 and *Council of Civil Service Unions v Minister for the Civil Service* [1985] 1 AC 374. Or, it may be an expectation arising from a representation or a past practice, as happened in *R v Secretary of State for the Home Department, Ex Parte Khan* [1985] 1 All ER 40, in which Parker LJ was willing to hold that a Home Office circular as respects adoption procedures for foreign children generated a legitimate expectation that the procedures therein would be followed and that the Minister could not resile from them without affording the Appellants a hearing and then only if the public interest demanded it. See also *R v Secretary of State for the Home Department, Ex Parte Ruddock* [1987] 2 All ER 518 and T S R Allan, 'Legislative Supremacy and the Rule of Law' [1985] CLJ 111 at page 129. It is my view that this theory lends itself readily for application to written constitutional provisions which embody the fundamental and organic law. I therefore accept the foregoing hypothesis and remark that my judgment has already indorsed the main pillars of it . . . [PP116–119] On the material facts here, it is reasonable to say of the Appellant that his legitimate expectation emanated from his experience of the fair treatment extended to him on two earlier occasions, when he was faced with complaints that could ultimately have led to loss of status, reputation, position, property, power and prestige; but that the JSC had employed a procedure by which he was able to repel those attacks. He, therefore, not speculatively, but reasonably, contemplated his third encounter before the JSC. His was a procedural expectation. From his own experience 'his knowledge of what [was] the general practice' (*O'Reilly v Mackman* [1982] 3 All ER 1124, *per* Lord Diplock) emerges as a factor of substantial weight in his favour. As Lord Fraser of Tullybelton said in *Council of Civil Service Unions v Minister for the Civil Service* [1985] 1 AC 374 at page 401: '[A legitimate expectation] may arise either from an express promise given on behalf of a public authority or from the existence of a regular practice which the claimant can reasonably expect to continue'. In view of the importance which the claim of legitimate expectation has assumed in Guyana within recent times, and the number of cases both at first instance and on appeal that are yet to be determined, it may be useful to emphasise that a legitimate expectation accords its claimant *locus standi* to seek judicial review of administrative action within the framework of public law. A number of decided cases permit the conclusion that legitimate expectation may be substantive or procedural in content: see *Cinnamond v British Airports Authority* [1979] RTR 331; affirmed, [1980] 2 All ER 368; and *Council of Civil Service Unions v Minister for the Civil Service* [1985] 1 AC 374. Here, the Appellant's notion is directed at the procedural aspect. Craig, *Administrative Law* (2 Edn) (1989) states under the heading 'Categorisation Rights, Privileges and Legitimate Expectation' (at page 206): 'The absence of a substantive right to a particular benefit should not lead to the conclusion that procedural rights are inapplicable, and the term legitimate expectation should not be manipulated to reach this end.' This statement perhaps provides an answer to the Solicitor-General's proposition and his misapplication of Persaud JA's judgment in *Attorney-General v KC Confectionery Ltd* (1985) 34 WIR 387. Craig continues: 'It is however also clear that the concept of legitimate expectations, like many legal concepts, can be used in more than one way; it does not have to be given a restrictive interpretation. Thus more recent cases have, in principle at least, given a broader meaning to that term, utilising it as the foundation for procedural consultation rights to be given to immigrants, workers and local authorities. Thus if an individual is to be deprived of a benefit which was enjoyed in the past, and which he could legitimately expect to continue, or he has received assurances from the decision-maker that such a benefit will not be withdrawn without giving him some opportunity to argue the contrary, then in either instance an opportunity for the individual to make representations will be accorded.' See also *Attorney-General of Hong Kong v Ng Yuen Shiu* [1983] 2 AC 629, *Council of Civil Service Unions v Minister for the Civil Service* [1985] 1 AC 374, *R v Secretary of State for Transport, Ex Parte Greater London Council* [1985] 3 All ER 300, and *Re Westmin-*

ster City Council [1986] 2 All ER 278 at pages 288, 289. Here, in the case of the Appellant, it was the Chairman himself, who, acting on his own responsibility, and without prior notice to the Appellant of his intention, discontinued the procedure the Appellant had come to know and rely on and, what is more, the members of the JSC did not, at the meeting convened by the Chairman, see fit to set aside the Chairman's decision. Had they done so, it ought not to have been seen by him as an affront to his otherwise able leadership, but instead as a timely and cautionary step to correct an act that was *ultra vires*, illegal, and strikingly inconsistent with what the Appellant had enjoyed before and must reasonably have expected to continue, if threatened by a complaint with respect to judicial misbehaviour. Foulkes, *Administrative Law* (7 Edn), summarises the position as regards legitimate expectation (at page 272): 'The right to a hearing, or to be consulted, or generally to put one's case, may also arise out of the action of the authority itself. This action may take one of two, or both, forms: a promise (or a statement or undertaking) or a regular *procedure*. Both the promise and the procedure are capable of giving rise to what is called a legitimate expectation, that is, an expectation of the kind which the Courts will enforce.' The subject 'legitimate expectation' has been treated in this judgment at some length, and there emerges from the discussion what may be labelled its historical element and justification, having due regard (*inter alia*) to past circumstances or experiences, touching the manner in which the authority or body dealt procedurally with certain questions. Professor William H Dray in *Philosophy of History* (1964) does not deal specifically with 'legitimate expectation', but what he offers adopting Hempel is directly relevant (at page 6): 'Historical explanation too, aims at showing that the event in question was not a "matter of chance" but was to be expected in view of certain antecedent or simultaneous conditions. The expectation referred to is not prophecy or divination, but rational scientific anticipation which rests on the assumption of general laws.' I welcome the foregoing theory and direct attention to the Guyanese case, *Kent Garment Factory Ltd v Attorney-General* (1991) 46 WIR 177, where the Court of Appeal may be understood to have given expression to it. There George C spoke on behalf of his brethren as follows on legitimate expectation (at page 187): 'It is a concept that is based on the desirability of, and indeed the necessity for, propriety and good faith on the part of a public official or authority towards a citizen, not to depart from a course of action which the latter had been led to believe or expect would be pursued or adopted and which departure would adversely affect his property or liberty, without due and adequate notice, and, if appropriate, providing for an opportunity to be heard.' See also *Stitch v Attorney-General of the Federation* [1987] LRC (Const) 948 and *Brandt v Attorney-General of Guyana* (1971) 17 WIR 448; and I say that the formulation of George C is both consummate and specifically referable to the relief sought by the Appellant here as regards his claim of legitimate expectation. And this follows from the type of promise, statement, undertaking or conduct upon which legitimate expectation can be established: the very facts may be enough to raise an estoppel against the decision-maker. Here, on the material facts, I so hold even though the point was not specifically argued. But it follows naturally as a corollary. Thus, it has been held that the enforcement of a legitimate expectation arising from a promise or previous practice is akin to the operation of estoppel; see *Robertson v Minister of Pensions* [1948] 2 All ER 767, *Lever (Finance) Ltd v Westminster Corporation* [1970] 3 All ER 496, *Western Fish Products Ltd v Penwith District Council* [1981] 2 All ER 204; see also *Brooks and Burton Ltd v Secretary of State for the Environment* [1978] 1 All ER 733. Dealing with the question of 'Estoppel and Public Authorities', Wade in *Administrative Law* (6 Edn) (1988) points out (at page 261), 'The basic principle of estoppel is that a person who by some statement or representation of fact causes another to act to his detriment in reliance on the truth of it is not allowed to deny it later, even though it is wrong. Justice here prevails over truth. Estoppel is often described as a rule of evidence, but more correctly it is a principle of law: *Canada & Dominion Sugar Co Ltd v Canadian National (West Indies) Steamship Ltd* [1947] AC 46 at page 56. As a principle of common law it applies only to representations about past or present facts. But there is also an equitable principle of "promissory estoppel" which can apply to public authorities.' See *A Roberts & Co Ltd v Leicester County Council* [1961] 2 All ER 545. Here, the claim of the Appellant to legitimate expectation is meritorious and I so declare, and enforcement of it gives rise to the operation of estoppel: see Foulkes, Administrative Law (7 Edn), pages 213, 214, 272, 273, and *R v Liverpool Corporation, Ex Parte Liverpool Taxi Fleet Operators' Association* [1972] 2 All ER 589. A consequence of the estoppel operating against the Respondents here is that it effectively prevents them from maintaining that the Appellant was not entitled to be treated the same way, in accordance with his knowledge and experience gained from the two earlier occasions. En passant, I say that even if the composition of the JSC was different on those two occasions from what it was in September 1989, the minutes of meetings should have revealed that a precedent of procedural expectation had been established in favour of the Appellant or any other judge accused of misbehaviour; see also *Perry v Sinderman*, 408 LJS 593 (1972) at page 601, and *Cabana v Bullock*, 474 LJS 376 (1986) at page 407 . . . [PP120–124] It is common knowledge to all students of administrative law that the duty to act fairly has been exhaustively discussed and its principles clearly stated. As usual, however, the problem lies, most times, in the application of the principles and identification of situations and circumstances that are to the purpose. But first this passage from Prof Riggs 'Legitimate Expectation and Procedural Fairness in English Law' (1988) 36 *Am Journal of Comparative Law* 395, which demonstrates the inter-relationship between legitimate expectation and the duty to act fairly: 'Since the landmark decision of *Ridge v Baldwin* [1964] AC 40, handed down by the House of Lords in 1963, English Courts have been in [the] process of imposing upon administrative decision-makers a general duty to act fairly. One result of this process is a body of case law holding that private interests of a status less than legal rights may be accorded procedural protections against administrative abuse and unfairness. As these cases teach, a person whose claim falls short of [a] legal right may nevertheless be entitled to some kind of hearing if the interest at stake rises to the level of a "legitimate expectation". The emerging doctrine of legitimate expectation is but one aspect of the "duty to act fairly" but its origin and development reflect many of the concerns and difficulties accompanying the broader judicial effort to promote administrative fairness. As such, it provides a useful window through which to view judicial attempts to mediate between individual interests and collective demands in the modern administrative State.' See also *Re Blake and Emanuel* (unreported), where Bishop JA addresses the duty of the Commissioner of Police to act fairly before taking an administrative decision. And Craig, Administrative Law (2 Edn), highlights the difficulty in applying the principles of law pertaining to the duty to act fairly (at page 207): 'The years since *Ridge v Baldwin* have not however been wholly marked by atavistic reasoning. Those years have also witnessed the development of new terminology. The case law is replete with mention of "fairness" or a "duty to act fairly". These terms make their initial appearance in Lord Parker CJ's judgment in *Re HK (an infant)* [1967] 2 QB 617 at page 630'. Since then their use has varied. Some Courts treat these terms in an omnibus fashion: natural justice is said to be but a manifestation of a broader concept of fairness; see *Wiseman v Borneman* [1969] 3 All ER 275 at pages 278, 279, *McInnes v Onslow-Fane* [1978] 3 All ER 211 at page 219, *O'Reilly v Mackman* [1982] 3 All ER 1124 at page 1127. In other cases the Courts will apply natural justice to judicial decisions and reserve a duty to act fairly for administrative or executive determinations; see *Re HK (an infant)* [1967] 1 All ER 226, *Pearlberg v Varty* [1972] 2 All ER 6 at pages 17, 19, 20, and *Bates v Lord Hailsham of St Marylebone* [1972] 3 All ER 1019 at pages 1023, 1024. It is not uncommon for different members of the Court to be in agreement as to the contents of the procedural duty, but to differ as to whether they describe this as resulting from natural justice or fairness; see *Re Pergamon Press Ltd* [1970] 3 All ER 535 at page 539, *per* Lord Denning MR ('fairly'), at pages 541, 542, *per* Sachs LJ ('natural justice') and at page 545, *per* Buckley LJ ('not a judicial function'). A third reference comes from Allen, Thompson and Walsh, *Cases & Materials on Constitutional and Administrative Law* (2 Edn), page 415 where the authors say: 'A related difficulty is whether there is any difference between the content of natural justice and the content of the duty to be fair. One view, which appears to be that of both Lord Roskill and Megarry VC [is that] there is no difference: the content of natural justice and the content of the duty to be fair are both flexible and depend on the circumstances of the case. Another view, however, is that the duty to be fair might include requirements which were not part of the traditional concept of natural justice, for example a duty to act on evidence (see *R v Deputy Industrial Injuries Commissioner, Ex Parte Moore* [1965] 1 QB 456).' Here in Guyana, Bollers CJ's pronouncement in *Brandt v Attorney-General of Guyana* (1971) 17 WIR 448 at page 484 is also of moment: 'An examination of these authorities leads me to the conclusion that where an administrative officer or body in the exercise of its administrative functions is called upon to decide questions affecting the rights of others, then he or they must act judicially or, as Lord Parker stated in the case of *Re HK (an infant)* [1967] 1 All ER 226, they must act fairly and observe the rules of natural justice. That can only be said to be done if they have listened to both sides.' Because of the declaration sought, with which I am now dealing, and its focus on a fair hearing and the duty to act fairly, I considered it opportune to introduce the interrelationship between legitimate expectation and the duty to act fairly, with a view to demonstrating ultimately that there are many kindred links that form an association of ideas whose treatment may be appropriate under the head 'natural justice', although I hope to show later that developments in administrative law have tended to assign to the relatively recent concept of fairness a more dynamic influence and role than the part played usually by natural justice. Indeed many of the well-known textbook writers and scholars appear to subscribe to this, as may be gathered from a brief acquaintance with their indexes; see, for example, Wade, *Administrative Law* (6 Edn), and de Smith, *Judicial Review of Administrative Action* (4 Edn) (1980). Professor Paul Jackson in his neat exposition on natural justice in his oft-cited work bearing that name (2 Edn) (1979) treats bias, the duty to act fairly, fairness, legitimate expectation and procedural irregularities. And, following his exordium to the effect that natural justice requirements may vary with modifications in societal norms, he says (at page 11): 'The English Courts . . . resort increasingly frequently to such alternatives to natural justice as "fair play in action": *Ridge v Baldwin* [1963] 1 QB 530 at page 578, *per* Harman LJ; *Wiseman v Borneman* [1969] 3 All ER 275 at page 279, *per* Lord Morris, "common fairness": *R v Secretary of State for the Home Department, Ex Parte Hosenball* [1977] 1 WLR 766 at page 784, *per* Geoffrey Lane LJ; "fairness of procedure": *Re Pergamon Press* [1971] Ch 388 at page 403, *per* Sachs LJ; "the fundamental principles of a fair trial": *Tameshwar v R* [1957] AC 476 at page 486, *per* Lord Denning; "a fair crack of the whip": *Fairmount Investments v Secretary of State for the Environment* [1976] 1 WLR 1255 at page 1266, *per* Lord Russell.' Then the author proposes an explanation which, when closely studied, suggests that the varying descriptions that he listed were employed by the Judges as they faced peculiar circumstances which demanded peculiar responses in terms of minimum procedural safeguards, when natural justice requirements were sought to be invoked. Professor Jackson continues: 'These phrases have the advantage of emphasising that requirements of natural justice vary with the circumstances of individual cases . . . ensuring that the Courts will not be led "into the trap of legalism": *Maxwell v Department of Trade and Industry* [1974] QB 523 at page 539; *R v Race Relations Board, Ex Parte Selvarajan* [1975] 1 WLR 1686 at page 1697. Such phrases may sometimes be used to refer not to the obligations to observe the principles of natural justice but, on the contrary, to refer to a standard of behaviour which, increasingly, the Courts require to be followed, even in circumstances where the duty to observe natural justice is inapplicable.' Professor Jackson's view is that procedural standards are implied in the duty to act fairly, as exemplified by Lord Pearson in *Pearlberg v Varty* [1972] 2 All ER 6 at page 17, and that fairness is not only used as a synonym for natural justice or 'to describe the minimal form of that concept as applies to administrative bodies', but also as a standard to guide Courts in many situations which cannot be described as raising questions of natural justice, unless the meaning of that term is to be stretched far beyond any rules related to the right to be heard before an impartial tribunal. The author (at page 108) refers to *Schmidt v Secretary of State for Home Affairs* [1969] 1 All ER 904 at pages 908, 909, where Lord Denning MR suggested that the ambit of natural justice extended not merely to protect rights but any 'legitimate expectation of which it would not be fair to deprive [a person] without hearing what he had to say'; see also *McInnes v Onslow-Fane* [1978] 3 All ER 211 at page 218, *per* Megarry VC. My having offered an appreciation of some features of what Prof Jackson has written on the subject of natural justice, I think an appropriate conclusion to this segment of my judgment, is provided by Foulkes, *Administrative Law* (7 Edn), page 269: 'We have therefore arrived at the position that in seeking to impose some procedural requirements on the administration it is not now (or ought not be) necessary to show that the body in question was in the particular circumstances acting judicially (or quasi-judicially), or to refer to rules of natural justice. It is enough to ask whether in all the circumstances of the case, it was acting fairly.' The exercise just concluded was aimed at showing that when discussing the subject 'natural justice' there are close and peripheral inter-relationships of meanings and purpose that reflect the varied approaches of the Courts in reacting to motions seeking judicial review of administrative action; and it may well be that at times there is overlapping, so much so that in the end some of the declarations pursued, whether out of abundant caution or inspired by a will to overwhelm the opposition, are superfluous ... [P125] In a general sense, natural justice may be seen as being concerned with those processes which were used or ought to have been by a public body or official to arrive at a decision which affects the interests of an aggrieved person. Within the parameters of that concern, there have developed special areas of consideration that include legitimate expectation and procedural requirements which are related to fairness of procedure and the duty to act fairly, although the latter may sometimes be seen or held to operate independently of the rules of natural justice. In 1975 Prof D J Mullan considered fairness to be 'The New Natural Justice' (1975) 25 *University of Toronto Law Journal*. Others must have held that view since, in the succeeding years, the concept has progressed to the stage where it seems to be treated in its own right, by some authors, as focusing on the rule against bias, the duty of fairness, and on fair hearing as being the right to fairness; see Allen, Thompson and Walsh, *Cases & Materials on Constitutional and Administrative Law* (2 Edn). See also Foulkes, *Administrative Law* (7 Edn), in which bias, fair hearing, the general duty to act fairly, legitimate expectation and procedural requirements are specifically discussed under the heading 'Fairness' ... [P133] It is correct to contend that the JSC was not an adjudicating body, but had been called upon to decide whether an adverse representation should be made against a high-ranking holder of a constitutional office who would be put at risk. His interests were unquestionably many to protect. In my view the principles of natural justice were at least impliedly to be invoked in the Appellant's favour, or procedural fairness accorded him and made manifest, thereby exemplifying the JSC's observance of its duty to act fairly. Instead, procedural fairness aimed at offering the protection which his several interests demanded of the JSC was withheld. The JSC, on the evidence, chose to adopt what the Chairman did on his own. I have already traced what his rulings were and suggest that, impelled by his view of the law, the Chairman asked himself certain questions. The answers he provided then set in train a course of events that was illegal. This was a special case; too much was at stake. Needed here was purposeful, protective and participative procedural engineering that reasonably matched the risks. Nothing of the sort occurred. Although the proceedings were non-adjudicative, I think the words of Taylor LJ in *R v Army Board of Defence, Ex Parte Anderson* [1991] 3 All ER 375 are of some assistance, since the JSC had a vital decision to make, and suspension of the Appellant and its associated disadvantages and deprivations were predictable consequences. His lordship advised (at page 387): 'There must be a proper hearing of the complaint in the sense that the Board must consider, as a single adjudicating body, all the relevant evidence and contentions before reaching its conclusions' ... [P140] Without doubt, the three aforementioned matters permitted the invoking of the *audi alteram partem* rule 'from first to last' here. The Appellant was first the holder of judicial office under the Constitution, was required to dispense justice according to law, and society held certain lofty and settled expectations of him as he discharged his duties. Secondly, had the JSC been convened to deal with the complaint in a manner that was fair in all the circumstances (*R v Commission for Racial Equality, Ex Parte Cottrell & Rothon (a firm)* [1980] 3 All ER 265, *per* Lord Lane CJ) and still had decided to make an adverse representation against the Appellant, it would there have been exercising the measure of control, in the circumstances contemplated as constituting the second criterion, in respect of natural justice rights, proposed by Lord Upjohn. Thirdly, the sanction following adverse representation was suspension, if the Chancellor (the Chairman of the JSC) so advised the President; see article 197(7) of the Constitution, which provides: 'In effecting any such suspension or any revocation of any such suspension, the President shall act in accordance with his own deliberate judgment in the case of the Chancellor or the Chief Justice and in accordance with the advice of the Chancellor in the case of any other judge.' It therefore seems correct to hold, and I so hold, that the judicial office-holder's participation is not only a pre-condition to be observed prior to the decision to make or not make the adverse representation, but he is entitled to be heard by the JSC after the adverse decision is taken ... [P141] ... certain duties devolved on the JSC; that related to them was a range of considerations, including appropriate procedural steps; and, because of its detrimental effects, suspension was an issue that required the office-holder's participation before a decision on it was made. It was a stage within the natural justice exercise ... [PP168–169] In my view, what took place before the JSC on 2 October 1989 can in no way be considered 'a fair hearing'. Apart from the absence of the Appellant from those proceedings, or anything in writing submitted by him, we have a situation where the Chancellor was not only an adjudicator but was also 'the prosecutor' and 'defence counsel'. In effect, the Appellant was never heard. In my humble opinion, the simple way in which the matter could have been properly handled by the JSC was either to read Miss la Bennett's letter of complaint to the Appellant or serve him with a copy of that letter, and then ask him what he had to say in answer to the allegation contained therein. The sum total of what I have been saying amounts to this: (1) the Appellant ought to have been heard by the JSC before it had made its representation to the President; and (2) the Appellant was never, in fact, heard by that body. I am not saying that it was absolutely necessary for the Appellant to have appeared personally before the JSC to answer the allegations. He could have submitted his explanation or answer in writing. There could have been a hearing by the presentation of documents, that is to say the JSC could have looked at written material submitted to it by the parties concerned. As Lord Denning MR said in *Kavanagh v Chief Constable of Devon and Cornwall* [1974] 2 All ER 697 at page 698: 'He need not hold any hearing. He can decide on paper'; see also Wade, *Administrative Law* (6 Edn), page 543, and *Lloyd v McMahon* [1987] 1 All ER 1118. In concluding this aspect, I could do no better than to echo the words of Bollers CJ in *Brandt v Attorney-General* (1971) 17 WIR 448, where the question to be decided was whether a German national had a right to be heard before a deportation order was made against him. Bollers CJ, citing Parke B in *Bonaker v Evans* [1850] 16 QB 162 at page 171, said (at page 477): 'No proposition can be more clearly established than that a man cannot incur the loss of liberty or property for an offence by a judicial or *quasi-judicial proceeding until he has had a fair opportunity of answering the case against him, unless indeed the legislature has expressly or impliedly given an authority to act without that necessary preliminary*' [emphasis supplied]. See also *Sheik Mohamed Hyden Ali v Public Service Commission* (unreported), *per* Luckhoo C (at pages 8, 16 of the transcript).

Having largely accepted that legitimate expection is based on procedural benefits, the courts have shown strong reluctance to use the doctrine of legitimate expectation to grant a substantive benefit.

In the Application of Vashti Sampson, Rajh Basdeo, Indar Samaroo, Grantley Prescott and James Chinapoo – Civil Appeal No 96 of 2003 (TT)
Nelson JA

[P28] It is trite law that a decision-maker cannot properly create a legitimate expectation that is beyond its statutory powers or in is breach of the law ... Even if counsel for the

Appellants could establish a legitimate expectation of a substantive benefit, it would on the present facts be affected by an overriding public interest i.e. the Authority's commitment to other persons in respect of these lands . . . What I have said about an overriding public interest would also annihilate any legitimate expectation of a procedural benefit.

***Re Gayman Jurisingh and Others* (1993) 48 WIR 301 (TT)**
Sharma JA

[P322] We think that it would be an usurpation of the functions of the executive, and contrary to the doctrine of the separation of powers, if legitimate expectation were to be used as a device for reversing or hindering the executive from carrying out its functions. They are the representatives of the people and are the most appropriate body to deal with Government policy. It seems to us that so long as there is no unlawfulness in executive actions, the Court ought not to interfere. We wish to sound a cautionary note that, if this doctrine were to develop to a point where it could give rise to substantive rights, it could lead not only to serious conflict between the executive and the judiciary but it would be contrary to the democratic principles of government, which would lead to chaos and could have the effect of crippling the executive. Matters of policy and any changes thereof are always, we repeat, for the executive. So long as the executive or the appropriate Minister does not act *ultra vires* the Courts ought not to interfere.

***In the Application of Balroop Ramlochand, Tara Ramroop, Jane Elahie, Ronald Ramdass, Jenny Lynn Diaz, Dennis Sampson, Balchan Samaroo, Dowin Alexander and Anne Alexander, Kenneth Coltrust, S. Ashook, Grace Gopaul, Terrance King and Cyntra Seepersad, Bansraj Harrilal, Patricia Austin, Kamraj Maharaj, Cindy Santoo, David Maharaj, Indar Samaroo, Ryan Headley, Rajh Basdeo, Chaitram Deonarine, Wendell Coltrust, Ashook Sookdeo, Junior Jackson, Sita Seelal, Mark Philbert, Hollister Peters* – Civil Appeal No 108 of 2003 (TT)**
Kangaloo JA

[P9] 11. Mr Maharaj contends from these undertakings that the Appellants were the beneficiaries of a legitimate expectation of a substantive benefit viz that they would be permitted to occupy their existing plots of land at Tarouba North until their occupation is regularized either on their existing plots or on alternative lands provided by the Respondents. He further contends that Rajnauth-Lee J. erred in law when she found there was no creation of a legitimate expectation of a substantive benefit. 12. I agree with the learned judge that there was no creation of a legitimate expectation of a substantive benefit as contended for by the Appellants because from the text of the speech set out, nowhere is that substantive benefit set out in terms which are 'clear, unambiguous and devoid of relevant qualification' one of the criteria necessary for a specific representation to be binding. (See *Judicial Review of Administration Action* 3rd Ed. de Smith, Woolf and Jowell pp 571–574 and the case of *R v Inland Revenue Commissioners, Ex Parte M.F.K. Underwriting Agencies Ltd* [1990] 1 WLR 1545, 1569, *per* Bingham L.J. cited therein).'

In an interesting judgment, Jamadar J seemed to have accepted that there can be legitimate expectation of a substantive benefit which is now becoming accepted in English law; however, on the facts of the particular case before him, he concluded that no such legitimate expectation was created.

***In the Application of Gillette Marina Ltd* – HCA No Cv S 1747 of 2002 (TT)**
Jamadar J

[P30] This because, if there were no representations made by PATT as alleged, then the very foundation of the Applicant's entire case is completely eroded and it falls to pieces . . . [P31] To adopt the words of Shiemann LJ in *R (Bibi) v Newman LBC* [2002] 1 WLR 237 at 244 D: 'if the public body has done nothing and said nothing which can legitimately have generated the expectation that is advanced to the Court, the case ends there'. In my opinion, this case ought to end at this point. Nevertheless, if I am wrong in the above, in my opinion, but for the representations made and actions taken by UDeCOTT in relation to the Applicant, an analysis of the other representations and/or actions taken by the other State departments cited by the Applicant (Land and Surveys, Town and Country, Ministry of Housing), show[s] that none of them (whether taken individually or collectively) were sufficiently clear, unambiguous or devoid of relevant qualification, so as to legitimately give rise to the expectations of substantive benefits claimed. None of these representations made by these other State departments were made overtly as agents of PATT and there is no evidence to suggest that any of them had any actual or ostensible authority to bind PATT (subject to the 'indivisibility of the State' for public law purposes argument to be considered later) . . . [P39] The Applicant has however raised a novel argument in this case, that of 'the indivisibility of the State' for Public Law purposes. The argument in a nutshell is, that from the perspective of the citizen, the acts of the State must be presumed to be consistent as between all 'State instrumentalities'. A 'State instrumentality' was defined as including any Ministry, State/Governmental Department, Statutory Corporation (PATT) or State owned private company (UDeCOTT). The argument advanced was that the representations, decisions and/or actions of one State instrumentality are binding on all others. And, to this extent they are all 'agents' *inter se* of the Government, and each is therefore compelled to give effect to representations, decisions and/or actions of the other, if any and/or all of same are capable of creating a legitimate expectation of a substantive benefit . . . [P41] In my opinion, given the nature of the democratic government that has been in existence in Trinidad and Tobago, since at least independence, and given its antecedents, there is no general principle, convention or practice that has been pointed to, that suggests a rule of State Corporations' and/or State owned private companies' subservience to execute policy, over and above the instruments (statutory or private) that establish these institutions. That is to say, PATT is established by statute and is obliged in law to conduct its business according to the duties, powers and responsibilities conferred on it by the enabling statute. Subject to this, PATT is an independent institution, and because of this, PATT is protected and insulated from arbitrary interference. PATT is therefore free to run its affairs as it sees fit, so long as it does so according to the provisions of the Port Authority Act and any other legislation that impacts on it. It is free, within this context, to disagree with the policies and/or actions of other statutory corporations.

2.12 FAILURE TO COMPLY WITH SETTLED PRACTICE

A public body may be judicially reviewed where it fails to follow a settled practice. This in fact is a manifestation of breach of a legitimate expectation.

In the Application of the Trinidad and Tobago Civil Rights Association –
HCA No 477 of 2004 (TT)
Dean-Armorer J

[PP59–60] I will now consider the argument that Cabinet had an obligation to employ a procedure similar to that adopted by its predecessor in appointing the first Commission. In my view, the obligation of the executive was to comply with the terms of the Environmental Management Act. They were not under an obligation to read any procedures into the statute or to be bound by procedures which had been used on a previous occasion. The authority of *AG v Whitman* (see *supra*) does not assist the Applicant. By definition a *settled practice* is one that has been observed for many years. The practice to which [the] Applicant has alluded was observed only once. Moreover, the alleged practice was not in existence at the date at which the Constitution came into effect and cannot therefore be regarded, as in *Whiteman*, as a procedural provision, envisaged by s 5(2)(h) of the Constitution . . . [P65] In the instant case the impugned decision was made by a group of persons, that is to say, the Cabinet. There is no cogent evidence of bad faith. The Court is required to infer the presence of bad faith and bias from the fact that the complaints of Justice Hosein were eventually followed by his replacement. In my view such an inference would be contrary to the preponderance of authority on bad faith and I am constrained to refuse to make it.

2.13 ACTING OUTSIDE OR IN EXCESS OF JURISDICTION

If a decision-maker acts outside, or in excess of, its jurisdiction then such a decision is reviewable, but where a decision-maker acts within its jurisdiction the courts are reluctant to review its decision. The acting outside, or in excess of, jurisdiction has also been articulated within the context of the doctrine of *ultra vires* to attack a decision of a public authority.

***In the Application of Ansarie Mohammed* – HCA No S-2089 of 2003 (TT)**
Moosai J

[P5] On the facts of this case, the power of the Commissioner of Prisons to cut the Applicant's hair and beard was circumscribed by the provisions of Rule 248, requiring the written order of the Medical Officer for the reasons set out therein, namely on account of vermin or dirt or on the grounds of health. No such written order was sought or obtained. The Commissioner of Prisons therefore acted outwith the powers conferred upon him by the Prison Rules. The decision of the Commissioner of Prisons in the circumstances was therefore unlawful.

***In the Application of Sabita Jagessar, Hazra Ramjohn, Nirmala Lokhai* – HCA No S 2053 of 2002 (TT)**
Dean-Armorer J

[P25] In the instance case, the Applicants, when they first occupied the lands, were mere squatters. They had no pretensions of holding a license from anyone and the land on which they constructed their original vending stalls had never been theirs. I am therefore of the view that the Applicants cannot be described as having occupied the land legitimately. Their original occupation from the years 1978–2000 was illegal and presents an unstable foundation for arguments as to fundamental rights ... [P43] The natural and inescapable inference from the foregoing is that the subject premises fell within the responsibility of the Director of Surveys, under the State Lands Act and that in the absence of some authorization emanating from the Director of Surveys ***neither*** the first Respondent nor Mr Dabideen had any right to enter or to evict anyone, including the Applicants ... [P45] I therefore hold that the actions and decisions of Mr Dabideen after the 12th of July, 2002 were *ultra vires* the powers, which have been conferred on him as Chairman under the Act, as amended by Act #13 of 2003.

***In the Application of the Public Service Association* – HCA No 784 of 2000 (TT)**
Smith J

[P21] No Minister can be expected personally to attend to every function or portfolio with which he is entrusted, therefore, the Courts have recognized that a Minister's power may 'devolve' upon (as opposed to being delegated to) his subordinates who in certain matters act as his alter ego and for whose actions he is responsible before Parliament ... [PP21–22] If the Carltona principle were to be held to straddle across Ministers and Ministries, without express legislation to that effect, it would make a sham of the doctrine of Ministerial responsibility to Parliament. It could result in difficult and embarrassing questions as to which Minister or Ministry is subordinate to the other or acts as the alter ego of the other. It could also cause confusion and uncertainty in cases where Ministerial functions overlap for then it may prove impossible to decide who is primarily responsible for a particular function of government and who should answer to Parliament for the area of government concerned. Ministers may also discover that they are saddled with responsibilities with which neither themselves nor their Ministries are equipped to deal, and which it was never intended to pass on to them. Likewise they may discover that another Minister or Ministry may be able to stake a better claim for an area over which they traditionally exercised control and with which they were better prepared to deal. Also, even Parliament, public servants and members of the public may not be able to ascertain who is the proper Minister to hold responsible for a particular branch or function of government ... [P22] Indeed, to simply apply the Carltona principle as between Ministers and Ministries would make a mockery of the principle of Ministerial responsibility, and I hold that it does not so apply ... [P23] (A) If one Minister purported to delegate a duty which was specifically imposed upon him to another Minister, or if he authorized another Minister to perform such a specific duty, he would be acting *ultra vires*; similarly, if one Minister abdicated his responsibility for such a specific duty and left it to another Minister he too would be acting *ultra vires* ... [PP24–25] (B) Even if it could not be proved that the Minister of Finance had delegated to or abdicated his duty under Section 24 in favour of the Minister of Health, if the Minister of Health purported to exercise that very duty which was imposed by statute specifically upon the Minister of Finance alone, he would have been acting without authority and outside of his lawful powers so that any direction given under such an illegal exercise of jurisdiction would also have been illegal ... [P25] Therefore, the simple argument that as a matter of law, the Minister of Health cannot be in breach of the duty of the Minister of Finance would not have been an answer to the *allegation* of illegality in this case.

***In the Application of the Public Service Association* – Civil Appeal No 123 of 2000 (TT)**
Warner JA

[P16] It is clear that if a Minister purports to carry out or interfere with statutory duties imposed on another Minister, the former will be acting in excess of authority, and not in breach of any statutory duty.

***In the Application of Ricky Sagram* – HCA No Cv299 of 1997 (TT)**
Jamadar J

[P14] In my opinion, by equal measure, the failure of the Magistrate to advise this Applicant of his right to apply for bail to a judge in chambers, and her decision to remand him in custody without bail or the opportunity to be granted bail, is so fundamental a breach that it amounts to the breach of a constitutional right, and *a fortiori*, undermined the Magistrate's jurisdiction to have made the remand order against the Applicant in this case (which by agreement is to be brought before this Court and quashed). I therefore hold that the Magistrate, in the circumstances of this case, acted outside of her jurisdiction and/or in excess of her jurisdiction, in remanding the Applicant into custody without bail on the 31st December, 1996 until the 3rd January, 1997 ... [P16] In my opinion therefore, the Magistrate is not entitled to the protection of Section 13 of the Magistrates Protection Act, as neither of the two conditions set out therein have been proven. (see *R v Manchester Ct., Ex Parte Davies* CA [1989] 1 QB 631). The Magistrate's liability to the Applicant for damages is therefore not limited to the sum of one cent. There is thus no bar to an assessment of the Applicant's damages, caused by the admitted illegal, unreasonable and unlawful decision of the Magistrate made on 31st December, 1996.

***In the Application of Delano Dennis* – HCA No 4143 of 1995 (TT)**
Blackman J

[P8] The PSC acts without its jurisdiction if it breaches provisions of the Constitution and such breaches may include a breach of the Applicant's right to be treated fairly, or his right to those fundamental principles of justice under our laws.

***In the Application of Josephine Millette* – Civil Appeal No 155 of 1995 (TT)**
de la Bastide CJ

[P16] In my view, if an order is made which the Court making it has no jurisdiction to make, it is open to any Court of competent jurisdiction to treat that order as void in any proceedings in which the validity of the order is relevant, even though that is not the purpose for which the proceedings were brought. Nor does it make any difference in my view that the order was made by consent, as it is well established that parties cannot by their consent confer on the Court a jurisdiction which it does not have.

***In the Application of the Aviation Communication and Allied Workers Union* –**
Civil Appeal No 35 of 1995 (TT)
Ibrahim JA

[P8] Sec. 23(7) excludes any Court from expounding on any matter touching the interpretation and application of the Act relating to the Board's functions and responsibilities and prohibits any legal proceedings concerning any matter touching the interpretation and application of the Act. It makes the Board the sole authority competent to deal with such matters. Once, therefore, it is a matter that falls within the functions and responsibilities of the Board then the Board can interpret and apply the Act in any way it thinks fit in relation to those functions and responsibilities. It may do so correctly or incorrectly and, if incorrectly, it is immune from being put right by any Court. If, however, the error made does affect the jurisdiction of the Board then it may be put right, as, for example, if it seeks to deal with a matter outside of its functions and responsibilities. Also, if it violates the rules of natural justice as for example, if it makes orders against a party without hearing that party or if one of its members has a real interest in the matter before it . . . [P9] In my view the matter is one that is properly before the Board for its determination. It is within its jurisdiction. The rules of natural justice are not breached. The learned judge came to a correct decision and for that reason the appeal would be dismissed.

***In the Application of the Aviation Communication and Allied Workers Union* –**
HCA No 2037 of 1993 (TT)
Sealey J

[P14] From the authorities, it would seem too, that once the tribunal is acting within its jurisdiction it is allowed to come to a right conclusion as well as wrong one. In such a case, that decision would not be reviewable, as the tribunal would have been acting within its jurisdiction. Having regard to the authorities, it is my view that the decisions of the Board are reviewable by the Court if the decision is made outside of the statutory functions and powers set out in Section 23(1) of the Act.

***In the Application of the Trinidad and Tobago Police Association* –**
HCA No 1946 of 1992 (TT)
Sealy J

[P12] Power given in an Act to make Regulations does not enable any authority to go beyond the 'scope or general operation of the enactment but is strictly ancillary. It will authorize the provision of subsidiary means of carrying into effect what is enacted in the statute itself and will cover what is incidental to the execution of its specific provisions. But such a power will not support attempts to widen the purposes of the Act, to add new and different means of carrying them out or to depart from or vary its ends'. *Utah Construction v Pataky* [1965] 3 All ER 650 at 653 *per* Lord Guest quoting from the Australian case of *Shanahan v Scott*. Clearly authorized persons are given power under specific legislative provisions to make Regulations in conformity with the particular statute, for the better management of the powers given under the statute; but they are not allowed to go beyond the intended scope of the statute.

***In the Application of the Board of Management Established Under the National Insurance Act* – HCA No 1272 of 1988 (TT)**
Ibrahim J

[PP2–3] Following the conclusions reached in that case I hold that the Respondent had no jurisdiction to hear and determine the matter.

***In the Application of Robert Fletcher* – HCA No 100 of 1987 (TT)**
Davis J

[P10] I am satisfied therefore that in this matter the learned Magistrate did exceed his jurisdiction under Section 10 of the Landlord and Tenant Ordinance Ch. 27, No. 16, and that there is no impediment in the way of my granting the relief sought.

***In the Application of the National Insurance Appeals Tribunal* – HCA No 5851 of 1985 (TT)**
Deyalsingh J

[P3] In my judgment, the issue involves the construction of the Act and is one of law and therefore, outside the jurisdiction of the Respondent.

***In the Application of Ramesh Lawrence Maharaj* – HCA No 2337 of 1986 (TT)**
Collymore J

[PP21–22] The important question now is, however, as to whether this error by the learned Magistrate is one which arises upon a question properly arising within her jurisdiction, or whether it is one in which she wrongly decided that she was without jurisdiction. The distinction is an important one, because as the cases show, an error of law as to a matter within jurisdiction is not reviewable by Certiorari, whereas the failure to exercise jurisdiction on the belief that it does not exist, is reviewable . . . [P25] Similarly, on the facts of this case, it is clear that Certiorari will lie on the ground that the learned Magistrate misconstrued the provision giving her power to act and so failed to deal with the question remitted to her, thus giving rise to a breach of the requirements of Natural Justice.

***R v The Industrial Disputes Tribunal ex parte Bank of Jamaica* – Supreme Court No M-116 of 2001 (JM)**
Pitter J

[PP19–20] I adopt the following extract taken from Benion *Statutory Interpretations*, second edition, Section 265: 'It is a principle of legal policy that law should be just, and that Court decisions should further the ends of justice. The Court when considering, in relation to the facts of the instant case, which of the opposing constructions of the enactment would give effect to the legislative intention, should presume that the legislation intended to observe this principle. The Court should therefore strive to avoid adopting a construction that leads to injustice.' Having regard to the foregoing, I am satisfied that the Tribunal in arriving at its decision to calculate Mrs. Steele's salary at level Grade 12 acted within its statutory jurisdiction and took due cognizance of and applied the provisions of the Employment (Termination and Redundancy Payments) Act and the Regulations thereunder. I am satisfied further that the Tribunal did not make the award inconsistent with any enactment of law, but acted within its powers and did not contravene Section 12(7)(a) of the Labour Relations and Industrial Disputes Act.

***In the Application of Carlton Brooks* – Supreme Court No M28 of 2001 (JM)**
Cooke J

[P4] It would seem to me that in the establishment of the Commission 'to regulate horseracing and the operation of racecourses' entitles that body to make such rules as in its opinion is necessary, or expedient or to facilitate the operation of the horseracing industry. I must say I would be loath to find any prescribed rule offensive unless it can be demonstrated that such rule is clearly outside of the Commission's competence.

***Regina v The Attorney General ex parte, The Jamaica Bar Association* – Supreme Court No M89 of 1999 (JM)**
Smith J

[P49] In light of the view I take that this involves the exercise of legislative power, in the circumstances, it would follow that only Parliament can alter the existing practice and procedure in respect of the hours within which the sittings take place. For the reasons which I have endeavoured to give I would answer the question posed by saying that the Chief Justice, in my respectful opinion, does not have the power to alter the hours of opening of the Courts aforementioned . . . [P85] So, in making his decision to alter the hours within which the daily sittings of the Resident Magistrate Court, The Family Court and Petty Sessions, the Family Court and the Resident Magistrate's Division of the Gun Court are to be conducted as of July 5, 1999, I would say, with respect, that the Chief Justice acted *ultra vires* his powers.

***In the Application of Cremo Ltd* – Supreme Court No M 122 of 1998 (JM)**
Walker J

[P7] Was the Minister here concerned with an industrial dispute within the contemplation of s 11A? I am not so persuaded. The Minister is not at large to act, and may not act, as arbiter in every instance where there is a dispute between an employer and a worker, even if such dispute be one that occurs in the course of employment. The Minister is not statutorily cast in such a role. The power given to the Minister by s 11A is properly invoked only in circumstances which are in conformity with the overall scheme of the Act, and after compliance with such conditions precedent as are prescribed in that section of the Act. In the instant case, it is clear that the Minister's reference was not prompted by a need to achieve or to preserve industrial peace, nor was it made in the public or national interest.

***Clifford Brown, Diana Brown and Ronald Williams v The Resident Magistrate of St. Catherine and the National Construction Company Ltd* (1995) 32 JLR 117 (JM)**
Carey JA

[P120] The function then of this Court is to examine the proceedings to discover whether the Full Court exercised its supervisory powers correctly. In my view, the Full Court was required in this matter to satisfy itself that the Resident Magistrate had not by some error of law exceeded her jurisdiction. The question was not simply whether she had erred in law because an appeal lies against any judgment which in the event she might have given. A resident Magistrate is permitted to fall into error but that does not necessarily make the judgment amenable to certiorari. It becomes so if and only if, the Magistrate can be said to be acting in excess of jurisdiction or without jurisdiction.

***The Minister of Foreign Affairs, Trade and Industry v Vehicles and Supplies Ltd and Northern Industrial Garage Ltd* (1991) 28 JLR 198 (JM)**
Lord Oliver

[P202] Their Lordships entertain no doubt that Ellis, J, was acting within his jurisdiction in making the order which he made on the Appellant's application and they have difficulty in understanding Carey, JA's, assertion that the Judge had before him no new material justifying his exercise of the jurisdiction. He had in fact most material evidence, adduced before the Court for the first time, first as to the supposed effect of the stay which Clarke J had purported to grant, and secondly that in fact the allocation had been made already and the instructions given to JCTC which, insofar as the 'stay' could have had effect, was not bound by the order and was not even a party to the proceedings. In their Lordship's judgment, Ellis, J, was entitled, on an application properly made, in his discretion to vary or revoke the *ex parte* order which had been made by Clarke, J, and no ground has been shown for any interference by an appellate Court with his exercise of discretion, which seems to their Lordships perfectly proper on the supposition, which everybody connected with the Court seems to have adopted, that the order for a stay had some inhibiting effect.

***Banana and Ramie Products Co Ltd v Ministry of Lands and Natural Resources* (1989) 41 WIR 76 (BZ)**
Henry P

[P76] It is conceded by Mr Hesse, counsel for the Respondents, that this part of the impugned order cannot stand as the determination so made was made by the Chairman alone and was not a determination of the Board. However, Mr Hesse has expressed the opinion that, had the Board itself made that determination, certiorari would not go as the determination as to the validity of title of a claimant is within the competence of a board under the Act . . . [P77] We disagree. While a board has implied power for the purpose of apportioning compensation to determine a claimant's interest in or right over property compulsorily acquired, it does not have power, express or implied, to determine title to property. It may only decide between competing claims of claimants for the purpose of apportioning compensation. Section 28 of the Act does not give the Board the power to determine title to land. That section provides that, where any question arises touching the title of any person to any land which may be entered upon or acquired for the purposes of the Act, or touching any estate or interest therein, the person having the ostensible possession or enjoyment of the rents and profits of such land should, for the purposes of the Act, be deemed to be the owner of the land until the contrary is proved. We do not find that section as authorising a board of assessment to determine the title of a claimant to the land compulsorily acquired. Such a determination is to be entrusted to the Supreme Court. Further, it is inconceivable that the legislature would entrust such a determination to an administrative tribunal the majority of the members of which might be persons without any legal qualifications.

***R v The Coroner for the Parish of St. Andrew ex parte Michael Alderidge* (1988) 25 JLR 195 (JM)**
Bingham J

[P196] It is abundantly clear that as the Learned Coroner was sitting without a Jury subsection (2) applied, and that if during the course of the hearing, having regard to the conclusion at which she arrived it must have operated in her mind at some stage of the proceedings that a finding adverse to the Applicant who was the driver of the motor car, may have been probable. Once that state was reached, there was no question of the Learned Coroner having a discretion in the matter as to whether to continue to stop the proceedings. The subsection mandates that this stage effectively results in what amounts to an ouster of the jurisdiction of the Coroner to continue the hearing without summoning a Jury. In so far as the Learned Coroner failed to have proper regard to provisions of Section 16 of the relevant Act, therefore, she acted in excess of her jurisdiction and the inquest held as well as the finding which followed was bad for want of jurisdiction.

***R v Commissioner of Income Tax ex parte Donald Panton* (1988) 25 JLR 448 (JM)**
Bingham J

[P454] Again, however, if I am wrong in so contending, in seeking to discover whether the actions of the Commissioner in requesting a sworn disclosure statement from the Applicant was lawful or not, an examination of the Act and in particular Section 75 discloses that the Commissioner although clothed with certain inquisitorial powers had no such authority. Section 75(5) merely empowers the Commissioner in her sole discretion to summon any person (which may include the Applicant) and to examine him on oath in respect [of] any assessment. This power does not extend to the request made of the Applicant in this case. It suffices to state that in this regard the Commissioner sought to arrogate unto herself powers which the Legislature had not given to her. In-so-far as her actions sought to make such a request of the Applicant, it was *ultra vires* and void. He was quite within his rights in refusing to comply with this request.

R v Commissioner of Police ex parte Howard Patrick Brown (1987) 24 JLR 53 (JM)
Wolfe J

[P55] An improperly constituted Court cannot be seized of jurisdiction and any action taken without being properly seized of jurisdiction is a nullity.

Glen Simms, Lincoln Ellis, Lynford Hue and Claud Thompson v Jamaica Racing Commission (1985) 22 JLR 264 (JM)
Kerr JA

[PP267–268] To have given the relevant provisions the narrow interpretation sought by Mr Rattray would be to ignore the primary purpose and functions for which the Commission was created, namely, to take over the reins of control from the Jockey Club and to have no less power than its predecessor to maintain discipline in the horse racing industry. Accordingly, I am of the opinion that rules, in particular Rules 247(XI) and 248 empowering the Commission to impose 'warning off' as a penalty, were in keeping with the legislative intent and *intra vires* rule making competence of the Commission. For these reasons, I concurred in dismissing the appeals and affirming the order of the Full Court.

R v Collector-General and the Licensing Authority for the Central Area ex parte Carroll Lawrence (1982) 19 JLR 396 (JM)
Smith CJ

[P399] In my opinion, the contention for the Collector-General is mis-conceived. In the first place, the Collector-General, to whom sales tax is payable, cannot lawfully authorize or direct the Collector of Taxes to make the issuance of a license under the Road Traffic Act subject to the payment of unpaid sales tax on a motor car. As provided in s 7 of this Act, the Collector of Taxes is, in this respect, the delegate of the Licensing Authority and is, therefore, subject only to the directions of that Authority. Secondly, in refusing to issue the temporary authority or a fresh license to the Applicant, the Collector of Taxes acted without lawful authority. Such discretion as he has was exercised for a reason for which was bad in law (see *Congreve v Home Office* [1976] 1 All ER 697 at 709). The Retail Sales Tax Act does not prohibit or restrict the resale of prescribed goods on which the original purchaser has not paid sales tax. Nor does it make a subsequent purchaser liable to pay that tax. The only sanctions imposed by the Act, where exempted goods are put to taxable use in breach of imposed terms or conditions, are liability on the original purchaser to pay the sales tax from which the goods were exempt and a penalty for commission of a criminal offence.

R v The Industrial Disputes Tribunal and Half Moon Bay Hotel Ltd (1979) 16 JLR 333 (JM)
Campbell J

[P342] I would respectfully adopt that statement and hold by analogy that whereas in this case the Act creates the right and prescribes the procedure to be followed leading to the creation of the right, no other method of creating the right is available, and the Tribunal would be exceeding its jurisdiction were it to declare the exercise of a right of recognition with the derivative right to negotiate which does not have its origin in the procedure prescribed in Section 5. I would accordingly allow the application of the Company on the ground that the facts do not constitute an industrial dispute and that accordingly the reference to the Tribunal is invalid also on the alternative ground that the dispute in question amounting as it does to a recognition dispute is expressly reserved for determination exclusively by the Minister under Section 5.

Parnell J

[P350] It seems to follow that where a pre-1975 collective agreement is relied on by a trade union, the employer is free—subject to his facing industrial action—to withdraw recognition of the union in question. This is a legal right which has not been affected by the Act. To submit such a claim which is made by an employer to a Tribunal for settlement is to ask the Tribunal to find whether a legal right which is crystallized before a reference is formulated, does or does not exist in fact.

***Aston Kane v Minister of Home Affairs and Justice* (1975) 13 JLR 109 (JM)**
Edun JA

[P111] In my view, the Appellant must satisfy us that the acting Chief Justice erred in principle or that he acted improperly, unjustly or wrongly. If he did act correctly, and exercised his discretion judicially, this Court should not and must not interfere with the discretion of a judge acting within his jurisdiction. Can we say from the facts and circumstances of the appeal before us that the acting Chief Justice was in any way wrong in the exercise of his discretion? . . . [P113] So too, despite the breach of the rule of natural justice it was well within the jurisdiction of the acting Chief Justice, to hold as he did, that the Appellant was not entitled to an extension of time within which to apply for leave to obtain a prerogative order, having regard to the facts and circumstances of the case before him.

2.14 PROPORTIONALITY

The courts have rejected the notion that, based on the principle of proportionality, a decision can be held to be reasonable where the harm incurred is minimal.

***In the Application of Seereeram Bros. Ltd* – HCA No 3123 of 1991 (TT)**
Jones J

[P23] The submissions of Attorneys for the Board and the Interested Party come close to an attempt to introduce into our law the principle of proportionality which had been rejected as being part of laws of England . . . [P25] As in the law of England, this doctrine has no place in the laws of Trinidad and Tobago and I decline any invitation to introduce it. To say that the decision of the Board is not unreasonable since the difference in price is less than 1% and there is the advantage of having the project completed in a shorter time, is to fall into the same error into which the Board fell by ignoring the possibility of there being extensions of time, which would trigger the fluctuation clause with the attendant increase or decrease in the price of the contract.

2.15 TAKING INTO ACCOUNT IRRELEVANT CONSIDERATIONS

Where a decision-maker takes into account irrelevant considerations in arriving at a decision, the courts may be inclined to condemn such decision. It must be emphasised that the decision-maker must have taken into account a factor he considered relevant but which, in fact, he ought not to have considered.

***In the Application of George Nicholas, Chairman of Mora Oil Ventures Ltd* –**
HCA No 2451 of 2004 and HCA No S516 of 2004 (TT)
Narine J

[P5] The High Court has always exercised a supervisory jurisdiction over proceedings of inferior Courts and tribunals. A Magistrate who conducts a preliminary inquiry for the purpose of deciding whether a person charged with an indictable offence should be committed for trial is performing a Ministerial and not a judicial function: *Amman v Wegener and Or* [1971] 129 CLR 415 (High Court of Australia). Administrative action is subject to control by judicial review where the decision-making authority has been guilty of an error of law, or has acted so unreasonably that no reasonable authority would have made such a decision, or where the decision-making authority has failed in its duty to act fairly. These grounds may be considered under the heads of illegality, irrationality and procedural impropriety. See: *Council of Civil Service Unions and Ors v Minister for the Civil Service* [1984] 3 All ER 935 at 937 . . . [P14] It appears on the face of his written reasons that the Magistrate considered irrelevant matters in coming to his decision. In particular the Magistrate took pains to consider the operating Agreement ('GN 9') and the Acquisition and Shareholder's Agreement ('GN 10') which have no bearing on the issue as to whether or not the signatories on Mora Oil's accounts were validly removed. Likewise, the Magistrate appears to have attached considerable significance to a certified copy of a Notice of Charge of Directors ('FS 2'), which has no relevance to any issue in the case.

In the Application of Caribbean Ispat Ltd – HCA No 458 of 1998 (TT)
Ventour J

[PP20–21] When Dr Mungrue, in his capacity as Secretary of the Council, wrote to Attorneys at Law for the Applicant on 5th December, 1997 stating that the '*Council can only proceed further when evidence of fraud has been established*' that statement demonstrates unequivocally in my view an abdication of the Council's responsibility under the provisions of the Act . . . [P21] The investigation being carried out by the police may or may not lead to the prosecution of anyone. And even if it does, a successful prosecution of Dr Dominique on indictment will provide a basis for disciplinary action separate and apart from infamous or disgraceful conduct in a professional respect in accordance with Section 24(1) of the Act. Therefore, to state that the Council can only proceed further in the matter when evidence of fraud has been established is to take into consideration extraneous matters in the exercise of its discretion.

In the Application of J. Astaphan and Co. (1970) Ltd – Civil Appeal No 5 of 1997 (DM)
Redhead JA

[P6] I agree entirely with this submission because if the Minister in exercising his discretion under S 4 of this Act were to take into consideration the resolutions of the Council of Ministers or the Treaty of Chaguaramas he would be taking into consideration irrelevant matters . . . [P9] It is quite clear from the affidavit evidence of Larocque that the Minister in exercising his discretion under S 4 of the Act took into consideration the Treaty of Chaguaramas and the resolutions of the Council of Ministers. He therefore took into consideration irrelevant considerations in making the impugned orders.

Barnwell v Attorney-General and Another (1993) 49 WIR 88 (GY)
Bishop CJ

[P103] In sum, the clear words of article 197(5) and the silence in the Constitution and elsewhere as to what pre-requisites, if any, were to be met by the JSC, or what matters it was to inform itself on, or be informed on or about, with or without the assistance or contribution of the Appellant, may have influenced the JSC to ask itself whether that silence or absence of guidelines was not intentional on the part of the framers of the Constitution and permitted it to conclude that there was no room for any implied procedure allowing an appearance of the Appellant before it. It would seem that the exclusion of the Appellant from appearing before the JSC reflects the question it asked itself and the answer it gave. If that exercise involved a misdirection in law or misconception of it or the taking 'into account of extraneous or irrelevant considerations', the influence on the decision to exclude the Appellant from appearing before the JSC would have been sufficiently substantial as to impair the decision and render it a nullity. In *Hanks v Minister of Housing and Local Government* [1963] 1 All ER 47 at page 55 Megaw J said: 'A "consideration", I apprehend, is something which one takes into account as a factor in arriving at a decision. I am prepared to assume, for the purposes of this case, that, if it be shown that an authority exercising a power has taken into account as a relevant factor something which it could not properly take into account in deciding whether or not to exercise the power, then the exercise of the power, normally at least, is bad. Similarly, if the authority fails to take into account as a relevant factor something which is relevant, and which is or ought to be known to it, and which it ought to have taken into account, the exercise of that power is normally bad. I say "normally" because I can conceive that there may be cases where the factor wrongly taken into account, or omitted, is insignificant, or where the wrong taking-into-account, or omission actually operated in favour of the person who later claims to be aggrieved by the decision' ... [P108] It may therefore be seen straight away that article 199 does not contemplate the situation of the Chairman acting on the JSC's behalf in a matter touching alleged misbehaviour of a member of the judiciary, and I can find no provision in the Constitution permitting him to so act. It therefore follows that, even if the members of the JSC were willing to receive the Chairman's report of what transpired first between himself and the Magistrate and (later) between himself and the Appellant, the Chairman's act could not be representative of the Constitutional body called the JSC, nor did its members possess the Constitutionally-endowed power to authorise, or ratify, or acquiesce in, any act of the Chairman himself, touching the misconduct alleged against the Appellant. The authors Keir, Lawson and Bentley in *Cases in Constitutional Law* (6 Edn) (1979) speak on the question of delegation (at page 413): 'Thus in *Allingham v Minister of Agriculture and Fisheries* [1948] 1 All ER 780, it was held that a county War Agricultural Executive Committee could not delegate to its executive officer the task of deciding what crops should be grown on particular plots of land; and that in consequence a notice issued by an executive officer ordering the Defendant to grow sugar-beet on a particular plot was ineffectual. But it seems clear, as is so often the case in problems of administrative law, that the question always depends on the construction of the empowering statute. In *Allingham's case*, the Defendant was held to be entitled to have the decision of the executive committee and of no-one else, and the executive officer was held to have acted on his own responsibility' ... [PP108–109] In the end, I am obliged to hold that, here, the Chairman's act of interviewing the Appellant was his own and not the JSC's; that if it is possible to call what transpired between the two a 'hearing', since that term has many connotations (de Smith's *Judicial Review of Administrative Action* (4 Edn) (1980) pages 201, 202), it still does not transform that act into any other person's. It has been said that each body is 'master of its own procedure' (*R v Race Relations Board, Ex Parte Selvarajan* [1976] 1 All ER 12 at page 19, *per* Lord Denning MR) but, in the final analysis, that mastership (as I understand it) would depend on the permissiveness that is yielded by a correct construction of the relevant statutory or constitutional provisions. If, therefore, the Chairman here intended to conduct a 'hearing' on behalf of the JSC or for its benefit, and the JSC thought that the Chairman's act could be adopted, the vote its members took was ineffectual because the Chairman's act was, in the first place, unauthorised, illegal, and a nullity. Further, by so acting, the Respondents displayed conspicuous ambivalence towards the Appellant's entitlement to a hearing, since while it was being strenuously resisted by them, it was none the less conceded, with equal force, to have been accorded him when the Chairman alone interviewed him ... [P110] After all has been said and done, it would be in order to state that the acts of the Chancellor and Chairman in his meetings with the Appellant, to the extent that they are understood to have been for, or on behalf of, the JSC, were acts of improperly assumed agency and *ultra vires*. They were acts performed on his own responsibility and inefficacious.

***In the Application of Leslie Mc Call* – HCA No 750 of 1992 (TT)**
Warner J

[P16] I find that Dr Beckles' Report, his amplifying statement and several exhibits thereto, touch and concern a wide range of matters not contained in his memoranda to the Applicant, and of which the Applicant had no notice ... I find therefore upon a balance of probabilities the Commission would have taken into account matters which it ought not to have taken into account.

***In the Application of Seereeram Bros. Ltd* – HCA No 3123 of 1991 (TT)**
Jones J

[P30] From the evidence it is beyond doubt that the Board had misdirected itself in its interpretation of the fluctuation clause in the contract . . . [PP30–31] The Board also misdirected itself by interpreting the comment of Mr Beache who was commissioned to evaluate the tenders, that the difference in the time stated for completion is not considered to be too significant to be that there was no significant difference in the time stated for completion between the Applicant Company and the Interested party. These matters show that the Board embarked upon a wrong course and made wrong assumptions which must have materially affected its judgment. Another matter which the Board took into consideration was the fact that Applicant Company had been granted other contracts which were ongoing at the time of consideration of the award. This was revealed by Mr Baboolal under cross-examination. That that was a matter totally irrelevant to the Board's consideration goes without saying . . . [P31] Attorney for the Board supported by Attorney for the Interested Party both emphasized that to be impugned the decision must be unreasonable in the sense of being absurd and outrageous as to defy logic. The authorities, however, suggest that the Court would view all lapses of administrative behaviour as being unreasonable. The concept of unreasonableness includes mistakes and misunderstandings.

***R v The Industrial Disputes Tribunal ex parte Jamaica Civil Service Association* – Supreme Court No M-36 of 2001 (JM)**
Pitter J

[PP15–16] There being no reason given by the Tribunal in arriving at its decision in making the award of $15,000 *per* month upkeep, this Court is constrained to review the evidence presented and the addresses made by the contending parties. At this stage this Court is concerned only to determine if the Tribunal fell into error. The question to be answered is whether the Tribunal acted on the evidence before it and if so whether it took irrelevant considerations into account, or failed to take relevant considerations into account or wrongfully excluded evidence.

The irresistible inference drawn results in my findings:

(1) That the Tribunal erred in law when it allowed the use of the Suzuki Baleno motor car to be adduced in evidence as the average car, or at all.
(2) That the Tribunal erred in law when it allowed evidence of budgetary constraints and national interest and acted upon these considerations.
(3) That the Tribunal erred in law when it took in consideration '**the reasonableness**' of the Government's offer.
(4) That the Tribunal erred in law when it disregarded the recommendation of Mr N Wilson, the Government's own expert.
(5) That the Tribunal erred in law when it failed to give effect to the provisions of Section 9.1 of the Staff Order by not making the award one of re-imbursement and acted instead on other considerations.
(6) These several errors render the award of the Tribunal a nullity.

***R v Commissioner of Customs and Excise, The Minister of Finance and The Resident Magistrate for the Parish of St. Andrew ex parte Machines and Allied Traders Ltd and Richard Khouri* (1993) 30 JLR 34 (JM)**
Clarke J

[P39] Our power to interfere with the Commissioner's decision is not that of an appellate body to override his decision. As a Court of review we are concerned only to see that he has not contravened the law by acting in excess of his statutory powers. Accordingly, on examining the affidavit evidence bearing upon his action we must determine whether he has taken into account irrelevant matters or has refused to take into account relevant matters. Even if he has so complied we can interfere if no reasonable authority could have decided to prosecute on the material he had before him: see *Associated Provincial Picture House Ltd. v Wednesbury Corporation (supra)*.

The party seeking judicial review must demonstrate that irrelevant considerations were considered by the decision-maker and not rely on unclear evidence of such irrelevant considerations.

***Dennie v The Chairman and Members of The Public Service Commission Saint Vincent and The Grenadines* – High Court Civil Suit No 196 of 1995 (VC)**
Adams J

[Para21] While I must acknowledge the principle that a tribunal's decision as the cases show, would in some cases he considered void because of the taking into account of matters extraneous to a proper adjudication upon the matter before it, I am of the view that this is not such a case. There is indeed very little evidence as to the questions actually asked. But, I accepted without hesitation the evidence of Dr Kenneth John, an Attorney-at-Law who as I have said presided as Chairman over the meeting of the Commission and swore that: '*The Plaintiff was asked a few questions which arose out of the main five questions*. I can see nothing wrong with that; everyone knows that the asking of the questions described as *main* may lead to relevant incidental questions, and incidental questions to the Plaintiff seem to suggest some answering on his part of preceeding questions'.

2.16 FAILURE TO CONSIDER RELEVANT MATTERS

A decision-maker must consider all relevant matters in arriving at a decision and its decision may be revoked on the ground that it has failed to consider a relevant matter.

***In the Application of Chandardaye Ramjitsingh* – HCA No 2744 of 2002 (TT)**
Mohammed J

[P20] There was in my view no rational basis for the decision of the Central Public Assistance Board. With respect to the medical reports before the Board where an opinion was expressed as to the nature, extent and effect of the Applicant's disabilities, they all pointed in the direction of the opposite conclusion than the one arrived at by the Board . . . [P21] There is therefore no indication that the Central Board took into account any irrelevant factors. Rather, the Board failed to give sufficient weight to relevant ones, the most important being the two reports from Dr Harry Singh and the further report from a different source, the St. Helena Health Centre, all of which spoke of the nature, extent and effect of the Applicant's disability in terms of her ability to earn a living.

***Dougnath Rajkumar* – Privy Council Appeal No 1 of 2001 (TT)**
Lord Mackay of Clashfern

[P14] 17. In the Court of Appeal the main judgment was given by Nelson JA, with whom Sharma JA and Ibrahim JA agreed, Sharma JA adding comments on the power of the Judge in judicial review applications to make the decision himself in substitution for a decision which he held to be flawed. In the principal judgment Nelson JA had reviewed the facts in some detail noting the Appellant's abiding sense of injustice that despite such protracted acting as Prison Officer II he has not been given the substantive post. He also states that, 'In the present case there is no evidence of any shortcomings or adverse comments in relation to the Respondent [now the Appellant]. Therefore none are to be assumed'. Later he went on: 'Since consideration of annual staff reports is only one of the many factors to be taken into account in assessing an officer's entitlement to promotion, all other factors having been considered I would hold that there was substantial compliance with the Regulations'. He also stated that the Appellant had intact his right of appeal to the Public Service Appeal Board. This is incorrect. The appeal referred to, is available only in disciplinary cases ... [PP14–15] 19. At the hearing before their Lordships, counsel for the Respondents accepted that having regard to the history of this matter this might well be a case in which reasons were required for the absence of promotion and he submitted that the reason was given in the evidence of the Commissioner that the Appellant was placed on the order of merit list prepared in 1995 and although he had not as yet secured promotion. 20. It is true as the Court of Appeal has said that the absence of staff reports was something that affected all Applicants for promotion, but not necessarily equally. For some the way they had done the work might commend them more effectively for promotion, than answering questions in an interview. 21. Their Lordships have reached the conclusion that in restricting consideration of the Appellant's promotion to the order of merit list of 1995—already three years old—and disregarding the other matters referred to in Regulation 172, in particular (e), an evaluation of the officer's overall performance as reflected in the annual staff reports, the approach taken to the decision on the Appellant's promotion was fundamentally flawed. 22. The Commissioner's account of the matter, which their Lordships have already quoted proceeds on the ability of the panel of interviewers to assess the officer on the basis of his response to their questions and makes no reference whatsoever to his experience or service in the office to which he was seeking promotion. Against that background to refuse him promotion because his turn as determined by the out-of-date merit list had not yet come is not substantial compliance with the terms of Regulation 172 and is unfair to the Appellant.

***In the Application of Air Caribbean Ltd* – HCA No 707 of 1998 (TT)**
Hosein J

[P29] This judgement has already adverted to the three matters raised by the Applicant to which the Respondent did not specifically give consideration namely BWIA's fianancial difficulties, the type of aircraft that it proposed to use and the uneconomic overlapping of BWIA's scheduled flights with those of the Applicant. In addition the Respondent gave consideration to a matter that was not relevant namely of the demand by the public for an additional airline. In the circumstances this Court holds that the Respondent acted illegally, in excess of its jurisdiction and committed an error of law.

***In the Application of Sumayyah Mohammed* – HCA No 3000A of 1994 (TT)**
Warner J

[P34] *Have the Respondents failed to take into account matters which they ought to have taken into account*? Again, the starting point is the acceptance of the sincerity of belief. However, the Respondents do not appear to have taken into account the psychological effect of insisting that the Applicant remove the hijab; the ripping away of traditions which she has observed for half of her life. Secondly, the official position of the Ministry of Education is that they do not object to the wearing of the hijab: the inference being that it is not considered to be an act of indiscipline in the several public schools in which they are worn.

***In the Application of Saga Trading Ltd* – HCA No Cv 1347 of 1993 (TT)**
Archie J

[P15] The test for an Applicant who seeks to impugn a decision is therefore very high. Reasonable people may differ as to the inferences to be drawn from a given set of facts ... [PP29–30] In effect, Mr Aching who was not an expert on speaker refurbishing brushed aside the purported transaction value on the basis of assumptions which on the evidence then before him were unwarranted. In doing so, he also failed to have regard to the statutory guidelines governing the exercise of his discretion. I therefore find that the decision to request a deposit was in the circumstances unreasonable and/or irrational.

In the Application of the Institute of Jamaica – Civil Appeal No 9 of 2002 (JM)
Bingham JA

[PP32–33] What the Tribunal ought to have focused its determination on, was its primary finding as to how it viewed the conduct of Mrs. Beecher in her removal of the staff chart, an act which it viewed as being a serious offence. It was that finding which ought to have ordered its determination of the matter. Had it proceeded along that path this would have led to the conclusion that the dismissal was clearly within the terms of Mrs. Beecher's contract. Her conditions of service given her conduct as a whole, made the actions of the Executive Director justifiable in all the circumstances of this case.

In the Application of the Grand Lido Negril – Supreme Court No M-98 of 1995 (JM)
Harrison J

[P32] I cannot say that the Tribunal has not acted within its jurisdiction. Its considerations were relevant and it cannot be said that its decision is tainted by unreasonableness. The Tribunal duly considered the interest of the hotel. It did not neglect to have regard to the national interest. It considered the interests of the dismissed workers. There is no reason why I should interfere with this decision.

Erlin Hall v Public Service Commission (1993) 30 JLR 442 (JM)
Langrin J

[P444] The Regulation did not give an absolute discretion to anyone to dispense with the services of the Applicant. In our view the discretion, although wide is not absolute. The Commission should have directed its mind to the criteria laid down in the Regulation in accordance with the principles of natural justice. This was not done and we think it was precisely because the Commission was advised that its discretion was absolute which led to the way the Applicant's case was treated.

Elwin v Public Service Commission Commonwealth of Dominica and the Attorney General of the Commonwealth of Dominica – High Court of Justice Civil Suit No 493 of 1998 (DM)
Cenac J

[Para27] The Commission's functions under the law respecting the appointment and promotion of public officers are of a public nature and quasi-judicial. As such, in exercise of its powers under the Regulations the Commission must be expected to act fairly. [Para28] In *Wiseman v Borneman* [1969] 3 All ER 275 at 277 Lord Reid said: 'Natural justice requires that the procedure before any tribunal which is acting judicially shall be fair in all the circumstances, and I would be sorry to see this fundamental general principle degenerate into a series of hard and fast rules. For a long time the Courts have, without objection from Parliament, supplemented procedure laid down in legislation where they have found that to be necessary for the purpose. But before this unusual kind of power is exercised it must be clear that the statutory procedure is insufficient to achieve justice and that to require additional steps would not frustrate the apparent purpose of the legislation'. [Para29] In *Public Service Board of New South Wales v Osmond* [1987] LRC 681 at p 698 Deane J repeating a statement of Kitto J in *Mobil Oil Australia Pty Ltd v Federal Commissioner of Taxation* [1963] 113 CLR 475 at p 504 said this: 'What the law requires in the discharge of a quasi-judicial function is judicial fairness. That is not a label for any fixed body of rules. What is fair in a given situation depends upon the circumstances'. [Para30] And as Lord Bridge put it in *Lloyd v McMahon* [1987] 1 All ER 1118 at 1161, [1987] AC 625 at 702–703: 'My Lords, the so-called rules of natural justice are not engraved on tablets of stone. To use the phrase which better expresses the underlying concept, what the requirements of fairness demand when any body, domestic, administrative or judicial, has to make a decision which will affect the rights of individuals depends on the character of the decision-making body, the kind of decision it has to make and the statutory or other framework in which it operates. In particular, it is well established that when a statute has conferred on any body the power to make decisions affecting individuals, the Courts will not only require the procedure prescribed by the statute to be followed, but will readily imply so much and no more to be introduced by way of additional procedural safeguards as will ensure the attainment of fairness'. [Para31] Was there unfairness in the procedure followed by the Commission under the Regulations? In other words has the Applicant made out a case of procedural unfairness? Where an Act of Parliament confers an administrative power there is a presumption that it will be exercised in a manner which is fair in all the circumstances. The standards of fairness are not immutable. They may change with the passage of time, both in the general and in their application to decisions of a particular type. The principles of fairness are not to be applied by rote identically in every situation. What fairness demands is dependent on the context of the decision, and this is to be taken account in all its aspects (*per* Lord Mustill in *Regina v Secretary of State for the Home Department, Ex Parte Doody* (HL) [1993] 3 WLR p 168). [Para40] Now here you have a situation where the Applicant, of the three names submitted to the Commission, although not the most senior but was senior to Angela Lawrence, was not less qualified than her, had acted in the post on more occasions before it became vacant, acted in the post after it became vacant and up to the time when the Commission made its decision to appoint Angela Lawrence. Further, the Applicant had been recommended by the Permanent Secretary to be appointed to the post. In spite of the foregoing, she was overlooked and Angela Lawrence was appointed. Obviously the Applicant must be left with a 'burning sense of grievance and a real feeling of injustice' . . . [Para42] Having regard to the facts and the law, I can only conclude that the Applicant's entitlement to appointment was far superior to that of the appointee. [Para43] I conclude also that the Commission could not have taken into account 'all the circumstances which it is statutorily required to take into account before selecting an officer for promotion' . . . [Para44] I am of the view that the Commission did not follow the procedure laid down in the Regulations. As Leggatt LJ said in *Cunningham* (*supra*) at p 958: 'One of the main areas in which supervision has to be exercised by way of judicial review is over procedural requirements, for the purpose of ensuring the right to a fair adjudication. The procedure of a public body is not only required to be fair in so far as an individual affected by its decisions has a legitimate expectation that it will be. Nor does natural justice or fairness require the giving of reasons for a decision only when an obligation to give them is imposed by statute.' [Para45] I am of the view that the decision taken by the Commission to appoint Angela Lawrence to the post over the Applicant in light of all the circumstances was so aberrant as to compel the inference that it must have been wrong, procedurally wrong and grossly unfair.

2.17 DECISIONS MUST NOT BE TAINTED BY BIAS

It is accepted in law that a decision tainted by bias will not be upheld by the courts. The real challenge however has been to find consistency in defining a test for bias. The test for bias is not subjective and this position has found favour with courts throughout the Caribbean. The case law on bias is heavily influenced by the House of Lords decision of *R v Gough* [1993] AC 643. However, there is now a question as to what the current test of bias is, in light of the House of Lords decision of *Porter v Magill* [2001] UKHL 67, which states 'whether the fair-minded and informed observer, having considered the facts, would conclude that there was a real possibility that the Tribunal was biased'.

***In the Application of Alvin Seereeram* – HCA No S-262 of 2001 (TT)**
Marcus J

[P49] Since the Permanent Secretary was biased in the legal sense of the word, and the disciplinary process was initiated by her, this Court is inclined to the view that the bias tainted the proceedings . . . [P50] This Court holds that the pronouncement regarding the obligation to apply the principles of natural justice by one entrusted to decide a preliminary point applies to the Permanent Secretary who took the initiatory decision to commence disciplinary proceedings. In this respect being the aggrieved party and complainant, she acted as a judge in her own cause . . . [P51] Having regard to the findings of this Court and to the decisions and pronouncements referred to, the Court holds that there has not been substantial compliance with the Regulations and the Applicant was not treated fairly in the institution of the disciplinary proceedings.

***In the Application of Private Nimchand Pittiman No 4195, Private Augustine Dharmoo, Private Rajaheswar Parsanlal No 31127 and Lance Corporal Winston Arnold* – Civil Appeal No 183 of 1984 (TT)**
Warner, JA

[PP10–11] It is settled law too that where persons having a direct interest in the subject matter of proceedings before an inferior Court take part in adjudicating upon it, the Tribunal is improperly constituted and the Court will grant an order of prohibition to prevent it from adjudicating. While disqualification is more readily incurred when an adjudicator has a direct pecuniary interest, it may also be incurred where his interest is not pecuniary but is such as may lead to an appearance or likelihood of bias on his part. The test of bias is not a subjective one. The Court will not seek to discover whether the mind of the person whom it is sought to disqualify was in fact affected by bias . . . [P14] He did not have to enquire whether the Judge Advocate was in fact biased but whether the ordinary spectator on the material available would reasonably suspect him of being biased. [PP14–15] The learned Judge having applied the wrong test, it is for this Court to see whether the circumstances are such that it can arrive at its own conclusion. Is there a real likelihood that a reasonable man with no inside knowledge will think that there might well be bias on the part of the Judge Advocate or in other words that he might favour the prosecution unfairly? The 'reasonable man' of whom we speak is not a lawyer whose training will make him conscious, as the learned Judge clearly was, of the ability of lawyers as a rule to divest themselves of prejudices and partisanship for such time as they are carrying out a judicial function. It would be going too far to attribute knowledge of this to the ordinary spectator sitting in at the hearing of the Court Martial. The reasonable man for our purposes here today is the ordinary listener sitting at Chaguaramas and following the proceedings of the Court Martial. I am satisfied that the reasonable man, asked if he thought that the Judge Advocate might be biased would have answered 'I am not sure that he is biased but he may very well be'.

The test for 'real danger of bias' (versus 'real likelihood') involves an examination by the courts of all the circumstances to determine whether there is in fact a real danger of bias on the part of the decision-maker and, if there is, that person is excluded altogether. Where the decision has already been made, it will be deemed null and void, whether correct or not. The courts seem to suggest that the greater the passage of time between the event relied on as illustrative of danger of bias, and the case in which the objection is raised, the weaker (other things being equal) the objection will be.

***Attorney-General v Caribbean Communications Network Ltd* (2001) 62 WIR 405 (TT)**
Hamel-Smith JA

[PP405–406] Bias is at the core of this appeal. The trial judge granted the Respondent ('CCN') constitutional relief when he found that its rights under the Constitution, viz the right to the protection of the law (s 4(b)) and the right to equality of treatment by a public authority (s 4(d)) had been infringed ... [PP416–418] The trial judge, however, appears to have overshot the mark. He made a finding of bias, both actual and apparent, and combined that finding with what he considered a failure to follow the evaluation procedure to arrive at the conclusion that there was a breach of both [ss] 4(b) and (d) of the Constitution. I do not think that it was necessary to make a finding of actual bias. The test of *real danger* will generally lead to the same result (see de Smith, *Constitutional and Administrative Law* (5th Edn, 1985) pp 584, 585) and counsel, in my view, was quite correct to confine his submissions to the finding of apparent bias only. The case of bias was premised on certain remarks made by the Prime Minister on a political platform over a period of some three years. The several remarks complained of are set out below. The first two occurred before the Prime Minister assumed responsibility for the Ministry of Telecommunications: (i) In delivering a speech at the Indian Arrival Day celebrations at Chandernagore on 29 May 1997, the Prime Minister referred to the CCN's Chairman, Ken Gordon, as a psuedo-racist who uses race to look after himself and who wants to maintain the monopolistic advantage over his competitors in the media. (ii) At another speech given at the Mid-Center Mall, Chaguanas, on 8 November 1998, to mark the commemoration of his party's third anniversary in office, he declared the Government was in a state of war with the media and called upon his supporters to target racist supporters and to 'do them before they do us' and called for a boycott by his party and its supporters of CCN's media houses and for the entire population to do likewise. After he had assumed the portfolio for telecommunications and about eleven weeks before seeking the advice of PWC, the Prime Minister publicly attacked CCN, describing it as one of the greatest enemies of the Government and again called for a boycott of it. His remarks were as follows: (iii) On 3 February, 2000 at a meeting of his party's supporters at North Eastern College, Sangre Grande, he accused the CCN group of companies of declaring war on his Government. He described the CCN newspaper, publishing company and television station as one of the greatest enemies of the Government. It had declared virtual war against the Government and [he] called on his supporters to defend themselves. He called for a boycott of the CCN newspaper publications and a boycott of those who advertise in them, and to organise [as] never before to fight 'the mother of all battles', the war that had been declared by CCN. And, (iv) At La Joya Auditorium, St Joseph, on 8 February 2000, at a meeting of his supporters, he said that the Government was being attacked in the newspapers and singled out CCN's Express newspaper as being biased and prejudiced. The trial judge found that the language used by the Prime Minister was 'impassionate and inflammatory' and that by his remarks he had displayed, what the Judge termed, obviously in an untypical betrayal of emotion, 'unbridled hostility'. He readily accepted that the Prime Minister was free to criticise anyone, including CCN whom he believed were his enemies or the enemies of the Government. He, however, found it 'inconceivable' that the Prime Minister, having publicly demonstrated such a degree of hostility for CCN, would 'so soon afterwards' sit in judgment in a matter involving the very company. The Prime Minister, he said, made no attempt to conceal his dislike for CCN and that 'such prejudice or predisposed position could easily have affected his decision to look with disfavour' on CCN and thereby exclude it from consideration for a grant of a special licence. In summary, it would be fair to say that the Judge was concerned that the remarks had reflected a degree of hostility against CCN and there was a real danger that that hostility would have affected the decision taken so soon afterwards. He then considered the circumstances surrounding the acceptance of the director's recommendation, as against the report of the King committee, and held that the Prime Minister was not only motivated by actual bias but there was a real danger of bias resulting from the Prime Minister's action. He believed that he was predisposed or prejudiced against CCN for reasons unconnected with CCN's application for a special licence ... [P421] The law appears to be clear that bias on the part of the decision-maker leads to his disqualification from the decision-making process. Lord Browne-Wilkinson, in *Ex Parte Pinochet Ugarte (No 2)* [1999] 1 All ER 577 at 586 revisited the fundamental principle that a man may not be a judge in his own cause. His lordship saw the principle as having two very similar, but not identical, implications; first, its literal application where the decision-maker has a financial or proprietary interest in the outcome; and, second, where his conduct or behaviour may give rise to a suspicion that he is not impartial. It is with this latter implication that we are concerned ... [P422] It needs to be said that, because the law is alive to the insidiousness of bias, a practical approach has been adopted to deal with it. It is not that a Court condemns the decision-maker or finds that he has done something unlawful in the criminal sense, but by disqualifying the decision-maker from taking part altogether, the integrity of the decision-maker and the decision-making process is secured. Bias, after all, is a human shortcoming that is sometimes difficult to recognise in oneself. It frequently happens that, when faced with a suggestion of apparent bias or even actual bias against a particular party, the average decision-maker may perceive that he is confident enough to approach the issue with an open mind in spite of the bias. That, too, is part of human nature simply because it is at times difficult to admit to such an imperfection. As a result a person may, with all good intentions, believe that he is acting impartially while the mind may unconsciously be affected by bias. Accordingly, in order to ensure that mere lip-service is not paid to the maxim 'justice must not only be done but be seen to be done' the Court looks at all the circumstances to determine whether there is a *real danger* of bias on the part of the decision-maker and, if there is, that person is excluded from taking part altogether. If the decision has been made already, it is not allowed to stand, whether correct or not. The approach is a reasonable and practical one that effectively gives life and purpose to the stated maxim. The trial judge in the instant appeal was fully aware of that rule and took it into account in arriving at his finding of apparent bias ... [PP424–425] The issue here, however, is not about the extent to which a politician (or any one for that matter) may or may not be permitted to go in for expression of views. In the final analysis, one has to examine the remarks to see whether they are capable of conveying to the Court that there is a real danger of bias on the part of the author against the person to whom they are directed. If there is such a danger, then it is sufficient to find apparent bias. On examination, the words cannot reasonably be said to be a measured response to criticism of the Government. They, as the trial Judge found, reflected a mind that was hostile and antagonistic to CCN and its Chairman and had been so for some time. In my view, whatever the nature of the response, it is not whether the Prime Minister was entitled to do so or to do so in the manner in which he chose to respond but it is more to the point whether in examining the response there is a distinct possibility that he betrayed a bias against CCN. That is the central issue and it seems that it can only be resolved against him. This much is evident because, in calling on the public at large to boycott the organisation or to do battle with the Government's greatest enemy or to expressly condemn someone as a pseudo-racist, the author would be hard pressed to deny that he has little use for that organisation. The judge was plainly concerned that since the remarks reflected a mind that was ill-disposed towards CCN, the Prime Minister ought not to have participated in the decision-making process for the single reason that such a person could not bring to bear an independent and open mind on the application at hand. They reflected the way he perceived the other party and the extent to which he would go or exhort his supporters to see it in ruin. What obviously added to this was the proximity of the remarks (made in February 2000) to the decision at hand. There was therefore sufficient material in these and other remarks referred to upon which the trial Judge could find that there was a real danger of bias ... The finding by the trial Judge of apparent bias was sufficient to disqualify the Prime Minister from participation in the decision-making process and it is from this perspective that the trial Judge came to the correct decision that the decision to exclude CCN from further consideration should be quashed.

In the Application of the Medical Council of Trinidad and Tobago – HCA No 481 of 1999 (TT) Smith J

[P25] In all the circumstances the Applicant has satisfied the real danger of bias test with respect to Dr Sinanan continuing to sit on the inquiry and it is in my view an abuse of power and/or unfair to allow the inquiry to continue with Dr Sinanan sitting as a member of the same . . . [PP25–26] The real danger of bias has been proved with respect to the other members of The Council and it would be an abuse of power and/or unfair to allow this inquiry to continue with the other members of The Council sitting upon the same. As a result, the application for judicial review is properly made at this stage since it is necessary to avoid an abuse of power and/or unfairness.

In the Application of Lt. Leon Chandler No 0115 – HCA No 2125 of 1998 (TT) Des Vignes J

[P42] Accordingly, in determining the issue of bias, I must ask myself, after ascertaining the relevant circumstances, whether, having regard to those circumstances, there was a real danger of bias on the part of the members of the Court-martial in the sense that they or any of them might unfairly regard or have unfairly regarded with favour or disfavour, the case of the Applicant . . . [P44] Taking all these circumstances into account, I am not satisfied that the Applicant has established that there is real danger of bias on the part of the Judge Advocate or any of the members of the Court-martial in the sense that they or any of them would unfairly regard or have unfairly regarded with disfavour the case of the Applicant. For me to make such a finding, it would be necessary for me to presume a lack of professionalism, independence and integrity on the part of the Respondents and I am not prepared so to do.

In the Application of Donald Panton and Janet Panton – Privy Council Appeal No 20 of 2000 (JM) Lord Clyde

[PP9–10] It has also to be recognized that the purity of the principle may require to give way to the exigencies and realities of life. In extreme cases the doctrine of necessity may require a judge to determine an issue even [though] he would otherwise be disqualified. An example can be found in *The Judges v the Attorney-General for the Province of Saskatchewan* (1937) 53 TLR 464 where this Board held that the Court in Saskatchewan was acting properly in deciding whether the salaries of Judges were liable to income tax. Such cases where resort has to be had to the doctrine of necessity are of course rare and special. But at a less extreme level it is right that account should be taken in assessing the independence of a judge of the likely responsibilities and interests which he or she will invariably have had during the course of a professional career which had preceded a judicial appointment. In those countries where there is not an exclusively career judiciary Judges are likely to have held offices or appointments in which they may have given public expression to particular points of view. This will necessarily be so where the career has involved an engagement in political life. Experience outside the law, whether in politics or elsewhere, may reasonably be regarded as enhancing a judicial qualification rather than disabling it. In countries where it is recognized and accepted that Judges may well have behind them a history of political affiliation or partisan interest it has also to be recognized that such historical associations can be put aside in the interest of performing a judicial duty with independence and impartiality. That has to be one of the considerations which should weigh in the mind of a reasonable or fair-minded person in deciding whether or not a Court may be biased or in deciding whether there is any real danger of bias. As was observed in *Kartinyeri* at p 304, para 33: 'Some members of this Court have come to it directly from a career in politics and in government. Inevitably, in Cabinet and in the Party Room, they must have had a very close association with members of the government whose legislation they have had from time to time to interpret. Sometimes the legislation may be in implementation of long-standing policy to which the former politician has subscribed and has perhaps even advocated. A particular association of itself, and even a current, proper one which observes the punctiliousness required in respect of a case and issues actually before, or which may be before, the Court should not ordinarily give rise to a reasonable apprehension of bias.'

In the Application of Pearson Small, Eric Rouse, Erskine Weekes, Philip Walters, Harry Greenidge, Grenville Toppin, Oliver Steele, Frank Butcher, Gairy Belgrave and Carl Jackson – Civil Appeal No 23 of 2000 (BB)
Chase JA, CJ (Ag.)

[P18] In the present case, the notices were issued after both counsel had addressed the Commission and the notices sought to give as much details as possible as to the allegations that were likely to be made against the Appellants on the evidence adduced at the hearings and the findings of misconduct that were possible without more before a final decision was made for incorporation into the Respondent's report. Indeed, Louis Blom-Cooper in his statement on the proposed procedures for conducting his inquiry notes that 'if there is any likelihood of criticism of any party, he or she is entitled to have advance notice of the nature of the potential criticism.' His statement further indicated that as soon as he thought that there was *prima facie* evidence of justifiable criticism a Salmon Letter setting out the particulars of any allegation or complaint would have been issued. It would appear therefore that the Respondent was purporting to adopt the Blom-Cooper procedure as his guidelines in dealing with the situation that confronted him ... [P22] It would seem that the language adopted has as its central purpose the fulfillment of the principle that if a person may in some way be adversely affected by an investigation and report, then he should be told the case made against him and be afforded a fair opportunity of answering it. (see *R v Race Relations Board, Ex Parte Selvarajan* [1976] 1 All ER 12 at p 19) ... [PP22–23] However, whatever may have influenced his mind in formulating the notices to the Appellants in the way he did, the Respondent certainly made a full disclosure to each of the Appellants as to what was operating in his mind as he sought to evaluate the evidence before him for the purposes of his report ... [P28] It is appropriate at this stage to note that the Canadian Court took the view that the 'hypothetical finding' set out in the notices to the persons concerned was one that a commissioner had the power to make as an actual finding in his report ... [P29] In the instant case, the Respondent's notices speak of 'likely findings'. All of these phrases would seem therefore to import the concept that the adjudicator had not taken a definite position on the evidence before him. In short, he had not yet made up his mind at the time of issuing the notices ... [PP36–37] On the basis of our examination of the cases and other materials referred to in the course of argument and on our analysis of the issues raised on this aspect of the appeal, we are of the view that the language adopted by the Respondent to formulate the notices to the Appellants cannot reasonably be construed as findings of misconduct within the contemplation of Section 23(2) of the Act. It is our further view that Section 23(2) contemplates that notice of allegations of misconduct must first be communicated to the persons concerned and that they be given an opportunity to respond before a commission may make formal findings on those allegations for inclusion in its report. Before any allegations may be formulated for notification to the person whose conduct is in question, it is manifestly clear that the evidence adduced before a commission would have to be the basis upon which the notices are constructed together with the commission's initial assessment of that evidence ... [PP48–50] One of the tests that Courts apply to determine whether or not there is bias on the part of an adjudicator appears in the judgment of Lord Goff in *R v Gough* [1993] 2 All ER 724 at 737 in these terms: ... I wish to express my understanding of the law as follows: I think it is possible, and desirable, that the same test should be applicable in all cases of apparent bias, whether concerned with justices or members of other inferior tribunals, or with jurors, or with arbitrators. Likewise, I consider that, in cases concerned with jurors, the same test should be applied by a judge to whose attention the possibility of bias on the part of a juror has been drawn in the course of a trial, and by the Court of Appeal when it considers such a question on appeal. Furthermore, I think it is unnecessary, in formulating the appropriate test, to require that the Court should look at the matter through the eyes of a reasonable man, because the Court in cases such as these personifies the reasonable man; and in any event the Court has first to ascertain the relevant circumstances from the available evidence, knowledge of which would not necessarily be available to an observer in Court at the relevant time. Finally, for the avoidance of doubt, I prefer to state the test in terms of real danger rather than likelihood, to ensure that the Court is thinking in terms of the possibility rather than probability of bias. Accordingly, having ascertained the relevant circumstances, the Court should ask itself whether, having regard to those circumstances, there was a real danger of bias on the part of the relevant member of the Tribunal in question, in the sense that he might unfairly regard (or have unfairly regarded) with favour, or disfavour, the case of a party to the issue under consideration by him. In seeking to resolve the issue of bias, it would seem that this Court has to consider whether in the circumstances and nature of this inquiry there is a real danger or possibility of bias on the part of the Respondent in that he might unfairly regard with disfavour the conduct of each of the Appellants in relation to the escape of the prisoner. As to real danger of bias, Lord Bingham CJ, in *Locabail Ltd v Bayfield Properties* [2000] 1 All ER 65 at p 77 indicated as follows: . . . a real danger of bias might well be thought to arise if there were personal friendship or animosity between the Judge and any member of the public involved in the case; or if the Judge were closely acquainted with any member of the public involved in the case, particularly if the credibility of that individual could be significant in the decision of the case; or if, in a case where the credibility of any individual were an issue to be decided by the Judge, he had in a previous case rejected the evidence of that person in such outspoken terms as to throw doubt on his ability to approach such person's evidence with an open mind on any later occasion; or if on any question at issue in the proceedings before him the Judge had expressed views, particularly in the course of the hearing, in such extreme and unbalanced terms as to throw doubt on his ability to try the issue with an objective judicial mind (see *Vakauta v Kelly* [1989] 167 CLR 568); or if, for any other reason, there were real grounds for doubting the ability of the Judge to ignore extraneous considerations, prejudices and predilections and bring an objective judgment to bear on the issues before him. The mere fact that a judge, earlier in the same case or in a previous case, had commented adversely on a party or witness, or found the evidence of a party or witness unreliable, would not without more found a sustainable objection . . . We repeat: every application must be decided on the facts and circumstances of the individual case. The greater the passage of time between the event relied on as showing danger of bias and the case in which the objection is raised, the weaker (other things being equal) the objection will be . . . It is, however, generally undesirable that hearings should be aborted unless the reality or appearance of justice requires that they should . . . [P55] Having regard to all of the above factors, we accordingly accept and find that the test and principles relating to the issue of bias must, in view of the special nature of the functions of a commissioner of inquiry, be applied flexibly, since the functions of a trial judge cannot be assimilated into the functions of an investigatory commission . . . [P59] Although the language adopted by the Respondent to elicit the evidence of the circumstances surrounding the escape of the prisoner was in some instances undoubtedly unfortunate we, however, do not find that the way in which he sought to express himself in his quest for truth gives rise to a real danger or real possibility or real apprehension of bias against the Appellants . . . [P60] In observing that the remarks made by the Respondent were in some instances unfortunate, we are nonetheless of the view that the terms in which they were expressed cannot necessarily be interpreted as disclosing an inability on the part of the Respondent to bring to bear an objective assessment of the weight of the evidence before him in a matter of public interest. In the event that we have misdirected ourselves in the assessment of the effect of the remarks made by the Respondent, we accept the principle of waiver and find that by not raising any objections to them at the hearings, the Appellants have waived their rights to object at this stage.

In the Application of Dr Vaughn Lewis – Civil Appeal No 12 of 1997 (LC)
Byron, CJ (ag.)

[P4] Without attempting to offer a full definition of bias, I think I can refer to it as being a predisposition to favour or disfavour a party or result, in a manner that is wrongful and which can lead to a denial of the judicial imperative of impartiality in the particular matter . . . [P5] In general, bias may fall into three categories: cases of actual bias; cases where the decision maker has a direct pecuniary interest in the outcome of the proceedings and other cases where the circumstances give rise to a presumption of bias . . . [P6] The law has now settled in *R v Gough* [1993] 2 All ER 724. Lord Goff having examined the principles and relevant cases in detail changed the focus of the test of bias . . . [PP6–7] He stated it in these terms: 'In my opinion, if, in the circumstances of the case (as ascertained by the Court), it appears that there is a real likelihood, in the sense of a real possibility, of bias on the part of a Justice or other member of an inferior tribunal, justice requires that the decision should not be allowed to stand.' As he was closing his opinion he emphasized the test in this succinct manner at page 737: 'Finally, for the avoidance of doubt, I prefer to state the test in terms of real danger rather than real likelihood, to ensure that the Court is thinking in terms of possibility rather that probability of bias. Accordingly, having ascertained the relevant circumstances, the Court should ask itself whether, having regard to those circumstances, there was a real danger of bias on the part of the relevant member of the Tribunal in question, in the sense that he might unfairly regard (or have unfairly regarded) with favour, or with disfavour, the case of a party to the issue under consideration by him' . . . [P10] The allegation in this case is that the Appellant has been associated with the taking of a decision which hurt or disappointed the Commissioner severely. The point being raised is about human nature, and I suppose it comes under the head of enmity, or a desire for revenge. Is this such a real and intrusive human quality that evidence of these circumstances raises the presumption that it may arise and present a real danger of bias? In my opinion, it is not highly probable that well intentioned people would be affected by malevolence in such circumstances. On the other hand it must be indisputable that there are some people who are driven by such motives. The legal test as I understand it does not permit an assessment of the Commissioner to determine how probable it is that she would be so driven. Lord Goff has stressed that the test is based on possibility not probability. Therefore, the question to be asked is whether a person could be driven by such motives. Not whether it is probable that this particular person would be. I find myself having to conclude that it is possible for a human being to be so driven. However, I think that I am required to go further and examine the circumstances to determine whether there is a real danger. In my judgment the danger would only exist if the Commissioner could conclude that the Appellant had unjustly caused her disappointment. It would be unreasonable to conclude that she could view anyone who was not identified as an architect of unjust [or] unfair disappointment with disfavour.

Redhead JA

[P25] Having regard to the fact there is an overriding interest that there should be confidence in the integrity of the administration of justice, and also having regard to the fact that it is of fundamental importance that justice should not only be done but should manifestly and undoubtedly be seen to be done, could the Court, possessed of all the facts as it has and the circumstances of the Appellant [also he is of course a member of the public] and [the Court] personifying the reasonable man say with confidence that there is no real danger of bias on the part of the Commissioner or Commission as presently constituted? I think not because bias is a perception concept. It is what people think. And the Court personifying the reasonable man must come to that conclusion.

In other instances, the courts have stated the test in terms of the real possibility of bias, which according to the decided cases would appear to be equivalent to the 'real danger of bias' test.

***In the Application of Fishermen and Friends of the Sea* – HCA Cv 2148 of 2003 (TT)**
Stollmeyer J

[P43] The further submission was that, in general, a relationship with an associated company of the same nature as would give rise to a real possibility of bias; if it was a relationship with the actual party, it was likely to give rise to the same real possibility of bias ... [P46] The allegations of DNV's bias and pecuniary connection are based upon nothing more than it, or its parent company, having provided services for an ALNG partner or shareholder. That evidence falls woefully short of what is required to demonstrate bias, whether real, actual or otherwise.

***In the Application of Anthony Lamsee* – HCA Cv S652 of 2002/Civil Appeal No 43 of 2002 (TT)**
Stollmeyer J

[P6] An appearance, but not merely a suspicion, of bias may suffice, either because a reasonable outsider may think there is a real likelihood that the issue could, or would, not be determined fairly on the merits, or because undue favour or partiality, or antipathy was demonstrated. The proper test in cases of apparent or unconscious bias is to determine whether there is a real danger or possibility of bias. The test is an objective one ... [P7] A reviewing Court must ascertain all the circumstances which have a bearing on the suggestion of bias, and must then decide whether those circumstances would lead a fair minded and informed observer to conclude that there was a real danger, a real possibility, that the Court was in fact biased ... See e.g. *Director General of Fair Trading v The Proprietary Association of Great Britain v The Proprietary Articles Trade Association* (C.A.) December 2000, Unreported).

***R v Office of Utilities Regulation ex parte World Telenet International Ltd* – Supreme Court No M81 of 2000 (JM)**
Clarke J

[P26] The whole question to be determined here is whether or not, as Mr Small puts it, past employment of an officer in a utility that is regulated by the Office disables that officer from participating in the functions, duties or activities of the Office in relation to that utility under the Office of Utilities Regulations Act or any other legislation ... [P27] The past employment by itself of Mr Jackson with Jamaica Telephone Company Limited cannot, in my view, raise the reality or appearance of bias on the part of Mr Jackson or the Office. Having examined the affidavits and the circumstances of the case before me I find that there is no evidence that would justify the application against the Office of the principles to protect against bias. Besides there being no evidence or circumstance to suggest a lack of impartiality, there is no evidential or legal basis to justify me to conclude that a risk or real danger or possibility of bias on the part of Mr Jackson or the Office occurred in this case.

Some courts have discussed the test for bias in terms of the real likelihood of bias which decreases the possibility, as in 'real danger of bias', to a mere probability.

***In the Application of Vishnudath Rooplal* – HCA No 929 of 1992 (TT)**
Lucky J

[P12] It seems to me that the question for consideration is this: would the reasonable man sitting as a spectator in Court think there was a likelihood of bias i.e. will the Magistrate commit the accused at the end of all the evidence in any event? Did it appear that he had already made up his mind to commit? ... [P14] There is no ambiguity in the words used; the meaning is clear and explicit. They can mean nothing else than there is sufficient evidence to commit you. The legally trained mind to which one attributes a degree of acquaintance with, and built-in confidence in, normal judicial detachment will conclude that the learned Magistrate was not prejudiced or biased but meant that a *prima facie* case had been made out, the evidence was not tenuous and the ingredients were proved. This ought not to suggest bias to any legally trained person, however, the test is not for such persons, but it is to be applied to the ordinary spectator, presuming him to be a reasonable man . . . [PP20–21] It seems to me that the reasonable man is not what English texts refer to as the man on the *Clapham Omnibus*, but here in Trinidad and Tobago he is the average, literate, fair minded and right minded man. I pose the question: would such a man knowing all the relevant facts have a reasonable suspicion that a fair hearing for the accused was not possible, because the Magistrate used the words in question? Could the reasonable man at that stage of the proceedings have felt that whatever occurred later on the Magistrate would have committed him for trial?

In the Application of Naresh Boodram – HCA No 3601 of 1990 (TT)
Wills J

[P14] From the circumstances of this case, I am of the opinion that the test to determine whether there is a real likelihood of bias is not subjective as it impinges on the mind of the Tribunal who is challenged. It is a question of public confidence in the administration of justice. Consequently in small communities, such as ours, one cannot be insensitive to the demonstrative insatiable appetite for gossips and half truths which may or may not affect the minds of some persons. It seems to me therefore, from the circumstances of this case the following questions are pertinent for the determination thereof:—

(a) Can it be said that the principle *nemo judex in causa sans* is in breach by the Magistrate presiding in the Preliminary Enquiry in the two matters concerning the Applicant?

(b) Would a reasonable and fair minded person sitting in a Trinidad and Tobago Court *knowing* all the facts, having read the Drug Report and in particular page 26 paragraph 4:33, have entertained a reasonable suspicion that a fair trial for the Applicant before the Learned Magistrate will be unlikely and or impossible? And finally

(c) Is there a real likelihood that a reasonable person, knowing all the facts, having read the Drug Report and in particular paragraph 4:33 at page 26 come to the conclusion that public confidence in the administration of justice will be lost and or undermined by the Learned Magistrate presiding over drug related cases?

There can be no doubt that a fair and public hearing by an independent impartial tribunal is a *sine qua non* in the proper administration of justice if public confidence is to be maintained.

In the Application of Nickson Mungroo, Feroze Mohammed, and John Gangadeen – HCA No 2386 of 1987 (TT)
Ibrahim J

[P22] I am of the opinion that if the question is asked, is there a real likelihood that a reasonable man with no inside knowledge will think that there might well be bias on the part of the Respondent bearing in mind the reasonable man is the ordinary listener sitting at Chaguanas in the Court and following the proceedings, he would have answered, 'I am sure that he is.' I must of course point out that this, however, does not mean that the Respondent was in fact biased. That is not an issue before me.

In the Application of Wishwa Maraj and Shanti Maraj – HCA No 2690 of 1986 (TT)
Koylass J

[P24] Indeed, as submitted by Dr Seepersad it is manifest that Mohess being a senior officer in the Inland Revenue Department a duty was imposed on him in the circumstances of the existing animosity between himself and the first-named Applicant to disqualify himself from any involvement in investigations pertaining to the Applicants' tax affairs. It is therefore quite unfortunate that he did not see fit so to do before the intervention of Mrs. Ali, at the request of Mr Roopnarine. Nevertheless, as I have already indicated, there is no evidence to sustain the argument that his involvement has resulted in the investigations being tainted with bias, spite or any unfairness, nor do I perceive any real likelihood of bias as was also contended.

***In the Application of Easton Wilberforce Grant* – Civil Appeal No 29 of 2003 (JM)**
Bingham JA

[PP24–25] Given the fact that the allegations of bias surfaced for the first time in these proceedings, there was no valid claim that it affected in any way the outcome of the proceedings before the learned trial judge. There was in effect no real likelihood or possibility of bias to have affected in any manner the decision arrived at by the learned judge. This ground therefore fails.

***R v Dr Auma Folkes, Principal Bellefield Comprehensive School ex parte Carmen Williams* (1995) 32 JLR 386 (JM)**
Langrin J

[PP388–389] Turning now to the third issue of whether there was a real likelihood of bias due to the presence of the Principal at the meeting which was convened to hear her charges. There is no evidence to substantiate the allegation that the Principal's presence was to influence any deliberation of the Board. It must be borne in mind that she was a witness and the actual hearing had not yet commenced. However when the hearing commences her presence at the hearing except as a witness should be discouraged.

There is precedent for the judicial position that a mere suspicion of bias may suffice.

***The Kingston and Saint Andrew Corporation ex parte Godfrey* (1934) 2 JLR 23 (JM)**
Lyall Grant CJ

[PP28–29] On the second point it appears to me that the present case comes within the rule which was applied in *R v The Essex Justices, Ex Parte Perkins* [1927] 2 KB 475. There objection was taken to a solicitor acting as clerk to the Justices on an application by a wife for maintenance, where his firm had previously been consulted by her in connection with a deed of separation. The solicitor when he so acted as clerk was quite unaware that his firm had ever advised the wife, and in fact advised the Court in favour of the husband. No objection was taken at the time to his advising the Justices. It was held that the Applicant had not waived his right to object, as at the time he was unaware of the right, and, further that he had a right to object, as the presence of the solicitor as clerk might raise in his mind the reasonable impression that justice was not being done. The principle stated by Lord Hewart C.J., in *Rex v Sussex Justices Ex Parte McCarthy* [1924] 1 KB 256 was acted upon. In Lord Hewart's wording: 'A long line of cases shows that it is not merely of some importance but is of fundamental importance that justice should not only be done but should manifestly and undoubtedly be seen to be done. The question therefore is whether the clerk was so related to the case in its civil aspect as to be unfit to act for the Justices in the criminal matter. The answer to that question depends not upon what actually was done but upon what might appear to be done. Nothing is to be done which creates even a suspicion that there has been an improper interference with the course of justice.' Avory J., in *Perkin's case* (*supra*) after quoting Lord Hewart as above, proceeded: 'I must conclude that though the clerk to the Justices did not know that his firm had acted for the Applicant's wife, the necessary or at least the reasonable impression on the mind of the Applicant would be that justice was not being done seeing that the solicitor for his wife was acting with the Justices and advising them on the hearing of the summons which she had taken against him.' It seems to us that the same principle is to be applied here. In the *Essex Justices* the solicitor was acting in perfect good faith and in ignorance of the fact that his firm had any connection with the matter on which he advised the Justices. Any action he took favoured the complainant. In spite of these circumstances, the fact of his taking part in the proceedings was held to invalidate them. I do not think we need go beyond the admitted facts in this case to see that on the authorities, however independently and fairly Mr Cargill might be acting, the mere fact of the connection of his firm with the previous applications, with the sale of the plot in question and with the loan of client's money on mortgage upon it on a value higher than the normal residential value of adjoining sites, might be sufficient to create an impression in the minds of people who objected to the application being granted, that Mr Cargill had some interest in the land and impartial justice was not being done.

Yet, other courts have stated that it must be a reasonable suspicion of bias.

***In the Application of Century Eslon Ltd* – HCA No 418 of 1992 (TT)**
Warner J

[P16] In effect therefore, the Court ought not to enquire whether the Authority favoured A & A, but the test to be applied is whether a reasonable man in possession of the facts would conclude that this was done . . . [P18] When compared fully with the procedure applied to the Applicant company's tender, the clear impression is that the Applicant company received less favourable treatment than Alex & Co. Ltd . . . All in all I conclude therefore that the Applicant has proven that a reasonable suspicion of bias attended the award.

***In the Application of Private Nimchand Pittiman No 4195, Private Augustine Dharmoo, Private Rajaheswar Parsanlal No 31127 and Lance Corporal Winston Arnold* – Civil Appeal No 183 of 1984 (TT)**
Kelsick CJ

[P5] The relevant tests to be applied in deciding whether a judge is incapacitated by bias from hearing a matter are as follows. Actual bias need not be established. There are two lines of authority—one in favour of the real likelihood of bias test and the other advocating the reasonable suspicion of bias test . . . [P7] I prefer the reasonable suspicion test which is more in harmony with the enjoyment of the right of the individual to liberty and security of the person and the right not to be deprived thereof except by due process of law conferred by s 4(a) of the Constitution as protected by s 5(2)(e), (f)(ii) and (h) of the Constitution. Applying that test I would hold that the Appellants and right minded members of the public would entertain a reasonable suspicion that the Judge Advocate because of his association with prosecuting counsel might not bring an impartial and unprejudiced mind to the performance of his advice and of his summing up of the evidence, to the members of the Court martial.

At times, the courts have articulated the presence of two tests for bias that can be applied in different circumstances, the real likelihood of bias test and the reasonable suspicion of bias test.

***Barnwell v Attorney-General and Another* (1993) 49 WIR 88 (GY)**
Bishop CJ

[PP176–179] Where an allegation of bias is made the burden of proof is clearly on the person making the allegation and this is on a balance of probabilities. Actual bias, however, does not have to be established in order to discharge the burden (see Wade, *Administrative Law* (6 Edn), page 477). In 1(1) *Halsbury's Laws of England* (4 Edn) (reissue) page 169, paragraph 89 puts the matter thus: '**Likelihood of bias**. It is generally unnecessary to establish the presence of actual bias, although the Courts are not precluded from entertaining such an allegation. It is enough to establish a real likelihood that in the circumstances of the case an adjudicator will be biased. *Alternatively, it may be sufficient to establish that a reasonable person acquainted with the outward appearance of the situation would have ground for suspecting bias*. In some situations a more exacting test will be adopted, and the Court may set aside a determination if justice has not been manifestly seen to be done; such a test has been applied in cases where a clerk to a tribunal has retired with the Tribunal and given the impression of participating in its decision' [emphasis supplied]. See *R v Sussex Justices, Ex Parte McCarthy* [1924] 1 KB 256. The above statement suggests that the correct test may very well be 'the reasonable suspicion test' and this seems to have support from what Lord Denning MR said in *Metropolitan Properties Co (FGC) Ltd v Lannon* [1968] 3 All ER 304 at page 310: 'in considering whether there was a real likelihood of bias, the Court does not look at the mind of the Justice himself or at the mind of the Chairman of the Tribunal, or whoever it may be, who sits in a judicial capacity. It does not look to see if there was a real likelihood that he would, or did, in fact favour one side at the expense of the other. *The Court looks at the impression which would be given to other people. Even if he was as impartial as could be, nevertheless, if right-minded persons would think that, in the circumstances, there was a real likelihood of bias on his part, then he should not sit. And if he does sit, his decision cannot stand*; see *R v Huggins* [1895] 1 QB 563, and *R v Sunderland Justices* [1901] 2 KB 357 at page 373, *per* Vaughan Williams LJ. Nevertheless, there must appear to be a real likelihood of bias. Surmise or conjecture is not enough; see *R v Camborne Justices, Ex Parte Pearce* [1954] 2 All ER 850 at page 858, and *R v Nailsworth Licensing Justices, Ex Parte Bird* [1953] 2 All ER 652. There must be circumstances from which a reasonable man would think it likely or probable that the Justice, or Chairman, as the case may be, would, or did, favour one side unfairly at the expense of the other. The Court will not inquire whether he did, in fact, favour one side unfairly. Suffice it that reasonable people might think he did. The reason is plain enough. Justice must be rooted in confidence; and confidence is destroyed when right-minded people go away thinking: 'The judge was biased' [emphasis supplied]. See also Wade, *Administrative Law* (6 Edn), page 484. The above dictum runs through the two tests of 'real likelihood of bias' and 'reasonable suspicion of bias' in a way which supports the view presently held by some that there is really now only one test, namely the 'reasonable suspicion test'. Should the Chancellor have participated in the meeting of the JSC of 2 October 1989 when he had previously suggested to the Appellant that he might consider 'resigning' or 'retiring'? Would a reasonable man, considering the behaviour of the Chancellor to the Appellant on 26 September 1989, conclude that the Chancellor might have been biased? Would he have suspected bias? In 1(1) *Halsbury's Laws of England* (4 Edn) (reissue), paragraph 88 under the heading 'Other forms of interest' reviews the situation in which the impression may be received that an adjudicator might be biased. The paragraph reads thus: 'In a wide range of other situations the impression may be received that an adjudicator is likely to be biased. A person ought not to participate or appear to participate in an appeal against his own decision, or act or appear to act as both prosecutor and judge; the general rule is that in such circumstances the decision will be set aside. Normally it will also be inappropriate for a member of the Tribunal to act as witness. Likelihood of bias may also arise because an adjudicator has already indicated partisanship by expressing opinions, antagonistic or favourable to the parties before him, or has made known his views about the merits of the very issue or issues of a similar nature in such a way as to suggest pre-judgment or because he is so actively associated with the institution or conduct of proceedings before him, either in his personal capacity or by virtue of his membership of an interested organisation, as to make himself in substance both judge and party ... or for other reasons. *It is not enough to show that the person adjudicating holds strong views on the general subject matter in respect of which he is adjudicating, or that he is a member of a trade union to which one of the parties belongs, where the matter is not one in which a trade dispute is involved. The fact that an administrator may incline towards deciding an issue before him one way rather than another, in the light of implementing a policy for which he is responsible, will not affect the validity of his decision, provided that he acts fairly and with a mind not closed to argument, and similar standards may be applied to other persons whose prior connection with the parties or the issues is liable to preclude them from acting with total detachment'* [emphasis supplied]. See also *Mitchell v Attorney-General* [1987] LRC (Const) 568, and *CREEDNZ Inc v Governor-General* [1981] 1 NZLR 172. Would any reasonable man sitting on the No 44 minibus and considering all that took place between the Appellant and the Chancellor on 26 September 1989, reasonably suspect that the Chancellor might have been biased? If the Chancellor might have been biased, then his bias would have affected the other members of the JSC. The result would have been that the proceedings before the JSC would be vitiated. Scott LJ said in *Cooper v Wilson* [1937] 2 All ER 726 at page 742: 'the risk that a Respondent may influence the Court is so abhorrent to English notions of justice that the possibility of it, or even the appearance of such a possibility, is sufficient to deprive the decision of all judicial force, and to render it a nullity'. However, there is a conflict between the Chancellor and the Appellant as to what took place between them at their meeting on 26 September 1989, a conflict which I cannot resolve by merely looking at the affidavits. Bearing in mind that the onus is on the Appellant to establish bias on the part of the Chancellor, and in view of the doubts surrounding the matter, I cannot make a positive finding on the issue. Bias cannot be founded on mere conjecture or surmise. For me to come down on the side of bias would mean that I would have to accept the Appellant's version, which, as I said, I do not think I can do. Even if I were to accept the Chancellor's version, I do not think that I can reasonably find bias, as the sum total of what the Chancellor told the Appellant was that he might consider retiring, if the allegations contained in the letter of complaint were true. When the contents of the Chancellor's affidavit of 24 November 1989 are read as a whole, as well as his later affidavits, the Chancellor did not indicate to the Appellant that he felt that the Appellant was guilty and, therefore, he must either resign (retire) or face the Tribunal which would be set up by the President. Whether one applies the test of 'real likelihood of bias' or the test of 'reasonable suspicion of bias' on the available material, I am inclined to the view that neither test has been satisfied in this case. The evidence did not go far enough.

***Griffith v Barbados Cricket Association; Byer and Another v Barbados Cricket Association* (1989) 41 WIR 48 (BB)**
Sir Denys Williams CJ

[PP62–63] Eve J in *Law v Chartered Institute of Patent Agents* [1919] 2 Ch 276 said: 'A person who has a judicial duty to perform is disqualified from performing it if he has a bias which renders him otherwise than an impartial judge or if he has so conducted himself in relation to the matters to be investigated as to create in the mind of a reasonable man a suspicion that he may have such a bias'. Mr Estwick's presence as a member of the Board at the final Board meeting offended the principles of natural justice. As the president of the BCL he had signed the complaint on its behalf; he had thereafter produced a tape to the Board and caused the matter to be remitted to the complaints committee; he had then appeared before the complaints committee in the capacity of complainant and presented the evidence provided by the tape; and he had then been present at the final meeting of the Board when the decision was taken. A reasonable suspicion of bias created by this conduct would have been reinforced by the coincidence between the action against St Catherine and Police which the complaint recommended and that which the Board in fact took. In the circumstances it is immaterial whether Mr Estwick did or did not take part in the discussions or decision at the Board's final meeting. Numerous cases can be cited to illustrate what the law is. In *Frome United Breweries Co v Bath Justices* [1926] AC 586 at pages 590, 591, Viscount Cave LC said: 'My Lords, if there is one principle which forms an integral part of the English law, it is that every member of a body engaged in a judicial proceeding must be able to act judicially; and it has been held over and over again that, if a member of such a body is subject to a bias (whether financial or other) in favour of or against either party to the dispute or is in such a position that a bias must be assumed, he ought not to take part in the decision or even to sit upon the Tribunal. This rule has been asserted not only in the case of Courts of justice and other judicial tribunals, but in the case of authorities which, though in no sense to be called Courts, have to act as Judges of the rights of others . . . From the above rule it necessarily follows that a member of such a body as I have described cannot be both a party and a judge in the same dispute and that if he has made himself a party he cannot sit or act as a judge and if he does so the decision of the whole body will be vitiated'. In the Bermudan case, *Hall v Bermuda Bar Council* (1983) 33 WIR 69 at page 94, da Costa JA said: 'in considering whether there was a real likelihood of bias, the Court does not look at the mind of the Justice himself or at the mind of the Chairman of the Tribunal, or whoever it may be, who sits in a judicial capacity. It does not look to see if there was a real likelihood that he would, or did, in fact favour one side at the expense of the other. The Court looks at the impression which would be given to other people. Even if he was as impartial as could be, nevertheless, if right-minded persons would think that, in the circumstances, there was a real likelihood of bias on his part, then he should not sit. And if he does sit, his decision cannot stand'.

***In the Application of Guyana Telephone and Telegraph Company Ltd* –**
HCSCJ No 13-M of 1999 (GY)
Singh J

[PP11–15] Prior to the year 1993, English Courts interchangeably applied two tests for the determination of bias. These were identified as 'the real likelihood of bias', and 'the reasonable suspicion of bias' tests. Much uncertainty surrounded the application of the tests in the determination of bias, which prompted Lord Justice Widgery in *Hannam v Bradford City Council* [1970] 1 WLR 937 at page 945 to remark that he 'did not wish to add to the somewhat confusing welter of authority on what is meant by bias.' While it was often argued that there was little difference between the two tests, the English Courts treated them as different from time to time and appeared to consider it necessary to make an election between them, so that in *R v Camborne Justices* [1995] 1 QB 41, the Divisional Court gave consideration to a number of authorities and firmly approved of the application of the real likelihood of bias test. However, in *Metropolitan Properties (FGC) Ltd. v Lannon* [1969] 1 QB 577, the Court of Appeal approved of the 'reasonable suspicion of bias' test, although as Professor Wade observed at page 411 of his test, *Administrative Law*, 4th edition, Lord Denning, MR 'interwove this with the other test' that it is, the real likelihood test. His Lordship at page 598–600 of the report observed: 'in considering whether there was a real likelihood of bias the Court does not look at the mind of the justice himself or at the mind of the Chairman of the Tribunal, or whoever it may be, who sits in a judicial capacity. It does not look to see if there was a real likelihood that he would, or did, in fact favour one side at the expense of the other. The Court looks at the impression which would be given to other people. Even if he was as impartial as could be, nevertheless if right-minded persons would think that, in the circumstances, there was a real likelihood of bias on his part, then he should not sit. And if he does sit, his decision cannot stand ... Nevertheless, there must appear to be a real likelihood of bias. Surmise or conjecture is not enough ... There must be circumstances from which a reasonable man would think it likely or probable that the Justice, or Chairman, as the case may be, would, or did, favour one side unfairly at the expense of the other. The Court will not inquire whether he did, in fact, favour one side unfairly. Suffice it that reasonable people might think he did. The reason is plain enough. Justice must be rooted in confidence: and confidence is destroyed when right-minded people go away thinking: "The judge was biased".' What Lord Denning sought to do in *Metropolitan Properties (FGC) Ltd. v Lannon* (*supra*) was to re-establish and re-enforce the celebrated dictum of Lord Hewart, C.J. in *R v Sussex Justices, Ex Parte McCarthy* [1924] 1 KB 256. In that case, His Lordship said that it is: 'of fundamental importance that justice should not only be done, but should manifestly and undoubtedly be seen to be done.' In 1993, the House of Lords in *R v Gough* [1993] 2 All ER 724, seemed to have finally settled, the interchangeable use, confusion and uncertainty of application of the 'real likelihood of bias' and the 'reasonable suspicion of bias' tests. The leading decision of the House was delivered by Lord Goff of Chieveley, who shifted the focus of the Court's scrutiny away from 'real likelihood' and 'reasonable suspicion' of bias to that of 'a real danger of bias'. His Lordship explained that in laying down 'the real danger' test the House was emphasizing 'the possibility' and not 'the probability' of bias. The Court also whittled away the need to ascertain the perceptions of the reasonable man and stressed that the views of the Court founded upon the facts must be imputed to the reasonable man personified by the Court. His Lordship explained at page 735: 'In my opinion, if in the circumstances of the case (as ascertained by the Court), it appears that there was a real likelihood, in the sense of a real possibility of bias on the part of a justice or other member of an inferior tribunal, justice requires that the decision should not be allowed to stand.' And in his concluding remarks, Lord Goff emphasized, at page 757: 'Finally, for the avoidance of doubt, I prefer to state the test in terms of real danger rather than real likelihood, to ensure that the Court is thinking in terms of possibility rather than probability of bias. Accordingly, having ascertained the relevant circumstances, the Court should ask itself whether, having regard to those circumstances, there was a real danger of bias on the part of the relevant member of the Tribunal in question, in the sense that he might unfairly regard (or have unfairly regarded) with favour, or with disfavour, the case of a party to the issue under consideration by him.' Given the very definitive pronouncements of Lord Goff in *R v Gough* (*supra*) it was to be expected that the confusion which surrounded the application of an appropriate test for the determination of bias had been settled once and for all, but many common law jurisdictions have refused to apply the test laid down in *R v Gough*. The House of Lords in *In Re Pinochet*, while not embarking upon a review of the test enunciated in *R v Gough*, certainly identified the reluctance to follow it or its rejection by some jurisdictions. Lord Brown-Wilkinson in that case observed: 'For the same reason, it is unnecessary to determine whether the test of apparent bias laid down in *Reg v Gough* ("is there in the view of the Court a real danger that the Judge was biased?") needs to be reviewed in the light of subsequent decisions. Decisions in Canada, Australia and New Zealand have either refused to apply the test in *Reg v Gough*, or modified it so as to make the relevant test the question whether the events in question give rise to a reasonable apprehension or suspicion on the part of a fair-minded and informed member of the public that the Judge was not impartial: see, for example, the High Court of Australia in *Webb v the Queen*. It has also been suggested that the test in *Reg v Gough* in some way impinges on the requirement of Lord Hewart's dictum that justice should appear to be done: see *Reg v Inner West London Coroner, Ex Parte Dallaglio* [1994] 4 All ER 139 at page 152 A to B. Since such a review is unnecessary for the determination of the present case, I prefer to express no view on it.' The real danger test has been applied in Commonwealth Caribbean jurisdictions. See for example: *Vaughn Lewis v AG of St. Lucia*, and *Compton v AG of St. Lucia*, Civil Appeals, Nos. 12 and 14 (OECS). *Rees v Crane* [1994] 1 All ER 833 . . . [P19] My own reflections on the matter lead me to the consideration that ours is a small society, and it is important for the proper administration of justice and for the maintenance of a higher level of confidence in the administration of justice, that the perceptions of fair-minded persons in our society be not ignored. I therefore find suitable and would adopt for application, whenever a test is required to be applied for the determination of allegations of bias, the test whether a fair-minded observer might reasonably suspect the existence of bias . . . [P28] I would conclude my discussion on the issue of bias by saying that bias really relates to the state of mind of the person against whom it is alleged. It is for this reason that the authorities are in unison on the impossibility of establishing actual bias. I certainly do not make any such finding here. However, it is usual to look at outward appearances, that is, things said or done by the person against whom bias is alleged. These are usually reflective of the state of mind of that person.

Bias is not only considered with respect to public bodies engaged in the exercise of judicial or quasi-judicial functions but also with respect to administrative tribunals.

Barnwell v Attorney-General and Another (1993) 49 WIR 88 (GY)
Bishop CJ

[P179] There is just one final matter which, I think, I need to address and that is whether an administrative tribunal is susceptible to the rules of bias. In my view, bias is not only applicable to bodies performing judicial or quasi-judicial functions but also to bodies performing administrative functions. These distinctions no longer exist and the true test is to determine what role or function is being performed by the particular tribunal.

2.18 ERRORS IN FORM OR PROCEDURE LACKING IN SUBSTANCE

The courts may decline an invitation to judicially review the decision of a public body where such a decision was tainted merely by an error in form or procedure, or where such an error can be considered as trivial and not of substance.

Herbert Charles – Privy Council Appeal No 26 of 2001 (TT)
Tipping J

[PP6–8] 9. The leading authority is the decision of the Privy Council in *Wang v Commissioner of Inland Revenue* [1994] 1 WLR 1286. At 1296 Lord Slynn of Hadley, who delivered the judgment of their Lordships, cited from the speech of Lord Hailsham of St Marylebone LC in *London & Clydeside Estates Ltd v Aberdeen District Council* [1980] 1 WLR 182 in which his Lordship had discouraged the use in this field of rigid legal classifications like mandatory and directory. Lord Slynn then said: 'their Lordships consider that when a question like the present one arises—an alleged failure to comply with a time provision—it is simpler and better to avoid these two words "mandatory" and "directory" and to ask two questions. The first is whether the legislature intended the person making the determination to comply with the time provision, whether a fixed time or a reasonable time. Secondly, if so, did the legislature intend that a failure to comply with such a time provision would deprive the decision maker of jurisdiction and render any decision which he purported to make null and void?' Some five years earlier the New Zealand Court of Appeal had taken much the same approach in *New Zealand Institute of Agriculture Science Inc v Ellesmere County* [1976] 1 NZLR 630. Cooke J (now Lord Cooke of Thorndon) speaking for the Court said at 636: 'Whether non-compliance with a procedural requirement is fatal turns less on attaching a perhaps indefinite label to that requirement than on considering its place in the scheme of the Act or Regulations and the degree and seriousness of the non-compliance.' 10. The approach evidenced by these cases was a development of earlier authority and was not in itself new. It can be traced back at least as far as the judgment of Lord Campbell, sitting as Lord Chancellor in *Liverpool Borough Bank v Turner* (1860) 29 LJ (Ch) 827; 2 DeGF & J 502, in which he said, in relation to the issue of implied nullification for disobedience of a statute, that the duty of the Courts was 'to try to get at the real intention of the legislature by carefully attending to the whole scope of the statute to be construed'. And in the well known case of *Howard v Bodington* (1877) 2 PD 203 at 210 Lord Penzance observed that he was not sure that the language of mandatory and directory was the most fortunate language that could have been adopted to express the idea that it was intended to convey. He continued: 'Still, whatever the language, the idea is a perfectly distinct one. There may be many provisions in Acts of Parliament which, although they are not strictly obeyed, yet do not appear to the Court to be of that material importance to the subject-matter to which they refer, as that the legislature could have intended that the non-observance of them should be followed by a total failure of the whole proceedings. On the other hand, there are some provisions in respect of which the Court would take an opposite view, and would feel that they are matters which must be strictly obeyed, otherwise the whole proceedings that subsequently follow must come to an end.' And a little later at 211, after citing from *Liverpool Borough Bank v Turner* (*supra*), Lord Penzance said: 'in each case you must look to the subject-matter; consider the importance of the provision that has been disregarded, and the relation of that provision to the general object intended to be secured by the Act; and upon a review of the case in that aspect decide whether the matter is what is called imperative or only directory.' It is quite clear that in context his Lordship was there using the words imperative and directory as shorthand for whether or not non-compliance with a particular provision should lead to a failure of the whole proceedings. 11. Their Lordships return to *Wang's case*. The answer to the first question posed there must be that the framers of Regulation 90, in this instance effectively the Commission itself (see the relevant notice in the Gazette of 23rd February 1984 in which the Commission adopted the Regulations), must have intended those involved to comply with the relevant time provisions. The answer to the second question involves an examination of (i) the role of Regulation 90, and its individual parts, in the overall regulatory scheme, (ii) the purpose and policy of the time provisions, and (iii) in the end a judgment as to whether those who promulgated the Regulations intended that breach of a time limit should deprive the Commission of jurisdiction, thus rendering any later purported decision or determination null and void. 12. The terms of Regulation 90 have already been set out. At the outset their Lordships observe that it seems highly unlikely that the Commission can have intended that breaches of time limits at the investigation stage would inevitably prevent it from discharging its public function and duty of inquiring into and, if appropriate, prosecuting relevant indiscipline or misconduct. A self imposed fetter of such a kind on the discharge of an important public function would seem inimical to the whole purpose of the investigation and disciplinary regime. The proposition that this was intended is also hard to reconcile with the then existence of Section 129(3) precluding inquiry into procedural irregularities not of a fundamental kind (see *Thomas v Attorney-General of Trinidad and Tobago* [1982] AC 113 PC). 13. The same picture emerges when reference is made to the text of Regulation 90 and subsequent Regulations. Regulations 90(1), 90(4) and 90(5) all use the phrase 'for the information of the Commission', thereby underlining that the inquiry function of the investigating officer is to gather material to enable the Commission to discharge its task of deciding whether the officer under investigation should be charged. Although the time limits in Regulation 90 are incidentally of benefit to that officer, their Lordships view them as designed primarily to expedite the investigation process for the benefit of the public interest in having matters of indiscipline or misconduct effectively investigated and dealt with. This makes it unlikely that breach of a time limit was intended to lead to the frustration of that ultimate purpose . . . [P9] 16. It is helpful to recall that in *London & Clydesdale Estates* Lord Hailsham at 189 spoke of the Courts having to decide in a particular case what should be the legal consequence of non-compliance with statutory or regulatory provisions like those in issue in the present case. The choice open to the Court is not a stark choice, as his Lordship put it. The issue is seldom black and white. His Lordship spoke of a spectrum of possibilities: 'At one end of this spectrum there may be cases in which a fundamental obligation may have been so outrageously and flagrantly ignored or defied that the subject may safely ignore what has been done and treat it as having no legal consequences upon himself. In such a case, if the defaulting authority seeks to rely on its action, it may be that the subject is entitled to use the defect in procedure simply as a shield or defence without having taken any positive action of his own. At the other end of the spectrum the defect in procedure may be so nugatory or trivial that the authority can safely proceed without remedial action, confident that, if the subject is so misguided as to rely on the fault, the Courts will decline to listen to his complaint.' 17. His Lordship added that most cases will fall somewhere in the middle and will be for the Courts to assess. If a complaint is made about the non-fulfilment of a time limit the giving of relief will usually be discretionary. This discretionary element to which Lord Hailsham referred underlines the fact that problems arising from breach of time limits and other like procedural flaws are not generally susceptible [to] rigid classification or black and white *a priori* rules. With this in mind their Lordships note that in the present case the delays were in good faith, they were not lengthy and they were entirely understandable. The Appellant suffered no material prejudice; no fair trial considerations were or could have been raised, and no fundamental human rights are in issue. 18. Bearing in mind the relevant aspects of Regulation 90 and its regulatory environment, and the other relevant circumstances of the case, including the lack of significant impact of the time defaults on the Appellant, their Lordships came to the clear view that the Regulations cannot have been framed with the intention that breaches of the kind in issue would deprive the Commission of jurisdiction to act as it thought fit on the investigating officer's report and thereby fulfil its public responsibilities.

***In the Application of Cecil Kennedy* – HCA No 653 of 2000 (TT)**
Ventour J

[P8] When, therefore, the Justice of the Peace allowed the proceedings to be instituted against the Applicant by a complaint involving more than one offence he was acting contrary to Section 39(4) of the Act. It is indeed an error on the part of the Justice of the Peace, but it is an error in form only, not substance, and therefore in my respectful view, it is not fatal. It is an error which the presiding Magistrate hearing the complaint has the power to correct prior to a plea being taken on this specific charge and no prejudice is caused to the Defendant at that stage of the proceedings. In my respectful view it would be wrong therefore to hold that such an error by the Justice of the Peace would nullify the complaint.

***In the Application of Balkaran Sinanan* – HCA No 3809 of 1984 (TT)**
Blackman J

[P8] It is not every trivial departure from procedure that will vitiate a hearing and unless an Applicant has been or is likely to be prejudiced thereby, the proceedings would not be invalidated. I think that in couching his language in the way he did, the Chairman of the Tribunal did not accurately express himself, but in my view the lapse was trivial in the circumstances.

***R v The Air Transport Licensing Board ex parte Tropical Airlines Ltd* (1996) 33 JLR 278 (JM)**
Langrin J

[P285] In any event, the mere breach of a procedural requirement in reaching an administrative decision will not necessarily result in it being quashed. The burden remains on the Applicant to show that substantial prejudice has been suffered as a consequence of the loss of this opportunity. This burden has not been discharged. The Board directed itself properly in law and called its own attention to the various matters it should consider and took all relevant matters into consideration. Consequently, the decision which was arrived at is one which a reasonable Board might reasonably have reached.

***R v Commissioner of Customs and Excise ex parte, A. & F. Farm Produce Company Ltd and Andre Chin* (1993) 30 JLR 462 (JM)**
Langrin J

[P469] In any event the mere breach of a procedural requirement in reaching an administrative decision will not necessarily result in it being quashed. Even if the affidavit evidence shows that a procedural irregularity has occurred the burden remains on the Applicant to show that substantial prejudice has been suffered.

The courts are prepared to hold that the failure to object to a procedural error may provide a defence for the decision-maker where the person adversely affected by the decision is seeking to have it judicially reviewed on the basis of the said procedural error.

***In the Application of Maniram Maharaj* – HCA No 1426 of 1999 (TT)**
Smith J

[P9] By participating in the meeting of the 28th June, 1999 without objection to the irregularity which he is deemed to have known about, the Applicant submitted to the jurisdiction of the Authority inspite of the procedural irregularity and cannot now seek to raise the point. Further, the irregularity complained of is a procedural matter and by participating in the meeting without objection, he waived the irregularity.

It must be emphasised however that failure to properly follow procedures may result in a decision being set aside, especially where the procedure enshrines the rules of natural justice.

***In the Application of Fishermen and Friends of the Sea* –**
Civil Appeal No 106 of 2002 (TT)
Lucky JA (dissenting judgment)

[P15] The crucial question is whether the EMA followed the procedure set out in the above sections before granting the certificate. It seems to me that the Judge did not address this issue because he had pre-empted the determination of those issues by refusing to grant an extension of time. I think that if he had he may not have exercised his discretion as he did without hearing the substantive matter because the following questions *inter alia* would have arisen: what specifically [is] the list of activities? What is the environmental impact assessment (the EIA)? Was the EIA submitted for public comment? (Section 28 of the EMA Act). What was the public response? Were there comments or representations made during the public comment period? If these statutory requirements were not followed and those could only be ascertained during the determination of the substantive matter, then the issuance of the CEC as exists at present was invalid and the decision ought to be reviewed.

***Roberts (Kemp) v Attorney-General* (1994) 52 WIR 273 (TT)**
Bernard JA

[P 277–278] In exercising the powers of dismissal or discharge of the Appellant as a constable in the police force conferred on him under the Constitution, the Commissioner was bound to observe the principles of natural justice and accord the Appellant the right to be heard. As was held in *Ridge v Baldwin*, compliance with the procedure laid down in the Police (Discipline) Act was a condition precedent to dismissal of the Appellant, and there was no room to circumvent it by having recourse to Section 35(1) of the Police Act . . . It is my view that the appeal turns on the failure of the Commissioner to invoke the procedure under the Police (Discipline) Act which accords with the principles of natural justice. In this regard I refer to the opinion of Lord Morris of Borth-y-Gest in *Ridge v Baldwin* [1963] 3 All ER at page 102: 'It is well established that the essential requirements of natural justice at least include that before someone is condemned he is to have an opportunity of defending himself and in order that he may do so that he is to be made aware of the charges or allegations or suggestions which he has to meet'. The principles of natural justice cannot be circumvented by utilising a short cut in achieving the desired objective of removing an employee from office. The errant constable or public servant is entitled to be heard before any disciplinary action is taken against him, especially if such action is likely to affect his ability to earn a living in the future and any financial entitlements. Dismissal is not an option to be exercised lightly by those who exercise disciplinary control over others. To emphasise the need to apply the *audi alteram partem* rule before any tribunal or person in an administrative position exercises the option of dismissal I refer to the *dictum* of Kelly CB in *Wood v Woad* (1874) LR 9 Exch 190 at page 196: 'This rule is not confined to the conduct of strictly legal tribunals but is applicable to every tribunal or body of persons invested with authority to adjudicate upon matters involving civil consequences to individuals.' The principles of natural justice and more specifically the *audi alteram partem* rule were applied recently and addressed extensively by all of the justices of this Court in *Barnwell v Attorney-General* (1993) 49 WIR 88 which concerned removal from office of a judge of the High Court. This Court was unanimous in its finding that the Judge ought to have been given an opportunity to be heard by the Judicial Service Commission before that body represented to the President that the question of his removal ought to be investigated as provided for under the Constitution. For all of the reasons stated above I find that the Commissioner of Police wrongly invoked his powers under Section 35(1) of the Police Act to discharge the Appellant from the Guyana Police Force instead of utilising the procedure laid down in the Police (Discipline) Act and as such deprived the Appellant of the right to be heard before he was dismissed. This rendered his actions void for failure to comply with the statutory provisions, as was held in *Ridge v Baldwin*.

R v Commissioner of Police ex parte Warren Douglas Turner **(1989) 26 JLR 263 (JM)**
Harrison J

[P266] The Regulations therefore contemplate a procedure as a condition precedent to the appointment of the Court of Enquiry. This is in the nature of a preliminary opportunity given to the Applicant to seek to exculpate himself. The Applicant should have been told at the time that charges were served on him that he had the right to state in writing 'before a specified date', that is, a date specifically named by the person serving the summons or the person issuing the summons, his reasons, sufficiently cogent, to excuse his alleged blameworthy conduct. If such explanation in writing was sufficiently excusable, the Commissioner would presumably refrain from appointing a Court of Enquiry. However, by paragraph (2)(c), if a member 'does not duly furnish such a statement as aforesaid or if he fails to exculpate himself the Commissioner shall appoint a Court of Enquiry' [P267]. In the instant case, the said Regulations contemplate a two-tier procedure. This procedure is formulated in order to ensure fairness to all parties concerned and more so to one who runs the risk of the penalty of loss of office or employment. The Regulations must be adhered to. Where one performs an administrative function *simpliciter* which is in the nature of a quasi-judicial act, such function takes unto itself the character of judicial proceedings and therefore attracts the strictures of the necessity that the principles of natural justice should be observed. When the Commissioner of Police on the 14th day of April 1989 ordered the assembly of a Court of Enquiry into the preferred charges against the Applicant, he did so on the basis that the pre-condition under paragraph 2(c) of Regulation 47 had been satisfied—the quasi-judicial act. In this case, the pre-condition was that the Applicant had been told of his right to seek to exculpate himself in writing, and he did 'not duly furnish such a statement'. No such basis existed. The Applicant was denied the opportunity of a preliminary review by the Commissioner of Police of his exculpatory statement, if any. This created a breach of the said Regulations and consequently a breach of natural justice. Accordingly, the Court of Enquiry which was subsequently assembled on this premise was not in accordance with the Regulations. The order of prohibition must issue.

R v The Rent Assessment Board for the Corporate Area ex parte Donald Glanville **(1988) 25 JLR 189 (JM)**
Bingham J

[P193] It is a cardinal rule of construction of statutes that where a specified period is fixed by the legislature for the doing of a particular act, then this must be strictly followed. It is also a principle of construction of general application that procedural requirements as laid down in statutes admit of a strict interpretation unless there are clear words which seek to alter or vary such an interpretation. Moreover, also of general application is the rule that statutes which seek to take away the rights of individuals or to fix obligations upon them are to be construed strictly ... [P194] We are of the view that this clearly mandates the Board to effect service in the manner as laid down by the rule. As it is common ground that the notices of claim were 'short served' in the light of the admitted facts, it follows that these notices were ineffectual and could only be cured by the commencement of the tenant's application *de novo*.

***Cecil Roy July v The Commissioner of Income Tax* (1988) 25 JLR 288 (JM)**
Rowe J

[P290] This case is not concerned with whether Mr July owes tax or does not owe tax. It is concerned with the procedure by which he was assessed and if he was assessed in a manner not permitted by the Income Tax Act then the Restriction Notice which was so intimately connected to the invalid Notices of Assessment is also of no validity.

***In the Application of David Commissiong* – Civil Appeal No 16 of 1998 (BB)**
Williams CJ

[P17] Both warrants recited, in terms of Section 70(1)(b) of the Act, that there were reasonable grounds for belief. Mr Shepherd for the Applicant submitted that the informations which were laid before the two Justices of the Peace did not justify the issuance of the search warrants since:

(A) they did not state with sufficient particularity the grounds upon which the deponent believed 'that there are reasonable grounds for believing that there is concealed on premises . . . certain articles of property to wit guns which would afford evidence as to the Commission of an offence to wit larceny';
(B) they did not state with sufficient particularity the grounds upon which the deponent believed that an offence had been committed;
(C) they did not state that the person who was actually swearing to the information himself believed that 'there are reasonable grounds for believing that there is concealed on premises . . . certain articles of property to wit guns which would afford evidence as to the Commission of an offence to wit larceny'; and
(D) they did not state with sufficient particularity the grounds upon which the deponent believed that an offence had been committed.

The Canadian cases relied on in support of these submissions disclose that search warrants were quashed because the informations on which they were issued did not state with sufficient particularity the grounds of belief of the deponents. Thus in *Rex v Binder* [1916] 30 DLR 520 Sutherland J said at p 523: 'In *Rex v Kehr* (1906) 11 OLR 517 it was held that the information necessary to justify the issuing of such warrant must disclose facts and circumstances showing the causes of suspicion, which tended to the belief of the Commission of the alleged offence, with regard to the alleged offence, with regard to which the warrant is deemed essential. The information herein being defective in this respect, the warrant was directed to be quashed.' The learned judge concluded (at p 524): 'It seems to me that I am bound by and should follow *Rex v Kehr* and hold that, as the information did not disclose facts and circumstances showing the causes of suspicion, the warrant issued thereupon must be deemed to have been improperly issued and must be quashed.' In *Rex v Kehr* the Code, section 569 form J, was the prescribed form of information and made provision for the causes of suspicion to be set out therein. (In Form 'J' to section 569 of the Code the words were: 'Hath just and reasonable cause to suspect and suspects (here add the causes of suspicion whatever they may be')). The causes of suspicion were not set out and led to the warrant being quashed. Clute J, with whose decision the other members of High Court of Ontario concurred, said ((1906) CCC 52 at p 60): 'I am of the opinion . . . that this information, being the basis of the subsequent proceedings and without which the Justice is not authorized to act must contain that which the statute contemplates, namely the causes of suspicion whatever they may be in order to satisfy the Justice that there is reasonable ground for believing that there is in the place to be searched anything which there is reasonable ground to believe will afford evidence as to the Commission of the offence charged.' In *Rev v Solloway and Mills* 53 CCC 271, a decision of the Ontario Supreme Court, Appellate Division, another case relied on by Mr Shepherd, Riddell JA said (at p 276) that there was not sufficient in the information for the Justice to have a 'satisfaction' upon; not to mention, he said, the vagueness and generality of the statements in the information, he does not even pledge his oath to his own belief, citing *Rex v Kehr*. Mr Shepherd also relied on *Re Borden & Elliot and the Queen* 30 CCC (2D) 337. In this case the Ontario Court of Appeal held that the information on which the warrant was issued did not set out a factual link between the alleged fraud and the trust account of the solicitors and the warrant was rightly quashed. This case does not appear to have any relevance to the issues in the present case. The Canadian cases relied on by Mr Shepherd are to be distinguished by the fact that whereas in those cases a statutory form was prescribed which detailed the particulars that were to be included in the informations on which the warrants were issued, there is in Barbados no corresponding statutory provision prescribing the details that are required to be included in the informations.

***In the Application of the Public Service Commission* – HCSCJ No 2610 of 1990 (GY)**
Singh J

[P8] It is my considered opinion that the principle would be the same and I therefore hold that the Commission had no power to dismiss the Appellant except it acted in accordance with the Rules which it did not do. Having taken this position regardless of the fact that it was erroneous—the Commission had rejected the Appellant's letter of resignation and regarded him as being under its jurisdiction.

2.19 FAILURE TO ASCERTAIN RELEVANT INFORMATION

Not only is a decision-maker required to consider all relevant matters, there is also a positive duty placed on a decision-maker to ascertain relevant information required for a proper decision.

***Barl Naraynsingh* – Privy Council Appeal No 42 of 2003 (TT)**
Lord Brown of Eaton-under-Heywood

[PP9–10] 23. Their Lordships do not say that it will always be necessary for the Commissioner to ascertain more about the circumstances of whatever it is which inclines him to revoke a licence than was ascertained here. Sometimes further information may simply not be available, or the facts may be plain enough. But where, as here, further information obviously *was* available, and where there are a number of puzzling features of the case (not least why so many people should have attended the Appellant's home to enforce a small debt), then a fair procedure demanded that further inquiries be made, particularly having regard to the abandonment of the criminal prosecution.

***In the Application of D.S. Maharaj Furniture and Applicances Ltd* –**
Civil Appeal No 6 of 1995 (TT)
de la Bastide CJ

[PP13–14] As has been pointed out, there is no evidence that the Trinidad and Tobago Customs ever communicated to the Appellant the contents of Marsheck's fax of November 10, or that the Appellant learnt of them from any other source prior to the issue of the second Notice of Query and Referral dated the 11th November, 1993—or indeed, prior to the commencement of these proceedings. It is clear therefore that the Appellant was given no opportunity to contradict or explain the vital piece of evidence which constituted the basis of Skerritt's decision of the 11th November. That decision was highly prejudicial to the Appellant as the effect of it was to make it necessary for the Appellant to make immediately quite a substantial payment which it had not catered for and which, according to the Appellant, it was unable to meet . . . The fact is that a decision was made by Skerritt which affected the Appellant adversely, on the basis of information which was not disclosed to the Appellant, and which it was given no opportunity to counter. That seems to me to be a clear breach of the rules of natural justice or, to use more modern terminology, a clear breach of procedural fairness. It is well established that the right to be heard includes the right to know the case against you . . . [PP16–17] Can a decision be quashed in judicial review proceedings on the ground that it was unreasonable to make it without first pursuing an obvious line of inquiry that was capable of producing relevant information? I have come across no authority which recognizes this as a ground for quashing an administrative decision . . . [P17] There is a growing support from text-book writers and judicially for recognizing as a ground on which an administrative decision may be quashed, not only the absence, but also the insufficiency, of evidence to support a finding of fact on which such decision was based . . . If an administrative decision can be quashed on the basis that it is founded on a factual premise which is patently flawed, what does one say about the unreasonable failure of the decision maker to provide himself by inquiry with a proper basis of fact for his decision? It strikes me as a legitimate extension on the ***Wednesbury*** unreasonableness to strike down a decision on the ground that no reasonable person would have taken it without first making some further inquiry. One may describe this as 'procedural unreasonableness', or simply, without a tag, as a form of procedural impropriety.

2.20 PURSUING IMPROPER OBJECTIVES

Although the *Jagroo Case* was ultimately determined by the Privy Council, it is noteworthy to mention an observation by Justice Warner at the High Court level—that a decision-maker must not exercise its power granted for a particular purpose in pursuit of a different objective.

***In the Application of Vinode Jhagroo* – HCA No 1147 of 1995 (TT)**
Warner J

[P5] The Court must not concern itself with the merits of the Commission's decision, but must examine the decision making process . . . [P8] Put another way, the principle in administrative law is that a power is not validly exercised when it is granted for one purpose, and the public body pursues some different or collateral object.

2.21 UNREASONABLE DELAY

An unreasonable delay on the part of a public body in making a decision may, in certain circumstances, lead to a successful judicial review action by the person affected by the delay.

***In the Application of Anthony Leach* – HCA No 1002 of 2004 (TT)**
Jones J

[PP15–16] 22. While I accept the submission of Counsel for the Applicant with respect to the Applicant's terms and conditions of employment, there are two factors which need to be considered, and which, in the instant case, will serve to qualify the above statement of the law. The first is the decision of the Privy Council in the *Herbert Charles case* where it was demonstrated that minor breaches in time limits will not serve to vitiate the disciplinary proceedings. The second and more fundamental is the fact that the Regulations do not provide a time frame for the making of the decision by the PSC. 23. In this regard I can do no more than go back to the judgment of de la Bastide CJ in the *Sookermany case* where he states: 'it has been said that in assessing whether a person's rights have been infringed by the delay in trying him on a criminal charge the touchstone is fairness.'

Page 354 letter b and the statements quoted earlier from the *Herbert Charles case* asks the questions: Were these delays in good faith? Were they lengthy? Were they entirely understandable? Did the Applicant suffer material prejudice? Are there any fair trial considerations or fundamental human rights in issue? These must, in my opinion, be the questions for the Court in circumstances like these. At the end of the day what this Court is called upon to determine is whether in all the circumstances it is fair, given the delay of over four years between the institution of the disciplinary procedure and the preferring of the charges, to allow the disciplinary proceedings to continue. It is in dealing with this question of fairness that both the reasons for the delay given by the PSC and the prejudice suffered by the Applicant are relevant . . . [P16] 25. The reasons given by the PSC for the delay cannot to my mind be acceptable. It cannot be reasonable for any public body, what ever its staffing situation, to take over three years to advise on whether or not to pursue disciplinary action against an officer and to draft charges. This is even more unacceptable when one looks at the charges as drafted . . . [P17] In the circumstances I find that the failure of the PSC to take a decision with respect to the bringing of disciplinary charges against the Applicant for a period of over four years from the commencement of the investigation constitutes an abuse of process. I find that it has caused prejudice to the Applicant in the presentation of his defense and generally, and affects his ability to get a fair hearing before any disciplinary tribunal which may be appointed to hear the charges.

In the Application of Rai Ramrattan – HCA No 1304 of 2003 (TT)
Best J

[PP4–6] The learned authors of de Smith, Woolf and Jowell's *Principles of Judicial Review* (London: Sweet & Maxwell, 1990) at paragraph 8–058 stated: 'This may be taken as a precise statement of the law. *Per* Turner J: "I have endeavored to explain why, within the Scheme as it exists there is a duty to give reasons which are proper sufficient and intelligible for the initial and review decisions of the Authority. It is also a requirement of fairness, or in accordance with the principles of natural justice, that a claimant who is appealing to the Appeals Panel should be provided, in advance of the day of the hearing, with access to the evidential material which the Authority, through its presenting officers, will be relying upon at the hearing of the Appeal".' Oliver LJ in the matter of *Amherst v James Walker* [1983] 2 AII ER 1066 at page 1075c stated: '*The expression "unreasonable delay" does I think, require some definition. It must . . . mean something more than "prolonged delay" and it may . . . be used to express the notion either of delay for which no acceptable reason can be advanced or delay which no reasonable man would incur acting in his own interest. But if this is its meaning then the absence of reason has no necessary relation to duration. If, on the other hand . . . the phrase is used to describe such delay as it would not in the circumstances be reasonable to expect the other party to put up with, then . . . that it contains within it, by necessary implication, the notion of hardship or prejudice, for how otherwise is the other party harmed by it?*' Although the said Regulation is lacking in this respect, it is hoped that in the future the Police Service Commission, as a requirement of fairness, would respond to an officer's representation without unreasonable delay so that he or his legal advisors are afforded sufficient time to consider whether or not to approach the Court. (iii) In the said letter the Police Service Commission gave a bald statement that it had 'indorsed' the recommendation of the Police Commissioner not to recommend the Applicant for promotion. Further, adopting the principles found in de Smith (*supra*), there is a duty placed upon the Police Service Commission not merely to '*endorse*' the decision of the Commissioner of Police but to give to the officer reasons for its endorsement, which are proper, sufficient and intelligent so that he or his legal advisors can determine whether or not to approach the Court. Messrs M. Supperstone QC and J. Goudie QC authors of *Judicial Review* (Butterworths, 2 Edn) at Chapter 7:15 stated: 'Consultation requires that the consultor must give careful consideration to the representations made, though obviously he is not bound to follow them.' Further, it must be clearly spelt out in their reasons that they gave due consideration to the officer's representations and why they adopted or rejected the endorsement of the Commissioner of Police.

***In the Application of Eusebio Cooper* – HCA No S-1264 of 2003 (TT)**[2]
Myers J

[P15] What, then, is an 'unreasonable delay'? In *Thornhill v The Attorney General of Trinidad and Tobago*, albeit in a different context, Lord Diplock, delivering the Advice to Her Majesty of the Judicial Committee of the Privy Council, defined 'delay' as a lapse of time that is longer than it should have been. Implicit in the analysis was the assumption that such a delay would be deemed unreasonable, if no good reason were given for it. That latter point is clear from the sentence reproduced in bold font in the following extract from Lord Diplock's words. 'Delay is a word which connotes not simply a lapse of time but one in the circumstances is longer [than] it should have been. Since the only hindrance to the processes of investigation which it was suggested by the police officers might be occasioned by Thornhill's being allowed to consult a lawyer at the time the requests were made was they would be less likely to succeed in obtaining self-criminating statements from him if he were advised about his legal right to decline to answer questions, **any delay for which this was the only reason was clearly an unreasonable delay** [my emphasis].' In other words, however one analysed the reason for that particular delay, it was plainly a bad (and cynical) one. Similarly, in *Amherst v Walker*, the English Court of Appeal held unreasonable delay to be delay for which no acceptable reason can be advanced, or which no one would incur if acting in his own interest.

***In the Application of Pancho's Ltd* – HCA No 3972 of 1992 (TT)**
Jones J

[P10] This Court must however point out that powers and duties are imposed on public authorities to be exercised without unreasonable delay.

***Regina v Board of the School of Physical Therapy ex parte Christopher Edwards* (1989) 26 JLR 400 (JM)**
Langrin J

[PP405–406] The House of Lords case of *Birkett v James* [1978] AC 297 makes reference to the appropriate principle to be applied in cases of delay. Lord Diplock in a speech which the other law Lords agreed, said that: 'That Court has an inherent jurisdiction to dismiss an action for want of prosecution if the delay was such as to involve a substantial risk that a fair trial of the issues would not be possible.' In the final analysis it is the totality of the delay from the alleged breach of discipline, from September 1985 to 15th August, 1988 when the charges were sent to the Applicant which matters and the ultimate question is: Has the total delay from the alleged breach of discipline down to the 15th August 1988 been such as to make a fair trial of the charges impossible? If one applies that test to the totality of the delay here, it seems to us that the delay is such that no fair trial of these charges is possible. We held that there is breach of natural justice on the part of the Board in not bringing the charges within a reasonable time. Accordingly, we would grant the application with costs to be taxed if not agreed.

***R v Commissioner of Police ex parte Joseph Maynard* (1986) 23 JLR 314 (JM)**
Gordon J

[PP322–323] We also accept the finding of the Board at p 585. Held (1) Regardless of the position at Common Law, the express words of section 20(1) of the Constitution of

2 This decision was reversed by the Court of Appeal. See *In the Application of Director of Personnel Administration and Police Service Commission*—Civil Appeal No 10 of 2004 and HCA No. S-1264 of 2003 (TT). However, the Privy Council upheld the first instance judgment of Myers J. in Privy Council Appeal No. 47 of 2005.

Jamaica plainly sufficed to consider on an accused the right to a fair hearing within a reasonable time. Furthermore, the accused did not have to show any specific prejudice before being entitled to have charges against him dismissed because of unreasonable delay in bringing him to trial. In determining whether the accused had been deprived of a fair trial by reason of unreasonable delay factors which were relevant were the length of the delay, the reasons given by the prosecution to justify the delay, the efforts made by the accused to assert his rights and the prejudice to the accused. The assessment of those factors would necessarily vary from jurisdiction to jurisdiction and case to case. The footnote on each summons served on the Applicant reads:—'THIS ENQUIRY MUST BE COMPLETED WITHIN TWENTY-ONE DAYS.' This pays lip service to the requirement that the hearing should be within a reasonable time: it was more honoured in the breach than in its observance. We do not accept the reasons for the delay advanced by the Respondent. In the ordinary Courts delays are occasioned by the absence of witnesses, and/or Attorneys-at-Law and occasionally by the state of the list. A special tribunal was appointed to hear the charges in the matter before us and there is no acceptable reason advanced why the hearing was so protracted. On March 7, 1986 we held that there was unreasonable delay in the prosecution of these cases and ordered that Prohibition should go to prohibit the Board of Enquiry from hearing the charges preferred against Sergeant Maynard. Costs were awarded to the Applicant against the Commissioner of Police.

***In the Application of David Commissiong* – Civil Appeal No 16 of 1998 (BB)**
Williams CJ

[PP19–20] The learned trial judge completed hearing of the case on May 6, 1996 and gave his decision just over 2 years later on June 19, 1998. Counsel's submission, relying on *Goose v Wilson Sanford & Co* Times Law Reports of February 19, 1998, is that the decision turned on a question of fact, the Judge holding that the Applicant had not shown that the Justices of the Peace had acted improperly, and that this Court must look with care at the finding of the fact. In *Goose v Wilson Sanford & Co*, Peter Gibson LJ, giving the decision of the Court of Appeal of England, said: 'The judge's tardiness in completing his judicial task denied justice to the winning party during the period of delay. It also undermined the loser's confidence in the correctness of the decision when it was eventually delivered. Compelling parties to await judgment for an indefinitely extended period prolonged, and probably increased, the stress and anxiety inevitably caused by litigation, and weakened public confidence in the whole judicial process. Left unchecked it would be ultimately subversive of the rule of law. A situation like this must never occur again. Because of the delay it was incumbent on their Lordships to look with special care at any finding of fact which was now challenged. In ordinary circumstances where there was a conflict of evidence a judge who had seen and heard the witness had an advantage denied to an appellate Court, which was likely to prove decisive an appeal unless it could be shown that he failed to use or misused his advantage. The very fact of the huge delay in itself weakened the Judge's advantage and that consideration had to be taken into account when their Lordships reviewed the material which was before the Judge. In a case as complex as this it was not uncommon for a judge to form an initial impression of the likely result at the end of the evidence, but when he came to study the evidence, both oral and written and the submissions with greater [c]are, he would then go back to consider the effect the witnesses made on him when they gave evidence about matters which were now troubling him. At a distance of 20 months Mr Justice Harman denied himself the opportunity of making that further check in any meaningful way.' In that case the appeal was allowed on the ground that a substantial miscarriage of justice would be occasioned to the plaintiff by allowing the Judge's decision to stand and it was not possible to rectify that miscarriage of justice without a retrial . . . [P21] In our view the circumstances do not require the extreme steps taken in *Goose v Wilson Sandford & Co* and the appeal is dismissed with costs.

Griffith v Commissioner of Police and the Attorney General **(1994) 30 Barb LR 416 (BB)**
Waterman J

[P434] However, I do accept Mr Simmons' submission that the Commission, to the detriment and prejudice of the Applicant did not, without delay, determine whether disciplinary proceedings ought to have been instituted against the Applicant and I find that the Commission has omitted to act with expedition in accordance with the proper construction of Regulation 13(2) of the Regulations. The matter continues to drag on to the detriment and prejudice of the Applicant. In that light, it is only fair and reasonable that the Applicant be paid, with all due dispatch, the full amount of the salary which he would have received if he had not been suspended until any disciplinary or other proceedings against him are completed. I so order.

It is important to note that the Jamaican courts have taken a more benevolent view on the impact of delay on the exercise of a statutory function.

Motor and General Insurance Company Ltd v The Superintendent of Insurance, The Minister of Finance and The Attorney-General **(1994) 31 JLR 74 (JM)**
Langrin J

[P76] The second question which we had to consider is: **whether there was a breach of the Rules of Natural Justice**. The ground initially gave us some concern, but on a closer examination we are unanimously of the view that any delay in carrying out a statutory function cannot amount to an abuse of a discretion.

The unreasonable delay in making subsidiary legislation has also been condemned by the courts.

In the Application of Chandresh Sharma **– HCA No S-1445 of 2004 (TT)**
Narine J

[P8] The delay of more than four years in making Regulations pursuant to Section 41(1) of the Act is in my view inordinate and unreasonable having regard to the circumstances. It is difficult to comprehend why the drafting of Regulations dealing with the matters contained in Section 41(1)(a), (b) and (c) should take such a long period of time. There is no evidence in the affidavit of Mr Alkins, as to what has transpired since the Commission took steps to enlist the assistance of consultants to draft the Regulations. There is no evidence that the Commission took any further steps to facilitate or speed up the process. There is no evidence that the Commission has acted with any urgency with a view to having the Regulations made and placed before Parliament. Accordingly, I find that there has been unreasonable delay on the part of the Respondent in making Regulations under Section 41(1)(a), (b), and (c) . . . [P14] Section 138(1) of the Constitution creates the Commission. Section 138(2) charges the Commission with the duty of receiving declarations in writing of the financial affairs of persons in public life, the supervision of and monitoring of standards of ethical conduct prescribed by Parliament to be observed by such persons, and the monitoring and investigating of conduct, practices and procedures which are dishonest or corrupt. Section 139 of the Constitution expressly empowers Parliament to make provision for such matters as the procedure of the Commission, conferring powers on the Commission as are necessary to enable the Commission to carry out its functions effectively and generally to give effect to Section 138 . . . In other words, the framers of the Constitution envisaged that Parliament has an important role in empowering the Commission so that it could carry out its functions effectively. If Parliament does not act, or acts slowly where legislative action is required, that may result in a toothless Commission, unable to perform its functions effectively. Having regard to the facts of this case, it appears that neither the Commission nor Parliament has acted with the urgency contemplated by the Constitution to put Regulations and prescribed forms in place so that the Commission could effectively carry out its constitutional role. This has led to the absurd result in this case where the Commission decided not to require persons to file declarations for the year 2002, thus nullifying the very function that it was created to carry out.

2.22 IMPROPER FINDINGS OF FACTS

The courts are obviously reluctant to interfere with findings of facts but such findings are subject to challenge, especially where there is no evidentiary basis for such findings.

In the Matter of an Inquest held under the Coroners Act Chapter 6 No 4 Touching the Death of Seepersad Lalla – **HCA No S-306 of 1993 (TT)**
Warner J

[P9] Irrationality. A material finding of fact is irrational in the absence of evidence capable of warranting such a finding. The flawed finding must be material to the decision maker's reasoning.

In the Application of Hamlet Dassrath – **Civil Appeal No S/168 of 1984 (TT)**
Hamel-Smith JA

[P6] In this case the record indicates that the Appellant did make a no case submission and that the prosecution answered that submission. The record does not indicate, however, that the Tribunal ruled on that no case submission as it was obliged to do. The effect of the failure to rule on the submission was to deprive the Appellant from electing to either stand on the submission or to call evidence in his defence. It was not absolutely necessary for the Tribunal to rule on the submission there and then. It could have deferred its decision. But, whatever course it adopted, it had to rule on the submission in order to allow the Appellant to exercise his option before it submitted its report of its findings of fact and expressions of opinion to the Commission. The record simply states, after the submission was made and answered by the prosecution, that 'the Chairman stated that the Tribunal will report its findings to the Commission. Matter concluded.'
[P7] Accordingly, any statement of fact contained in that report must be reflected in the record. If, as in this case, the report states that the Appellant had rested on his no case submission such a statement must be supported by the record of proceedings. Unfortunately, the record does not support the statement that the Appellant had rested on his submission. It would be improper, in my view, for a tribunal to state in its report that a Defendant had rested on his no case submission if such a statement cannot be supported by the record. The Regulations lay down a procedure to be followed and the record must at all times reflect as accurately as possible what transpired at the hearing before the Tribunal . . . The Appellant was accordingly deprived of his right to either rest on the submission or to call evidence in his defence. There is therefore an error on the face of the record which error establishes that there has been a breach of the rules of natural justice.

Wadinambiaratchi v Hakeem Ahmad and Others **(1985) 35 WIR 325 (TT)**
Bernard JA

[P340] It would appear from the affidavits filed on their behalf that they omitted so to do due to a mistaken understanding of the true position. But this is not the fault of the university. The blame must lie where it has fallen! For the foregoing reasons and with due respect to the trial Judge I am of the opinion that his findings and conclusions were not justified on the evidence that was before him.

***In the Application of Jamaica Public Service Co. Ltd* – Supreme Court No HCV 01742 of 2003 (JM)**
Sinclair-Haynes J (Ag.)

[P6] Assuming the error is a factual one, the reliance upon an erroneous factual conclusion may itself offend the principles of legality and rationality thus rendering the decision *ultra vires*.

***In the Application of the Attorney General for Jamaica* – Civil Appeal No 56 of 2002 (JM)**
Harrison JA

[PP12–13] A reviewing body may not therefore allow a challenge to the findings of fact of a tribunal where there was some relevant evidence on which the Tribunal could and did act. The fact that the reviewing body would have come to a different conclusion is irrelevant and constitutes the wrong test. It is only if the findings of fact are of such a nature that they could be labeled irrational, that is, a finding that no reasonable tribunal could have come to, that the challenge may succeed, as a point of law: (*Associated Provincial Picture Houses Ltd. v Wednesbury Corporation* [1948] 1 KB 223). A tribunal would have erred if in coming to its decision it took into consideration matters which it should not have, or ignored matters that it ought to have considered. Proceedings before a review Court are supervisory and not by way of an appeal. Such proceedings are concerned with the propriety of the method by which the decision is arrived at, as distinct from the substance of the decision itself . . . [PP17–18] Although the brief of the Government of Jamaica and the closing submissions of counsel for the Appellant, before the IDT, both referred to 'budgetary restraints' and 'national interest', there was no evidence in support of such issues. One cannot therefore conclude as the learned judge did, that the IDT took such matters into consideration in making its award. This is more so in the absence of reasons and the nature of the evidence.

***In the Matter of 15 South Avenue, Registered at Volume 1127 Folio 105 of the Register Book of Titles* – Supreme Court No M101 of 1996 (JM)**
Woolfe CJ

[P17] These are findings of fact. Certiorari in these circumstances will only lie if there is no evidence to support these factual findings. There is no submission that there is no evidence to support the findings, rather, the submission is that the reasons given are invalid . . . [PP20–21] In the instant case the Applicant has admittedly breached the statute by not applying for permission prior to building or developing the land. There was no need for consultation prior to the service of the notice. There was no understanding between himself and the decision making authorities which could lead him to reasonably expect that he would be consulted before notice was served upon him for any breach which he might have committed . . . [P26] The orders sought, to wit, Certiorari and Prohibition are discretionary remedies. Even where a person may be awarded a certiorari *ex debito justitiae* the Court retains a discretion to refuse his application, if his conduct has been such as to disentitle him to relief. The Court is entitled to have regard generally to the conduct of the Applicant and to the special circumstances of the case in deciding whether to grant him the remedy he seeks. In the instant case the Applicant was served a notice to cease building, in that he had no permission so to do. He deliberately refused to obey the lawful order of the prescribed authorities. His conduct, if I may borrow the words of Singleton LJ in *Ex Parte Fry* [1954] 1 WLR (CA) 730 at p 735 'was extra-ordinarily foolish.' The discretion of the Court ought not to be exercised in the favour of one who has behaved so unreasonably. This type of conduct militates against the development of a well organized society and makes governance extremely difficult. Persons who flout the law so flagrantly must not expect the Court to come to their aid. The Court takes judicial notice of the number of persons prosecuted in the Courts of the island for erecting buildings without first obtaining permission so to do. This kind of disregard for the law has had the effect of ruining many neighbourhoods causing extensive economic loss to owners of property.

***Regina v The Jamaica Racing Commission ex parte Harold Clemetson* (1994) 31 JLR 390 (JM)**
Langrin J

[P395] The procedure invoked by the Supreme Court to deal with cases of injustice by Domestic Tribunals is by way of certiorari. The tribunals are concerned with questions of fact and this Court is constrained to accept those findings of fact unless there is no basis for them.

2.23 WRONG ADHERENCE TO POLICY

A decision-maker must not adopt and adhere to a policy that disables it from properly exercising its functions.

***In the Application of Pancho's Ltd* – HCA No 3972 of 1992 (TT)**
Jones J

[P10] On the facts of this case the shipment of oil filters has not been duly reported and entered and the Comptroller has acted lawfully in withholding delivery . . . The Comptroller of Customs and Excise is not justified in retaining goods on the basis of some practice within his Department but can only do so under the powers vested in him and in the manner authorized by the Customs Laws. In the premises, he must take immediate steps to pursue whatever remedies are available to him under the law or release the goods upon payment of the appropriate duties and taxes.

***Clayton Southwell v The Attorney-General and the Licencing Authority* – Civil Appeal No 1 of 1999 (KN)**
Matthew JA

[P6] The Administrative Law issues under this head the Appellant submitted that the discretionary power vested by Section 67 was not lawfully or properly exercised by the Licensing Authority because, among other things, he was not given an opportunity to be heard in accordance with the rules of natural justice. I agree with the submission of learned Counsel for the Appellant that there has been a large number of authorities which support the principle that the Courts can declare a public authority's exercise of its power improper, null and void whether the impugned decision is one which is executive, administrative, judicial or quasi-judicial. *Ridge v Baldwin* [1963] 2 All ER 66; *Burroughs v Katwaroo* (1985) 40 WIR 287; *Sukhlal v Collector, Santa* [1969] AIR 176. In *R v Gaming Board, Ex Parte Benaim* [1970] 2 All ER 528, Lord Denning, in delivering the judgment of the Court stated: 'At one time it was said that the principle of natural justice only applies to judicial proceedings and not to administrative proceedings. That heresy was scotched in *Ridge v Baldwin*'. And in *Burroughs' case* Bernard JA who gave the leading judgment stated at page 307: 'If one accepts that "natural justice" is a flexible term which imposes different requirements in different cases, it is capable of applying appropriately to the whole range of situations indicated by terms such as "judicial", "quasi-judicial" and "administrative". Nevertheless, the further the situation is away from anything that resembles a judicial or quasi-judicial situation, and the further the question is removed from what may reasonably be called a justiciable question, the more appropriate it is to reject an expression which includes the word "justice" and to use instead terms such as "fairness" or "the duty to act fairly".' [PP7–8] Learned Counsel for the Appellant submitted that the Licensing Authority's policy of suspending the driver's licence of all persons charged with the offence of causing death by dangerous driving is unlawful since the adoption of a fixed policy in this regard is an abdication of the exercise of flexible discretion which Section 67 expressly contemplates. In this context reference was made to the works of two leading authorities on Administrative Law, one of whom I had the privilege to know very well, in his lifetime. In his sixth edition on *Administrative Law*, Professor Wade wrote at page 370: 'An authority can fail to give its mind to a case, and thus fail to exercise its discretion lawfully, by blindly following a policy laid down in advance. It is a fundamental rule for the exercise of discretionary power that discretion must be brought to bear on every case: each one must be considered on its own merits and decided as the public interest requires at the time'. And Professor de Smith was to the same effect in his fourth edition of *Judicial Review of Administrative Action* at page 311 where he wrote: 'A tribunal entrusted with a discretion must not, by the adoption of a fixed rule of policy, disable itself from exercising its discretion in individual cases.' [PP9–10] Learned Counsel for the Respondent was in some difficulty relying on *Bahadur's case* on the second day of the appeal especially as learned Counsel for the Appellant had on the first day submitted that the right of appeal to the Board may be more illusory than real as it did not appear that the Traffic Safety Board provided for in the Vehicles and Road and Road Traffic (Amendment) Act 1989 [No. 9 of 1989] was ever established. Learned Counsel for the Respondent told the Court he could not say that a Board had ever been appointed. It follows that the automatic suspension of the Appellant's driving licence without giving him a chance to be heard was wrong in law.

2.24 FAILURE TO COMPLY WITH ADOPTED OR PUBLISHED PROCEDURES

A public authority must comply with published or adopted procedures because the public is entitled to rely on published or adopted procedures in its interaction with a public authority.

***The National Water Commission ex parte Desmond Alexander Reid* (1984) 21 JLR 62 (JM)**
Smith CJ

[P65] The Water Commission was a statutory corporation established for public purposes. Having adopted and published procedures to be followed in the exercise of its powers of disciplinary control over its employees, it was, in my judgment, bound thenceforward by the principles of administrative law to follow those procedures until they were validly altered. Thus, if an employee was dismissed in breach of the procedural requirements he would have a right to challenge the decision by seeking a judicial declaration or an order of certiorari, as appropriate.

2.25 RE-HEARING OF ISSUE

A public body cannot re-hear an issue that it has already determined on the same subject matter unless clothed with the statutory authority to so do.

***R v Bustamante Industrial Trade Union and The National Workers Union and The Industrial Disputes Tribunal ex parte Jamaica Public Service Co. Ltd* (1986) 23 JLR 309 (JM)**
Downer J

[P312] It is undisputed that when a statutory Tribunal has completed its functions, it cannot undertake any further hearing and determining on the same subject matter, unless a statute so permits . . . [P313] Certiorari therefore should issue to quash the second interpretation on the ground that there was an error of law on the face of it.

2.26 RIGHTS MUST BE CONSTRUED AS MEANINGFUL

In construing that a right exists, it is important that procedures are followed that would ensure that such a right would have meaningful application.

***In the Application of Innis Frederick* – Civil Appeal No 144 of 1986 (TT)**
Davis JA

[P8] These rules, literally construed, seem to me to emphasize that a police officer facing a charge has the right to make a no-case submission to the Tribunal before whom he appears. It seems to me, therefore, that the Tribunal must equally be under an obligation where such a submission is made to rule upon that submission. The exercise of the right would be meaningless if the Tribunal was under no obligation to rule upon that submission. The right to make a no-case submission is, in my view, a procedural right, and it seems to me that Regulation 92(2) is preserving that right.

***In the Application of Hamlet Dassrath* – Civil Appeal No S/168 of 1984 (TT)**
Hamel-Smith JA

[P6] In this case the record indicates that the Appellant did make a no case submission and that the prosecution answered that submission. The record does not indicate, however, that the Tribunal ruled on that no case submission as it was obliged to do. The effect of the failure to rule on the submission was to deprive the Appellant from electing to either stand on the submission or to call evidence in his defence. It was not absolutely necessary for the Tribunal to rule on the submission there and then. It could have deferred its decision. But, whatever course it adopted, it had to rule on the submission in order to allow the Appellant to exercise his option before it submitted its report of its findings of fact and expressions of opinion to the Commission. The record simply states, after the submission was made and answered by the prosecution, that 'the Chairman stated that the Tribunal will report its findings to the Commission. Matter concluded.'
[P7] Accordingly, any statement of fact contained in that report must be reflected in the record. If, as in this case, the report states that the Appellant had rested on his no case submission such a statement must be supported by the record of proceedings. Unfortunately, the record does not support the statement that the Appellant had rested on his submission. It would be improper, in my view, for a tribunal to state in its report that a Defendant had rested on his no case submission if such a statement cannot be supported by the record. The Regulations lay down a procedure to be followed and the record must at all times reflect as accurately as possible what transpired at the hearing before the Tribunal . . . The Appellant was accordingly deprived of his right to either rest on the submission or to call evidence in his defence. There is therefore an error on the face of the record which error establishes that there has been a breach of the rules of natural justice.

3

NATURAL JUSTICE

The rules of natural justice are so profoundly central to judicial review that as a ground for judicial review, it merits separate examination. It must be noted that although there are several rules that fall under the umbrella of natural justice, the concept of natural justice is not fixed and constantly evolves depending on the demands of justice in a particular case.

3.1 OBSERVANCE OF THE PRINCIPLES OF NATURAL JUSTICE

The rules of natural justice are there to ensure fairness in the decision-making process and these rules are not to be taken lightly.

***In the Application of Vashti Sampson, Rajh Basdeo, Indar Samaroo, Grantley Prescott and James Chinapoo* – Civil Appeal No 96 of 2003 (TT)**
Nelson JA

[P30] While it is true that a public authority equipped with power to affect adversely a person's rights has a duty to exercise that power only after a fair hearing of the party adversely affected, this principle does not apply in cases relating to private law rights. For example, no individual notices need be served on each occupier by a private landowner who seeks summary possession of his estate under Order 94 of the Rules of the Supreme Court 1975 . . . [P31] In the instant case the Authority did give notice to the squatters, but there is no requirement that an inquiry be held into each case before a notice to quit is served.

***In the Application of Maniram Maharaj* – HCA No 1426 of 1999 (TT)**
Smith J

[PP26–27] I agreed with the Respondent's submission that where, as here, there were no specified or established procedures to be followed in the holding of an inquiry, the requirements of natural justice varied from case to case. As was stated in *Wiseman v Borneman* [1969] 3 All ER 275 at 277–278 and repeated by Mc Pherson J in *R v Monopolies and Mergers Commission, Ex Parte Matthew Brown plc* [1987] 1 All ER 463 at 467 e.g. As Lord Reid said in *Wiseman v Borneman* [1969] 3 All ER 257 at 277–278: 'Natural justice requires that the procedure before any tribunal which is acting judicially shall be fair in all the circumstances, and I would be sorry to see this fundamental general priciple degenerate into a series of hard-and-fast rules . . . Even where the decision is to be reached by a body acting judicially there must be a balance between the need for expedition and the need to give full opportunity to the Defendant to see the material against him'. 'We often speak of the rules of natural justice. But there is nothing rigid or mechanical about them . . . The principles and procedures are to be applied which, in any particular set of circumstances are right and just and fair'. Natural justice it has been said is only 'fair play action'. The question as Lord Morris posed it later, is 'whether in the particular circumstances of a case a tribunal acted unfairly so that it could be said that their procedure did not match with what justice demanded?'.

***In the Application of Ishwar Galbaransingh and Northern Construction Ltd* – HCA No. 1202 of 1997 (TT)**
Warner J

[P16] With the utmost of deference to Senior Counsel, I venture to say, that whether or not the report had been for Cabinet consumption only, that the concept of natural justice is a fundamental doctrine of the common law . . . [P21] While it is true that the Committee had no power to subpoena witnesses, it seems to me that it was necessary to identify all the persons likely to be affected by the Committee's actions and to afford them the opportunity of expressing their views . . . [PP21–22] I do not at all suggest that there should necessarily have been an oral hearing, or that the technicalities associated with criminal trial ought to have been observed. The over-riding principle is that justice must be done. There are no hard and fast rules; but the climate tended to suggest that all the '**relevant parties**' were willing to co-operate. The Applicants, not having been invited, would not have known what was being alleged nor what information had been brought forward and what procedure the Committee had adopted. I must therefore reject the submission that the Applicant ought to have asked to be heard.

In the Application of Clarissa Gonzales **– HCA No 5194 of 1996 (TT)**
Warner J

[P8] I now proceed to examine the decision-making process . . . The essential features of the letter are these. The statement of offences; a comment; an intention to terminate; and the indication that the Commissioner intended to hear her representations against dismissal . . . [P10] The Applicant's right, was to expect a *bona fide* decision by the Commissioner on her suitability to continue her training. The principles of natural justice were indeed applicable and they were in fact observed.

In the Application of Misai Ali **– HCA No 2247 of 1993 (TT)**
Warner J

[P7] The elements of fairness may be summarized as follows, in so far as they relate to the present case:

1. there must be notification of the case to be met.
2. there must be a fair opportunity to correct or contradict the case.
3. there must be adequate time to prepare one's case in answer.
4. there must be the opportunity to present one's case . . .

[P10] The Court fully appreciates the need for Applicants to observe the provisions of Order 53 Rule 4, however in my view it would be unjust to dismiss this claim on the ground of delay when the letter of 10th July 1992, in effect 'invited' the Applicant to await further developments. Moreover, there is no evidence of prejudice occasioned by the Respondent.

In the Application of Saga Trading Ltd **– HCA No Cv 1347 of 1993 (TT)**
Archie J

[P30] It is clear that while judicial precedents are of some value in illustrating the correct approach, the practical requirements imposed on a decision maker by the rules of natural justice must be determined with reference to the facts and circumstances of the particular case under consideration and against the backdrop of the statutory framework under which the decision maker operates.

In the Application of Bickram Ramnanan **– Civil Appeal No 149 of 1993 (TT)**
Hamel-Smith JA

[P4] Nevertheless, this appeal proceeded on the basis that the Appellant was entitled to withdraw Ground (ii) of his application and to proceed solely on Ground (i), namely, the alleged breach of the rules of natural justice. As profound and necessary as these rules are, there is little mystery to them. They exist to ensure that a party is given a fair hearing before a decision adverse to him is made. What constitutes a fair hearing depends upon the circumstances of the particular case or charge and, while a party is entitled to be heard, it is not in every instance that a 'trial' must be held to determine the issue. I would think that, given the circumstances of this case, the holding of an enquiry at which the aggrieved party is present, at which he is made aware of the allegations against him and then afforded, first, the opportunity to orally explain his actions and then to consult his attorney with a view to providing a more comprehensive explanation was sufficiently adequate to satisfy the rules of natural justice, provided, of course, that the decision taken was honestly arrived at by the bank.

***In the Application of Juan Mosca* – HCA No 407 of 1989 (TT)**
Blackman J

[P6] Sometimes the principle of natural justice is expressed to be a fair hearing. What constitutes a fair hearing is not always easy to determine . . . [P20] The principle of natural justice is a flexible concept, but however flexible this concept may be proceedings by which a decision affecting the rights of others is reached, must not only be fair and just but must manifestly and undoubtedly appear to be so.

***In the Application of Gaynell Mc Donald* – HCA No 4098 of 1987 (TT)**
Ibrahim J

[P9] There is no express statutory provision for the student nurse to be heard or for any opportunity to be afforded the student nurse to make any explanation or suggestion as to how the issue may be resolved . . . [P10] The principles of natural justice have been applied as a fundamental rule for many centuries last past. The rules and the application thereof were clear and consistent . . . [P12] In such a case, I am of the view that the principles stated in *O'Reilly v Macman*, *supra*, are applicable here and the Applicant should have been afforded a fair opportunity of hearing what is alleged and of presenting her own case. This is especially so where the power to act is discretionary. I am of the opinion that the Respondent Council acted contrary to law and the decision to remove the name of the Applicant from the Register is null and void and of no effect whatever. But this is not the kind of case where the Court on its own can easily reinstate the name of the Applicant on the Register . . . The matter is, therefore, referred back to the parties for further consideration and determination, but failing which, the Court will finally decide the issues . . .

***In the Application of Police Inspector Rudolph Steele, Police Sgt. Michael Lambert, Cpl. Willard Gibbs, PC. Fitzgerald Pritchard, PC. Burt Liverpoole, PC. Desmond Bharat and PC. Wayne Lewis* – HCA No 1780 of 1987 (TT)**
Edoo J

[P5] A number of instances are then given in which the Rule has been excluded. Thus, where an act or proposal is only the first step in a sequence of measures which may culminate in a decision detrimental to a person's interests, the Courts will generally decline to accede to that person's submission that he is entitled to be heard in opposition to this initial act, particularly if he is entitled to be heard at a later stage . . . [P7] In my opinion, the rules of natural justice, i.e. the right of the Applicants to be heard before suspension, was not breached as they were not entitled to be heard at this stage.

***In the Application of Doekie Singh* – HCA No 1300 of 1981 (TT)**
Deyalsingh J

[P7] Although it was merely an 'application' case, the Court held that the rules of natural justice were applicable as a refusal of the certificate of fitness would be a slur on the Applicant. In the 'forfeiture' category, the law is now well-established and again I quote from the Judgement of Megarry J (*supra*): 'It seems plain that there is a substantial difference between the forfeiture cases and the application cases. In the forfeiture cases there is a threat to take something away for some reasons; and in such cases, the right to an unbiased tribunal, the right to notice of the charges and the right to be heard in answer to the charges (which in *Ridge v Baldwin* [1963] 2 All ER 66 at 114 Lord Hudson said were the three features of natural justice which stood out) are plainly apt . . .' [P7] It is not in dispute that the Commissioner of Police gave no opportunity to the Plaintiff to meet the case against her ... [PP8–9] Next, [do] the reasons although belatedly given 'cure the procedural wrong' as Mr Beckles submits? I certainly do not think so—and for two reasons. As said before, the Plaintiff 'contests', albeit in part, the reasons advanced by the first Defendant. She must therefore, in justice, be given an opportunity to persuade the first Defendant that he is wrong. Secondly, to accept the submission would be to violate two principles fundamental to our law, principles enshrined in the phrases *'audi alteram partem'* and 'justice must not only be done but must be seen to be done'. These principles find place among the foundation stones upon which the edifice of justice stands and they must never lightly be ignored. *'Justitia firmatur solium'* (Justice strengthens the throne). It is upon such principles aforesaid that a country and its government stand firm. One last matter, I have considered whether the rules of natural justice should apply in firearm cases. Mr Beckles did not make any such point and I think he would have, if there was merit in it. Suffice it to say that I take the view that the rules of natural justice should not be excluded only because firearms are the subject matter.

Auburn Court Ltd – Privy Council Appeal No 76 of 2002 (JM)
Lord Hope of Craighead

[PP16–18] 45. The argument under this heading is directed to the events that preceded the service of the second enforcement notice. It will be recalled that it was preceded by a meeting of the building and planning committee of KASC at which the committee decided to refuse the Appellant's application for building approval and planning permission for the building which it was erecting at 15 South Avenue. The Appellant was not present or represented at that meeting. Mr Codlin said that the fact that the Appellant was not given an opportunity to be heard at this meeting was a breach of the principle of natural justice. He referred to the dispute as to what had been said by Mr White at the meeting which took place on site on 25 March 1996. Mr White was present at the meeting. He was not there just as an expert, said Mr Codlin. He was intimately involved in the whole matter. So fairness demanded that before any decision was taken the committee should hear both sides of the argument as to whether, in view of the road-widening proposal, permission should be given for the development. 46. There is no doubt that the principles of natural justice require that before a decision is taken by a tribunal that is acting judicially the person against whom it is taken must be given a fair opportunity of setting out the facts which he thinks are relevant and the arguments on which he relies. But, as Lord Reid observed in *Ridge v Baldwin* [1964] AC 40, 65, attention needs to be paid to the great difference between the various cases in which it has been sought to apply this principle. He elaborated upon this point in *Wiseman v Borneman* [1971] AC 297, 308: 'Natural justice requires that the procedure before any tribunal which is acting judicially shall be fair in all the circumstances, and I would be sorry to see this fundamental general principle degenerate into a series of hard-and-fast rules. For a long time the Courts have, without objection from Parliament, supplemented procedure laid down in legislation where they have found that to be necessary for this purpose. But before this unusual kind of power is exercised it must be clear that the statutory procedure is insufficient to achieve justice and that to require additional steps would not frustrate the apparent purpose of the legislation.' 47. The legislation under which the committee were acting in this case does not require the Applicant to be present at the meeting at which the decision is to be taken as to whether or not to grant his application. He has, of course, an opportunity to set out his case that permission should be granted in his application. It must be accompanied with plans and such other details as the authority may require. Regulation of the Kingston and St Andrew Building (Notices and Objections) Regulations 1938 provides that a hearing may be held if there are objections to the proposal, at which both sides may appear or be represented. It is obvious that the principle requires that, if an objector is to be heard by the committee, the committee ought to give the Applicant an opportunity of being heard also. In a contest of that kind, one side cannot properly be heard without hearing the other. 48. But there were no objections for the committee to consider in this case. The meeting was, of course, attended by officials such as Mr White, whose function it was to provide the advice and information that the committee needed before the decision was taken. The question whether the Appellant should be present too and given an opportunity of being heard when that advice was given was at the discretion of the committee. 49. Megarry J set the Appellant's argument into its proper context when in *Gaiam v National Association for Mental Health* [1971] Ch 317, 333C he said: 'local planning authorities refuse thousands of planning applications each year without giving the Applicant any hearing, leaving him to his remedy by way of appeal to the Minister, when a full hearing is given; yet I know of no suggestion that local planning authorities are thereby universally acting in contravention of the principles of natural justice.' As that observation indicates, the question of fairness must be answered by looking to the whole of the procedure which is provided by the statute, including the provision that is made for the Applicant to be heard by way of an appeal. 50. Provision is made both in the Building Act and in the Planning Act for an Applicant who is aggrieved by a decision taken by the committee to appeal against it. Every person whose plans or drawings have been refused permission by the building authority may appeal to the Tribunal of Appeal under the Kingston and St Andrew Building (Tribunal of Appeal) Regulations 1932. Every person who is aggrieved by an enforcement notice could, as the law stood at the date of the service of the second enforcement notice, appeal to the Tribunal established under the Planning Act under Section 23A. There was a further right of appeal under Section 23(8) to the Court of Appeal. It has not been suggested that the remedies that were available to the Appellant by way of appeal were inadequate. 51. Their Lordships have concluded that, when account is taken of the whole of the procedure which the statutes lay down, including the opportunities for appeal, the rules of natural justice were not breached in this case.

***In the Application of Easton Wilberforce Grant* – Supreme Court No M107 of 2000 (JM)**
Cooke J

[PP13–14] What took place at the second hearing was an entirely new hearing despite the fact the substance of the allegations against the Applicant were the same. There was no finding in respect of the first hearing. At that time there was no personnel committee in place. Having realized the mistake a new hearing was convened. Here the Applicant was given every opportunity to respond to the charges. He refused to be persuaded so to do. In these particular circumstances the fact that the composition of the personnel committee was identical did not make the second hearing unfair.

***In the Application of Owen Vhandel* – Civil Appeal No 72 of 2000 (JM)**
Downer JA

[P18] In fact, the wording of the Regulation implies that there is a right to a hearing. It obliges the Board to give reasons coupled with the payment of one month's salary or a month's notice. The necessary implication from the obligation to give reasons is that a hearing from both sides is mandatory. If this were not so, why is the delivery of reasons obligatory? The Appellant, although 'a temporary (acting)' teacher holds an office recognized by statute and the principle of natural justice, is the essential ingredient of judicial review. Further, judicial review is enshrined in the Constitution Sec. 1(9) of Chapter 1 reads: '(9) No provision of this Constitution that any person or authority shall not be subject to the direction or control of any other person or authority in exercising any functions under this Constitution shall be construed as precluding a Court from exercising jurisdiction in relation to any question whether that person or authority has performed those functions in accordance with this Constitution or any other law.' This provision in the Constitution brings into play Lord Diplock's classic summary of judicial review on procedural fairness referred to earlier. The Constitutional provision and the evolving principles of judicial review demonstrate the interplay between constitutional provisions and the common law ... [P21] We should point out that even before the recent amendment to the Judicature (Civil Procedure Code) Law of August 5, 1998, which provided for discovery of documents in Judicial Review Proceedings, the Court on its own motion secured the production of documents vital to the outcome of a case . . . This Court is empowered to ask for further evidence because the issue goes to jurisdiction . . . [P29] As it is, the Appellant has made a clear and compelling case that the Board of Management which dismissed him was not properly constituted, as the Principal, himself the accuser, was present and took part in the decision to dismiss him. The decision to dismiss him was also invalid because the Board of Management gave him no opportunity to make representation on the charges in the letter . . . [P30] No reasons which flowed from the Board's decision could have any validity. The Board of Management should also have realized that its obligation to give reasons means that even if the reasons were validly issued, they can be challenged to ascertain if the punishment is proportionate to the breach of discipline . . . [P37] The principles of natural justice are recognized by the common law as an entitlement of every citizen. Any tribunal or institution purporting to conduct disciplinary proceedings must do so acting judicially and not in breach of natural justice. Natural justice embraces, *inter alia*, the right to be heard in defence of a charge, as also a prohibition against an accuser being an adjudicator in the same cause. The right to be heard was recognized quite long ago . . . [P38] The presumption of a right to be heard can properly be denied in some circumstances, for example in instances of urgency, where the hearing is granted later in the appeal process.

***Clarke (Glenroy) v Commissioner of Police and Another* (1996) 52 WIR 306 (JM)**
Carey JA

[P310] The rules of natural justice which are not inflexible must be applied having regard to all the circumstances of the case . . . The absence of any inquiry, or request, inclines me to think that the Appellant and his attorney were satisfied that the reports contained nothing about which the Appellant was ignorant. This leads me to conclude that there was never any belief on the Appellant's part that the Commissioner had taken into account any material which he ought not to have done . . . [P312] For these reasons, I am not persuaded that any good or sufficient cause has been shown to hold that the Full Court came to a determination with which this Court ought to interfere. I would dismiss the appeal.

***R v Commissioner of Police ex parte Glenroy Clarke* (1994) 31 JLR 570 (JM)**
Ellis J

[P583] Fairness in exercising a discretion involves an obedience to the rules of Natural Justice and in particular the right to a fair hearing.

***Danhai Williams v The Attorney-General, the Minister of National Security and the Superintendent of Police, St. Andrew Division* (1990) 27 JLR 512 (JM)**
Carey JA

[P515] The Minister is clearly called upon to adjudicate, to hear both sides and to give a decision. He is in the position akin to a judge holding an '*inter partes*' hearing after the grant of an *ex parte* injunction. Although the aggrieved party has no right to be present, it seems to me he should know the date on which the hearing of the appeal is to take place. It will enable him to decide whether he should retain counsel to apply to be present. He may wish to apply for further time to submit further representations. Further if the aggrieved person is to be able to appeal the decision, he should be in a position to know the basis of the revocation seeing that the reasons for revocation are categorized in specific and general terms . . . I would hold that it would be wholly unreasonable to assert that an aggrieved person against whom serious allegations could be made as affecting his reputation or good name, is fairly treated if he is expected to appeal a decision founded upon charges, the nature of which has never been vouchsafed to him . . . [P517] In the result, I am of the opinion that there was a breach of the rules of natural justice. The Minster ought to have indicated to the Appellant—

(i) the nature of the charges against him to enable him fairly to meet them;

(ii) the date of the hearing so that he was afforded a time frame within which to apply to make further representations; and

(iii) that although a request was made for the Appellant to be present or represented that request was not considered by the Minister.

***Banana and Ramie Products Co. Ltd v Ministry of Lands and Natural Resources* (1989) 41 WIR 76 (BZ)**
Henry P

[P77] Before leaving this aspect of the matter it is to be noted that the Chairman of the Board in making his determination did not give the parties affected thereby any opportunity to deal with or refute such matters of fact or inferences therefrom as arose from his investigations of the Appellants' title to the land, thereby breaching the rules of natural justice.

***Maria A. Smith v The Commissioner of Police* (1981) 18 JLR 154 (JM)**
Carberry JA

[P168] The Lord Chancellor went on to observe that many bodies have been entrusted by Parliament with the duty of hearing appeals in matters which really pertain to administration rather than to the exercise of the judicial functions of an ordinary Court, and that such bodies were administrative rather than 'judicial' in the ordinary sense. Nevertheless in deciding such matters those bodies were subject to the *audi alteram partem* rule as set out in *Board of Education v Rice* (*ante*). [PP186–187] We are of the opinion that, both on the ordinary rules of statutory interpretation and on authority, Section 43(2) of the C.I. Traffic Law, Law 16 of 1973, vests in the Commissioner a *discretion* as to whether he will revoke a taxi driver's license or not: the vast range of offences which may give rise to the occasion to exercise that discretion points unerringly to the conclusion that the power to revoke is not intended to be automatic but discretionary. It is primarily intended to cover cases in which the Court does not have the power to revoke, but considerations of the need to protect those who use public transport make it desirable that the original grantor of the license should have the power to revoke the taxi driver's license, as for example in the case of a taxi driver who is convicted of rape of a female passenger. We are further of the opinion that the statute being silent on the matter, the common law imports into the exercise of the Commissioner's powers in this respect the need to observe the tenets of natural justice, and in particular the three features which stand out:

(1) the right to be heard by an unbiased tribunal;

(2) the right to have notice of charges of misconduct;

(3) the right to be heard in answer to these charges.

Per Lord Hodson in *Ridge v Baldwin* [1964] AC at page 132. The Commissioner's powers are clearly to be exercised in a 'judicial' manner. The licensee ought to have had notice of his intention to invoke Section 43(2) of the Act, and of the reasons or charges, in this case it would be conviction for the possession of ganja on a given date, time and place. The licensee ought also to have had the opportunity of appearing before the Commissioner and answering those charges, or putting forward circumstances in mitigation of the offence. As we do not know the details of the original case it is not easy to forecast what these might be . . . The Commissioner 'may' revoke, on being satisfied of the conviction, but the licensee has the opportunity of attempting to show by other evidence if it can be got, that there ought not to be a revocation. Naturally, such evidence may be viewed with great suspicion but it may prove useful. In *Spackman's case* Viscount Simon, LC observed at page 636: 'What matters is that the accused should not be condemned without being given a fair chance of exculpation. This does not mean that the Council has to rehear the whole case by endeavoring to get the previous witnesses to appear before it, though in special circumstances the recalling of a particular witness, in the light of what the accused or his witnesses assert, may, if feasible, be desirable. The council will primarily rely on the sworn evidence already given at the trial'. The licensee may of course admit the conviction and attempt to advance mitigating factors only; in any event there seems to be no reason why the Commissioner's own inquiry should be unduly onerous or burdensome, provided that the licensee gets a fair opportunity of putting forward his case or any mitigating aspects that he may wish to urge.

***R v Commissioner of Police ex parte Tennant* (1977) 15 JLR 79 (JM)**
Vanderpump J

[P83] If he is to be dismissed 'with all the odium which a dismissal carries' then he should know beforehand the ground on which such a strong decision is to be based and natural justice demands that he should be given an opportunity to defend himself. The Applicant who has twelve years of service was told about 48 hours before his summary dismissal what was going to happen. Benignity did not extend beyond the '48 hours notice'. Execution was carried out in the manner told to him. The Applicant was given no opportunity to have a fair run before the axe fell. To decide an important matter which seriously affects a man without a hearing is arbitrary and unreasonable. Despite the persistency and valiance which Mr Ellis displayed in his arguments, I can find nothing in the Act or in the Regulations which supports the stand taken by the Commissioner of Police. And I would be surprised if an Act of Parliament can be found in these modern days which would support a contention that the rules of natural justice can be relegated to a furnace by a tribunal when a man's reputation, his right to work, and his right to property are at stake.

***Aris v Chin* (1972) 19 WIR 459 (JM)**
Fox JA

[P464] Admittedly, the function of the Solicitors Committee at the hearing of a complaint against a solicitor is judicial in character. It follows, therefore, that in the conduct of such proceedings, the committee must adhere to the code of natural justice. In other words, the Committee was required to observe that principle in the maxim *audi alteram partem;* 'hear both sides.' But the doctrine of that maxim does not imply that there must always be a hearing, or a hearing of both sides, but only that each party must be afforded an adeqate opportunity of advancing his case. In short, natural justice is nothing more than fair play. To be understood in this realistic and straight-forward manner, a definition of natural justice presents no problem. The real difficulty is one of application. This demands the ability to recognize when in any particular factual situation natural justice has been honoured or denied. Fair play then is nothing more than what seems to be fair to a given Court in a given case. Shorn of its outwardly objective habiliments, natural justice is, therefore, in actuality, a subjective concept. It is 'the length of the Chancellor's foot' still, it is, as well, the modern equity.

***Griffith v Barbados Cricket Association; Byer and Another v Barbados Cricket Association* (1989) 41 WIR 48 (BB)**
Williams CJ

[P58] The rules of natural justice: what is fair? The rules of natural justice (i.e. that a man should know what is alleged against him, and be given a reasonable opportunity to rebut the allegations, and that no man should be a judge in his own cause) have been the basis on which the Courts have over the years controlled the decisions of statutory and contractual tribunals and bodies exercising judicial or quasi-judicial functions. In recent years as administrative law has developed and the scope of the Court's power of review [has] been broadened, the rules of natural justice have tended to become part of a concept of fairness to which bodies that can by their decisions affect the lives of men and women are required to conform.

Public Disclosure Commission v Isaacs (1988) 37 WIR 1 (BS)
Lord Bridge of Harwich

[PP6–7] The Respondent succeeded in the Court of Appeal on the alternative ground that the so-called *audi alteram partem* rule applied. The principle underlying the rule is clearly expressed in the judgment of Lord Denning MR in *R v Race Relations Board, Ex Parte Selvarajan* [1975] 1 WLR 1686 at pages 1693, 1694, where he said: 'In recent years we have had to consider the procedure of many bodies who are required to make an investigation and form an opinion . . . In all these cases it has been held that the investigating body is under a duty to act fairly: but that which fairness requires depends on the nature of the investigation and the consequences which it may have on persons affected by it. The fundamental rule is that, if a person may be subjected to pains or penalties, or be exposed to prosecution or proceedings, or deprived of remedies or redress, or in some such way adversely afflicted by the investigation and report, then he should be told the case made against him and be afforded a fair opportunity of answering it.' With respect to the Court of Appeal, their Lordships do not think that this principle has any application to a complainant under the Act, save in the case already considered and not here applicable where the Commission are minded to report to the Attorney-General under Section 8(3) that the complaint was groundless. In any other case, the complainant is not liable to be subjected to any pains or penalties or exposed to prosecution. He is not seeking to enforce any private right, so there is no question of depriving him of any remedies or redress to which he may be entitled. He is acting as a public-spirited citizen in giving information to the Commission to assist them in the performance of their public duty. Any personal or political interest he may have in the outcome is irrelevant. He cannot be 'told the case made against him and afforded a fair opportunity of answering it' because no case is made against him; it is he who makes a case against the declarant. It was submitted for the Respondent that he was adversely affected by the publication in the *Gazette* of the Commission's conclusion that his complaint was not substantiated. Their Lordships cannot accept that this is a matter of sufficient weight to prevail against the countervailing considerations to which attention has already been directed. The language used in the statute distinguishing between complaints which are frivolous, vexatious or groundless on the one hand and complaints which are not substantiated on the other may be open to misunderstanding by uninformed members of the public. But on the true construction of the statute a finding that a complaint has not been substantiated connotes no more than that, when investigated and considered in the light of all available evidence, the complaint was not made out. Such a finding casts no adverse reflection on the complainant. Any person making a complaint under Section 7(1)(b) must be presumed to know that, although made in good faith and on sufficient grounds, his complaint may fail because it can be successfully rebutted and that this will lead to a published statement by the Commission that it was not substantiated.

Dennie v The Chairman and Members of The Public Service Commission Saint Vincent and The Grenadines – High Court Civil Suit No 196 of 1995 (VC)
Adams J

[Para11] It is important to note that Regulation 37 involves what are notoriously known as 'the rules of natural justice' which in so far as they are applicable to this case would require the Officer to know the grounds on which his retirement is being contemplated, and provide him with an opportunity of being heard by the Commission in relation to that matter. These rules make up what has been described as the 'Court's code of fair procedure' and failure to observe them in the decision making process of bodies such as the Public Service Commission may lead to the nullification of their decisions . . . [Para17] The acknowledgement of the need for adherence to the rules of natural justice seems to be deeply imbedded in the jurisprudence which our Courts have inherited from England. What this case is concerned with is the removal of the Plaintiff from office and the application of the rules of natural justice thereto. Those rules were as early as 1615 being applied in *Bagg's case* 1615 11 Co. Rep 93 (b) where the question was whether a man could be deprived of his status of a burgess of Plymouth without being heard. In *R v Gaskin* 1799 8 Term Report 209 it was the issue of the dismissal of a parish clerk that invoked consideration of the rules, and led to the description by Lord Kenyon CJ of the principle *audi alteram partem* as one of the first principles of justice. In the case of *R v Smith* 1844 5 PB 614 Lord Denman held that even the personal knowledge of the offence was no substitute for hearing the officer; his explanation might disprove criminal motives or intent and bring forward other facts in the mitigation and in any event delaying to hear him would prevent yielding too hastily to first impressions. The need for adherence to the rules of natural justice found expression in a case where the citizen's house was ordered to be pulled down: see *Hopkins v Smethwick* [1890] 24 QBD at pp 714 and 715. In *Osgood and Nelson* 1872 L.R 5 HL 36, objection was taken to the way in which the corporation of the City of London had removed the Clerk to the Sherriffs Court and Hatherley LC said: 'I apprehend my Lords that as has been stated by the learned Baron who has delivered in the name of the Judges their unanimous opinion, the Court of Queens Bench has always considered that it has been open to that Court, as in this case it appears to have considered, to consult any Court or tribunal or body of men who may have a power of this description, a power of removing from office, if it should be found such persons have disregarded any of the essentials of justice in the course of their enquiry before making that removal or if it should be found that in the place of reasonable cause those persons have acted obviously upon mere individual caprice'. Finally *De Vertuil v Knaggs* [1918] AC 557 was a case in which the Governor of Trinidad was entitled to remove immigrants from an estate 'on sufficient ground shown to his satisfaction.' In the course of his judgment Lord Parmoor had this to say: 'the acting Governor was not called upon to give a decision on an appeal between parties and it is not suggested that he holds the position of a judge or that the Appellant is entitled to insist on the forms used in ordinary judicial procedure . . .' but he had 'a duty of giving to any person against whom the complaint is made a fair opportunity to make any relevant statement which he may desire to bring forward and a fair opportunity to correct or controvert any relevant statement brought forward to his prejudice'.

Elwin v Public Service Commission Commonwealth of Dominica and The Attorney General of the Commonwealth of Dominica – High Court of Justice Civil Suit No 493 of 1998 (DM)
Cenac J

[Para27] The Commission's functions under the law respecting the appointment and promotion of public officers are of a public nature and quasi-judicial. As such, in exercise of its powers under the Regulations the Commission must be expected to act fairly. [Para28] In *Wiseman v Borneman* [1969] 3 All ER 275 at 277 Lord Reid said: 'Natural justice requires that the procedure before any tribunal which is acting judicially shall be fair in all the circumstances, and I would be sorry to see this fundamental general principle degenerate into a series of hard and fast rules. For a long time the Courts have, without objection from Parliament, supplemented procedure laid down in legislation where they have found that to be necessary for the purpose. But before this unusual kind of power is exercised it must be clear that the statutory procedure is insufficient to achieve justice and that to require additional steps would not frustrate the apparent purpose of the legislation'. [Para29] In *Public Service Board of New South Wales v Osmond* [1987] LRC 681 at p 698 Deane J repeating a statement of Kitto J in *Mobil Oil Australia Pty Ltd v Federal Commissioner of Taxation* [1963] 113 CLR 475 at p 504 said this: 'What the law requires in the discharge of a quasi-judicial function is judicial fairness. That is not a label for any fixed body of rules. What is fair in a given situation depends upon the circumstances'. [Para30] And as Lord Bridge put it in *Lloyd v McMahon* [1987] 1 All ER 1118 at 1161, [1987] AC 625 at 702–703: 'My Lords, the so-called rules of natural justice are not engraved on tablets of stone. To use the phrase which better expresses the underlying concept, what the requirements of fairness demand when any body, domestic, administrative or judicial, has to make a decision which will affect the rights of individuals depends on the character of the decision-making body, the kind of decision it has to make and the statutory or other framework in which it operates. In particular, it is well established that when a statute has conferred on any body the power to make decisions affecting individuals, the Courts will not only require the procedure prescribed by the statute to be followed, but will readily imply so much and no more to be introduced by way of additional procedural safeguards as will ensure the attainment of fairness'. [Para31] Was there unfairness in the procedure followed by the Commission under the Regulations? In other words has the Applicant made out a case of procedural unfairness? Where an Act of Parliament confers an administrative power there is a presumption that it will be exercised in a manner which is fair in all the circumstances. The standards of fairness are not immutable. They may change with the passage of time, both in the general and in their application to decisions of a particular type. The principles of fairness are not to be applied by rote identically in every situation. What fairness demands is dependent on the context of the decision, and this is to be taken account in all its aspects (*per* Lord Mustill in *Regina v Secretary of State for the Home Department, Ex Parte Doody* (HL) [1993] 3 WLR p 168). [Para40] Now here you have a situation where the Applicant, of the three names submitted to the Commission, although not the most senior but was senior to Angela Lawrence, was not less qualified than her, had acted in the post on more occasions before it became vacant, acted in the post after it became vacant and up to the time when the Commission made its decision to appoint Angela Lawrence. Further, the Applicant had been recommended by the Permanent Secretary to be appointed to the post. In spite of the foregoing, she was overlooked and Angela Lawrence was appointed. Obviously the Applicant must be left with a 'burning sense of grievance and a real feeling of injustice'. [Para42] Having regard to the facts and the law, I can only conclude that the Applicant's entitlement to appointment was far superior to that of the appointee. [Para43] I conclude also that the Commission could not have taken into account 'all the circumstances which it is statutorily required to take into account before selecting an officer for promotion'. [Para44] I am of the view that the Commission did not follow the procedure laid down in the Regulations. As Leggatt LJ said in *Cunningham* (*supra*) at p 958: 'One of the main areas in which supervision has to be exercised by way of judicial review is over procedural requirements, for the purpose of ensuring the right to a fair adjudication. The procedure of a public body is not only required to be fair in so far as an individual affected by its decisions has a legitimate expectation that it will be. Nor does natural justice or fairness require the giving of reasons for a decision only when an obligation to give them is imposed by statute.' [Para45] I am of the view that the decision taken by the Commission to appoint Angela Lawrence to the post over the Applicant in light of all the circumstances was so aberrant as to compel the inference that it must have been wrong, procedurally wrong and grossly unfair.

***In the Application of the Chief Immigration Officer* – Civil Appeal No 7 of 1994 (BVI)**
Floissac CJ

[PP9–10] According to the '*audi alteram partem*' rule, where any authority (person or body of persons) intends to exercise a constitutional, statutory or prerogative power and thereby to make or take a judicial, quasi-judicial or administrative decision or action which will adversely affect the status, rights, interests or legitimate expectations of any other person (the complainant), the authority is under a common law duty (and may also be under a constitutional or statutory duty) to observe certain formalities and the complainant has a correlative common law right (and may also have a correlative constitutional or statutory right) to the observance of those formalities before such decision or action is made or taken. Those formalities may include notice to the complainant of the specific allegations made against him and a fair and reasonable opportunity for the complainant to answer or rebut those allegations and to make representations in regard to the intended decision or action. In the present case, the Respondent may not have had any legal right to enter and remain in the Territory. But in the special circumstances of this case, he certainly had legitimate expectations that he would be granted permission to do so and that at least some of the formalities required by the *'audi alteram partem'* rule of natural justice would have been observed before any decision or action was made or taken by way of refusal of such permission.

3.1.1 Right to a Fair Hearing

A right to a fair hearing commonly suggests that such a hearing be an oral hearing. There are clear instances, however, where written representations and the exchange of correspondence have led to the conclusion that an aggrieved party was in fact afforded a fair hearing.

***In the Application of the Trinidad and Tobago Civil Rights Association* – HCA No 477 of 2004 (TT)**
Dean-Armorer J

[P67] Having held that Cabinet acted in breach of natural justice in failing to afford Justice Hosein an opportunity to be heard either before or immediately after its decision not to re-appoint him, it is now necessary to consider whether the residents of Tortuga were invested with sufficient interest in respect of a breach of natural justice committed against Justice Hosein.

***In the Application of Roland Gokool* – HCA No 1246 of 2001 (TT)**
Bereaux J

[P4] As to the issue of procedural impropriety and the lack of opportunity to be heard neither Section 8 or 9 provide that an application to vary must be made to the Magistrate by either side and I do not consider that any right can be implied. No doubt it was advisable for the Magistrate to invite the submissions of both sides if she were minded to vary bail but there was no breach of natural justice by her failure to do so.

***In the Application of A.P.I. Pipeline Construction Co. Ltd* – HCA No 74 of 1999 (TT)**
Ventour J

[P24] It seems very clear to me, and indeed I agree with Counsel for the Respondent that the Tax Appeal Board does have the power to deal with procedural issues in matters coming before it as has been so clearly demonstrated by the authorities referred to by Counsel. However, I must point out that there is nothing to prevent a taxpayer from coming before this Court to challenge a decision of the Respondent if the Applicant could show that the Respondent has failed to discharge its statutory duty toward him or that they have abused their powers . . . [PP24–25] I have therefore found on a balance of probability that the Respondent treated the Applicant unfairly and acted contrary to the principles of natural justice when it denied the taxpayer the right to challenge the assessment prior to taking recovery action. In the view of this Court the Respondent's conduct amounts to an abuse of process.

***In the Application of Globe Detective & Protective Agency Ltd* – HCA No 3812 of 1996 (TT)**
Jairam J

[P19] These cases and Professor Sir William Wade's words are clear and high authority for the proposition that the Applicants in this case need not have had an oral hearing especially given the statutory framework of the enactment. A limit has to be implied and I so hold . . . [P21] The facts in each case must be looked at very carefully and an assessment of these facts must be made before one seeks to apply these hallowed principles of law, whether or not they are immutable. The *fons et origo* of the Applicants' problem appear to be that they are of the view that they ought to have had a full scale hearing as a Court of law. This is an extravagance or luxury which the law does not permit. In my judgment, there has been substantial fairness from the beginning to the end of this matter between the COP and the Applicants.

In the Application of Jason Roberts – **HCA No S554 of 1995 (TT)**
Moosai J

[P8] Regulation 123 is silent as to the procedure to be followed where the **suspension** of a temporary officer is contemplated ... [P12] In effect the Applicant's suspension was lifted without there being any disciplinary proceedings. Additionally the Applicant was suspended on full pay and suffered no financial loss. Suspension in the instant case seemed to me only the first step in a sequence of measures which **might** have culminated in a decision detrimental to the Applicant's interests. I am therefore of the view that the suspension of the Applicant was not inflicted by way of punishment but was made as a holding operation designed to protect the public interest and repute of the Statutory Authority. In those circumstances the Applicant did not have a right to be heard before being suspended.

In the Application of Buena Vista Nursing Homes Ltd and Grace Clifton, Managing Director – **HCA No 2215 of 1993 (TT)**
Warner J

[P10] In this application the appointment of the investigating Team was prompted by the letter of 15th March 1993, a complaint of two private citizens. The Applicants were not informed of this complaint ... The licence was revoked without notice; the Applicants were not afforded the opportunity of showing cause ... [P11] Numerous judicial dicta recognize that refusal to renew a licence may involve interference with the citizen's ability to earn his livelihood. There is also the important aspect of reputation; refusal to renew may cast doubts as to the individual's reputation. The Applicant's case was no exception ... [P13] In my view, even if Section 10 of the Act applied and not Section 9, the Applicants would have had a right to be heard. The decision to revoke or to refuse the renewal was exercised in an unfair and arbitrary manner, and resulted in a deprivation of the Applicants' right to a fair hearing: guaranteed by Section 4(b) and 5(2)(e) and (h) of the Constitution.

In the Application of Jules Bernard – **Civil Appeal No 13 of 1993 (TT)**
Ibrahim JA

[P9] By that I mean that unless there are clear words excluding the right to an oral hearing (and there are none) then I would expect that the Commission would afford the Applicant an oral hearing before so serious a matter is determined. To do otherwise would be to act unfairly towards him.

The Commissioner of Police v Charles Mitchell – **Civil Appeal No 1 of 1992 (TT)**
de la Bastide CJ

[P6] It is well established that it is not essential in every case that a person should be given an oral hearing. It depends on the circumstances of each case. In the circumstances of this case, for reasons which will become clearer, an oral hearing was not, in my view, essential. So that by giving the Respondent an opportunity to make representations in writing, the Commissioner did satisfy the requirements of natural justice, provided it is understood what the basis of the Commissioner's proposed action really was.

In the Application of Gaynell Mc Donald – **HCA No 4098 of 1987 (TT)**
Ibrahim J

[P9] It will be observed that under Section 11(1), the power to remove the name is discretionary. The Regulation states: 'The name of a student nurse may be removed ...' There is no express statutory provision for the student nurse to be heard or for any opportunity to be afforded the student nurse to make any explanation or suggestion as to how the issue may be resolved ... The Respondent Council is vested with duties and responsibilities which, when exercised, can have far reaching and serious and sometimes disastrous consequences for student nurses ... [P12] In such a case, I am of the view that the principles stated in *O'Reilly v Mackman, supra*, are applicable here and the Applicant should have been afforded a fair opportunity of hearing what is alleged and of presenting her own case. This is especially so where the power to act is discretionary. I am of the opinion that the Respondent Council acted contrary to law and the decision to remove the name of the Applicant from the Register is null and void and of no effect whatever.

***In the Application of Karine Martin, Karl Dunkley, Michael Brady, Millicent Williams, Carlton Rowe, Gloria Salmon, Hermine Campbell and Marva Phillips* – Supreme Court Nos M 02–08, 18–20 of 2001 (JM)**
Harrison J

[P12] The facts presented in the instant case reveal that following the issuing of letters to the teachers, meetings were convened between the JTA and officials of the Ministry at which the letters were discussed. A process of review was implemented. The hearings were attended by the affected teachers and representatives of the relevant school management Boards. In each case the teacher was represented by a member of the JTA. Some of the teachers to whom letters were issued had in fact accepted retirement and were now retired from the teaching profession. Others had accepted relocations. The records further reveal that the Applicants before this Court were aware of the review process undertaken by the Ministry. Both Michael Brady and Gloria Salmon had requested a review but they had also filed suit. Marva Phillips and Lorna Jackson had requested a review of their cases. This review was scheduled for hearing but they subsequently declined and filed suit. The other Applicants had not requested reviews but filed suit instead. It is my considered view that the Applicants were given an opportunity for a hearing.

***R v Coffee Industry ex parte Supreme Coffee Corp. Ltd* – Supreme Court No M124 of 1997 (JM)**
Clarke J

[P9] Therefore, this is an application case in which Supreme Coffee seeks to obtain a licence that it never held and had no legitimate expectation of holding. I accept Mr Braham's submission that all that the Board was required to do was to reach an honest conclusion without bias, and without caprice (See *McInnes v Onslow Fane and Another* [1978] 3 All ER 211). I find that the Board met that requirement. Indeed, before reaching its decision the Board wrote to Supreme Coffee (at least twice) raising issues which it considered important to which Supreme Coffee responded. Even if a hearing were required that, in my judgment, would have been sufficient for the purpose of the case before this Court to constitute a hearing.

***R v Commissioner of Customs ex parte Vons Japanese Imports Ltd* (1997) 34 JLR 342 (JM)**
Clarke J

[P344] In our opinion, the Commissioner's power of revocation of permission was properly exercisable only after scrupulous observance of the *audi alteram partem* rule ... The evidence clearly shows that the Applicant was afforded no opportunity to be heard before the decision to revoke was taken by the Commissioner. We find that this decision was taken even though the Applicant had a legitimate expectation that the permission to use the premises as a bonded warehouse would continue for a reasonable time ... [P345] Von Strolley was called to the meeting only so that the decision which had already been made could be communicated to him. It is our view that that decision should not have been reached prior to that meeting which should have been used to provide the opportunity for the Applicant to be heard.

***Paul Jennings v Director of Civil Aviation* (1997) 34 JLR 60 (JM)**
Carey JA

[P62] It can be said with a degree of certainty that, if therefore, misconduct is the basis for dismissal then procedural fairness demands that a temporary employee cannot be dismissed without the holding of an enquiry. It would be entirely impermissible to send him off, albeit with the appropriate notice or pay in lieu thereof . . . [P63] The Appellant who as a temporary employee had his appointment terminated, should not and cannot have on his file any record that he was dismissed for misconduct.

***R v Commissioner of Police ex parte Keith A. Pickering* (1995) 32 JLR 123 (JM)**
Langrin J

[P127] This Court regards this rule as fundamental in circumstances of this nature when deprivation of office is in question. *A fortiori* when the manner in which the Applicants' appointments were revoked *casts a slur on the reputation of the Applicants*. Notwithstanding the remarkable silence of the Respondent in his affidavit evidence pertaining to the allegation of the 'Indian Racket', in my view those allegations provided the impetus to the revocation of the Applicants' appointment. The law therefore contemplates a hearing prior to the deprivation of the office held by the Applicants and any failure to allow the said hearing would amount to a procedural impropriety and accordingly a breach of Natural Justice. The ingredients of a fair hearing may be divided into three categories:

(1) Advance notice of charges or accusations
(2) Right to see factual evidence in the possession of the decision-maker
(3) Right to make representations

Whichever of these processes is adopted will depend upon the particular circumstances of each case. A formal hearing may well be unnecessary but an enquiry on the facts should be carried out and common prudence should dictate that the report or at least its substance should be shown to the Applicants and an opportunity afforded them to comment on it before the final decision was taken by the Respondents. The Applicants have shown that they have all suffered injustice. In the final analysis fairness is what is necessary to do justice in the particular context and nothing more. Fairness prevails over administrative convenience, except in cases of confidentiality and national security and leans heavily upon the notion of depriving individuals of rights e.g. depriving the Applicants of their office or making accusations of misconduct e.g. being involved in a 'racket'.

***Regina v Minister of Labour and Employment and Ocean Textiles Ltd ex parte Robert Agutaya and Godfredo Fernando (on behalf of Thirteen (13) Fellow Employees of East Ocean Textiles Ltd)* (1989) 26 JLR 148 (JM)**
Bingham J

[P152] It is further clear from what transpired at the meeting and from the subsequent press release that the Honorable Minister met with the representatives of the company and heard their side of the matter. It is further clear and beyond question that he did not hear from the legal representatives acting on behalf of the dismissed workers. He merely summoned them in his presence to advise them as to his decision to cancel their work permits. In so acting the Honorable Minister acted unfairly and in clear breach of the principles of natural justice in breach of the *audi alteram partem* rule in particular.

***In the Application of Aubrey Roberts* – Civil Appeal No 53 of 1998 (GY)**
Chang JA

[P26] The issue as to the Commission's jurisdiction is a pure question of law which an administrative tribunal is usually unequipped to deal with and is essentially a matter for a Court of law. As such, while a right to be heard may exist in relation to a hearing of the substantive matter, I doubt whether such a right exists in relation to a preliminary issue of the administrative tribunal's jurisdiction to hear the matter. I have no doubt that the Appellant could have been entertained on the issue of the Commission's jurisdiction. But I have extreme doubt whether he enjoyed a **right** to be heard before the Commission in relation to the legal issue of the Commission's jurisdiction in contradistinction to the substantive matter.

***In the Application of Vieira Communications Ltd* – HCSCJ No 4787 of 1993 (GY)**
Singh J

[PP7–8] Senior Counsel went on to submit that licensing is a drastic power which greatly affects the rights and liberties of citizens and in particular their livelihood, and demands fair administrative procedure. In the case of *R v Wear Valley DC, Ex Parte Binks* [1985] 2 All ER 699. In this case, the Applicant, a street trader, operated a hot food take-away caravan from a market place. The business was her livelihood. She had no written licence but had, since September 1982, operated an informal arrangement with the Respondent council under which she paid the council three pounds fifty pence *per* night **for the right to station** the caravan in the market place on at least three evenings a week. In November 1983, without giving her any notifications, the council gave her notice to quit. The Applicant sought an order of certiorari to quash the council's decision on the ground that it was contrary to the rules of natural justice. The council contended *inter alia,* that a local authority's duty to observe the rules of natural justice when regulating public rights in connection with market trading only arose—where a statutory market was involved, and not where there was simply a single grant of a licence to a single person to trade on council's land. The Court held that the question, whether the council was regulating a statutory market or an informal market was irrelevant to the application of natural justice, since the exercise of the council's powers and the performance of its duties as a local authority [were] governed by the same principles, including the rules of natural justice. Moreover, since the Applicant had been given permission to trade in a place to which the public had access at all times and the council had a discretion whether to allow street trading in the market place, the situation was akin to an informal market and, furthermore, since the Applicant would be deprived of her livelihood, it followed that for both those reasons the rules of natural justice applied to the ending of the arrangement under which the Applicant was allowed to trade. The Court in this particular case stressed the duty of fairness where livelihood is at stake. In comparing this case with the present it is important to note that Ms Binks only had a permission, she had no license as **Ex VCT** embodying a condition similar to condition 5. To hold that the Applicant company is not entitled to be heard before its license is revoked would be saying a person with less rights as Ms Binks would be in a better position and such a situation would be rather absurd . . . [P19] The **NFMU** had a duty to act fairly, in that, before the decision was taken to reallocate the Applicant, it ought to have been informed and given an opportunity to be heard.

It has sometimes been argued that a right to a hearing, when an initial disciplinary step is taken (such as suspension), ought to be granted even when the person being disciplined is not adversely affected financially. This proposition is not without opposition and courts are prepared to decline judicial review when someone is suspended on full pay.

***In the Application of Rodwell Murray* – HCA No 1973 of 1992 (TT)**
Ramlogan J

[P15] Mr Ramesh Maharaj submitted further that the Applicant ought to have been given a hearing before he was suspended . . . [PP17–18] Mr Thorne further submitted that he was suspended on full pay and therefore the suspension is not a penalty and he had the right to be heard later. In my view financial loss may be of little consequence when weighed against the embarrassment, frustration and mental agony which a suspended person may have to undergo. It is true that the public interest may in most circumstances be best served by the suspension of the Officer without a hearing because he has an opportunity to be heard at a later stage. The public interest and that of the Public Service may however be far better served if the Officer is given a hearing in circumstances like these. The suspension of an Officer without a hearing, upon tenuous evidence, may be inimical to the public interest and even in violent collision with it. I am of the opinion that the Officer ought to have been given a hearing and the failure to do so in these circumstances was unfair. This does not necessarily mean a full scale hearing.

***In the Application of Andy Allan* – HCA No 1617 of 1990 (TT)**
Blackman J

[P14] I think I should make it quite clear at the outset that it is not, in my view, an unfailing rule that because an aggrieved person will at some later stage be given an opportunity to be heard that he should not be heard before that later stage is reached. But I think it is one of the factors to be considered in deciding whether at the earlier stage he should be heard. I think that it will depend on the circumstances of each case ...
[PP21–22] It seems to me that the purpose of the Regulation, and in this instance Regulation 79, is to provide for a holding operation prior to the officer being given a hearing. The suspension is done in the interest of the service and it must be done forthwith. It is not meant as a punishment, nor does it have that effect as the officer suffers no loss. The fact that he is suspended on full pay supports this conclusion, that is, that the suspension is merely a holding operation. The procedure which follows Regulation 79 and the tenor of the Regulation also indicate, in my view, that natural justice in the sense of a hearing does not arise at that stage and therefore the rules with regard to natural justice were not breached when the Applicant was not given an opportunity to be heard. It must be borne in mind that fairness does not necessarily require a plurality of hearings or representations and counter-representations (see *Furness v Whangarei High Schools Bd* [1973] AC 681 (E-F)). There is therefore no ground, in my view, for supplementing the procedure under Regulation 79.

***Griffith v Commissioner of Police and the Attorney General* (1994) 30 Barb LR 416 (BB)**
Waterman J

[P432] I agree with Mr Browne's submissions that the suspension of the Applicant was done in the interest of good administration. It was not done to punish him, but was merely a holding operation until the Commission determined whether or not disciplinary charges ought to be instituted (see *Lewis v Heffer*) (*supra*). As I see it there was certainly no question of punishing the Applicant. The suspension was made as soon as possible after the incident of March 14, 1991 in the interest of the public, the Police Service and the Applicant himself. There is no need for the Court to imply that there is a right to be heard at the stage before the recommendation was made by the Commission to the Governor-General to suspend the Applicant as there was no unfairness in my view at that stage. There was also no unfairness when the Commissioner formed his opinion. In my judgment, the principles of natural justice do not apply at the suspension stage. They apply at the tribunal stage. I also find that the provisions of Part IV of Regulations are adequate to protect the Applicant's rights and ensure fair play at the suspension stage.

The court seemed, however, to be sensitive to the plight of a suspended person who may suffer more than financial consequences, such as loss of reputation, and is inclined to include a requirement of natural justice at the stage of suspension.

***In the Application of Rafael Mitchell* – HCA No 3211 of 2000 (TT)**
Ventour J

[P15] The question that arises for determination is whether, having regard to the financial detriment the officer is made to suffer, it is necessary to supplement the procedure by importing into Regulation 89 a right to be heard prior to the Commission exercising its power to interdict the officer. Clearly, there is nothing expressed in the Regulation which affords the officer the opportunity to be heard before the loss of any portion of his salary ... [P18] A closer examination of Regulation 89 would reveal that Parliament intended that the power of interdiction ought to be exercised only after careful consideration of all the circumstances ... [P21] Having regard to the adverse effects interdiction would have on the Applicant and the likelihood of emotional stress and personal embarrassment I would conclude that in the absence of any clear legislative intent to the contrary that the rules of natural justice and fairness would apply in the circumstances where the Applicant, in addition to having to suffer the indignity of being suspended from performing the duties of his office, is being made to suffer financial losses ... In all the circumstances of the case I think that to import into Regulation 89 the rules of natural justice which would afford the Applicant a right to be heard prior to interdiction would be just and fair and would in no way 'frustrate the apparent purpose of the legislation'.

Although the exact nature of a hearing is not cast in concrete, courts have adopted an amazing flexability as to what consists of a hearing. In the case of *Mohan Redoy*, the court ruled that a casual discussion with an employee of a decision-maker amounts to a hearing.

***In the Application of Mohan Redoy* – HCA No 2895 of 1992 (TT)**
Sealey J

[PP14–15] It is clear that a hearing is not necessarily an oral hearing, and moreso when a Commission can regulate its own procedure, it can determine how it carries out its functions one of them being to appoint persons to be teachers. I am of the view that the Applicant has not shown on the evidence or by means of any interpretation of the Regulations, that he is entitled to the interview, but howsoever, if one ought to have been held, the interview by a representative of the Commission was sufficient to satisfy any such requirement. The employees at the Commission spoke to him, and he told them his story, the same story which is told to the Court, and some of which is corroborated by the said employees. His story was relayed to the powers that be ... In all the circumstances, I find that the Applicant is not entitled to judicial review based upon the lack of statutory restrictions, and even if he did he has failed to show that he was entitled to a second interview, that the Commission lacked jurisdiction to deal with the matter or that it acted in excess of jurisdiction or that the Commission took irrelevant or extraneous matters into consideration in making its findings. He also failed to show that he was entitled to the interview, as a hearing on the production of the letter or that even if he did, he did have a hearing. The motion is dismissed with costs.

The Court of Appeal of Trinidad and Tobago also would appear to have adopted a more casual approach as to what constitutes a right to a hearing, but this did not find favour with the Privy Council.

***In the Application of Barl Naraynsingh* – Civil Appeal No 98 of 2000 (TT)**
Kangaloo JA

[P17] It is this Court's view that the series of correspondence passing between the Appellant and the Respondent afforded a sufficient hearing to the Appellant and amounted to an inquiry reasonable in the circumstances.

Barl Naraynsingh Privy Council Appeal No 42 of 2003 (TT)
Lord Brown of Eaton-under-Heywood

[PP6–7] 16. So much for the facts. The question for the Board's determination is whether the Commissioner acted fairly in those circumstances in reaching his conclusion that the Appellant's licence should be revoked. Could he properly 'think [it] fit' to revoke the licence without making any further enquiry into the matter and without giving the

Appellant any further or better opportunity of contesting the allegation that a second firearm had indeed been found at his house rather than, as he himself was alleging, been planted there? As for the demands of fairness in any particular case, their Lordships, not for the first time, are assisted by the following passage from Lord Mustill's speech in *R v Secretary of State for the Home Secretary, Ex Parte Doody* [1994] 1 AC 531, 560: 'What does fairness require in the present case? My Lords, I think it unnecessary to refer by name or to quote from, any of the often-cited authorities in which the Courts have explained what is essentially an intuitive judgment. They are far too well known. From them, I derive that (1) where an Act of Parliament confers an administrative power there is a presumption that it will be exercised in a manner which is fair in all the circumstances. (2) The standards of fairness are not immutable. They may change with the passage of time, both in the general and in their application to decisions of a particular type. (3) The principles of fairness are not to be applied by rote identically in every situation. What fairness demands is dependent on the context of the decision, and this is to be taken into account in all its aspects. (4) An essential feature of the context is the statute which creates the discretion, as regards both its language and the shape of the legal and administrative system within which the decision is taken. (5) Fairness will very often require that a person who may be adversely affected by the decision will have an opportunity to make representations on his own behalf either before the decision is taken with a view to producing a favourable result; or after it is taken, with a view to procuring its modification; or both. (6) Since the person affected usually cannot make worthwhile representations without knowing what factors may weigh against his interests fairness will very often require that he is informed of the gist of the case which he has to answer.' [P8] 19. Notwithstanding the absence of any right of appeal from the Commissioner's decision, their Lordships would unhesitatingly reject this submission. Rather they would accept in this regard the correctness of two earlier decisions of the Courts of Trinidad and Tobago concerning the exercise of this section 21(d) power of revocation of a firearm user's licence: *Burroughs v Katwaroo* (1985) 40 WIR 287, CA, and *Globe Detective and Protective Agency Ltd v Commissioner of Police* (an unreported first instance decision dated 11 June 1997). The Commissioner, in short, is not required to convene an oral hearing before exercising this power: he can adopt an exclusively written procedure.

It must be pointed out that the right to a hearing does not carry with it an automatic right to an oral hearing, as the opportunity to make written submissions may satisfy the requirement for an oral hearing.

***In the Application of Nyoka Segree* – Civil Appeal No 142 of 2001 (JM)**
Downer JA

[PP24–25] It is surprising that at this stage of our jurisprudential development, it is being thought that to be heard means that evidence has to be taken *viva voce*. This Court has said on several occasions, for example in respect of disciplinary proceedings such as the instant matter as well as in relation to applications for licences, that the right to be heard is not confined or restricted to a *viva voce* hearing. The management of public affairs in this regard would be too hamstrung if all proceedings of this nature had to be done completely *viva voce*. The unbridled fact is that the Appellant was given ample information as to what was being alleged, and was given generous opportunities to respond.

***In the Application of the Trinidad and Tobago Police Association* –**
HCA No 1946 of 1992 (TT)
Sealy J

[P16] In the present case, the Applicants were indeed given an opportunity to be heard; they were asked to produce books and records to support their objection to the new association's application for recognition . . . Instead, they sought an oral hearing because their objection could not be adequately presented in writing or the mere production of documents alone. Even if they were correct in seeking the oral hearing, given what the letter said, and what was requested, it was incumbent on them to supply the books and say at the same time, that they wished an oral hearing . . . [P17] The Applicants had a responsibility to supply the documents sought; they did not do so. They were given an opportunity to be heard and they failed to respond.

3.1.2 Right to Full Particulars

A person must be given full notification of the case he is required to meet and allegations that are being considered by a decision-maker must be drawn to the attention of the adversely affected party.

In the Application of Malcolm Johnatty – **HCA No 707 of 1997 (TT)**
Warner J

[P7] The point taken by the Applicant does seem to have merit. I hold the view that the charge as drafted is vague and imprecise, and admits of several interpretations. The scope of the natural justice principle does include the right to be told precisely the nature of the charge.

In the Application of Ronald Narine – **HCA No 1274 of 1994 (TT)**
Warner J

[P10] In the instant case, the Respondent had undoubtedly throughout the ten year period, been in communication with the Applicant about aspects of his work; there were however times when his superior officers wrote of improvement; there were letters of commendation, and above all, a disciplinary inquiry was begun and from the evidence never concluded. Against that background, was this officer adequately notified in either of the letters of the case he had to meet? I think not. I therefore find that the Applicant was not given proper notification of the case he had to meet.

In the Application of Jules Bernard – **Civil Appeal No 13 of 1993 (TT)**
Ibrahim J

[P9] The second matter is that those allegations which are broad and general should be so treated and if the Commission intends to consider specific facts occurring on specific dates then the full particulars of those facts should be given to the Applicant and he should be afforded an opportunity to be heard on those facts before it considers them finally.

In the Application of Mahadeo Singh – **HCA No 451 of 1992 (TT)**
Jones J

[PP6–7] In this Court's view the report of Supt. Dennis was by its nature a report by a Head of Division on the conduct of one of his men and should have been acted upon by the Commissioner of Police as such. If upon consideration of the report, the Commissioner of Police was of the view that it merited the revocation of the Applicant's appointment, it was his duty to bring the allegations to the Applicant's attention and give him an opportunity to make any representations he might wish.

In the Application of Ronald Narine – **HCA No 1273 of 1984 (TT)**
Davies J

[P7] Neither Regulation 54 nor any of the other Regulations of the Public Service Commission Regulations lay down any format for the setting out of the grounds referred to in Regulation 54 and the conveying of those grounds to the officer concerned. It seems to me, therefore, that the Public Service Commission, once it particularizes the basis on which it proposes to retire the officer in the public interest, and conveys that information to the officer in a manner which enables him to understand what is alleged against him, then this would be a sufficient compliance with Regulation 54, so as to enable the officer to reply to the grounds on which his retirement is contemplated. In my view, therefore, one cannot lay down any hard and fast rule for compliance with Regulation 54 in this connection. Each case will have to be considered on its own merits. Indeed the very case of *Wilson and Others v Secretary of State for the Environment and Another* makes the point that where no specific provision is made as to the method of giving public notice, then there are various ways in which such notice could properly be given.

***Regina v Medical Council ex parte Dr Mohammed N. Baza* (1987) 24 JLR 443 (JM)**
Harrison J

[P447] The Courts have always recognized that there is an implied duty on administrative tribunals to act fairly, i.e. to apply the rules of natural justice . . . The Medical Council is the body that has been given the statutory responsibility to specially register Medical Practitioners. They are under no obligation to give reasons for their decision, however, if allegations or complaints are made against an Applicant to the Council in respect of the Applicant's professional competence or ethical conduct, such complaints or allegations should be brought to the attention of the Applicant and he should be given an opportunity to answer such charges. When the Medical Council, an Administrative body, embarked upon an enquiry into 'reports adverse to the Applicant in his professional capacity', the Council was then performing the duties of a quasi-judicial tribunal and as a consequence had a duty to act fairly . . . [P448] We find that mandamus is the appropriate remedy to direct the Council to properly hear and determine the application giving to the Applicant—details of allegations adverse to him thereby affording to him the opportunity to be heard in his defence.

An interesting dimension of full disclosure that the courts must now address pertains to information deemed confidential for reasons such as national security.

***R v Commissioner of Police ex parte Keith A. Pickering* (1995) 32 JLR 123 (JM)**
Langrin J

[P127] In the final analysis, fairness is what is necessary to do justice in the particular context and nothing more. Fairness prevails over administrative convenience, except in cases of confidentiality and national security and leans heavily upon the notion of depriving individuals of rights e.g. depriving the Applicants of their office or making accusations of misconduct e.g. being involved in a 'racket'.

***R v Commissioner of Police ex parte Glenroy Clarke* (1994) 31 JLR 570 (JM)**
Patterson J

[P577] That case must be considered on its own facts. I know of no rule of law which specifically binds the Courts as to when the *audi alteram partem* rule must be applied. The circumstances of each case must be looked at to determine whether the procedure adopted at each stage requires the application of the rule. The over-riding principle is, in my view, that where the circumstances are such that fairness is required, then the rule applies . . . [PP577–578] I do not share the view that in such circumstances it is incumbent on the Commissioner to disclose any confidential reports that he has received and used in arriving at a decision whether or not to re-enlist or employ the Applicant . . . [P578] In the instant case, it is my judgment that the Commissioner's decision not to approve the Applicant's application for re-enlistment is not void because he took into account 'certain intelligence reports' which were not made known to the Applicant. The Applicant was afforded ample opportunity to press his case for re-enlistment, and the Commissioner must have come to his decision after taking into consideration all relevant factors. I found that the rules of natural justice had not been infringed.

Re Blake **(1994) 47 WIR 174 (KN)**
Floissac CJ

[P178] The ultimate question which arises is whether a Court can properly rule against a decision of a Head of State or other public authority without giving to the authority prior notice of the grounds of objection to the decision and a reasonable opportunity to make representations and to be heard on those grounds before the decision is condemned. According to the '*audi alteram partem*' rule of natural justice, the answer is in the negative. The Attorney-General (representing the Governor-General) should have been given that notice and opportunity. In the absence of such notice and opportunity, any order made by the High Court on the Appellant's originating summons would have been irregular and liable to be set aside . . . [PP179–180] The decision to appoint a Prime Minister or any other Minister of Government is one of the many decisions which [is] made in the exercise of prerogative powers and which [is] not justiciable or subject to judicial review for the simple reason that the subject matter of the decision is not amenable to the judicial process. In *Council of Civil Service Unions v Minister for the Civil Service* [1985] AC 374 at page 418, Lord Roskill said: 'Many examples were given during the argument of prerogative powers which as at present advised I do not think could properly be made the subject of judicial review. Prerogative powers such as those relating to the making of treaties, the defence of the realm, the prerogative of mercy, the grant of honours, the dissolution of Parliament and the appointment of Ministers as well as others are not, I think, susceptible to judicial review because their nature and subject matter are such as not to be amenable to the judicial process. The Courts are not the place wherein to determine whether a treaty should be concluded or the armed forces disposed in a particular manner or Parliament dissolved on one date rather than another.' In his assessment as to whether a proposed Prime Minister is likely to command the support of the majority of the Representatives, the Governor-General is free to consult not only the Representatives themselves but other persons who should know how the Representatives are likely to behave under certain pressures and circumstances. In *Adegbenro v Akintola* [1963] AC 614 at page 629, Viscount Radcliffe (delivering the judgment of the Privy Council in an appeal from the Federal Supreme Court of Nigeria) said: 'By the words they have employed in their formula, "it appears to him", the judgment as to the support enjoyed by a Premier is left to the Governor's own assessment and there is no limitation as to the material on which he is to base his judgment or the contacts to which he may resort for the purpose. There would have been no difficulty at all in so limiting him if it had been intended to do so'. If the decision of the Governor-General to appoint a Prime Minister was made subject to judicial review, the results could be horrendous. It would mean that the Head of State might be required to divulge sensitive confidential opinions and information imparted by the Representatives and other persons and would be exposed to all the undesirable consequences of such disclosure. Public policy dictates that the Head of State should be spared those consequences.

3.1.3 Right to Consultation

It has been argued that a basic tenet of natural justice is the right to consultation before a decision is made by an administrative body. The courts have been reluctant to grant such a wide ranging right in the absence of statutory compulsion.

In the Application of Fishermen and Friends of the Sea **– HCA Cv 2148 of 2003 (TT)**
Stollmeyer J

[P64] The rules of natural justice do not necessarily require that there be a formal, oral, hearing in public. It is sufficient if those affected, or likely to be affected, are put into a position that allows their views and opinions to be heard, to be ventilated fully, and that those views and opinions be considered properly in the decision making process. There is no requirement for ongoing public debate.

In the Application of Rai Ramrattan – **HCA No 1304 of 2003 (TT)**
Best J

[PP4–6] The learned authors of de Smith, Woolf and Jowell's *Principles of Judicial Review* (London: Sweet & Maxwell, 1990) at paragraph 8–058 stated: 'This may be taken as a precise statement of the law. *Per* Turner J: "I have endeavored to explain why, within the Scheme as it exists there is a duty to give reasons which are proper sufficient and intelligible for the initial and review decisions of the Authority. It is also a requirement of fairness, or in accordance with the principles of natural justice, that a claimant who is appealing to the Appeals Panel should be provided, in advance of the day of the hearing, with access to the evidential material which the Authority, through its presenting officers, will be relying upon at the hearing of the Appeal".' Oliver LJ in the matter of *Amherst v James Walker* [1983] 2 AII ER 1066 at page 1075c stated: *'The expression "unreasonable delay" does I think, require some definition. It must . . . mean something more than "prolonged delay" and it may . . . be used to express the notion either of delay for which no acceptable reason can be advanced or delay which no reasonable man would incur acting in his own interest. But if this is its meaning then the absence of reason has no necessary relation to duration. If, on the other hand . . . the phrase is used to describe such delay as it would not in the circumstances be reasonable to expect the other party to put up with, then . . . that it contains within it, by necessary implication, the notion of hardship or prejudice, for how otherwise is the other party harmed by it?'* Although the said Regulation is lacking in this respect, it is hoped that in the future the Police Service Commission, as a requirement of fairness, would respond to an officer's representation without unreasonable delay so that he or his legal advisors are afforded sufficient time to consider whether or not to approach the Court. (iii) In the said letter the Police Service Commission gave a bald statement that it had 'indorsed' the recommendation of the Police Commissioner not to recommend the Applicant for promotion. Further, adopting the principles found in de Smith (*supra*), there is a duty placed upon the Police Service Commission not merely to '*endorse*' the decision of the Commissioner of Police but to give to the officer reasons for its endorsement, which are proper, sufficient and intelligent so that he or his legal advisors can determine whether or not to approach the Court. Messrs M. Supperstone QC and J. Goudie QC authors of *Judicial Review* (Butterworths, 2 Edn) at Chapter 7:15 stated: 'Consultation requires that the consultor must give careful consideration to the representations made, though obviously he is not bound to follow them.' Further, it must be clearly spelt out in their reasons that they gave due consideration to the officer's representations and why they adopted or rejected the endorsement of the Commissioner of Police.

In the Application of Ajodha Persad – **HCA No 323 of 2003 (TT)**
Mohammed J

[P16] Although there is no duty imposed on the Comptroller by statute to consult the affected officer in the case of an intended rescission of an assignment to an outposting (and one would not in any event expect a statutorily imposed duty in cases of this sort), I am of the view that the basic requirements of procedural fairness necessitate consultation on the part of the Comptroller with the affected officer. Consultation would allow the officer to hear the reasons why the intended assignment is being reviewed, which is important in the interests of the transparency and the consistency of the review process—in short, in the interests of good and orderly departmental administration. Equally, consultation would give the officer concerned an opportunity to advance any reasons as to why his assignment to the outpost ought not to be rescinded. The officer's position on the matter and preference would thus be appropriately factored into account in the final decision. I accordingly hold that the Respondent had a duty to consult with the Applicant in the matter of the intended rescission of his assignment to Tobago. The Courts have steered away from prescribing a minimum content for consultation since so much would be dependent on the circumstances of the particular case. Not every failure to follow what may be termed 'the best practice' as far as consultation is required will lead to the grant of judicial review. It must be demonstrated by the Applicant that the failure to consult at all or the failure to consult adequately amounts to a failure on the part of the public officer or authority to act fairly ... [P19] I accordingly conclude that the Ag. Comptroller of Customs and Excise fulfilled his duty to act fairly toward the Applicant by engaging in consultation with him on the issue of the revocation of his outposting to Tobago. It may not have been the 'best practice' for consultation but it cannot be demonstrated that the Respondent failed to treat with the Applicant in an essentially fair manner.

***In the Application of the Medical Council of Trinidad and Tobago* – HCA No 481 of 1999 (TT)**
Smith J

[P20] I find that the principles of natural justice or fairness did not mandate that the Applicant ought to have been consulted or to have been given the opportunity to rebut the allegations against him before the decision to hold the inquiry.

***In the Application of Steve Ramsaroop, Ramnarine Beharrylal, Sham Mohammed, Francis Seebarran and Deonarine Jawahir* – HCA No S–1569 of 1996 (TT)**
Mendonca J

[P9] The Applicants also contend that they had a right to be consulted prior to the implementation of the traffic changes and they were not ... There is no express provision in the Act giving to the Applicants a right to be consulted and in my view there is no room for any such implication.

***In the Application of The Teaching Service Commission sued by its members Trevor Lee, Beulah Meghu, Gloria Valere, Martuza Baksa And Arthur Maul* – Civil Appeal No 49 of 1996 (TT)**
Permanand J

[P16] On the facts of this case, Counsel contends that the expectation to which the Respondent lays claim is a substantive as well as a procedural right. The substantive claim he contends is that the Respondent was entitled to have a further renewal of his contract and procedurally the Respondent had a legitimate expectation of consultation, that is, he was entitled to be heard when the Commission decided that there would be no further renewal of his contract ... [P17] The simple point is that the Respondent was well aware of the appointment he held, in accordance with the clear and unambiguous terms of the letters of appointment. There was no representation to him express or implied that his appointments will continue indefinitely. The contention that he had a legitimate expectation to continued temporary appointments or a right to be heard before the appointment was terminated if accepted would be to introduce new concepts in the well established doctrine of legitimate expectation which are not sustainable in the circumstances of this case.

***In the Application of Carl Hanoman* – HCSCJ No 23M of 1999 (GY)**
Bernard CJ

[P9] However, modern trends indicate that the consultation process embraces more than just affording an opportunity to express views and receive advice. It involves meaningful participation and overall fairness, and although it inevitably involves the exercise of a discretion inherent in that discretion is the obligation to act fairly and reasonably within the boundaries of the statute authorizing the exercise of the discretion ... [PP11–12] In the present case although the Respondent began the consultation process by requesting the Medical Association to submit the names of its nominees for consideration for appointment to the Medical Council, he later rejected two of the nominees and consulted other bodies and persons claiming that the statute does not give exclusive rights to consultation to the Medical Association. The question arises as to whether the consultation process would not have been more meaningful if the Association had been given an opportunity to state their views when two of their nominees were rejected had they known the reasons for the rejection.

3.1.4 Right To Respond/Make Representations

A person affected by a decision of a public body has a right to respond, by means of representations, to allegations or statements that may have influenced the decision-maker.

***In the Application of Mahadeo Singh* – HCA No 451 of 1992 (TT)**
Jones J

[PP6–7] In this Court's view the report of Supt. Dennis was by its nature a report by a Head of Division on the conduct of one of his men and should have been acted upon by the Commissioner of Police as such. If upon consideration of the report, the Commissioner of Police was of the view that it merited the revocation of the Applicant's appointment, it was his duty to bring the allegations to the Applicant's attention and give him an opportunity to make any representations he might wish.

***In the Application of Luxsam Industries Ltd* – HCA No 2719 of 1988 (TT)**
Warner J

[P36] Taking into account on the one hand the need for judicial review proceedings to be brought promptly as stressed in the various authorities cited and the rights of AML which may be affected and on the other the realities of negotiating with public authorities in the hope of avoiding litigation, I extend the time for making application for leave to apply for judicial review so as to permit the commencement of these proceedings on 8th June, 1988 . . . [P38] The justifiable conclusion is that no consideration was given to the questions raised in the letter, even though its content was such as to make it obvious that the Applicant was being put at a disadvantage by AML being allowed terms which were not enjoyed by Luxsam, and that this could have disastrous effect on Luxsam's business and on the employment of persons then employed by Luxsam. As can be seen from the judgment of McNeill J in *R v Secretary of State, Ex Parte Greater London Council* [1985] 3 All ER 300 even where the decision-making power is statutory, the statute itself not providing for consultation expressly or by implication, and there is no evidence of a benefit enjoyment of which was previously permitted and which the Applicant legitimately could expect to continue, whatever phrase be used, natural justice may entitle the party whose interests are thus affected to make representations against such adverse effect. I would apply the same principle to an administrative decision leading up to the formal exercise of statutory power and I hold that considering the peculiar circumstances in which the decision fell to be made, the Applicant was entitled to a fair hearing. The Applicant in this case had interests which could be affected by the decision. It made representations. Was it given a fair hearing? As I have already indicated, no consideration was given to the representations, but the decision was taken.

***In the Application of Hugh Graham* (1995) 32 JLR 426 (JM)**
Langrin J

[P429] The doctrine of legitimate expectation is in practice procedural and only confers an expectation to be provided with an opportunity to be heard. The principle is that of fairness, the denial of which lies at the heart of procedural impropriety and which has traditionally been referred to as natural justice . . . How then can a reluctance on the part of the Applicant to attend further interviews be regarded as a waiver of his right to a hearing? Within the context of this case the highest intention which can be accorded to the proposed interviews is an attempt to further the investigation pertaining to the aborted seizure. This conclusion is derived from the withdrawal by the Revenue

Protection Division of the criminal charge against the Applicant on the basis of insufficient evidence. What was necessary in this case was for the decision making process to unequivocally afford the Applicant an opportunity to respond to the allegations before the duty concession was revoked. This in our view was not done . . . [P430] The failure of the Respondent to give the Applicant a hearing before the benefit was revoked is sufficient to dispose of Mr Campbell's submission. Although a seemingly narrow point it is fundamental to the principle of fairness which must reside in any concept of justice in this country.

***Erlin Hall v Public Service Commission* (1993) 30 JLR 442 (JM)**
Langrin J

[PP444–445] We must make certain observations on the law as we understand it. The *locus classicus* in this area of the law is the decision of the House of Lords in *Ridge v Baldwin* [1963] 2 All ER 66, [1964] AC 40, where we find useful guidance on the proper approach to this type of case. Lord Reid in delivering his judgment said there is an unbroken line of authority to the effect that an officer cannot lawfully be dismissed without first telling him what is alleged against him and hearing his defence or explanation. We regard this rule as fundamental in cases of this kind when deprivation of office is in question. *A fortiori* when the officer has served over 20 years. A formal hearing may well be unnecessary but an enquiry on the facts should be carried out and common prudence should dictate that the report or at least its substance should be shown to the officer and an opportunity afforded to him to comment on it before the final decision was taken by the Respondent. There must have been a particular date on which this Commission considered and arrived at its decision, yet there is no evidence before us that this date was notified to the Applicant. Indeed, there is not one thread of evidence that any attempt was made by the Respondents to invite the Applicant to attend at an informal hearing of the charge which had such disastrous results. We do not doubt the good faith of the Commission but in the end it seems to us that largely as a result of a mistaken notion of the law the Rules of Natural Justice were breached. The proper approach to this type of case was that the Commission was bound to act fairly in exercising its statutory power under Regulation 37(4). The decision which was reached did not accord with the standard of fairness because the Applicant was not given an opportunity to answer the accusation which led the Commission to the conclusion which was reached.

Narsham Insurance (Barbados) Ltd v Supervisor of Insurance and Another
(1999) 56 WIR 101 (BB)
Williams CJ

[PP122–123] We accept Chase J's finding on the evidence that the concerns of the office of the Supervisor were well founded and that the Supervisor had reasonable grounds for proposing an investigation into the business of Narsham under s 37. We also accept the finding that Narsham was afforded an opportunity to explain the reasons for its non-compliance with the conditions of its registration, which were referred to in the notice requiring the company to show cause. We accept too that the Supervisor's refusal to grant an extension of time was, in the circumstances, a reasonable exercise of his discretion. However, we do not agree with the opinion of the Judge that the Insurance Act is constituted as a special Act so as to exclude the application of the Administrative Justice Act, nor that the acts or omissions of the Supervisor are not susceptible to review under that Act. We do not accept that Parliament intended that the acts or omissions of the Supervisor under the Insurance Act should be outside the scope of review of the Administrative Justice Act . . . [PP124–125] It is in our opinion relevant to note that motor vehicle insurance was Narsham's only business. So that the directions to cease writing new business were in effect an order to cease doing all of its income-generating business. And by virtue of s 148(1) of the Insurance Act, it would have been an offence for Narsham to contravene the directions. It is to be observed that a proposal to cancel

Narsham's registration would, pursuant to s 16 of the Act, have required Narsham to be notified in writing and Narsham would have had a right to review of the proposal under s 141. Narsham's sole activity being the transaction of motor vehicle insurance business, the directions to cease that business under pain of criminal sanctions were virtually a cancellation of the registration, without an opportunity being given by the Supervisor for a review of his proposal before confirmation was given to what he intended to do. In our opinion, Narsham should have been given an opportunity to respond to the conclusions (i.e. the findings) resulting from the investigation before the Supervisor issued the directions that he did issue. This is not to say that we are making any judgment on the merits. But as a matter of procedural fairness it should have been given that opportunity. We hold that the act of the Supervisor is reviewable by virtue of s 16(1)(a) of the Administrative Justice Act as an act modifying, and virtually revoking, Narsham's 'licence, permission, qualification or authority' to transact motor vehicle insurance business. Even if it can be said that the Supervisor's act does not fall within s 16(1)(a), s 16(2) would operate to enable the Court to say that in the circumstances the Supervisor had a common-law duty to accord procedural fairness to Narsham and that he failed in that duty.

***In the Application of Oscar Peters* – HCSCJ No 4347 of 1996 (GY)**
Biscessar J

[P4] As a general rule the authority must give the individual concerned a fair opportunity of dealing with the matters raised in the case, including evidence raised by the authority or others, and to give the individual sufficient indication of any objections or any allegation raised against him or her such as to enable him or her to answer them . . . [PP13–14] I am of the view, and so hold, that there is nothing in the Mining legislation which expressly excludes to the Applicant the right to be heard, nor do I consider that to so hold would be to frustrate the purposes of the Mining Act. The Act is concerned with mining for metals and minerals, etc. by persons generally and with the protection of the interests of the State and of private persons. Hence in so far as the interest of persons under the Act will be affected by any decision of the Commissioner it must be a requirement that he should hear the person to be affected before making his decision.

***In the Application of Lindsworth Castello, Terry Dean and Conrad Lyttle* –**
HCSCJ No 3292 of 1995 (GY)
Singh J

[P4] It was incumbent on the Public Service Commission to make the Applicants aware of the cause or reasons for the termination of their services and to give them an opportunity to make a specific and appropriate response. This, the Commission did not do . . . The position of the Courts is understandable and is to be readily appreciated. The power of removal from the Public Service conferred upon the Public Service Commission by the Constitution is one which touches 'bread and butter issues' for those affected and its exercise must therefore meet the basic procedural safeguards prescribed by law . . . [P5] The opportunity afforded to the Applicants to make comments on the recommendation for their removal from the Public Service, was a shortcut to achieving the desired objective of their dismissal and was a cosmetic dressing of the requirements of natural justice. It is therefore, my view that in this regard the Commission fell into substantial procedural error and the decision of the Public Service Commission to remove the Applicants from employment in the Public Service, which was communicated to them by the Permanent Secretary is therefore, a nullity and must accordingly be quashed and I so rule.

3.1.5 Duty Not to Make Decision Before Hearing

A decision-maker cannot arrive at a decision prior to having a hearing to determine a particular matter.

In the Application of the Medical Board of Trinidad and Tobago – Civil Appeal No 123 of 1999 (TT)
de la Bastide CJ

[P10] Turning to the text-books in Wade and Forsyth on *Administrative Law* (7th edition), there is quoted from an old case the following passage, 'Preconceived opinions—though it is unfortunate that a Judge should have any—do not constitute such a bias nor even the expression of such opinions, for it does not follow that the evidence will be disregarded'. [P11] In these circumstances, I regard it as a matter on which the Council of the Board was entitled to take and to declare a position, even six days before the resumption of the enquiry into the Respondent's case. Their position is not like that of a Judge who can only make law (if he can make it at all) in the context of an actual case which comes before him. By contrast it was open to the Board, in my view, to make and state its policy outside the context of any particular case with which it was dealing. This is what it did in this statement insofar as the issue of whether or not Forensic Pathology was a separate specialty is concerned . . . [P15] The matter was treated by the Judge as a case of bias and predetermination seems traditionally to have been so special and different from other types of bias, since it does not involve the adjudicator having an interest in the outcome or of having any particular affinity or hostility to one of the parties. That is not what creates the objection. The objection really arises from the fundamental rule '*audi altarem partem*'. It is a breach of that rule because it is a statement in advance of your decision on an issue on which you have not yet heard one of the parties, the party against whom the issue is resolved. Therefore, it does not matter whether or not the conclusion you have come to, is [a] reasonable one or the correct one, or even the only one. The rule is really an application of the principle that justice must not only be done but must manifestly be seen to be done. Therefore it is not acceptable for a Court, or any adjudicator to state in advance of the hearing, his conclusion on a specific issue which is peculiar to the case that he is about to hear. The statement of the Council in my view, went to the limit of what was permissible. Dr Sinanan went beyond it.

In the Application of Web Communications Ltd – Supreme Court No M030 of 2002 (JM)
Smith J

[PP16–17] I have made the following findings: . . . 2. That the Applicant is only entitled to Judicial Review prior to the hearing being convened where the Tribunal acts in excess of its jurisdiction or contrary to law. In this case, I am of the opinion that the Tribunal at no time exceeded its jurisdiction by being biased as alleged by the Applicant in predetermining the outcome of the hearing proposed under the 'Cease and Desist Notice' dated the 21st of January 2002. The Court accepted the Respondent's submission, that what took place were preliminary investigations which did not involve the rules of natural justice so as to result in an excess of jurisdiction. No final decisions had been taken which affected the rights and interests of the Applicant. Having so concluded the Applicant is not entitled to Judicial Review in those circumstances.

Corporal Glenroy Clarke v Commissioner of Police and the Attorney General of Jamaica (1996) 33 JLR 50 (JM)
Carey JA

[P53] Where the Commissioner has taken a decision not to approve reenlistment, then, upon any application of the member for re-enlistment the Commissioner is obliged, in fairness, to supply the reasons for his decision and allow the officer affected, an opportunity to be heard in relation to that material if the officer requests it. In the instant case, the gravamen of the attack on the decision is that the Commissioner intimated to the Chairman of the Police Federation his intention not to change his decision to refuse approval upon receipt of the Appellant's application. Presumably, it is being said that the Commissioner should await the application before giving a ruling. I have already endeavoured to show that the Commissioner was not acting unfairly if he acted in the way it is said he did. Any right which the Appellant had to be heard could only arise after the Appellant had been advised of the decision not to approve and the reasons therefore. The opportunity afforded to the Appellant to be heard allowed the Commissioner to review his decision in the light of any submissions made to him by the officer or his attorney. The reasons having been supplied, must then be answered by the attorney.

3.1.6 Right to Reasons

There would appear to be no automatic right vested in natural justice for a person to be provided with reasons for a decision by a public authority that may adversely affect such person. If required by statute, reasons must be provided but where statute is silent, reasons are discretionary. Notwithstanding the discretionary nature of the right to reasons, it must be emphasised that the modern imperatives of good administration is creating a greater willingness on the part of courts to make the refusal to provide reasons the exception rather than the norm.

***In the Application of Kenneth Lalla, Henley Wooding, Corinre Mohammed, Carlyle Walters, Sakal Seemungal (Members of the Public Service Commission)* – Civil Appeal No 128 of 1999 (TT)**

Sharma JA

[PP2–3] If a tribunal is properly entertaining an application before it, there is no general principle that reasons should be given for its decision. In some cases, however, the relevant legislation may so provide, and then the Tribunal would be obliged to do so. In some cases, the Courts may insist and order that reasons be given, even though the particular legislation does not say so. In the instant case, the failure of the Commission to give reasons does not constitute a denial of natural justice. In my respectful view to insist that the Tribunal should have given reasons for the decision not to promote the Respondent is not in the interest of good administration.

Nelson JA

[P25] Based on these authorities I hold that there was no duty imposed on the Commission to give reasons to the Respondent for his non-promotion. There was therefore no breach of the rules of natural justice. Accordingly the Constitutional ouster clause applies to preclude the Courts from inquiring into his non-promotion in the present circumstances.

***In the Application of Air Caribbean Ltd* – HCA No 707 of 1998 (TT)**

Hosein J

[P7] The law does not recognize any general duty that compels decision makers to give reasons for their decisions.

***In the Application of Everest Big Ben Jr* – HCA No 2466 of 1997 (TT)**

Sinanan J

[P11] Nothing is to be added or to be taken away from a statute unless there are adequate grounds to justify the inference that the legislature intended something which it omitted to express . . . [P14] However, there is no express obligation upon the Minister to give reasons for his decision. I disagree with Attorney for the Applicant that there exists a common law duty on the decision maker to give reasons . . . [P20] I come to the conclusion then that in the circumstances of this case, the Minister of National Security was obliged to provide the Applicant with reasons for the decision not to grant resident status . . . [P22] The right to be given reasons for the refusal does not necessarily import a right to be heard before or on the refusal.

In the Application of Caribbean Book Distributors (1996) Ltd – HCA No S 764 of 1997 (TT)
Ramlogan J

[PP7–8] While it is desirable that reasons should be given in the interest of good administration and good management if it were the general rule that the administration should give reasons for everything that it does to all those who may be affected by its decision, administration would come to a standstill. The Applicant must show that in the circumstances there was a duty to give reasons to him. That duty would arise if there were special circumstances. The Applicant has shown none and no authority has been produced to support the contention that confidential data should be given to him.

In the Application of Randolph Burroughs and the Attorney General of Trinidad and Tobago – Civil Appeal No 63 of 1981 (TT)
Kelsick CJ

[P2] In the circumstances of this case, including the relevant provisions of the Firearms Act, the Respondent was entitled to be supplied with reasons for the revocation of his licence.

In the Application of Leonie Marshall – Civil Appeal No 39 of 2003 (JM)
Forte P

[P5] The Director of Public Prosecutions is an officer created by the Constitution and whose powers are set out therein. Some may say he has awesome powers, being able to determine whether to initiate criminal proceedings against any citizen, as also to bring to an end any such proceedings which have been commenced. He is not subject to the direction of control of any other authority, and can only be questioned in the context of judicial review in Court by virtue of Section 1(9) of the Constitution. He is however accountable to the people of Jamaica whom he serves, and should be expected, except in cases where it is not in the public interest, to be open in respect to the processes by which he makes his decisions. Cases like the subject matter of this appeal, where a Coroner's Inquest has concluded that persons are criminally responsible, and where police officers of the State are the likely persons to be so responsible, place even a greater burden on the Director of Public Prosecutions to declare publicly the reasons for coming to his conclusion that no one should be charged. The necessity to do so, in my view, became even more so, when the Full Court granted leave for judicial review of his decision . . . [PP11–12] Smith, JA has done a detailed analysis of that evidence, and has concluded that on that evidence it cannot be said that the Director acted outside of his powers. That is an opinion with which I agree and it is therefore unnecessary for me to enter into my own examination of the available evidence or to reiterate what Smith, JA has said in relation to the test to be applied in such circumstances. In the event, although in my view the DPP should have given fuller reasons to facilitate the proper examination of his decision, in the circumstances of this case, having regard to the evidence that would be led at a trial and our conclusion thereon, I would also refrain from granting the orders prayed.

Regina v the Commissioner of Police ex parte Owen Wright – Supreme Court No M144 of 2002 (JM)
Brooks J

[P5] Although this is not a ground of complaint by the Applicant, I am of the view that such a decision by the Commissioner ought to have been communicated in writing directly to the Applicant. It seems that Rule 36 of the Police Service Regulations 1961 have been complied with in that the Applicant has been supplied (no doubt at his request) with a copy of the Notes of Evidence. The Regulation provides for the supply of the Notes within thirty days of the decision of the Court of Enquiry upon the request for same being made within that time. It is therefore ordered that the application for leave to apply for judicial review is refused. Since the application was made *ex parte* the Commissioner of Police (despite the presence of Counsel on his behalf), I am unable to include as part of the order a direction to the Commissioner.

***Regina v the Minister of Finance and Planning and the Director of the Revenue Protection Division ex parte Linton Lloyd Simpson* – Supreme Court No M150 of 1998 (JM)**
Cooke J

[P6] It is recognized that the modern trend is towards greater openness and fairness may demand the giving of reasons . . . However, there are no definitive guidelines as yet. It would seem that where a decision affects a right as opposed to a privilege it is incumbent on the decision maker to give reasons. In this case the 20% concession was a privilege. I hold that the Minister was not in fairness obliged to give any reasons for his inevitable decision.

***In the Application of Acting Corporal Brian Elletson Baker* – Supreme Court No M 129 of 1996 (JM)**
Panton J

[PP3–4] In Supreme Court Civil Appeal No. 84/94, *Corporal Glenroy Clarke v Commissioner of Police and the Attorney General for Jamaica* (March 11, 1996), Carey, JA said: 'Where the Commissioner has taken a decision not to approve re-enlistment, then, upon any application of the member for re-enlistment the Commissioner is obliged, in fairness, to supply the reasons for his decision and allow the officer affected, an opportunity to be heard in relation to that material if the officer requests it.' In the instant case, the Applicant was not informed of the decision and so did not get an opportunity to appear before the Commissioner.

***Danhai Williams v The Attorney-General, the Minister of National Security and the Superintendent of Police, St. Andrew Division* (1990) 27 JLR 512 (JM)**
Gordon JA

[P520] The law gives the aggrieved party the right to appeal against the decision revoking his license. It also gives him a right to a hearing for the first time and it would seem in these circumstances that there should be conformity with the rules of natural justice; he must be told what he has to meet. If the right to appeal is real and not illusory then the grounds of appeal should relate to a specific basis of complaint for revocation of the license . . . The right to appeal involves the right to the legitimate expectation that the rules of natural justice will apply. These rules subscribe to a right to fairness. How can one submit meaningful grounds of appeal if he is unaware of the basis for the revocation? In my view the Appellant should have been informed of the basis of complaint.

***Raymond Clough v Superintendent Greyson and Attorney-General* (1989) 26 JLR 292 (JM)**
Carey JA

[P297] I have already indicated that it is now accepted that where executive action is concerned, there is a duty to act fairly. Mr Grant's arguments as to legitimate expectation being disappointed adds nothing. There is little doubt that the holder of a firearm licence has a legitimate expectation that it will not be arbitrarily withdrawn but I am not attracted by that principle as a basis for saying that the 'appropriate authority' must act fairly. If the Court is to intervene, it must be shown that the statutory procedure is insufficient to achieve justice and that to require additional steps would not frustrate the apparent purpose of the legislation . . . If it is being suggested that because the function exercised by the appropriate authority is administrative and thus the Court could not judicially review it, such a view is wholly misconceived. The modern attitude is that judicial review, that is, an application for an order of certiorari, mandamus or prohibition, is no longer limited to bodies exercising some judicial or quasi-judicial function but extends to administrative proceedings . . . [P299] Before parting with this case, I desire to observe that when a Superintendent of Police is exercising his power of revocation of a Firearm User's License, he is not required to act judicially; he is required to act fairly but that does not involve either hearing the holder or giving him reasons. For all practical purposes, it means having a *prima facie* case, or acting *bona fide*. He is obliged to give his reasons only to the Minister if the holder is aggrieved by the decision. But the Minister is bound to hear him or his legal representative and the Minister is bound to provide him with the reasons for the decision to enable the holder, as an aggrieved party, to rebut any allegations made against him. The Minister, it seems to me, must act fairly, but I have no need to consider Ministerial action any further for the Appellant chose not to prosecute his appeal to finality.

***In the Application of Errol E. Niles (2)* – Civil Appeal 2003 (BB)**
Simmons CJ

[PP36–37] It is unarguable that if there is a statutory duty to give reasons they must satisfy a minimum standard of clarity and explanation. Parliament in this case provided that reasons be given and it seems to us that that must mean that proper, intelligible and adequate reasons be given.

***In the Application of Carl Hanoman* – HCSCJ No 23M of 1999 (GY)**
Bernard CJ

[PP11–12] This brings me to the next issue to be considered—the need for a public functionary to give reasons for the exercise of his discretion . . . [P12] There is no definitive position on the question of need for reasons, and opinions differ depending on the particular case and circumstances, e.g. in *R v Higher Education Funding Council, Ex Parte Institute of Dental Surgery* [1994] 1 All ER 651, it was held that there was no duty on administrative bodies to give reasons for their decisions either on general grounds of fairness or simply to enable any grounds for judicial review of a decision to be exposed, but as the law stood, whether such a duty existed depended on where, in the particular circumstances the decision fell in the spectrum between decisions which obviously demanded reasons and decisions where reasons were entirely inapposite. In the absence of specific legislation obligating a public functionary to give reasons for a decision, many cases indicate that the modern trend is towards openness, fairness and transparency regardless of the right that is infringed—personal, vested, public or rights acquired under schemes or plans. The overall objective is fairness based on the long-established principle of natural justice . . . [PP13–15] This leads me to consider now what I refer to as the Caribbean position on the giving of reasons. In 1970 Parnell, J. in *R v Licensing Authority for the Western Area, Ex Parte LS Panton Ltd.* (1970) 15 WIR 380, lamented the absence of reasons in writing, and felt impelled to make a recommendation that having regard to the proliferation of statutory bodies and other tribunals which are given power to hear and determine causes affecting the rights of citizens, Parliament should require that these tribunals give reasons for any order or judgment made by them. Reference was made by both Counsel for the Applicant and the Respondent to Professor Albert Fiadjoe's *Commonwealth Caribbean Public Law*, 2nd Edition, where he reviewed the position in the United Kingdom concerning the duty to give reasons for administrative decisions. He regarded it as being fraught with raging controversy, but admitted that serious inroads have been made. At page 56 he made this observation with regard to the Caribbean: 'But one is emboldened to argue that in the Caribbean today, a failure to state reasons for administrative decisions ought to be regarded as wrongful in law for the fact of the Constitutional prescription of fairness which natural justice now imports in Caribbean public law in the context of fundamental rights infringements. Thus far, Caribbean Courts have tended to favour the "error approach" and hold that a failure to give reasons amounts *per se* to an error of law.' Professor Fiadjoe went on to state that fortunately Barbados has brought about a profound change in the law by settling the controversy in favour of a conditional duty imposed on any person or body making a decision to give reasons. He observed that apart from Barbados no other Caribbean territory has a legislative definition of a solution, and the common law holds sway in these jurisdictions with all the attendant uncertainties. However, he opined that it should be possible to argue for a duty to state reasons based on the argument that the common law now accepts that persons with the power to make discretionary decisions ought to provide reasons for those decisions, especially when demanded, and suggested that recent developments in this area of the law represent the increasing recognition by the Courts that the giving of reasons is one of the requirements of procedural fairness and of the principles of good administration. Within the Caribbean the case of *Burroughs and Another v Rampargat Katwaroo* (1992) 40 WIR 287, exemplifies the approach of the Courts to the giving of reasons for administrative decisions, and in the course of his judgment Bernard, J.A. of the Court of Appeal of Trinidad & Tobago, made this observation: 'But albeit that Parliament may have empowered a competent authority to take such action "as it thinks fit" the Courts today would not necessarily allow this formula to debar them from their power of review of the exercise of the competent authority's discretion even though it is purely an executive one.' This case involved the revocation of a firearm licence by the Commissioner of Police without giving reasons for the revocation. The Court of Appeal made a declaration that the aggrieved person was entitled to know the reasons for the revocation, and ordered the Commissioner to give the reasons within a stipulated time. Public officials who are charged with the responsibility of making decisions particularly those which involve the exercise of a discretion whether by acting on advice or consulting must do so with fairness and give reasons for the exercise of the discretion in a particular way so that it can be ascertained whether the discretion was exercised reasonably and according to Lord Greene, MR in *Wednesbury* (*supra*) 'within the four corners of the principles' he enumerated. The exercise of a discretion is rooted and grounded in the need and duty to act fairly. This does not mean that the Courts must decide whether the decision of the decision-maker is fair; this is solely the function of the person exercising the discretion. What the Courts are concerned with is the decision-making process and the manner in which the discretion was exercised, and whether it was exercised fairly . . . [P16] Certiorari is usually sought to bring up before the High Court the decision of an authority to have it investigated, and if found to be unlawful to have it quashed. Mandamus is usually sought to enforce the performance of a public duty, and Prohibition to forbid an authority from acting or continuing to act unlawfully . . . [P18] In this regard although I do not find the conduct of the Respondent illegal, I find it to be unfair and procedurally improper. It indicated interference in the internal affairs of the Guyana Medical Association. If the Minister was of the view that the nominees did not reflect what he had in mind he ought to have laid down criteria for selection initially and so inform the Association. He also failed to respond to the Association's request for reasons for the rejection of two of their nominees thereby denying them an opportunity to convince him about the suitability of the two nominees who are competent and highly skilled members of the medical profession.

***Elwin v Public Service Commission Commonwealth of Dominica and the Attorney General of The Commonwealth of Dominica* –**
High Court of Justice Civil Suit No 493 of 1998 (DM)
Cenac J

[Para49] I deal now with the right to reasons. 'The principles of public law require that those affected by decisions are given the reasons for the decisions in some cases but not in others' *per* Lord Donaldson MR in *R v Civil Service appeal Board, Ex Parte Cunningham* [1992] LRC (Const) 941 at 948. [Para50] In *Public Service Board of New South Wales v Osmond* [1987] LRC (Const) 681, the High Court of Australia held, following authoritative judicial precedents from England, Canada and New Zealand, that there is no general rule of common law and no principle of natural justice which requires an administrative authority to give reasons for all its decisions. This view is also confirmed by leading textbook writers; that natural justice or procedural fair play required reasons to be given

> for administrative decisions in special, exceptional circumstances only. [Para51] I refer to the judgment of Gibbs CJ in that case at page 687, where he states the following: 'With the greatest respect to the learned Judges in the majority in the Court of Appeal, the conclusion which they have reached is opposed to overwhelming authority. There is no general rule of the common law, or principle of natural justice, that requires reasons to be given for administrative decisions, even decisions which have been made in the exercise of a statutory discretion and which may adversely affect the interests, or defeat the legitimate or reasonable expectations, of other persons. That this is so has been recognized in the House of Lords (*Sharp v Wakefield* [1891] AC 173 at p 183; *Padfield v Minister of Agriculture, Fisheries and Food* [1968] AC 997, at pp 1032–1033, 1049, 1050–1054 and 1061–1062) and the Privy Council (*Minister of National Revenue v Wrights' Canadian Ropes Ltd* [1947] AC 109 at p 123); in those cases, the proposition that the common law does not require reasons to be given for administrative decisions seems to have been regarded as so clear as hardly to warrant discussion. More recently, in considered judgments, the Court of Appeal in England has held that neither the common law nor the rules of natural justice require reasons to be given for decisions of that kind: *R v Gaming Board for Great Britain, Ex Parte Beniam and Khaida* [1970] 2 QB 417, at pp 430–431; Payne v Lord Harris [1981] 1 WLR 754 at pp 764, 765. It has similarly been held that domestic tribunals are not bound to give reasons for their decisions; see *McInnes v Onslow-Fane* [1978] 1 WLR 1520 and earlier authorities collected in *Pure Spring Co Ltd v Minister of National Revenue* [1947] 1 DLR 501, at pp 534–535'. [Para52] In the more recent case of *Cunningham* (*supra*), Lord Donaldson MR had a different view. He said at page 949: 'a tribunal exercising a jurisdiction which mirrors that of the industrial tribunals which are required to give reasons and further or alternatively a tribunal which is exercising a judicial function from which there is no appeal should give sufficient reasons to enable a party to know why he has failed to secure any or, as the case may be, all of the relief which he sought and above all to be satisfied that the decision was unlawful'. [Para53] In the recently decided case by the Privy Council, *Dr Martha Stefan v The General Medical Council* (Privy Council Appeal No. 16 of 1998), their Lordships were of the view that the trend of the law has been towards an increased recognition of the duty upon decision-makers of many kinds to give reasons. This trend is consistent with current developments towards an increased openness in matters of government and administration. [Para54] At page 11 of that judgment their Lordships held: But it is well established that there are exceptions where the giving of reasons will be required as a matter of fairness and openness. These may occur through the particular circumstances of a particular case. Or, as was recognized in *Reg v Higher Education Funding Council, Ex Parte Institute of Dental Surgery* [1994] 1 WLR 242, 263, there may be classes of cases where the duty to give reasons may exist in all cases of that class. Those classes may be defined by factors relating to the particular character or quality of the decisions, as where they appear aberrant, or to factors relating to the particular character or particular jurisdiction of a decision-making body, as where it is concerned with matters of special importance, such as personal liberty. There is certainly a strong argument for the view that what were once seen as exceptions to a rule may now be becoming examples of the norm, and the cases where reasons are not required may be taking on the appearance of exceptions. [Para55] Having regard to the above, the circumstances make this case a special case in which natural justice required reasons to be given. I am of the view that the Commission should give reasons to the Applicant, even succinct reasons, if only to put her mind at rest.

The courts are prepared to uphold reasons that are bad in law, provided that the decision-maker would have reached the same decision on the basis of other valid reasons.

***R v The Air Transport Licensing Board ex parte Tropical Airlines Ltd* (1996)**
33 JLR 278 (JM)
Langrin J

[P284] In our view, where the reasons given by a statutory body for taking or not taking a particular course of action are not mixed and can be separated and where the Court is satisfied that even though one reason may be bad in law, nevertheless the statutory body would have reached the same decision on the other valid reasons, then the Court will not interfere by way of judicial review.

3.1.7 Right to Know of Investigation

With the activities of public authorities coming under increasing judicial scrutiny, the courts are now increasingly prepared to lift the veil that traditionally surrounded investigations and demand that such investigations be subjected to the rules of natural justice. Persons should have a right to know of investigations that may adversely affect them.

***In the Application of Krishna Rampersadsingh* – HCA No Cv S 637 of 2004 (TT)**
Jamadar J

[P8] In my opinion, fundamental fairness demands that this Applicant be told, with sufficient particularity of the allegations against him, of the persons making them and of any investigations conducted. The failure to do so, in the circumstances of this case, especially where a written request for same was made since 1st March, 2004 amounts to a breach of the principles of fundamental fairness and natural justice; as also would any future actions against the Applicant related to appointments based on this letter of 31st October, 2003 . . . [P9] This kind of conduct by a CMO and/or a Permanent Secretary is not conducive to good public administration. Such conduct can only undermine public trust and confidence in Public Administration, and demotivate and discourage public servants. Though true for all the Public Service, it is critically imperative that in the Health Care Sector, the highest standards of Public Administration are maintained—for here, what is at stake are the lives and limbs of the Nation's people.

3.1.8 Right to Participate Fully in Hearing

A person has a right to participate fully in a hearing which may lead to adverse findings against him.

***In the Application of Maniram Maharaj* – HCA No 1426 of 1999 (TT)**
Smith J

[P28] In these circumstances, I find that while the procedure of allowing Mr Govia to address the inquiry in the absence of the Applicant on the opening of the inquiry was not one to be recommended, on the special facts of this case, the procedure was not one which produced unfairness to the Applicant and was not in itself a breach of the rules of natural justice.

3.1.9 Right to Know of Potential Adverse Findings

In conducting a hearing, natural justice demands that parties to such a hearing must be warned very early as to whether they are in fact subjects of the hearing and whether or not adverse findings may be made against them.

***R v The Jamaica Racing Commission ex parte Anthony Subratie* (1984) 21 JLR 100 (JM Malcolm J**

[P109] Natural justice is fair play in action. A man's livelihood is at stake—The Tribunal through its Chairman intimates—'there is no charge laid against anybody, so that Mr Subratie's position can in no way be affected' then at the end a pronouncement of conspiracy. [P110] Subratie given the early assurance that he would not be adversely affected could never have imagined that this evidence would have affected him and would have resulted in a finding prejudicial to him. [P 110–111] On such a finding of conspiracy which involved not only the Applicant but another party to the conspiracy, it was imperative, if the principles of natural justice were to be followed, that the Applicant be alerted at the very inception of the investigation or at the earliest possible moment of the nature of the charge . . . A tribunal on reading Section 25(i) of the Jamaica Racing Commission Act may pardonably experience a 'heady' feeling of limitless power. They should always remember however that they must act within the limits of natural justice. In my view the Tribunal failed to apply the rules of natural justice and in addition made a finding of conspiracy which was totally unwarranted. It is for the foregoing reasons that I agreed that the application be granted and that certiorari should go to quash the order of the Jamaica Racing Commission.

3.1.10 Right to Legal Representation

There is no inflexible principle of natural justice that prescribes a right to legal representation. However, depending on the facts and circumstances of an inquiry, a court may be prepared to find that natural justice includes a right to legal representation, especially where it is founded on a legitimate expectation.

***In the Application of Desmond Harvey* – Supreme Court No M 53 of 1997 (JM) Panton J**

[P3] The factual position, therefore, is that the Minister heard and decided the appeal without any input from the Applicant, whether in person or in writing. Indeed, the Applicant was not made aware of the complaints against him; and he never had the opportunity to attempt to answer them. He was not even advised of the date of the hearing . . . [PP6–7] In the instant case, the irresistible conclusion based on the correspondence passing between the Applicant's attorneys-at-law and the Ministry of National Security and Justice is that the Applicant was led to believe that he would have been afforded an opportunity to be legally represented at the hearing of his appeal to the Minister. The inescapable inference to be drawn from the several letters from the Applicant's attorneys-at-law is that the Applicant was requesting such an opportunity which, in the result, he was denied. Even if one were to accept Miss Johnson's submission that the Applicant's request was never expressly granted by the Minister, the fact of the matter is that neither was that request ever expressly refused. In such circumstances, the best that can be said is that the Applicant's request was ignored by the Minister in which event such conduct would, in itself, amount to such a breach of the rules of natural justice as was recognized by the Court in the *Danhai Williams case* (*supra*).

A tribunal providing a right to legal representation must not unnecessarily attack the legal representatives of the person who is the subject of the inquiry.

***R v The Jamaica Racing Commission ex parte Anthony Subratie* (1984) 21 JLR 100 (JM) Malcolm J**

[P111] May I make this passing comment that when persons are clothed with quasi-judicial functions it is not in the least helpful or necessary as the Chairman did in the instant case to cry 'utter rubbish' to objections and comments made by participating attorneys—it is far more desirable to bring a balanced and fair approach to bear on the proceedings.

4

OBSTACLES TO A JUDICIAL DETERMINATION OF THE MERITS OF A JUDICIAL REVIEW APPLICATION

Judicial review is not an automatic entitlement and there are several preliminary objects that can disentitle a person from having a hearing on the substantive merits of a claim for the judicial review of decisions of public bodies. The attitude of the courts vary with respect to taking preliminary objections, with some judges showing reluctance to decline judicial review simply on a technicality, while others show greater willingness to refuse to entertain a judicial review application on the basis of preliminary objections.

***In the Application of Harricrete Ltd* – HCA No 1254 of 2000 (TT)**
Myers J

[PP14–15] It is clear that a trial judge has to exercise caution in deciding whether to allow a party to litigation to take a preliminary point. This is patent from the passage (at page 5) from the judgment of the learned Chief Justice in *Felix Augustus Durity v The Attorney General of Trinidad and Tobago* CV No. 140/1998 expressing reservations about 'splitting a case' and dealing with it 'on the basis of a preliminary objection.' This [is] because, 'the taking of what appears to be a shortcut often results in considerable lengthening of the road that leads to final determination.' However, while the learned Chief Justice plainly had doubts about adopting such a course, he expressly declined to say anything more about it. Therefore, I did not conclude that His Lordship intended to say that a trial judge should never allow a party to take a preliminary point. In fact, ultimately such a decision should be left up to the trial Judge, and unless plainly wrong, it should be left undisturbed by an appellate Court; *Ashmore & Ors v Corporation of Lloyds* [1992] 1 WLR 446, at page 454 *per* Lord Templeman. In *Tilling v Whiteman* [1979] 2 WLR 401, Lord Wilberforce (at page 403) was plainly not enamoured of the practice of allowing preliminary points to be taken 'since this course frequently adds to the difficulties of Courts of appeal and tends to increase the cost and time of legal proceedings.' His Lordship went on to say that '[i]f this practice cannot be confined to cases where the facts are complicated and the legal issue short and easily decided, cases outside this guiding principle should at least be exceptional.' Two points need to be made about this. First, and like the learned Chief Justice in *Durity, supra,* Lord Wilberforce was not expressing a blanket prohibition on the granting of leave to take preliminary points. He was simply indicating that such leave should not be granted often, and preferably only where the facts were complicated and the legal issues short and easily decided. Secondly, in that case, Lord Wilberforce was dealing with a situation where no evidence at all appears to have been before the trial Court on the taking of the preliminary point. The judge had been dealing with assumed facts, which had not been the subject of proof . . . [P19] I test the position in this manner: if I had determined not to try the preliminary questions and proceeded with the trial as a whole, at the end of that trial, I would have felt entirely free (as there is no authority to compel a contrary conclusion) to have simply set aside the grant of leave on the basis that an effective alternative remedy was provided in the legislation. If that is correct, and given that I have already held that I should take the preliminary issues, not least of all because (1) there is much evidence into which I can chew, so I am not embarking on an exercise of expensive and theoretical futility; and (2) in the circumstances of the present case, I am content that there is a real prospect that costs would be saved and that was to everyone's advantage, I cannot as a matter of principle see why it would be too late for me to consider an application seeking an order setting aside the grant of leave. That is a conclusion to which, in the peculiar circumstances of this case, I do not find myself driven to by the authorities cited by

Mr Martineau SC. In the result, in my judgment, in the circumstances of the present case, it is not too late to mount an attack on the allegedly *per incuriam* grant of leave to bring the judicial review proceeding.

***In the Application of Ramnath Guptar* – HCA No S-1096 of 1988 (TT)**
Wills J

[P8] In my view when a litigant seeks redress from a Court of Law he ought not to be shut out without being heard merely on technical grounds except in circumstances where there is a clear evidence from which the Court is satisfied that the process is being abused. However in circumstances where the Court is asked to exercise its jurisdiction *ex parte* the Court is entitled to expect conduct of candour.

4.1 SUFFICIENT INTEREST

The person or entity launching a judicial review action must have sufficient standing or interest in the matter to justify the courts intervening on their behalf with respect to the decision of a public body. The courts will not allow mere busybodies to bring proceedings to question decisions of public bodies. The sufficiency of interest in a matter supplies the vital *locus standi* that the courts require before they would contemplate intervention in judicial review proceedings.

***In the Application of the Trinidad and Tobago Civil Rights Association* –**
HCA No 477 of 2004 (TT)
Dean-Armorer J

[P67] Having held that Cabinet acted in breach of natural justice in failing to afford Justice Hosein an opportunity to be heard either before or immediately after its decision not to re-appoint him, it is now necessary to consider whether the residents of Tortuga were invested with sufficient interest in respect of a breach of natural justice committed against Justice Hosein ... [P68] In keeping with this authoritative ruling, I am of the view and I hold that although Justice Hosein should have been given the opportunity of being heard he chose not to complain and took no step to protest against Cabinet's decision to appoint another to replace him and accordingly the residents of Tortuga do not have the right to interfere independently of Justice Hosein.

***In the Application of Chandresh Sharma* – Civil Appeal No 115 of 2003 (TT)**
Nelson JA

[P13] The trend in judicial review is towards a liberal interpretation of standing.

***In the Application of Ishwar Galbaransingh and Northern Construction Ltd* –**
HCA No 1202 of 1997 (TT)
Warner J

[P22] I think I ought to re-address the question of the Applicant's standing at this stage merely to say that the weight of authority supports a finding that the Applicants are not busy-bodies, cranks or mischief makers. I have already held that the Committee acted in a public law capacity, and is amenable to judicial review, since it was established to undertake a public function.

***In the Application of the Trinidad and Tobago Unified Teachers' Association* –**
HCA No 414 of 1996 (TT)
Jairam J

[P17] 'Sufficient interest' is a mixed question of fact and law—a question of fact and degree and the relationship between the Applicant and the matter to which the application relates, having regard to all the circumstances (see *Per* Lord Roskill in *R v IRC, Ex*

Parte National Federation of Self-Employed and Small Businesses Ltd. [1982] AC 617, HL at 658H–659B; The Supreme Court Practice (1997) Vol. 1 para 53/1–14/11). The authorities further show an increasingly liberal approach to standing on the part of the Courts during the last 12 years because (a) the merits of the challenge are an important, if not dominant, factor when considering standing; (b) the importance of vindicating the rule of law; (c) the likely absence of any other responsible challenger; (d) whether the Applicant can show some substantial default or abuse; and (e) the nature of the breach of duty against which relief is sought (see *Per* Rose LJ in *R v Secretary of State for Foreign Affairs, Ex Parte World Development Movement Ltd.* [1995] 1 All ER 611 at 620b-j).

In the Application of Globe Detective and Protective Agency Ltd –
HCA No 3812 of 1996 (TT)
Jairam J

[PP12–13] In my judgment the rule governing the standing of an Applicant to apply for judicial review is that the Court must consider 'that the Applicant has a **sufficient interest** in the matter to which the application relates' (see Order 53 Rule 3(5) of the Rules of the Supreme Court, 1975). In *R v IRC, Ex Parte National Federation of Self-Employed and Small Businesses Ltd.* [1982] AC 617, HL at 658H–659B, Lord Roskill cited with approval a passage appearing in the Supreme Court Practice (1979) Vol. 1 under Order 53 note 14/21 which he said was admirably concise and with which he agreed. That passage reads as follows: 'The question of what is a "sufficient interest in the matter to which the application relates" appears to be a mixed question of fact and law; a question of fact and degree and the relationship between the Applicant and the matter to which the application relates, having regard to all the circumstances of the case.' (See also The Supreme Court Practice (1997) vol. 1 para. 53/1–14/11 at p 854.) For the purposes of this case in general and for the *locus standi* point in particular, the best and most apt exposition on the question of **sufficient interest** is contained in the judgment of Rose LJ in *R v Secretary of State for Foreign Affairs, Ex Parte World Development Movement Ltd.* [1995] 1 All ER 611, QBD at 620b-j where His Lordship said: 'The authorities referred to seem to me to indicate ***an increasingly liberal approach to standing on the part of the Courts during the last 12 years***. It is also clear from *R v IRC, Ex Parte National Federation of Self-Employed and Small Businesses Ltd.* [*supra*] that standing should not be treated as a preliminary issue, but must be taken in the legal and factual context of the whole case (see [1981] 2 All ER 93 at 96, 110, 113, [1982] AC 617 at 630, 649, 653 *Per* Lord Wilberforce, Lord Fraser and Lord Scarman). Furthermore, the merits of the challenge are an important, if not dominant, factor when considering standing. In Professor Sir William Wade's words in *Administrative Law* (7th edn, 1994) p 712: "*. . .* ***the real question is whether the Applicant can show some substantial default or abuse, and not whether his personal rights or interests are involved***". Leaving merits aside for a moment, there seem to me to be a number of factors of significance in the present case: ***the importance of vindicating the rule of law***, as Lord Diplock emphasized in *IRC v National Federation of Self-Employed and Small Businesses Ltd.* [1981] 2 All ER 93 at 107, [1982] AC 617 at 644; the importance of the issue raised, as in *Ex Parte Child Poverty Action Group* [1990] 2 QB 540, CA; the likely absence of any other responsible challenger, as in *Ex Parte Child Poverty Action Group* [*supra*] and *Ex Parte Greenpeace* Ltd [1994] 4 All ER 329; ***the nature of the breach of duty against which relief is sought*** (see *IRC v National Federation of Self-Employed and Small Businesses Ltd.* [1981] 2 All ER 93 at 96; [1982] AC 617 at 630 *per* Lord Wilberforce); and the prominent role of these Applicants in giving advice, guidance and assistance with regard to aid (see *Ex Parte Child Poverty Action Group* [1989] 1 All ER 1047 at 1048, [1990] 2 QB 540 at 546). All, in my judgment, point in the present case, to the conclusion that the Applicants here do have a sufficient interest in the matter to which the application relates within s 31(3) of the 1981 Act and Order 53, Rule 3(7). It seems pertinent to add this, that if the Divisional Court in *Ex Parte Rees-Moog* eight years after *Ex Parte Argyll Group* was able to accept that the Applicant in that case had standing in the light of his "sincere concern for constitutional issues", *a fortiori*, it seems to me that the present

Applicants, with their national and international expertise and interest in promoting and protecting aid to underdeveloped nations, should have standing in the present application' [emphasis supplied]. Leaving aside merits for a while, I am of the opinion that, based on the modern authorities and given the proximity of the relationship between the Applicants, the nexus between the FUL and the company's business, and the history of the company's business, the company has satisfied the requirement of Rule 3(5) (*supra*) that it has a sufficient interest in the matter to which this application relates and I so hold. I am also fortified in this conclusion by the above-mentioned passage from The Supreme Court Practice (1997) (*supra*).

***In the Application of East Caribbean Liquid Gas Ltd* – HCA No 5848 of 1988 (TT)**
Gopeesingh J

[P23] In the light of the foregoing, therefore, I hold that the instant application is not frivolous or vexatious, that the Applicant is not a busy body or a crank and that an arguable or *prima facie* case of reasonable suspicion has been established, on the evidence before me. I hold that it is not the function of the Court, at this threshold stage, without evidence from both parties, to decide the questions addressed by Attorney for the Respondents in his submissions. I hold that, at this stage, I cannot come to the conclusion that the Applicant has no interest at all or no sufficient interest in the matter, and therefore, I should not refuse leave. Accordingly, I order that leave be granted and the same is hereby granted to the Applicant to apply for judicial review.

***In the Application of Carl Hanoman* – HCSCJ No 23M of 1999 (GY)**
Bernard CJ

[PP6–7] Counsel for the Applicant referred the Court to 'Wade on *Administrative Law*', 7th Edition, which I have found most instructive. At page 623 the author states that unlike private law remedies, the prerogative remedies have never been dependent on the Applicant showing a specific personal right. Application for judicial review was introduced in the Courts of England in 1977 with new rules of procedure. Therefore the old procedure is more relevant to our practice, and in this regard I refer to an excerpt on page 702 of Wade with regard to standing under the prerogative writs of certiorari and prohibition: 'The prerogative remedies being of a "public" character . . . have always had more liberal rules about standing than the remedies of private law. Prerogative remedies are granted at the suit of the Crown, as the title of the cases shows; and the Crown always has standing to take action against public authorities, including its own Ministers, who act or threaten to act unlawfully . . . Consequently the Court is prepared to act at the instance of a mere stranger, though it retains discretion to refuse to do so if it considers that no good would be done to the public. Every citizen has standing to invite the Court to prevent some abuse of power, and in doing so he may claim to be regarded not as a meddlesome busybody but as a public benefactor'. The Applicant herein cannot be regarded as a 'meddlesome busybody', being the President of the Guyana Medical Association, and even though he personally was appointed to the Medical Council, the interests of the Medical Association are affected by what has been done, and in these circumstances, as stated by Denning, MR in *R v Paddington Valuation Officer, Ex Parte Peachey Property Corporation Ltd.* [1965] 2 All ER 836, 'the Court will listen to anybody whose interests are affected by what has been done'.

***In the Application of the Chief Immigration Officer* – Civil Appeal No 7 of 1994 (BVI)**
Floissac CJ

[PP5–6] A complainant will be held to have *locus standi* by way of a relevant or sufficient interest in an actual or intended decision or action of a public authority (1) if the decision or action infringed or threatens to infringe any constitutional, statutory or common law right whatsoever vested in the complainant or (2) if the decision or action infringed or threatens to infringe the complainant's specific constitutional, statutory or common law right to the observance of the formalities required by the '*audi alteram partem*' rule of natural justice or (3) if the decision or action disappointed or threatens to disappoint the complainant's legitimate expectation that certain benefits or privileges will be granted to him or that certain rules of natural justice or fairness would be observed in relation to him before the decision or action is made or taken.

It must be emphasised that demonstrating sufficient interest does not lift the burden of establishing an arguable case as a prerequisite to obtaining leave for judicial review.

***In the Application of the Sawmillers Co-operative Society Ltd* – HCA No S426 of 2000 (TT)**
Smith J

[P5] With respect to the test to be applied as to who is a 'proper person' for the purposes of Judicial Review, I agree with Counsel for the interveners that the private law test for giving leave to intervene is inapposite to public law proceedings where Applicants seek to challenge decisions on grounds which would otherwise not apply to private law proceedings such as illegality, irrationality, or procedural impropriety and can seek declarations without necessarily pursuing a right to compensation for pecuniary loss. On the other hand, not every busybody can seek judicial review of a decision, and while I do not propose to define or categorise the classes of persons who may be proper persons to intervene in an application for Judicial Review, I think it must include those persons whose interest are directly and adversely affected by the decisions of the relevant body.

***In the Application of Robert Perekebena Naidike* – HCA No 1162 of 1996 (TT)**
Warner J

[P6] In my view, the Applicant has on those bare facts, not made out an arguable case. The position is not simply as Mr Mobota has submitted, merely to show a sufficient interest.

4.2 LEAVE GRANTED WHERE THERE IS AN ARGUABLE CASE

The purpose of the requirement of leave for judicial review is to facilitate a judicial filtering of hopeless cases. An applicant must establish at least an arguable case that merits detailed examination at the substantive hearing of the judicial review application.

***In the Application of Balroop Ramlochan, Kamraj Maharaj, Tara Ramroop, Cindy Santoo, Jane Elahie, Davie Maharaj, Ronald Ramdass, Indar Samaroo, Jenny Lynn Diaz, Ryan Headley, Dennis Sampson, Rajh Basdeo, Balchan Samaroo, Chaitram Deonarine, Dowin Alexander and Anne Alexander, Wendell Coltrust, Kenneth Coltrust, Ashook Sookdeo, S. Ashook, Junior Jackson, Grace Gopaul, Sita Seelal, Terrance King and Cyntra Seepersad, Mark Philbert, Bansraj Harrilal, Hollister Peters, Patricia Austin* – HCA No S1475 of 2003 (TT)**
Rajnauth-Lee J

[P8] The requirement for the grant of leave prior to the commencement of judicial review proceedings is designed to filter out applications which are either groundless or hopeless ... Although the threshold is low, the Applicants must demonstrate that there is an arguable case that a ground for seeking judicial review exists.

***In the Application of Zimmern Beharry* – HCA No 3212 of 1996 (TT)**
Sealey J

[PP3–4] At this stage of the proceedings the Court is not expected to go into the matter in any depth, even on an opposed *ex parte* application for leave. The Applicant should have sufficient interest in the matter to which the application relates and he must show that he has an arguable case ... Once the Applicant achieves these requirements, leave ought properly to be granted [to] him to seek judicial review of the action of which he complains.

***In the Application of Juan Mosca* – HCA No 2295 of 1993 (TT)**
Sealey J

[P9] The arguments have shown the divergent views of the two parties. This alone is not sufficient to ground a case for leave for judicial review, but the Applicant must show that he has an arguable case and it seems to me that this Applicant has done so and that I should give the leave for the Applicant to apply for judicial review. To do otherwise at this threshold stage with the evidence of only one side available to the Court, and with the conflict as to the correctness of procedure, would not be consistent with what is required of a Court at the stage of leave for judicial review. The Court at this stage seeks to screen applications which might be groundless or baseless and to prevent a wastage of judicial time with misguided or trivial complaints of administrative error.

***In the Application of Lolita Saroop* – HCA No 2115 of 1993 (TT)**
Sealey J

[P4] The factor with which we are most concerned at the moment is whether the Applicant has an arguable case. This has been the subject of judicial consideration in many cases, including *Regina v Secretary of State For the Home Department, Ex Parte Swati* [1986] 1 WLR 477 at page 485 letter A: 'an Applicant must show more than that it is not impossible that grounds for judicial review exist. To say that he must show a *prima facie* case that such grounds do in fact exist may be putting it too high, but he must at least show that it is a real, as opposed to a theoretical, possibility. In other words, he must have an arguable case.' *Per* Sir John Donaldson, MR.

***In the Application of Felix Augustus Durity* – Civil Appeal No 49 of 1993 (TT)**
Gopeesingh JA

[PP10–11] It is clear that the purpose of requiring leave of the Court as a precondition to making a substantive application for judicial review is to weed out the hopeless cases. The value of that purpose would, therefore, in my view, be greatly diminished if appeals are entertained from a refusal to grant such leave or perhaps even from the grant of such leave. This requirement that leave be granted before a substantive application may be made for judicial review is consequently akin to the requirement (discussed in *Lane v Esdaile*) of obtaining leave to appeal. In the same way that that requirement of obtaining leave to appeal was intended to serve as a check to unnecessary or frivolous appeals, the requirement for leave under Order 53 Rule 3(1) is intended to weed out the hopeless cases. Accordingly, to permit an appeal against the refusal to grant such leave would be to render nugatory the very nature, object and purpose of the requirement for leave ... [P11] In the result, therefore, it is my considered judgement, that the expression, 'decisions' appearing in Section 109(1)(a), 109(1)(c) and 109(2)(a), rather than being given the wide interpretation urged by Attorney for the Applicant, should be construed narrowly and strictly to exclude from its ambit a refusal by this Court, on a renewed *ex parte* application, of the grant of leave to apply for judicial review.

***In the Application of Jules Bernard* – Civil Appeal No 13 of 1993 (TT)**
Ibrahim JA

[PP9–10] Leave should be granted if upon the material then available the Court thinks without going into the matter in depth that there is an arguable case for granting the relief claimed by the Applicant. In *R v Secretary of State for the Home Department, Ex Parte Rukshanda Begum* (1990) COD 107, the Court of Appeal held that the test to be applied in deciding whether to grant leave to move for judicial review is whether the Judge is satisfied that there is a case fit for further investigation at full *inter partes* hearing of a substantive application for judicial review.

***In the Application of Millicent Forbes* – Supreme Court No HCV – 01386 of 2004 (JM)**
Smith J

[P7] In keeping with the practice where the purpose of the requirement for leave is to eliminate at an early stage claims which are hopeless, frivolous or vexatious and to ensure that a claim only proceeds to a substantive hearing if the Court is satisfied that there is a case fit for consideration, I find that as regrettable as the surrounding circumstances may have been in this case, to grant Judicial Review would be without merit. The application for leave is refused.

***Regina v The Commissioner of Police ex parte Carvel Anthony Williams* –**
Supreme Court No HCV 0741 of 2003 (JM)
Brooks J

[P8] Although I have been at pains to set out the facts of the case, I have borne in mind the words of Lord Diplock in the *IRC case* (*supra*) at p 106 f and when he said: 'the whole purpose of requiring that leave should first be obtained to make the application for Judicial Review would be defeated if the Court were to go into the matter in any depth at that stage.' I however am of the view that the issue involved here is an uncomplicated one, which is, whether the Commissioner in deciding a straight-forward question of fact, exceeded his authority, committed an error of law or a breach of natural justice, reached a decision which no reasonable tribunal could have or in any way abused his powers. (See the words of Lord Templeton in *Preston v Inland Revenue Commissioners* [1985] 2 All ER 327 at p 337). As I have indicated, I find that Constable Williams has not made out an arguable case showing that the Commissioner was guilty of any of those breaches. As a result the Application for Leave is refused.

***Maria A. Smith v The Commissioner of Police* (1981) 18 JLR 154 (JM)**
Carberry JA

[PP158–159] The procedure to be followed in applying for an Order of Certiorari, or of Prohibition, is laid down in The Grand Court (Applications for Orders of Mandamus, Prohibition, Certiorari and Habeas Corpus) Rules, made in March 1977. Those rules were modeled on the corresponding rules in the United Kingdom Supreme Court Rules, Order 53: *Applications for Orders of Mandamus, Prohibition, Certiorari etc*. (The UK Rules have recently been altered into Applications for judicial review, enabling Applicants to seek in one and the same application one or more claims for relief). These rules in effect provide for two stages in the making of such an application: (a) an application for leave to make the application, and, if leave is given, (b) the actual application before the Grand Court. The first stage is *ex parte*, and is conducted before the Judge in Chambers. At this stage all that is necessary to show is that there is some arguable case or claim which is not obviously untenable, vexatious or frivolous. The original application is supported by a short *statement* setting out the bare grounds on which the relief is sought, with an affidavit verifying the facts relied on. (Useful reference can be made to the pre–1979 White Book, e.g. see the 1970 or 1976 White Book: note 53/1/7). It ought normally to be rare for the application to be refused at this stage, unless it is obviously untenable. Any defence or answer to the application is to be made at the second stage, when leave having been granted, the Applicant proceeds to file a Notice of Motion and to serve the parties against whom he seeks relief, with copies of the Notice of Motion (or summons), the Statement, and any affidavits accompanying the original application for leave, together with any other additional material. The Respondent in his turn may file affidavits in reply *et cetera* . . . [P159] In our view, Mr Donaldson had no right of audience at this stage of the application: it was *ex parte*, and unlike *Bazie's case, supra*, we have no idea how he came to be there. In our view there was sufficient material before the learned Judge in Chambers for leave to have been granted to proceed with the application in the normal way.

4.3 DELAY

Judicial review proceedings must be brought promptly, and in most jurisdictions within the Caribbean, such proceedings must be brought not later than three months from the date of the decision that is being questioned. This three month period is an upper limit and an application for leave within the three month period can be defeated when not brought promptly. In an application for leave for judicial review, where delay is raised as a bar to the grant of leave, the courts will consider whether the grant of leave to apply for judicial review, in light of any delay, would be detrimental to good administration or would cause substantial prejudice or substantial hardship to third parties. Nonetheless, there is a discretion vested in the courts to extend time for filing the action for judicial review, once good reason for the delay is provided.

***In the Application of Clyde de Coteau* – HCA No Cv S 2108 of 2003 (TT)**
Jamadar J

[P6] In the principal affidavit of the Applicant, no good reason is given for this delay. The statement at paragraph 12 that: 'From the time that I received notice that the Commission declared that I had resigned my office in the Fire Service until the present time, I did not have the necessary funds available to me to retain an Attorney at Law to obtain the necessary legal advice on the matter or to file the necessary Court proceedings necessary to vindicate my rights,' is not credible . . . In the realm of Public Law, good administration requires timeliness, finality and certainty. Those who wish to challenge decisions and/or failures to make decisions must be prepared to act promptly if they are to assert their rights. Thus, it is only for good reasons, which must mean credible and *bona fide* reasons, that this statutory requirement will be extended.

***In the Application of Deborah Thomas-Felix* – HCA No 1988 of 2003 (TT)**
Mohammed J

[P3] According to Section 11(1) of the Judicial Review Act, No. 60 of 2000, an application for judicial review is to be made promptly and in any event within three (3) months from the date when the grounds for the application first arose, unless the Court considers that there is good reason for extending the period within which the application should have been made . . . [P5] In the three month period, between 08 January to 08 April 2003 and shortly thereafter, there was every indication that the situation was not going to be resolved, notwithstanding the further correspondence on the subject. In any event, such a highly subjective 'hope' on the part of the Applicant could hardly be said to constitute good reason as is required by the Act to justify an extension of the period of time. A private 'hope' that an issue might be resolved without ultimate recourse to legal action probably exists on the part of very many concerned parties involved in all different types of contemplated litigation but it cannot be advanced, in my view, as a good reason to excuse the delay in this case . . . [PP6–7] The Applicant is a judicial officer of considerable experience who had the benefit of advice from Senior Counsel very early on in the three month period—see Exhibit D.T.F. 17. During and shortly after that period, there was no indication that the issue in dispute could be resolved internally without proceeding further or that the Applicant's medical condition would or might resolve itself in the short term of three months or thereabouts, as opposed to a longer term. It ought to have been readily apparent to the Applicant therefore, within the three month period, and in a situation where time was very much of the essence, that the passage of more time was not going to bring about an internal resolution of the various issues. Yet the Application is brought about some six and a half (6½) months after the decision of which complaint is made. I do not accept that in this context, the Applicant has behaved reasonably, sensibly and rationally by allowing such time to pass, on the 'hope' that the various situations, including the medical one, would resolve themselves. In determining whether to grant an extension of time, I have also viewed the strength of the challenge and I am of the view that the Applicant has not crossed the threshold of what was described in *R v Press Complaints Commission* 31 July 2001 (unreported) . . . An overview of the various issues raised in the Application does not lead me to conclude that the Applicant has demonstrated a prospect of success on any of the grounds. I conclude therefore that none of the reasons advanced are good reasons for extending the period within which the application should have been made. There has been undue delay in the making of this application . . . [P8] Good administration, in the circumstances of this case, would have required the very timely institution of action so as to conduce to the orderly and more settled administration of the Magistracy, in this regard with reference to the assignment of Magistrates by the Chief Magistrate and the need for certainty and finality with respect to such assignments.

***In the Application of Gillette Marina Ltd* – HCA No Cv S 1747 of 2002 (TT)**
Jamadar J

[PP49–50) Thus, though *Jones v Solomon* was a case dealing with certiorari (which is not the relief sought in the instant matter), in my opinion, on the issue of delay in applying for judicial review (Bernard CJ at page 316 a), it establishes the following:

a. 'where an application for judicial review is sought, it is fundamental and critical' that the application be made promptly (Sharma J.A., *Jones v Solomon*, page 334 j).
b. where an application is out of time, that is there is a delay, at the leave stage, the first step is to have time extended and then only if time is extended the application for leave will be dealt with (Sharma J.A., *Jones v Solomon*, page 335 f).
c. where there is undue delay, 'in the interest of justice and fair play' and 'despite the absence of any rule to the effect', the Court should order that the application for an extension of time should be made and notice given to the proposed Respondent (Bernard J.A., *Jones v Solomon*, pages 318e – 319c). [This was not done in the instant matter.]
d. on the hearing of the substantive matter, the Respondent is entitled to show that time ought not to have been extended at all (presumably, provided no opportunity was afforded at the leave stage to do so), which if successful would result in the application being dismissed (Bernard C.J., *Jones v Solomon*, page 319g, and Sharma J.A., page 335g).
e. at the substantive hearing, the Respondent is also entitled to show, even where there may have been 'good and valid reasons for the extension of time', that the 'delay still remains "undue" and it is still open to the Respondent . . . to show . . . that the granting of the relief sought would be likely to cause any one of the situations specified in Rule 4(1)', in which event, if successful, the leave obtained may be set aside or the relief sought refused (Sharma J.A., *Jones v Solomon*, page 335h–j).
f. that there is no requirement of proof, by a Respondent, of substantial hardship, prejudice or detriment to good administration, as a condition precedent to the refusal of relief (or presumably to the refusal of leave)—(Bernard C.J., *Jones v Solomon*, page 318d).
g. that though there is 'no onus' on the Respondent 'to show positively that there is prejudice or hardship, etc', if the Respondent is 'able to show on a balance of probabilities that there is likely to be hardship (or presumably, prejudice or detriment), that would be enough' (Sharma J.A., *Jones v Solomon*, page 540e).

It is clear, on the basis of the doctrine of *stare decisis*, that this Court is bound by the decisions of the Court of Appeal of Trinidad and Tobago, and that decisions of the House of Lords are only persuasive, even if highly so . . . [P56] In the light of this Court's view that the changes effected by the Act now necessitate affirmative evidence of any detriment to good administration once time has been extended and where there is undue delay. And that, the only discretion the Court has, pursuant to Section 11(2) of the Act (where there is undue delay), is to refuse leave to apply for judicial review (and no longer to refuse to grant any relief sought). And, given that the substantive law proclaimed by the Act takes precedence over the procedural law as contained in Order 53, Rule 4(1) RSC (where there is a conflict between the two, the substantive law must prevail). And, that the order made granting leave in this case could only have reserved the right to raise delay under Section 11(2) of the Act. Then, given the absence of any affirmative evidence of detriment to good administration, this Court is of the view that the Respondent's submissions on delay must fail.

***In the Application of Fishermen and Friends of the Sea* – Civil Appeal No 106 of 2002 (TT)**

Nelson JA[1]

[P10] I must bear in mind the policy of the JRA was to have a filtering mechanism for applications for judicial review, and, further, where such applications are not prompt or later than three months from the impugned decision a second filter, a discretionary extension of time, must be put in place. Thereafter, under our law, if the time for applying for leave is extended, by Section 11(2), which deals only with the leave stage, the application for leave may be defeated if undue delay would cause substantial hardship to third parties or detriment to good administration. Against the background of these multi-tiered discretions I bear in mind the words of Lord Diplock in *Hadmor Productions v Hamilton* [1982] 2 WLR 322 at 325: '[An appellate Court] must defer to the Judge's exercise of his discretion and must not interfere with it merely upon the ground that the members of the appellate Court would have exercised the discretion differently. The function of the appellate Court is initially one of review only.' 'It is only where the decision exceeds the generous ambit within which reasonable disagreement is possible, and is, in fact, plainly wrong, that an appellate body is entitled to interfere': *per* Lord Fraser of Tullybelton in *G v G* [1985] 1 WLR 647, at p 651. See also *Jones v Solomon* (1989) 41 WIR 299, 336B–337H *per* Sharma J.A. (as he then was) . . . [PP11–13] Section 11 deals with delay in applying for judicial review. In its Amended Statement, the Appellant sought 'leave of the Court to extend the period of time within which to make this application as there is good reason for extending the period.'

Section 11 of the Judicial Review Act, 2000 reads in part:

'11. (1) An application for judicial review shall be made promptly and in any event within three months from the date when grounds for the application first arose unless the Court considers that there is good reason for extending the period within which the application shall be made.

(2) The Court may refuse to grant leave to apply for judicial review if it considers that there has been undue delay in making the application, and that the grant of any relief would cause substantial hardship to, or substantially prejudice the rights of any person, or would be detrimental to good administration.

(3) In forming an opinion for the purpose of this section, the Court shall have regard to the time when the Applicant became aware of the making of the decision, and may have regard to such other matters as it considers relevant.'

1 The decision of the Court of Appeal was endorsed by the Privy Council. *Fishermen and Friends of the Sea – Privy Council Appeal No 30 of 2004.*

Until the enactment of the JRA the law on delay in judicial review proceedings was based on the Rules of the Supreme Court 1975, particularly Order 53 Rule 4(1), which was copied from the English Order 53 Rule 4(1) as it existed in 1977. That rule gave the Court power to refuse preliminary leave and to refuse any relief sought on the application where there was undue delay in making the application. In England Rule 4(1) was revoked in 1980 and replaced by a new Rule 4(1) based on lack of promptness unless there was good reason for extending the time for applying for leave to apply for judicial review. That 1980 rule has been enacted in Trinidad and Tobago as Section 11(1) of the JRA. Thus, in Trinidad and Tobago we have both the old Order 53 Rule 4(1) and the 1980 replacement of it. However, since the 1980 UK Rule 4(1) has been enacted as substantive law in Section 11(1) it must prevail over our existing Rule 4(1), which is subordinate legislation. In 1981, the UK Parliament enacted Section 31(6) of the Supreme Court Act, 1981, which reverted to the concept of undue delay but yet preserved the 1980 rule with its three-month time limit subject to extension for good reason. In Trinidad and Tobago we have copied Section 31(6) of the UK Supreme Court Act in our Section 11(2), but with substantial changes. The effect of the changes is to disapply the concept of undue delay to applications for substantive judicial review. Section 11(2) deals only with leave applications and not substantive applications. Section 11(3) has no parallel in the UK principal or subordinate legislation. Subsection (3) gives the Court a wide discretion to take any relevant matters into consideration including the time when the Applicant became aware of the making of the decision in forming the good reason opinion for overriding lack of promptness or in arriving at a decision to refuse leave on the grounds that because of undue delay the grant of any relief would cause substantial hardship or substantial prejudice to the rights of any person or would be detrimental to good administration. In my judgment the phrase 'an application for judicial review' in Section 11(1) of the JRA should be read as referring to an application for leave to apply for judicial review: see *R v Stratford-on-Avon DC, Ex Parte Jackson* [1985] 1 WLR 1319 (CA) and *R v Dairy Produce Quota Tribunal, Ex Parte Caswell* [1990] 2 WLR 1320 (HL). The effect of Section 11(1) was that an application for leave must be made promptly and in any event within three months of the making of the impugned decision: see *Ex Parte Caswell* (*supra*). In such a case, the Court may refuse leave unless it considers that there is good reason for extending the period: see Section 11(1) of the JRA. When read with Section 11(1), Section 11(3) gives the Court the power to consider a wide range of factors in arriving at its opinion on good reason. The chief relevant factor is the time when the Applicant became aware of the making of the decision . . . [P20] It must not be forgotten that the English provisions are different from ours. In Trinidad and Tobago the structure of Section 11 of the JRA requires an application more than three months late to pass the test of an extension of time and thereafter the test of substantial hardship or prejudice to third parties or detriment to good administration. On these tests while merits in the sense of an arguable case rather than the outcome of the case are relevant, at the undue delay stage even substantial merits can be defeated by third party considerations or detriment to good administration. A consideration of merits on an extension of time application may well be otiose . . . [P21] Suffice it to say that neither case lays down a rule of law that merits would inexorably lead to an extension of time. The most that can be said is that merit is a factor to be considered in the Judge's exercise of his discretion . . . [PP22–23] The learned judge in considering other matters relevant to his decision under Section 11(1) of the JRA assessed the detriment to good administration if he were to extend time and allow the action to proceed. The learned judge properly called to mind a passage from *Ex Parte Caswell* (*supra* at p 1328): 'In asking whether the grant of such relief would be detrimental to good administration, the Court is at that stage looking at the interest in good administration independently of matters such as these. In the present context, that interest lies essentially in a regular flow of consistent decisions . . . in citizens knowing where they stand, and how they can order their affairs in the light of the relevant decision.' He further relied on *O'Reilly v Mackman* [1983] 2 AC 237 at p 280 *per* Lord Diplock.

Lucky JA

[P7] As I alluded to earlier an extension of time should have been granted. Therefore the learned judge should have made a more than 'quick perusal' of the merits. In his judgment at p 21 the Judge said: [PP7–8] . . . Mr Maharaj submitted and I agree that the Judge ought to have done more. He ought to have said why he did not accept the evidence produced by the Appellant and why the '**lack of promptness**' weighed more in favour of '**the public interest**'. The long-term effects any project will have on the communities and ecosystems of this country require prime consideration and attention, moreso where there may be risks to health. The judge said he acquainted himself with the material put before him. In other words he familiarized himself then he gave his decision. I do not think the foregoing is sufficient or adequate in these circumstances. I do not think the evidence was sufficiently assessed. This is a complex matter, a '***class action***', filed by a public spirited organization comprising many persons of different walks of life. Certainly it required more than acquaintance with the material, it necessitated a proper assessment of material and evidence and findings in respect of them and to ascertain whether the public interest balance comes down in favour of extending the time and therefore in my opinion there was sufficient cause to hear the substantive action. His reasons at page 21 clearly indicate a greater concern with two activities of BPTT and the presumption of correctness of the grant of the CEC rather than to the public interest balance to which I have alluded by reference to *Greenpeace* (*vide* paragraph 3 page 7 *supra*) . . . [P9] As I said earlier, I think the trial Judge ought to have extended time. This is a complex matter of '***public interest***' and environmental concern and should have been fully addressed . . . [P12] It is my view that Section 11 should be construed as a whole. The provisions of subsections (1), (2) and (3) are all inclusive in its construction and application. Subsection 3 begins with the words: '***In forming an opinion for purpose of this section the Court shall have regard to . . . such other matters as it considers relevant***' [emphasis mine]. So in exercising his discretion the learned judge ought to have given full consideration to the merits and indicate why he preferred one to the other or others which could only be achieved by the hearing of the substantive action.

***In the Application of Yuclan Balwant* – HCA No. 402 of 2001 (TT)**
Hamel-Smith J

[PP5–6] Section 11(1) expressly requires that an application for Judicial Review be made promptly and in any event within 3 months from the date when grounds for the application first arose. This requirement is, however, made subject to the Court's jurisdiction to extend the period for making an application if the Court considers that there is good reason to do so. The language of Section 11 is closely based on the language of the English Order 53 Rule 4(1). The English Rule refers to an application for leave to apply for Judicial Review, while the local Act refers to an application for Judicial Review. Since, however, the first step in an application for Judicial Review is to apply for leave this one variation in language makes no difference. Cases which have been decided on the basis of the English Rule are relevant therefore to a construction of our Section 11(1) . . . [P6] It is clear that Section 11(1) lays down a primary requirement that the application be made promptly, followed by the secondary requirement that it be made, in any event, within 3 months. Accordingly, it is quite possible that an application made within 3 months may not have been made promptly, in which case leave to apply should not be granted by the Court unless it considers that there is good reason for extending the time for such application.

***In the Application of Walkerwell Ltd* – HCA No Cv 342 of 2000 (TT)**
Jamadar J

[PP12–13] There is no question that judicial review is a discretionary jurisdiction (see in this regard, *Ex Parte Argyll Plc.* [1986] 1 WLR 763 at 774–775). Thus, a Court may in its discretion refuse to grant a remedy, even if it is convinced that there has been some procedural impropriety, illegality or unreasonableness in the decision making process. The consequence of a refusal to grant a relief sought, for example, that an act or decision is unlawful, *ultra vires*, null and void and of no effect, is that the act or decision remains effective and valid.

Though delay is one consideration for the exercise of the discretion to refuse relief (Order 53 Rule 4), there are others also related to the particular circumstances of each case. These other considerations include:

i. regard for the wider public interest;
ii. whether the relief sought would be of any practical value;
iii. the impact on third parties; and
iv. the impact on administration.

Clearly more than one consideration may be present in any single case. Ultimately however, the decision whether or not to grant relief must be made in light of the circumstances existing at the time of the hearing and not of the original decision (see *Ex Parte Everett* [1989] QB 811). In this Court's opinion, apart from the consideration of delay and the application of Order 53 Rule 4(1)(b), this Court would refuse the relief sought having considered its likely impact on:

i. the Contractor,
ii. the due administration of WASA,
iii. the wider public interest,

and also because, once the relief of certiorari is refused, there is no useful or practical value in granting any of the declarations sought (see in this regard *Williams Construction v Blackman* (1994) 45 WIR 94 at 101 d–h) . . . [P16] It is noteworthy that the Applicant in its affidavits in support of the application for leave to seek judicial review did not specifically set out any explanations for its delay in commencing these proceedings. The onus and obligation is on the Applicant to explain any delay, to give good reasons for same and to seek an extension of time (*Jones v Solomon* at 317 j, 318 g–h and 335 f–h) . . . [P17] In my opinion, in this case, in the context of the subject nine month contract, in view of the Applicant's knowledge of the award of the contract and of its nature and duration, in light of the Applicant's choice not to notify the Respondent or the Contractor of the bringing [of] these proceedings and given the performance that would have occurred by the time these proceedings were initiated, it cannot be said that this Applicant acted promptly. There has therefore been unexplained undue delay in the making of this application for judicial review . . . [P18] That being the case, has there been substantial hardship, prejudice or detriment to good administration, as contemplated by Order 53 Rule 4(1). In my opinion yes . . . The question is therefore, whether on a balance of probabilities, if the relief sought is granted, there is likely to be substantial hardship to or it will substantially prejudice the rights of, any person or it would be detrimental to good administration . . . [PP19–20] The result is that both the Respondent and a third party (the Contractor) have taken steps on the faith of the subject decision. Considerable time, human resources and expenses have been expended by other persons while the Applicant slept on its rights and [chose] to give no indication to the affected parties of its intentions to challenge the subject decision and award (see in this regard, *Ex Parte Argyll Plc.* [1986] 1 WLR 763 at 778 H and 783 A). Furthermore, indirectly the lives of citizens of Tobago and of industry and tourism in Tobago (the wider public interest) stand to be adversely affected if the relief sought by the Applicant is granted. In my opinion, to quash the decision to award the contract to the Contractor and/or to grant a declaration stating that the subject decision or award is *ultra vires*, null and void and of no effect at this point, would result in substantial hardship and prejudice to both the Respondent and the Contractor and also to the people of Tobago. What would happen to the work done and the monies expended to date? What of the rights of the Contractor to enforce the terms of a contract under which he has been performing these works and incurring these expenses? Who is to benefit from the exploratory work done, and the water resources discovered? In my opinion this contract is at this stage, one (1) month before completion, irreversible. The Applicant must accept full responsibility for finding itself in this position, brought about by its undue delay in commencing these proceedings and conducting them as it has chosen to do . . . [P21] So also here, in my opinion given the knowledge of the Applicant, the failure to obtain a 'stay,' the duration of the contract, the evidence of the Respondent, the extent to which the contract has been performed and the obvious likelihood of hardship and prejudice to all concerned, it must have been apparent at the commencement of the hearing before this Court in July, 2000, that quashing the decision or the award was unlikely. And consequently, that obtaining a declaration that the contract was null and void and of no effect was improbable. Yet the Applicant has persisted in this action . . . The public interest in good administration requires that there be finality and decisiveness once a decision has been reached. That is, public authorities and third parties (such as in this case) should not be kept in suspense as to the legal validity of a decision. Thus, the length of the delay, the extent and effect of the decision under challenge, and the impact if it were to be quashed are all relevant considerations in determining whether there is detriment . . . [P22] In this case, as I have explained, the length of the delay by the Applicant in bringing this application and in seeking to 'stay' the performance of the contract, has resulted in the contract being virtually completed at the time of hearing. The requirements of finality and decisiveness demand that this decision and award remain. Also, the subject decision and award (contract) directly affect the lives of the people on the island of Tobago and the viability of industry and tourism there. If this decision and award were quashed now and/or declared null and void and of no effect, the negative impact on the people of Tobago and on the duty of WASA to meet their needs for an adequate supply of water would be adversely affected. Not only will there be considerable delay in achieving the goal of supplying an additional essential two million imperial gallons of water *per* day, but also there may be a considerable cost incurred in litigation and/or compensation as the rights and entitlements of the Contractor are sorted out. Furthermore, what is to happen to the process? Is it to be reopened? How? To whom? Thus, there is no doubt in my mind that to grant the relief of certiorari and/or the declaration that the decision and/or award is null and void and of no effect would have been by the date of hearing detrimental to good administration . . . [PP23–24] What then is the purpose or usefulness of making this declaration? And, in any event, what does this declaration have to do with the subject decision and/or award? All of the relief sought including the declaration with respect to notification became purely academic and of no practical significance by the hearing date. In this case there are no new or novel points of law raised, about which it may be argued there is some need to clarify the law or give general guidance for future decision makers (in this regard compare, *Ex Parte Ruddock* [1987] 2 All ER 518 at 521 j) . . . In these circumstances, in my opinion, there is no point in granting any of the relief sought. To quash the subject decision and re-open bids would necessarily: impose heavy administrative burdens on the Respondent (see paragraphs 8 and 18 of the affidavit of U. Maharaj, filed on the 12th April, 2000), result in the diversion of resources towards possibly repeating the entire process, and lead to increased and no doubt unbudgeted expenditure. To what avail? No other bidder has challenged the subject decision or award. The Applicant has not qualified for stage II and has not stated that given its bid of $25M it could or would be able to perform the contract for $15M. And, on the face of it, reconsideration would likely result in the same decision being made. Thus, to grant the relief sought would, in these circumstances, be entirely useless and would have a disproportionately negative impact on good administration and third parties . . . [P24] This Court has disposed of the Applicant's case in the exercise of its discretion on the grounds of: undue delay resulting in prejudice and hardship to other persons and detriment to good administration; the relief sought being of no practical use; and the impact on third parties and administration. All of these were considerations which were clearly foreseeable before the actual hearing of the substantive motion began and especially in light of the affidavits filed on behalf of the Respondent.

***In the Application of Luxsam Industries Ltd* – HCA No 2719 of 1988 (TT)**
Warner J

[P36] Taking into account on the one hand the need for judicial review proceedings to be brought promptly as stressed in the various authorities cited and the rights of AML which may be affected and on the other the realities of negotiating with public authorities in the hope of avoiding litigation, I extend the time for making application for leave to apply for judicial review so as to permit the commencement of these proceedings on 8th June, 1988 . . . [P38] The justifiable conclusion is that no consideration was given to the questions raised in the letter, even though its content was such as to make it obvious that the Applicant was being put at a disadvantage by AML being allowed terms which were not enjoyed by Luxsam, and that this could have disastrous effect on Luxsam's business and on the employment of persons then employed by Luxsam. As can be seen from the judgment of McNeill J in *R v Secretary of State, Ex Parte Greater London Council* [1985] 3 All ER 300 even where the decision-making power is statutory, the statute itself not providing for consultation expressly or by implication, and there is no evidence of a benefit enjoyment of which was previously permitted and which the Applicant legitimately could expect to continue, whatever phrase be used, natural justice may entitle the party whose interests are thus affected to make representations against such adverse effect. I would apply the same principle to an administrative decision leading up to the formal exercise of statutory power and I hold that considering the peculiar circumstances in which the decision fell to be made, the Applicant was entitled to a fair hearing. The Applicant in this case had interests which could be affected by the decision. It made representations. Was it given a fair hearing? As I have already indicated, no consideration was given to the representations, but the decision was taken.

***In the Application of Winston Braithwaite* – HCA No 2305 of 1994 (TT)**
Hosein J

[P18] In his Statement filed the Applicant sought to explain the lapse of time between the date of the decision and the commencement of these proceedings on two grounds. Firstly that the Applicant did not abandon his claim against the Respondent . . . Secondly the Applicant sought to advance a case of what was described as 'personal impecuniosity' . . . A mere recital of correspondence between the Applicant and his representatives and the Respondent is not a sufficient explanation of the lapse of time . . . [P19] In addition it is well-settled law that a mere assertion of financial hardship is hardly enough to relieve a party from fulfilling a requirement imposed on him by law . . . Further this Court would hasten to add that financial hardship by itself is only one factor in determining whether there has been undue delay. It would be rare indeed for a party asserting this argument by itself, to be able to justify any delay on his part . . . [P20] The presence of undue delay by itself would not enable a Court to refuse relief. On the hearing of a substantive application a Court may exercise its discretion and may refuse the relief sought on the grounds of undue delay if it concludes that granting of relief would cause substantial hardship to or substantially prejudice the rights of, any person or would be detrimental to good administration . . . [P21] The Courts should be allowed a great degree of flexibility in determining what amounts to hardship, prejudice or is detrimental to good administration. Each case has to be decided on its own facts.

***In the Application of Leslie Mc Call* – HCA No 750 of 1992 (TT)**
Warner J

[P9] On the evidence before me, I find that the Commission was dilatory in dealing with the Applicant's representations, and had replied to her Attorney's letters. Further, upon a balance of probabilities the Applicant may have been led to believe that the decision would have been reversed in the light of the action taken in the *Phipps'* decision.

In the Application of Clyde Dipnarine – HCA No 3494 of 1991 (TT)
Wills J

[P7] The effect of the cases cited and or referred to by Attorney, when put succinctly, amount to no more than saying that one must not sleep on one's rights to the detriment of others and or to good administration ... [P9] What for this purpose is meant by 'undue delay'? In my view it means delay which is not justified and or excessive and or excusable having regard to all the circumstances. To establish whether a period of delay is justified and or excessive and excusable, a Court must examine all the circumstances in conjunction with any explanation given, if any. Explanation would, in my view, be a condition precedent for justification of the delay. Where however the reasons for the delay are apparent or patent from the circumstances as a whole, I am of the view that the tenets of justice would require a Court to act upon such findings of fact as are apparent or patent, from the records before it. From the admitted facts in this case, it seems clear that when the decision was taken to hear the matter *de novo* no communication was addressed to the Applicant until the charges were preferred for the second time nor was any thought given to the legislative intent of the draftsman of the Regulations ... [PP13–14] Good administration in this context would, in my opinion, mean the *proper and or efficient co-ordination* of a body or group of employed persons in any establishment or organization, *within the context prescribed by rules for the effective achievement*, realization and or maximization of the establishment's or organisation's full potential. In this regard it would require that the administrators and or his agents recognize and or appreciate the almost unlimited sensitivities of the human personality to real or perceived injustice and or unfair practices. This is particularly so when apparent reasonable choices can be made but yet ignored by the Administrator or his agents. It is in this context that one would expect Regulations or rules which have been made and which admit of discretion to apply to contingencies such as those which are now before the Court ... [P14] On the issue of undue delay, I find, and so hold that such delay as there had been was contributed to by the Respondent. In the result, I am of the opinion that I ought to determine this case on its merits, since one ought not to be permitted to excuse oneself from performing a statutory duty by undue delay which arise[s] mainly by his own act or contributed thereto by him.

In the Application of Cecil Kennedy – HCA No 4196 of 1990 (TT)
Jones J

[P4] In this case there had been no formal application for an extension of time by the Applicant when he made his application for leave approximately 1 month after the time stipulated in Order 53 of the Rules of the Supreme Court expired. The Respondents were admittedly not present at this *ex parte* stage and had not taken steps subsequently to have the leave set aside on the ground of delay. However, as is open to the Respondents at this hearing of the substantive application Attorney for the Respondents took an objection *in limine* claiming that the application was not maintainable on the ground that there had been undue delay in commencing these proceedings ... [P5] The principle derived from the rule it seems to me is that leave having been granted and not set aside the Court may now refuse any relief sought on the application on the ground of delay if it considers that the granting of relief would be likely to cause substantial hardship to or substantially prejudice the rights of any person, or would be detrimental to good administration. Whether or not relief was likely to cause substantial hardship to or substantially prejudice the rights of any person, or would be detrimental to good administration are matters of evidence ... However, no attempt was made by Attorney for the Respondent to point to any factor which will influence the Court's decision whether to grant the reliefs. Attorney felt content to rely solely on the one month's delay. It seems to me that having arrived at the stage of the hearing of the substantive application, the presence or absence of the factors set out in the rule becomes relevant and the Court must therefore consider the substantive application to determine whether or not such factors exist or whether the Applicant has made out a case for the reliefs claimed in which latter instance the Court will consider whether to exercise its general discretion to grant the reliefs having regard to the unexplained delay.

***In the Application of Harold Barcoo* – HCA No 1599 of 1990 (TT)**
Jones J

[P17] If indeed a litigant ought not to be prejudiced by the default whatever it might be of his legal adviser, can time be extended indefinitely? What period must elapse before the Court stops the clock? In this case 11 months had elapsed. The Applicant had placed the matter in the ample hands of his legal adviser. Indeed there are many situations in which litigants have been left without remedies through failure of their legal advisers e.g. judgments in default and actions dismissed for want of prosecution. I hold that in this case the Applicant must therefore bear the consequences of the 'error' of his legal adviser and as a result in my view no sufficient reason for the delay in bringing these proceedings had been advanced. This should put an end to the matter but since the question was argued forcefully before me, I will proceed to consider whether the Applicant should be granted the reliefs claimed in the event the delay ought to be excused . . . The onus is on the Respondent to establish that the grant of the relief is likely to cause substantial hardship or substantially prejudice the right of any person or would be detrimental to good administration . . . [PP18–19] The Court of Appeal held that to grant relief would have been detrimental to good administration since a significant number of claims would have had to be reopened or if not the Applicants would have enjoyed an advantage over the other unsuccessful claimants.

***In the Application of Nixie Quashie* – HCA No 1220 of 1990 (TT)**
Jones J

[P5] One common theme runs throughout the authorities and that is relief is for the vigilant . . . [PP5–6] This to my mind is offering no explanation for the delay and amounts to a failure by the Applicant to discharge the burden of showing that in all the circumstances despite the undue delay he is deserving of the Court's discretion in his favour. It is the application for judicial review which must be made promptly and where there is delay the Applicant must show that the delay was through no fault of his. I hold, in the circumstances, that there has been undue delay in bringing these proceedings. One other matter deserves attention. The Applicant in this case has sought not only certiorari but mandamus both of which are available under Order 53. Unlike the present English rule, where the three month time limit is applicable to all reliefs sought under Order 53, our Order 53 stipulates that the time limit of three months is applicable only to applications for certiorari. It is conceivable therefore that an Applicant for madamus can be refused leave or substantive relief even if his application is brought before the expiration of three months. In such circumstances, the sole question is, has it been made promptly, that is, without undue delay . . . [P8] In the instant case no direct evidence has been adduced by the Respondent to show that the granting of the relief would be likely to cause hardship, or prejudice to any person or be detrimental to good administration . . . I hold, in the circumstances that it would be detrimental to good administration for the Authority to be hindered in the pursuit of its objectives on account of the dilatoriness of persons against whom it has had cause to take action or persons against whom it might consider similar action necessary.

***In the Application of Tilson Webb* – HCA No 3835 of 1988 (TT)**
Brooks J

[P24] In the instant case, Webb did not apply promptly for his remedy, i.e. an order of certiorari. He allowed approximately 2½ months to elapse after receiving notice of the directive before applying for same. Certiorari was important to his cause—and he went to sleep—so to speak, on his remedy. The resulting delay would in my view cause substantial prejudice to the other Prison Officers who went ahead and sat 'The Promotion Examination' in good faith . . . [P25] It has been clearly demonstrated by these cases that certiorari would only be granted where due diligence is shown by an Applicant in real need of the remedy. In my view, to grant the remedy at this stage would also be prejudicial to good administration in the Prison Service.

In the Application of Lennie Campo – **HCA No 5925 of 1987 (TT)**
Hamel-Smith J

[PP5–6] I am of the view that when an Applicant is seeking a discretionary remedy he must put forward substantial and good reasons for his delay. To simply ignore the issue and tell the Court 'forget about the delay, there is a substantive issue to be determined here' is not good enough. Attorney for the Applicant himself concedes that an explanation for the delay should have been given.

In the Application of Industrial Sawmilling and Pallet Manufacturing Ltd –
HCA No 4336 of 1987 (TT)
Blackman J

[P29] The next question is whether the company should be refused the reliefs it has claimed on the ground of delay in seeking redress . . . [P34] It is my respectful view that when an Applicant seeks judicial review and there has been a delay of the nature such as there has been in this case, he must give satisfactory reasons to explain the delay especially when that period of delay is substantial and in the case of certiorari beyond the period of three months. The reasons must be ample and cogent . . . [P35] Therefore although I find that the Parliamentary Secretary's acts were *ultra vires* and illegal I would refuse to grant the company the reliefs sought on the ground of undue delay on the part of the Applicant.

In the Application of the Attorney General – **HCA No 3260 of 1987 (TT)**
Blackman J

[P5] Leave to apply for judicial review was sought on 12th June, 1987, that is over five months after due publication of the appointments of which complaint has been made by the Attorney General. No reason has been given by the Attorney General for such a delay . . . [P7] However, the Court has a discretion in the matter. The exercise of that discretion I will base on the principle described by Lord Wilberforce in *Wong supra* at p 560 where he said: . . . the Courts are somewhat slower to deny the Attorney General, as the custodian of the public right, relief on this ground (SC. delay) than in the case of an individual. The injury to a public interest by denial of relief, its extent and degree of irremediability must be weighed against any loss which the Defendant may have sustained by the plaintiff standing by while the Defendant incurs expense or if such is the case misleading the Defendant into supposing that its activities were or would be permitted. I will therefore not deny the Attorney General relief on the ground of undue delay in the circumstances.

In the Application of Gladstone Solomon – **Civil Appeal No 85 of 1986 (TT)**
Sharma JA

[P23] It is well established, and all the authorities speak with one voice, that where an application for judicial review is sought, it is fundamental and critical to this sort of relief that it should be made promptly—and that the power to grant leave is discretionary and not as of right . . . [P24] Before seeking leave for judicial review if an Applicant is out of time, there is delay. The first step he must take is to have that time extended to the date of the application. This must not be confused with the application *for leave* [my emphasis] which will *only* be dealt with when the time has been extended. An application for an extension of time in this jurisdiction is made on the hearing of the application for leave. In the affidavits in support of this application, the Applicant normally sets out facts from which the Court will determine whether it will exercise its discretion to extend time or not. It must be noted that all this takes place in the absence of the Respondent. On the hearing of the substantive matter however, the Respondent is entitled to show that the time ought not have been extended at all. If he does this successfully, then in my judgment, the Applicant's application must be dismissed. In other cases however, there might have been good and valid reasons for the extension of time, nevertheless the delay still remains 'undue' and it is still open to the Respondent to show that if the Court is of the view that the granting of the relief sought would be likely to cause any one of the situations specified in Rule 4(1), then the leave obtained may be set aside or the Court may refuse to grant any of the relief sought on the application ... [P25] In my opinion, this was a case in which the Judge ought to have specifically addressed the question of delay. Be that as it may, he exercised his discretion favourably, and the question now arises, whether this Court ought to interfere with the exercise of that discretion when he extended the time after some two and a half years ... [P30] Accordingly, I am of the view that the Judge in extending the time to some two and a half years later from the decision to retire the Respondent, fell into error. At this stage, what I have said so far is enough to dispose of this appeal. I am, however, prepared to proceed further for two reasons, firstly, in the event I have erred in holding that the Judge had wrongly exercised his discretion, and secondly, out of deference to attorney for the Respondent who made certain submissions on Order 53 Rule 4(1)(a)(b) ... [P31] I emphasise the word 'likely' here, because in my judgment, there is no onus on the Appellant to show positively that there is prejudice or hardship, etc. In my judgment, if the Appellant is able to show on a balance of probabilities that there is likely to be hardship, that would be enough. In the instant case, admittedly there was no evidence from the Appellant, but I think that having regard to the special circumstances of this particular case, the Appellant has shown that there is a likelihood of prejudice.

***In the Application of Maniram Ramnarine* – HCA No 1044 of 1985 (TT)**
Davis J

[P5] I am led to the conclusion that in the circumstances of this case the Applicant slept on his right to and is guilty of undue delay in pursuing his remedy by way of judicial review. He elected to pursue another remedy which failed, viz, representation through his Association.

***In the Application of Carol Lena Winston Churchill* – Supreme Court No C.L. M/104 of 2002 (JM)**
Brown J

[PP4–5] At the commencement of proceedings the Court advised the Applicant that the application for leave for Judicial Review was filed out of time. She conceded that there was a delay but asserted that there was good reason for the Court to extend the period within which the application be made. She said the delay was as a result of her attempt to obtain a corrected certificate of convection from England. She then sought to have time extended without filing for an extension of time. This was fatal to her case. The proper procedure would be for the Applicant to:

1. Make an application to have the time extended to the date of the filing of the application for leave for Judicial Review.
2. In the affidavit in support of the application she then sets out the facts from which the Court will determine whether or not it will exercise its discretion to extend.
3. Notice be given to the proposed Respondent who is entitled to be heard on the question of whether leave should be granted for making the application.

In the instant case, there was no application before this Court for an extension of time.

***Regina v The Minister of Agriculture ex parte D.Y.C. Fishing Ltd* – Supreme Court No M-069 and M-146 of 2002 (JM)**
Anderson J

[P13] I have come to the conclusion that I should uphold the preliminary point and hold that, to the extent that the Applicant relies as the basis or ground for application for leave upon the fact of the lack of integrity of the licensing system and the issue of the licences in May 2001 under this system, that the Applicant is guilty of undue delay. That having determined that there has been undue delay, the burden for showing that time ought to be extended for filing the application for leave is upon the Applicant. The Applicant has failed to discharge that burden . . . [P15] Accordingly, my order is that this application for leave is out of time as the Applicant is guilty of undue delay; application for extension of time is refused on the basis that it would be contrary to good administration and prejudicial to other persons, including non-conch processing interests of the fishing industry, such as the Intervenor in this case.

***In the Application of Tulloch Estate Ltd* – Supreme Court No M130 of 2001 (JM)**
Campbell J

[P8] The award which is sought to be impugned is dated 28th June 2001. Although filed within the time allowed by the rules that govern these applications, it was not filed until 24th September 2001. It should be noted that because of the nature of these applications expedition is an essential feature, and delay should be avoided. The need for certainty in public administration dictates that decisions of public bodies be expeditiously reviewed . . . Lord Goff in examining the question of delay, intimated that an application although filed within the time stipulated by the rules may still fail to satisfy the criteria for promptness.

***In the Application of Anthony Daley* – Supreme Court No M 152 of 1995 (JM)**
McIntosh J

[PP3–4] The inordinate and inexcusable delay of the Applicant in pursuing his application amounts to an abuse of the process of the Court. During the period of delay, the Cement Company would have reorganized their affairs as a result of Respondent's confirmation of the termination of Applicant's employment. Applicant's delay would likely cause damage to the Cement Company, an affected but unnamed party to these proceedings. This Court found that the reasons given for Applicant's delay were inexcusable, spurious and even farcical.

***In the Application of Castel Gordon* – Supreme Court No M111 of 1995 (JM)**
Harris J

[PP4–5] There has been non-compliance on the part of the Applicant in making his application for leave to apply for an order of certiorari within one month of the decision of the School Board, which is sought to be quashed. No application for extension of time to make the application was presented, nor was any notice of intention to extend time given to the Respondent. Although leave was granted to apply for the order to issue the writ of certiorari, the notice of motion was not filed within 14 days as prescribed and the leave would have therefore lapsed.

***In the Application of Judy Lloyd* – Civil Appeal No 9 of 1998 (BB)**
Williams CJ

[PP8–11] In England the grant of leave by the Court is necessary before a person may pursue an application for judicial review. A provision to that effect is absent from Section 8 of the Administrative Justice Act and it must, we think, be assumed that such a provision was deliberately omitted so as not to impose any fetter on the adjudication by the High Court of complaints by Applicants against the administrative acts and omissions of public officials and authorities. In this case the application was struck out by the Court acting under Section 8 on what counsel referred to as an *in limine* objection. The Court construed the section as giving the Court a discretion to strike out an application but in the cases to which I have been referred in which Section 31(6) of the English Act came under consideration, the provision of that subsection corresponding to Section 8 of the Administrative Justice Act was construed as enabling the Court to refuse relief on the hearing of the substantive application. Thus the words of Ackner LJ, delivering the judgment of the Court of Appeal in England in *R v Stratford-on-Avon District Council and another, Ex Parte Jackson* [1985] 3 All ER 769 at 774: 'However applying the objective test which we have indicated as being the correct one, we accept that there has been undue delay in the present case within the meaning of s 31(6) and so hold. We therefore emphasise that on the hearing of the substantive application the Respondents will have liberty to argue that, even though we have found that there was good reason for the failure to act promptly, the Court should still refuse to grant the relief sought on the hearing on the grounds referred to in s 31(6); the discretion to refuse relief conferred on the Judge by that subsection will not be fettered in any way by our decision.' And in *Caswell and Another v Dairy Produce Quota Tribunal for England and Wales* [1990] 2 AC 738 at 747, Lord Goff said: 'Section 31(6) simply contains particular grounds for refusing leave or substantive relief, not referred to in Rule 4(1), to which the Court is bound to give effect, independently of any rule of Court.' The textbook, *Principles of Judicial Review* by de Smith, Woolf and Jowell, 1999 at 15–047 is to the same effect: 'Delay is distinct from the other grounds upon which the Court may withhold a remedy in that it is expressly recognized in Section 31(6) of the Supreme Court Act 1981 which provides that where there has been undue delay in making an application for judicial review: "the Court may refuse to grant leave [i.e. permission] for making the application or (b) any relief sought on the application if it considers that the grant of the relief sought would be likely to cause substantial hardship to, or substantial prejudice to the rights of any person or would be detrimental to good administration. Order 53, Rule 4(1) states that applications for permission must be made promptly and in any event within three months from the date when grounds for the application first arose." Delay is thus relevant both at the permission stage and in relation to the grant of relief after the Court had determined the merits of the Applicant's case.' The language of Section 8 has to be unreasonably and excessively strained, in order to support a construction of the section as enabling a Court to strike out *in limine* an application for review under the Act. The grant or refusal of relief is not a matter that falls to be determined at the initial or preliminary stage of a trial. The appropriate relief in a particular case is decided upon after a substantive hearing. To strike out *in limine* such an application is in effect to reinsert in the section a provision requiring leave to make the application which Parliament must be taken to have deliberately excluded. In striking out the notice of motion the learned judge said: 'Where public officials take a decision it is not in the interest of good administration for those officials and third parties to be left in suspense as to whether the legal validity of that decision will be challenged several years later by a person who thinks himself aggrieved by the decision. There must be a point at which public officials can act with the assurance that a decision is final. In my opinion that is precisely the sort of mischief that Parliament was minded to exclude when it enacted the provision in Section 8 of the Administrative Justice Act relating to the detriment to good administration. It is my opinion that to allow this application to proceed after such a lapse of time would be detrimental to good administration.' These considerations may have weight when the substantive matter is heard and the Court has to decide whether to grant relief. But the fact is that Section 8 makes no provision for the Court to take such considerations into account before it is called upon to decide the question of substantive relief. In any case, in the opinion of this Court, whether the grant of relief sought would cause [substantial] hardship to, or would substantially prejudice the rights of, any person, or would be detrimental to good administration are questions that are more appropriately decided after a full hearing. As Bingham LJ said in *R v Chief Constable of the Thames Valley Police, Ex Parte Cotton* [1999] 1 RLR 345 at 352, unless the subject of the decision has had an opportunity to put his case it may not be easy to know what case he could or would have put if he had had the chance.

***Re Young* (1993) 47 WIR 60 (BB)**
Waterman J

[PP64–65] In the instant case, the Applicant seeks to have the conduct of the commanding officer in relation to his conduct of the summary trial and his award of punishment and the conduct of the Chief of Staff in relation to his review of the summary trial and award reviewed under the provisions of the Administrative Justice Act. As I see it, the orders of certiorari and mandamus ought not to be granted under the Administrative Justice Act in this case. The High Court ought not to intervene in matters relating to military law and discipline. The Applicant by becoming a soldier, and receiving his pay as such, agreed and consented to be subject to military discipline. In the present case, he was found 'Guilty' by his commanding officer of conduct prejudicial to the good order and discipline of the Defence Force. He considered himself wronged by his commanding officer. He sought redress in his case by petitioning the Chief of Staff under Section 116 of the Act for a review. The grounds on which he sought relief from the Chief of Staff under the Defence Act are the same grounds on which he now seeks relief from this Court. The Chief of Staff examined each ground of his petition, reviewed the evidence and confirmed the finding of the summary trial. The Applicant has no reason to complain, for he has all which the law military, to which he engaged to submit when he entered that service, entitles him to have. This Court will not now intervene and grant him relief under the Administrative Justice Act and Order 53 of the Rules of the Supreme Court.

***Sowatilall v Kalika Persaud et al* (1971) 18 WIR 186 (GY)**
Crane JA

[PP191–192] My opinion, however, is that neither the original appellate nor the supervisory jurisdiction of the High Court can properly be attracted in this case, simply because both these jurisdictions are intended by the Ordinance to be exercised by a procedure that is strictly mandatory. The powers of review by the High Court are thus circumscribed, and, as I see it, that Court may properly exercise its supervisory jurisdiction only when the Commissioner has decided the dispute himself under s 49(2)(a), or when there is an adjudication by him on an appeal from the arbitrators' award. In either event, such review lies only when he acts in excess of jurisdiction or contravenes the principles of natural justice. But it cannot be too strongly stressed that review by the High Court can only be in respect of the Commissioner's decision; not against the arbitrators' award, nor, it would seem, against the order of reference, nor against the arbitration proceedings. Such is the extent of the supervisory jurisdiction of the High Court in the light of the finality and privative provisions in s 49(4): see *Sowatilall v Fraser and Anor* ((1960) 3 WIR 70). Section 49(5), however, is quite definite. It says that if there is no appeal to the Commissioner the arbitrator's award is final, and that it shall not be questioned in any civil Court. Here, I think the legislature, by making use of such clear and unequivocal privative language, has put beyond peradventure its intention to oust the appellate jurisdiction of the High Court, having conferred that exclusively in the first instance on the Commissioner for Co-operative Development. We have seen that the object and intention of s 49(3) is to make it obligatory on an aggrieved party to appeal from the arbitrators' award directly to the Commissioner; also that s 49(5) precludes questioning the award in any civil Court if no appeal is preferred to him. But does the fact that, in this case, the Appellant is also challenging two matters preliminary to the award, namely, the Commissioner's order of reference and the arbitration proceedings, give him the right to circumvent an appeal to the Commissioner by directly invoking the jurisdiction of the High Court in an action for a declaration and injunction? As I see it, the prohibition against the award, being questioned in any civil Court must, by necessary implication, also include questioning the Commissioner's order of reference to the arbitrators, for the reason that the award being the creature of that order, any attack on the order can only be an oblique attack on, and, in effect, an appeal against the award itself, a thing which is forbidden when there is no appeal to the Commissioner. Moreover, objection to both the Commissioner's terms of reference and the arbitration proceedings was taken and overruled in the arbitration proceedings that led to the award from which there has been no appeal to the Commissioner, the Tribunal designated for that purpose. In such circumstances, it appears to me authority is not wanting for the view that when the legislature has supplied a code of procedure for obtaining judicial review, an award of arbitrators ought not to be impugned by action for a declaration when that code of procedure has not been followed.

***Sundry Workers v Antigua Hotel and Tourist Association* (1993) 42 WIR 145 (AG)**
Lord Bridge of Harwich

[PP147–148] Section 17(4) confines an appeal from the Industrial Court to the Court of Appeal to the grounds set out in subsection (1) and precludes any collateral challenge to a decision of the Industrial Court by judicial review or otherwise. But once the Court of Appeal has entertained an appeal from the Industrial Court and given its decision thereupon, Section 17(4) ceases to be of any relevance. The question whether an appeal lies from the decision of the Court of Appeal to Her Majesty in Council then falls to be determined in accordance with Section 122 of the Constitution and their Lordships can see no arguable ground for excluding such a decision from the ambit of the phrase 'any decision of the Court of Appeal in any civil or criminal matter' in Section 122(4) from which an appeal lies with the special leave of Her Majesty . . . [P155] It appears to their lordships that when the Industrial Court has found that employees have been unfairly dismissed the necessary implication of such a finding is that the dismissals were in circumstances that were 'not in accordance with the principles of good industrial relations practice'. From this it must follow that no appeal lies against the awards of compensation made by the Industrial Court in this case.

Where there is delay and a party successfully obtains leave at an *ex parte* hearing of an application for leave for judicial review, the court retains the right at the substantive hearing of the application, to re-examine the grant of leave and to set aside the order of leave in specific circumstances.

***In the Application of Sanatan Dharma Maha Sabha of Trinidad and Tobago* – HCA No S 1095 of 2004 (TT)**
Gobin J

[P4] 11. I find that in a case of alleged continuing illegality, the issue of delay cannot be so stringently regarded. 12. I find further that the issue raised by the Applicant is one of resolving sufficient importance and one which requires a resolution by the Court. The delay notwithstanding, I exercised my discretion to grant leave.

Judith Jones J

[PP7–9] Section 11(2) of the Act mandates the Court at the stage of the application for leave, if it considers that there has been undue delay in bringing the application, to consider whether the grant of leave would cause substantial hardship to or substantially prejudice the rights of any person, or would be detrimental to good administration. To my mind therefore, once the Court considers that there has been undue delay it is entitled to receive facts relevant to a determination as to whether the grant of leave would cause substantial hardship, prejudice the rights of any person or be detrimental to good administration. It is unrealistic to assume that these facts could or would be placed before the Court by an Applicant for leave. It is hardly likely that an Applicant seeking leave to review a decision of a Respondent would be in a position to place before the Court facts showing that the grant of such relief would cause substantial hardship etc. or indeed be expected to do more than answer any such queries put to them by the Judge on their *ex parte* application. To expect an Applicant to do more than this would, to my mind, be an extremely unfair burden to place on an Applicant. How then is the Judge to be informed of facts relating to the risk of substantial hardship to or the likelihood that the granting of the order would substantially prejudice the rights of any person or would be detrimental to good administration? This question is of particular importance since Section 11 mandates that this be considered at the stage of the grant of leave. It must be that the legislature anticipated that a Respondent would be given the opportunity to put evidence relevant to those issues before the Court and/or be entitled to address the Court on the said issues. This, it would seem, can only be achieved where the Court on the *ex parte* application being made defers the granting of the leave until the Respondent has been served with the documents, or specifically reserves the question of delay to the Judge hearing the substantive application as was done in the case of *Fishermen and Friends of the Sea v The Environmental Management Authority and BP Trinidad and Tobago LLC* CA No 106 of 2002 or if the Respondent is allowed to adduce such evidence and/or to address the Court on the point on an application to set aside the leave granted. This course of action, suggested by Sharma JA in the case of *Jones v Solomon* (1989) 41 WIR 299, and Lord Slynn in *R v The Criminal Injuries Compensation Board, Ex Parte A* [1999] 2 AC 330 was accepted by Hamel-Smith J in the *Balwant case*. To my mind the latter course must be an option available to a Respondent in circumstances where there has been undue delay in applying for leave to seek judicial review and leave has been granted on an *ex parte* application, even in circumstances where the Court has expressly extended the time for the filing of the application. In the circumstances I am of the opinion that the Court has jurisdiction to set aside the grant of leave made *ex parte* in circumstances where

1. It is plainly unjustified; or
2. It is vitiated by non-disclosure of relevant facts; or
3. Where there has been undue delay and the Respondent wishes to bring to the Court new facts and/or to address the Court on matters within the ambit of Section 11(2) of the Act.

[PP12–13] The Act does not define what is good administration. Is it merely the smooth running of a particular body or must it have a 'public aspect' to it? In the case of *Caswell and Another v Dairy Produce Quota Tribunal for England and Wales* [1990] AC 738 Lord Goff in dealing with the equivalent English section quoted from the case of *O'Reilly v Mackman* [1983] 2 AC 237 at page 280–281 where Lord Diplock stated: 'The public interest in good administration requires that public authorities and third parties should not be kept in suspense as to the legal validity of a decision the authority has reached in purported exercise of decision-making powers for any longer period than is absolutely necessary in fairness to the person affected by the decision.' Lord Goff goes on to say at page 749 E of the judgment in Caswell: 'I do not consider that it would be wise to attempt to formulate any precise definition or description of what constitutes detriment to good administration. This is because applications for judicial review may occur in different situations, and the need for finality may be greater in one context than in another. But it is of importance to observe that Section 31(6) recognizes that there is an interest in good administration independently of hardship, or of prejudice to the rights of third parties, and that the harm suffered by the Applicant by reason of the decision which has been impugned is a matter which can be taken into account by the Court in deciding whether or not to exercise its discretion under Section 31(6) to refuse the relief sought by the Applicant. In asking the question whether the grant of such relief would be detrimental to good administration, the Court is at this stage looking at the interest in good administration independently of matters such as these.' To my mind the fact that the Act seeks to draw a distinction between substantial hardship, substantial prejudice and detriment to good administration suggests that what is required in order to show a detriment to good administration would be more than merely a deleterious effect on the day to day administration of a particular body, in this case the Central Bank. A Respondent would have to show that if the relief was to be granted, in the circumstances of the undue delay, that it is the public interest in good administration that would suffer. This public interest may be directly related to a particular institution or it may be in respect of general public policy but it cannot be found on facts which merely show hardship or prejudice to the rights of a particular person or body, these situations are already covered by the first two grounds stated in the section.

4.4 MATERIAL DISCLOSURE

A person seeking judicial review must make all material disclosures pertinent to the action under review, as the failure to make such disclosures may result in a court electing not to examine the substantial merits of a judicial review application and dismiss it. It should be noted that while this is generally the law, it seems that courts inevitably look at the merits of the matter even though they may have already signalled an intention to dismiss the judicial review application because of the failure to make all material disclosures.

***In the Application of Dennis Graham* – HCA No S-156 of 2005 (TT)**
Pemberton J

[P14] The ACP Graham did not fulfill the duty of candour at the leave stage, not having disclosed fully the provisions of the MVRTA. This is a material non-disclosure of law and is sufficient to set aside the leave granted. Further ACP Graham did not, on the face of his application demonstrate a sufficient interest as required by Section 6(2) of the Act or that he was adversely affected by the Traffic Regulations as is required by Section 5(2)(a) of the Act.

***In the Application of Sabita Jagessar, Hazra Ramjohn, Nirmala Lokhai* –**
HCA No S 2053 of 2002 (TT)
Dean-Armorer J

[P48] The test of what is material is whether the Court which granted leave would have done so if the disclosure in question had been made . . . [P49] I am mindful that the second and third Respondents have been the unfortunate and innocent victims in this case of a series of errors and I express the hope that they might be able to recover redress at some later date.

***In the Application of Nigel Rajcoomar* – HCA No S 1008 of 2000 (TT)**
Dean-Armorer J

[P12] 18. I am of the view that this lack of frankness was material in that it would have been clear to the learned trial Judge who heard the application for leave, if the truth were told, that the Applicant chose not to avail himself of his right to approach a Judge in Chambers for his bail to be reviewed. The Applicant's lack of frankness operated, in all probability, quite deliberately, to conceal his failure to use an effective available alternative remedy. 19. A material non-disclosure entitles the Court to dismiss the Application without enquiring into the merits thereof. I am also inclined to refuse the Application because the Applicant had at his disposal an effective alternative remedy and no special circumstances have been revealed.

***In the Application of Star Telecommunications Company Ltd* –**
HCA No Cv 1713 of 1999 (TT)
Jamadar J

[PP18–20] Finally, a lot of argument took place on the relevance to judicial review proceedings of the principles of non-disclosure as stated by Ralf-Gibson LJ in *Brink's Mat*

Ltd. [1988] WLR 1350 at 1356F to 1357F: In considering whether there has been relevant non-disclosure and what consequence the Court should [attach] to any failure to comply with the duty to make full and frank disclosure, the principles relevant to the issues in these appeals appear to me to include the following:

1. The Duty of the Applicant is to make 'a full and fair disclosure of all the material facts:' see *Rex v Kensington Income Tax Commissioners, Ex Parte Princess Edmond de Polignac* [1917] 1 KB 486, 514, *per* Scrutton L.J.
2. The material facts are those which it is material for the Judge to know in dealing with the application as made: materiality is to be decided by the Court and not by the assessment of the Applicant or his legal advisers: see *Rex v Kensington Income Tax Commissioners, per* Lord Cozens-Hardy MR, at p 504, citing *Dalglish v Jarvie* (1850) 2 Mac, & G. 231, 238, and *Browne-Wilkinson J. Thermax Ltd. v Schott Industrial Glass Ltd.* [1981] FSR 289, 295.
3. The Applicant must make proper inquiries before making the application: see *Bank Mellat v Nikpour* [1985] FSR 87. The duty of disclosure therefore applies not only to material facts known to the Applicant but also to any additional facts which he would have known if he had made such inquiries.
4. The extent of the inquiries which will be held to be proper, and therefore necessary, must depend on all the circumstances of the case including (a) the nature of the case which the Applicant is making when he makes the application; and (b) the order for which application is made and the probable effect of the order on the Defendant: see, for example, the examination by Scott J of the possible effect of an Anton Piller order in *Columbia Picture Industries Inc. v Robinson* [1987] Ch 38; and (c) the degree of legitimate urgency and the time available for the making of inquiries: see *per* Slade L.J. in *Bank Mellat v Nikpour* [1985] FSR 87, 92–93.
5. If material non-disclosure is established the Court will be 'astute to ensure that a plaintiff who obtains [an *ex parte* injunction] without full disclosure . . . is deprived of any advantage he may have derived by that breach of duty': see *Per* Donaldson L.J. in *Bank Mellat v Nikpour*, at p 91, citing Warrington L.J. in the *Kensington Income Tax Commissioners' case* [1917] 1 KB 486, 509.
6. Whether the fact not disclosed is of sufficient materiality to justify or require immediate discharge of the order without examination of the merits depends on the importance of the fact to the issues which were to be decided by the Judge on the application. The answer to the question whether the non-disclosure was innocent, in the sense that the fact was not known to the Applicant or that its relevance was not perceived, is an important consideration but not decisive by reason of the duty on the Applicant to make all proper inquiries and to give careful consideration to the case being presented.
7. Finally, it 'is not for every omission that the injunction will be automatically discharged. A *locus poenitentiae* may sometimes be afforded': *Per* Lord Denning MR in *Bank Mellat v Nikpour* [1985] FSR 87, 90. The Court has a discretion notwithstanding proof of material non-disclosure which justifies or requires the immediate discharge of the *ex parte* order, nevertheless to continue the order, or to make a new order on terms.

> 'when the whole of the facts, including that of the original non-disclosure, are before [the Court, it] may well grant . . . a second injunction if the original non-disclosure was innocent and if an injunction could properly be granted even had the facts been disclosed': *Per* Glidewell L.J. in *Lloyds Bowmaker Ltd. v Britannia Arrow Holdings Plc*, ante, pp 1343H–1344A.

[P21] Nevertheless, I think the statements in *Brink's Mat* as to the compelling duty to make proper inquires and to disclose all material facts, are relevant to and support the approach of the public law Courts in dealing with the issue of non-disclosure and the exercise of the discretionary power to refuse relief on that ground . . . [P22] In my opinion, the weight of authority is for proper inquiries and full disclosure in discharge of an ineluctable duty of candour to the Court. I am also inclined to the view that StarTel has failed to demonstrate the degree of candour that is required in cases such as these and that the non-disclosure complained of is of a sufficient materiality and importance to the issues to be determined in this case, to justify the refusal of any relief in this matter. However, I will reserve final comment on this issue until a full consideration of all other issues that have been raised.

***In the Application of Charmaine Johnson* – HCA No 949 of 1999 (TT)**
Mendonca J

[P10] It is not in dispute that the Applicant did not disclose that there was an enquiry conducted by Mr Lewis when she gave him a statement. But it is not every non-disclosure that will result in the guilty party being shut out . . . [PP11–12] In HCA No. 3123 of 1991 *Seereeram Brothers Limited v Central Tenders Board*, Jones J after reviewing certain of the authorities on non disclosure including the *Brink's Mat Case*, concluded (at p 29), with which I concur, 'The approach suggests that not every omission would result in the offending party being shut out; the circumstances of each case must be fully examined. The Court must consider whether the facts not disclosed are of sufficient materiality to justify or require immediate discharge of the order without examination of the merits. This would depend on the importance of the fact to the issues which are to be decided on this application'.

***In the Application of Air Caribbean Ltd* – HCA No 707 of 1998 (TT)**
Hosein J

[P8] It is the duty of a Respondent to make full disclosure to a public law Court if an Applicant can satisfy such a Court that the facts are sufficient to entitle it to apply for judicial review or relief under the Constitution . . . [P10] A Court engaged in reviewing a decision of the Respondent in circumstances where an Applicant satisfies it that the facts are sufficient to entitle it to apply for judicial review, expects the Respondent to fully comply with the strictures enunciated by Lord Donaldson in *Ex Parte Huddleston*. Indeed this Court asserts, that in circumstances such as these, a Respondent is obliged to give a public law Court a full and fair disclosure as to how the Respondent arrived at its decision. Moreover its affidavits should depose with particularity to the decision making process. This level of disclosure is necessary so as to enable a Court whilst reviewing the process to have the benefit of all the relevant information regarding the process . . . [P11] It is not good enough for the Respondent to have made on its behalf, an affidavit that is bare on the details and which states that the Respondent had considered the Applicant's representations and was satisfied that it would not adversely affect the Applicant. The requirement of disclosure is founded on the notion that decision makers more often than not have access to information that is not within the knowledge or even the reach of an Applicant. Therefore once an Applicant crosses the evidential threshold required to apply for judicial review it is now the duty of the decision maker to explain 'what has occurred and why'. The highest standards of public administration demanded that the Respondent now faced with those allegations had a duty to place 'all the cards upwards on the table'.

***In the Application of Rapid Response Security Services Company Ltd* –**
HCA No 373 of 1996 (TT)
Stollmeyer J

[P9] The disclosure of facts in an application such as this is not, as was so correctly pointed out by both Advocates appearing in this matter, something for the Applicant to decide, nor is it something for its Attorneys to decide. It is for the Court to decide and there is ample authority to be cited in support of this proposition . . . [P10] As to whether the facts not disclosed were material to such a degree that the Applicant should be denied the relief it seeks is not perhaps so easily determined. Upon the totality of all that is before me, however, it is my view that the non-disclosure was sufficiently material . . . [PP10–11] Having so ordered it is therefore not necessary for me to deal with other issues. Suffice it to say, however, I am of the view that the first-named Respondent afforded the Applicant the opportunity, and sufficient opportunity at that, to put to the first-named Respondent full and detailed reasons, supported by the opinions of experts where necessary or desirable, in an effort to persuade the first-named Respondent that the firearm users' licence should not be revoked upon the grounds which the first-named Respondent proposed to do so . . . [P11] Further, there is nothing before me to persuade me that the first-named Respondent's decision was manifestly unreasonable given what was before him at the time he made his decision not that he acted capriciously, improperly or otherwise other than he might have been reasonably expected to decide on the facts and matters before them.

***In the Application of Ashmeed Mohammed* – HCA No 3924 of 1992 (TT)**
Warner J

[PP16–17] Moreover, that apart, can this Court come to the aid of the litigant who has admitted that he consciously and deliberately inserted an incorrect date on an affidavit? Was not the purpose to place his application in a light, which he conceived to be more favourable to him? I am of the view therefore, that the Applicant's misconduct would disentitle him to relief.

***In the Application of Michael Brasse* – HCA No 734 of 1992 (TT)**
Jones J

[P11] I agree with the interpretation placed by Attorney for the Respondent on paragraph 12 of the Applicant's affidavit set out earlier in this judgment, the Courts have a function to examine the effect of such non disclosure before taking any step to shut out the opposite party. To produce that result the non disclosure must go to the root of the issue before the Court . . . [PP11–12] In *Brink's Mat. Ltd. v Elcombe* (1988), Slade LJ, having said that the principle of full disclosure is an extremely important one, continued at page 194–195: 'Nevertheless, the nature of the principle, as I see it, is essentially penal and in its application the practical realities of any case before the Court cannot be overlooked. By their very nature, *ex parte* applications usually necessitate the giving and taking of instructions and the preparation of the requisite drafts in some haste. Particularly in heavy commercial cases, the borderline between material facts and non-material facts may be a somewhat uncertain one. While in no way discounting the heavy duty of candour and care which falls on persons making *ex parte* applications, I do not think the application of the principle should be carried to extreme lengths. In one or two other recent cases coming before the Court, I have suspected signs of a growing tendency on the part of some litigants against whom *ex parte* injunctions have been granted, or of their legal advisers, to rush to the *R v Kensington Tax Comrs* principle as a *tabula in naufragio*, alleging material non-disclosure on sometimes rather slender grounds, as representing substantially the only hope of obtaining the discharge of injunctions in cases where there is little hope of doing so on the substantial merits of the case or on the balance of convenience.' While I am in no way attributing conduct as cited above to the Respondent's Attorney, I have cited the above passage to demonstrate the new approach of the Courts to the question of non disclosure. The rigid position taken in the *Kensington Tax Commissioners case* [1917] 1 KB 436 is no longer applied.

***In the Application of Ramnath Guptar* – HCA No S–1096 of 1988 (TT)**
Wills J

[PP8–9] It follows therefore that an Applicant for Judicial Review has a duty *uberrimae fidei* to disclose all relevant information available to him. And recent developments in this regard have shown that whilst such duty rests primarily upon the Applicant it also applies to attorneys advising such Applicants since they owe a duty to the Court to be frank in making *ex parte* applications; consequently attorneys as advisers should satisfy themselves that they are fully aware of all the material facts which ought to be disclosed ... [P9] In the result therefore, the law is that, where an *ex parte* application has been made to the Court for a rule *nisi* or other process, if the Court comes to the conclusion that the affidavit in support of the application was not candid and did not fairly state the facts, but stated in such a way as to mislead the Court as to the true facts, the Court ought for its own protection and to prevent an abuse of its process, to refuse to proceed any further with the examination of the merits. The power of the Court not to enquire into the merits ought only to be exercised in circumstances where the Court is satisfied that there is deception. However, a Court should only come to the conclusion that there has been deception after careful examination of the facts as they are and as they have been stated in the Applicant's affidavit.

***In the Application of Carson Haynes* – HCA No 1039 of 1988 (TT)**
Hosein J

[P10] The failure by the Applicant to disclose the allegations made against him and his letter of response thereto constitutes a suppression of material facts and I consider that a gross deception had been practiced on this Court by the Applicant at the time of his *ex parte* application. For this reason alone it would be proper, in my view, to dismiss the application.

***In the Application of Matthew Joseph, Asad Ali, Soogrim Bhaggan, Gunness Bhagewandeen, Rampersad Ragoo, Reeka Rampersad, Francis Gopaul, Clement Brizan, Radhay Kissoon, Jankinath Sookdeo, Ian Johnson, Seepersad Singh* – HCA No S–611 of 1988 (TT)**
Blackman J

[P27] I have already dealt in detail with the marked divergence between what was stated in the affidavits of the Applicants particularly when leave was sought and the facts that later came to light in the affidavit of Victoria Mendez-Charles and in the cross-examination of the Applicants. There is a clear conclusion in my view from what was later disclosed that the Applicants misled the Court in their application for leave by concealing their true position. They made it appear that they were enclosed and had no other means of egress except by going onto the Highway and hence their reason for erecting the structures. I think that their affidavits were so worded to make their application for leave attractive and convincing. In so doing the Court was deceived. Reeka Rampersad may be considered an exception but in this regard all the other Applicants acted with a glaring display of lack of *uberrima fides*. In their case therefore, although I have dealt with the other submissions and concluded that they were not well founded, on the ground of non-disclosure of material facts alone, I would have followed the same course in any event as had been adopted by Viscount Reading C.J. in the *De Polignac case* and dismiss their applications.

***In the Application of Republic Bank Ltd* – HCA No 6921 of 1987 (TT)**
Deyalsingh J

[P8] It is clear that on application for leave to apply for judicial review the Applicant must show *uberrima fides*, and if leave is obtained on false statements or a suppression of material facts in the affidavit, the Court may refuse an order on this ground alone ... [PP9–10] It is a very serious matter to deny a litigant a hearing on the merits and the Courts will not do so merely on the ground of non-disclosure. The authorities bear out the proposition that:

i. the non-disclosure must be of material facts which lead to the clear inference (if not directly established) that the Applicant has tried to conceal something which might work to his advantage, if disclosed. Mere non-disclosure is not enough. It must amount to a suppression of material facts with an element of *mala fides*;

ii. where the non-disclosure is of facts found not to be material, there must be clear evidence of an intention to mislead or deceive the Court. The Court simply will not assist an Applicant in an interlocutory matter who has deliberately set out to mislead or deceive it; and

iii. where the non-disclosure is inadvertent the question arises whether, if disclosure had been made, the *ex parte* order would have been granted. If the Order would not have been granted then the subsequent proceedings would be dismissed because the Applicant would have misled the Court, albeit innocently, and obtained an Order which he should not have obtained in the first place.

Although material non-disclosures are usually grounds for rejection of an application for judicial review, the application may still be allowed where the judicial review of the decision of a public body ought to be examined by the courts in the public interest.

***In the Application of Chandresh Sharma* – HCA No Cv S2005 of 2004 (TT)**
Jamadar J

[P16] In all of these circumstances I hold that the Applicant had available to him an alternative form of redress (Section 38A of the FOIA) and was obliged pursuant to Section 9 of the JRA and Order 53 Rule 3(2)(a)(vi) to at least disclose this. No doubt, if this had been disclosed, a Court would have been put on notice and may have requested submissions from the Applicant; or may have convened an *inter partes* hearing for leave; or may have stayed the proceeding; or even refused leave *ex parte*. This Court frowns upon this sort of non-disclosure, as it undermines the very basis upon which judicial review proceedings are founded—the exercise of judicial discretion in the realm of public administration. It cannot be overstated that in judicial review, relief is not as of right, but is a matter of discretion. Even where public administration may be shown to be flawed, relief can be refused. This process of discernment and of the exercise of discretion is intended to begin at the leave stage—and for good reason, because judicial review is a remedy of last resort, not a weapon of first strike. The implications of this non-disclosure for this case will be dealt with below . . . [P17] In light of the above, what effect should the non-pursuit and/or non-disclosure of the alternative form of redress prescribed by Section 38A of the FOIA have on this case? In my opinion the issues raised in this case are of public importance. Of prime importance is the public's right of access pursuant to the FOIA to information held by the IC. Also of general importance is the approach to be taken by the Courts and public authorities to the interpretation and application of the FOIA. In this context one cannot lose sight of the history, reality and aspirations of the community in relation to persons in public life, public authorities, the IC and the State's needs and concerns with respect to these. In this regard the role and function of the Court includes ensuring that the intention of Parliament and the will of the people are not frustrated. For these reasons, in the special circumstances of this case, this Court in the exercise of its discretion will not deem these proceedings an abuse of process and will allow the Applicant limited relief (set out below). However, the non-pursuit and non-disclosure of the alternative redress to the Ombudsman will affect this Court's order for costs, as also explained below.

4.5 PRIVATE VERSUS PUBLIC FUNCTION

Judicial review will not lie against an administrative body engaged in a private act but only where the decision complained of was taken as part of the exercise by the public body of a public function. Typically, cases that involve breach of contract, either employment contracts or otherwise, are treated as being more appropriate for private law.

In the Application of Seebalack Singh – HCA No S430 of 2003 (TT)
Tiwary-Reddy J

[P14] Having reviewed the authorities cited and the statutory provisions and considering that the MD is charged with the day to day administration and control of the business of the Bank and is answerable to the Board which is itself charged with managing the Bank, I hold that the Board was exercising functions of a public nature when it hired the Applicant and that this is not a pure master and servant situation . . . [P16] In the result, I hold also that the Board was exercising a public law function when it terminated the Applicant's employment for failing to implement the Board's decision.

In the Application of Vashti Sampson, Rajh Basdeo, Indar Samaroo, Grantly Prescott and James Chinapoo – HCA No S–157 of 2003 (TT)
Bereaux J

[P23] The legality of the Respondent's resort to self-help (if in fact undertaken by the Respondent) is an issue of private law between the Respondent and the occupier so affected. If the Applicants or any of them claim some licence or interest consequent upon acquiescence, then they can pursue it in the ordinary way . . . [P25] They are squatters. However sympathetic one may be of their plight the law recognizes the right of the lawful owner to evict them. In deciding to evict them, the lawful owner is not bound to give them a hearing. The fact that the owner is a statutory corporation makes it no less entitled to do so. Nor is its action unreasonable or improper. If the Applicants claim to have acquired rights by reason of their occupation, the common law will accommodate an action in pursuit of those rights and to that extent they will have the protection of the law.

In the Application of Sabita Jagessar, Hazra Ramjohn, Nirmala Lokhai –
HCA No S 2053 of 2002 (TT)
Dean-Armorer J

[P47] The matter does not end there. The Court is now required to consider whether the Applicants are entitled in public law to any relief . . . In my judgment the compelling answer to this question must be in the affirmative. Mr Dabideen, in both acts of eviction and of allocation, was acting in his capacity as Chairman and was recognized as such by all concerned, including the Applicants. It is also beyond dispute that by his actions he was seeking to achieve a benefit for the residents of the municipality, by stimulating trade and creating avenues of employment to those whom he perceived as disadvantaged. Whether his actions were unfortunately misguided raises other issues. I therefore hold that there is an adequate presence of a public law element in this case to empower the Court to exercise its supervisory jurisdiction.

In the Application of Star Telecommunications Company Ltd –
HCA No Cv 1713 of 1999 (TT)
Jamadar J

[P10] First, he raised the question whether this application is rooted in public law and suggested that there was no sufficient public law element to bring the case within the scope of the Court's public law jurisdiction. Thus, the application should be dismissed . . . [PP12–13] It is clear therefore, that in determining whether there is a public law element, *the source of the power* is not the only consideration and the Courts will consider other relevant circumstances, such as *the nature of the function* and *the subject matter of the claim*. So far as the source of the power is concerned and so far as is relevant to this case, '**powers** derived from the royal prerogative are classed as public, and to the extent that such powers are reviewable at all, are reviewable by way of application for judicial review,' (Lewis, page 13) . . . [PP15–16] I am of the view that in a developing democracy such as Trinidad and Tobago, where the state, acting by the central government through one of its Ministries, chooses to exercise its prerogative or common law power to contract and where the nature of that function is clearly public (as it is in this case), it cannot hide behind the veil of the 'contractual nature' of the exercise of its power. This is so, especially where (as in this case) what is being challenged, are alleged criteria laid down in advance by The Ministry and the exercise of the Minister's powers in relation to same in the context of procedural fairness. To my mind, the fact that if in these circumstances there was some statutory underpinning, there would have been a sufficient public law element to justify judicial review proceedings, operates in favour of concluding that there is a sufficient public law element in this case to bring it within the scope of judicial review proceedings ... In this post modern era, when the principles of transparency, openness and accountability are the increasing norm for the conduct of public affairs and the maintenance of a free and democratic society, there is no good reason why the exercise of central government's prerogative or common law power to contract should enjoy an exemption from judicial review of procedural impropriety, whether the challenge is on the basis of illegality, irrationality, abuse or excess of power or otherwise.

***In the Application of the Chairman, Alderman, Councillors and Electors of the Region of Tunapuna/Piarco Regional Corp.* – HCA No 1066 of 1999 (TT)**
Bereaux J

[P20] The true test of the Court's jurisdiction under Order 53 is whether the powers and functions of the Respondent are public in nature. It is that which determines the issue of jurisdiction. Whether the function arises out of statute or under a contract is no longer of singular significance. The question of reviewability is no longer answered only by identifying the source of the power being exercised by the decision-maker whose action is being challenged, although this remains a relevant consideration. The recent approach is to identify the type of functions performed by the public authority and to determine whether they are functions of a public law system, are of a public law character or have public law consequences.

***In the Application of Charmaine Johnson* – HCA No 949 of 1999 (TT)**
Mendonca J

[P21] The Respondent contends that if I should find that there is no sufficient public law remedy that I should not order that these proceedings be continued as if begun by writ pursuant to Order 53 Rule 9 of the Rules of the Supreme Court, 1975. The Applicant did not address this point and it seems to me unnecessary to decide it ... Firstly an order under Order 53 Rule 9 can only be made where there has been a breach of a public law obligation one of the consequences of which is to give rise to an entitlement of damages ... With respect therefore to the Applicant's removal from the band and choir that case is against the Applicant. Secondly the power to order the proceedings to continue as if begun by writ is discretionary. With respect to Applicant's claim that the warning letter has damaged her reputation, the claim in libel needs to be properly pleaded. This can more conveniently be done in new proceedings which, it appears to me, would result in an overall savings of costs.

***In the Application of Emmanuel Romain* – HCA No 2605 of 1996 (TT)**
Ramlogan J

[PP4–5] The issue in this case is whether the Applicant's employment had an element of public law which would entitle him to bring proceedings for Judicial Review or whether he ought to seek his redress by way of private law ... [P8] I do not agree with this for it is clear that the doctrine of legitimate expectation can only arise if there is a public law element. The doctrine cannot give rise to a public law element. The doctrine was developed in the area of public law for the control of the exercise of discretion by a public body performing a public function ... [P9] The dismissal of the Applicant was concerned with an employer and its employee. The Respondents in terminating the Applicant's services were not performing a public function even if it were decided that the Statutory Regulations which were abolished in 1980 applied by agreement.

***In the Application of Leo Cowie* – HCA No 124 of 1996 (TT)**
Sealey J

[P4] The issue then arises whether the cutting off of water supply from premises is a matter for public law. 'Public authorities may exceed or abuse their statutory, prerogative or other powers, or may fail properly to fulfill their statutory duties. These issues raise questions of public law, suitable for resolution by way of the judicial review procedure. The activities of public authorities may also raise questions of civil liability. In the course of exercising statutory powers public bodies may commit torts such as negligence, nuisance or trespass. In so far as these acts are not authorized by statute, the public authority may be liable in damages to the individual concerned. In addition, certain statutory duties give rise to liability in damages in the event of a breach of that duty. Public authorities may also enter into contracts which may give rise to disputes as to whether the terms of the contract have been breached.' (*Judicial Remedies In Public Law*—Clive Lewis, pages 48–49) . . . [P5] Notwithstanding the fact that the plaintiff is seeking damages for trespass it is clear to me that the acts complained of arise from the acts of the servants and/or agents in the exercise of their statutory function of cutting off the water supply of an allegedly delinquent ratepayer. It is not sufficient to simply couch the reliefs in the form of a private law action to bring the action within the realm of private law. One has to look at the acts complained of and determine whether they fall with the confines of the statutory powers of the Authority. I am not persuaded by any argument to the contrary . . . In the circumstances I find that the plaintiff cannot obtain judgment against the Defendant for its failure to file and serve a defence as this action should have been brought by way of leave for judicial view.

***In the Application of Sumayyah Mohammed* – HCA No 3000A of 1994 (TT)**
Warner J

[P14] So that, while not all of the activities of the Board may be of a governmental nature, I am of the view that when the Principal and the Board took a decision to refuse admission to the Applicant (dressed as she was) they were exercising functions of a governmental nature and of a coercive nature. Clearly neither was exercising a private function . . . [P33] In my view, there is no material to justify the conclusion which appears to be lurking in the minds of the Respondents that indiscipline would result if exemption were granted, or that the sense of loyalty to school and sense of tradition would in any way be eroded. While it is true that the Respondents have heard the Applicant's request for an exemption, their contention that they would have to accede to other requests suggests to me that they adhered to a fixed policy, paying little regard to the Applicant's reasons for the application for exemption . . . [P34] The Respondents clearly entertain the notion that the rules of the school are inflexible and that no accommodation can be made for a genuinely held religious belief. Each case must however be decided according to its factual background . . . *Have the Respondents failed to take into account matters which they ought to have taken into account*? Again, the starting point is the acceptance of the sincerity of belief. However, the Respondents do not appear to have taken into account the psychological effect of insisting that the Applicant remove the hijab; the ripping away of traditions which she has observed for half of her life. Secondly, the official position of the Ministry of Education is that they do not object to the wearing of the hijab: the inference being that it is not considered to be an act of indiscipline in the several public schools in which they are worn.

***In the Application of Daniel Chookolingo and Anne Marie Chookolingo* –**
HCA No 342 of 1993 (TT)
Sealey J

[P25] Does this fall under the umbrella of public law or is it a private law matter, considering that it refers to a change of user? It is my view that it arises solely from the relationship of landlord and tenant. The landlord/corporation has to ensure that the covenants under the lease are kept . . . [P26] The Corporation is a public authority, and it is my view that even though the contractual situation could as it has done here, effectively prevent the public law aspect from arising, one must ask one's self whether the first is so inextricably bound up with the other, that even though it is a private law issue, the prerogative writs should come into operation? . . . [P29] The Applicants in this case wish to impugn not a statutory determination of the Corporation, but a contractual decision. There is sufficient remedy in private law for this. I find therefore, that this is not an apt case for judicial review and the motion must fail.

***In the Application of Jessica Clarke* – HCA No 1048 of 1991 (TT)**
Permanand J

[P9] I have already pointed out that the fact of employment by a public authority does not *per se* render such employment subject to public law remedies as there must be statutory restrictions on dismissal which 'underpinned the employees' position' and thus allowing the decision making process to be questioned and thereby enabling an Applicant to be entitled to seek judicial review . . . [PP9–10] It is to be noted that where the Court considers that relief sought in judicial review proceedings should not be granted on an application for judicial review but might have been granted if it was sought in an action begun by Writ, the Court may instead of refusing the application order the proceedings to continue as if they had in fact been commenced by Writ of Summons. However, there is no converse power under the Rules of the Supreme Court to permit an action begun by Writ to continue as if it were an application for judicial review. The proceedings must be commenced afresh by an application for judicial review. See *O'Reilly v Mackman* (*supra*) at 1109—also Order 53/1–14/19 RS.C., the Supreme Court Practice 1985.

***In the Application of Jamaat Al Muslimeen* – HCA No 540 of 1990 (San F'do)/HCA No 2195 of 1990 (PoS) (TT)**
Blackman J

[P10] In my respectful and humble view, this appears to me to be the effect of Section 14 of the Constitution. In judicial review proceedings a person has no such choice. His remedy must be one in public law alone. There is no question of his having a remedy both in private law and in public law . . . Although, therefore, cases under the Constitution fall within the realm of public law, and judicial review cases are also within the realm of public, these two procedures are not necessarily interchangeable . . . [P13] It is manifest from the above principles that the source of the decision-making power in judicial review proceedings may emanate from: (a) a statute; (b) subordinate legislation made under a statute; or (c) the prerogative i.e. the common law. Decisions issuing from these sources of power are public law decisions amenable to judicial review . . . [P15] The question as to whether the Applicant is in lawful or unlawful occupation of the lands of the State is in my view a matter of private law not public law. A public law right only arises where the source of power purported to be exercised by the decision-maker is derived from statute, subordinate legislation, or the prerogative . . . [P16] The proper test of whether a body is subject to judicial review is not that it is a public authority, or that it is endowed with coercive power; the proper test as to whether a public body as decision maker is amenable to judicial review is that it must purport to act under a Statute, under subsidiary legislation or under prerogative . . . [P17] Attorney for the Applicant argued that even if the Court finds that the matter involves private law and not public law, the Court should make an order under Rule 9(5) of Order 53 ordering that proceedings should be continued as if begun by Writ . . . In any event even if the Court has the power under Rule 9(5) to order the proceedings to continue as if begun by writ, such a power is discretionary. In this case it seems to me that the best course would be to refuse the application leaving the Applicant to proceed in private law. In such circumstances, it will have an opportunity of properly formulating its case in an action commenced by writ. This will make for a tidier and proper way of dealing with the pleadings. I think the ends of justice will be better served in this way.

In the Application of the All Trinidad Sugar and General Workers Trade Union, Sultan Khan, Hilton Ramharrack, Rabindranath Seetahal, Cyril Tom and Pooran Rattan – **HCA No 437 of 1990 (TT)**
Permanand J

[P35] It is my opinion then that when Ministers perform executive acts they are performed by the Government and are either under statutory authority, for example Public Transport Service Corporation Act, Chap 48:02, Water and Sewerage Authority Act, Chap 54:40, National Insurance Act, Chap 32:01, Housing Act, Chap 33:01 or unwritten powers derived from the common law or prerogative as H.W.R. Wade describes it, namely, 'legal powers which appertains to the Crown but not to its subjects' . . . [P41] It is accepted that the Ministers perform public law functions towards Caroni (1975) Limited, so that, with regard to an important policy change as to the formation of a subsidiary Company of Caroni (1975) Limited and transfer of assets from Caroni (1975) Limited, it is my opinion that such a step would have a public law element sufficient, in my view for the Applicants to expect that there will be consultation . . . [P42] It is my opinion then that 'legitimate expectation' is entwined with the right to be heard and must therefore be determined on the surrounding relevant circumstances.

In the Application of Roland de Verteuil – **HCA No 4424 of 1987 (TT)**
Warner J

[P12] It would follow that the matter being a master and servant question there is no room for judicial review and that if there has been any wrong, it is in the field of contract and if there is to be any remedy, it must be sought by proceedings for breach of contract. However, in view of developments in more recent times in the field of public law and in the light of the distinction sought to be drawn between ordinary cases of breach of contract and the instant case, I shall see whether these developments or the particular distinction affect the position . . . [PP13–14] In the instant case far from underpinning the position of estate constables vis-à-vis their employers, Parliament has provided that the employer may dismiss them at any time. I therefore conclude that there is no public law element in the dismissal of Mr De Verteuil which could give rise to any entitlement to administrative law remedies.

In the Application of Republic Telecommunications Ltd – **HCA No 2253 of 1987 (TT)**
Gopeesingh J

[P14] I do not think it can be disputed that, in the instant matter, the plaintiff is seeking to challenge an administrative act or omission of a public authority charged with the performance of public acts and duties. He is complaining of the infringement, therefore, of a public law right . . . [PP17–18] It seems to me, therefore, that since the plaintiff is seeking to challenge the decision (an administrative act or omission) of a public authority charged with the performance of public acts and duties and consequently, he is complaining of the infringement of a public law right and all the remedies for the protection of this right, including that of a declaration, could have been obtained by an application for judicial review, having regard to all the circumstances of this matter, it would be contrary to public policy and an abuse of the process of the Court for the plaintiff to be permitted to seek redress by way of an originating summons. It matters not in my respectful view, that it is not an adjudication by a public authority but rather an administrative decision by that authority which is being challenged . . . [PP18–19] In my judgment, therefore, since the plaintiff in beginning these proceedings, failed to adopt the proper procedure, this failure amounts to an irregularity. And since the Defendants have chosen to seek that the Court so finds and no amendment can in fact cure such defect, and the Court cannot, in the circumstances, order that the proceedings be continued as if it had been begun under Order 53 and to allow it to continue as if it had begun under any other procedure would not avail the plaintiff, the provisions of Order 2 Rule 1(3) are not available to the plaintiff under the circumstances.

***In the Application of Tyrone Karran* – HCA No 1111 of 1987 (TT)**
Davis J

[P6] I have therefore to consider whether and to what extent the Applicant's complaints involve an element of public law sufficient to attract public law remedies, and in particular, whether certiorari would lie in this case or not . . . [P10] In my view this is not a case upon which the Court's Supervisory functions can be focused. It is a case in which mere private contractual rights are involved, and I accordingly have no jurisdiction to deal with it under Order 53 of the Rules of the Supreme Court.

***In the Application of Glen Adolphus Grant* – HCA No S. 2567 of 1986 (TT)**
Hosein J

[P13] The question therefore arises as to what extent the complaints made by the Applicants contain an element of public law sufficient to attract public law remedies. There is no doubt that the Applicants here were employed by a public statutory authority in which there is an element of public employment or service, even though their status is not one protected by statute as is, for example, that of Judges . . . [P18] In my view when one looks at the development of the rights of employees and the parallel revolution which took place in the Statutory provisions governing the relationship between the employers and employees, it must have been the intention to create a separate forum for the resolution of industrial disputes of any nature and to remove from the realm of public law situations like those in the instant case.

***In the Application of Shoeila Hadeed* – HCA No 3961 of 1985 (TT)**
Blackman J

[P20] In other words, the relationship here is one of master and servant and therefore no issue of administrative law arises. I cannot say that Parliament has underpinned the employment of the Applicant restricting the freedom of the Authority to dismiss the Applicant so as to give her public law rights. Therefore the procedure under Order 53 is inapplicable . . . [P27] I will grant the amendment in terms of the declaration and order that the proceedings continue as if begun by writ, also that the Applicant deliver her Statement of Claim within 21 days of the date hereof; that the defence be delivered within 21 days of the date of delivery of the Statement of Claim; and that the reply if necessary be delivered within 14 days of delivery of the defence.

***In the Application of Apprentice Jockey Flores* – HCA No 3564 of 1985 (TT)**
Permanand J

[PP7–8] From the above mentioned authorities it is clear that in order that there should be a remedy which makes available the relief granted under Order 53 there must be something more than a mere contractual right on which the Court's supervisory functions can be focused, as Certiorari is available to impugn a decision of a domestic tribunal which was performing a public duty. It is my view that the Rules of the Racing Authority under which the Authority operates are of a domestic character and regulate conditions under which licences are granted and withdrawn and discipline administered. The grant of a licence to the Applicant in my judgment constitutes a contract between the Authority and the Applicant and there is no element of public law involved when the disciplinary procedure laid down in the Rules are invoked which would attract administrative law remedies. The fact that the Applicant holds a licence issued by the Authority established under the Act or the fact the Authority under its Rules exercises discipline over the Applicant do not in my view give the Applicant any public law remedy arising out of the public rights and duties imposed on the Authority by the Act.

***In the Application of Trinidad and Tobago Racing Authority* – Civil Appeal No 63 of 1985 (TT)**
Davis JA

[P6] The determination of the question whether the issue before the Court was one founded in contract (a private law matter) or whether the issue involved a public law matter, viz, the derivation of the power of the Appellant to take disciplinary action against persons who breached its rules, was obviously of primary importance. If the Appellant, in carrying out its disciplinary functions, exercised a power derived from statute, then, *prima facie*, it was exercising a public law function, and all that would then have to be established was that the Appellant was, in addition, a public authority. The learned trial judge, while not stating definitively that the Appellant was not a public authority, appeared to me to have concluded that it was not . . . On the other hand, he also pointed out that even in case of a public authority where the cause of action truly lies in contract or tort or an analogous case, then a person is entitled to bring proceedings by writ or originating summons as if the public authority were not a public body . . . [P7] So the question must be faced. Is the Appellant a public authority or not? Courts of law wisely refrained from laying down any general definition of what is or is not a public authority. A public authority does have certain characteristics. Those characteristics have been set out in *Halsbury's Laws of England*, 3rd Ed., Vol. 30 para. 1317 as follows: 'A public authority is a body, not necessarily a county council, Municipal Corporation or other local authority, which has public or statutory duties to perform, and which perfoms those duties and carries out its transactions for the benefit of the public and not for private profit. Such an authority is not precluded from making a profit for the public benefit, but commercial undertakings acting for profit and trading corporations making profits for their corporators are not public authorities even if conducting undertakings of public utility.' Bearing those characteristics in mind, I now turn to consider whether the Trinidad and Tobago Racing Authority (the Authority) incorporated by Act of Parliament, namely the Trinidad and Tobago Racing Authority Act, Ch. 21 No. 50 (the Act) is or is not a public authority . . . [P8] I am satisfied, therefore, that the Racing Authority is not a trading corporation set up for the purpose of making a commercial profit. In my view, the Racing Authority has public and statutory duties to perform, and performs those duties for the benefit of public. The Authority, therefore, has the characteristics of a public authority, and I would hold that it is in fact a public authority . . . [P9] This was a public law matter which ought to have been commenced against the Racing Authority, a public authority, by invoking the Court's jurisdiction under Order 53 of the Rules of the Supreme Court.

***In the Application of Charles Ganga-Singh* – Supreme Court No M-156 of 2002 (JM)**
Mangatal J

[P4] It was common ground on both sides that for the decision of the Commission to be amenable to judicial review there has to be an issue of public law involved in this case . . . [PP26–28] To decide this issue it is important to review the principles concerning the relationship of master and servant:

(a) Whether a dismissal from employment by a public authority is subject to public law remedies depends on whether there were special statutory restrictions on dismissal which underpinned the employee's position, and not on the fact of employment by a public authority or the interest of the public in the functioning of the authority—*R v East Berkshire Health Authority, Ex Parte Walsh; R v Civil Service Appeal Board, Ex Parte Bruce.*

(b) The statutory underpinning may arise by implication under the principal Statute or Regulations—*Malloch's case* [1971] 2 All ER 1278, as explained by May LJ at 435f–436h of *East Berks Health Authority.*

(c) Some of the earlier decisions in this general field, such as in *Malloch's case* were decided before the enactment of any of the modern employment protection legislation. The concept of natural justice involved in many of these cases is now subsumed in that of an unfair dismissal—May LJ 434g and 436f in the *East Berkshire case*. In Jamaica we have extensive modern legislation in the form of the Labour Relations and Industrial Disputes Act and Code dealing with industrial disputes and unfair dismissal.

(d) If there are statutory restrictions requiring the employer, a statutory body, to contract with the employee in a certain way and the employer fails to secure those private rights for the employee, then the employee of a statutory authority who does not receive those rights has an administrative law remedy by way of judicial review—Sir John Donaldson MR—431 b-*East Berks Health Authority*.

(e) However, where he is the recipient of these rights, or conditions but his complaint is that under those conditions he was deprived of certain rights or was not afforded natural justice, then his complaint is really one of unfair dismissal to be directed to an industrial disputes tribunal—431 c–d and 436f–437b *East Berks Health Authority*.

(f) There are four distinct areas of law potentially involved in the cases dealing with master and servant relationships between employees and statutory bodies. These are the common law, the law of contract, the law dealing with unfair dismissal, dealt with by an industrial disputes tribunal and administrative law in the form of judicial review. '*The ordinary employer is free to act in breach of his contracts of employment and if he does so his employee will acquire certain private law rights and remedies in damages for wrongful dismissal, compensation for unfair dismissal, an order for reinstatement or reengagement and so on. Parliament can underpin the position of public authority employees by restricting the freedom of the public authority to dismiss, thus giving the employee "public law" rights and at least making him a potential candidate for administrative law remedies. Alternatively, it can require the authority to contract with its employees upon specified terms with a view to the employee acquiring "private law" rights under the terms of the contract of employment. If the authority fails or refuses thus to create "private law" rights for the employee, the employee will have "public law" rights to compel compliance, the remedy being mandamus requiring the authority so to contract or a declaration that the employee has those rights. If, however, the authority gives the employee the required contractual protection, a breach of that contract is not a matter of "public law" and gives rise to no administrative law remedies*—Donaldson MR—*East Berks Health Authority*—430 e–g.

(g) Where a public authority has acted in breach of its own dismissal procedures but these procedures are not statutorily underpinned, the employee may succeed in an unfair dismissal application. Judicial Review will not in those circumstances be appropriate.

[PP29–30] As I have indicated, the central issue in determining this preliminary point involves a finding as to whether there is any public law issue. I have found that there is none. The application on behalf of the Commission is for the proceedings to be struck out. There is however power to transfer proceedings from one division of the Court to another. Indeed, under the CPR this is to be encouraged, since, provided a transfer is appropriate, it may result in the saving of time and expense for the parties. Under Rule 56.10 of the CPR which deals with administrative claims, and is headed 'Joinder of Claims for other relief' the Court may direct that the whole application be dealt with as a claim, as opposed to an administrative law claim, and give appropriate directions under Parts 26 and 27 of the CPR. These Parts deal with case management of private law claims. Also, Rule 26.9(3) states that where there has been an error of procedure the Court may make an order to put things right. However, it is to be noted that in this case there is no claim by the Applicant for relief, which has as its proper basis, private law rather than public law. The relief claimed here is principally for certiorari/mandamus, and the declaration and injunction claimed stand or fall on the appropriateness of judicial review. There is here no claim for damages. Further, any issues of unfair dismissal have to be dealt with by the Industrial Disputes Tribunal and cannot be dealt with by the Supreme Court. It would therefore seem to me that this would not be an appropriate case to order the proceedings to continue as a claim. See *East Berks Health Authority* paragraph 2 of the Headnote and the pages of the Judgment there cited. Like Sir John Donaldson MR at 429a of *East Berks Health Authority*, I take the view that the term 'abuse' has offensive overtones and 'misuse' is a more appropriate term to use when making a ruling in relation to the continuance of the application for judicial review. The preliminary point succeeds. My ruling is that the remedy of judicial review is wholly inappropriate and the continuation of the application for judicial review would be a misuse of the process of the Court. Accordingly the application for judicial review is dismissed.

***Regina v The Principal of the Norman Manley Law School ex parte Janet Mignott* – Supreme Court No M-9 of 2002 (JM)**
Daye J (Ag.)

[PP6–7] Just to say from the outset that, in my view, if on an *ex parte* application for leave, the application cannot survive a preliminary objection or an objection *in limine* such as the Court has no jurisdiction to hear it because it is founded in private Law, i.e. contract, tort, or any private right conferred by statute and not in public law, then it will fail the test that there is a *prima facie* arguable case . . . [P21] Mr Justice Carey Judge of Appeal in *Binger's case* (*supra*) emphasized that the remedies for judicial review are discretionary. They were subject to the common law, especially the rule in contract that a Court will not grant specific performance of a contract of employment 'in the absence of special circumstances'. He said if the effect of granting the remedy of Certiorari of Declaration would be to enforce specific performance of contract of employment then either remedy would not be granted. The effect of asking to obtain Certiorari or Mandamus by the Applicant in respect to her position as Course Director would be to enforce specific performance of an implied [term] of the contract of employment. This would not be entertained or granted in public law or administrative law. The contract of the Applicant is a simple contract of employment. It is not buttressed by any statutory or special procedure about assignment or re-assignment of her duties. Her contract is not injected with or is underpinned by any public law element. Therefore the preliminary objection to her *ex parte* or *inter partes* application for leave in our Court will be upheld.

***Bryan Sykes v The Minister of National Security and Justice and the Attorney-General; Legal Officers Staff Association v The Minister of National Security and Justice and the Attorney-General* (1993) 30 JLR 76 (JM)**
Downer JA

[P79] It is settled law that the remedies by way of prerogative orders are discretionary. Leave has to be sought to institute proceedings. By such provisions, the common law provides effective means of challenging public authorities while at the same time recognizing that, for the executive to function properly, the law must provide some protection. No such protection need be accorded to the executive when there is a claim for salaries for services rendered pursuant to a contract of employment. Such a claim is governed by the ordinary common law and the provisions of the Crown Proceedings Act.

Patterson JA (Ag.)

[P88] Since wages arise from a contract the claimant must prove his entitlement. Remuneration is always a matter of private law . . . [P92] It is clear that on the facts of this, that the substance of the officers' claim was an assertion of their rights in private law, and accordingly, I agree with Mr Chin See that those proceedings for prerogative remedies amount to an abuse of the process of the Court. For these reasons above, the Appellant is not entitled to the relief sought.

***R v Binger, N.J. Vaughan and Scientific Research Council ex parte Chris Bobo Squire* (1984) 21 JLR 118 (JM)**
Carberry JA

[P151] As to the argument at (b) I have already discussed the status of the Council: It is an ordinary corporation set up for the job of fostering and co-ordinating scientific research in this island: (sec. 5(1)). The Appellant's contract of employment lacks even the 'statutory flavour' existing in a case such as *Barber v Manchester Regional Hospital Board* and the mere fact that it is a statutory corporation does not give to its employees any particular status: See the *Vidyodaya University case.* I have been unable in this case to find anything that would lead to the conclusion that the Appellant enjoyed or occupied a 'Public Office' within the meaning in which those words are used in this context. It was in my view a simple master and servant or employer and employee relationship. The result is that neither certiorari nor a declaration could be made in this case. And I therefore see no reason to disagree with the judgment of the Chief Justice who decided the case on this issue. So too did Orr, J, though for the reasons indicated above I do not find it necessary to decide that the decision to terminate the contract was that of the Council. Whether it was or was not certiorari will not issue.

***R v Binger & N.J. Vaughan ex parte Chris Bobo Squire* (1983) 20 JLR 114 (JM)**
Orr J

[P124] I adopt this as an accurate statement of the law. In the light of the authorities cited and the position of the Applicant referred to above, I am of the opinion that the relationship between the Applicant and the Scientific Research Council was that of master and servant and therefore certiorari does not lie in respect of the decision to dismiss him.

***Barbados Cricket Association and Others v Peirce* (1999) 57 WIR 29 (BB)**
Williams CJ

[P33] Order 53 of the Rules of the Supreme Court relates to applications for mandamus, prohibition and certiorari, and provides that no application for such an order shall be made unless leave therefore has been granted in accordance with Rule 1 of the Order . . . [P37] Notwithstanding the exclusive control which the Jockey Club exercised over horse racing in Great Britain, it was held not to be amenable to judicial review. In contrast, the BCA has never had sole control over cricket in Barbados, it being common knowledge that for very many years another body (the Barbados Cricket League) has organised cricket competitions in Barbados concurrently with the BCA; indeed, the BCA's very Act of incorporation had and has built-in restrictions on its powers and authority, in that s 4 provides (*inter alia*) that its bye-laws, ordinances, orders, rules and Regulations 'shall not in any manner affect any other person or persons but those who are or may become members of the [BCA]'. It follows, *a fortiori*, that the BCA is likewise not amenable to judicial review. So that, the BCA being a domestic body and the nature of the function that is under challenge not being public or governmental, Wanderers' remedy lay in private law. The application under Order 53, being misconceived and in error, must fail; and the interlocutory injunction which was granted on that application and the relief sought therein, must be discharged.

***Griffith v Barbados Cricket Association; Byer and Another v Barbados Cricket Association* (1989) 41 WIR 48 (BB)**
Williams CJ

[PP57–58] Most Barbadians enjoy cricket. Many play it, others just watch and talk about it and follow the fortunes of their favourite teams. A few players reach international level and play for Barbados or the West Indies. Some become professionals. Mr Short, the association's president, agreed with counsel that, if the reputation of any player is called into question by the association, it can affect his cricketing life. About seven years ago the association introduced monetary prizes into its First Division cricket competition. The winners of the 1987 competition were to receive about $6000 in addition to the winners' trophy. The association is given power by its acts and decisions to affect the cricketing lives of those who play for the member clubs and to deprive those clubs of the awards which they claim to have won according to the competition rules. These are good reasons why the Court cannot close its doors to cricketers and clubs who complain against the exercise of that power. As long ago as *Scott v Avery* (1856) 5 HL Cas 811 it was decided that it is a principle of law that parties cannot by contract oust the jurisdiction of the Courts. Lord Campbell said (at page 852): 'When an action is indispensable, you cannot oust the Court of its jurisdiction over the subject because justice cannot be done without the exercise of that jurisdiction. That is all and there is no doubt about it. This is the foundation of the doctrine that Courts are not to be ousted of their jurisdiction'. In a more recent case *Lee v Showman's Guild of Great Britain* [1952] 2 QB 239 at page 254 Romer LJ said: 'The proper tribunals for the determination of legal disputes in this country are the Courts, and they are the only tribunals which, by training and experience, and assisted by properly qualified advocates are fitted for the task. The Courts jealously uphold and safeguard the *prima facie* privilege of every man to resort to them for the determination and enforcement of his legal rights'. In the same case Lord Denning MR said (at page 242) that, if the parties should seek, by agreement, to take the law out of the hands of the Courts and put it into the hands of a tribunal without any recourse to the Courts in case of error of law, the agreement is to that extent contrary to public policy and void. And in *Baker v Jones* [1954] 2 All ER 553 at pages 558, 559, Lynskey J said that the parties can make a tribunal or council the final arbiter on questions of fact but, although they can leave questions of law to the decision of a tribunal, they cannot prevent its decision being examined by the Courts.

***In the Application of Anthony Willis* – HCSCJ No 522 of 1996 (GY)**
Biscessar J

[P7] 4. The University is a public body and would be subject to judicial review if in breach of their statutory public duties. 5. There is no breach of their public duties. 6. This is clearly a master/servant relationship to which private law remedies apply if there is a breach of the terms of employment. Accordingly in the circumstances of this case, I find that the Applicant is not entitled to an order of certiorari and must vindicate his grievance on the basis of the private law remedies available to him.

A challenging situation for the courts arises in instances where the decision complained about flows from the conduct of a private body that is controlled by the state, eg a state-owned privately registered company.

***In the Application of NH International (Caribbean) Ltd* – HCA No Cv 3181 of 2004 (TT)**
Stollmeyer J

[PP4–5] Given the clear state of the law that hearsay evidence is generally not admissible on the hearing of a motion in judicial review, I exercised my discretion with reluctance, but found that given all the circumstances the scales were tipped very finely in favour of doing so because the justice of the case required it ... [P17] There is no contention of UDECOTT being a public authority or a public body. It is clearly a private entity ... [PP20–21] I accept that public bodies can perform private functions and provide private services as well as enter into private contracts i.e. those that are purely commercial and without a public flavour. That is clearly the case where a government ministry sells one of its motor vehicles, if I may give just a trite example. I accept also that the contract between the government and UDECOTT may not be one with a public flavour. It is after all is said and done, akin to no more than one party agreeing with another that the latter will construct and deliver a completely outfitted building for immediate use. UDECOTT is not shown to be an agent of the government for this purpose. Moreover, I accept that the challenged decision concerns a construction contract, and that there is nothing inherent in a construction contract that gives it a public flavour or includes a public function—not in the usual course of events, at any rate. Further, this was not a case of an 'open tender'. All four bidders had been pre-qualified and submitted their bids on that basis. Additionally, there was no statutory underpinning for the tender procedure or which governed the manner in which UDECOTT went about considering those bids. That was done based upon purely what might be called 'private law' considerations and principles, more particularly those in contract. UDECOTT is not a 'creature of statute' from which it derives its power, nor is it bound by any statutory requirements or constraints (see e.g. *Mercury Energy Ltd. v Electricity Corporation of New Zealand Ltd.* [1994] 1 WLR 521), nor is the process by which it enters into any contract pursuant or subject to any statutory obligations or restraints. It is clear that UDECOTT was pursuing what it perceived to be a strategy of obtaining the best value for its money. That is both perfectly legitimate and correct, and it appears well accepted that it is not appropriate for a Court to interfere in that process, not being best placed (when expressed at a minimum) to judge what is best value. And, negotiating the final terms of a contract or, in this case, further investigating certain areas of the bid, would not alter the private law element (see *Mass Energy Ltd. v Birmingham City Council* [1994] 2 Env LR 298). As in that case, this is in reality a battle between two tenderers to be awarded the contract for the Project, UDECOTT having sought voluntarily to enter into a contract *via* the tender route. Public funding or the public purse being imposed upon, is not of itself sufficient to give the required element of public flavour, nor is the fact that UDECOTT may have been carrying out what might otherwise be regarded as governmental function (*see R v Lord Chancellor, Ex Parte Hibits and Saunders* [1993] COD 326). Something more is needed than merely negotiating a contract for the Project to bring this decision within the scope and supervision of public law (see *Mercury Energy*). In the circumstances, I have come to the conclusion that the contract for the Project is not one that attracts a public law element, and the decision-making process is therefore not susceptible to judicial review. That is not to say that the UDECOTT's functions are generally and necessarily totally outside the purview or scope of public law, or sufficiently so as to remove it and its decisions totally from amenability to judicial review. Its functions are certainly capable of bringing it within the scope of judicial review, as was found to be the case in *Oropune Village Multipurpose Co-operative Society Ltd.* HCA 483 of 2002, but I make no finding as to whether that is so in the present instance: it is sufficient to say that the nature of the contract is such that it falls within private and not public law.

In the Application of Oropune Village Multipurpose Co-operative Society Ltd –
HCA No 483 of 2002 (TT)
Smith J

[P20] Even assuming that UDECOTT and ODL were exercising public functions, they were not departments of government under the control of a Permanent Secretary. They had no privileges or immunities of the State, their property was not State property, their employees were not members of the public service and like any other private corporation they were not exempt from the general laws of the land and especially so from the payment of tax. For whatever the reason, the government preferred to have these entities run as private companies under the Companies Act and the Companies would therefore also benefit from insulation from the government. Perhaps this in itself was a reason why government divested itself of some aspects of its powers, namely, that a private corporation, being free from the bureaucracy of the public service may be able to perform such functions more efficiently, and probably more profitably than the public service. If, however, it were alleged that the divestment of government functions were a sham and that a private company was merely a front for the government itself exercising its power, then that would itself raise justiciable issues and be subject to challenge ... [P22] In all the circumstances, I find that UDECOTT and ODL were not bound as a matter of law to follow any Ministerial or Cabinet directive (if indeed any such directive existed) to vest the 46 acre parcel of land in the Applicant and the challenge to UDECOTT and ODL's actions on this issue must fail.

***In the Application of Industrial Risks Consultants Ltd and Consolidated Insurance Consultants Ltd* – HCA No 536 of 1995 (TT)**
Bharath J

[P4] The first issue to be decided in this case is whether Petrotrin is a public body performing or exercising a public function and therefore susceptible to judicial review ... [PP5–6] In determining whether Petrotrin is a public body or public Authority I have to apply the definition set out in *Halsbury's Laws of England* (3rd Ed) 682 paragraph 1317:—

> **'A public authority is a body not necessarily a County Council, municipal corporation, or other local authority which has public or statutory duties to perform and carries out its transactions for the benefit of the public and not for private profit'.**

This definition was applied by (1) Lawton LJ in *R v Manners* ([1976] 2 All ER 96) in determining whether North Thames Gas Board was a public body, (2) by Ibrahim JA in Civil Appeal No. 132/88 *Shastri Moonan and DPP and the Commissioner of Police* when determining whether Telco was a public body for the purpose of the Prevention of Corruption Act (11 of 1987) and (3) by Justice Best in HCA no S 1947/92 in *Bruno Maharaj & Ors. v National Fisheries* where he had to consider whether National Fisheries Company Limited was a public authority and susceptible to judicial review in charging the Applicants a throughput fee of 10 cents plus VAT *per* litre of gas. Justice Best had the same issues to deal with in that case and came to the conclusion that National Fisheries was a private company operating commercially and that its decision to charge a throughput fee was not susceptible to judicial review. To determine whether Petrotrin is exercising a public function I must examine its source of power, the nature of its functions and the nature of the Applicant's dispute or challenge. Petrorin's source of power is the Memorandum and Articles of Association. It is contractual in nature and not statutory ... [P6] It should be noted that the shareholders, whether Government or its nominees, are bound to observe all the provisions of the Memorandum and Articles as if they individually covenanted to do so. Its activities of providing refining and marketing petroleum and other oils are commercial for making profits and not for the benefit of the public ... [P7] It was after the stage of offer by means of written tender and oral presentation but there was no acceptance by Petrotrin and therefore no constituted contract. The dispute is therefore a private law dispute and not justifiable under common law ... In contrast Petrotrin is not a self regulating body and its powers are derived from a contractual source. It has acted within the powers authorized by the Memorandum and Articles of Association. The Court must decline jurisdiction for the above reasons ... [P8] I am adopting the authorities cited by Justice Best in the matter of *Bruno Maharaj & Ors. v National Fisheries Company Limited* and following his decision. I am of the view that Petrotrin is not a public body performing a public function and is not amenable to judicial review. It exercises contractual powers in awarding contracts. It operates for profits and not for the benefit of the public.

***In the Application of Bruno Maharaj, Basdeo Manmohansingh, Herbert Roberts, Horace Baksh, Tyrone Karan, Dipnarine Tewarie, Hosein Khan, Hatim Gardner, Hannif Mohammed, Nazir Mohammed, John Lanser, David Lanser, Enterprise Sea Foods Ltd* – No S-1947 of 1992 (TT)**
Best J

[P5] Thus it would seem that the test to be applied as to whether an entity is susceptible to judicial review is to determine the nature and purpose of its functions, as well as the source of its power. In applying this test, it would seem that one will have to concern oneself with elucidating whether the entity concerned dealt with matters that redound to benefit of the public or are concerned with matters, merely commercial in nature ...

[PP6–7] Thus, in the view of this Court, it is jurisprudentially possible for a public body to make decisions that have both public and private law impact. Also, in the view of this Court, it is jurisprudentially possible for a statutory body, involved in a purely commercial enterprise, to attract the Court's supervisory jurisdiction by making a decision which has a public law impact . . . [P8] In the view of this Court, upon a review of the authorities cited that the National Fisheries Company, despite being a private trading body operating under the Companies Ordinance, with its Memorandum and Articles of Association, its decision may or may not have a public law impact i.e. amenable to judicial review. It is possible for the Respondent Company to make decisions that are essentially commercial or managerial in nature, and which fall outside the supervisory jurisdiction of the Court. The decision disputed herein I hold, was essentially a management decision relating to the economic survival of the Company and cannot be the subject of this Court's scrutiny. There were other arguments raised herein, but having decided as I have I see no need to go on to them. In the premises the Applicant's application for judicial review is refused.

***In the Application of East Caribbean Liquid Gas Ltd* – HCA No 5848 of 1988 (TT)**
Warner J

[P11] The first question for determination is whether the decision of the Respondent company and the concurrence of the Minister are matters which attract judicial review. It was not disputed that a decision of a state enterprise such as the Respondent company is one on which the supervisory jurisdiction of the Court may be focused . . . [P12] The question with which this Court is faced is whether there is a public law element when a state enterprise and a private individual or body corporate are negotiating with a view to entering into a contract.

***In the Application of Shastri Moonan* – Civil Appeal No 132 of 1988 (TT)**
Ibrahim JA

[P48] In England, companies acting for profit although conducting undertakings of public utility are not regarded as public authorities. Even though its duties and functions in relation to the telephone service that it operates are for the benefit of the public it is in my opinion not a public utility like water and sewerage, and electricity. It was submitted that it is a state enterprise and by virtue of the provisions of the Constitution, secs. 116 and 119, the Auditor General is empowered to carry out audits of its accounts, balance sheets and other financial statements . . . [PP48–49] In my opinion, these provisions became necessary from 1976 solely because of the necessity of having Parliament oversee the accounts of companies that are owned wholly or partly by the State. This does not make them public authorities or public bodies.

***In the Application of Julian Gooding* – HCA No 3076 of 1987 (TT)**
Lucky J

[P9] The Trinidad and Tobago Electricity Commission (T&TEC) was established by the Trinidad and Tobago Electricity Commission, Act Chap 54:70 to provide electricity to the public, in a safe, reliable and efficient manner. This in my view sums up its duties to the public . . . [P10] I think this exclusion gives T&TEC more of an independent corporate personality and gives it more of the qualities of a limited liability company incorporated under the Companies Ordinance. Such a company is not a public authority . . . [P13] The fact that Trinidad and Tobago Electricity Commission is a 'public authority' does not *per se* make the claim a matter of public law. There is, I think, a dichotomy in the functions of a public authority. This is found in its relationship with the public and its contractual obligations with its employees . . . [P14] This certainly arises from a contract of employment which established a relationship of master and servant, and is a private right. To my mind, the Applicant's right, assuming he has one, is in private law . . . [P15] In the light of the authorities, I have come to the conclusion that the Applicant's case involves no arguable complaint in public law and I agree that seeking relief by way of judicial review is an abuse of procedure.

4.6 OUSTER OF JURISDICTION

On many occasions, parliament may elect to oust the jurisdiction of the courts to judicially review a decision of a public body. This ouster may be embedded in constitutional provisions or in legislation itself. The courts must comply with an ouster provision but will generally not hold its jurisdiction to review a decision of a public body where (1) the decision involves a breach of the principles of natural justice; (2) the decision-maker acted outside of its jurisdiction; or (3) it can be shown that fraud influenced the decision of the public body.

In the Application of Alvin Seereeram – **HCA No S-262 of 2001 (TT)**
Marcus J

[P51] Section 129(3) of the Constitution ('the ouster clause') prohibits the Courts enquiring into whether a Service Commission, any member of the Commission or other person or authority has validly performed any function vested or delegated or relating to the work of the Commission, as the case may be . . . [P52] The ouster clause was abolished by Section 3 of the Constitution (Amendment) Act, No. 43 of 2000 with effect from 25th September, 2000, the date it received the Presidential assent.

In the Application of Herbert Charles – **HCA No Cv 1308 of 1999/HCA No SCv 531 of 1999 (TT)**
Kangaloo J

[P21] It is clear from the quoted passage that the ouster clause bites, once the function being performed by the Commission and for the purposes of this case, by any person doing work in relation to the work of the Commission, is within the Constitutional jurisdiction of the Commission. There are however two exceptions when the ouster clause would not apply viz if the Commission did something that lay outside its functions or where there is a challenge to the validity of an order made by a commission against an individual officer based upon a contravention of his right to a fair hearing in accordance with the principles of fundamental justice for the determination of his rights and obligations.

In the Application of Suresh Rampersad – **Civil Appeal No 186 of 1997**
Warner JA

[PP12–13] There has been no complaint that the Respondent was denied a fair hearing, or that the Commission had no jurisdiction to hear the matter. In the absence of any such complaint, the ouster clause in Section 129(3) of the Constitution operated to preclude the Court from enquiring into whether the Public Service Commission had validly performed its functions. (See *Endell Thomas v The Attorney General* [1982] AC 113).

In the Application of the Port Authority of Trinidad and Tobago – **HCA No 14 of 1997**
Jairam J

[P6] Most crucially, any award, order or other determination of the Special Tribunal is final **(see Section 42(2) of the Act; Section 21(4) of the Civil Service Act)** which is a concept generally given to 'specialized Courts' exercising jurisdiction of a superior Court of record. On this ground alone, namely, judicial review would not lie against a superior Court of record such as the Special Tribunal.

***In the Application of Vinode Jhagroo* – HCA No 1147 of 1995 (TT)**
Warner J

[P8] Put another way, the principle in administrative law is that a power is not validly exercised when it is granted for one purpose, and the public body pursues some different or collateral object . . . [P10] As I have stated before, the Commission is not precluded from making a series of fixed term appointments. Despite the structure of the letters however, it is clear that the decision making authority in failing to consider this Applicant's eligibility for permanent appointment as an Assistant Teacher III, based on the evidence before me did not correctly understand the law regulating its decision-making power . . . [PP11–12] Miss Hernandez relied on the ouster provision under Section 129(3) of the Constitution which would prevent the Court from reviewing the decision of the Teaching Service Commission. In the instant case however, the Applicant in his grounds and his affidavit alleged a breach of natural justice in that the Commission refused to continue his employment as an Assistant Teacher III without giving him any notice of its intention to do so, and without giving him a hearing or any reason for not continuing his employment. He also challenged the validity of the order on the ground that the Commission had acted outside its jurisdiction. (See *The Thomas case*) . . . [P12] The Applicant has made [the] application within the 3 month period, and I see no reason to impute delay . . . [P13] I hold therefore that on the evidence adduced, the Commission exceeded the terms of the power which authorized the making of the decision.

***In the Application of Ronald Narine* – HCA No 1274 of 1994 (TT)**
Warner J

[P10] I have found that there has been a breach of fundamental justice, so that according to the dictum of Lord Diplock in *Thomas v Attorney General* (1981) 32 WIR 375 at pages 393–394, the Court's jurisdiction is not ousted.

***In the Application of Lynette Maharaj* – Civil Appeal No 157 of 1994 (TT)**
Hamel-Smith JA

[P6] The section, in effect, prevents any inquiry by a Court of law to determine whether the Commission has validly performed any of its functions under the Constitution unless it can be shown that in exercising its power the Commission acted outside its jurisdiction or in breach of the rules of natural justice . . . [P7] Since the limited grounds upon which the Court can intervene are lack of jurisdiction and breach of the rules of natural justice, it follows that the issue of irrationality could not arise. On the issue of procedural impropriety, unless the Commission was under an obligation to give the Respondent an opportunity to be heard before it exercised its power of appointment that too could not be an issue. The main issue for determination therefore, was that of jurisdiction and the application of the ouster clause in the event that the Commission had failed to follow the Regulations . . . [P8] Even if counsel for the Respondent is correct and the assumption could be made that the Commission had failed to comply with the Regulations, could it be said that the Commission was acting outside of its jurisdiction? The answer must be 'no'. The Commission, in exercising its power of appointment, was appointing Mr Beepath to the post of principal and that was something it was empowered to do by virtue of Section 125. The fact that failure to comply with a particular Regulation or to construe or apply it properly may result in a function vested in it not being validly performed is precisely the purpose of the ouster clause. It prohibits a challenge to a decision of the Commission in a Court of law on that basis. Accordingly, there could be no challenge to the decision of the Commission in the circumstances of this case . . . [P9] It is because of the failure of the Respondent to establish that the Commission acted outside its jurisdiction or in breach of the rules of natural justice that the appeal must be allowed.

In the Application of Juan Mosca – HCA No 2295 of 1993 (TT)
Sealey J

[P16] Nowhere in the rules of racing is there any procedure laid out for the conduct of these inquiries, therefore, it is incumbent on the Respondent authority to use a procedure which it feels adequately meets the situation and which provides the Applicant with all the opportunities of putting forward his case. The Respondent's procedure of allowing the Applicant to question witnesses was entirely proper in those circumstances. The Applicant fails on this ground . . . [P32] Attorney-at-law for the Respondent suggested that Courts should be reluctant to interfere in decisions of sporting bodies, and in support thereof . . . [P33] I find in those sentiments much to commend themselves, especially having regard to what I have expressed as the intention of the legislature in seeking to control the sport of horse racing and to put in place rules which ought to control the behaviour of all who have to take part in the sport from a management as well as a participant point of view.

In the Application of Codrington Waldron – HCA No 3512 of 1991 (TT)
Wills J

[P19] I hold that there is, in this case, a breach of the principles of natural justice, in that the Applicant was not afforded any or any reasonable opportunity to be heard before the decision to revoke his appointment as a Police Inspector and/or to demote him to his former rank of Police Sergeant. In my opinion, Statutory Commissions or similar bodies which are charged by the legislature with functions which by their actions can affect or are likely to affect adversely, the rights, livelihood and or positions of the persons over whom they have authority or jurisdiction must observe the principles of natural justice. Statutory provisions such as are contained in Section 129(3) of the Constitution do not deprive the Court of its supervisory power whenever the circumstances warrant it. The right to be heard is, in addition, implicit and need not to be expressed as attorney for the Respondent would seem to suggest. In any democratic and or civilized society, delegated statutory powers must be exercised with scrupulous adherence to the principles of natural justice which cannot be satisfied by a compulsive appearance before the statutory body exercising them.

In the Application of John Barrow – HCA No S-514 of 1987 (TT)
Crane J

[P8] From these pronouncements, there appears to be at least two instances in which the 'ouster clause' (which expression is used to describe s 129(3) and any other similar provision such as s 80(2) of the Constitution) would not operate. The first is where the Commission acts outside the functions vested in it by the Constitution, the second where there is a breach of 'the right to a fair hearing in accordance with the principles of fundamental justice for the determination of his rights and obligations' that is secured to him by s 5(2)(e) of the Constitution. This would arise where there is a breach of the principles of natural justice—one principle of which is *audi alterem partem*. A third instance may well arise where fraud can be shown to have influenced the decision of the Commission.

In the Application of the Public Service Appeal Board – Civil Appeal No 52 of 1985 (TT)
des Iles JA

[P13] I wish most respectfully to adopt the language of the learned Law Lords quoted above and I would accordingly hold that the Teaching Service Commission was in breach of the rules of natural justice by having failed to afford the Respondent an opportunity to be heard orally before dismissing him, especially in the light of the fact that he had requested to be heard . . . [P14] '(3) The question whether,

(a) A Service Commission has validly performed any function vested in it by the Constitution;

may not be enquired into by any Court . . .'

In any event, the ouster of the Court's jurisdiction is only effective where there has been no breach of natural justice, but in this appeal, there have been flagrant breaches of the rules of natural justice by the Teaching Service Commission. To argue, as was done for the Appellants before this Court, that the fact the Respondent had been given fourteen days in which to show cause why he should not be dismissed, without stating by whom it had been reported that he failed to submit his scheme of work, and in complete disregard of his denial of the allegations and his production of copies of the relevant documents from official custody, the ignoring of his imputation of bias against him by the Principal of the relevant school as well as the failure of the Commission to provide the Respondent with an opportunity to be heard orally in answer to the report made against him, as he had requested, was compliance with the rules of natural justice, indicates a complete misunderstanding of what is required in matters of this kind, and makes a mockery of justice.

***In the Application of James Munroe* – Civil Appeal No 56 of 1997 (JM)**
Rattray J

[P22] It is in our view and indeed well established that despite clauses of this nature referred to in some cases as 'no certiorari' clauses, found in the statutory instruments or in the Constitution of the nation if the determination made affecting the rights of the subject is challenged on the ground that it is a nullity, the existence of a 'no certiorari' clause cannot debar the aggrieved person from questioning in a Court of law a decision adverse to him. It is no longer doubted that prerogative powers are capable of being subject to judicial review once they are justiciable (see *Council of Civil Service Union and Others v Minister of the Civil Service* [1984] 4 All ER 935.) Nor can it be now arguable that 'no certiorari' clauses in a statute or a Constitution can in an appropriate case debar the Court from having jurisdiction, and prevent it from embarking upon the determination of an issue involving a breach of the principles of natural justice. These principles are well established in the cases cited to us including *Anisminic Ltd. v The Foreign Compensation Commission and Another* [1969] 1 All ER 208; and *Thomas v Attorney-General* [1981] 32 WIR 375. We have to examine the circumstances of each case to determine whether jurisdiction is ousted or not. In our view the jurisdiction in this appeal is not ousted and full argument has been allowed. We therefore conclude that the determination of the Governor-General acting on the advice of the Public Service Commission was not wrong in law as misconduct was proved as required by the Pensions Act. Furthermore the Governor-General's decision on the advice of the Public Service Commission not to pay the Appellant the salary withheld from him during his interdiction was likewise not wrong in law as the proceedings against him had not resulted in his exculpation but in the imposition of a punishment.

***In the Application of Aubrey Norton* – HCCJ No 5932 of 1997 (GY)**
Bernard CJ

[P13] This reasoning suggests that Courts should lean towards interpreting literally exclusionary or ouster clauses in statutes relating to parliamentary affairs thus leaving no room for liberal or expansive interpretations. Such interpretations may give rise to varying and variable opinions leading to uncertainty in matters relating to our parliamentary system which ought not to be constricted by a plethora of judicial dicta.

***Thomas d'Arcy Ryan* – Privy Council Appeal No 29 of 1977 (BS)**
Lord Diplock

[PP9–10] The relevant ouster provisions of Section 16 of The Bahamas Nationality Act 1973 are: '. . . the decision of the Minister on any such application [sc. for registration as a citizen of The Bahamas] . . . shall not be subject to appeal or review in any Court.' 'Appeal' in the context of an ouster clause means re-examination by a superior judicial authority of both findings of fact and conclusions of law as to the legal consequences of those facts made by an inferior tribunal in the exercise of a jurisdiction conferred upon it by statute to decide questions affecting the legal rights of others, and the substitution of the superior judicial authority's own findings of fact and conclusions of law for those of the inferior tribunal. In 'review' the function of the superior judicial authority is limited to re-examining the inferior tribunal's conclusions of law as to the legal consequences of the facts as they have been found by the inferior tribunal. It is by now well-established law that to come within the prohibition of appeal or review by an ouster clause of this type the decision must be one which the decision-making authority, under this Act the Minister, had jurisdiction to make. If in purporting to make it he has gone outside his jurisdiction, it is *ultra vires* and is not a 'decision' under the Act. The Supreme Court, in the exercise of its supervisory jurisdiction over inferior tribunals, which include executive authorities exercising quasi-judicial powers, may, in appropriate proceedings, either set it aside or declare it to be a nullity: *Anisminic Ltd. v Foreign Compensation Commission* [1969] 2 AC 147. It has long been settled law that a decision affecting the legal rights of an individual which is arrived at by a procedure which offends against the principles of natural justice is outside the jurisdiction of the decision making authority. As Lord Selborne said as long ago as 1885, in *Spackman v Plumstead District Board of Works* (1885) 10 AppCas. 229, 240: 'There would be no decision within the meaning of the statute if there were anything . . . done contrary to the essence of justice.' See also *Rigde v Baldwin*. Their Lordships, in agreement with all the Judges in the Courts below, would therefore conclude that the ouster clause in Section 16 of The Bahamas Nationality Act 1973 does not prevent the Court from inquiring into the validity of the Minister's decision on the ground that it was made without jurisdiction and is *ultra vires*.

***The Constituency Boundaries Commission v The Attorney-General of the Commonwealth of Dominica and Urban Baron* in the Eastern Caribbean Supreme Court of Appeal Civil Appeal No 12 of 1998 (DM)**
Satrohan Singh JA

[P5] In considering the question of ouster of jurisdiction, it is important to focus on the fact that the House of Assembly has not as yet approved of the draft order submitted by the President . . . [PP6–8] I do not agree that the authorities aforementioned support these submissions of the Learned Attorney General: In the *Rediffusion case* Lord Diplock said at page 1157: The immunity from control by the Courts, which is enjoyed by members of a legislative assembly while exercising their deliberative functions is founded on necessity. The question of the extent of the immunity which is necessary raises a conflict of public policy between the desirability of freedom of deliberation in the legislature and the observance by its members of the rule of law of which the Courts are the guardians. If there will be no remedy when the legislative process is complete and the unlawful conduct in the course of the legislative process will by then have achieved its object, the argument founded on necessity in their Lordships view leads to the conclusion that there must be a remedy available in a Court of justice before the result has been achieved which was intended to be prevented by the law from which a legislature which is not fully sovereign derives its powers. I accept this opinion as a correct proposition of the law. It demolishes the submission of Mr LaRonde. I also do not agree with the reasoning of the learned Attorney General on S 57(8) of the Constitution. The absence of a right of appeal *per se* has never precluded the supervisory jurisdiction of the Court. As I see it, the intention or purpose of the Constitution at S 57(8) was to allow access to the Court. Mr LaRonde in his submissions impressed upon this Court, quite correctly, to give a generous and purposive construction to the provisions of the Constitution, avoiding what has been called the austerity of tabulated legalism. [*Donovan v The Attorney General* [1961] IR 114: *Minister of Home Affairs v Fisher* [1980] AC 319.] If then that was the purpose of S 57(8), I would conclude that the inaction on the part of Parliament to make the required appellate provision, was nothing more than an attempt at frustrating that provision of the Constitution. There is no merit in this submission. The Court must construe the Constitution so as to give to the individual the full benefit of the rights and freedoms so protected. In my judgment, there is supervisory jurisdiction in the Courts in the context of this matter. Nowhere in S 57 of the Constitution is the jurisdiction of the Court specifically excluded except for S 57(7), and this is at the stage of the proceedings when the draft order of the President has been approved by the House, a stage not yet reached in this matter. In my view, when S 103 specifically excepted only S 57(7) from its application, the clear implication was that every other aspect of S 57 was justiciable. Until the S 57(7) stage is reached therefore, there is jurisdiction in the Courts to enquire into the matter and to grant relief. Without this jurisdiction to grant relief before the resulting act is completed, the citizen intended to be protected would be deprived of any remedy. It is clear from the unchallenged evidence of the Respondent, that the report of the Commission, if accepted as is, would seriously affect his future political career. In this context, to exclude the jurisdiction of Court to inquire into it, in order to decide whether to grant relief to the Respondent, the Appellants had to show that the challenge of bias was purely an abstract question, the answer to which would be incapable of affecting any existing or future legal rights of the Respondent. This they have not done. Just as it is the duty of the Court to attribute autonomy of decision to the approval of the Order of the President, so the counterpart of this autonomy is to ensure that the Constitutional provisions were observed by the Commission. [*Anisminic Foreign Compensation Commission* [1969] 2 AC 147.] For these reasons, I hold that the submission of the learned Attorney General on ouster of jurisdiction is without merit and accordingly overruled.

4.7 MIXING OF CONSTITUTIONAL AND JUDICIAL REVIEW MATTERS

While both residing in the realm of public law, the courts are not prepared to allow judicial review proceedings that in essence involve constitutional matters. It is accepted that, at times, decisions by public bodies may infringe constitutional rights while also offending principles that attract judicial review; however, the preferred position of courts is not to engage in the co-mingling of issues dealing with constitutional and administrative law.

***In the Application of Corporal No 10089 Christopher Holder* – HCA No 2581 of 1993 (TT)**
Bharath J

[PP7–8] In my view, commingling of constitutional matters with errors in administrative decisions [is] inappropriate in Judicial Review proceedings and should be struck out. The proper procedure to be followed where there are mixed questions of constitutional and administrative law is to file separate proceedings for review of administrative decisions and constitutional matters for infringement of the Constitution and then consolidate them to be heard together. All proper reliefs with damages can then be granted. Although I hold that constitutional matters are inappropriate and should be struck out, I heard full arguments in these proceedings and will treat this matter as an exception but dealing with the infringement of constitutional rights on the basis of denial of fairness or breach of natural justice and not otherwise. For the future I do not propose that this exception should be used as a precedent.

***In the Application of Seereeram Bros. Ltd* – HCA No 3123 of 1991 (TT)**
Jones J

[P38] The Constitution it was contended had its own special place. By Section 14, a particular procedure was laid down for the enforcement of the rights enshrined therein. Judicial Review proceedings on the other hand they say are not proceedings for the enforcement of rights as such but for the review of administrative action. The two remedies being distinct and apart, a breach of the Constitution must be challenged in a separate action and cannot be relied on as founding a basis of challenge to unlawful administrative decisions . . . [PP38–39] While on a further consideration of the matter I might have gone too far in my treatment of the Applicant's grounds in the particular case, I am still of the view that where for instance the only complaint an Applicant has against a public authority is that the authority had breached his constitutional rights, a Court in this jurisdiction ought not to be called upon to embark upon an enquiry into a breach of constitutional rights in order to determine whether an administrative discretion has been properly exercised. In the present case the complaints are not limited to a constitutional breach and the breach of the Constitution had been cited as an instance of illegal action on the part of the Board.

Kemrajh Harrikissoon – Privy Council Appeal No 40 of 1977 (TT)
Lord Diplock

[P268] The notion that whenever there is a failure by an organ of government or a public authority or public officer to comply with the law this necessarily entails the contravention of some human right or fundamental freedom guaranteed to individuals by Chapter 1 of the Constitution is fallacious. The right to apply to the High Court under Section 6 of the Constitution for redress when any human right or fundamental freedom is or is likely to be contravened, is an important safeguard of those rights and freedoms; but its value will be diminished if it is allowed to be misused as a general substitute for the normal procedures for invoking judicial control of administrative action. In an originating application to the High Court under Section 6(1), the mere allegation that a human right or fundamental freedom of the Applicant has been or is likely to be contravened is not of itself sufficient to entitle the Applicant to invoke the jurisdiction of the Court under the subsection if it is apparent that the allegation is frivolous or vexatious or an abuse of the process of the Court as being made solely for the purpose of avoiding the necessity of applying in the normal way for the appropriate judicial remedy for unlawful administrative action which involves no contravention of any human right or fundamental freedom. The instant case concerns and concerns only the right of a holder of a public office not to be transferred against his will from one place to another. In their Lordships' view it is manifest that this is not included among the human rights and fundamental freedoms specified in Chapter 1 of the Constitution . . . [P272] The ouster of the Court's jurisdiction effected by this section is in terms absolute. In their Lordships' view it is clearly wide enough to deprive all Courts of jurisdiction to entertain a challenge to the validity of an order of transfer on either of the grounds alleged by the Appellant in the instant case; and that is sufficient to support the dismissal of the Appellant's claim on this ground also. In all the judgments below, however, there is considerable discussion of recent English cases dealing with 'ouster of jurisdiction clauses' contained in Acts of Parliament. Section 102(4) does not form part of an Act of Parliament; it is part of the Constitution itself. Their Lordships do not think that the instant appeal provides an appropriate occasion for considering whether Section 102(4) of the Constitution, despite its unqualified language, is nevertheless subject to the same limited kind of implicit exception as was held by the House of Lords, in *Anisminic Ltd. v Foreign Compensation Commission* [1969] 2 AC 147, to apply to an ouster of jurisdiction clause in very similar terms contained in an Act of Parliament. This question is best left to be decided in some future case if one should arise, in which the facts provide a concrete example of the kind of circumstances that were discussed in the judgments in the *Anisminic case*. The facts in the instant appeal do not. The appeal is dismissed with costs.

4.8 ALTERNATIVE PROCEEDINGS

Judicial review may be refused when an applicant has alternative remedies and cannot establish the existence of exceptional circumstances that would justify the court ignoring the alternative remedies and acquiescing to judicial review proceedings.

In the Application of Celia Balroop – HCA No S-463 of 2005 (TT)
Pemberton J

[PP7–8] [17] . . . (1) Section 39 of the FOI Act does not enable an Applicant to approach the Court for Judicial Review as of right. The Judicial Review Act and Order 53 RSC govern Judicial Review proceedings notwithstanding a direct reference to such proceedings. This is so in any statute unless the statute expresses otherwise. Freedom of Information Act does not enable an Applicant to approach the Court for Judicial Review as of right. (2) The Ombudsman is an alternative remedy available to an Applicant under the Act provided there is an active refusal by the Public Authority to satisfy the request for information and notice of that refusal is communicated in accordance with the Act. This is the conjoined effect of Section 23(1) and 38A of the Judicial Review Act [and the FOI Act respectively]. (3) Judicial Review proceedings are not an abuse of process once the Ombudsman's jurisdiction cannot be invoked. (4) Judicial Review proceedings may be invoked once Section 39 is satisfied. [18] In this instance the inaction of the Ministry of Works puts the Applicant in the position of being a suitable candidate to seek Judicial Review. [19] Having come to those conclusions, I entertain favourably Mr Ramlogan's application to add a party to these proceedings. I therefore find that the Minister of Works ought to be made a Respondent in these proceedings, that the proceedings be amended to reflect same and that leave be granted to the Applicant to pursue her relief.

In the Application of Anthony Leach – HCA No 1002 of 2004 (TT)
Judith Jones J

[P18] 29. It is trite law that the judicial review jurisdiction will not normally be exercised where there is an alternate remedy available. In the instant case Counsel for the PSC submits that it is at this stage open to the Applicant to raise all the submissions made before me at the disciplinary hearing. Whereas there is no doubt that this is possible the difficulty with this argument is that at the time these proceedings were brought no charges had as yet been brought against the Applicant. There would, therefore, have been no other forum open to the Applicant to air these issues. 30. In *Caverley's case* in dealing with this issue Sir John Donaldson MR, at page 433 letter F referred to a statement of Glidewell LJ in *Ex Parte Waldron* [1985] 3 WLR 1090 at page 1108 where he stated: 'Whether the alternative remedy will resolve the question at issue fully and directly; whether the statutory procedure would be quicker, or slower than procedure by way of judicial review; whether the matter depends on some particular or technical knowledge which is more readily available to the alternative appellate body; these are amongst the matters which a Court should take into account when deciding whether to grant relief by judicial review when an alternate remedy is available.' . . . [P19] 32. In all the circumstances of this case I am of the view that the alternative remedy will not resolve the issue at hand nearly as quickly as the judicial relief procedure neither will it be anywhere so convenient, beneficial or effectual as these proceedings.

In the Application of Harricrete Ltd – HCA No 1254 of 2000 (TT)
Myers J

[P20] A passage from the judgment of my learned brother Mr Justice Archie in *Saga Trading Limited v The Comptroller of Customs and Excise* HCA No. CV 1347 of 1993 (at page 33), provides a useful starting, and ultimately finishing, point: 'There is now a substantial body of judicial authority which supports the proposition that where there is an ***effective*** [my emphasis] alternative remedy, the ***discretion*** [my emphasis] to grant judicial review will only be exercised in "exceptional circumstances".' I gratefully and respectfully adopt that passage. It succinctly and accurately summarises the effect of all the authorities which had been cited to my brother in that case, and those additionally cited to me in this case. Applying this, seized as I am of an application for judicial review where there is an alternative remedy, I must ask:

1. Is the alternative remedy provided under Section 27 of the Anti-Dumping Act effective? . . .

[P21] 2. Are there any 'exceptional circumstances' present to warrant the exercise of my discretion to keep the application before me, and not cede jurisdiction to the Tax Appeal Board? . . .

[P34] In view of the above, I do not consider that it would be appropriate for me, sitting as a trial judge to attempt to do anything more than decide (citing the absolute minimum of authority necessary) the very narrow issue which has now emerged: where there is a highly efficacious alternative remedy, comprising a statutory appeal to a specialist superior Court of record set up for the express purpose of dealing with exactly the type of matter sought to be ventilated before the public law Court, how exceptional must the circumstances be to persuade the public law Court to exercise its discretion to maintain its jurisdiction? During the course of his submissions, Mr Martineau SC eventually came to a quiet place where he accepted that the burden upon him was a very heavy one. Mr Daly SC's formulation was that, in order for Mr Martineau SC to bring Harricrete within 'exceptional circumstances', he had to show 'something more' which could be further broken down as (1) abuse of power; and (2) grave circumstances disturbing the conscience of the Court.

In the Application of Selwyn Patrovanie – **HCA No 431 of 1999 (TT)**
Bereaux J

[P6] As a general proposition the Courts will refuse to grant judicial review where there is an alternative remedy by way of appeal which has not been exhausted. They will not grant judicial review merely because it is more effective and correct to do so. There must be exceptional circumstances . . . [P8] The Applicant must produce compelling reasons why he chose to come to the High Court rather than to pursue his remedy under the statute. He stated that he was unable to file an appeal because he was proceeding with the support of his fellow villagers, at least three of whom are in Court on the very issue . . . The Applicant has not persuaded me that there are exceptional circumstances justifying the non-pursuit of his statutory remedy. The application should be dismissed on this ground alone.

In the Application of Kenneth Lalla, Henley Wooding, Corinre Mohammed, Carlyle Walters, Sakal Seemungal (Members of the Public Service Commission) –
Civil Appeal No 128 of 1999 (TT)
Nelson JA

[PP25–26] Generally the Courts will not grant judicial review where an Applicant has not pursued all his rights to challenge a decision under a statute: see *R v Chief Constable of Merseyside, Ex Parte Calveley* [1986] 1 All ER 257 (CA). In the present case the Applicant has intact his right of appeal to the Public Service Appeal Board: see Section 132 of the Constitution.

In the Application of the Director of Public Prosecutions – **HCA No 1361 of 1998 (TT)**
Ventour J

[P14] I think it is to the credit of the law that exceptions to many a general principle have been created to meet the ends of justice and with such objective in mind the Courts have been able to grant judicial review in many a case where the Applicant has, for one reason or another, not exhausted the alternative remedy available. It appears to me that each case would depend upon the particular set of circumstances . . . [P16] What I have gleaned from the several authorities which I have been invited to examine is that while the general principle as expressed is clearly defined, nevertheless its application to any particular set of facts will vary depending upon the circumstances of each case. For example, there are many cases where given the particular set of circumstances the Court has found that the alternative statutory remedy was neither effective nor convenient and the Court proceeded to grant judicial review reliefs to the Applicant notwithstanding the fact that alternative statutory remedies were not exhausted.

***In the Application of Trevor Bailey* – Civil Appeal No 204 of 1997 (TT)**
Nelson J

[P13] Further, no arguments have been addressed to us which would justify overturning the Judge's exercise of his discretion not to grant judicial review remedies on the basis that the Appellant had an alternative remedy of making a no case submission at the trial.

***In the Application of Margaret Chuckaree* – Civil Appeal No 21 of 1994 (TT)**
de la Bastide CJ

[P3] There are a number of other factors however that caused us to take time over the decision whether or not to permit these proceedings to continue. These have to do with the fact firstly that it is clearly and essentially an industrial relations dispute, and the Union which represents these Applicants has taken steps to bring their grievances before the Industrial Court and to obtain a remedy for them in that forum. It may be argued that the remedies which are available in that Court are more flexible and can be more easily structured so as to meet the justice and merits of this case assuming that it is a proper case for intervention. On the other hand, we cannot ignore the fact that the objection which is being taken is one based on an allegation of nullity arising out of a legal question as to whether or not the employers had the authority in law to terminate the employment of the Applicants. Clearly, the Supreme Court is the proper forum for the determination of such a question.

***In the Application of Lolita Saroop* – HCA No 2115 of 1993 (TT)**
Sealey J

[PP13–14] It seems to me if I understand Baker LJ in the *Swati case*, the Applicant ought to say whether there was an alternative remedy and whether it was a proper one in the circumstances, and it would be for the Court then to decide whether the circumstances outlined were the proper ones to ignore the other alternative remedy.

***In the Application of Saga Trading Ltd* – HCA No Cv 1347 of 1993 (TT)**
Archie J

[P33] There is now a substantial body of judicial authority which supports the proposition that where there is an effective alternative remedy available, the discretion to grant judicial review will only be exercised in 'exceptional circumstances' . . . [PP34–35] The criteria which Courts adopt in the exercise of this discretion are further illustrated by the decided cases, e.g. in *Ex Parte Waldron* [1986] QB 824 at 852 G. Glidwell LJ considered: 'Whether the alternative statutory remedy will resolve the question at issue fully and directly; whether the statutory procedure would be quicker or slower than procedure by way of judicial review; whether the matter depends on some particular or technical knowledge which is more readily available to the alternative appellate body'. The element of public interest is also a relevant factor as the same judge observed in *R v Huntingdon DC, Ex Parte Cowan* [1984] 1 WLR 501 at 507: . . . The nature of the central issue to be resolved and the appropriateness of the remedies available are also factors.

***In the Application of Nixie Quashie* – HCA No T 89 of 1992 (TT)**
Permanand J

[P15] Section 132 of the Act provides adequate remedies for the Applicant and he has shown no exceptional circumstances exist for the Court to exercise its discretion to proceed and hear the application for judicial review.

In the Application of Kool Temp Trading Co. – HCA No 3875 of 1991 (TT)
Warner J

[P28] Recent cases demonstrate that as a general rule an Applicant should exhaust alternative remedies rather than apply for judicial review. In *R v Epping and Harlow General Commissioners, Ex Parte Goldstraw* [1983] 3 All ER 257, it was held *inter alia* that the application for judicial review was within the residual jurisdiction of the Court, but save in exceptional circumstances, that jurisdiction would not be exercised where other remedies were available and had not been used ... [P30] I hold that there are no exceptional circumstances which would justify the bringing of this application for judicial review. The Applicant Company has an alternative remedy which it has chosen not to pursue.

In the Application of Construction Marketeers and Services Ltd –
HCA No 1761 of 1989 (TT)
Hosein J

[P2] Where the Legislature has created a Court to deal with specific matters, the Applicant ought to have recourse to that Court.

Wadinambiaratchi v Hakeem Ahmad and Others (1985) 35 WIR 325 (TT)
Bernard JA

[PP345–346] In my opinion, the facts and circumstances of this case fall squarely within the principles laid down in *Thomson v University of London* (1864) 33 LJ Ch 625 and *Thorne v University of London* [1966] 2 All ER 338. The signatories to the charter deliberately and consciously chose Her Majesty to be the visitor. In this regard, I take the view that having regard to the broad terms of Section 6 of the charter, Her Majesty's appointment was not ceremonial but one of general visitatorial jurisdiction. As I see it, it was open to the Respondents to petition Her Majesty through Her Privy Council by way of appeal (see *Ex Parte Kirby Ravensworth Hospital* (1808) 15 Ves 305; *R v Dean and Chapter of Chester* [1850] 15 QB 513; and the cases cited at footnote 37 at page 614 of Dr Peter Smith's article at 97 LQR 610). Alternatively, they could have sought Her Majesty's permission to resit the examination in the event that they had failed. If so, it would have been open to Her Majesty to consider the representations herself or appoint a delegate, if she so chose, to consider and decide upon the prayer on her behalf. This, in my view, was the better and proper course. It may well be that, had this course been pursued, the latter prayer at least may well have struck a responsive chord in the mind of Her Majesty or her delegate. The Respondents instead chose to come to the Courts. In my view, on the facts and the law, as I see it, they had no right of query in our legal forum. The matter, in my opinion, was a purely domestic affair which fell within the exclusive jurisdiction of the visitor or her delegate. Accordingly, for this and the other reasons which I have sought to show their summons, in my opinion, should have been struck out by the trial Judge.

In the Application of Web Communications Ltd – Supreme Court No M030 of 2002 (JM)
Smith J

[P17] On the issue of whether the Applicant should be allowed to proceed to Judicial Review without reference to alternative mechanisms or statutory scheme, it is my opinion that the Courts must never be too anxious or too eager to engage in Judicial Review, unless it is absolutely necessary. Where Parliament legislates and proper procedures are put in place for the implementation of those provisions the Court should have due regard for the legislation. It should bear in mind what was the intent and purpose of that legislation. In this case the Telecommunications Act 2000 sets out the framework for the carrying out of the functions of the Office of Utilities Regulation. If it is to operate to its optimum and carry out its functions as envisaged, then it ought not to be fettered by whimsical challenges to its authority. If Judicial Review were to be granted in all such circumstances then the Office of Utilities Regulation would be rendered ineffective and powerless and this to my mind would certainly defeat the whole purpose and intent of the Act.

In the Application of Harry Persaud – **HCSCJ No 795 of 1995 (GY)**
Biscessar J

[P6] Apart from appeal, where there are other alternative remedies which are more appropriate the Court ought to refuse certiorari . . . [P7] In the determination of this submission I have considered these principles again and being convinced that the appeal procedure in the instant case is not as expeditious as an application for certiorari I find, therefore, that it is not a ground for refusing the instant application.

In the Application of Winston Hermanstyne – **HCSCJ No 4805 of 1997 (GY)**
Biscessar J

[P5] I am convinced that the appeal procedure in the instant case is not as expeditious as an application for certiorari and therefore is not a ground for refusing the instant application.

4.9 REMEDY SOUGHT MUST BE MEANINGFUL

Judges have generally adopted the position that a judicial review proceeding must be capable of producing a meaningful remedy and in the absence of such, the court will not be lightly engaged in what might merely be an academic exercise. Further remedies granted must not cause adverse hardship to third parties.

In the Application of Dennis Graham – **HCA No S-156 of 2005 (TT)**
Pemberton J

[P13] [32] DECLATORY RELIEF. The **Act** is clear—declatory relief in and of itself can be granted on an application for Judicial Review once it is just and convenient. [33] ACADEMIC INTEREST. Courts do not like making orders in vain, but will not shy away from making prospective declarations should the need arise to do so. This does not arise in this case.

In the Application of Trinidad And Tobago Information Access –
HCA No Cv 1054 of 2004 (TT)
Jamadar J

[P3] In these circumstances, this Court opined that the essential order sought for access and disclosure of information was too vague, general and unspecific, and to make such an order would be unjustifiably onerous and oppressive . . . In the exercise of this Court's discretion it was considered inappropriate to make an order that would be oppressive, otiose, unenforceable or impossible to police.

In the Application of Florence Bobb and Girlie Moses – **Civil No 2663 of 2002 (TT)**
Mohammed J

[P8] Declaratory relief in judicial review will not be granted if the issues raised are academic, hypothetical and/or premature and, moreover, a combination of all three . . . [P9] Dependent on what transpires in the Parliament, the House of Representatives may well become duly constituted by the election of a Speaker and the passage of a budget, or the Prime Minister may be left with no practical choice but to call a General Election, a matter for his political judgment. It may well be called before the time suggested by the Applicants. The issues raised in this application are of therefore academic significance at this stage, and are also raised prematurely.

***In the Application of Florence Bobb and Girlie Moses* – Civil Appeal No 97 of 2002 (TT)[1]**
Nelson JA

[PP22–23] The true basis for the discretion to hear academic disputes was stated by Lord Slynn in *R v Home Secretary, Ex Parte Salem* [1999] 1 AC 450, 457: 'The discretion to hear disputes, even in the area of public law, must, however, be exercised with caution and appeals which are academic between the parties should not be heard unless there is a good reason in the public interest for doing so, as for example (but only by way of example) when a discrete point of statutory construction arises which does not involve detailed consideration of facts and where a large number of similar cases exist or are anticipated so that the issue will most likely need to be resolved in the near future.' I am satisfied that the restated questions of constitutional importance have already been decided. Nothing has been put forward to indicate that tied elections in a matrix of identical or even similar facts are likely to recur in the near future. In exercising his discretion whether or not to grant leave the learned judge was entitled to consider that a Court hearing an academic issue in a substantive hearing might then decline to rule in the matter: see *Hilly v Governor-General of the Solomon Islands* [1994] 2 LRC 27, 46F–47A . . . [P23] For these reasons, I consider that the learned judge correctly exercised his discretion not to grant leave on the basis that the issues left at the hearing were at that stage academic and premature. The post-application events confirm the Judge's decision and further support his decision not to grant leave.

***Vinode Jhagroo* – Privy Council Appeal No 35 of 2001 (TT)**
Lord Walker of Gestingthorpe

[PP14–15] 38. Mr Fitzgerald's primary submission was that the Appellant was not merely an employee, but was also an office-holder, and that there had never been any valid decision of the TSC which brought his tenure of office to an end. The appropriate remedy, therefore, was a declaration, and so far as monetary compensation was concerned, the Appellant's claim was not a claim for damages, but was founded in debt. Mr Fitzgerald relied on the decision of the House of Lords in *Malloch v Aberdeen Corporation* [1971] 1 WLR 1578 and the decision of the Constitution Court of South Africa in *Hoffmann v South African Airways* [2001] 2 LRC 277 (especially at pp 297–8) . . . [P15] 41. This is not an appropriate case for their Lordships to embark on a full analysis of the sometimes obscure border between tenure of a statutory office and employment under a contract of service. Even if the position is regarded in terms of a statutory office regulated by public law, it is a matter of judicial discretion whether a litigant, who has been unlawfully dismissed (or compelled to resign), and has in fact ceased to perform any of the duties of the office, should be granted an order for reinstatement: see *Chief Constable of the North Wales Police v Evans* [1982] 1 WLR 1155. [PP15–16] 42. In the present case, there would be a high degree of unreality in a declaration that the Appellant is still a member of the Teaching Service, or in an order directing the TSC to reappoint him to the Teaching Service. It is now over eight years since the Appellant last taught at Fyzabad ASS. He is now 50 years of age. Since he was forced to stop teaching he has had very serious health problems which have resulted in the amputation of both his legs. [P16] 43. Their Lordships feel great sympathy for the Appellant in these grave misfortunes. But it would not be appropriate to make an order which had the practical effect of requiring the TSC to appoint the Appellant (who may not be well enough to discharge his duties) to an office which is no doubt now held by another history teacher. The Appellant himself seems to have recognised, in his first affidavit, that his employment had effectively been terminated.

1 Decision of the Court of Appeal upheld by the Privy Council in Privy Council Appeal No. 50 of 2004.

In the Application of Dr Mentor Melville – HCA No 191 of 1998 / HCA No T 35 of 1998 (TT)
Kangaloo J

[P11] It is trite law that the grant of relief in judicial review proceedings is discretionary and would not be granted where the same is useless.

In the Application of Rodwell Murray – HCA No 5534 of 1996 (TT)
Ramlogan J

[P11] The remedy is discretionary and the Court would not grant an order for certiorari if no good would result. If an order of certiorari is granted then Mr Guy's appointment would thereby be quashed, someone would have to be appointed in his place and the process for appointment of a Deputy Commissioner would have to start all over again. More than this, even if the Commission were able to reconsider its appointment before the Applicant's date of retirement on the 2nd June, 1997, it is hardly likely that the Applicant would be appointed to the post at this stage. An order for certiorari or a declaration would serve no useful purpose. Failure to comply with the Regulations may well have deprived the Applicant of promotion and benefits following from it.

In the Application of Steve Ramsaroop, Ramnarine Beharrylal, Sham Mohammed, Francis Seebarran and Deonarine Jawahir – HCA No S-1569 of 1996 (TT)
Mendonca J

[P11] It has been stated in a number of authorities that the function of the Courts are, *inter alia*, to decide only live practical questions and they are not concerned with hypothetical, premature or academic questions. In *Marco's Leisure v West Lothian District Licensing Board*, the Times Law Reports (14 January 1993) relief was refused since to grant it would be academic or of no practical use. In my view this application is subject to the same criticism.

In the Application of Maharaj Trading and Transport Company Ltd – HCA No 2057 of 1993 (TT)
Warner J

[P14] The author Clive Lewis in his work *Judicial Remedies in Public Law* at pages 186 to 190, treats with the topic of 'restrictions on the grant of declaratory relief.' While he recognizes that the Court's jurisdiction is extremely broad, he refers to the Court's reluctance to grant relief where the matter is hypothetical; for example where the issue is raised prematurely. Mrs. Allahar has pointed out that in England, the Town Planning Act 1971 provides for the grant of an 'established use certificate' to a person who claims that a particular use of land in which he has an interest has become established. There is no parallel provision in the local Act. I am of the view that it is not to be assumed that the Respondent will fail to pay heed to the judgment; so that no declaratory or prohibitory order will be granted.

In the Application of Joyce Marshall – HCA No 5161 of 1989 (TT)
Warner J

[P4] It was contended that the burden rests on the Applicant for judicial review to surmount the hurdle created by delay. Where despite delay the Court has granted leave to make the application, it is still open to the Respondent to object *in limine* that there has been undue delay . . . [PP10–11] It is also clear from the same judgment that it is not for the Respondent on the application for judicial review to prove substantial hardship or substantial prejudice, the burden to prove that neither of these will result is on the Applicant if the issue is raised. Again, from the judgment of Edoo JA, it can be seen that it is desirable that before leave is given where *prima facie* there has been undue delay and in particular in certiorari applications where three months have passed, the Respondent be given an opportunity to be heard on the question. In the instant case, I did not before granting leave give an opportunity to the Respondents to be heard. Nevertheless at the time I did give some consideration to the lapse of time before exercising my discretion to grant the leave to apply for judicial review. The Respondents were however entitled to take a preliminary objection on the question of delay and the Court had to decide it on the material available and on the arguments on both sides . . . [PP11–12] The discretion in respect of leave had already been exercised, the discretion in respect of relief failed to be exercised. As I saw it, two courses were open to me. One was to reserve the question of exercising discretion whether or not to grant the relief in the light of the undue delay to the end of the hearing of the merits, the second was to decide at that stage that it was unnecessary to proceed with a hearing on the merits and to dismiss the application on the ground of the Applicants' undue delay in applying for leave to pursue certiorari proceedings . . . [P13] Having found that there was undue delay, and that the Applicants had failed to establish that granting the relief sought would not be likely to cause substantial hardship or prejudice the rights of the Respondents and was not detrimental to good administration, I declined to grant an extension of time for the making of the application and dismissed the motion on the ground of undue delay.

***Regina v The Minister of Agriculture ex parte D.Y.C. Fishing Ltd* – Supreme Court No M-069 and M-146 of 2002 (JM)**
Reid J

[PP5–6] Judicial Review being a discretionary remedy must take account of whether impugned activities were substantially unlawful or were in substance, lawful but exhibiting deficiencies in strict compliance with the Act and Regulations. To the extent that the reliefs seek statutory interpretations of the provisions a Court should selectively avoid mere academic exercises unless there are some points of public importance demanding a determination. Moreover, where orders would involve a day-to-day supervision of the activities, in this case, of the Competent Authority and by extension that of the Veterinary Committee in its role as advisor to the CA, the making of such orders would be superfluous. Consideration must be had to orders which if granted would be detrimental to good administration having regard to events long past and the *status quo* on which the public in general, and in this case, the international community, would have relied. The interval of two years between the grant of leave to proceed to Judicial Review and the commencement of this hearing (even without ascribing fault to the Claimant) must render certain issues, stale or otiose. Since, however there is a difference in the interpretation as to who is a qualified engineer, a declaration is called for, notwithstanding the CA and the VC agreeing that an engineer's report would henceforth be required. Agreement on this, as well as other items, demonstrates the commitment to strict compliance with the provisions of the Act notwithstanding deficiencies that have been demonstrated. As to relief 2(i), instead of a prohibiting order, a declaration is hereby made that the licensing of a processing establishment requires the statement from a qualified refrigeration engineer. Such certification will provide proper determination of capacities and sufficiency of facilities postulated in reliefs 2(a), 2(o) and 2(p) and determine the issue of requiring separate refrigeration, freezer and storage compartments as variations in configuration obtain.

***In the Application of ICWI Investments Ltd, Patrick Rosseau and Ivor Campbell* – Supreme Court No M-08 of 2002 (JM)**
Wolfe CJ

[PP3–4] The hallowed principle comes to mind viz, a Court must never act in vain. To do so is to make a mockery of the Court's jurisdiction. The offer having been made, the exemption granted by the Commission ceases to be of any effect. What then is the purpose of an order to quash the decision granting the exemption? The making of the offer is a clear indication by Life of Jamaica Holdings Limited that it is no longer relying on the exemption granted by the Commission. The offer is an admission by Life of Jamaica Holdings Limited that the Applicants are entitled to be offered the option of selling their shares in the company. I am satisfied that to grant the order sought is an exercise in futility. Further the refusal to grant the order will in no way prejudice the Applicants. If the Applicants have sustained any loss, because of the offer not having been made at the correct time, such loss is recoverable in an action for damages. It must be borne in mind that certiorari is a discretionary remedy. The fact that a person aggrieved is entitled to certiorari *ex debito justitiae* does not alter the fact that the Court has power to exercise its discretion against him, as it may in the case of any discretionary remedy. I am not unmindful that the greatest care must be taken in the exercise of this discretion. For the reasons stated, I would refuse the application for an order of certiorari.

4.10 PREJUDICE TO THIRD PARTIES

The courts may decline leave for judicial review where there is prejudice to third parties. Even where an order for leave has been obtained, the remedies that may be granted against a decision-maker could be withheld if it may have an adverse impact on third parties.

***In the Application of Fishermen and Friends of the Sea* – HCA No 1715 of 2002 (TT)**
Bereaux J

[P19] BPTT has invested heavily in the construction of the Project, since December 2001 shortly after the grant of the CEC. Even though I accept that Mr Aboud did not have concrete information of the grant of the CEC until March 2002, the fact is that more than five and a half months elapsed before the application for judicial review was filed. In the interim BPTT, acting on the decision of the Respondent, has proceeded apace with the construction of the project at considerable expense and without any notice from the Applicant of its intention to mount a legal challenge to the grant of the CEC. It was not until the day of the filing of the application for judicial review that BPTT was informed. More appropriate notice would have been at least from mid March 2001 when the grant of the CEC was confirmed. The Applicant's conduct in the light of its failure to warn both BPTT and the Respondent of its intended action is a factor to be considered in deciding whether to exercise its discretion to grant leave or not.

The decision of Bereaux J in the *Fishermen and Friends of the Sea* action was endorsed by the majority decision of the Court of Appeal.

***In the Application of Fishermen and Friends of the Sea* –**
Civil Appeal No 106 of 2002 (TT)
Nelson JA

[P14] In the light of his own findings and the evidence before the learned judge he was entitled to exercise his discretion by refusing to extend the time for applying for leave to bring judicial review proceedings.

***In the Application of Gulf Insurance Ltd* – Civil Appeal No 32 of 2000 (TT)**
Nelson JA

[P46] In my judgment, even if the decisions were *ultra vires*, the Court could properly withhold remedies for unlawful administrative action including declaratory relief because the grant of such remedies might have an adverse impact on third parties.

4.11 GOOD ADMINISTRATION

Like the position on prejudice to third parties, the courts are also reluctant to grant leave for judicial review or provide certain remedies where it may prove inimical to the imperatives of good administration.

***In the Application of Clyde de Coteau* – HCA No Cv S 2108 of 2003 (TT)**
Jamadar J

[P6] In the principal affidavit of the Applicant, no good reason is given for this delay. The statement at paragraph 12 that: 'From the time that I received notice that the Commission declared that I had resigned my office in the Fire Service until the present time, I did not have the necessary funds available to me to retain an Attorney at Law to obtain the necessary legal advice on the matter or to file the necessary Court proceedings necessary to vindicate my rights,' is not credible . . . In the realm of Public Law, good administration requires timeliness, finality and certainty. Those who wish to challenge decisions and/or failures to make decisions must be prepared to act promptly if they are to assert their rights. Thus, it is only for good reasons, which must mean credible and *bona fide* reasons, that this statutory requirement will be extended.

***In the Application of Fishermen and Friends of the Sea* –**
Civil Appeal No 106 of 2002 (TT)
Nelson JA

[P24] At least five other companies in the oil and gas sector of the economy are affected. If the EMA's decision on the Project were re-opened it would lead to other applications to review EMA clearances in respect of those projects. I can take judicial notice of the importance of the oil and gas sector to the economy of Trinidad and Tobago. In the circumstances I would agree with the learned judge for these additional reasons that it would be detrimental to good administration not to treat the EMA's decision on November 29, 2001 as final in the face of the Appellant's delay.

4.12 GRANTING REVIEW OR SUBSTITUTING DECISION

While the court will exercise supervisory jurisdiction and may find a decision to be wrong, it will set aside the decision but will not substitute its own decision for that of the decision-maker.

***Dougnath Rajkumar* – Privy Council Appeal No 1 of 2001 (TT)**
Lord Mackay of Clashfern

[PP15–16] 23. While there may be cases in which the result of a successful judicial review is that the legal considerations provide a unique admissible decision which the statutory authority could lawfully give in the circumstances, that is not the position in the present case since promotion to Prison Officer II is necessarily competitive. For this reason the decision of Lucky J cannot be supported. In the circumstances their Lordships are of the view that the Appellant is entitled to a decision that insofar as the decisions impugned did not promote him they are flawed, but on the other hand their Lordships cannot accede to setting aside these decisions insofar as they appoint others whose promotion their Lordships are not empowered to question. The appropriate relief accordingly is that the case should be remitted to the Public Service Commission urgently to review the Appellant's application for promotion, to take account in that consideration of the length of time for which the Appellant has served in the position of acting Prison Officer II without complaint or adverse comment, to take account of all the other matters mentioned in Regulation 172 and in the light of that to decide whether the Applicant's present position as acting Prison Officer II should be upgraded to a full substantive appointment as Prison Officer II; and if the Commission decides not to award the promotion it shall give its reasons for doing so under each of the applicable heads of Regulation 172.

***In the Application of Charles Vernon Frederick, Mookish Pulliah Shamshudeen Mohammed, Adrian Pascal, Wilbert Lovell and Kundan Nancoo* – HCA No S 111 of 2003 (TT)**
Dean-Armorer J

[P10] This Court, of course, on an application for judicial review has no power to order that the Public Service Commission make the promotions, of which the Applicants are hopeful. This Court is however invested with the power to order, following the Judicial Committee of the Privy Council in the case of *Dou[g]nath Rajkumar v Lalla and Others*, that the Public Service Commission consider and act upon the original list of the Commissioner of Prisons and if the Public Service Commission decides against awarding the promotions to the Applicants, it shall provide reasons to the Applicants for their unsuitability for promotion ... In the absence of an agreed position, I can find no basis for stipulating a time-frame from a body such as a Service Commission. I can go no further than to order that the issue be reviewed urgently and to urge the Public Service Commission to be mindful of the colossal disadvantage with which the Applicants now contend.

***In the Application of Kenneth Lalla, Henley Wooding, Corinre Mohammed, Carlyle Walters, Sakal Seemungal (Members of the Public Service Commission)* – Civil Appeal No 128 of 1999 (TT)**
Sharma JA

[P2] It is important to appreciate that a power of a judge in judicial review proceedings is not unlimited. It is not for him to make the decision. It is for the person entrusted with the power to do so. He must, in my respectful view resist every temptation to supplant his decision for that of the tribunal, even though he perceives the latter is unfair or unjust. The judge can quash the decision, either because it is illegal or wrong or for some other reason, he cannot remake the decision. The quashed decision is remitted to the tribunal, in the light of any guidance given by the Court, so that any decision thereafter made does not have the taint of being illegal or wrongful.

Nelson JA

[P26] Secondly, in *Chief Constable of North Wales v Evans* [1982] 1 WLR 1155 (HL) Lord Hailsham reminded Judges at 1160G that 'it is no part of that purpose [sc. of the remedies of judicial review] to substitute the opinion of the judiciary or of individual Judges for that of the authority constituted by law to decide the matters in question.' It is clear therefore that in the present case there was no jurisdiction in the Courts to promote the Applicant.

***In the Application of Roland de Verteuil* – Civil Appeal No 55 of 1989 (TT)**
de la Bastide CJ

[P7] We have no doubt that if this failure to conform to good industrial relations practice had been brought to the attention of the Industrial Court in appropriate proceedings, the Appellant would not have gone without redress. But for the reasons I have given, we are not in a position to offer any such redress. I would express the hope, I trust not merely a pious one, that the Authority may see it fit even at this stage to provide some compensation for what I regard as its unfair treatment of the Appellant.

***R v Resident Magistrate for St. Andrew ex parte Ervin Walker* (1981) 18 JLR 6 (JM)**
Parnell J

[P8] Now, where a statute gives a person power to do something coupled with a discretion a very strong case would have to be made out to say that Mandamus should go to that person to do his duty, if that person has exercised the discretion given judiciously. In other words, where there was no application of a wrong principle; or there was no consideration of any irrelevant matter what has been done cannot be controverted. And, even if the Court were to take the view that it would not have exercised its discretion in the way it was done, if that is the only thing, then mandamus cannot go because there could be no question of compelling a person to do what he honestly thinks, by the exercise of his discretion, should not be done at all. It seems that that is what happened in this case.

It is accepted that the courts will not usurp the authority of a decision-maker.

***In the Application of Ishwar Galbaransingh and Northern Construction Ltd* – HCA No 1202 of 1997 (TT)**
Warner J

[P24] It is not at all the Court's business to usurp the authority of the Cabinet or any public body in this matter. I am content to make clear what I have been convinced is the Applicants' position in the eyes of the law.

***In the Application of Ramesh Lawrence Maharaj* – HCA No 2337 of 1986 (TT)**
Collymore J

[P57] I consider next the submission by Mr Sedley that the proceedings show that so insufficient a case has been made out by the prosecution that it would be in the interest of justice if this Court should now discharge him. He then carried out a searching analysis of the facts in support of his point. In my judgment, Mr Alexander was right in his reply that for this Court to do so would be for me to usurp the function of the Magistrate. There has been no finding on the enquiry for this Court to review. This is all the more so in light of my decision that the case should now continue for the purpose of taking further evidence of the handwriting experts. I must, therefore, refrain from making any comment whatever on the nature of that evidence.

***R v The Town and Country Planning Authority ex parte Auburn Court Ltd and Delbert Perrier* (1988) 25 JLR 223 (JM)**
Malcolm J

[P225] This Court does not act in the capacity of a reviewing body as it is not clothed with appellate powers. It is not for us to decide whether the facts before us we would have come to a conclusion contrary to that of the Authority as to do so would be tantamount to a usurpation of the functions of the Authority. Neither can we say that based upon the facts before us and the reasons given by the Authority for its refusal that such a responsible body acted illegally, irrationally, or with procedural impropriety.

***In the Application of Edgar Aaron* – Civil Appeal No 41 of 1997 (GY)**
Kennard C

[P8] The order of discharge issued by the Commissioner of Police having been set aside by the trial Judge, the Appellant is quite free to pursue such other course of action as he may be advised by Counsel but we cannot make an order directing the Commissioner of Police to re-instate him in the Police Force which as Lord Hailsham had stated might border on the usurpation of the powers of the Commissioner of Police, which is to be avoided.

Notwithstanding the general principle of law whereby courts would not substitute their decision for that of a decision-maker, there are times when courts, in delivering their orders, have come perilously close to so doing.

***In the Application of Gaynell Mc Donald* – HCA No 4098 of 1987 (TT)**
Ibrahim J

[P12] The matter is, therefore, referred back to the parties for further consideration and determination, but failing which, the Court will finally decide the issues.

***In the Application of Earl Lewis* – HCA No 3847 of 1985 (TT)**
Collymore J

[P13] I find, therefore, that so far as concerns the allegations at (a) to (c) of the grounds which were supplied in the Commission's letters of 20/1/84 there has been shown to have occurred a breach of the rules of Natural Justice in that the Applicant was condemned without having been given any impartial hearing in his defence. Justice was manifestly not seen to have been done in these instances . . . [P14] If an officer's work and conduct has been unsatisfactory over any period, then good administration and fair dealing would demand that the short-comings observed by his superiors be pointed out to him with the appropriate warning as to the possible consequences to him in the future if there was no improvement in his performance. To leave such a matter unspoken and then to take the cumulative effect of ten such reports is manifestly unjust . . . [P16] In effect therefore, the result of this decision is that not only is the dismissal order of the Commission quashed, but I must now direct the Commission to—'reach a decision in accordance with the findings of the Court.' This I interpret to mean that the Court is empowered in effect to order the re-instatement of the officer and I now so order.

4.13 WRONG PARTY

It is important that a person seeking judicial review of a decision from a public body ensure that the proper party is brought before the court.

***In the Application of Sanatan Dharma Maha Sabha of Trinidad and Tobago* –**
HCA No 438 of 2004 (TT)
Best J

[P8] Applying the foregoing to the extant matter, I have formed the view and so hold that an application, under the FOIA for documentary information, concerning the activities of a director of the Central Bank, must be made to the Responsible Minister and not to the Governor of the said Bank.

***In the Application of Beshpati Gunness* – HCA No S-1999 of 1986 (TT)**
Blackman J

[P4] It is clear to me that upon a reading of Sections 128 and 132 of the Summary Act together with Sections 13, 44 and 47 of the Act that a statutory appeal procedure was available to the Applicant . . . [PP7–8] I can see nothing in the grounds put forward by the Applicant or in his affidavit which takes his case beyond the remedies available to him under the statutory appeal procedure. Further no good reason has been advanced by the Applicant to justify my coming to the conclusion that any exceptional circumstances exist for by-passing the appeal procedures provided for under the Summary Act . . . [P11] From the judgments in the Canadian jurisdiction it is not quite clear whether there are such statutory provisions as exist in Trinidad and Tobago for example provisions analogous to Section 19(2) of the State Liability and Proceedings Act. Further there is nothing to distinguish the instant point from the one raised in *Sooknanan*. I must therefore follow *Sooknanan*. In consequence I hold that the Attorney General has been improperly joined in these proceedings.

***Wadinambiaratchi v Hakeem Ahmad and Others* (1985) 35 WIR 325 (TT)**
Bernard JA

[PP335–336] It is a matter of undisputed record that the institution first came into being as the University College of the West Indies under royal charter granted on 9th January 1949, and that it was later granted university status under a royal charter of incorporation made by letters patent on 22nd April 1962. The first charter provided that the reigning monarch would always be visitor to the college and the second one provided for HM

Queen Elizabeth II to fill that position . . . [P337] The power to grant a declaratory relief is discretionary. The discretion should be exercised with due care and caution and judicially with regard to all the circumstances of the case. Hence, it is necessary that the proper parties should be before the Court. The law on the point is succinctly stated in de Smith's *Judicial Review of Administrative Action* (4th Edn) page 510. There the author in reliance upon the cases cited in the appropriate footnotes states: 'Not only must there be a plaintiff whose legal interests are affected sufficiently to enable him to sue; the Defendant must be one whose legal interests are sufficiently affected by the plaintiff's claim (or whose conduct could be sufficiently affected by judgment in the plaintiff's favour) to render him a competent party to defend the action. And even if a competent Defendant is before the Court, the Court will, save in exceptional circumstances, decline to make a declaration affecting the interests of persons who are not before it; all those whose interests are liable to be affected should be made parties to the action.' . . . [PP337–338] In my opinion, the facts and circumstances fall squarely within the principles stated above. The Appellant had no 'interests' in the matter. He was a servant of the university and was merely carrying out the lawful directions of the Board for Higher Degrees. The notice said so. The decision was that of the Board, not his. The actual contents of the notice were later confirmed by Mr Draper, the Vice-Dean of the Social Sciences Faculty, who at the time was likewise acting on the direction of the Board. The Appellant was, in my view, not the proper party to the action . . . [PP338–339] It is to be recorded that before this Court, it was acknowledged (indeed it was conceded) that no rule of natural justice had been breached here. Natural justice was not in issue. What was in issue was the interpretation and/or clarification of Regulation 52. The clarification of a rule could not in the circumstances involve a breach of natural justice. Regulation 52 is discretionary and in any event its provisions are subordinate to those of the charter. In the result, I take the view that under the provisions of the laws regulating the day-to-day management of the university, the latter is under no duty to communicate to the students concerned its system of marking, as distinct from the method of examination. This was the crux of the contention of the Appellant and my examination of the relevant provisions of the charter and of Regulation 52 impels me to the conclusion that his contention is correct. That apart, it seems to me that the decision of the Board (as conveyed in the notice) was in the nature of a facility to the students more particularly at that stage; and as I see it, far from being detrimental, it was of necessity beneficial to them. What the Respondents in effect sought to achieve was the grant in the end of an indulgence to them which, by its very nature, would have done violence to the declared objects and powers of the university as set out in Sections 2 and 3 of the charter, which is the supreme law.

***In the Application of Millicent Forbes* – Supreme Court No HCV – 01386 of 2004 (JM) Smith J**

[P7] The Attorney General is not a proper Defendant to Judicial Review proceedings, as an order for certiorari is a Prerogative Remedy and thus cannot lie against the Crown.

4.14 ADJOURNMENTS

In an interesting decision, the court had to determine whether to grant an adjournment because of rulings made on preliminary issues in a judicial review application so as to allow the aggrieved party to appeal the rulings on the preliminary issues. The court took the view that such adjournments are not likely to be granted and refused the same.

In the Application of Gillette Marina Ltd – **HCA No Cv S 1747 of 2002 (TT)**
Jamadar J

[PP5–6] In my opinion, the weight of authority suggests that barring some special or exceptional grounds or circumstances, a Court should not readily adjourn the hearing of a trial to facilitate an appeal on matters raised during the course of the trial or even at an interlocutory stage. The reasons for this approach are stated in the cited cases . . . [PP6–7] As I have explained, largely for the sake of good management of the proceedings and in order to ensure a measure of certainty for the hearing of the substantive motion, the Respondent's application to strike out was treated as an interlocutory application. If these applications were heard during the substantive hearing, there would be no doubt, that barring special grounds or exceptional circumstances, it would be an abuse of process to adjourn the substantive hearing pending the determination of an appeal against a ruling on the admissibility of evidence. Certainly, in an ordinary civil trial context, when evidence is objected to and excluded, such an application for an adjournment is unlikely to succeed . . . [P7] Also, even though novel points were raised which may be of some importance in the realm of Public Law, that in and of itself cannot justify the adjournment sought. Part and parcel of the Court's function is to hear and determine novel and important issues of law. The Court's duty is to rule impartially and in a timely manner on the issues and so facilitate the judicial process.

4.15 NATURE OF DECISION

It is often the case in judicial review proceedings that the question arises as to what constitutes a decision. The courts have agreed that a liberal meaning ought to be given to the meaning of decision.

In the Application of Dr Colin Furlonge – **HCA No Cv 2098 of 2003 (TT)**
Jamadar J

[P15] The decision under review is a recommendation of the Respondent. As such it is a preliminary decision to the 'final' decision of the PSC with respect to the appointment of an officer to an acting appointment. A preliminary decision such as this is amenable to judicial review. It is reviewable to ensure that:

i. there has been a lawful exercise of power, and
ii. the relevant procedural requirements have been observed.

It is also reviewable because this preliminary decision can affect the career of an officer, as in this case to the Applicant's detriment. And also because, a recommendation, such as the one under consideration, is a precondition to the exercise of the statutory power in the PSC to appoint an officer to an acting position. In any event, a recommendation such as this is likely to be taken into account by the PSC before making its decision. To this extent, a recommendation can be considered advice likely in practice to be followed or considered by the final decision-maker (and certainly 'advice' given pursuant to a statutory power—Regulation 27) . . . [PP16–17] The declared policy is that as a general rule acting appointments under Regulation 26 are to be made in favour of the most senior eligible officer. There is an established system for ranking officers according to seniority, which is purposeful. Thus, procedurally, the Regulations require that all eligible officers be notified where an acting appointment falls to be made. And, that before a recommendation is made seven days be allowed to elapse to facilitate independent representations by any such officers. Further, where any officers are being passed over, that reasons for same be given accompanying the recommendations. This Court has added a further procedural requirement, that, generally, where an eligible officer is passed over the reasons for same are to be given to him/her no less than seven (7) clear days before the date on which a decision is likely to be made by the PSC. There is no good reason why, in the context of this regime, if the person recommended is 'the most able and competent officer,' who also happens to be junior to other eligible officers, that this reason with adequate particulars cannot be given, both to the PSC and the officer(s) passed over. As indeed they should. Lord Slynn has pointed out (in Ex Parte Salem (1999) 2 WIR 483 at 488): 'reviews which are academic should not be heard unless there is good reason in the public interest for doing so.' As I have sought to demonstrate, in this case, given the erroneous practice being followed by the Respondent and the issues under review, and given the wide ranging implications of a flawed procedure being perpetuated, there is every good reason in the public interest to adjudicate on these matters . . . [P18] Clearly the Applicant felt aggrieved by the approach of the Respondent in this matter and the victim of a history of prejudicial treatment. The Applicant, through his attorneys, took every step to bring to the Respondent's attention the errors in the approach being adopted, but to no avail. Before this Court, the attorneys for the Respondent and the Attorney General have accepted the illegality and procedural impropriety of the Respondent's conduct. Costs must, therefore, follow the event.

In the Application of Chandresh Sharma – Civil Appeal No 115 of 2003 (TT)
Nelson JA

[P13] The word 'decision' in section 5 is not to be given a narrow meaning. It covers any deliberate acts or omissions amounting to unlawful administration.

Of course, it depends on the facts of individual cases and, in some instances, a judicial review application, with respect to a preliminary decision, may be held to be premature.

In the Application of Jules Bernard – HCA No 2361 of 1993 (TT)
Ramlogan J

[PP14–15] There is nothing to indicate that anything has been done or not done which taints the process. The letter, in my view, does not constitute a decision to retire the Applicant. It merely says that the Commission would be considering whether it ought to retire the Applicant. The Applicant's contention seems to be that the Commission has indicated its intention to retire him. That is a very different thing from what the letter says. The letter is seeking to get information so that the Commission could consider whether the Applicant should be retired. It is a mere preliminary step. In any case, how has the Commission erred in arriving at the decision that it ought to consider whether the Applicant should be retired? There is no breach of the rules of natural justice. What is there to be reviewed? The Court should not interfere unless some injustice has been done or injustice is inevitable. Whether or not that is so must be determined by looking at the matter as a whole. One cannot look at just one step. There is nothing to suggest that any injustice has been done or that injustice is inevitable. The Commission should not be bogged down by mere technicalities emanating from flights of the imagination. At this stage the Court must do what it can to ensure that Judicial Review is not used to stultify the *bona fide* efforts of the Commission. It seems to me that if this application for leave were to be granted, it would be an unnecessary interference with the Commission in the performance of its duties. The public interest demands that the issue as to whether the Applicant ought to be retired or not be expeditiously dealt with. In these matters private rights must be protected but the public interest cannot be ignored. If there is ground for intervention by the Court, at a later stage the Applicant can be heard. But the Police Service Commission must be allowed to continue with its work.

In the Application of Infochannel Ltd **– Supreme Court No M40 of 2001 (JM)**
Harris J

[P28] The OUR dealt only with incoming bypass. It had not fully inquired into the complaints from C&WJ with respect to both incoming and outgoing calls and had not reached a conclusion that the Applicant had engaged in bypass activities. The Applicant was informed that the ruling of March 12 was of an interim nature. The Applicant complained that it did not obtain certain documents, in particular those with respect to the Group B lines which it declared it had not received prior to the February 21 hearing. It is now in possession of those documents. The proposed hearing will afford the Applicant an opportunity to make submissions and to be heard. The intended Inquiry by the OUR will not amount to a new hearing of a complaint upon which the OUR had already adjudicated and will not in any way prove prejudicial to the Applicant.

The Commissioner of Police v Leslie Harper **(1994) 31 JLR 24 (JM)**
Carey JA

[P26] With all respect to the learned judge, I am quite unable to discover from any reading of that directive any facts from which any inference could be drawn that '*quasi-judicial* proceedings with respect to the Applicant, were either pending or in progress.' The letter I suggest, did no more than give directives or what are, in fact, orders to a subordinate officer. These directives gave no indication whatever as to what action was contemplated. It would be the merest speculation as to what the Commissioner's future actions would be. There was no evidence either inferential or direct, in the affidavit or in the directive that proceedings of any kind were either pending or in progress. One would have expected if such proceedings there were that such evidence would be adduced before the Judge. In the absence of any such evidence the challenged order could not be made and it is in that respect that the Judge fell into error. That is, in my view, enough to dispose of the appeal.

R v Commissioner of Customs and Excise ex parte, A. & F. Farm Produce Company Ltd and Andre Chin **(1993) 30 JLR 462 (JM)**
Langrin J

[P469] The rules of natural justice did not render a decision invalid where that decision is only the first step in a sequence which may culminate in a decision detrimental to that person's interest, bearing in mind that the law lays down the procedure for a hearing at a later stage.

4.16 REVIEWING EXECUTIVE ACTIONS

While decisions of administrative bodies and other public bodies exercising quasi-judicial and judicial functions have attracted judicial review, there is a marked divergence in Caribbean Commonwealth courts to judicially review executive actions.

England and Another v Attorney-General of St. Lucia **(1985) 35 WIR 171 (LC)**
Bishop JA

[PP180–182] Perhaps it should have read 'before the Governor-General made the Order' instead of 'when the Governor-General was making the Orders'; but I have interpreted what Mitchell J said there to mean that neither natural justice nor the *audi alteram partem* rule applied to the Englands' case when considered under Section 4(3)(b). I am fortified in my conclusions by findings made in two cases to which I wish to make but brief reference. In *Musson v Rodriguez* [1953] AC 530, an appeal from a judgment of the Supreme Court of Trinidad and Tobago, the Judicial Committee of the Privy Council was invited to consider Section 4 (as amended) of the Immigration (Restriction) Ordinance, which, as will be seen, was expressed in terms not dissimilar from those of Section 4(3)(b) of the Immigration Ordinance (as amended). The former read: '(1) The following persons . . . are prohibited immigrants . . . (h) any person who from information or advice which in the opinion of the Governor-in-Council is reliable information or advice is deemed by the Governor-in-Council to be an undesirable inhabitant of, or visitor to the colony . . . (3) No appeal shall lie against the decision of the Governor-in-Council in regard to any person mentioned in paragraphs . . . (h) . . . unless such appeal be directed to the identity only of the person affected by the decision.' I have already quoted Section 4(3)(b) and (5) of the Immigration Ordinance of St Lucia. In *Musson's case*, after stating that the basis for the whole proceedings was Section 4 (as amended) Lord Normand, who delivered the advice of their Lordships, quoted the section and said: 'The drastic power given to the Governor-in-Council by Section 4(1)(h) to interfere with personal liberty may be exercised without any antecedent judicial inquiry, and without the persons who are affected having had any opportunity of making representations. It is not subject to any appeal to a Court of law or to any form of review at the instance of the affected persons.' Then Lord Normand went on to explain that in such a situation there must be the strictest compliance with the provisions by which such a power is given. The other case, *Brandt v Attorney-General and Austin* (1971) 17 WIR 448, was decided in the Court of Appeal of Guyana. There, the President of Guyana, acting under Section 4 of the Expulsion of Undesirables Ordinance, made an expulsion order against an alien of the Federal Republic of Germany who was at all relevant times lawfully resident in Guyana. It was held that Brandt had no right to have representations by him heard before a deportation order was made, and that the rules of natural justice were of no avail to him. Sir Edward Luckhoo C in his judgment adhered to the principle that had been established by the *Venicoff case*, and he further stressed that the purpose of the Ordinance would be defeated and the necessity for promptitude without previous warning would be frustrated. Bollers CJ also followed the authority of the *Venicoff case* and expressed the opinion that any hearing before the Order was made would have the effect of defeating the purpose of the legislation. Persaud JA was of the view that the President was not performing a judicial or quasi-judicial function when he acted under Section 4 of the Expulsion of Undesirables Ordinance. Cummings JA dealt with the purpose of the relevant Ordinance and pointed out that there was no express provision or necessary implication that there be a hearing at the pre-Order stage, since that could very well have defeated the purpose of the Ordinance and afforded an opportunity for the person affected to go into hiding or abscond. Crane JA stressed that executive authority in Guyana was vested solely in the President and when he made the expulsion Order it was an act of prerogative power, neither curtailed nor abridged by any expressed or implied obligation to afford a hearing before making the Order. At the time of the Order which affected the Englands, the immigrant was a person who had entered St Lucia from a place outside St Lucia and the immigration into St Lucia of any person specified in an Order made by the Governor-General in Council under Section 4(3) of the Immigration Ordinance was prohibited. The Englands (who were not citizens of St Lucia) were such persons. They may have been desirous of becoming registered as citizens of St Lucia, but they had not applied for registration nor been granted registration of citizenship. They were declared to be prohibited immigrants and directed to be removed from the Island. I have found no cause to disturb the decision of the trial Judge and would therefore dismiss the appeal.

Re Blake (1994) 47 WIR 174 (KN)

Floissac CJ

[P178] The ultimate question which arises is whether a Court can properly rule against a decision of a Head of State or other public authority without giving to the authority prior notice of the grounds of objection to the decision and a reasonable opportunity to make representations and to be heard on those grounds before the decision is condemned. According to the '*audi alteram partem*' rule of natural justice, the answer is in the negative.

The Attorney-General (representing the Governor-General) should have been given that notice and opportunity. In the absence of such notice and opportunity, any order made by the High Court on the Appellant's originating summons would have been irregular and liable to be set aside . . . [PP179–180] The decision to appoint a Prime Minister or any other Minister of Government is one of the many decisions which [is] made in the exercise of prerogative powers and which [is] not justiciable or subject to judicial review for the simple reason that the subject matter of the decision is not amenable to the judicial process. In *Council of Civil Service Unions v Minister for the Civil Service* [1985] AC 374 at page 418, Lord Roskill said: 'Many examples were given during the argument of prerogative powers which as at present advised I do not think could properly be made the subject of judicial review. Prerogative powers such as those relating to the making of treaties, the defence of the realm, the prerogative of mercy, the grant of honours, the dissolution of Parliament and the appointment of Ministers as well as others are not, I think, susceptible to judicial review because their nature and subject matter are such as not to be amenable to the judicial process. The Courts are not the place wherein to determine whether a treaty should be concluded or the armed forces disposed in a particular manner or Parliament dissolved on one date rather than another.' In his assessment as to whether a proposed Prime Minister is likely to command the support of the majority of the Representatives, the Governor-General is free to consult not only the Representatives themselves but other persons who should know how the Representatives are likely to behave under certain pressures and circumstances. In *Adegbenro v Akintola* [1963] AC 614 at page 629, Viscount Radcliffe (delivering the judgment of the Privy Council in an appeal from the Federal Supreme Court of Nigeria) said: 'By the words they have employed in their formula, "it appears to him", the judgment as to the support enjoyed by a Premier is left to the Governor's own assessment and there is no limitation as to the material on which he is to base his judgment or the contacts to which he may resort for the purpose. There would have been no difficulty at all in so limiting him if it had been intended to do so'. If the decision of the Governor-General to appoint a Prime Minister was made subject to judicial review, the results could be horrendous. It would mean that the Head of State might be required to divulge sensitive confidential opinions and information imparted by the Representatives and other persons and would be exposed to all the undesirable consequences of such disclosure. Public policy dictates that the Head of State should be spared those consequences. The answer to the question who is 'likely to command the support of the majority of the Representatives' is subjective and the Constitution makes it subjective to the Governor-General's personal judgment. The answer is an elusive issue which is not justiciable. As Lord Brightman said in *R v Hillingdon London Borough Council, Ex Parte Puhlhofer* [1986] 1 AC 484 at page 518: 'Where the existence or non-existence of a fact is left to the judgment and discretion of a public body and that fact involves a broad spectrum ranging from the obvious to the debatable to the just conceivable, it is the duty of the Court to leave the decision of that fact to the public body to whom Parliament has entrusted the decision-making power save in a case where it is obvious that the public body, consciously or unconsciously, is acting perversely'. The Constitution itself provides the procedure for determining whether the Governor-General's decision and the opinion on which the decision was based were correct. That procedure is a motion of no confidence in the Government. The outcome of such a motion would establish conclusively whether or not the Prime Minister in fact commands the support of the majority of the representatives . . . [PP181–182] There is no evidence or justification for the conclusion that the Governor-General's decision was 'so outrageous in its defiance of logic or of accepted moral standards that no sensible person who had applied his mind to the question to be decided could have arrived at it'. There is therefore no valid ground for impugning the Governor-General's decision at a judicial review. But even if the Appellant had proved that the Governor-General's decision was illegal, irrational or procedurally improper, the appropriate remedy would have been a declaration of nullity of the decision and an order of certiorari quashing the decision. The order of mandamus sought could not have been made because such an order would have gone beyond the bounds of judicial review. A Court (hearing an application for judicial review of the decision of a public authority) is not empowered to usurp the powers of the authority by substituting its own opinion or decision for the decision of the authority which is the constitutionally, statutorily or legally authorised decision-maker. The purposes of a judicial review of a public authority's decision are merely to determine whether the decision is legal, rational and procedurally proper, and if not, to make such orders as may be necessary to protect individuals affected by the decision from the illegality, irrationality or procedural impropriety of the decision. In *Chief Constable of the North Wales Police v Evans* [1982] 3 All ER 141 at page 154, Lord Brightman said: 'Judicial review is concerned, not with the decision, but with the decision-making process. Unless that restriction on the power of the Court is observed, the Court will, in my view, under the guise of preventing the abuse of power, be itself guilty of usurping power'. In *Re Amin* [1983] 2 AC 818 at page 829, Lord Fraser of Tullybelton said: 'Judicial review is entirely different from an ordinary appeal. It is made effective by the Court quashing an administrative decision without substituting its own decision, and is to be contrasted with an appeal where the appellate tribunal substitutes its own decision on the merits for that of the administrative officer'. The decisions to remove the Prime Minister, to dissolve Parliament and to issue new writs for general elections are decisions made in the exercise of prerogative powers and discretions which the Constitution has specifically conferred upon the Governor-General. The grant of the mandamus sought would be a usurpation of those powers. It would amount to the making or dictation by the Court of those decisions which the Constitution has reserved specially for the Governor-General as Head of State. The application for the mandamus implied in the Appellant's originating summons was therefore correctly refused.

4.17 REVIEWING JUDICIAL ACTIONS

Superior courts are reluctant to review the exercise of a discretion by an inferior court where the exercise of such a discretion has not been shown to be palpably or plainly wrong. It is not sufficient for the superior court to make a finding that it would have exercised the discretion differently.

***In the Application of Balroop Ramlochand, Tara Ramroop, Jane Elahie, Ronald Ramdass, Jenny Lynn Diaz, Dennis Sampson, Balchan Samaroo, Dowin Alexander and Anne Alexander, Kenneth Coltrust, S. Ashook, Grace Gopaul, Terrance King and Cyntra Seepersad, Bansraj Harrilal, Patricia Austin, Kamraj Maharaj, Cindy Santoo, David Maharaj, Indar Samaroo, Ryan Headley, Rajh Basdeo, Chaitram Deonarine, Wendell Coltrust, Ashook Sookdeo, Junior Jackson, Sita Seelal, Mark Philbert, Hollister Peters* – Civil Appeal No 108 of 2003 (TT)**
Kangaloo JA

[P13] 19. In the circumstances, I am of the view that it has not been demonstrated that the learned judge misapprehended either the relevant principles of law or the facts in this matter, neither has it been shown that the exercise of her discretion was plainly or palpably wrong. It must be remembered that any of these conditions must be met before an appellate Court can interfere with the exercise of a judge's discretion, even though the appellate Court would have exercised its discretion differently from that of the first instance judge.

***In the Application of NH International (Caribbean) Ltd* –**
Civil Appeal No 17 of 2004 (TT)
Archie JA

[PP4–5] **What is the correct approach to the review of the Judge's exercise of discretion?** 14. No written reasons of the learned High Court Judge were available at the hearing of this appeal. The basis upon which she exercised her discretion to refuse leave is discernable only from the affidavit of Mr Byrne who had conduct of the matter on behalf of the Applicant/Appellant. This placed the Court at a considerable disadvantage. Counsel for the Appellant urged us to regard the appeal as a 'rehearing in the truest sense' i.e. to treat it as a fresh application and to exercise our independent discretion on the grant of leave. That approach, he argued, would give some meaning to the curious language of Order 59 Rule 5 which does not speak of 'an appeal' but of 'an application for a similar purpose'. 15. There is some logic in that argument and indeed many of the authorities usually referred to on this point do not specifically deal with *ex parte* applications. However, this Court has recently reaffirmed the approach to be taken in such applications and the Appellant has not demonstrated that those decisions were made *per incuriam*. In any event, it is not necessary to give further consideration to that point at this stage because even on the more stringent test set out in the recent authorities, the result in this matter would be the same. 16. That test was succinctly set out by Nelson, JA in *Fisherman and Friends of the Sea v The Environmental Management Authority and BP Trinidad & Tobago Ltd* Civil App No. 106 of 2002 in which he quoted *Hadmoor Productions v Hamilton* [1982] 2 WLR 322 at 325: '[An appellate Court] must defer to the Judge's exercise of his discretion and must not interfere with it merely on the ground that the members of the appellate Court would have exercised the discretion differently. The function of the appellate Court is initially one of review only' and later: 'It is only where the decision exceeds the generous ambit within which reasonable disagreement is possible and is, in fact, plainly wrong, that an appellate body is entitled to interfere.' 17. A similar view was expressed by Kangaloo, JA in *Balroop Ramlochan et al v The National Housing Authority* Civil App No. 108 of 2003 when he said: 'The issue in the appeal therefore is whether the Appellants have been able to demonstrate that [the learned judge's] refusal to exercise her discretion to grant leave was based on some wrong principle of law or on a misapprehension of the facts or alternatively that her decision was so plainly wrong that it could be said that she must have exercised her discretion wrongly.' The *Hadmoor case*, which was concerned with the grant of an injunction, also provides further guidance on the approach where the trial Judge's reasons may be 'sketchy': 'there may also be occasional cases where even though no erroneous assumption of law or fact can be identified the Judge's decision to grant or refuse the injunction is so aberrant that it must be set aside on the ground that no reasonable judge regardful of his duty to act judiciously could have reached it.' 18. Assuming those cases to have correctly stated the law, I now turn to its application in the present context. It must be borne in mind that the learned judge was not required to consider whether there had been a decision by UDECOTT to award the contract and/or whether it was a public body exercising a public duty or function. She had to determine, on the material before her, whether there was an arguable case that all of those circumstances existed. Since we are an appellate tribunal and operating, like the trial Judge, with incomplete information, I will be cautious in what follows not to express a final view on the matter. It is preferable to have the benefit of the considered ruling of a trial judge before pronouncing an opinion ... [P8] 31. During the hearing of this appeal a letter was placed before the Court on the instructions of UDECOTT which indicated that it had 'provisionally' awarded the contract to the lowest bidder subject to a number of unspecified matters being looked into. It stated that after completion of that exercise, the matter of whether and to whom an award should be made would be considered. That did not improve the position as it still left unanswered why and upon what basis any 'provisional' award (whatever that means) was made. 32. It is not contended by the Appellant that UDECOTT is bound to accept the advice of its advisors. It may well have good reasons for not doing so. However, in the absence of any rational explanation, the departure from the advice of all its experts is *prima facie* irrational. There is at least an arguable case for irrationality which will have to be heard and determined by a trial judge after all affidavits including the Respondent's have been filed. 33. I would therefore allow this appeal and direct that leave be granted to NH International to apply for judicial review. I would further direct that the matter be listed for urgent hearing in view of the fact that the anticipated time for commencement of the project was the end of February 2005.

A court of equal jurisdiction will not judicially review the decision of a superior court.

In the Application of Millicent Forbes **– Supreme Court No HCV—01386 of 2004 (JM)**
Smith J

[P7] It is my considered view that the very basis upon which the Applicant was relying to say what took place in the Portland Circuit Court is void *ab initio* has evaporated. I am therefore of the opinion that the acquittal of Rohan Allen at the sitting of the Portland Circuit on the 15th day of March 2004 is not open to Judicial Review and cannot be quashed by certiorari, as a decision of a Superior Court is not subject to Judicial Review by a Court of equal jurisdiction.

4.18 REVIEWING PROSECUTORIAL AUTHORITY

As in the case of reviewing executive and judicial authority, the court is cautious in reviewing the exercise of prosecutorial authority.

In the Application of Leonie Marshall **– Civil Appeal No 39 of 2003 (JM)**
Smith JA

[PP29–30] In considering whether to institute criminal proceedings the Director of Public Prosecutions must first have regard to the sufficiency of evidence test. If there is sufficient evidence then he may go on to determine whether it is in the public interest to prosecute. In this appeal the public interest criterion is not relevant. We are here only concerned with the evidential sufficiency criterion. In this regard, if the available and admissible evidence is indubitably sufficient, bearing in mind any defence which is clearly open to the police officers, then the Director of Public Prosecutions' decision not to prosecute would be unreasonable and therefore bad in law. It is only in such an event that the Court may interfere with his decision. In other words, unless the Appellant shows that the Director of Public Prosecutions' decision not to prosecute is bad in law there will be no basis for the Court to interfere . . . [P42] However, the authorities clearly establish that although a decision of the Director of Public Prosecutions not to prosecute is subject to judicial review, the power of review should be sparingly exercised. The sufficiency or otherwise of evidence to prosecute as a matter of law is within the purview of the Director of Public Prosecutions' discretion. For that discretion to be overturned on judicial review it would have to be shown that the discretion was unreasonably exercised within the meaning of the rule in the *Wednesbury case*. If there is no realistic prospect of a conviction then a decision not to prosecute is reasonable and is not bad in law. The authorities also establish that the prosecutor should have regard not only to the defence indicated by the alleged offender but also to any defence which is plainly open to him.

4.19 REVOCATION OF LEAVE

There is a discretion vested in the courts to vary or revoke leave for judicial review when such leave has been granted on the basis of an ex parte order.

In the Application of Sanatan Dharma Maha Sabha of Trinidad and Tobago **–**
HCA No S 1095 of 2004 (TT)
Judith Jones J

[P9] In the circumstances I am of the opinion that the Court has jurisdiction to set aside the grant of leave made *ex parte* in circumstances where

1. It is plainly unjustified; or
2. It is vitiated by non-disclosure of relevant facts; or
3. Where there has been undue delay and the Respondent wishes to bring to the Court new facts and/or to address the Court on matters within the ambit of Section 11(2) of the Act.

***In the Application of Web Communications Ltd* – Supreme Court No M030 of 2002 (JM)**
Smith J

[P18] On the issue of leave having been granted for Judicial Review by another Court, there is authority which states that a Judge of the Supreme Court has the discretion to vary or revoke an *ex parte* order which has been made by another Judge of the Supreme Court. This was enunciated by the Privy Council in the case of *The Ministry of Foreign Affairs, Trade and Industry v Vehicles and Supplies Limited and another* [1991] 28 JLR 198.

4.20 PRESUMPTION OF REGULARITY

The courts are reluctant to permit a successful judicial review application in the absence of any evidence of *mala fides* on the part of the administrative body or evidence that the administrative body has acted without jurisdiction. This reluctance is based on a presumption of regularity made in favour of public bodies in the decision-making process.

***Mohanlal Bhagwandeen* – Privy Council Appeal No 45 of 2003 (TT)**
Lord Carswell

[PP8–9] 20. . . . It is to be noted, however, that at first instance in that case Deyalsingh J reasoned cogently at pages 15 to 20 of his judgment (HCA No 1279 of 1982), which was reversed by the Court of Appeal, that both the presumption of regularity and the necessity for proof of *mala fides* rested on unsatisfactory foundations and should not be accepted as correct. 21. Their Lordships would require detailed argument on the issue before attempting to express any definite conclusion on the correctness of the propositions accepted by the Court of Appeal on this issue and would wish to give fuller consideration to the Indian authorities on which the Court of Appeal relied. Subject to that, however, they are inclined to the view that there may have been a degree of confusion between two distinct concepts, the presumption of regularity and the necessity for proof of deliberate intention to discriminate in a claim of inequality of treatment. 22. The presumption of regularity comes into play in this context when there is no evidence either way whether a public authority or official has taken into account the correct considerations in reaching an administrative decision. In such case the decider is entitled to the benefit of the presumption of regularity and is not obliged to adduce evidence to establish that he took only the correct factors into account. In consequence, in the absence of contrary evidence, the application for judicial review will fail.

***In the Application of the Sawmillers Co-operative Society Ltd* –**
HCA No S426 of 2000 (TT)
Archie J

[P20] On the contrary there is a presumption of regularity. Unless that presumption is displaced by some evidence to the contrary it would be pure speculation and wrong in law to draw the conclusion that the requirements of Rule 2 were not met.

***In The Application of Gulf Insurance Ltd* – HCA No 3036 of 1993 (TT)**
Barnes J

[P5] There is a rebuttable presumption in law that all things are done correctly and properly. So that where a duty is imposed by law on an office-holder to report to the Board or to the Governor there is a presumption that it has been properly done. The presumption is all the more strong when action has been taken ostensibly in keeping with or in furtherance of the report.[2]

***In the Application of Lolita Saroop* – HCA No 2115 of 1993 (TT)**
Sealy J

[PP10–11] Having said that I must add that judicial review is concerned with the decision making process only, and not with the decision, the Court is not a Court of appeal against the decision of the Magistrate acting as he was. Additionally, in this decision making process which is challenged, the presumption of regularity must apply and unless the Applicant can bring a case to rebut this presumption, this Court cannot confer any jurisdiction on itself if this presumption is not discharged.

***In the Application of Carson Haynes* – HCA No 1039 of 1988 (TT)**
Hosein J

[P14] I am therefore of the view that the Court is precluded from enquiring into the validity of the exercise by the Commission of the power under Regulation 88. Further the presumption of regularity of action by the State and its officials would apply in the absence of any allegation that the State either acted *mala fides* or without jurisdiction in the method and form adopted in communicating its decision to the Applicant.

4.21 PREMATURE PROCEEDINGS

Proceedings brought prematurely may not find favour with courts and litigants must be careful not to launch legal challenges before there is real cause to so do.

***In the Application of Junior Khan* – HCA Cv 357 of 2005 (TT)**
Stollmeyer J

[P2] The Applicant's appeal was due to be heard by the Public Services Appeal Board on 8th March 2005, about two weeks after the date on which his application for leave was being argued *ex parte* . . . [P4] His appeal to the Public Services Appeal Board was due to be heard within a matter of two weeks . . . Further, it is clear that if his dismissal were to stand then, equally, the resignation could not be effective. That appeal being pending, the application before me was clearly premature.

***In the Application of NH International (Caribbean) Ltd* – HCA No Cv 3181 of 2004 (TT)**
Stollmeyer J

[P23] In my view, and with the greatest deference to the view expressed by the Court of Appeal in its judgment on the appeal from the refusal of leave (at para. 29), the decision was not final in the sense that HK would be awarded the contract come what may. It was, if anything, a conditional award, and if UDECOTT was not satisfied with the results of its investigations then it was free to take up the matter with any other bidder, or proceed otherwise, if it so chose . . . [P24] Given my conclusion as to the nature of the decision, it is my further conclusion that these proceedings were premature, although I

2 This decision has been reversed by the Privy Council.

accept that review can take place of a decision that is not final (see e.g. Fordham: *Judicial Review Handbook* 4th Ed. para. 4.7.1 *et seq*). The contract had not been awarded, and there was no guarantee or assurance that it would be awarded to HK. The decision-making process was interrupted by these proceedings and on what is before me. I am not persuaded that it would be appropriate for a Court to intervene at this juncture, assuming the decision to be susceptible to judicial review (see *R v Broadcasting Complaints Commission, Ex Parte BBC* (1994) 6 Admin LR 714; Lewis: Judicial Remedies in Public Law 3rd Ed. at para. 11:15).

***In the Application of Wishma Maraj and Shanti Maraj* – Civil Appeal No 4 of 1989 (TT)**
de la Bastide CJ

[P5] There are two reasons why, in my view, this appeal cannot succeed. One is that the 'decision' which is under challenge is not an assessment of the Appellants at all but only an indication that the Revenue was proposing to make an assessment along the lines mentioned in the letter. In my view, if the Appellants wished to mount a challenge to what the Revenue were doing by way of judicial review, then they ought to have waited at least until the assessment was made and then challenged that assessment. They did not do so. In my opinion, the challenge was mounted prematurely.

***In the Application of Republic Bank Ltd* – HCA No 6921 of 1987 (TT)**
Deyalsingh J

[P13] A review of the cases cited by Mr Daly on this point makes it quite clear that judicial review is available even before a decision is made by the decision making authority . . . [P14] That in my view is sound and common sense law. If a party is saying that a decision making authority is entertaining an issue in law which is clear cut, why should it wait until the authority makes a wrong decision with grave consequences to it before challenging the Authority . . . [P17] What clearly emerges from these authorities is this proposition: Where a decision making authority is in the process of considering a matter which does not involve a finding of material facts (either because it involves a clear matter of law or the facts are not in dispute) and there is a reasonable possibility that in reaching its decision it will fall into an error of law, the Courts will on an application for prohibition, prohibit it from making a decision which will be erroneous in law or from acting in a manner which will be contrary to the law.

***In the Application of Sir John Compton* – Civil Appeal No 14 of 1997 (LC)**
Redhead JA

[P7] This to my mind clearly demonstrates that there is a real possibility that adverse findings can be and may be made against the Appellant. He does not have to wait until these findings are made to say that he is a person identified as being [probably] culpable. In my judgment, the Appellant is the subject of the inquiry. Having regard to the foregoing in my judgment, if the inquiry goes ahead against the Applicant as presently constituted there is a real danger of bias.

4.22 SPECIAL TRIBUNALS

The courts have accepted that certain public bodies, such as military tribunals, ought to be afforded special status due to the sensitive nature of their duties.

***Re Ian Hugh Clarke* (1994) 31 JLR 432 (JM)**
Rattray CJ

[PP435–436] Although no submissions were made to us by either party on the question of the Court's jurisdiction in relation to the decisions of military authorities, we consider it appropriate to take the opportunity in this judgment to indicate our views particularly as the previous application for an Order for Certiorari in Suit M94 of 1992 had been granted by a Full Court. In *Council of Civil Service Workers and Others v Minister of the Civil Service* [1984] 3 All ER 935 it was made clear that the question whether a decision or action was necessitated by the requirements of national security was non-justiciable. (Lord Fisher at page 942, Lord Scarman at page 949) more directly, however, as is stated in *Judicial Review of Administrative Action* by S.A. De Smith (4th Edition page 146)—'Special considerations apply where procedural errors have been committed by authorities administering military discipline. The Courts have always shown a marked aversion from seeming to interfere with the proceedings of military authorities except where the civil rights of an individual have been infringed . . .' There is abundant authority of respectable vintage and sufficient consistency to support this proposition.

4.23 RIGHT TO INTERVENE

Although having an interest creates an interest to intervene in a matter, intervention by a third party is not automatic and where a third party is seeking to preserve a decision of a public body, such third party ought not to have a right to intervene as such right is properly vested in the public body whose decision is under question.

***In the Application of Chandresh Sharma* – HCA No S-109 of 2005 (TT)**
Pemberton J

[PP15–16] Is it justifiable for this Court to allow the application to intervene in the circumstances of this case, a member of parliament seeking to preserve his position before the law? One cannot classify Dr Rowley as a mere busybody as far as this action is concerned. As I have stated already, he does have a genuine interest in the matter and the issue to be determined is of importance. However, can any other of the other considerations mentioned at Section 5(7) be satisfied? I do not think that there is any suggestion of vindicating the rule of law. The nature of the decision against which relief is sought is one that, as it stands benefits Dr Rowley. I ask the question: does the Judicial Review Act contemplate an intervention by any person for the preservation or protection of the decision sought to be impugned? Judicial Review is an action in public law. The only person who can seek to protect the existing decision is the public authority that is under question. I do not think that the Act contemplated that that function or role or that that right can be vested in any person or body other than the public authority called to bar. It does not lie to a private person to occupy that space.

4.24 JUDICIAL REVIEW AS FINAL PROCEEDINGS

Despite efforts to view judicial review as interlocutory proceedings and not final in light of the fact that the courts do not ultimately determine the final outcome of the decision of a public body, the courts are clear that judicial review proceedings are not interlocutory and must be treated as final proceedings.

***In the Application of Felix Augustus Durity* – HCA No S-283 of 1993/Civil Appeal No 49 of 1993 (TT)**
Sharma JA

[PP10–11] I now turn to the second issue—namely whether these proceedings are final. Procedurally speaking the determination of whether a matter was either final or interlocutory has always been a vexed question. Judges have at different periods suggested different approaches or tests in seeking to resolve this problem. [P11] In this jurisdiction, however, we are still guided by the test laid down in *White v Brunton* [1984] QB 570. The test propounded in that case is what is described as the application test as opposed to the order test. If the application is capable of determining the matter finally either way, the matter is to be regarded as final. It is one of those matters which would not involve the application of any test. Brunton or otherwise. It is obviously NOT final ... [P12] Matters of a Constitutional nature, especially where judicial officers are suspended by the appropriate authorities while performing official functions are by their nature inherently matters of public importance. I can therefore see no reason why this application would not easily pass the test laid down in the appropriate section.

In the Application of Seereeram Bros. Ltd – HCA No 3123 of 1991 (TT)
Jones J

[P7] Attorney for the Applicant submitted that judicial review proceedings are interlocutory, they are not as he put it 'free standing' and therefore statements of information and belief are admissible in such matters ... [PP8–9] Rules of Court relating to Judicial Review are themselves silent as to the sources and types of evidence permitted on applications for Judicial Review. It is necessary therefore to examine Order 41 and the rules relaying to affidavits generally. By Order 41 Rule 5 if the proceedings in question are interlocutory affidavits may contain statements of information or belief. If, however, the proceedings are final it would seem the general rule that an affidavit may only contain such facts as the deponent is able of his own knowledge to prove obtains. To determine whether Judicial Review proceedings are interlocutory or final one must consider the nature of a decision in Judicial Review proceedings. While it is true that the effect of the proceedings will usually not be to determine the ultimate right of the parties, to consider that Judicial Review proceedings are interlocutory in view of this is to my mind to consider the outcome of the proceedings rather than the proceedings themselves. In other words to say that Judicial Review may not be finally determinative of ultimate questions or right is *not* to say that the proceedings themselves are not final. Speaking for myself it is my view that the proper interpretation to be placed on the decision of the reviewing Court is that it is final as regards the validity of the decision under review i.e. the decision as reached but not necessarily determinative of the matter to be decided upon. In other words the reviewing Court may finally rule that a decision of a tribunal is invalid on account of a procedural failure in the decision making process but it does not necessarily in so doing make any finding as to the decision which would have been reached had the correct procedure been adopted ... [P10] I hold in the premises that Judicial Review proceedings are final proceedings. It is a distinct and self contained remedy and the outcome of an application is final as regards the status of the authority, or tribunal's decision.

Kemper Reinsurance Co. Appellant v Minister of Finance and Others –
Privy Council Appeal No 67 of 1997 (BM)
Lord Hoffman

[P9] Their Lordships' jurisdiction is wholly appellate and it is not their practice to decide new points of law without the benefit of the judgments in the Courts below: see *Pillai v Comptroller of Income Tax* [1970] AC 1124, 1130. Lord Neill's application was therefore refused. Their Lordships therefore turn to the single issue in the appeal ... [P11] '... Now just let us consider what that means, that an appeal shall not be given unless some particular body consents to its being given. Surely, if that is intended as a check to unnecessary or frivolous appeals it becomes absolutely illusory if you can appeal from that decision or leave, or whatever it is to be called itself. How could any Court of Review determine whether leave ought to be given or not without hearing and determining upon the hearing whether it was a fit case for an appeal? And if the intermediate Court could enter and must enter into that question, then the Court which is the ultimate Court of Appeal must do so also. The result of that would be that in construing this order, which as I have said is obviously intended to prevent frivolous and unnecessary appeals, you might in truth have two appeals in every case in which, following the ordinary course of things, there would be only one; because if there is a power to appeal when the order has been refused, it would seem to follow as a necessary consequence that you must have a right to appeal when leave has been granted, the result of which is that the person against whom the leave has been granted might appeal from that, and inasmuch as this is no stay of proceeding the Court of Appeal might be entertaining an appeal upon the very same question when this House was entertaining the question whether the Court of Appeal ought ever to have granted the appeal. My Lords, it seems to me that that would reduce the provision to such an absurdity that even if the language were more clear than is contended on the other side one really ought to give it a reasonable construction.' . . . [PP14–15] In principle, however, judicial review is quite different from an appeal. It is concerned with the legality rather than the merits of the decision, with the jurisdiction of the decision-maker and the fairness of the decision-making process rather than whether the decision was correct. In the case of a restriction on the right of appeal, the policy is to limit the number of times which a litigant may require the same question to be decided. The Court is specifically given power to decide that a decision on a particular question should be final. There is obviously a strong case for saying that in the absence of express contrary language, such a decision should itself be final. But judicial review seldom involves deciding a question which someone else has already decided. In many cases, the decision-maker will not have addressed his mind to the question at all. The application for leave may be the first time that the issue of the legality of the decision is raised and their Lordships think it is by no means obvious that a refusal of leave to challenge its legality should be final. The law reports reveal a number of important points of administrative law which have been decided by the Court of Appeal or House of Lords in cases in which leave was refused at first instance. In principle, therefore, their Lordships do not think it possible to say that the very nature of the leave requirement for an order of certiorari excludes, or makes absurd, the possibility of an appeal. But unless such a conclusion can be drawn, their Lordships consider it very difficult to find the necessary intendment restricting the general right of appeal conferred by Section 12. It may be appropriate, as a matter of policy, to restrict that right of appeal, but their Lordships consider that this is a matter for legislation rather than judicial interpretation . . . [P19] Their Lordships therefore consider that the Court of Appeal had jurisdiction to hear the appeal and will humbly advise Her Majesty that the appeal should be allowed. The Respondents must pay Kemper's costs in the Court of Appeal and before their Lordships' Board.

However, the Privy Council has made it clear that judicial review proceedings are not summary proceedings.

***Dougnath Rajkumar* – Privy Council Appeal No 1 of 2001 (TT)**
Lord Mackay of Clashfern

[P4] 8. The Appellant founded on the decision of McMillan JA (Ag) in *Jones v Solomon* (Civil Appeal No. 11 of 1986) in the Court of Appeal of Trinidad and Tobago which is based on the view that judicial review proceedings do not involve the full trial process, and are therefore summary. In this connection the learned Justice of Appeal relied upon an observation of Lord Scarman, in *R v Inland Revenue Commissioners, Ex Parte Rossminster* [1980] AC 952 at page 1025 where Lord Scarman indicates that in a judicial review, 'If issues of fact, or law and fact, are raised which it is neither just or convenient to decide without the full trial process, the Court may dismiss the application or order, in effect, a trial'. The later decision in *O'Reilly v Mackman* makes clear that the option referred to by Lord Scarman is no longer available if it was intended to suggest that the trial was not in the judicial review process. While therefore some proceedings for judicial review may require more elaborate procedures than others, judicial review is in no sense an optional procedure to be contrasted with some more formal procedure. Accordingly the Board is of opinion that judicial review proceedings are not summary proceedings and do not constitute a summary proceeding within the meaning of Section 38(2)(c) of the Supreme Court of Judicature Act Chapter 4:01. Therefore no leave is required from a final order in such proceedings. This accords with the tentative view of the Court of Appeal of Trinidad and Tobago in *Romain v Water and Sewerage Authority* [1997] No 24 where the point was not argued.

5

CONDUCT OF JUDICIAL REVIEW PROCEEDINGS

It is important to examine the attitude of the courts in the actual conduct of judicial review proceedings, particularly in dealing with evidentiary matters. The emerging picture is that of conservative views with marked inflexibility being shown, much to the benefit of the State.

***In the Application of Ameena Ali* – HCA No S-1812 of 2003 (TT)**
Ventour J

[P14] Indeed, it is well established that Judicial Review proceedings are final proceedings and hearsay evidence are therefore inadmissible. Moreover, none of the statements to which counsel has taken objection fall within any of the exceptions to the hearsay rule. Accordingly, I am left with no alternative but to order that the said statements be struck out as being inadmissible.

This is not to say, however, that courts have not urged a more flexible approach to the receipt of evidence.

***In the Application of Alvin Seereeram* – HCA No S-262 of 2001 (TT)**
Marcus J

[PP21–22] The remaining objection was made by Mr Thorne as to the admissibility of the exhibit 'A.S.4', a memorandum dated 18th January, 2000 purportedly from the Permanent Secretary, Ministry of Finance, Planning and Development to the Permanent Secretary, Ministry of Agriculture, Land and Marine Resources. Mr Thorne's grounds of objection were that the Applicant did not state how he came by it, that on its face the Applicant did not appear to have had any personal knowledge of its contents and accordingly Order 41, Rule 5 of the Rules of the Supreme [Court] was being infringed. The Court admitted 'A.S.4.' for the following reasons . . . [P23] . . . the Court was mindful of the modern relaxed approach to the admissibility of documents which have bearing on issues in a case even though there has not been strict compliance with the rules of Court or other technical rules relating to admissibility . . . [PP23–24] Had the document been certified in accordance with Section 22 of the Evidence Act as 'being a record in any . . . Government department' there could not have been any valid objection to its admissibility. This Court is of the view that the Attorney for the State, Government Department, Statutory corporation or other State agency in matters in which the citizen is pitched in legal battle against the machinery of the State or any of its agencies stands in a similar position to and carries similar responsibilities as prosecuting counsel in criminal prosecutions. As such he or she is akin to, if not entirely so, a Minister of justice. In a situation such as the present, the ends of justice would be better served if the authenticity of the document is established—a matter which, in the Court's view, is easy of ascertainment or verification—and the technical objection waived . . . [P24] It is an observation with which I respectfully agree and adapt to the situation in hand by saying that once an official document on which a citizen relies in his suit against the State or State agency is ascertained to be authentic—a matter, hopefully, within easy reach of any State Attorney—the ends of justice would be better served if technical objections are not taken against its admissibility. Excluding it for technical reasons is, in this Court's view, tantamount to not bringing it forward.

In the Application of Shastri Moonan – HCA No S-18 of 1988 (TT)
Hamel-Smith J

[P30] Before I close I wish to make reference to the application made by the Respondent with respect to striking out certain paragraphs of the Applicant's affidavit on the grounds that they were, *inter alia*, 'hearsay' and/or irrelevant. I deferred my ruling on that application, preferring instead to follow the ruling in *Re J* [1960] 1 WLR 253 where in the light of the numerous paragraphs brought into question, the Court decided to defer striking the paragraphs until such time as the Applicant attempted to make use of them. In this instance, very few paragraphs were relied on by the Applicant and, where necessary, a ruling was given. The Applicant has not relied on certain other paragraphs and so there was no need to rule formally on them.

5.1 NEWSPAPER ARTICLES AS EVIDENCE

The approach of the courts to newspaper articles as evidence reflects an emerging but unfortunate inconsistency in the acceptability of these articles as evidence.

In the Application of Star Telecommunications Company Ltd – HCA No Cv 1713 of 1999 (TT)
Jamadar J

[P5] In my opinion, paragraph 10 of the affidavit of Keith Ramnath contains evidence which is properly within the knowledge of the deponent, to wit:—that on the 14th July, 1999 he had a telephone conversation with one Davendra Ramnarine; that in that conversation he was told certain things about a newspaper article appearing in the 14th July, 1999 edition of the '*Newsday*' newspaper; that Davendra Ramnarine sent him a copy of that article by facsimile transmission which he received on the 14th July 1999; and that the exhibit 'KR-4' is a copy of the article that was sent to and received by him. Further, in my opinion this evidence is relevant to the issues raised in this case, as what transpired on the 14th July, 1999 forms the basis for what Keith Ramnath subsequently did, as set out at paragraph 11 of his said affidavit (some of which is disputed by the Respondents). However, it is equally clear to me, that though the evidence at paragraph 10, including exhibit 'KR-4', is admissible for the facts of what transpired on the 14th July, 1999, 'KR-4' is not admissible for the truth of its contents, which is hearsay evidence and offends the provisions of Order 41 Rule 5. In the circumstances, I will order that the evidence at paragraph 10 of the affidavit of Keith Ramnath is admissible for the facts outlined above but not for the truth of the contents of the *Newsday* article referred to therein and exhibited as 'KR-4'. There will be no order as to the costs of this application.

In the Application of Air Caribbean Ltd – HCA No 707 of 1998 (TT)
Hosein J

[P24] Leading counsel for BWIA Mr Thorne with his usual erudition objected to the use of these newspaper articles as evidence and applied to have them struck out as exhibits on the grounds that they are irrelevant and in any event their contents cannot amount to any reliable evidence. This Court is not concerned about the truth of the contents of these articles. Those were matters that ought to have occupied the attention of the Respondent in arriving at the March and April decisions ... These are matters for the Respondent. All the Applicant did was to bring to the attention of the Respondent these articles and it was for the Respondent to investigate these matters and determine their value in the decision making process. In the circumstances this Court declines the invitation to strike out the exhibits.

***In the Application of Caribbean Book Distributors (1996) Ltd* – HCA No S 764 of 1997 (TT)**
Ramlogan J

[PP6–7] I agree with the submission that these Newspaper reports put before me by the Applicant are evidentially valueless and suspect. Even a cursory look at the Newspaper reports indicate[s] they cannot survive closer examination. I place no reliance on them and hold that there is no evidence of bias whatsoever.

***In the Application of Richard Alfred Crane* – HCA No 3961 of 1990 (TT)**
Jones J

[P11] In the first place this Newspaper article is not evidence. It is nothing but hearsay. However, I allowed the Newspaper articles to be read into the proceedings *'de bene esse'* and heard submissions on the admissibility ... [P13] What is complained of in the instant matter is a breach of natural justice. It is by its very nature a final act and bears no resemblance to a continuing wrong. In the circumstances I hold that the articles published in the *Newsday* of the 26th and 27th June 1994 are hearsay, irrelevant and inadmissible.

The courts have in fact taken judicial notice of newspaper reports and given credibility to their evidential value.

***In the Application of Chandresh Sharma* – Civil Appeal No 115 of 2003 (TT)**
Nelson JA

[P8] A local newspaper, the *Daily Express*, which carried the press release, pinpoints the source of the press release as coming from within the Caricom Secretariat, the CCJ Project Co-ordinating Unit.

***In the Application of Gulf Insurance Ltd* – Civil Appeal No 32 of 2000 (TT)**
Nelson JA

[P30] Against that background there appeared the page one article in the weekly newspaper, *The Bomb*. The article contained in the top right hand corner the logos of NCB, TCB and the Workers' Bank. Beneath the logos was the banner headline '$1b NCB DEBT HEADACHE'. The article stated that NCB had bad debts conservatively estimated at $1 billion. The Workers' Bank bad debts were put at $800 million. The writer reported the view of 'one well-placed banker' that a write-off of the alleged billion dollar NCB bad debts could cause a run on the merged Bank, FCB, when it belatedly opened its doors for business. These facts constituted sufficient material upon which the Central Bank might conclude that the financial system was in danger of disruption as a result of a possible run on the three banks prompted by *The Bomb* article. What was envisaged was a tremor whose epicentre was NCB. The force of the tremor would send shock waves through the system, which TCB, propped up by Central Bank funding over the years, could not withstand.

***In the Application of Harry Sooknanan* – HCA No 225 of 1989 (TT)**
Warner J

[PP15–16] The two newspaper reports fall for consideration. That neither report was *ipso facto* evidence of the truth of its contents, appears to be axiomatic. At this point, what is being considered is whether either Mr Sooknanan or Dr Rennie was or both were aware that the 1988 salaries were going to be paid in January without any cut. Did either newspaper publication come to the notice either of Dr Rennie or Mr Sooknanan at any time before the hearing of the *ex parte* application for leave? If yes, what is the effect of this on the question whether the Applicant knew of the arrangements set out in this circular? The Court has been asked to draw the inference of such knowledge. No direct evidence has been provided that either deponent saw or read either of the particular newspaper reports between 13th and 19th January or at all. It is a notorious fact that the *Trinidad*

> *Guardian* and the *Daily Express* are in daily circulation throughout Trinidad and Tobago and that they are the only two morning newspapers in such circulation. It cannot be that the law of evidence imposes such a degree of artificiality upon Judges as to require them to ignore such a notorious fact. I take judicial notice that these two newspapers are the only morning newspapers in daily circulation throughout Trinidad and Tobago. From the copies of the reports annexed to the affidavit of Mr Andrews, I find that each of the reports indicated that salaries of public servants for January would be paid without being reduced by ten *per* cent . . . [P17] Nevertheless, I am bound by the rules of evidence. My conclusion is that the fact of the publication in the newspapers and the fact that one or both reports would have come to their notice during the relevant period, do not amount to evidence that either of them knew as a fact that no cut would be made in January.

In the Application of Fishermen and Friends of the Sea – HCA Cv 2148 of 2003 (TT), Stollmeyer J accepted the objections to important newspaper articles that would have supported the argument of the applicant for judicial review, that the decision-maker may have abdicated its responsibility. What was noteworthy is that the decision-maker, in its extensive filing of affidavits, made no attempt to disclaim what was reported in the articles but merely elected to rely on the strict adherence to the evidentiary rule of hearsay to have the articles removed from the judicial attention of the court.

5.2 WAIVER OF IRREGULARITY

The courts are prepared at times to entertain the argument that the non-objection to an irregularity, especially a procedural irregularity, will operate as a waiver to objecting to the said irregularity during the course of judicial review proceedings.

In the Application of Maniram Maharaj – HCA No 1426 of 1999 (TT)
Smith J

> [P9] By participating in the meeting of the 28th June, 1999 without objection to the irregularity which he is deemed to have known about, the Applicant submitted to the jurisdiction of the Authority inspite of the procedural irregularity and cannot now seek to raise the point. Further, the irregularity complained of is a procedural matter and by participating in the meeting without objection, he waived the irregularity.

5.3 FRESH EVIDENCE AND *EX POST FACTO* REASONS

The courts will only allow fresh evidence to be introduced by a decision maker or *ex post facto* reasons for a decision under limited circumstances.

In the Application of Reynold Makhan – HCA No 562 of 2003 (TT)
Narine J

> [P8] Of course, it is permissible for a decision maker to clarify or supplement his reasons, where there is genuine confusion as to what his reasons for the decision actually are. However, the Court will not admit affidavit evidence which seeks to show that the basis of the decision was in fact different from that expressed in the original decision.

In the Application of Vashti Sampson, Rajh Basdeo, Indar Samaroo, Grantley Prescott and James Chinapoo – Civil Appeal No 96 of 2003 (TT)
Nelson JA

> [P32] The statement of the Executive Director was never before Bereaux J. No application was made to introduce it as fresh evidence on this appeal. Nor was the statement before

the decision maker. There is therefore no basis on which this Court can take into account or consider the statement of the Executive Director.

In the Application of Mohanlal Bhagwandeen – HCA No 37 of 2000 (TT)
Narine J

[PP27–28] It seems to me that if I accept the evidence of the Commissioner of Police on this issue, certain inexorable conclusions must follow. The first of these is that he did not apply his mind to Section 20 of the Regulations at all, that is, he did not consider the criteria listed thereunder. The evaluation of the officer's overall performance as reflected in his performance appraisal reports is only one of those criteria. The second conclusion to be drawn is that the real reason for the omission of the Applicant was the absence of a performance appraisal report for the year preceding the omission. This reason was not communicated to the Applicant by the Commissioner of Police, so that the Applicant would know why he had not been recommended for promotion, and have the opportunity to make representations to the Commission, or possibly to bring to the attention of the Commissioner of Police material upon which the Commissioner of Police could base his considerations . . . [P29] However, I cannot permit the Commissioner of Police to provide further reasons *ex post facto*, in order to justify his decision, where by his own admission he did not consider those matters at the material time.

In the Application of Aldric Tudor – HCA No 5461 of 1984 (TT)
Permanand J

[P13] I find it appropriate at this stage to rule on the admissibility of the affidavit of Wilfred Mc Kell . . . [P14] In *R v Secretary of State for the Environment and another, Ex Parte Powis* [1981] 1 All ER 788, the Court of Appeal in England considered the categories of fresh evidence admissible on judicial review and Dunn LJ stated the following at p 797:—'what are the principles on which fresh evidence should be admitted on judicial review? They are: (1) that the Court can receive evidence to show what material was before the Minister or inferior tribunal (see *per* Lord Denning MR in *Ashbridge Investments Ltd. v Minister of Housing and Local Government* [1963] 3 All ER 371 at 274; (1965) 1 WLR 1320 at 1327); (2) where the jurisdiction of the Minister or inferior tribunal depends on a question of fact, or where the question is whether essential procedural requirements were observed, the Court may receive and consider additional evidence to determine the jurisdictional fact or procedural error (see de Smith's *Judicial Review of Administrative Action* (4th Edition, 1980, pp 140–141 and cases there cited); (3) where the proceedings are tainted by misconduct on the part of the Minister or member of the inferior tribunal or the parties before it. Examples of such misconduct are biased by the decision-making body, or fraud or perjury by a party. In each case fresh evidence is admissible to prove the particular misconduct alleged (see *R v West Sussex Quarter Session* [1973] 3 All ER 289 at 298, 301, (1974) QB 24 at 39, 42 *per* Orr and Lawton L.J.)'. [P15] In the matter before this Court, Counsel's objection is restricted to paragraph 5 of the affidavit. The effect of paragraph 5 is to explain the terminology 'seconded for duty'; it is not new evidence and is therefore admissible merely as being explanatory. See *R v Secretary of State for the Home Department, Ex Parte Mc Anoy* 1984 3 All ER 417 at p 423.

In the Application of Auburn Court Ltd – Civil Appeal No 99 of 1997,
Suit Nos M101 and M102 of 1996 (JM)[1]
Harrison JA

[P73] Generally, the bases on which the Court will exercise its discretion to admit fresh evidence are that the fresh evidence was not available at the first trial, that is credible

1 This decision was endorsed by the Privy Council, *Auburn Court Ltd—Privy Council Appeal No. 76 of 2002 (JM)*.

and probably would have affected the outcome if it had been called at the trial: *Reg v West Sussex Quarter Sessions, Ex Parte Johnson Trust Ltd. et al* [1974] 1 QB 24, applying the *ratio* of *Ladd v Marshall* [1954] 1 WLR 1489 ... [P74] Judicial review is concerned with the propriety of the decision-making body and not the decision itself, and therefore the admission of fresh evidence in an effort to influence the decision based on the facts is inappropriate in certiorari proceedings: (*R v Secretary of State for the Environment, Ex Parte Powis* [1981] 1 All ER 788). I maintain that the application to lead fresh evidence should be refused.

5.4 RAISING NEW GROUNDS

The courts will not allow a party to raise new grounds in judicial review proceedings to attack a decision maker when such grounds were not placed before the decision-maker at the time of the making of the decision for consideration.

***The Jamaica Public Service Co. v Bancroft Smikle* (1985) 22 JLR 244 (JM)**
Carey J

[P250] This misconception of their powers in my opinion induced all the Judges in the Court below to fall into error. As I have earlier remarked the Full Court granted the order on the basis that the Appellant had not complied with a condition precedent to dismissal, viz, suspension. That was a matter before the Tribunal. It was not raised in the briefs, nor was evidence led to deal with it, and it never surfaced until the hearing before the Full Court where it was mentioned in the Respondent's counsel's reply. No later point in the proceedings could have been chosen. By no manner or means could it be said that this point was an error of law on the face of the record. The record shows plainly what the issue joined between the parties was, viz, the conduct of the Respondent such as would entitle the Appellants to dismiss him. The Respondent said he did nothing to warrant dismissal while the Appellants argued contra. There was no question that the dismissal was unjustified because some procedural rule had been breached. Had their lordships in the Court below appreciated the limited scope of their functions, they could not have rested their decision on any such footing.

Campbell J

[PP261–262] It is an accepted and well established principle that a party who has not raised or otherwise canvassed before a Tribunal of fact an issue of fact in the determination of which the opposing party would have been entitled to adduce evidence will not generally be permitted to raise this issue on appeal as a basis for depriving the successful party of the fruits of his victory. This principle is in my view equally applicable where the decision of the Tribunal of fact is sought to be impeached in certiorari proceedings. In the absence of such a principle a party would be able to go into a trial Court on one footing and on failing to prove his case there come to the appellate or supervisory Court and succeed on an altogether different footing. This would result in great prejudice and injustice to the other party who would have been deprived of the opportunity of meeting by relevant and appropriate evidence in the trial Court the new case of his adversary on which he has succeeded in the higher Court ... [P262] For the above reasons, it is my view that the Full Court fell into error in allowing submissions to be made to it on the non-compliance with the procedural requirement of suspension and in upholding this submission and using it as the principal basis for quashing the Tribunal's award.

5.5 IRRELEVANT EVIDENCE

The courts are vigilant to ensure that, in judicial review proceedings, evidence is not introduced that is irrelevant or scandalous.

***In the Application of Marilin Sammy-Wallace* – HCA No Cv S-623 of 2003 (TT)**
Jamadar J

[P3] In these circumstances, and given that the core issue to be determined involves the decision of the JLSC, I am of the opinion that the narrative in the subject paragraphs is irrelevant to the relevant issues to be determined in this case. Moreover, several of the assertions in the subject narrative are scandalous of the person and the office of the President of the Industrial Court and warrant a reply. Such a course would involve additional expense and an increased volume of paper and affidavits. It has been indicated to this Court, that all of these allegations will be contested if they stand. If this is the case, the result would be hard swearing about matters which this Court would not be called upon to resolve, as their truth or untruth is irrelevant to the issues raised concerning the JLSC.

5.6 DISCOVERY

The attitude of the courts towards discovery is very clear, in that, discovery will only be allowed in limited circumstances.

***In the Application of Spancrete Caribbean Ltd* – HCA No 3129 of 2001 (TT)**
Mohammed J

[PP8–9] Applications for Discovery and Inspection may be relatively rare in applications for Judicial Review since the Court is functioning in its supervisory jurisdiction and is in many cases concerned exclusively or primarily with issues of law rather than with issues of fact. In such cases, an order for discovery should be quite exceptional. This is a practical consequence of the nature of the jurisdiction. It would lead, in my view, to the creation of an artificial and unwarranted distinction were it to be decided as a general principle that discovery in Judicial Review proceedings is subject to a higher standard than in Writ actions. Judicial Review is directed at ensuring compliance with high standards of public administration. In an era of increasing paper bureaucracy, there is almost certain to be a level of disparity between the access which an Applicant in Judicial Review proceedings has to documents which are under the control and in the possession of public authorities and the level of control which public authorities have over such documents. Of course, this is not to say that the duty on an Applicant to establish the relevance of the documents sought and the necessity for their production for inspection in order to fairly dispose of the issues in this case should in any way be mitigated as a concession to the existence of any such disparity. Rather, the existence of a disparity in access is a persuasive reason why in my view there is no acceptable basis for stating as a general principle that discovery in Judicial Review proceedings should operate on a more restricted basis than in Writ actions, once the documents have been otherwise shown to be relevant to the issues raised, within the terms of the test laid down in the *Peruvian Guano case*, and also necessary for the fair disposition of the case . . . [P10] In an application for Discovery and Inspection of documents, it is in my view necessary for the Applicant to show that the documents sought are not only relevant, but as well necessary for the fair disposition of the case.

In the Application of Walkerwell Ltd – HCA No Cv 342 of 2000 (TT)
Stollmeyer J

[PP8–10] Discovery is available in judicial review proceedings but there is no inherent right to an order for same and such an order is more difficult to obtain than in a writ action, being seen as less appropriate, and is likely to be circumscribed in scope. This reflects the principle that the Court is functioning in a supervisory role, concerned largely with matters of law and not fact, but there are instances in which it may be necessary to investigate the facts of the case, to some extent, at least. See *Khawaja v Secretary of State for the Home Department* [1983] All ER 765. Generally, discovery should not be ordered unless a Court is satisfied that the evidence reveals reasonable grounds for believing there has been a breach of public duty and, if ordered, discovery should be limited strictly to documents relevant to the issue which emerges from the affidavits, although this was said in the context of the duty of confidence owed by the revenue to the taxpayer. See *Inland Revenue Commissioners v National Federation of Self-Employed and Small Businesses Ltd.* at 654. Discovery is obtainable, however, whenever and to the extent that the justice of the case requires. See *O'Reilly v Mackman* [1983] 2 AC 237 at 282. Orders for discovery will not, at least usually, be made to make good a defect in the Applicant's evidence, and it seems that there will seldom be orders for discovery of a full private law nature where the review proceedings are based on a '*Wednesbury*' challenge. Discovery, however, will be ordered where it is required so that the justice of the case may be advanced and where it is necessary for disposing fairly of the matter. It will also be ordered even if the effect of doing so is to go behind the contents of an affidavit if there is some matter before the Court which suggests that the contents of that affidavit are not accurate, or that it is in some respect incorrect. Additionally, if an affidavit only deals partially and not sufficiently or adequately with an issue, it may be appropriate to order discovery to supplement the affidavit, as compared to challenging the accuracy of what has been said there. Ultimately, it will depend on the nature of the issue which the Court is required to consider. See *R v Secretary of State for Foreign Affairs, Ex Parte World Development Movement Limited* [1995] All ER 611 at 621. Additionally, in deciding whether discovery should be ordered, it is necessary to determine positively that the document is needed for the determination of an issue. If this is not needed, or the Court cannot say that it is needed given what is before it, then discovery should not be ordered. Further, if a party raises a factual issue of sufficient substance which leads the Court to conclude that it may or will not be able to resolve the issue fairly to all parties without discovery, then the discovery may be ordered. See *R v Secretary of State for Health, Ex Parte London Borough of Hackney per* Bingham MR, referred to in 'Judicial Review Update' Vol. 1 paragraph U.48.4.14. Mrs Alcala stressed in her submissions the necessity of public authorities maintaining the highest standards of public administration and transparency. I think that this is correct. The post-war development of administrative and public law, and of judicial review, continues and there is no doubt that it will continue to do so in order to meet the needs of a society as it [evolves] and [changes]. As a corollary to that, there will also of necessity be developments in the law and rules relating to discovery, but of course, any such developments must be as are appropriate and proper in all circumstances of the particular case. See, for example, *O'Reilly v Mackman* at 281, 285 where Lord Diplock refers to the (new) Order 53 made in 1977 having removed the disadvantages faced by those seeking a public law remedy 'particularly in relation to discovery'. Mr Martineau, on the other hand, stressed the restricted, or restrictive and circumscribed nature of discovery as it now exists. He made detailed submissions as to either or both the absence of relevance and necessity of each of the documents in respect to which discovery was sought when they were considered in the light of each of the Grounds set out in the Motion and the issues raised in the affidavits. In essence, he submitted that those documents which might have some relevance were not in any event needed to enable a Court to determine the issues when the Motion was heard. The application was best characterized, in his view, as being in the nature of a 'fishing' or 'Micawber' expedition. I was not persuaded that this was so, at least in relation to all the documents.

***In the Application of Gladstone Solomon* – Civil Appeal No 11 of 1986 (TT)**
Mc Millan JA (Ag.)

[P4] Clearly, the proceedings are not interlocutory, and any order granting or refusing a substantive application for judicial review is a final order . . . [P6] Indeed, although both discovery and cross-examination may be permitted in proceedings under Order 53 they are both limited.

***In the Application of Francis Eustace Bernard and Nydia Bernard* –**
HCA No 4771 of 1983 (TT)
Douglin M

[P2] There is no dispute that discovery may be ordered against the State, but the Respondents resist disclosure on the ground that the said documents are protected by legal professional privilege . . . [P3] The authorities establish that in order to claim legal privilege there has to be a clear indication that the documents in question were materials required for the brief . . . [PP4–5] The question here is whether the documents of which inspection is sought are within the legal professional privilege. I think that they are not. It is not clear that they were documents containing information which had been obtained by the Respondents with a view to consulting their legal advisers . . . The following remarks of Cotton LJ in *Southwark and Vauxhall Water Co. v Quick* [1878] at p 321 *supra* are apposite. 'We are now dealing with the production of documents and the question is whether the documents do or do not come within what is called privilege. Privilege only extends to communications with legal advisers or in some way connected with legal advisers; communications with a most confidential agent are not protected if that confidential agent happens not to be a solicitor. And this proceeds on the principle that laymen (by which I mean persons not learned in the law) cannot be expected to conduct their defence or litigation without the assistance of professional advisers; and, for the purpose of having the litigation conducted properly, the law has said that communications between the client and the solicitor shall be privileged, and that no one shall be entitled to call for the production of a document which has been submitted to the solicitor for the purpose of obtaining his advice, or for the purpose of enabling him to institute or to defend proceedings. There must be the freest possible communication between solicitor and client, and it is on this ground that professional communications are entitled to privilege, which excepts them from the general rule. The most obvious form of claiming privilege is when any litigant sends either directly or indirectly to his solicitor a document for the purpose of obtaining his advice, or for the purpose of enabling him to institute or defend an action'. I can do no better than end with the dicta of Lord Justice James at p 655 in the case of *Anderson v Bank of British Columbia* 1876 2 Ch. Division. 'Notwithstanding the great length of the arguments addressed to us and the number of cases cited I think that this is a document which ought to be produced. Looking at the dicta and the judgments cited they might require to be fully considered but I think they may possibly all be based upon this which is an intelligible principle that as you have no right to see your adversary's brief you have no right to see that which comes into existence merely as the materials for the brief. But that seems to have no application whatever to communication between a principal and his agent in the matter of the agency giving information of the facts and circumstances of the very transaction which is the subject matter of the litigation. Such a communication is above all others, the very thing which ought to be produced'.

5.7 INTERROGATORIES

Interrogatories are permitted in judicial review proceedings where demanded by the justice of a particular application.

***In the Application of NH International (Caribbean) Ltd* – HCA No Cv 3181 of 2004 (TT)**
Stollmeyer J

[PP2–3] The present position insofar as seeking interrogatories in judicial review motions is concerned appears to me to be as follows: first, applications can be and are increasingly made for interrogatories in judicial review; second, although relatively rare, such orders can and are made; third, the long held, generally accepted, view I have referred to above has been ameliorated, to some extent at least; fourth, the prevailing view now is that cross-examination in judicial review should be permitted whenever the justice of the particular case so requires, although such instances may remain relatively rare. I see no reason why the same principles should not apply to discovery and interrogatories. Like cross-examination they go to the facts of the cause or matter and I have already expressed this view in relation to discovery; fifth, an order for interrogatories must depend on the circumstances of each individual case, and it must be remembered that as a general rule the purpose of judicial review is to review the decision-making process rather than the decision itself; sixth and finally, the Courts now generally require parties to put all their cards on the table—to make a full and frank disclosure of their respective cases without it having to be prised out of them. The interrogatories sought here can in general be said to relate to the issues I have already outlined. In deciding those issues (which I am not required to do here) and in particular whether the Respondent was performing a public function when making the challenged decision, the Court will need to consider a variety of factors. They include, but are not limited in any way to, ownership of the Respondent; its policy and any policy directions which may be given to it; the nature of the work it performs generally as well as in this particular instance; the source of its funding, because the question of the public purse is important; the expenditure of funds on its work; its relationship to government; and of course, in this particular instance, ownership of the parcel of land in question.

5.8 CROSS EXAMINATION

Cross examination is important in judicial review cases where there are conflicts of facts contained in the affidavits filed in the action. In judicial review, the onus is on the applicant to establish his case and, where there is a dispute of fact, the court will proceed on the basis of the affidavit evidence supporting the respondent.

***In the Application of Malcolm Johnatty* – HCA No 2016 of 2004 (TT)**
Narine J

[P5] The onus is on the Applicant to establish the facts on which he relies to make out his case for judicial review. Where there is conflict in the affidavit evidence on critical issues which are not resolved by oral evidence and cross-examination, the Court will proceed on the basis of the Respondent's evidence. See: *Judicial Remedies in Public Law*, Clive Lewis (2004 edition Paragraph 9–096 page 354).

***In the Application of Vashti Sampson, Rajh Basdeo, Indar Samaroo, Grantly Prescott and James Chinapoo* – HCA No S-157 of 2003 (TT)**
Bereaux J

[P15] There has been no cross-examination on the affidavits and the question is whom should I believe . . . [P16] It seems to me therefore that I must accept the evidence of the

Respondent in the case. The onus of proof lies on the plaintiff and there has been no cross-examination sought by either side.

In the Application of Sabita Jagessar, Hazra Ramjohn, Nirmala Lokhai – **HCA No S 2053 of 2002 (TT)**
Dean-Armorer J

[P12] I respectfully agree with the law as stated by the learned first instance Judge in the case of *Adolphus Mondesir v AG* HCA No. 1903 of 1997. The failure to cross-examine does not produce an automatic effect and certainly not one in favour of the Respondent. Where however, there are direct conflicts of evidence, without cross-examination and the Court derives no assistance from flaws in the evidence of either party, it is my view that the Court can allude to a litigant's failure to cross-examine and therefore to discharge their burden of proof by cross-examination and find in favour of the party which does not carry the burden of proof. It requires emphasis that the burden of proof, in respect of any given allegation, rests on the party who substantially asserts the affirmative of the issue. See Phipson on *Evidence* (12th Edition) paragraph 91. Where the allegation is made by the Respondent, the burden of proof also lies on the Respondent and in the event of a direct conflict, it will, in my view, be the obligation of the Respondent to call the other side to be cross-examined. In such cases, the available authorities suggest that the Court may take into account the failure of the Respondent to cross-examine and find in favour of the Applicant.

In the Application of Gillette Marina Ltd – **HCA No Cv S 1747 of 2002 (TT)**
Jamadar J

[P20] One matter that arises in this case, is what is the proper approach to the assessment of evidence, where the same is on affidavit and where there are conflicts in the evidence which are untested by cross-examination . . . [P21] In the instant case, though this Court inquired whether there was a need for cross-examination or whether any such application was intended to be made, both sides took the decision not to seek cross-examination of any of the deponents to any of the affidavits relied on . . . [P23] For myself, I hesitate to apply, as a rule of law, to ever[y] circumstance of an unresolved conflict of evidence in judicial review, the statement of Lewis cited by the Respondent above. It would appear, that if the onus is on an Applicant to establish certain facts/issues and there is a clear unresolved conflict of evidence on that fact/issue, then the fact/issue should be deemed to have not been established, the onus of proof not having been satisfied. For this reason, the relevant issue should be resolved against the party on whom the onus lies. However, to take the further step and accept as established the evidence of the other party, when that very evidence is necessarily also in dispute, seems to be taking a step beyond what is jurisprudentially justifiable.

In the Application of the Chairman, Alderman, Councillors and Electors of the Region of Tunapuna/Piarco Regional Corporation – **HCA No 1066 of 1999 (TT)**
Bereaux J

[P33] Cross-examination in cases of judicial review is rare. The Court is normally required to resolve the issues on the affidavit evidence . . . [P34] Cross-examination is usually ordered where the Court is called upon, as it is in this case, to resolve issues of fact . . . [P35] I have not had the benefit of cross-examination in this case. With hindsight, it ought to have been ordered so as to assist me in deciding whether the Respondent gave the instruction or not. Consequently, I do not find myself able to resolve the conflict in the Applicant's favour. The presumption is that public officials will conduct themselves honestly and in accordance with the rules of law and the evidence in this case is not of sufficient quality to have displaced it. In any event the Respondent accepts that he has no power to give the instruction and that any such instruction would be illegal.

***In the Application of Steve Ramsaroop, Ramnarine Beharrylal, Sham Mohammed, Francis Seebarran and Deonarine Jawahir* – HCA No S-1569 of 1996 (TT)**
Mendonca J

[P8] In this matter there has been no cross examination of the deponents. Where there is a dispute of fact in cases such as this the Courts will proceed on the basis of the affidavit evidence presented by the person who does not have the onus of proof . . . In this case the onus is clearly on the Applicants to make out their case for judicial review. I will proceed on the basis of the Respondent's affidavit.

***In the Application of Richard Toby* – HCA No S-1276 of 1992 (TT)**
Lucky J

[P13] It is trite law that where there is a dispute of fact and there has been no cross-examination, a Court must proceed on the basis of the affidavit evidence of the person who does not have the onus of proof; in this matter, the Respondent.

***In the Application of Seereeram Bros. Ltd* – HCA No 3123 of 1991 (TT)**
Jones J

[P15] There is no doubt wisdom in the guidelines set out by the Judges in the above statements, as it seems to me to be only just and right that an Applicant or other party to judicial review proceedings (bearing in mind the nature of such proceedings) ought not to be allowed to use cross-examination as a means of luring his opponent to make admissions in order to bolster his own case. An example comes to mind. An Applicant cannot allege that the Tribunal had taken extraneous matters not apparent on the record into consideration and seek through cross-examination to ascertain what those matters might be. He must in my view set out in his affidavit in as clear terms as possible what extraneous matters were in fact taken into account. It is another matter, however, where on the face of the affidavits matters arise which in the light of the expressed case of either party, further enquiry becomes necessary.

5.9 ANONYMOUS EVIDENCE

The courts in certain circumstances may permit the tendering of evidence by persons whose identity are not made available to an applicant for judicial review proceedings.

***Regina v Director of Public Prosecutions and Director of Correctional Services ex parte Vivian Blake* (1996) 33 JLR 299 (JM)**
Smith J

[P304] Are anonymous depositions evidence upon which a committal Court in this country can act? In other words can a Magistrate attach any weight to depositions so taken? We can safely say that, in this regard, the law applicable in England is the law applicable in this jurisdiction. As there is a dearth of cases on this point in the country, we must see how the English Courts deal with the reception of anonymous evidence . . . [P306] From the cases mentioned above it may be deduced that as to whether the identity of a witness should be withheld is a matter for the exercise of the discretion of the Magistrates. The exercise of this discretion will only be interfered with if it was shown that 'it was so unreasonable that no Magistrate properly considering it and properly directing himself could have reached that conclusion.' In the instant case the witnesses John Doe #1 and John Doe #2 deponed before a judge of The United States District Court for the Eastern District of Virginia. Both swore that they used pseudonyms because of fear of threat of bodily injury, given the reputation for violence of the accused. It is for the Magistrate to decide whether the rights of the Applicant particularly his ability to prepare and conduct his defence to the charges, [were] thereby prejudiced. He must balance the interests of the Applicant and the interest of justice in deciding, whether based on such evidence, he should commit the Applicant to custody to await his extradition. In coming to this decision the Magistrate would no doubt give careful consideration to the submissions of the Applicant's Attorney-at-Law that the withholding of the identity of the witnesses deprived the Applicant of the opportunity of calling witnesses to rebut the specific allegations made against him. We cannot in the circumstances of this case conclude that the Magistrate acted unreasonably in relying on the evidence of those two anonymous witnesses. This ground also fails.

5.10 NATURE OF REPLY

The reply in judicial review proceedings should not be used to re-argue a specific point, but generally to reply to new cases.

***In the Application of Veron Simpson* – Civil Appeal No 28 of 1999 (JM)**
Downer JA

[P24] Mr Macaulay QC attempted to reply to all the points raised by Ms. Davis for the Respondent. He was stopped. The practice and procedure in this Court is that the Appellant only has a right to reply to new cases cited by the Respondent. This Court may ask counsel for the Appellant to reply to specific points which it raises. Further, counsel may seek leave to reply on a specific point or points which may be granted. This is the practice and procedure which has guided this Court at least since 1971 when I appeared as counsel for the Crown and this practice has continued since I have been a member of the Court in 1986. No good reasons have been advanced why this flexible procedure should be altered. We think it is appropriate to reiterate this stance in writing for the guidance of counsel, particularly, as counsel has raised it for the second time. It is fair and of great assistance in the prompt dispatch of business. The power to regulate our own procedure in the absence of statutory rules flows from the Court's inherent power as a Superior Court of Record. We use this power in the interests of justice.

5.11 RE-OPENING CASES

The courts will only, in exceptional cases, re-open a matter, such as where procedural unfairness has been established through no fault of a party to the proceedings, as there is a public interest in having an end to litigation.

***In the Application of Errol E. Niles (2)* – Civil Appeal 2003 (BB)**
Simmons CJ

[PP7–10] The law has long insisted that there is a public interest in having an end to litigation. That insistence is exemplified in the Latin maxim *interest rei publicae ut sit finis litium*. Yet, in order to ensure justice, the law has to invest a Court with power to respond to special or exceptional circumstances which will arise from time to time and necessitate relaxation of the principle providing for finality of litigation. The law reports show that the House of Lords has sparingly and reluctantly exercised a power to re-open a previous decision—see *R v Bow Street Metropolitan Stipendiary Magistrate, Ex Parte Pinochet Ugarte* [1991] 1 All ER 577 where in the special circumstances of that case bias was alleged against Lord Hoffmann who was a member of a previous panel of Law Lords. It is our understanding of that case that their Lordships were at pains to emphasise that the exceptional use of power to re-open previous litigation in the House of Lords was because, as Lord Browne-Wilkinson stressed at p 585: 'In principle it must be that your Lordships, *as the ultimate Court of Appeal*, have power to correct any injustice caused by an earlier order of this House . . . However, it should be made clear that the House will not reopen any appeal save in circumstances where, through no fault of a party, he or she has been subjected to an unfair procedure.' In *Taylor v Lawrence*, Lord Woolf CJ distinguished the special position of the House of Lords as a final appellate Court vis-à-vis the Court of Appeal and warned that the observations of Lord Browne-Wilkinson (*supra*) could not 'automatically be applied to' the Court of Appeal. We are equally conscious of the status of the Barbados Court of Appeal relative to the Privy Council in the Barbadian hierarchy of Courts. *Taylor v Lawrence* was a case where the Applicants were relying upon fresh evidence alleging bias as the ground for re-opening a previous decision of the Court of Appeal. They applied to re-open the appeal which had been previously dismissed. The second Court of Appeal dismissed that application but granted leave to appeal to the House of Lords to enable the judgment of Woolf CJ to be further considered. In delivering the judgment of the Court of 5 Judges, Lord Woolf made a number of useful pronouncements. *Inter alia*, His Lordship explained that a Court of Appeal is established with two principal objectives. 'The first is a private objective of correcting wrong decisions so as to ensure justice between the litigants involved. The second is a public objective, to ensure public confidence in the administration of justice not only by remedying wrong decisions but also by clarifying and developing the law and setting precedents.'—paragraph [26]. As the head note reads: 'The Court of Appeal had a residual jurisdiction to re-open an appeal in order to avoid real injustice in exceptional circumstances. The Court had implicit powers to do that which was necessary to achieve the dual objectives of an appellate Court. The residual jurisdiction to re-open appeals was linked to a discretion which enabled the Court of Appeal *to confine its use to cases in which it was appropriate for the jurisdiction to be exercised*.' [Our emphasis]. Clearly the need to maintain confidence in the administration of justice makes it imperative that there should be a remedy where procedural unfairness has been *established*. If such impropriety is indeed established, this Court would be justified in re-opening the proceedings previously heard and determined by the original Court of Appeal . . . [PP11–12] We think that a Court of Appeal has a residual jurisdiction to re-open an appeal which it had already determined in order to avoid real injustice. Serious injustice may occur if there is no power to re-open an appeal.

6

REMEDIES

As noted in Chapter 1, the principal remedies in judicial review proceedings are mandamus, *certiorari*, prohibition and declarations.

In the Application of Bob Sooknanan – Civil Appeal No 109 of 1985 (TT)
Persaud JA

[P4] It seems clear, therefore, that the proceedings brought by the Appellant in the instant matter are not caught by sec. 19(2) of Chap 8 whereby the Attorney General must, subject to any other written law, be made a Defendant in proceedings against the State. The learned judge was therefore in my view in error in ordering that the Attorney General be substituted as the Defendant in these proceedings . . . [P7] The first is that an order for judicial review may be obtained to protect rights in public law, and where upon such an application a breach of a person's right in private law has been established instead, such a person may nevertheless obtain an appropriate order as is provided for in Order 53, Rule 9(5). The second is that where there is an allegation of an infringement of a right by a public authority (and that expression must include a person holding public office by virtue of any law) the proper procedure is to come for judicial review. But who must be the Respondents to such application? . . . [PP10–11] Dealing with the historical development of certiorari, prohibition, and mandamus under the caption 'Judicial Remedies' in 1 *Halsbury's Laws of England, (4th ed.)* at para. 81, the learned authors state—'Mandamus will lie to any person or body in respect of anything that appertains to his or their office and is in the nature of a public duty. It has never been limited to, or indeed primarily concerned with persons or bodies whose office is judicial or who have a duty to act judicially. The breach of duty may be a failure to exercise a statutory discretion, or a failure to exercise it according to proper legal principles. Orders of prohibition and certiorari, on the other hand, issue primarily to inferior Courts and other persons and bodies having legal authority to determine questions affecting the rights of subjects and having the duty to act judicially, where there has been an actual or threatened usurpation of jurisdiction, or a breach of the rules of natural justice, or an error of law on the fact of the proceedings. The legal authority in question is normally one [derived] from statute, but the orders are also available to control the exercise of jurisdiction by non-statutory bodies performing functions of a public, as a distinct from a private, nature.' And in para. 80 (*opas cit.*) certiorari, prohibition, mandamus, and declaratory orders have all been described as the principal non-statutory remedies. It seems to me therefore, from the more recent authorities, that in matters which were formerly on the Crown side where the Attorney General may not be made a Defendant, the proper party should be the relevant officer *eo nomine* . . . [P15] In my judgment the Respondents were the proper parties and the Judge was wrong to remove them from the motion paper and [substitute] the Attorney General. The result is that in my view, this appeal succeeds with costs to the Appellant.

In the Application of Francis Eustace Bernard and Nydia Bernard –
HCA No 4771 of 1983 (TT)
Permanand J

[P7] The application before this Court is made in the field of public law. Public law regulates the affairs between subjects and public authorities. For centuries there have existed special remedies available in public law namely the Writs of Certiorari, Mandamus and prohibition . . . [P26] The remedies of certiorari, mandamus and prohibition are of the greatest importance for the purpose of compelling tribunals, Ministers and other government bodies to act lawfully and to perform their duties. Since the end of the

16th century those remedies had become generally available to ordinary litigants, before they were only available to the Crown and not to the subject . . . Certiorari will lie where there is excess of jurisdiction or error on the face of the record. There is excess of jurisdiction where there is a neglect of mandatory conditions, consideration of irrelevant grounds, unlawful purposes, breach of natural justice, fraud . . . [P27] Originally certiorari lay to control the functions of inferior Courts i.e. judicial functions but now this remedy is used to control all kinds of administrative as well as judicial acts . . . [P29] The scope of certiorari extends to the correctness of excess of jurisdiction. It has been held that where decisions have been arrived at in the absence of evidence, same amounts to acting without jurisdiction.

R v Binger, N.J. Vaughan, and Scientific Research Council ex parte Chris Bobo Squire
(1984) 21 JLR 118 (JM)
Carberry JA

[PP120–123] Some preliminary observations are in order. The growth of the common law has been largely shaped by the development of the remedies that it provides. Judicial control of the process of local government and what we now call administrative law was largely exercised and developed through the use of the prerogative writs, and as much of the local government law was administered by Justice of the Peace it was perhaps inevitable that such attempts as were made to secure uniformity of administration and the proper observance of the limits of the power entrusted to them should have been exercised by the superior Courts, principally by the Court of King's Bench. Control tended to be developed through litigation, on a case to case basis, and a principle area of concern was with the issue of jurisdiction. The pre-eminent remedies of this period were the prerogative writs of certiorari, prohibition and mandamus. *Halsbury's Laws of England*, 1st Edn. (1909), Vol 10: Crown Practice, Proceedings on the Crown side of the King's Bench Division, sec., 7: page 155, para 310: Certiorari: the nature of the writ: states:- 'The writ of certiorari issues out of a superior Court, and is directed to the Judge or other officer of an inferior Court of record. It requires that the proceedings in some cause or matter pending before such inferior Court shall be transmitted into the superior Court to be dealt with, in order to insure that the application for the writ may have the more sure and speedy justice . . . The object of the writ, particularly in civil proceedings, is to give relief from some inconvenience supposed, in the particular case, to arise from the matter being disposed of before an inferior Court less capable than the High Court of rendering complete and effectual justice.' At page 160 para 320 of the same work: Certiorari to quash: It is said: 'Certiorari lies at common law to remove the proceedings of inferior Courts or judicial bodies for the purpose of quashing such proceedings where the writ of error did not lie. Certiorari also lies to remove for the purpose of quashing, the determination *of persons or bodies who are by status at charter entrusted with judicial functions out of the ordinary course of legal procedure, but within the general scope of the common law* . . .' [emphasis supplied]. No indication is given for the test or touchstone to be applied to see whether the body or the decision in question falls within the reach of certiorari, but, as usual in attempts to define the common law, a number of example cases are given. It is apparent that there was at least one common factor, that is that the body was exercising a power in the field of public law, and a second factor (later to be challenged) was that the nature of the power was 'judicial' in character, in that it involved the making of a decision to apply the power to an ordinary citizen, and that in the decision making process law was to be applied to facts in a considered way, and to anticipate, that the person involved in its application should have a chance to be heard by the deciders before or during the decision making process. The Courts were concerned with two main aspects: had the decision makers acted within their powers and secondly, was it the sort of decision that required from its nature that the persons affected should have a chance to be heard. Certiorari was to lie where the normal process of judicial review did not run, whether by way of the writ of error or by appeal, but certainly whatever the test, there was never any doubt that it lay in the field of public law, as opposed to that of private law where the common law remedies such as the action for damages was available. As to the early history of the prerogative writs see generally Holdsworth's *History of English Law* Volume 10 page 243 *et seq*, and Vol. 14 page 245 *et seq*. It should be observed that in general the Courts did not canvass the merits of the actual decisions, but concentrated principally on whether the decision was within the jurisdiction, and on whether the situation was one in which the principles of natural justice (the opportunity to be heard) should be applied. With regard to the former a considerable volume of learning was built up as to whether the error appeared on the face of the record, or not, and [if] not as to whether it could be proved *aliunde*. The Courts also refrained from interfering in 'administrative' decisions. The test of the difference between 'administrative' and 'judicial' was on a case to case basis. By the time of the appearance of the Third Edition of *Halsbury's Laws of England*, in 1955: Volume 11 still under the title of Crown Proceedings, the writs had become orders (save from *habeas corpus*), but still issued out of the superior Court (usually King's Bench). The nature of the orders remained the same: See *Halsbury*. 3rd Edn. Page 52 para 107: Nature of the three orders: (mandamus, prohibition and certiorari). So far as certiorari was concerned, the scope of the order had widened in respect of the persons to whom the order would issue. More and more cases or situations had been added to the list. An attempt had been made in the celebrated dictum of Lord Atkin in *R v Electricity Commissioners, Ex Parte London Electricity Joint Committee Company (1920) Ltd.* [1924] 1 KB 171 (CA) to distinguish those cases which would be treated as vulnerable to certiorari proceedings, and those which would not. In that case the proceedings had been brought to test the validity of a proposed scheme published by the Commissioners for effecting an improvement of the existing organization for the supply of electricity in the London and Home [counties] district. The Commissioners were a statutory body set up by Act of Parliament to effect rationalization and formulate schemes for unification of the supply of electricity in various districts (then supplied by a variety of private enterprises). The Applicants were existing suppliers of electricity who would be affected adversely by the proposed scheme. They challenged the Commissioners by certiorari, alleging that they had exceeded their jurisdiction by not hearing them before publishing the scheme. The Commissioner replied in effect that they were exercising 'administrative' powers, and thus not within the reach of certiorari. At pages 204–205 Atkin, LJ, said: 'The question now arises whether the persons interested are entitled to the remedy which they now claim in order to put a stop to the unauthorized proceedings of the Commissioners. The matter comes before or upon rules for writ of prohibition and certiorari which have been discharged by the Divisional Court. Both writs are of great antiquity, forming part of the process by which the King's Courts restrained Courts of inferior jurisdiction from exceeding their powers. Prohibition restrains the tribunal from proceeding further in excess of jurisdiction; certiorari requires the record or [order] of the Court to be sent up to the King's Bench Division, to have its legality inquired into, and, if necessary, to have the order quashed. It is to be noted that both writs deal with questions of excessive jurisdiction, and doubtless in their origin dealt almost exclusively with the jurisdiction of what it described in ordinary parlance as a Court of Justice. But the operation of the writs has extended to control the proceedings of bodies which do not claim to be and would not be recognized as, Courts of Justice. *Wherever any body of persons having legal authority to determine questions affecting the rights of subjects, and having the duty to act judicially, act in excess of their legal authority they are subject to the controlling jurisdiction of the King's Bench Division exercised in these writs*' [emphasis supplied]. Atkin LJ then proceeded to give examples of cases in which the Courts had held bodies subject to the control of these writs, and others in which they had not. He and the other members of the Court of Appeal decided that prohibition would lie to the Commissioners. All of these examples came from the field of public law, they related to statutory bodies of one sort or another exercising control of and making decisions which affected individual members of the public. It seems clear that this element is what is being referred to in the first part of the dictum. As to the second part, 'having the duty to act judicially', no clear test was formulated as to when such a duty would arise, and it remained, and still remains, a problem, addressed by Lord Reid, amongst others, in *Ridge v Baldwin* [1964] AC 40 at pages 74 *et seq*. Lord Reid was of the view that the 'duty to act judicially' is to be inferred from the nature of the power, and he was content to indicate certain fields in which from the nature of the power the duty to act judicially would not be inferred, as for instance a considerable body of wartime legislation. *Ridge v Baldwin* apart from this is of special importance in the case before us, as it dealt with the exercise of the power of dismissal of a chief constable by the local watch committee which had such a power of dismissal, but were held to be obliged to exercise it in accordance with the rules of natural justice. Apart from a consideration of the general nature and scope of certiorari as a remedy, it should be noted as another factor from the growth of the remedy of 'declaration'; in which the Courts are asked to make declarations as to the rights of the parties before them, or to be more accurate 'declaratory judgments' a remedy that grew and developed as the result of the amendment in 1883 of the former Order 25 Rule 5, to the effect that such declarations could be made 'whether or not any consequential relief is sought or could be claimed'. The learning in regard to this remedy is to be found in the notes in the White Book dealing with Order 15 Rule 17, and more recently with those dealing with Order 15 Rule 16. The Jamaican equivalent is to be found in sec. 239 of the Judicature (Civil Procedure) Code. The declaration, or declaratory judgment, together with the injunction have become increasingly popular because they are not hedged about with the restrictions applicable to the prerogative writs or orders; thus no leave is required to bring such an action [if] it is begun by writ, and had procedural advantages in that discovery *et cetera* could be obtained. Further the remedy was available in the field of both public and private law and there was therefore a considerable overlap with certiorari, as it was possible to invoke the principles of natural justice when seeking a declaration. One result had been to assimilate the two remedies to a considerable extent, so that if a declaration cannot or ought not to be made a similar ruling is likely to be made in similar circumstances with regard to certiorari. Nevertheless the converse is not true, there are cases in which certiorari will not lie (because it applies only in the field of public law), but in which an application for a declaration might have succeeded: see for example *Hannam v Bradford City Council* [1970] 2 All ER 690; [1970] 1 WLR 937. Perhaps one way of looking at the distinction is to observe that in certiorari the Applicant is asserting as a matter of general public law that the rules of natural justice apply, whereas in the action for a declaration he tends to be relying on specific contractual provisions arising in the field of private law, which involve the application of the natural justice principles.

6.1 MANDAMUS

In deciding whether mandamus is an appropriate remedy, the court will consider the public interest in making such an order.

***In the Application of the Chairman, Alderman, Councillors and Electors of the Region of Tunapuna/Piarco Regional Corp.* – HCA No 1066 of 1999 (TT)**
Bereaux J

[P37] Among the reliefs sought by the Applicant is mandamus to compel the Respondent's attendance and certiorari to quash the actions taken in pursuance of the Minister's illegal instructions. Given Mr Mahabir's obvious recalcitrance and the rancour flowing between the parties, the grant of mandamus will not serve the public interest. Indeed it may be inimical to it. As to the grant of certiorari, the roads in question have already been paved and it is of no practical value. I shall confine myself to declarations.

6.2 DAMAGES

Damages are obtainable in judicial review proceedings in Trinidad and Tobago.

***In the Application of Cecil Kennedy* – Civil Appeal No 653 of 2000 (TT)**
Sharma CJ

[PP13–14] [32] In support of this decision, the Judge reviewed several local and English cases, the more pertinent one being *Millette v McNicolls* Civ App 155/95. In that case it was held by the then Chief Justice that Order 53 Rule 7 is *intra vires* and valid so that it grants power to award damages in judicial review proceedings subject to the fulfillment of the three said conditions. It was quoted: 'The claim to damages in an application for judicial review is not the creation of a new substantive right but must be one which could have been made in an action commenced by writ.' (see page 12 of judgment of de la Bastide, CJ). [33] This position supports the basic principle of judicial review that mere careless performance of a statutory duty will not of itself give rise to any cause of action in the absence of a common law duty of care in negligence or a right of action for breach of statutory duty: *Geddis v Proprietors of Bann Reservoir* [1878] 3 AC 430. Liability for damages in judicial review proceedings must therefore rest on the same tenets as claims in private law actions. Thus, in the absence of negligence, malice or misfeasance in public duty, there could be no liability for damages under proceedings for judicial review.

***In the Application of Ronnie Samaroo* – HCA No S. Cv 536 of 1998 (TT)**
Jamadar J

[P4] It is agreed that in order for the Applicant to be awarded damages in judicial review proceedings, three pre-conditions must be satisfied (see *Millette's case* at pp 7–8). These are:

1. there must be a claim for damages included in the statement, which is a pleading requirement.
2. the claim for damages must arise from the same matter that forms the basis of the application for judicial review.
3. the Applicant could have been awarded damages had he brought an action for same at the time when the application for judicial review was made (whether at common law or on a constitutional motion).

[P8] By the Constitution, Section 4(f) provides by implication the right of a child to be educated in a school of choice . . . Moreover, since as I have already stated, implicit in the conduct of proper inquiries is the entitlement of the suspendee to be given the opportunity to be heard, the failure to afford the Applicant any such opportunity and to continue his suspension nevertheless, is a contravention of that right. A contravention which amounts to a breach of his constitutional right to the protection of the law (see *Rees v Crane* [1994] 43 WIR 444 at 453(j) and Section 4(b) of the Constitution). Implicit in the right to natural justice is the concept of fairness, antithesis of which is arbitrariness. In my opinion this Applicant could have succeeded on the matters raised in these proceedings in a claim under the Constitution for breach of his fundamental right to the protection of the law and would have been entitled to damages for same.

***In the Application of Josephine Millette* – Civil Appeal No 155 of 1995 (TT)**
Hosein JA

[PP5–6] Order 53 was substantially revamped by an amendment of the rules which took effect in January, 1983 . . . The basic element in the reform was the grouping together of what were formerly the prerogative orders of mandamus, certiorari and prohibition, under the general heading of judicial review and the prescription of a standardized procedure for applying for these orders, which eliminated the risk of losing one's remedy as a result of choosing the wrong procedure or for some other technical reason. The rule also added to the arsenal of remedies available to the Court dealing with applications for judicial review, the power to award damages and make declarations ... [PP7–8] If one analyses Order 53 Rule 7, one notes that it imposes three conditions for the award of damages in judicial review proceedings viz:

[1] there must be a claim for damages included in the statement ...

[2] the claim for damages must arise from the same matter that forms the basis for the application for judicial review ...

[3] if the Applicant had brought an action for damages at the time when he made his application for judicial review, he could have been awarded damages ...

[P13] Before the new Order 53 was made, it had not been possible (or at least not advisable) for a claim for damages to be filed until the judicial review proceedings had first [been] concluded. It is only at that stage that the claimant having established the public law wrong could file his writ to enforce his private law right to damages, by which time the relevant period of limitation might well have run out (particularly in Trinidad and Tobago where there was a specially short limitation period of one year for actions against public authorities) ... [P14] The abbreviated review which I have made of the English authorities indicates that they are overwhelmingly in favour of upholding the validity of Order 53 Rule 7, even without any statutory backing, on the ground that the facility which it provides of combining a claim for damages with an application for judicial review does not make any alteration in the substantive law, but is a reform that is wholly procedural. I have no doubt whatever that that is the correct view of the rule. It creates no new cause of action. Damages are only recoverable in judicial review proceedings if they would have been recoverable in an ordinary action brought either by writ or by some other form of originating process e.g. constitutional motion. What the new rule does is to obviate the necessity for a fresh and separate action in order to enforce the right to damages and thus avoid a multiplicity of actions ... [PP15–16] For these reasons I have come firmly to the conclusion that Order 53 Rule 7 is *intra vires* and valid and that there is power to award damages in judicial review proceedings subject to the fulfillment of the three conditions examined earlier in this judgment ... [P16] In my view, if an order is made which the Court making it has no jurisdiction to make, it is open to any Court of competent jurisdiction to treat that order as void in any proceedings in which the validity of the order is relevant, even though that is not the purpose for which the proceedings were brought. Nor does it make any difference in my view that the order was made by consent, as it is well established that parties cannot by their consent confer on the Court a jurisdiction which it does not have.

In the Application of Cleavon Frank Joseph – HCA No 1740 of 1994 (TT)
Best J

[PP4–5] It was never disputed by either of the parties before the Court that prior to the passing of Rules of the Supreme Court 1975 it was possible to obtain relief by way of a Originating Motion/Summons for judicial review and to obtain damages if successful—See, The Supreme Court Practice 1985 (53/1–14/20): 'The claim to damages in an application for judicial review is not the creation of a new substantive right, but must be one which could have been made in an action commenced by writ.' Section 20 of the Supreme Court of Judicature Act enjoined the High Court to do all such things to avoid a '... multiplicity of legal proceedings ...'. The end result, was the introduction of Order 53; its revocation and its replacement by the Amendment Rule (*supra*), which came into operation on 17th January, 1983. This activity by the Rules Committee, in the view of this Court was an attempt to remove the inconvenience caused by a dual system of remedies which co-existed in an uneasy manner. The Rules Committee did not legislate into operation a legal Right, that Right existed before the Rules of the Supreme Court—thus Subrule 07 states: 'On an application for judicial review the Court may ... award damages to the Applicant if . . . the Court is satisfied that, if the claim had been made in an action begun by the Applicant at the time of making his application, he could have been awarded damages'.

6.3 *CERTIORARI*

Certiorari is a specialised remedy which operates in the area of public law and is essentially a discretionary remedy which will only be granted where the conditions for the grant exists.

***In the Application of Seebalack Singh* – HCA No S430 of 2003 (TT)**
Tiwary-Reddy J

[P12] Certiorari is technically an order bringing a decision of a public body to the High Court so that the Court may determine whether the decision is valid.

***In the Application of the Minister of Commerce and Technology* –**
Civil Appeal No 18 of 1998 (JM)
Downer JA

[PP5–6] The procedural rules governing an application for an order of certiorari must take into account the special nature of the proceedings. These proceedings are markedly different from ordinary adversarial proceedings commenced by writ of summons. In the first place remedy is discretionary, but it will not be refused where the interests of justice are in favour of the Applicant. Secondly, it is a public law remedy and so its issue is generally against the order of a Tribunal or a member of the Executive. Thirdly, there is an initial scrutiny or filtering process to eliminate worthless applications. Fourthly, promptitude is a necessary feature of certiorari proceedings as proceedings may be stayed until the merits are determined by the Full Court. In the case of a Minister, an important administrative decision may be quashed so the Minister may consider it prudent and suspend action until the merits of the case are determined. Fifthly, certiorari is a remedy in proceedings for judicial review. In judicial review proceedings the merits of the Tribunal's decision or the prudence of the Minister's policy is not an issue. It is the legality of procedure that is being tested. It is whether the proceedings were in accordance with law not whether the decision was right. Sixthly, there is a distinction between judicial review and an appeal. An appeal is concerned with the merits of a decision and is always on a statutory basis. Judicial review has its origin in the common law. It is the exercise of the supervisory jurisdiction of the Supreme Court. Seventhly, judicial review is recognized in the Constitution in Chapter 1 Section 1(9) which reads: 'No provision of this Constitution that any person or authority shall not be subject to the direction or control of any other person or authority in exercising any functions under this Constitution shall be construed as precluding a Court from exercising jurisdiction in relation to any question whether that person or authority has performed those functions in accordance with this Constitution or any other law'. Eighthly, it is always the private person who seeks the remedy of certiorari. The Tribunal or Ministry is always the Respondent. Where two public authorities have a dispute they resort to the remedy of a declaration to determine their respective rights. These special features of the remedy of certiorari are not meant to be exhaustive but they are sufficient to form the background to consider the jurisdictional issue.

***Brown and Others v Resident Magistrate, Spanish Town Resident Magistrate's Court, St. Catherine* (1995) 48 WIR 232 (JM)**
Carey JA

[PP235–236] The function of this Court is to examine the proceedings to discover whether the Full Court exercised its supervisory powers correctly. In my view, the Full

Court was required in this matter to satisfy itself that the resident Magistrate had not by some error of law exceeded her jurisdiction. The question was not simply whether she had erred in law, because an appeal lies against any judgment which in the event she might have given. A resident Magistrate is permitted to fall into error but that does not necessarily make the judgment amenable to certiorari. It becomes so if, and only if, the Magistrate can be said to be acting in excess of jurisdiction or without jurisdiction. I am reinforced in my thinking by the observations of Lord Reid in *Anisminic Ltd v Foreign Compensation Commission* [1969] 1 All ER 208 at page 213 when in dealing with the term 'jurisdiction' he said: 'It has sometimes been said that it is only where a tribunal acts without jurisdiction that its decision is a nullity. But in such cases the word "jurisdiction" has been used in a very wide sense, and I have come to the conclusion that it is better not to use the term except in the narrow and original sense of the Tribunal being entitled to enter on the inquiry in question. But there are many cases where, although the Tribunal had jurisdiction to enter on the inquiry, it has done or failed to do something in the course of the inquiry which is of such a nature that its decision is a nullity. It may have given its decision in bad faith. It may have made a decision which it had no power to make. It may have failed in the course of the inquiry to comply with the requirements of natural justice. It may in perfect good faith have misconstrued the provisions giving it power to act so that it failed to deal with the question remitted to it and decided some question which was not remitted to it. It may have refused to take into account something which it was required to take into account. Or it may have based its decision on some matter which, under the provisions setting it up, it had no right to take into account. I do not intend this list to be exhaustive. But if it decides a question remitted to it for decision without committing any of these errors it is as much entitled to decide that question wrongly as it is to decide it rightly. I understand that some confusion has been caused by my having said in *Armah v Government of Ghana* [1966] 3 All ER 177 at page 187 that, if a tribunal has jurisdiction to go right, it has jurisdiction to wrong. So it has if one uses "jurisdiction" in the narrow original sense. If it is entitled to enter on the inquiry and does not do any of those things which I have mentioned in the course of the proceedings, then its decision is equally valid whether it is right or wrong subject only to the power of the Court in certain circumstances to correct an error of law.' Certiorari is a specialised remedy which operates in the area of public law and is essentially a discretionary remedy. Where the conditions for its exercise do not exist, it ought not to be invoked. These conditions are those suggested by Lord Reid. It cannot in my judgment, be invoked by creating a record to show an error of law, which is what occurred in the instant case. At the end of the second Respondent's (i.e. the plaintiff's) case, the Magistrate should have made an order either requiring the Appellants (i.e. the Defendants) to elect to stand on their submissions or she should call upon them to make their defence. Doubtless, in the course of a finding for either party, her reasons would show that she had either accepted or rejected the submissions made. An order consistent with her finding or ruling might be wrong in law, but that would not affect her jurisdiction. An error in law would not in those circumstances, I suggest, amount to a nullity and thus be amenable to judicial review. For these reasons, I conclude that it would be a sleeveless errand to embark on an inquiry into whether or not the Magistrate was in point of law wrong in her ruling and I decline therefore to follow Mr Macaulay into such an exercise. In the fulfilling of its supervisory powers, the Full Court had no such mandate.

***In the Application of Aubrey Roberts* – Civil Appeal No 53 of 1998 (GY)**
Chang JA

[P4] It is instructive to note that, generally, Certiorari does not lie to determine whether an inferior tribunal acted rightly or wrongly in a matter but rather whether it acted lawfully or unlawfully ... [P5] Lord Brightman captured the point when he succinctly stated in *Chief Constable of North Wales Police v Evans* [1982] 3 All ER 141 at 154: 'Judicial review is concerned not with the decision but with the decision making process. Unless restriction on that power of the Court is observed, the Court will, in my view, under the

> guise of preventing an abuse of power, be itself guilty of usurping power.' ... [P6] Every tribunal has the jurisdiction to determine the extent of its own jurisdiction. The law has not given the tribunal the right to make a wrong determination on this question of jurisdiction. Therefore, the determination of such a jurisdictional question must necessarily be reviewable by the Court as a matter of law. The determination of this jurisdictional question of law may depend on a preliminary or collateral issue of law. Both issues of law are reviewable by the Court ... [P8] It should be noted, *per curiam*, that judicial review does lie against a wrong finding of jurisdictional *fact*. [PP8–9] It is essential that where the exercise of administrative power depends on the prior establishment of an objective fact, the Court will be the final arbiter as to whether that requirement has been satisfied. Otherwise, the Court will be surrendering the rule of law to the rule of administrative discretion. In my view, whether a collateral jurisdictional question of fact or law or of mixed fact and law arises and is determined by an administrative tribunal whether positively or negatively either in conferment of jurisdiction or in denial of it, the Court has the power to quash the preliminary ruling as to jurisdiction if such a question has been wrongly decided by the administrative tribunal.

***In the Application of Aubrey Norton* – HCCJ No 5932 of 1997 (GY)**
Bernard CJ

> [P6] The discretionary remedies of certiorari and prohibition were employed primarily for the control of inferior Courts, tribunals and administrative or other public authorities. It was a form of judicial review whereby the acts of these Courts, tribunals or public authorities could be quashed if it was found that they had acted outside of their mandate or unfairly even within their mandate or jurisdiction. Over the years judicial review has undergone tremendous changes particularly in England where nearly every tribunal or authority which exercises administrative functions in one form or another is subject to judicial review. These functions are no longer confined to judicial or quasi-judicial functions, and the decisions of Ministers have often been brought before the Courts to be quashed. Whereas we are lagging far behind in this branch of administrative law the English Rules of Court expressly provide for judicial review, and lay down the procedure to be followed. The writs of certiorari and prohibition in their old forms are still available in our legal system. Certiorari is used to bring before the High Court the decision of some inferior Court or tribunal in order that it may be investigated ... [PP8–9] There is no longer any distinction between judicial and administrative decisions which can be the subject of a writ of certiorari.

The courts will not make an order of *certiorari* where such an award is detrimental to good administration or unfair to a third party.

***In the Application of Chester Polo* – HCA No S 1203 of 2002 (TT)**
Dean-Armorer J

> [P20] In the instant case, the illegality of the impugned decision of the Public Service Commission is glaring. Whereas the terms of s 121(1) and (7) of the Constitution are general in their application, the terms of s 5 of the Act are specific. The former cannot therefore derogate from the latter and s 5 must be interpreted as investing in the Minister of Health, and no one else, the power to designate the Registrar. The natural result of such a finding is that the impugned decision is *ultra vires*, null and void ... [P23] The Court is inclined to refrain from granting an Order of certiorari. Such an Order, in the Court's view, would nullify an appointment in respect of which there has already been service by and remuneration to the benefit of Mr Kerr. This appeared to be both unfair to a third party and detrimental to good administration, since, in the capacity of acting Registrar, even if pursuant to an *ultra vires* appointment, Mr Kerr would have performed duties, the validity of which could be called into question. The Court may have held a different view if at the outset the Applicant had obtained an injunction restraining the

appointment of Mr Kerr. The remedies which are available in judicial review are granted according to the discretion of the Court.

In the Application of Caribbean Book Distributors (1996) Ltd – **HCA No S 764 of 1997 (TT)**
Ramlogan J

[PP9–10] An order of certiorari is a discretionary remedy. The Court must consider all the factors including how its Order would affect third parties. In this case even if there were good grounds and I hold that there is none, I would not grant an order for certiorari. Schools have opened more than a week ago and parents must have bought books based on the final list. To quash that list now would mean that these parents might have to purchase new books which would not only place an intolerable burden on them but be grossly unfair.

Certiorari will be granted where the decision-maker arrived at its decision on the basis of fraud or perjured evidence.

In the Application of Castus John – **HCA No 6658 of 1987 (TT)**
Hamel-Simth J

[P6] Certiorari is a remedy of a very special character. In most cases it is moved and granted on the question whether or not an inferior Court or tribunal has jurisdiction. Where it is shown that the inferior Court either has no jurisdiction in a particular matter or has exceeded its jurisdiction, certiorari will be granted. It is sometimes granted where there is an error of law on the face of the record. Then there are cases, and they have been few, where certiorari will be granted where the decision of the inferior Court has been obtained by the fraud or on the perjured evidence of the person invoking the jurisdiction ... [P11] I find that the fraud here is sufficiently clear and manifest to warrant the Court in exercising its discretionary jurisdiction ... It is true that it is a principle that certiorari will go only where there is no other effective and convenient remedy. But cases for judicial review can arise even where appeal procedures are provided by Parliament ... [P13] I find that this case is one of exceptional circumstances. A fraud has been perpetrated against the Applicant and as a result he has been denied both his right to be heard in defence and on appeal. And in any event, an application for Certiorari was the speediest and cheapest method and in my view the most preferred one in the circumstances.

Certiorari is a discretionary remedy and the courts will often consider the conduct of the party seeking the remedy before making an order.

In the Application of Easton Wilberforce Grant – **Supreme Court No M107 of 2000 (JM)**
Cooke J

[P14] Before departing from this application, perhaps I should add that the remedy of certiorari is discretionary. In this matter the behaviour of the Applicant was so unmeritorious, that even if there had been a failing in any aspect of the proceedings I doubt that I would grant the relief sought.

Regina v the Minister of Finance and Planning and the Director of the Revenue Protection Division ex parte Linton Lloyd Simpson – **Supreme Court No M150 of 1998 (JM)**
Cooke J

[P5] Even to the most non-discerning, a cursory review of the circumstances outlined above reveals an exercise of chicanery. The lack of sincerity on the part of the Applicant is to be strongly deplored. It is indeed a barefaced Applicant who would seek relief from a Court when it is palpably obvious that the application is most unmeritorious ... The reliefs sought—Certiorari and Mandamus—are discretionary in nature.

In the Application of Auburn Court Ltd – **Civil Appeal No 99 of 1997, Suit Nos M101 and M102 of 1996 (JM)**
Harrison JA

[P96] The Appellant's conduct was one of a persistent disregard for the law. It commenced and continued construction of the building on South Avenue knowingly without permission. It defiantly continued construction even after it was instructed to cease. Such conduct cannot be ignored by a Court. The Full Court recognized its discretionary powers exercisable in consideration of the grant of the orders of certiorari and prohibition and declined to favour the Appellant. This approach of the Full Court cannot be faulted. I agree with its conclusions.

6.4 INJUNCTION

Injunctive relief is available in judicial review proceedings where an order of a court may be rendered nugatory if it fails to maintain the status quo. However, injunctive relief is not to be lightly exercised and will only be done in the clearest circumstances. Indeed, injunctive relief will not be granted where there is delay on the part of the person seeking the remedy and the decision complained of is in the process of actual implementation.

In the Application of Garvin Thomas et al – **HCA No 1946 of 2003 (TT)**
Bereaux J

[P8] In *Belize Alliance of Conservation Non-Governmental Organisations v Department of the Environment & Another* (Belize) UKPC 63 (13 August 2003), the Judicial Committee of the Privy Council refused an interim injunction because it did not consider the Appellants in that case to have had 'a strong case on which to seek, without an undertaking in damages, an injunction which could halt a major construction project for four months'. Lord Walker of Gestingthorpe at para 40 in his judgment considered that: ***'A delay of four months with about 300 men and large quantities of vehicles and plant now on site, would be bound to cause severe disruption and significant loss.'*** On the facts of this case, entry was made in late April, 2003 and certainly by the 2nd of May, 2003. The application for judicial review was made on 15th July. Leave was granted on 18th July, 2003 but an application for a stay was refused. The application for an interim injunction was not made until 10th September, 2003, almost two months after the application for judicial review. Mr Noel Garcia, Executive Director of the Respondent Authority has deposed that the Government has agreed to vest the lands in the Respondent and the Director of Surveys authorized the Respondent to take possession of the lands for the construction of a middle income housing development pending the transfer of title to the Respondent . . . [P9] Having regard to the evidence of both the Applicants and the Respondent, it appears to me that the project is well advanced and it would not be appropriate to grant injunctive relief at this stage. Workmen and equipment have already been mobilized and building supplies procured. The Applicants were obliged to move swiftly once the Respondent had taken possession of the lands. They did not seek injunctive relief until four and a half months after work was commenced on the lands by the contractor. An injunction will cause severe disruption and financial loss to the project which the Applicants will not be able to offset by any undertaking in damages. Moreover the strength of the Applicants' challenge to the Respondent's action is not sufficient to warrant the grant of interim injunctive relief.

In the Application of Walkerwell Ltd – **Civil Appeal No 94 of 2000 (TT)**
Hamel-Smith JA

[P4] While the application was filed within three months of the Appellant learning of the award, no interim relief was sought at the leave stage, as is the general practice. The

Appellant opted to seek it at the hearing of the substantive application. It filed the summons for that relief on April 7, 2000 and the hearing took place on April 13 when relief was refused. As a result some two more months were allowed to lapse before the stay was sought. The relevance of this delay is that the contract was well underway when the application for a stay was filed. It is true that the Appellant was not privy to the precise date when the contract was implemented. The only information available to it was the photograph in the newspaper. It had no official word as to when the contract was implemented but it is reasonable to assume that within a relatively short space of time implementation would take place. There was an obligation on the part of the Appellant to move swiftly if it wished to challenge the award and have the contract stopped in the interim. When it filed its application for interim relief in April 2000, it sought a stay of the implementation of the contract. But it must have been apparent at that stage (i.e. before that application was actually heard) from the Respondent's affidavits that the contract was well underway by then. The Appellant must therefore have appreciated that its application could not be pursued in the form in which it was filed but had to be varied to a stay of further progress of the works under the contract until the determination of the substantive matter. I think that in those circumstances very different considerations applied. Had the application been made before the contract was taken up and acted upon the position certainly may have been different. But that is not the case. No longer had the Court to consider the issues between the 'parties' but it had the additional burden of having to consider the prejudice and hardship that may be occasioned to the contractor who was not joined in the suit. This required the trial Judge to balance on the one hand the fact that the contractor was already on site in Tobago, performing the contract and the serious prejudice to him if he were stopped in midstream so to speak and, on the other hand, the right of the Appellant to be treated fairly and afforded equal treatment by the Respondent in making its award ... [P5] We are not persuaded that the trial Judge wrongly exercised his discretion in refusing to grant the stay. He must have taken into account the considerable delay in making the application, one that should generally be made at the leave stage, and the more important factor, that the contract was well underway by the time the application was made.

***In the Application of General Earth Movers Ltd* – HCA No 585 of 1997 (TT)**
Persad-Maharaj J

[P18] Further, I hold that the decisions of the Respondent are not decisions of a Court of law or Tribunal and that the narrow meaning is the correct approach taken by this Court. That the Applicant's case falls squarely within the case of Vehicles and Supplies. That the Applicant is not entitled to a Stay of the Proceedings or in the nature as suggested by the Applicant's Attorney ... [P19] If I am wrong to hold that the narrow meaning is the correct meaning and that the wider meaning is appropriate, then in such circumstances and in the exercise of my discretion, I am of the view that a Stay should not be granted. Further the Stay sought by the Applicant has far reaching consequences for the Government of Trinidad and Tobago, Phase III Rehabilitation Programme. It would bring the entire project to a halt until the principal matter is decided and other pre qualifying contractors of the Respondent will not be able to be awarded contracts in so far as the whole project is concerned. The grant of a Stay of Proceedings would be too wide in its term.

***In the Application of Anne-Marie Lequay, Lydia J. Baah, Merilee Barrow, Wilma Collins, Shirley Bland, Helen Alleyne, Patsy Ali, Sheila Sirju, Gail Lans and Tayiff Deen* – HCA No 6512 of 1988 (TT)**
Blackman J

[P12] The issue as to whether the Court has the jurisdiction to grant an interim injunction in judicial review proceedings was not agitated. Again the case can be distinguished from the instant one. (ii) *Attorney General of Trinidad and Tobago v Sumair Hansraj & Others* Civil Appeal No 77/83 is also a case which offers no assistance. As I understand that case it decided that an interlocutory injunction cannot be obtained against the State or officers of the State acting as such in an application for redress under the Constitution. This is because the Constitution expressly so states. The judgment does not affect applications for judicial review . . . [P13] Here the Court is called upon to deal with a different kettle of fish. What has to be determined is whether in judicial review proceedings the Court has jurisdiction to grant an interim injunction against the State or servants of the State acting as such . . . [P17] It seems to me that interim relief under Rule 3(8) can only be granted if such relief is permissible in an ordinary action. But in an ordinary action against the State an interim injunction may not be granted against the State or a servant of the State . . . [P19] In the circumstances my conclusion must be that neither an interim injunction nor interim declaration could be granted against the State or an officer of the State in Judicial Review Proceedings.

***Infochannel Ltd v Cable & Wireless Jamaica Ltd* (2000) 62 WIR 176 (JM)**
Downer JA

[P196] In my view, the Supreme Court has no direct jurisdiction pursuant to s 51 of the Act, save by way of judicial review, and therefore the redress sought by way of interlocutory injunction cannot be granted.

Harrison JA

[P232] In all the circumstances, on the evidence, I agree with Reckord J when he found that he did not feel that 'high degree of assurance' that the Appellant would succeed at the trial and refused to grant any injunctive relief. In any event, Cable & Wireless can rely on an acceptable defence to the suit, namely that it acted under the directions of the OUR, a statutory authority, within the provisions of s 51 of the Act. The right which the Appellant claims does not appear on the evidence to be a clear, unchallenged right that survives the strictures of s 76 and to be preserved to continue in Phase I, by the transitional provisions of s 85 of the Act, as contended for by the Appellant. The evidence discloses that the Appellant may well have been engaged in bypass operations, that is reducing into the local Cable & Wireless lines incoming international calls, thereby evading the international gateway, to Cable & Wireless's detriment. The recipients of these calls (for example, Hamilton and Manning) were Cable & Wireless customers and not the Appellant's Internet subscribers. Cable & Wireless may, therefore, have properly discontinued service to the Appellant in respect of the offending telephone lines, under the provisions of s 51 of the Act. There is a serious question to be resolved at a trial. However, the facts and circumstances do not favour the grant of an injunction, as Reckord J found. Damages will be an adequate remedy in the event that the Appellant should succeed at the trial. The proportionate increase in current business and the projected expansion reduced by the loss of clientele to the Appellant by the refusal to grant the injunction is ascertainable and can be quantified as damages. The remedy of injunctive relief obtained at the *ex parte* stage by the Appellant was correctly discontinued and the interlocutory injunction sought was properly refused. I would dismiss this appeal with costs.

Belize Alliance of Conservation Non-Governmental Organizations –
Privy Council Appeal No 47 of 2003 (BZ)[1]
Lord Walker of Gestingthorpe

[PP16–19] 33. It is unnecessary to pursue that point since their Lordships are satisfied that the Board itself has jurisdiction to grant interim relief, where appropriate, in order to ensure that any order which it makes on the eventual hearing of the appeal should not be rendered nugatory. The clearest and most obvious instance of this is in staying execu-

1 Judgment upon a Petition for a Conservatory order of the Lords of the Judicial Committee of the Privy Council, delivered on 13 August 2003.

tion of a death sentence: see *Reckley v Minister of Public Safety and Immigration* [1995] 2 AC 491. Their Lordships are not aware of any reported decision in which the jurisdiction has been discussed and exercised in a civil case, but they are satisfied that it exists, and has been exercised from time to time. The jurisdiction depends on the power of any superior Court to supervise and protect its own procedures (see *Attorney General v Punch* [2003] 2 WLR 49, especially the observations of Lord Nicholls of Birkenhead at page 58). The power may be termed an inherent power, but that is not to say that its origins are devoid of statutory foundation. When Parliament established the Judicial Committee of the Privy Council and then extended its powers by the Judicial Committee Acts of 1833 and 1843 it must be taken to have intended to confer on the Board all the powers necessary for the proper exercise of its appellate jurisdiction . . . 35. Counsel were agreed (in the most general terms) that when the Court is asked to grant an interim injunction in a public law case, it should approach the matter on the lines indicated by the House of Lords in *American Cyanamid Company v Ethicon Limited* [1975] AC 396, but with modifications appropriate to the public law element of the case. The public law element is one of the possible 'special factors' referred to by Lord Diplock in that case (at page 409). Another special factor might be if the grant or refusal of interim relief were likely to be, in practical terms, decisive of the whole case; but neither side suggested that the present case is in that category. 36. The Court's approach to the grant of injunctive relief in public law cases was discussed (in particularly striking circumstances) by Lord Goff of Chieveley in *Queen v Secretary of State for Transport, Ex Parte Factortame Limited (No 2)* [1991] AC 603, 671–4. The whole passage calls for careful study. Lord Goff stated at page 672 that where the Crown is seeking to enforce the law, it may not be thought right to impose upon the Crown the usual undertaking in damages as a condition of the grant of injunctive relief. Lord Goff concluded (at page 674): 'I myself am of the opinion that in these cases, as in others, the discretion conferred upon the Court cannot be fettered by a rule; I respectfully doubt whether there is any rule that, in cases such as these, a party challenging the validity of a law must—to resist an application for an interim injunction against him, or to obtain an interim injunction restraining the enforcement of the law—show a strong *prima facie* case that the law is invalid. It is impossible to foresee what cases may yet come before the Courts; I cannot dismiss from my mind the possibility (no doubt remote) that such a party may suffer such serious and irreparable harm in the event of the law being enforced against him that it may be just or convenient to restrain its enforcement by an interim injunction even though so heavy a burden has not been discharged by him. In the end, the matter is one for the discretion of the Court, taking into account all the circumstances of the case. Even so, the Court should not restrain a public authority by interim injunction from enforcing an apparently authentic law unless it is satisfied, having regard to all the circumstances, that the challenge to the validity of the law is, *prima facie*, so firmly based as to justify so exceptional a course being taken.' 37. In some public law cases (such as *Queen v Servite Houses and Wandsworth LBC, Ex Parte Goldsmith* (2000) 3 CCLR 354) the issue is a straightforward dispute between a public or quasi-public body (in that case, a charity providing care services on behalf of a local authority) and citizens to whom the services are being provided. In such a case an injunction may be granted to the citizen, without any undertaking in damages, if justice requires that course. Swinton Thomas LJ took into consideration the public importance of the case, involving the closure of a residential care home; the very serious consequences for the elderly and infirm residents who would be moved from accommodation in which they were settled; their prospect of success at the full hearing; and the relatively short period for which the injunction would be in force pending the hearing of the appeal. 38. In *Queen v Inspectorate of Pollution, Ex Parte Greenpeace Limited* [1994] 1 WLR 570, on the other hand, a campaigning organisation was challenging an official decision which, if stayed, would have adverse financial implications for a commercial company (British Nuclear Fuels PLC) which was not a party to the proceedings. Brooke J had refused a stay and the Court of Appeal upheld this decision. Glidewell LJ said at page 574: 'At the hearing before Brooke J no offer was made by Greenpeace to give an undertaking as to damages suffered by BNFL should they suffer any; the sort of undertaking that would normally be required if an interlocutory injunction were to be granted. I bear in mind that the Judge said that he was influenced by the evidence about Greenpeace's likely inability to pay for that financial loss, but he had earlier remarked that he had not been offered an undertaking. If we were dealing with this matter purely on the material which was before the Judge, I would find no difficulty at all. This was essentially a matter for the discretion of the Judge.' Scott LJ said at page 577: 'But if the purpose of the interlocutory stay is, as here, to prevent executive action by a third party in pursuance of rights which have been granted by the decision under attack, then, in my judgment, to require a cross-undertaking in damages to be given is, as a matter of discretion, an entirely permissible condition for the grant of interlocutory relief and in general, I would think, unless some special feature be present, a condition that should be expected to be imposed.' A similar approach has been taken by the Land and Environment Court of New South Wales in *Jarasius v Forestry Commission of New South Wales* (19 December 1989). Some observations of Lord Jauncey of Tullichettle in *Queen v Secretary of State for the Environment, Ex Parte The Royal Society for the Protection of Birds* [1997] Env LR 431, 440 are also consistent with the view that an undertaking in damages should normally be required, even in a public law case with environmental implications, if the commercial interests of a third party are engaged. 39. Both sides rightly submitted that (because the range of public law cases is so wide) the Court has a wide discretion to take the course which seems most likely to produce a just result (or to put the matter less ambitiously, to minimise the risk of an unjust result). In the context Mr Clayton referred to the well-known decision of the Court of Appeal in *Allen v Jambo Holdings* [1980] 1 WLR 1252, which has had the result that in England a very large class of litigants (that is, legally assisted persons) are as a matter of course excepted from the need to give a cross-undertaking in damages. However their Lordships (without casting any doubt on the practice initiated by that case) do not think that it can be taken too far. The Court is never exempted from the duty to do its best, on interlocutory applications with far-reaching financial implications, to minimise the risk of injustice. In *Allen v Jambo Holdings* Lord Denning MR said (at page 1257), 'I do not see why a poor plaintiff should be denied a Mareva injunction just because he is poor, whereas a rich plaintiff would get it'. On the facts of that case, that was an appropriate comment. But there may be cases where the risk of serious and uncompensated detriment to the Defendant cannot be ignored. The rich plaintiff may find, if ultimately unsuccessful, that he has to pay out a very large sum as the price of having obtained an injunction which (with hindsight) ought not to have been granted to him. Counsel were right to agree (in line with all the authorities referred to above) that the Court has a wide discretion.

6.5 COSTS

While costs are awarded in judicial review proceedings, they will not readily be granted to third parties appearing in such proceedings. It is incumbent on an intervenor to demonstrate how its participation in a judicial review application went beyond that of the principal parties to the judicial review proceedings.

***In the Application of NH International (Caribbean) Ltd* – HCA No Cv 3181 of 2004 (TT) Stollmeyer J**

[P31] As to the latter, it is clear that UDECOTT should have its costs. There is authority, however, for the proposition that an intervenor is not always in the same position, particularly when the issues it raises are in reality no different to those raised by a Respondent (see e.g. *Judicial Review Handbook* para. 18.1.7 *et seq.*). I accept, however, that the submissions on behalf of HK went further than those on behalf of UDECOTT in some instances.

***In the Application of Cable & Wireless Jamaica Ltd –* Supreme Court No M-89 of 1998 (JM) Woolfe CJ**

> [PP4–5] I am settled in the view that it was unnecessary to hear from Counsel for the Third Parties. The arguments which they advanced were merely supportive of the full arguments by the Learned Solicitor General. Counsel for the Third Parties broke no new ground in their arguments. The other Third Parties could easily have adopted the position which Mr Christopher Cheddar adopted in respect of his client Comtech Ltd. He announced that he was only holding a watching brief. He filed no affidavits and advanced no arguments. No doubt he realized that the validity of the licence which he held depended entirely upon whether or not the Minister had the authority to grant the licence. The position of Comtech Ltd. was essentially the same as that of the other Third Parties. The arguments of the Learned Solicitor General were exhaustive. The arguments proffered by the Third Parties, with respect, were no more than *'a gilding of the [lily]'*. For the reasons mentioned I would not make an order for costs in favour of the Third Parties.

The issue of security for costs in judicial review proceedings is also important and the court has regard to the public interest involved.

***In the Application of Quality Trading Company Ltd* – HCA No S-916 of 1993 (TT) Persad-Maharaj J**

> [P20] Although the Applicant's case is not based on any trade practice, I cannot close my eyes to the fact that the public interest element in litigation is significant in the Court's decision to allow or refuse security for costs. Nothing in the Applicant's notice of motion shows, however, that the claim is a novel one.

7

BREAKING NEW GROUNDS

Judicial review has been attaining great prominence in the Commonwealth Caribbean, particularly in Trinidad and Tobago, as the weapon of choice in attacking decisions of public bodies. Judicial review is now moving into many critical areas and it is important to note judicial trends in the treatment of these often controversial matters.

7.1 EQUALITY OF TREATMENT

The political divide in Trinidad and Tobago, with the dominant political forces having their respective bases in the two major population groups, those of African descent and those of East Indian descent, has translated into allegations of discrimination whenever one group is not enjoying political power. Judicial review is the available mechanism to deal with alleged abuses by decision-makers seen as being under political influence.

***In the Application of Dr Colin Furlonge* – HCA No Cv 2098 of 2003 (TT)**
Jamadar J

[P15] The decision under review is a recommendation of the Respondent. As such it is a preliminary decision to the 'final' decision of the PSC with respect to the appointment of an officer to an acting appointment. A preliminary decision such as this is amenable to judicial review. It is reviewable to ensure that:

i. there has been a lawful exercise of power, and

ii. the relevant procedural requirements have been observed.

It is also reviewable because this preliminary decision can affect the career of an officer, as in this case to the Applicant's detriment. And also because, a recommendation, such as the one under consideration, is a precondition to the exercise of the statutory power in the PSC to appoint an officer to an acting position. In any event, a recommendation such as this is likely to be taken into account by the PSC before making its decision. To this extent, a recommendation can be considered advice likely in practice to be followed or considered by the final decision-maker (and certainly 'advice' given pursuant to a statutory power—Regulation 27) . . . [PP16–17] The declared policy is that as a general rule acting appointments under Regulation 26 are to be made in favour of the most senior eligible officer. There is an established system for ranking officers according to seniority, which is purposeful. Thus, procedurally, the Regulations require that all eligible officers be notified where an acting appointment falls to be made. And, that before a recommendation is made seven days be allowed to elapse to facilitate independent representations by any such officers. Further, where any officers are being passed over, that reasons for same be given accompanying the recommendations. This Court has added a further procedural requirement, that, generally, where an eligible officer is passed over the reasons for same are to be given to him/her no less than seven (7) clear days before the date on which a decision is likely to be made by the PSC. There is no good reason why, in the context of this regime, if the person recommended is 'the most able and competent officer,' who also happens to be junior to other eligible officers, that this reason with adequate particulars cannot be given, both to the PSC and the officer(s) passed over. As indeed they should. Lord Slynn has pointed out (in Ex Parte Salem (1999) 2 WIR 483 at 488): 'reviews which are academic should not be heard unless there is good reason in the public interest for doing so.' As I have sought to demonstrate, in this case, given the erroneous practice being followed by the Respondent and the issues under review, and given the wide ranging implications of a flawed procedure being perpetuated, there is every good reason in the public interest to adjudicate on these matters ... [P18] Clearly the Applicant felt aggrieved by the approach of the Respondent in this matter and the victim of a history of prejudicial treatment. The Applicant, through his attorneys, took every step to bring to the Respondent's attention the errors in the approach being adopted, but to no avail. Before this Court, the attorneys for the Respondent and the Attorney General have accepted the illegality and procedural impropriety of the Respondent's conduct. Costs must, therefore, follow the event. It is hoped that there will be proper compliance with the provisions of the Public Service Commission Regulations in the future. Such compliance is necessary if there is to be public confidence in the Public Service and the Public Service Commission. Failure to do so invariably results in a warranted suspicion of arbitrariness, discrimination, bias, partiality and even political interference. This is especially so in a small 'rumourmongering' society like Trinidad and Tobago, where divisions along ethnic and political lines are often determinative of the perception of reality. As it turns out, this Applicant has quite legitimately felt aggrieved.

***Mohanlal Bhagwandeen* – Privy Council Appeal No 45 of 2003 (TT)**[1]
Lord Carswell

[PP3–4] 8. The Appellant on 6 August 1999 brought a constitutional motion in the High Court, in which he claimed a declaration that the Commissioner had discriminated against him by failing and/or refusing to recommend him for promotion because of his suspension from duty, contrary to Section 4(b) and (d) of the Constitution of Trinidad and Tobago, together with an order directing the Commissioner to reconsider his promotional prospects. In paragraph 8 of his replying affidavit sworn on 28 December 1999 the Commissioner stated: 'The reason why the Applicant was not recommended for promotion was not because he had been suspended *per se*, but rather because there were no performance appraisal reports for the Applicant for the period under review. There was therefore, nothing upon which I could make a proper and/or fair decision to recommend the Applicant for promotion. This is what I meant in my letter to the Applicant dated July 5, 1999 when I stated that he was not found to be suitable to be recommended at that point in time for promotion because of his long period of suspension from duty. In other words, it was not because of the actual fact of the suspension but rather, by reason of his absence from duty as a result of his being on suspension, there was no material upon which the Applicant could have been recommended.' 9. The Appellant then on 11 January 2000 commenced proceedings for judicial review, seeking to set aside the Commissioner's decision not to recommend him for promotion and various declarations ... 10. The two matters were heard together by Narine J, who in a written judgment given on 31 January 2001 found in favour of the Appellant on both the Constitutional motion and the judicial review application. He made a declaration that his right to equality of treatment by a public authority had been infringed, directed the Commissioner to reconsider his promotional prospects and awarded him the sum of $7500 for breach of

1 This decision reversed a strong first instance judgment. *In the Application of Mohanlal Bhagwandeen – HCA No 37 of 2000 (TT), Narine J*, [P36] 'The concept of equal treatment by a public authority assumes that that authority will treat those who come before it in the same way. The authority will be impartial and unbiased. It will apply the same standards, and same considerations in deliberating upon the matters entrusted to it, in relation to those who come before it. The presumption of regularity applies to all its actions. It will be presumed in its favour that it acted rationally, and took into consideration all matters that it is enjoined by statute to consider. It is presumed that it will take all such steps that it is enjoined by the general law to take and will not act in breach of the principles of natural justice. And, of course, it will carry out its functions in good faith. Can it be said that in this case the Applicant received equal treatment from the Commissioner of Police, in so far as his decision not to recommend the Applicant is concerned? Having considered the evidence of the Commissioner of Police himself, my conclusion is that the Applicant did not'.

his constitutional rights under Section 4(d) of the Constitution . . . 11. The Commissioner appealed to the Court of Appeal against the Judge's decision on the Constitutional motion, but not against that given on the application for judicial review. [PP7–8] 18. A claimant who alleges inequality of treatment or its synonym discrimination must ordinarily establish that he has been or would be treated differently from some other similarly circumstanced person or persons, described by Lord Hutton in *Shamoon v Chief Constable of the Royal Ulster Constabulary* [2003] 2 All ER 26 at paragraph 71 as actual or hypothetical comparators. The phrase which is common to the anti-discrimination provisions in the legislation of the United Kingdom is that the comparison must be such that the relevant circumstances in the one case are the same, or not materially different, in the other. The Appellant in the present case relied on an actual comparator, Sergeant Fitzgerald George, who was promoted some seven and three quarter months after his reinstatement following a long period of suspension. That interval of time is the only real similarity between their cases. In his affidavit sworn on 28 December 1999 the Commissioner compared the history and record of the Appellant and Sergeant George in some detail, which it is not necessary to set out in detail in this judgment. Their Lordships are satisfied on this evidence, which was not controverted, that the Court of Appeal was correct in rejecting Sergeant George as a true comparator. Since the Appellant had to concede that none of the other officers to whom he referred in his affidavit sworn on 5 August 1999 as having been promoted following periods of suspension was similarly circumstanced to himself, he is left without a foundation for his claim of unequal treatment. 19. That conclusion is sufficient to determine the appeal in favour of the Respondent and it is not necessary for the Board to decide the second issue, that of *mala fides*. Since it was dealt with in some detail in the judgment of Kangaloo JA, however, they propose to add a few observations on this topic. 20. The proposition that to establish a case of discrimination by a public official it is necessary to prove *mala fides* on his part appears in several cases in the Courts of Trinidad and Tobago, notably the judgment at first instance in *Smith v LJ Williams Ltd* (1980) 32 WIR 395 and that of the Court of Appeal in *Attorney General v KC Confectionery Ltd* (1985) 34 WIR 387. In the former case Bernard J considered Indian and United States authorities and stated at page 411: 'In so far as official acts are concerned, the nub of the matter is, in my view, that the section both guarantees and is intended to ensure that where parties are similarly placed under the law they are entitled to like treatment under that law. However, there is a presumption of regularity in the acts and conducts of officials. Consequently, the burden of proof is upon the aggrieved party to establish *mala fides* in the administration of the enactment.' In *Attorney General v KC Confectionery Ltd* the Court of Appeal adopted a similar approach, accepting as correct the propositions that there is a presumption of regularity in the acts of officials and that it is necessary to show a clear and intentional discrimination when a claimant alleges unequal treatment at the hands of a public official or authority. Bernard JA, as he had then become, said at page 415: 'Having held that the presumption of regularity in the acts of public officials exists in this jurisdiction, I entertain the view that it can only be discharged by proof of *mala fides* on a balance of probability.' . . . [P9] 23. The need for proof of deliberate intention to discriminate is quite a different question. The Court of Appeal of Trinidad and Tobago accepted in *Attorney General v KC Confectionery Ltd* that a party complaining of discrimination must prove, in the same terms as it was formulated in the US authorities, 'intentional and purposeful' acts of unequal treatment. Persaud JA said at page 403 that the complainant must show a clear and intentional discrimination, 'which in turn connotes *mala fides*'. That this is not required in discrimination cases in the United Kingdom was established by the House of Lords in *James v Eastleigh Borough Council* [1990] 2 AC 751, when the majority preferred what Lord Lowry termed the causative to the subjective construction and held that discrimination could be established even though the Respondent council had not intended to discriminate between men and women. Accordingly the law of Trinidad and Tobago relating to discrimination by public officials may require further consideration in the light of these observations. 24. In the light of the conclusions reached in paragraph 18 and the reservations expressed in paragraph 23 above it is unnecessary for their Lordships to consider whether on the facts of this case *mala fides* has been established. They would, however, share the unwillingness of the Court of Appeal to regard a case of *mala fides* or hostile acts as having been made out where a complainant has not sought to cross-examine the party against whom the allegation is made.

***In the Application of Robert Matthews* – HCA No 972 of 1999 (TT)**
Ventour J

[P16] In the view of this Court the general policy of the Licensing Authority seems to introduce into the process of issuing permits for public service vehicles a discrimination which the provisions of the Act do not contemplate at all. I would also venture to say that the application of such a discriminatory policy can lead to unfair results as has been clearly demonstrated in the instant case, in the processing of applications for permits for public service vehicles. The Licensing Authority may instead wish to consider each application on its merits . . . [P21] Counsel for the Applicant invited this Court to take judicial notice of the United Nations Declaration on the Rights of Disabled persons proclaimed by General Assembly resolution 3447(XXX) of 9th December, 1975. That resolution calls for national and international action to ensure that it will be used as a common basis and frame of reference for the protection of those Rights. Two of those Rights appear to be very relevant to the issue before this Court . . . [P22] This Court is of the view that every opportunity should be afforded to the physically challenged person to realize his/her fullest potential in the same way that opportunities are afforded to the ordinary citizen. This is particularly so having regard to the advanced state of technological development in the world today . . . [P25] On the totality of the evidence I have found on a balance of probability that the Applicant was not treated fairly; that the first Respondent acted with procedural impropriety in that he failed to follow the procedure clearly set out in Regulation 111(3) of the Motor Vehicles and Road Traffic Regulations, Chapter 48:50; that the second Respondent acted in breach of the rules of natural justice when it failed to afford the Applicant an opportunity to be heard and to make representations on his own behalf on the hearing of the appeal. It is trite law that where a tribunal adopts a procedure which is unfair to a litigant then the Court may, in the exercise of its discretion, quash the resulting decision by applying the rules of natural justice. While quashing the decision of the Superintendent in the *Re Lewis' case* (*supra*) Justice Taylor cautioned that it is not for the Court to substitute its judgment for that of the Superintendent and thereby take on the function of deciding whether or not the Applicant should receive the class 1 licence.

***In the Application of Matthew Joseph, Asad Ali, Soogrim Bhaggan, Gunness Bhagewandeen, Rampersad Ragoo, Reeka Rampersad, Francis Gopaul, Clement Brizan, Radhay Kissoon, Jankinath Sookdeo, Ian Johnson, Seepersad Singh* –**
HCA No S-611 of 1988 (TT)
Blackman J

[P25] Attorney for the Applicants also argued that there was inequality in the treatment of his clients in relation to others. He contended that this element was introduced in order to support his ground of unreasonableness on the part of the Minister. If the Applicants are right it would in my view show that the Minister did not act *bona fide* or that there may be some ulterior motive in his action. In this sense the Minister's act would have been unreasonable in the legal sense. But what are the facts? Mr Charles under cross-examination though admitting that there were other structures on the highway explained that it was the intention of the State to remove the others as well but that Government was awaiting the outcome of this action as it was advised to hold its hands until then. I accept Mr Charles' explanation and therefore I do not find that there has been any inequality of treatment. This ground of unreasonableness is therefore also rejected.

***Elwin v Public Service Commission Commonwealth of Dominica and the Attorney General of the Commonwealth of Dominica* – High Court of Justice Civil Suit No 493 of 1998 (DM)**
Cenac J

[Para27] The Commission's functions under the law respecting the appointment and promotion of public officers are of a public nature and quasi-judicial. As such, in exercise of its powers under the Regulations the Commission must be expected to act fairly. [Para28] In *Wiseman v Borneman* [1969] 3 All ER 275 at 277 Lord Reid said: 'Natural justice requires that the procedure before any tribunal which is acting judicially shall be fair in all the circumstances, and I would be sorry to see this fundamental general principle degenerate into a series of hard and fast rules. For a long time the Courts have, without objection from Parliament, supplemented procedure laid down in legislation where they have found that to be necessary for the purpose. But before this unusual kind of power is exercised it must be clear that the statutory procedure is insufficient to achieve justice and that to require additional steps would not frustrate the apparent purpose of the legislation'. [Para29] In *Public Service Board of New South Wales v Osmond* [1987] LRC 681 at p 698 Deane J repeating a statement of Kitto J in *Mobil Oil Australia Pty Ltd v Federal Commissioner of Taxation* [1963] 113 CLR 475 at p 504 said this: 'What the law requires in the discharge of a quasi-judicial function is judicial fairness. That is not a label for any fixed body of rules. What is fair in a given situation depends upon the circumstances'. [Para30] And as Lord Bridge put it in *Lloyd v McMahon* [1987] 1 All ER 1118 at 1161, [1987] AC 625 at 702–703: 'My Lords, the so-called rules of natural justice are not engraved on tablets of stone. To use the phrase which better expresses the underlying concept, what the requirements of fairness demand when any body, domestic, administrative or judicial, has to make a decision which will affect the rights of individuals depends on the character of the decision-making body, the kind of decision it has to make and the statutory or other framework in which it operates. In particular, it is well established that when a statute has conferred on any body the power to make decisions affecting individuals, the Courts will not only require the procedure prescribed by the statute to be followed, but will readily imply so much and no more to be introduced by way of additional procedural safeguards as will ensure the attainment of fairness'. [Para31] Was there unfairness in the procedure followed by the Commission under the Regulations? In other words has the Applicant made out a case of procedural unfairness? Where an Act of Parliament confers an administrative power there is a presumption that it will be exercised in a manner which is fair in all the circumstances. The standards of fairness are not immutable. They may change with the passage of time, both in the general and in their application to decisions of a particular type. The principles of fairness are not to be applied by rote identically in every situation. What fairness demands is dependent on the context of the decision, and this is to be taken account in all its aspects (*per* Lord Mustill in *Regina v Secretary of State for the Home Department, Ex Parte Doody* (HL) [1993] 3 WLR p 168). [Para40] Now here you have a situation where the Applicant, of the three names submitted to the Commission, although not the most senior but was senior to Angela Lawrence, was not less qualified than her, had acted in the post on more occasions before it became vacant, acted in the post after it became vacant and up to the time when the Commission made its decision to appoint Angela Lawrence. Further, the Applicant had been recommended by the Permanent Secretary to be appointed to the post. In spite of the foregoing, she was overlooked and Angela Lawrence was appointed. Obviously the Applicant must be left with a 'burning sense of grievance and a real feeling of injustice' . . . [Para42] Having regard to the facts and the law, I can only conclude that the Applicant's entitlement to appointment was far superior to that of the appointee. [Para43] I conclude also that the Commission could not have taken into account 'all the circumstances which it is statutorily required to take into account before selecting an officer for promotion' . . . [Para44] I am of the view that the Commission did not follow the procedure laid down in the Regulations. As Leggatt LJ said in *Cunningham* (*supra*) at p 958: 'One of the main areas in which supervision has to be exercised by way of judicial review is over procedural requirements, for the purpose of ensuring the right to a fair adjudication. The procedure of a public body is not only required to be fair in so far as an individual affected by its decisions has a legitimate expectation that it will be. Nor does natural justice or fairness require the giving of reasons for a decision only when an obligation to give them is imposed by statute.' [Para45] I am of the view that the decision taken by the Commission to appoint Angela Lawrence to the post over the Applicant in light of all the circumstances was so aberrant as to compel the inference that it must have been wrong, procedurally wrong and grossly unfair.

7.2 SQUATTERS

Squatters have sought to use judicial review to attack the decision of the State to remove them from State lands.

***In the Application of Vashti Sampson, Rajh Basdeo, Indar Samaroo, Grantley Prescott and James Chinapoo* – Civil Appeal No 96 of 2003 (TT)**
Nelson JA

[PP11–12] Although necessity is a defence to trespass to land, homelessness does not constitute necessity: see *Southwark LBC v Williams* [1971] Ch. 734. Nor are the so-called landless, if proved to be such, entitled to rely on the defence of necessity to resist a landowner's claim for recovery of possession. A trespasser who evicts the person in possession does not obtain possession against the person evicted seeking to re-enter unless the person evicted acquiesces by delaying steps to remove the trespasser: *Browne v Dawson* (1840) 12 A&E 624; *Mc Phail v Persons Unknown* (1973) Ch. 447. The consequence of being a trespasser who has not obtained possession, sometimes referred to as 'a mere trespasser', is that such trespasser cannot maintain an action in trespass: see *Browne v Dawson* (*supra*) at p 629 . . . [P18] The learned judge correctly states the law on forcible entry on the part of a true owner as follows: 'It cannot be doubted that an owner of lands at common law has the right to evict trespassers. If he uses no more force than is necessary, he is not civilly or criminally liable. If he uses more force than is necessary he may be civilly liable in assault or criminally liable for assault and battery and/or under the Statutes of Forcible Entry' . . . [P20] In my view the common law privilege of forcible entry should be sparingly exercised by public bodies, and then only as a last resort . . . [P30] While it is true that a public authority equipped with power to affect adversely a person's rights has a duty to exercise that power only after a fair hearing of the party adversely affected, this principle does not apply in cases relating to private law rights. For example, no individual notices need be served on each occupier by a private landowner who seeks summary possession of his estate under Order 94 of the Rules of the Supreme Court 1975 . . . [P31] In the instant case the Authority did give notice to the squatters, but there is no requirement that an inquiry be held into each case before a notice to quit is served.

***In the Application of Michael Jones and Gregor Armstrong* – HCA No T 70 of 2003 (TT)**
Volney J

[P8] Equally, Counsel's argument that self-help was unlawful in the circumstances of this case appears to be unsound. If the Applicant is a squatter, and the lands not subject to statutory strictures for his removal, then the employment of self help in order to repossess is not unlawful. There is in my judgment no viable argument on the affidavit of the Applicants to suggest that they were entitled to be treated in any structured manner provided by law and accordingly, there is no merit in the Applicant's claim to procedural legitimate expectation which was denied them.

7.3 POLITICAL PROCESS

There has always been reluctance on the part of the courts to intervene in matters involving political questions. Indeed, this is part of the reticence of the courts to interfere in matters deemed to fall within the purview of executive action. Notwithstanding the reluctance of the courts to address matters with political implications, this has not stopped the litigatants from employing judicial review to have the judiciary pronounce on matters that in the past never came before the courts.

In the Application of Chandresh Sharma – **HCA No Cv S. 1537 of 2003 (TT)**
Jamadar J

[P5] There can be no illegality of a swearing in that is purely ceremonial. And, there can be no challenge to the appointment of persons by reason of such a swearing in, where such a swearing in was not required for the validity of the appointments ... [PP6–7] Thus, there could be no arguable case that the Chief Justice of Trinidad and Tobago acted in any manner that could have either undermined the perception of the independence of the Judiciary, or offended the doctrine of the Separation of Powers as it ought to exist between the Executive and Judiciary in Trinidad and Tobago. In performing this non judicial function, the Chief Justice did not act subject to any executive control or direction or engage in something that was more usual or appropriate to another branch of government or exercise a discretion on grounds of policy that could implicate the citizens of Trinidad and Tobago. Thus, in my opinion, it is not arguable that the decision and/or action of the Chief Justice of Trinidad and Tobago to mark the appointment of the members of the RJLSC by a purely ceremonial installation accompanied by swearing in, occurring as it did on the evidence in this case, can be reviewable as being *ultra vires* the powers of the Chief Justice or unconstitutional by reason of offending the doctrine of the Separation of Powers.

In the Application of Director of Personnel Administration and Police Service Commission – **Civil Appeal No 10 of 2004 and HCA No S-1264 of 2003 (TT)**[2]
Sharma CJ

[PP12–14] [31] The Judge stated at paragraph 60 of his judgment: '*If Cabinet can eviscerate the Public Service Examinations Board at a whim by firing its members and changing the composition of its membership, thereby turning it into a ventriloquist's dummy, a cipher, in my*

2 This decision was a firm reversal of the postion adopted by the first instant judge: *In the Application of Eusebio Cooper – HCA No S-1264 of 2003 (TT), Myers J*, [PP26–27] 'That being so, however laudable the aims Cabinet sought, and seeks, to achieve by appointing the Public Service Examinations Board, and however squarely those aims might arguably sit within the "general direction and control of the government", Cabinet were and are not entitled to act in the manner that they did. A power derived from an inferior Act of Parliament cannot be construed in a manner which entitles Cabinet to act in breach of the checks and balances imposed upon Executive power by the framers of the Constitution. That this assertion is correct is implicit in the vigorous attempts of the Respondents to confine the effect of Lord Diplock's dicta in *Thomas* to political interference exercised directly upon the Service Commissions. It is clear to me that the Respondents recognized that their submission regarding the empowerment of Cabinet by §75 of the Constitution and §45(2) of the Interpretation Act, could only survive if they could persuade me that the vesting of this power in Cabinet, and its exercise by Cabinet, did not breach the headline principle enunciated in *Thomas*. To achieve that end, they sought to narrow that headline principle. In the next section, I explain why, in my judgment, the Respondents' efforts in this regard are misconceived . . . [P28] Thus motivated, the framers vested in autonomous Service Commissions, to the exclusion of any other person or authority, power to make appointments to the relevant service, *promotions* and transfers within the service, and power to remove and exercise disciplinary control over members of the service. Though the Police Service Commission may delegate any of its powers to an officer of the Police Force, the right to delegate (although it requires the approval of the Prime Minister) is [its] alone and any power so delegated is exercised under the control of the Police Service Commission and on its behalf and not on behalf of the State,

judgment, the consequence would be that any potential influence that Cabinet might exercise on the examiners, and the promotion process would be direct, not indirect.' [32] On the facts, there was no scope, in my respectful view, for such an application of the doctrine. The Board had independent members who in turn selected persons on their own merit to sit as examiners without the influence of Cabinet. This arrangement did not violate the doctrine of the separation of powers since Board members were sufficiently insulated from any undue political influence from the Executive (Cabinet). [33] There is an inherent danger in having power reposed in only one organ of the State, be it the Executive, Legislature or Judiciary. To avoid this mischief, and to act as a check and balance on the particular organization, power may often be diffused in the hands of independent bodies. Judging from the very appointment of persons to high office under the Constitution it is clear that politics often plays an important if not an underlying role. In fact, the Constitutions of the Commonwealth Caribbean contemplate such diffusion and interplay by allowing the overlap of these three-fold categories. Thus similar instances of political infusion are evident in the appointment of persons to the offices under the Constitution such as the President, the Prime Minister, the Chief Justice and the Speaker of the House. [34] The President is elected as the Head of State under Section 29 of the Constitution by majority voting of the Electoral College (all members of Senate and House of Representatives). In the past the nominee of the party who commands the majority becomes the President. What can be more political than that? Yet his office is independent. The Prime Minister's appointment under the Constitution is of course wholly political and governed by Section 76(1). He is appointed by the President and must be a member of the House of Representatives capable of commanding majority support from the other members. The Chief Justice is appointed by the President in consultation with the Prime Minister and the Leader of the Opposition pursuant to Section 102 of the Constitution. The Speaker of the House is elected from among members of the House of Representatives under Section 50 and is also an entirely political appointment. [35] Appointments to these positions of high office under the Constitution all involve some measure of political/executive input and overlap. In these appointments, there is no insulation or buffer as in the instant case with the appointed Board responsible for choosing its own panel of examiners. The integrity of holders of high office must be presumed in order to have a functional working Constitution. [36] If

---

or of any other person or authority, including the Executive . . . [PP29–30] So, the Doomsday scenario of potential direct political influence over the Police Service in the form of dismissal at pleasure is the potential transformation of the Police Service into a private political army. As a small democracy, the political and philosophical culture of Trinidad and Tobago is such that this was not a risk that the framers of either of the two Constitutions were willing to run. In the ordering of priorities, our framers put the insulation from political influence of certain officer holders and institutions provided for in the Constitution, above the accountability of those office holders and institutions to the citizenry through the Executive, and through them, to the electorate. I do not propose speculating on the reason or reasons, but the Constitution is littered with examples of that thinking, including the provisions relating to the Service Commissions . . . [PP31–32] The difficulty is in constructing an analytical template to provide guidance in approaching any particular set of facts. It is difficult, on the basis of one set of facts in one case, to derive a universally applicable template for every possible permutation of a particular situation. However, I diffidently offer the following as one possible approach, read against the background of this generally applicable comment: it should be noted that there is no burden on the complaining party to prove that, in fact, direct or indirect political influence was actually being exercised, although, where such facts could be proved, the complaining party would be in a very strong position. All that is necessary is for the complaining party to show that, on the face of what was being done, the possibility of the exercise of direct or indirect political influence was not too far-fetched. This is clear from the approach adopted by Lord Diplock in *Thomas* when he made it plain that no-one was actually suggesting that there was any likelihood that the extreme consequence of the political directorate converting the Police Service into a private army would occur'.

The Privy Council however upheld the first instance decision of Myers J. and reversed the Court of Appeal in Privy Council Appeal No. 47 of 2005.

the Judge were correct in his reasoning, it could be plausibly argued that the appointment of the President, without the insulation as is evident in this instant case with the Board (so-called independent) is also a political appointment and as such, the President would be directly influenced by the Executive. In fact, all appointments under the Constitution could be condemned for violation of the separation of powers, involving as they do, the necessary input from the Executive. To adopt such an inflexible approach to the application of the doctrine is simply to thwart the true intention of the Constitution and would render it unworkable. It would be a recipe for chaos. Presumed Integrity of Holders of High Office. [37] As a further point, Cabinet has appointed the Board without impropriety over the years under its general mandate to govern the country. To suggest, in the absence of definite evidence, that the Cabinet-appointed Board would succumb to political interference or fail to insulate its members from undue political interference would be to presume ... 'a lack of professionalism, independence and integrity' ... on the part of its members ... [P15] [39] In presuming impropriety from holders of high office and basing his entire decision on the threat or potential for such impropriety, the Learned Judge, with greatest respect, stretched this doctrine to unrealistic lengths and would render the Constitution practically unworkable ... [P22] [61] The Cabinet appointed Board did not violate any principle of the Constitution. It is my respectful view that the Judge was not justified in restricting further promotions in the Police Service. Neither was he justified in imposing time limits since the PSC was not the body responsible for appointing the Board.

Kangaloo JA

[P7] 19. Finally on the question of the overlap of the powers of the Executive, the Legislature and the Judiciary in the Constitution, I need only say that there can never be in a Constitution modeled along Westminster lines any complete, distinct and surgically precise delineation of those powers. In respect of the Executive and the Public Service Commission and the PSC one only has to look at Sections 121 and 123 of the Constitution to see the involvement of the Prime Minister in the first instance enjoying a veto power in respect of the appointment by the Public Service Commission of several key personnel and in the second, a similar privilege with respect to the appointment of the Commissioner of Police or his deputy. As Mr Hosein submitted '*An inflexible and dogmatic application of the doctrine is inimical to an efficacious and workable government*'. With this submission I agree. 20. I also think that the potential for interference must exist once there is this overlap of powers and that at the end of the day it becomes a question of the degree of influence or interference that is permissible in a functioning democratic society with proper regard for the rights of individuals. A proper balance has to be struck between these competing estates of government and once the evidence does not reveal undue influence by one estate over another, any questioned acts ought to pass constitutional muster.

In the Application of Florence Bobb and Girlie Moses –
Civil Appeal No 97 of 2002 (TT)[3]
Nelson JA

[PP8–9] The learned judge held:

(a) that the naming of a date for a general election involved political policy, political strategy and other political considerations, which at this stage were not justiciable;

3 The Court of Appeal endorsed the position adopted by the first instant judge: *In the Application of Florence Bobb and Girlie Moses – Civil No 2663 of 2002 (TT), Mohammed J*, [PP4–5] 'The first issue that arises is whether the Court has the jurisdiction to entertain this application. From the several Commonwealth cases cited by Mr Maharaj for the Applicants, it can be readily deduced that the Courts will not shirk from examining issues with a distinct political flavour which, by their substantive nature however, involve the need to examine the Constitution, statute law or the common law, to see whether what is broadly described as a

(b) that the Court had no jurisdiction because it would be an unwarranted incursion into the purely political jurisdiction of the Prime Minister and that violated the principle of the separation of powers.

[P12] . . . I would prefer to support the learned judge's decision on the basis of the general principle informing the political question doctrine he refers to, i.e., the doctrine of the separation of powers . . . In my judgment therefore the Judge was not obliged to defer non-justiciability to the substantive stage of the proceedings. To do so would be otiose . . . I am firmly of the view that the statement was not a decision, but that is not a bar to judicial review . . . [PP12–13] The learned judge held that the statement of July 3, 2002 was not a decision, in the public law sense, affecting or capable of affecting the rights of the Appellants. The Respondents endorse this approach. I agree with counsel for the Appellants that this is too narrow an approach and hold that judicial review would lie in respect of any unlawful use of power, whether a deliberate act or omission to act. Unlawful administration is the subject-matter of judicial review. However, in the instant case the real object of the Appellant's attack was the Respondent's failure or refusal to give the President dissolution advice in the face of a perceived lack of a majority and the non-election of a Speaker as well as remaining in office without a majority.

***In the Application of Ramesh Lawrence Maharaj, Unanan Persad, Indiria Lisa Bolai, Ralph Maraj, Archbishop Barbara Gray Burke, Garnet Mungalsingh, Hosein Mohammed, Morgril Polson, Muriel Helena Amoroso, Peter Carasquero, Saieed Mohammed and Joseph Theodore* – HCA No 3293 of 2001 (TT)**
Mendonca J

[P13] The UNC is a voluntary society and its constitution contains provisions regulating its internal affairs. Save for the due disposal and administration of property, which is not the issue here, Courts do not take cognizance of the rules of a voluntary society entered into for the Regulation of its own affairs . . . [PP13–14] If the EBC is not subject to the direction or control of any other person or authority, then to say it must be guided by the Constitution of the UNC does not follow. It follows that it is not subject to the party's constitution. It is certainly not the function of the EBC to construe the Constitution of the UNC. However if it had considered the Constitution there is no provision there that provides for the National Executive of the UNC to submit to the EBC a list of party candidates. What the UNC constitution does provide is for the National Executive to approve candidates to contest elections to the House of Representatives after consultation with the party's organs and institutions. This is not the same thing as submitting a

---

"political power," has been exercised within the ambit of the relevant law. The Court will however have no jurisdiction if the issue raised is wholly or very substantially a political one, which by its nature in reality involves the exercise of a political judgment, as opposed to a legal one . . . [PP5–6] In my view, the naming of a date for a General Election pre-eminently involves political policy, political strategy and other political considerations which at this stage are non-justiciable. In a matter such as this, the Court would be making an unwarranted incursion into the purely political jurisdiction of the Prime Minister and the Executive, and thereby violate the principle of the separation of powers, were it to accede to the granting of the reliefs sought . . . [P7] Apart from my conclusion on the political question issue, I am of the further view that because of the practical constitutional checks and balances provided, together with the specific mechanism for the removal from Office of a Prime Minister and the vacation of Office of a Prime Minister, this Court does not have the jurisdiction in public law at this stage to direct a Prime Minister to announce a date for a General Election by a certain period, failing which the Office of Prime Minister would be declared vacant. That is not to say however, that in the case of an abuse of the essential constitutional checks and balances themselves, judicial review cannot be sought to review arguably illegal and unreasonable administrative acts and decisions. Vindication of the rule of law would warrant the intervention of the Court in such an extreme circumstance'.

The Privy Council upheld the decision of the lower courts in Privy Council Appeal No. 50 of 2004.

list of party candidates to the EBC . . . [PP14–15] To simply rely on the authority purportedly given by any of these bodies to anyone would be reckless unless the EBC were to attempt to properly construe the UNC constitution. To do so the EBC would have to constitute itself a Court of Law and determine questions of mixed law and fact which it has no business in doing. In those circumstances it does not appear to me to be unreasonable for the EBC, which is charged with the responsibility for the smooth conduct of elections, to say that it will act on a list supplied by the leader of the party where there is no dispute as to the holder of that office.

***In the Application of Aubrey Norton* – HCCJ No 5932 of 1997 (GY)**
Bernard CJ

[P20] Judges strive to dispense justice under severe pressures and less than favourable conditions. Very often they make decisions which are not always popular; it is one of the occupational hazards, and we learn to live with it providing always that we know we have decided fairly and in accordance with the law. However, we hope, and I trust that I speak for all members of the judiciary, that we do not have to carry the additional burden of political pressure from any quarter. We are here to dispense justice fairly and to hold the scales evenly. Any political party or citizen must feel free to approach the Courts and have their cases decided according to law. To put it simplistically if the law is on your side regardless of the identity of the litigant you will win; if the law and judicial precedent is against you, you will lose. Justice must never be tied to political considerations and affiliations if we as a democratic nation believe in the separation of powers, i.e. the legislative, the executive and the judiciary. The independence of the judiciary must be maintained at all times.

***R v Commissioner of Customs and Excise ex parte, A. & F. Farm Produce Company Ltd and Andre Chin* (1993) 30 JLR 462 (JM)**
Langrin J

[P466] A fundamental principle of public law as enshrined in constitution is the principle of separation of powers of the Legislature, the Executive and the Judiciary. Consistent with the principle the exercise of powers entrusted to the Executive are matters for the Executive and the Judiciary cannot in the exercise of its supervisory jurisdiction in matters falling under judicial review substitute its view for those of the Executive.

***R v Alvan S. Williams (Returning Officer for St. Andrew, West Rural Constituency) ex parte Seth George Ramocan* (1993) 30 JLR 223 (JM)**
Harrison J (Ag.)

[P226] Certiorari is usually invoked to quash an order which has been made without jurisdiction or in defiance of the rules of natural justice. While it is only applicable to review a judicial act, 'judicial' must be used in the widest sense. The power of obtaining an order of certiorari is not limited to judicial acts or orders in a strict sense, that is to say, acts or orders of a Court of law sitting in a judicial capacity. It extends to the acts and orders of a competent authority which has power to impose liability or to give a decision which determines the rights or property of the affected parties (see *Local Government Board v Arlridge* [1915] AC 120). This therefore leads to the question, what then is the legal status of the Returning Officer? Is he acting Ministerially or judicially? The true view as expressed by the authorities is that he partakes of both characters; that whilst for some purposes—such as giving notices or providing polling stations he is merely a Ministerial officer; for others such as determining objections to ballot papers he is a judicial officer. In considering any question which he is empowered to deal with in respect of enquiries to ballot boxes, Section 46 of the Representation of the People Act clearly defines his judicial functions. He shall have all the powers of and be deemed to be a Commissioner appointed under the Commission of Enquiry Act. Turning now to the facts before me, it is apparent from the affidavits filed, that the Returning Officer had directed his attention to the provisions of Section 46 of the Representation of the People

Act. He had commenced his enquiries but these were short-lived as he felt that he had a deadline to meet. He was of the view that he had to finalise his count before Parliament opened. It is also deposed in the affidavit evidence where he stated that if he had more time he would probably have rejected more boxes. In light of the above disclosures, I have no hesitation in saying that these allegations levelled serious charges or complaints against the conduct of the Returning Officer in relation to his management of the election and as such this brings him in my view within the spirit and intendment of Section 18 of the Election Petition Act. It is the general duty of the Returning Officer at a parliamentary election to do all such acts and things as may be necessary for effectively conducting the election by the rules and law governing such an election. Although he was not expected to take upon himself the onerous responsibility of deciding nice questions of law or fact upon the spur of the moment he is indeed the Superintendent or Steward of the election in his constituency and he must therefore account for his stewardship. It was therefore my considered view that the proper forum for these complaints should be and ought to be the Election Petition Court rather than a Full Court.

***Regina v Minister of Labour and Employment and Ocean Textiles Ltd ex parte Robert Agutaya and Godfredo Fernando (on behalf of Thirteen (13) Fellow Employees of East Ocean Textiles Ltd)* (1989) 26 JLR 148 (JM)**

Bingham J

[P152] It is of some significance that the affidavits sworn by the Applicants and their Attorney, Donovan Jackson, have not evoked the slightest response from the Respondents. The Honorable Minister can be presumed, therefore, to have sought to rest his case for seeking to justify his decision upon it being that of an executive or Ministerial order. It may be a timely reminder which bears repeating that such acts in so far as they relate to even prerogative orders do not exclude the power of the Courts to review the basis for the order.

***The Constituency Boundaries Commission v The Attorney-General of the Commonwealth of Dominica and Urban Baron in the Eastern Caribbean Supreme Court of Appeal Civil Appeal* No. 12 of 1998 (DM)**

Satrohan Singh JA

[P8] The rule against bias is one of the pillars of the principles of natural justice. It is [a] rule that is concerned, not only to prevent the distorting influence of bias, but also to protect the integrity of the decision making process by ensuring that, however disinterested the decision maker is in fact, the circumstances should not give rise to the risk of bias. [De Smith, Woolf and Jowitt *Judicial Review of Administrative Action* 5th Edition page 52]. The law on this concept is settled and I do not propose to have another discussion on it here. The accepted principle relied on in this matter by the Respondent, was that there existed in the Commission, a real danger of bias or prejudice. If the evidence relied on by the Judge supports this principle, then the learned trial judge would be found to be correct in his finding of bias in favour of the Respondent. [See *Vaughan Lewis v Attorney General of St. Lucia* and *Compton v Attorney General of St. Lucia* Civil Appeals 12 and 14 of 1997] . . . [PP10–13] The learned Attorney General submitted that the report was not conclusive, it only made recommendations which recommendations need not be acted upon by the House. I do not disagree. However, only someone who does not have his feet firmly planted on the earth, will not see that such a proposition is mere rhetoric and that there was real danger of bias from the accepted evidence in this matter. The reality of the situation is that when such a Commission is being set up, the respective sides will recommend members whom they are satisfied will look after each side's respective interests. Their concentration will be more on political advantage than constitutional requirement. I agree that the Speaker as the Commission Chairman stands in the middle. But again one has to be real. The Speaker was elected by the Government majority. It is my considered opinion that such a Commission, will always lean more towards political loyalty than constitutional integrity. What would assist in order to avoid the appearance of this mischief of bias, is that if, when members are to be recommended to the President, the respective politicians give names of those who are less politically conspicuous. Life would be so much simpler. S 56(4) of the Constitution precludes from membership to the Commission, a member of the House. The obvious purpose of this provision was to avoid this very danger of bias. In this context, it is my opinion that there is very little difference between members of the House and political activists. The Constitutional importance of a Boundaries Commission cannot be overstated. It plays a pivotal role in ensuring free and fair elections. The right to vote as contemplated by the Constitution is a right to vote in a constituency without gerrymandering. Gerrymandering, or any unfair attempt to alter the boundaries of any constituency, contrary to the provisions of the Constitution, violates the very fabric of our Parliamentary system of democracy. It is my view that the evidence shows real risk of bias with respect to all four nominated members of the Commission, but more so, of those on the side of the Government. That was not the intention or purpose of the aforementioned Constitutional provisions. When the evidence as it related to the alleged bias is looked at in its entirety, I therefore can find no justifiable reason to dilute the finding of the trial Judge that it appeared as if the whole exercise by the Commission was deliberately engineered so as to favour one political party over another. As a result, there appears to be, what can be described as an imposition of the paramountcy of the Government's party or its political will on the Commission. In my view, the appearance of such an imposition is completely alien and repugnant to the Constitution and will have to be rejected as an insidious contravention of the Constitution. I do not wish what I am saying to be misunderstood or misinterpreted. The fact that the Commission was appointed in accordance with S 56 of the Constitution, triggered the presumption of impartiality in favour of the members regardless of their personal affiliations. That means that the onus was then placed on the Respondent to rebut that presumption by cogent evidence on a balance of probabilities. In doing so the Respondent did not have to prove actual bias. All he was required to prove was a real danger of bias or prejudice and that was all the Court was required to find. Bias has a legal meaning but it is basically a human concept. Byron CJ in *Vaughan Lewis* (*supra*), defined it as a predisposition to favour or disfavour a party or result, in a manner that is wrongful, and which can lead to a denial of the judicial imperative of impartiality in the particular matter. Given the accepted evidence in this matter, (1) four political activists in the Commission (2) no consultations (3) no documentary readings (4) all the constituencies to be altered not represented by any Government member (5) all votes taken at the second meeting split down the middle with the Speaker giving the casting vote at all times in favour of the Government nominees (6) Petite Savanne, an already small opposition constituency, being made smaller so that the Government won constituency of Grand Bay can become larger, what, in all probability, would the man on the Pais Bouche bus think? The Speaker might have cast his vote with all the honesty and integrity becoming his very high office. But, that is not the issue. The fact is that he voted at all times with the Government side and the man on the bus knows he was elected by a Government majority in the House. Even if in fact the report was prepared with honesty and in the spirit of the Constitution, because of these facts, the ordinary reasonable man would be hard put to accept that. On these facts he will see a possible invasion of his Constitutional rights. Bias is such an insidious thing, that a person, while he may in good faith believe he was acting impartially, his mind may unconsciously be affected by bias. Nothing should be done which could create a real danger of bias [*R v Gough* [1983] AC 646]. For these reasons, I agree with the judgment of Cenac J. The appeal is dismissed with costs to the Respondent to be taxed if not agreed.

7.4 THE ENVIRONMENT

In the Caribbean, the traditional apathy held by government for the environment is now being subject to judicial review and although results in the courts have not been encouraging, the use of judicial review to assess the decision of environmental regulatory bodies is now firmly entrenched in the judicial landscape.

In the Application of Fishermen and Friends of the Sea –
Civil Appeal No 106 of 2002 (TT)
Nelson JA

> [P16] The Act, however, is silent as to whether such 'old law' applications already in the system had to be started all over afresh or continued and taken over by the EMA with the benefit of the process already completed. In my judgment this was a practical matter for the EMA. It could not have been the intention of Parliament that the huge outlays in time, effort and money involved in such applications should be thrown away, and be incurred all over again . . . [P24] At least five other companies in the oil and gas sector of the economy are affected. If the EMA's decision on the Project were re-opened it would lead to other applications to review EMA clearances in respect of those projects. I can take judicial notice of the importance of the oil and gas sector to the economy of Trinidad and Tobago. In the circumstances I would agree with the learned judge for these additional reasons that it would be detrimental to good administration not to treat the EMA's decision on November 29, 2001 as final in the face of the Appellant's delay.

In this case, there was a powerful dissent by Lucky JA.[4]

---

4 However, the Privy Council endorsed the majority decision of the Court of Appeal: *Fishermen and Friends of the Sea, Privy Council Appeal No 30 of 2004, Lord Walker of Gestingthorpe* [P13–15] '27. Their Lordships do not accept that (as Lucky JA thought) the judge, by refusing an extension of time, pre-empted the determination of the most important issues in the case. He recognised that he could have carried forward the issue of delay to a substantive hearing. But he had in the course of a six-day hearing done far more than make a "quick perusal" of the merits. As their Lordships read his judgment he expressed a definite preliminary view against granting an extension of time, because of the unjustifiable delay on the part of FFS, but then went on to test that conclusion against other issues, including the public interest and the strengths and weaknesses of FFS's case. His consideration of those other matters did not alter his preliminary view. On the contrary, they confirmed his view that an extension should not be granted. 28. In their Lordships' view there is only one significant criticism to be made of the judge's careful and thorough judgment. In the penultimate paragraph of his judgment (set out in paragraph 26 above) the judge emphasised that the Authority had taken an informed decision, but the judge paid insufficient attention to the need for public consultation and involvement in the decision-making process (his reference to "consultation by technocrats" does not seem to refer to public consultation). Public consultation and involvement in decisions on environmental issues are matters of high importance in a democracy. In *Berkeley v Secretary of State for the Environment* [2001] 2 AC 603, 615, 616, Lord Hoffmann said, "The directly enforceable right of the citizen which is accorded by the Directive is not merely a right to a fully informed decision on the substantive issue. It must have been adopted on an appropriate basis and that requires the inclusive and democratic procedure prescribed by the Directive in which the public, however misguided or wrong-headed its views may be, is given an opportunity to express its opinion on the environmental issues. A Court is therefore not entitled retrospectively to dispense with the requirement of an EIA on the ground that the outcome would have been the same or that the local planning authority or Secretary of State had all the information necessary to enable them to reach a proper decision on the environmental issues." 29. These passages refer to the requirements of legislation of the European Union. But similar principles underlie the EMA 2000, as appears from the detailed requirements of section 28. The doctrine of "substantial compliance" must therefore be treated with considerable caution in environmental cases of this sort: see *Berkeley* at pp 616–7. 30. Before their Lordships, Mr Herberg (for BPTT) accepted that there was an arguable case that the Authority had not fully complied with the requirements of the EMA 2000 and the secondary legislation made under it. Mr Daly SC (for the Authority), while rejecting the submission of

In the Application of Fishermen and Friends of the Sea –
Civil Appeal No 106 of 2002 (TT)
Lucky JA

[P7] As I alluded to earlier an extension of time should have been granted. Therefore the learned judge should have made a more than 'quick perusal' of the merits. In his judgment at p 21 the Judge said: [PP7–8] . . . Mr Maharaj submitted and I agree that the Judge ought to have done more. He ought to have said why he did not accept the evidence produced by the Appellant and why the '**lack of promptness**' weighed more in favour of '**the public interest**'. The long-term effects any project will have on the communities and ecosystems of this country require prime consideration and attention, moreso where there may be risks to health. The judge said he acquainted himself with the material put before him. In other words he familiarized himself then he gave his decision. I do not think the foregoing is sufficient or adequate in these circumstances. I do not think the evidence was sufficiently assessed. This is a complex matter, a '***class action***', filed by a public spirited organization comprising many persons of different walks of life. Certainly it required more than acquaintance with the material, it necessitated a proper assessment of material and evidence and findings in respect of them and to ascertain whether the public interest balance comes down in favour of extending the time and therefore in my opinion there was sufficient cause to hear the substantive action. His reasons at page 21 clearly indicate a greater concern with two activities of BPTT and the presumption of correctness of the grant of the CEC rather than to the public interest balance to which I have alluded by reference to *Greenpeace* (*vide* paragraph 3 page 7 *supra*) . . . [P9] As I said earlier, I think the trial Judge ought to have extended time. This is a complex matter of '***public interest***' and environmental concern and should have been fully addressed. It seems to me that citizens should prevent destruction of the environment for industrial development which involves the extraction of the non-renewable resources of the country or if for sustained economic development necessary safeguards and guarantees should be put in place with the necessary checks and balances to protect the environment. Necessary Legislation has been passed to ensure the foregoing. Hence the establishment of the EMA . . . [P11] The public interest in situations such as this is very important. There is evidence of letters from Mr Aboud and news releases which

---

Mr Maharaj SC as to "clear" or "naked" illegality, did not contend that there had been no procedural irregularity. Had the irregularity significantly affected the process of public consultation it is very doubtful whether it would be right, in a case of so much public interest, to treat the Authority as having substantially complied with its obligations. 31. In this case, however, the procedural irregularities arose primarily from shortcomings in the transitional provisions of the EMA 2000. The Authority's human and financial resources were no doubt limited and its officers were understandably reluctant to spend time and money in reconsidering EIAs which had already been carefully considered after their submission to the TCPD and the Ministry of Energy. But any shortcuts which were taken did not interfere with the processes of public consultation. A lengthy and detailed EIA on the Bombax project, including the risk assessment in section 8, was delivered to Mr Aboud of FFS on or about 26 July 2001, and at the same time it was made available for public inspection at various locations, and public comment was invited. The same EIA, shorn of section 8, was republished on or about 15 October 2001, and again public comment was invited. FFS responded on 5 November 2001, during the statutory consultation period. The omission (which dealt specifically with the safety of the 36 inch pipeline) was ill-advised. But Mr Aboud already had that information, and he used the full EIA to obtain advice at the end of August 2001. The concerns about the 36 inch pipeline were fully aired. 32. In these circumstances the judge's exercise of his discretion was not flawed. There is no reason to interfere with his decision not to grant an extension of time, and the appeal must be dismissed. The Appellants must pay the Respondents' costs before the Board and in the Court of Appeal. The Court of Appeal was not bound by section 7(8) of the JRA, which applies only at first instance, and there is no reason to interfere with the Court of Appeal's discretion in awarding costs against FFS. It was entitled to make its first-instance application without being at risk as to costs, but it acted at its own risk in taking the matter to appeal.'

were used to demonstrate that he knew there was an application for a CEC and that one had been granted months before the application was filed. But if the EMA was aware of this, the question must be posed: Why the haste? In carrying out the ***'balancing act'*** to exercise his discretion I think the learned judge should have given further consideration to the application and examined carefully whether the procedure adopted by the EMA before the grant of the CEC was correct . . . [P13] As I alluded to earlier the application before the Judge could not have been an *inter partes* hearing on the merits. The rights of BPTT were considered in some detail but not those of the Appellant and by extension the public interest of the 'class' in turn to which he was compelled to find the appropriate balance. As I said, in my view, acquainting oneself with material is not sufficient. The crucial question is whether the EMA followed the proceedings set out in Law for the grant of a CEC.

***In the Application of Fishermen and Friends of the Sea* – HCA Cv 2148 of 2003 (TT) Stollmeyer J**

[PP49–50] The precautionary principle is included in the National Environmental Policy but only as a general statement of principle. It is difficult to translate it into specific commitments or requirements because it contemplates enormous financial burdens and foregone opportunities with no clear scientific justification. It must be directed to achieving sustainable development in a manner that is cost effective and not completely divorced from economic realities. Sustainable development is the ultimate goal of the National Environmental Policy. Sustainable development is accepted internationally as an article of faith in environmental policy decisions. It refers to . . . 'development that meets the needs of the present without compromising the ability of the future generations to meet their own needs' . . . (See the accepted international definition—The Brundtland Report—1987 Report of the World Commission on Environment & Development, Our Common Future). This is the overriding consideration in all matters involving the implementation of the precautionary principle . . . [P52] First, before the precautionary principle is invoked, there must be a comprehensive scientific evaluation of any potential risk. The precautionary principle is usually invoked if, following this risk assessment, serious or irreversible threats of environmental damage are discovered. The risk assessment is a critical requirement as its purpose is to calculate the degree of probability of the threats of serious irreversible environmental damage. There must be an assessment of the severity of the impact on human health and the environment were the threat to occur, the extent to which there may be possible adverse effects, the reversibility of any adverse effects and the possibility of delayed effects . . . [P53] Second, the precautionary principle is only invoked where scientific opinion conflicts [with] the potential threat. Scientific uncertainty on the nature and severity of the threat is the second condition for the application of the principle. The principle places the burden of proof on developers to prove that their actions will not cause serious or irreversible harm to the environment. It is therefore placed on the party who threatens the environmental status quo. Third, where there is scientific uncertainty as to the existence or extent of the threats to the environment the authority or agency (in this case the EMA) may, by reason of the precautionary principle, take protective measures without having to wait until the reality and the seriousness of those threats become fully apparent. Measures aimed at preventing or containing the threats may be adopted. There are no hard and fast rules on when to take action. Each case has to be considered on its own facts . . . [P59] It is well accepted that if there has been, or may be, a breach of a constitutional right, the remedy lies against the State, not a private individual or corporation. There can therefore be no remedy obtained in these proceedings against the EMA for breach of a constitutional right. That is sufficient to dispose of this ground . . . [P60] While I accept the existence of certain common law environmental rights (to which I have already referred), I am reluctant to elevate them or categorise them together with those rights entrenched in the Constitution, despite also accepting that the latter is a living document which should be interpreted generously. The position remains, however, as acknowledged in Europe and

India, for example, that these 'rights' are subject to other considerations. I do not wish to embark here on an investigation as to whether the rights of an individual should prevail over those of the society generally, or vice versa. It is sufficient to say that issues of environmental control often involve the delicate balancing of competing social and economic interests, as well as the application of specialized expertise. Furthermore, the inevitable trade-off between economic and ecological values is a subject matter which is inherently political. It is not for a Court to rewrite the Constitution. I am not persuaded that I should attempt to do so in this instance. This is best left to the legislature . . . [PP91–93] An analysis of the major Canadian and American authorities reveals that the Court's role in judicial review of environmental assessment is clearly circumscribed. The scope of judicial review of the agency's discretions is narrow because of policy concerns which militate in favour of a more deferential approach, as recognized in *Iverhuron & District Ratepayers Ass'n v Canadian (Minister of the Environment)* (2001) 272 NR 62 para 53. 'The extent to which certain factors are considered, and the weight given to the various factors on the overall assessment of environmental effects, are matters for those who have expertise to make such judgments, and not for the Court.' The Court limits itself to mainly procedural review seeking to ensure that the statutory requirements have been [complied] with and the legislative purpose is achieved. Courts only intervene to overturn the agency's findings if they are arbitrary and capricious. It is clear from these decisions that the Court's function in judicial review proceedings is not to act as an 'academy of science' (see Steyn J in *Vancouver Island Peace Society v Canada* [1992] 3 FC 42, 51) or a 'legislative upper chamber'. To turn the reviewing Court into an 'academy of science' would be both inefficient and contrary to the scheme of the Act (see Sexton JA in *Iverhuron*). As long as the agency complies with the statutory process, the Court must defer to their substantive determinations, but this deference is not absolute. The Court of Appeal in *Iverhuron* made it clear that the Court's approach should not 'be so deferential as to exclude all inquiry into the substantive adequacy of the environmental assessment. To adopt this approach would risk turning the right to judicial review of the decision into a hollow one.' *Neighbours of Cuddy Mountain, Blue Mountains Biodiversity Project v Blackwood* 161 F.3d 1208 (9th Cir. 1998) and *Muckleshoot Indian Tribe v Forest Service* 177 F.3d 800 (9th Cir. 1999) develop an approach to judicial review in which the Court's mandate is to verify two things:

1. procedural compliance—a demonstrated carrying-out of regulatory detail shows that the mechanics of the Regulation have been followed by the agency.
2. substantive compliance—a sufficiently detailed regulatory compliance demonstrates fulfillment of the Act's mandate as a whole. Information supplied in response to these Regulations succeeds only to the extent that it evidences a carrying out of the statutory goal.

The approach to judicial review of cumulative impact assessment in these cases is referred to as the 'hard look doctrine' and originated in the context of Court review of administrative decisions. The approach adopted by these Courts does not in substance differ from the approach adopted in this jurisidiction when considering applications for judicial review of an administrative decision. The 'hard look' [test] requires the agency to take its statutory responsibilities seriously and take a 'hard look' at all the relevant circumstances. It calls only for the Court 'to ensure that the agency took a hard look at the cumulative environmental consequences' (see *NRDC v Morton* 485 F.2d. 827). Once the agency has taken 'a hard look' by complying procedurally and substantively with the legislative intent, the Court cannot impose its views or interject into the agency's discretion as to the action to be taken. The Court applies this doctrine by scrutinizing the record to satisfy itself that the agency has exercised a reasoned discretion with reasons that do not deviate from or ignore the ascertainable legislative intent (see *Greater Boston Television Corporation v FCC* 444 F2d. 841 (DC Cir 1970)). The agency's hard look must be supported by substantial evidence and the Court should only set aside the agency's decision if it is not supported by substantial evidence (see Harold Leventhal, *Environmental Decision Making and the Role of the Courts*).

Belize Alliance of Conservation Non-Governmental Organizations –
Privy Council Appeal No 47 of 2003 (BZ)
Lord Hoffman

[PP18–19] 69. The ground upon which the Appellants submit that they can satisfy this demanding requirement is that the DOE postponed consideration of matters which should have been contained in the EIA. But, as their Lordships have observed, that only raises the question of what should have been in the EIA. Both the Chief Justice and the Court of Appeal cited with approval the remarks of Cripps J in the Land and Environment Court of New South Wales in *Prineas v Forestry Commission of New South Wales* (1983) 49 LGRA 402, 417: 'I do not think the [statute] . . . imposes on a determining authority when preparing an environmental impact statement a standard of absolute perfection or a standard of compliance measured by no consideration other than whether it is possible in fact to carry out the investigation. I do not think the legislature directed determining authorities to ignore such matters as money, time, manpower etc. In my opinion, there must be imported into the statutory obligation a concept of reasonableness . . . [P]rovided an environmental impact statement is comprehensive in its treatment of the subject matter, objective in its approach and meets the requirement that it alerts the decision maker and members of the public . . . to the effect of the activity on the environment and the consequences to the community inherent in the carrying out or not carrying out of the activity, it meets the standards imposed by the Regulations. The fact that the environmental impact statement does not cover every topic and explore every avenue advocated by experts does not necessarily invalidate it or require a finding that it does not substantially comply with the statute and the Regulations.' Their Lordships also respectfully adopt these observations. It is not necessary that an EIA should pursue investigations to resolve every issue. This is not only common sense but contemplated by the terms of the Belize legislation itself. Thus Regulation 5(f) says that an EIA should include an indication of 'gaps in knowledge and uncertainty which may be encountered in computing the required information' and Regulation 19(b), prescribing the form of an EIA, says it should contain a summary which highlights the 'conclusions, areas of controversy and issues remaining to be resolved'.

7.5 CARIBBEAN COURT OF JUSTICE

This issue of governance in Trinidad and Tobago is critical and the Caribbean Court of Justice has been caught in the middle of the battle for transparency. Although Guyana had similar issues to Trinidad and Tobago as it currently faces, in the period of the 1960s to the 1980s, judicial review was hardly used by those of Indian descent to fight state sponsored abuse. Guyanese attorneys, in interviews, indicated that they had no faith in the national courts, especially as Guyana had abolished the Privy Council as its final Court of Appeal. Accordingly, judicial review was not a weapon of choice to fight the state. The situation in Trinidad and Tobago is quite different and the proliferation of judicial review matters partly has its genesis in the fact that there is a perception that having the Privy Council as a final Court of Appeal is a guarantee of impartial justice. It is clear that significant work has to be done to convince a major section of the population of Trinidad and Tobago that the Caribbean Court of Justice will be just as effective and impartial a final Court of Appeal as the Privy Council was.

In the Application of Chandresh Sharma **– Civil Appeal No 115 of 2003 (TT)**
Nelson JA

[P16] The implementation of the CCJ Agreement was pursuant to obligations in international law. None of the acts complained of in the application alters or purports to alter the domestic law of Trinidad and Tobago. The appointment of the first Commission by letter by the Heads of Judiciary; the swearing in or installation of members of the first Commission; the expenditure of monies to defray the cost of the installation of the members of the Commission—none of these acts has any resonance in the domestic law of Trinidad and Tobago . . . [P20] Arising out of these two principles I derive the following proposition. The creation of the CCJ and the Commission as international institutions was an act done *jure imperii*. Participation in the proceedings of these international institutions by *personae designatae*, whether the Chief Justice of a contracting state or otherwise, takes place on the international law plane and is not amenable to the processes of our Courts. It is precisely because the CCJ Agreement and protocols form no part of Trinidad and Tobago law at the present time and neither grant nor deprive citizens of rights or obligations in domestic law, that the application before the learned judge was grossly misconceived . . . [P21] There is no express prohibition in the Constitution or any other law which prevents the Chief Justice from performing extra-judicial duties outside the judicature . . . [P22] The role of the Chief Justice at this stage was purely transitional i.e. to appoint the members of the first Commission. The contracting parties were anxious that not even at the outset should the Executive (the Heads of Government) have a say in selecting the body to appoint Judges of the CCJ. Thus, the Chief Justices were not performing any acts on behalf of the Executive; and there could be no question of incompatibility with the office of Chief Justice . . . [P23] On the view I have formed that the actions of the Chief Justice were on the international plane outside the orbit of judicial review, there is no need to examine further the contentions of the Appellant on this point. However, out of deference to the arguments presented I examine their validity . . . [P26] In these passages the Judges of the High Court of Australia recognize that the power of Parliament to confer functions of an executive or administrative nature on a person who may be a judge and who consents is an exception to the separation of the judicature from the other branches of government . . . [P27] Thus, if, which is not admitted, the Executive conferred a power on the Chief Justice to act as he did, the grant of that power would be by way of exception to the separation of powers. Again, the doctrine of the separation of powers may be relaxed where 'the exigencies of government' have made it necessary to designate a judge to carry out certain functions . . . [P29] Accordingly, if it were necessary, I would hold that where Trinidad and Tobago is bound by a treaty in international law even though not in domestic law, the exigencies of that Treaty may require the Chief Justice to carry out certain non-judicial functions in the national interest.

7.6 RIGHT TO INFORMATION

Increasingly in the Commonwealth Caribbean, there is the battle to obtain access to information held by public bodies so as to scrutinise the manner in which they exercise their functions. In Trinidad and Tobago, this battle has intensified with forces in opposition to the policies and practices of the government of the PNM, using the provisions of the Freedom of Information Act, No 26 of 1999, in the attempt to access information. The response of public bodies has not always been in the manner contemplated by the Freedom of Information Act and numerous judicial challenges have resulted.

In the Application of Chandresh Sharma – HCA No Cv S2005 of 2004 (TT)
Jamadar J

[P9] In my opinion it would be an unduly rigid approach, in the circumstances of this case (where no responsible Minister exists), to treat the Applicant's request/application as misconceived because it was made pursuant to Section 13(1) of the FOIA. Such a formalistic approach fails to give effect to the obvious and declared intention of Parliament. A more reasonable, realistic and pragmatic approach, that would further the intention of Parliament, would be to recognize that where there is no responsible Minister (for the purpose of a (k)(i) public authority) that a request pursuant to Section 13(1) of the FOIA is permissible. Indeed, given the mandate 'to facilitate and promote, promptly and at the lowest reasonable cost, the disclosure of information' (Section 3(2) FOIA), Parliament could not have reasonably intended that in the absence of a responsible Minister an Applicant must first take steps (legal if necessary) to have a responsible Minister appointed/declared and then make his/her request for information. No practical system of laws could intend anything so unreasonable. I therefore hold that the Applicant's request for information, made directly to the IC pursuant to Section 13(1) of the FOIA, was not so misconceived in the circumstances of this case such as to warrant a dismissal of this application or a refusal to grant access to the information requested . . . [P11] I accept that the IC is under a duty to keep and have records and information of *all persons who are required to file both declarations and statements of registrable interests*. Section 11(6) clearly presupposes this. It would be most remarkable if the IC, entrusted with the responsibilities that the IPLA gives it, were not to know who were the persons in public life who were expected to comply with the provisions of the IPLA. The presumption of regularity leads to the assumption that the IC has that information . . . [P13] Thus, in light of all of the above, I am of the opinion that none of the information requested is deemed secret or confidential pursuant to Section 20 of the IPLA or exempt pursuant to Part IV and Section 34 of the FOIA. And, that on the available evidence the said information is held by the IC in connection with its functions as a public authority, and is as such a 'document' and an 'official document' for the purposes of the FOIA.

8

CONCLUSION: JUSTICE IN THE FUTURE

Judicial review is about obtaining justice in the face of adverse decisions by public bodies and therefore it is hardly surprising that in some Commonwealth Caribbean countries such as Trinidad and Tobago, judicial review is increasingly being viewed with much suspicion by the executive power. In light of the proliferation of the number of cases filed by persons and groups seeking to review decisions of public bodies, especially decisions with political undertones, the tabling of a Judicial Review (Amendment) Bill in 2005 by the Government of Trinidad and Tobago, to limit the intent of the original JR Act by removing the ability of persons and groups to engage in public interest litigation, comes as no surprise to the public.

As noted, the very existence of the Caribbean Court of Justice, particularly with regard to Trinidad and Tobago, has become embroiled in the forward march of judicial review as a weapon for fighting perceived state oppression. The faith in the Privy Council as opposed to home grown justice continues to dominate the views of those using judicial review in the struggle against acts of the State. Despite robust views on the role of judges, there is still a lingering perception (often misguided) that our judges are much too conservative and would appear to favour the State in judicial review proceedings. This makes it imperative to some that the Privy Council be retained to ensure the continuing engendering of hope in the judicial system.

***In the Application of Ramesh Lawrence Maharaj* – Civil Appeal No 131 of 1986 (TT)**
Warner JA

> [P45] Every effort has been made, and quite properly, on the part of the Appellant herein to have this Court stop these prosecutions. Mr Turner Samuels QC for the Appellant, after inviting us to make a great contribution to Commonwealth jurisprudence later and towards the end of his submission, informed us that he had been reading the History of the Bar by Francis Bacon in which it was said that Judges should be like lions, and we were told that if we did what the Respondent asks us to do we would be acting like lambs. In other words, if we did what the Appellant asked of us we should be considered strong but if we held against him we would be considered weak. The first error in this submission is that the meekness of the lamb is mistakenly identified with weakness, an error that has occurred before. But lest the role of this Court be misunderstood, I wish to state categorically that my brothers and I consider it a matter of no concern whatever to us who thinks that we are strong or who thinks that we are weak in deciding this or any matter before us. We are not participants in a popularity contest, but rather conceive our function as being to determine matters before us on the evidence and according to law by the grace of God and with the courage of our convictions without fear or favour, affection or ill-will, with a view to ensuring true justice in our land, and I must confess to being surprised at what I consider to have been a most unfortunate submission.

While it is commendable to exhort the virtues of the lamb, in confronting the challenges of the twenty-first century in the Commonwealth Caribbean, judges must strive to exhibit courage in the face of growing public scepticism and ever present fears of politically tainted decisions. The situation is even more complex in countries such as Guyana and Trinidad and Tobago where ethnic concerns are significant. The twenty-first century reality of judicial review involves new challenges involving political questions, the environment and social issues such as squatting and the right to equality of treatment. Therefore, judges must rise above the tensions inherent in many Caribbean societies and deliver brave judgements that are prepared to challenge traditional dogma and allay fears that are resonating throughout the Caribbean. When a judiciary is strong and fearless, democracy becomes emboldened and tyranny can be confronted, however, when the judiciary is perceived as lacking the judicial fortitude to confront the excesses of the State, the very fabric of democracy starts to unravel and the people ultimately bear the brunt of the anarchy that follows. Caribbean jurists must step forward with boldness and vigour and play their role in moving Caribbean societies into the twenty-first century so as to ensure that judicial review does not become an exercise in futility, but rather that judicial review is transformed into an effective weapon to combat those who seek to wield public power in a manner inimical to all principles of fairplay and justice.

APPENDIX A

TRINIDAD AND TOBAGO

The Judicial Review Act, No. 60 of 2000

ENACTED by the Parliament of Trinidad and Tobago as follows:

PART I
PRELIMINARY

1.—This Act may be cited as the Judicial Review Act, 2000.

2.—This Act shall come into force on such date as is fixed by the President by Proclamation.

3.—This Act binds the State.

4.—In this Act—

"Court" means the High Court of the Supreme Court of Judicature;

"action" includes inaction.

PART 2
JUDICIAL REVIEW PROCEDURE

5.—(1) An application for judicial review of a decision of an inferior Court, tribunal, public body, public authority or a person acting in the exercise of a public duty or function in accordance with any law shall be made to the Court in accordance with this Act and in such manner as may be prescribed by rules of Court.

(2) The Court may, on an application for judicial review, grant relief in accordance with this Act—

(a) to a person whose interests are adversely affected by a decision; or

(b) to a person or a group of persons if the Court is satisfied that the application is justifiable in the public interest in the circumstances of the case.

(3) The grounds upon which the Court may grant relief to a person who filed an application for judicial review includes the following:

(a) that the decision was in any way unauthorised or contrary to law;

(b) excess of jurisdiction;

(c) failure to satisfy or observe conditions or procedures required by law;

(d) breach of the principles of natural justice;

(e) unreasonable, irregular or improper exercise of discretion;

(f) abuse of power;

(g) fraud, bad faith, improper purpose or irrelevant consideration;

(h) acting on instructions from an unauthorised person;

(i) conflict with the policy of an Act;

(j) error of law, whether or not apparent on the face of the record;

(k) absence of evidence on which a finding or assumption of fact could reasonably be based;

(l) breach of or omission to perform a duty;

(m) deprivation of a legitimate expectation;

(n) a defect in form or a technical irregularity resulting in a substantial wrong or miscarriage of justice; or

(o) an exercise of a power in a manner that is so unreasonable that no reasonable person could have so exercised the power.

(4) An Applicant is not limited to the grounds set out in the application for judicial review but if the Applicant wishes to rely on any other ground not so set out, the Court may, on such terms as it thinks fit, direct that the application be amended to specify such other ground.

(5) Subject to subsection (1), sections 6(1) and 11, a person is entitled, when making an application for judicial review under subsection (2)(b) or (6), to make the application in any written or recorded form or manner and by any means.

(6) Where a person or group of persons aggrieved or injured by reason of any ground referred to in paragraphs (a) to (o) of subsection (3), is unable to file an application for judicial review under this Act on account of poverty, disability, or socially or economically disadvantaged position, any other person or group of persons acting *bona fide* can move the Court under this section for relief under this Act.

5A.—(1) Where an application is filed under section 5(2)(b) or (6), the Court may suspend the hearing of the matter for such time as it considers just, and appoint a person or such number of persons possessing such training or qualifications as the Court considers just and as the circumstances warrant, to investigate the facts of the complaint or matter and to submit a report on its finding to the Court within such time as is specified by the Court.

(2) Such report shall be made available to the parties to the action who shall be entitled to be heard in respect of the report and make whatever application to the Court in respect of the report that they consider just.

6.—(1) No application for judicial review shall be made unless leave of the Court has been obtained in accordance with rules of Court.

(2) The Court shall not grant such leave unless it considers that the Applicant has a sufficient interest in the matter to which the application relates.

7.—(1) Notwithstanding section 6, where the Court is satisfied that an application for judicial review is justifiable in the public interest, it may, in accordance with this section, grant leave to apply for judicial review of a decision to an Applicant whether or not he has a sufficient interest in the matter to which the decision relates.

(2) Upon the filing of an application for leave under subsection (1), the Registrar shall immediately cause notice of the application to be published on two days in each of two daily newspapers circulating in Trinidad and Tobago.

(3) A notice under subsection (2) shall name the Applicant, state the decision which is the subject matter of the application, describe the nature of the relief being sought, and any other relevant matter, and invite any person with a more direct interest in the matter to file a similar application, or to apply to be joined as a party to the proceedings, within fourteen days of the last publication of the notice.

(4) Where no one files a similar application or applies to be joined as a party within the time specified in subsection (3), the Court may grant leave to the Applicant.

(5) Where an application is filed within the time specified in subsection (3) and the Court is satisfied that—

(a) the person applying ("the second Applicant") has a more direct interest in the matter than the first Applicant; and

(b) the first Applicant does not possess any special expertise or ability that will materially enhance the presentation of the case,

the Court may refuse to grant leave to the first Applicant and grant leave instead to the second Applicant, but in that event the second Applicant shall not be liable to pay the costs of the first Applicant.

(6) Where an application to be joined as a party is made by more than one person within the time specified in subsection (3), the Court may grant leave to such Applicant or Applicants as it thinks fit.

(7) In determining whether an application is justifiable in the public interest the Court may take into account any relevant factor, including—
(a) the need to exclude the mere busybody;
(b) the importance of vindicating the rule of law;
(c) the importance of the issue raised;
(d) the genuine interest of the Applicant in the matter;
(e) the expertise of the Applicant and the Applicant's ability to adequately present the case; and
(f) the nature of the decision against which relief is sought.
(8) Where an application is filed under section 5(6), the Court may not make an award of costs against an unsuccessful Applicant, except where the application is held to be frivolous or vexatious.

8.—(1) On an application for judicial review, the Court may grant the following forms of relief:
(a) an order of mandamus, prohibition or certiorari;
(b) a declaration or injunction;
(c) an injunction under section 19; or
(d) such other orders, directions or writs as it considers just and as the circumstances warrant.
(2) A declaration may be made or an injunction granted under this subsection in any case where an application for judicial review seeking such relief has been made, and the Court considers that, having regard to—
(a) the nature of the matters in respect of which relief may be granted by orders of mandamus, prohibition or certiorari;
(b) the nature of the persons and bodies against whom relief may be granted by such order; and
(c) all the circumstances of the case, it would be just and convenient for the declaration to be made or injunction to be granted, as the case may be.
(3) In any law—
(a) reference to a writ of mandamus, prohibition or certiorari shall be read as reference to the corresponding order; and
(b) reference to the issue or award of any such writ shall be read as reference to the making of the corresponding order.
(4) On an application for judicial review, the Court may award damages to the Applicant if—
(a) the Applicant has included in the application a claim for damages arising from any matter to which the application relates; and
(b) the Court is satisfied that, if the claim has been made in an action begun by the Applicant at the time of making the application, the Applicant could have been awarded damages.
(5) The Court, having regard to all the circumstances, may grant in addition or alternatively an order for restitution or for the return of property, real or personal.

9.—The Court shall not grant leave to an Applicant for judicial review of a decision where any other written law provides an alternative procedure to question, review or appeal that decision, save in exceptional circumstances.

10.—(1) An interlocutory application may be made in an application for judicial review and the Court may make any interlocutory order, including an order for discovery of documents, interrogatories or crossexamination, and may grant any interim relief as it thinks fit.
(2) The Court may, at any stage of the application for judicial review, direct that the proceedings to which such application relates shall be stayed until further notice.

11.—(1) An application for judicial review shall be made promptly and in any event within three months from the date when grounds for the application first arose unless the Court considers that there is good reason for extending the period within which the application shall be made.

(2) The Court may refuse to grant leave to apply for judicial review if it considers that there has been undue delay in making the application, and that the grant of any relief would cause substantial hardship to, or substantially prejudice the rights of any person, or would be detrimental to good administration.

(3) In forming an opinion for the purpose of this section, the Court shall have regard to the time when the Applicant became aware of the making of the decision, and may have regard to such other matters as it considers relevant.

(4) Where the relief sought is an order of certiorari in respect of a judgment, order, conviction or other decision, the date when the ground for the application first arose shall be taken to be the date of that judgment, order, conviction or decision.

12.—Where the Court is of the opinion that an inferior Court, tribunal, public body or public authority against which or a person against whom an application for judicial review is made is not subject to judicial review, the Court may allow the proceedings to continue, with any necessary amendments, as proceedings not governed by this Act and not seeking any remedy by way of orders of mandamus, prohibition or certiorari, and subject to such terms and conditions as the Court thinks fit.

13.—Where the Court is of the opinion that a decision of an inferior Court, tribunal, public body or public authority against which or a person against whom a writ of summons has been filed should be subject to judicial review, the Court may give such directions and make such orders as it considers just to allow the proceedings to continue as proceedings governed by this Act.

14.—(1) Any person who has an interest in a decision which is the subject of an application for judicial review may apply to the Court to be made a party to the proceedings.

(2) The Court may—

(a) grant the application either unconditionally or subject to such terms and conditions as it thinks just;

(b) refuse the application; or

(c) refuse the application but allow the person to make written or oral submissions at the hearing.

15.—(1) Where—

(a) a person has a duty to make a decision to which this Act applies;

(b) there is no law that prescribes a period within which the person is required to make that decision; and

(c) the person has failed to make that decision,

a person who is adversely affected by such failure may file an application for judicial review in respect of that failure on the ground that there has been unreasonable delay in making that decision.

(2) Where—

(a) a person has a duty to make a decision to which this Act applies;

(b) a law prescribes a period within which the person is required to make that decision; and

(c) the person has failed to make that decision before the expiration of that period,

a person who is adversely affected by such failure may file an application for judicial review in respect of that failure on the ground that the decision-maker has a duty to make that decision, notwithstanding the expiration of that period.

(3) Without prejudice to section 8, on an application for judicial review under this section, the Court may make all or any of the following orders:

(a) an order directing the making of the decision;
(b) an order declaring the rights of the parties in relation to the making of the decision;
(c) an order directing any of the parties to do, or to refrain from doing, any act or thing, the doing, or the refraining from the doing, of which the Court considers necessary to do justice between the parties.

16.—(1) Where a person is adversely affected by a decision to which this Act applies, he may request from the decision-maker a statement of the reasons for the decision.
(2) Where a person makes a request under subsection (1), he shall make the request—
(a) on the date of the giving of the decision or of the notification to him thereof; or
(b) within twenty-eight clear days after that date, whichever is later, and in writing.
(3) Where the decision-maker fails to comply with a request under subsection (1), the Court may, upon granting leave under section 5 or 6, make an order to compel such compliance upon such terms and conditions as it thinks just.

Part 3
Miscellaneous

17.—The Court may at any stage direct that proceedings to which an application for judicial review relates shall be stayed until further order on such terms and conditions as the Court may direct.

18.—(1) Where a person brings proceedings alleging that another person is not entitled to act in an office to which this section applies, the Court may—
(a) grant an injunction restraining that other person from so acting; and
(b) if the case so warrants, declare the office to be vacant.
(2) This section applies to—
(a) a public office;
(b) an office created by any written law;
(c) an office in which the public has an interest; and
(d) any other office as the Court considers it is in the public interest to grant relief.

19.—(1) The Court may, at any time before the proceedings are concluded, of its own motion or on the application of any party, revoke, vary or suspend the operation of any order made by it under this Act.
(2) Without prejudice to any other law, the Court shall have such incidental or ancillary powers to enforce any order or judgment it makes under this Act.

20.—An inferior Court, tribunal, public body, public authority or a person acting in the exercise of a public duty or function in accordance with any law shall exercise that duty or perform that function in accordance with the principles of natural justice or in a fair manner.

21.—If, on an application for judicial review seeking an order of certiorari, the Court quashes the decision to which the application relates, the Court may remit the matter to the Court, tribunal, public body, public authority or person concerned, with a directive to reconsider it and reach a decision in accordance with the findings of the Court.

22.—(1) Subject to subjection (2), where an order has been made or a judgment given in favour of a person who brought an application under section 5(2)(b) or (6) and who, for any reason, is unable to enforce the order or judgment, any other person is entitled to enforce that order or judgment on behalf of that person.
(2) Where a person seeks to enforce a judgment or order under subsection (1) on behalf of a successful Applicant, he shall first obtain leave of the Court.

23.—(1) A person aggrieved by a decision of the Court, including an interlocutory order, under this Act is entitled to appeal that decision as of right to the Court of Appeal.

(2) An appeal shall lie from a decision of the Court of Appeal referred to in subsection (1), as of right to the Judicial Committee of the Privy Council.

24.—The Rules Committee, established under section 77 of the Supreme Court of Judicature Act, may make rules to give effect to this Act.

25.—Nothing in this Act shall apply to proceedings which began before the commencement of this Act.

Legal Notice No. 184: The Supreme Court of Judicature (Judicial Review) (Amendment) Rules, 2002

REPUBLIC OF TRINIDAD AND TOBAGO

THE SUPREME COURT OF JUDICATURE ACT, CHAP 4:01

RULES OF COURT

MADE BY THE RULES COMMITTEE UNDER SECTION 78 OF THE SUPREME COURT OF JUDICATURE ACT AND PURSUANT TO SECTION 24 OF THE JUDICIAL REVIEW ACT, 2000

THE SUPREME COURT OF JUDICATURE (JUDICIAL REVIEW) (AMENDMENT) RULES, 2002

1. These Rules may be cited as the Supreme Court of Judicature Citation (Judicial Review) (Amendment) Rules, 2002, and shall be read as one with the Rules of the Supreme Court, 1975.
2. Order 53 is revoked and replaced by the following:

ORDER 53

APPLICATIONS FOR JUDICIAL REVIEW

1.—In this Order "the Act" means the Judicial Review Act, 2000.

2.—An application for judicial review shall be made in accordance with this Order.

Grant of leave to apply for judicial review

3.—(1) Subject to section 5(5) of the Act, no application for judicial review shall be made unless the leave of the Court has been obtained in accordance with this rule.

(2) An application for leave shall be made *Ex Parte* to the High Court, except in vacation when it may be made to a Judge in Chambers, and be supported –

(a) by a statement setting out –
   (i) the name and description of the Applicant;
   (ii) the Applicant's address for service;
   (iii) the relief sought, including any interim relief;
   (iv) the grounds on which it is sought;
   (v) particulars of damages, where appropriate;
   (vi) whether or not an alternative form of redress exists and, if so, why leave should be granted;
   (vii) the reason for the delay, if any, in making the application; and
   (viii) the facts which entitle the Applicant to make the application; and

(b) by affidavit to be filed before the application is made, verifying the facts relied on.

(3) The Applicant shall file his application for leave not later than the day before the application is made and at the same time lodge with the Registrar or appropriate Assistant Registrar copies of the statement and every affidavit in support.

(4) Without prejudice to its powers under Order 20, Rule 8, the Court hearing an application for leave may allow the Applicant's statement to be amended, whether by specifying different or additional grounds or relief or otherwise, on such terms, if any, as it thinks fit.

(5) Where leave is sought to apply for judicial review of any judgment, order, conviction or other proceeding which is subject to appeal and a time is limited for the bringing of the appeal, the Court may adjourn the application for leave until the appeal is determined or the time for appealing has expired.

(6) Where the Court grants leave, it may impose such terms as to costs and the giving of security as it thinks fit.

(7) Where leave to apply for judicial review is granted, then –

(a) if the relief sought is an order of prohibition or certiorari and the Court so directs, the grant shall operate as a stay of the proceedings to which the application relates until the determination of the application or until the Court otherwise orders;

(b) if any other relief is sought, the Court may at any time grant in the proceedings such interim relief as could be granted in an action begun by writ.

Mode of applying for judicial review

4.—(1) Subject to section 5(5) of the Act, when leave has been granted to make an application for judicial review, the application shall be made by originating motion to the High Court, except in vacation when it may be made by originating summons to a Judge in Chambers.

(2) The notice of motion or summons shall be served on all persons directly affected and where it relates to any proceedings in or before a Court and the object of the application is either to compel the Court or an officer of the Court to do any act in relation to the proceedings or to quash them or an order made therein, the notice or summons shall also be served on the clerk or other appropriate officer of the Court and, where any objection to the conduct of the Judge or other person presiding over such Court is to be made, on the Judge or other person.

(3) Unless the Court granting leave has otherwise directed, there shall be at least ten days between the service of the notice of motion or summons and the day named therein for the hearing.

(4) A motion shall be entered for hearing within fourteen days after the grant of leave.

(5) An affidavit giving the names and addresses of, and the places and dates of service on all persons who have been served with the notice of motion or summons shall be filed before the motion or summons is entered for hearing and, if any person who ought to be served under this rule has not been served, the affidavit shall state that fact and the reason for it; and the affidavit shall be before the Court on the hearing of the motion or summons.

(6) If on the hearing of the motion or summons the Court is of the opinion that any person who ought, whether under this rule or otherwise, to have been served has not been served, the Court may adjourn the hearing on such terms, if any, as it may direct in order that the notice or summons may be served on that person.

Statements and affidavits

5.—(1) Copies of the statement in support of an application for leave under Rule 3 shall be served with the notice of motion or summons and, subject to subrule (2), no grounds shall be relied upon or any relief sought at the hearing except the grounds and relief set out in the statement.

(2) The Court may on the hearing of the motion or summons allow the Applicant to amend his statement, whether by specifying different or additional grounds or relief, or otherwise, on such terms, if any, as it thinks fit, and may allow further affidavits to be used by him.

(3) Where the Applicant intends to seek leave to amend his statement or to use further affidavits, he shall give notice of his intention and of any proposed amendment to every other party.

(4) Any Respondent who intends to use an affidavit at the hearing shall file it in the Registry or appropriate Sub-Registry and give notice thereof to the Applicant as soon as practicable and in any event unless the Court otherwise directs, within twenty-eight days after service upon him of the documents required to be served by subrule (1).

(5) Each party to the application shall supply to every other party on demand and on payment of the proper charges, copies of every affidavit which he proposes to use at the hearing, including, in the case of the Applicant, the affidavit in support of the application for leave under Rule 3.

Interlocutory applications

6.—(1) Subject to Rule 3(2), unless the Court otherwise directs, any interlocutory application in proceedings on an application for judicial review may be made to a Judge in Chambers.

(2) This rule is without prejudice to any statutory provision or rule of law restricting the making of an order against the State.

Hearing of application for judicial review

7.—(1) On the hearing of any motion or summons under Rule 4, any person who desires to be heard in opposition to the motion or summons and appears to the Court to be a proper person to be heard, shall be heard, notwithstanding that he has not been served with notice of the motion or the summons.

(a) Where the relief sought is or includes an order of certiorari to remove any proceedings for the purpose of quashing them, the Applicant may not question the validity of any order, warrant, commitment, conviction, inquisition or record unless before the hearing of the motion or summons he has lodged with the Registrar a copy thereof verified by affidavit or accounts for his failure to do so to the satisfaction of the Court hearing the motion or summons.

(b) Where an order of certiorari is made in any such case as is referred to in subrule (2), the order shall, subject to subrule (4), direct that the proceedings shall be quashed forthwith on their removal into the High Court.

(c) Where the relief sought is an order of certiorari and the Court is satisfied that there are grounds for quashing the decision to which the application relates, the Court may, in addition to quashing it, remit the matter to the Court, tribunal or authority concerned with a direction to reconsider it and reach a decision in accordance with the findings of the Court.

(d) Where the redress sought is capable of being provided by a declaration, injunction or damages and the Court considers that for the reasons mentioned in section 12 of the Act or for any other reason, such redress should not or cannot be granted on an application for judicial review but might have been granted in an action begun by writ by the Applicant at the time of making his application, order the proceddings to continue as if begun by writ; and Order 28, Rule 8, shall apply, as if, in the case of an application made by motion, it had been made by summons.

Saving for person acting in obedience to mandamus

8.—No action or proceedings shall be commenced or prosecuted against any person in respect of anything done in obedience to an order of mandamus.

Consolidation of Applicants

9.—Where there is more than one application pending under section 18 of the Act against several persons in respect of the same office, and on the same grounds, the Court may order the applications to be consolidated.

Entry of motion

10.—(1) Entry of a motion in proceedings to which this Order applies shall be made when a copy of the notice of motion and any other documents required to be lodged before entry, have been lodged in the Registry or appropriate Sub-Registry, as the case may be.

(2) The party entering the motion for hearing shall leave a copy of the proceedings for the use of the Judge.

Directions

11.—Nothing herein contained shall prevent the Court from making such orders or giving such directions as may be appropriate in the circumstances for the just, convenient and expeditious hearing and determination of any application for judicial review.

Meaning of "Court"

12.—In relation to the hearing by a Judge of an application for leave under Rule 3 or of an application for judicial review, any reference in this Order to "the Court" shall, unless the context otherwise requires, be construed as a reference to "the Judge."

The Judicial Review (Amendment) Bill, 2005

Explanatory Note

(These notes form no part of the Bill but are intended only to indicate its general purport.)

The purpose of this Bill is to limit the categories of persons who may apply to the High Court for relief respecting a decision of an inferior Court, tribunal, public body, public authority or person acting in the exercise of a public duty or function in accordance with any law. The Bill seeks to accomplish its purpose by repealing the provision permitting persons to apply for judicial review under the Judicial Review Act, 2000 where the relief sought would be justifiable in the public interest and by making the consequential amendments.

A Bill

AN ACT to amend the Judicial Review Act, No. 60 of 2000

ENACTED by the Parliament of Trinidad and Tobago as follows:

1. This Act may be cited as the Judicial Review (Amendment) Bill, 2005.
2. In this Act, "the Act" means the Judicial Review Act, 2000.
3. Section 5 of the Act is amended—
   (a) by repealing subsection (2) and substituting the following subsection:

   "(2) The Court may, on application for judicial review, grant relief in accordance with this Act to a person whose interests are adversely affected by a decision."; and

   (b) in subsection (5) by deleting the words "(2)(b) or".
4. Section 5A(1) of the Act is amended by deleting the words "5(2)(b) or (6)" and substituting the word "5(6)".
5. Section 7 of the Act is repealed.
6. Section 22(1) of the Act is amended by deleting the words "5(2)(b) or (6)" and substituting the words "5(6)".

APPENDIX B

JAMAICA

Supreme Court of Jamaica Civil Procedure Rules 2002

PART 56

ADMINISTRATIVE LAW

Contents of the Part

Scope of this part

56.1—(1) This Part deals with applications—

(a) for judicial review;

(b) by way of originating motion or otherwise for relief under the Constitution;

(c) for a declaration or an interim declaration in which a party is the State, a Court, a tribunal or any other public body; and

(d) where the Court has power by virtue of any enactment to quash any order, scheme, certificate or plan, any amendment or approval of any plan, any decision of a Minister of government department or any action on the part of a Minister of government department.

(2) In this part such applications are referred to generally as "**applications for an administrative** order".

(3) "**Judicial Review**" includes the remedies (whether by way of writ of order) of—

(a) certiorari, for quashing unlawful acts;

(b) prohibition, for prohibiting unlawful acts; and

(c) mandamus, for requiring performance of a public duty, including a duty to make a decision or determination or to hear and determine any case.

(4) In addition to or instead of an administrative order the Court may, without requiring the issue of any further proceedings, grant—

(a) an injunction;

(b) restitution or damages; or

(c) an order for the return of any property, real or personal.

Who may apply for judicial review

56.2—(1) An application for judicial review may be made by any person, group or body which has sufficient interest in the subject matter of the application.

(2) This includes—

(a) any person who has been adversely affected by the decision which is the subject of the application;

(b) any body or group acting at the request of a person or persons who would be entitled to apply under paragraph (a);

(c) any body or group that represents the views of its members who may have been adversely affected by the decision which is the subject of the application;

(d) any statutory body where the subject matters falls within its statutory remit;

(e) any body or group that can show that the matter is of public interest and that the body or group possesses expertise in the subject matter of the application;

(f) any other person or body who has a right to be heard under the terms of any relevant enactment or the Constitution.

Judicial Review—application for leave

56.3—(1) A person wishing to apply for judicial review must first obtain leave.

(2) An application for leave may be made without notice.

(3) The application must state—

(a) the name, address and description of the Applicant and Respondent;

(b) the relief, including in particular details of any interim relief, sought;

(c) the grounds on which such relief is sought;

(d) whether an alternative form of redress exists and, if so, why judicial review is more appropriate or why the alternative has not been pursued;

(e) details of any consideration which the Applicant knows the Respondent has given to the matter in question in response to a complaint made by or on behalf of the Applicant;

(f) whether any time limit for making the application has been exceeded and, if so, why;

(g) whether the Applicant is personally or directly affected by the decision about which complaint is made; or

(h) where the Applicant is not personally or directly affected, what public or other interest the Applicant has in the matter;

(i) the name and address of the Applicant's attorney-at-law (if applicable); and

(j) the Applicant's address for service.

(4) The application must be verified by evidence on affidavit which must include a short statement of all the facts relied on.

Judicial Review—hearing of application for leave

56.4—(1) An application for leave to make a claim for judicial review must be considered forthwith by a judge of the Court.

(2) The Judge may give leave without hearing the Applicant.

(3) However, if—

(a) the Judge is minded to refuse the application;

(b) the application includes a claim for immediate interim relief; or

(c) it appears that a hearing is desirable in the interests of justice.

the Judge must direct that a hearing in open Court be fixed.

(4) The judge may direct that notice of the hearing be given to the Respondent or the Attorney General.

(5) Where the application relates to any judgment, order, conviction or other proceedings which are subject to appeal, the Judge may adjourn consideration of the application to a date after the appeal has been determined.
(6) The judge may allow the application to be amended.
(7) Where the Applicant seeks an order for certiorari relating to any matter in respect of which there is a right of appeal subject to a time limit, the Judge may adjourn the application for leave until the appeal is determined or the time for appealing has expired.
(8) The judge may grant leave on such conditions or terms as appear just.
(9) Where the application is for an order (or writ) of prohibition or certiorari, the Judge must direct whether or not the grant of leave operates as a stay of proceedings.
(10) The judge may grant such interim relief as operates just.
(11) On granting leave the Judge must direct when the first hearing or, in case of urgency, the full hearing of the claim for a judicial review should take place.
(12) Leave must be conditional on the Applicant making a claim for judicial review within 14 days of receipt of the order granting leave.

Where leave refused or granted on terms

56.5—(1) Where the application for leave is refused by the Judge or is granted on terms (other than under Rule 56.4 (12)), the Applicant may renew it by applying—
(a) in any matter involving the liberty of the subject or in any criminal cause or matter, to a full Court; or
(b) in any other case to a single judge sitting in open Court.
(2) A single judge may refer the application to a full Court.
(3) No application not involving the liberty of the subject or a criminal cause or matter may be renewed after a hearing.
(4) An Applicant may renew his application by lodging in the registry notice of his intention.
(5) The notice under paragraph (4) must be lodged within 10 days of service of the Judge's refusal or conditional leave on the Applicant.
(6) The Court hearing an application for leave may permit the application under Rule 56.3 to be amended.

Delay

56.6—(1) An application for leave to apply for judicial review must be made promptly and in any event within three months from the date when grounds for the application first arose.
(2) However the Court may extend the time if good reason for doing so is shown.
(3) Where leave is sought to apply for an order of certiorari in respect of any judgment, order, conviction or other proceeding, the date on which grounds for the application first arose shall be taken to be the date of that judgment, order, conviction or other proceeding.
(4) Paragraphs (1) to (3) are without prejudice to any time limits imposed by an enactment.
(5) When considering whether to refuse leave or to grant relief because of delay the Judge must consider whether the granting of leave or relief would be likely to—
(a) cause substantial hardship to or substantially prejudice the rights of any person; or
(b) be detrimental to good administration.

Proceedings by way of claim which should be application for administrative order

56.7—(1) This rule applies where a claimant issues a claim for damages or other relief other than an administrative order but where the facts supporting such claim are such that only or main relief is an administrative order.

(2) The Court may at any stage direct that the claim is to proceed by way of an application for an administrative order.
(3) Where the appropriate administrative order would be for judicial review the Court may give leave for the matter to proceed as if an application had been made under Rule 56.3.
(4) Where the Court makes an order under paragraph (2) it must give such directions as are necessary to enable the claim to proceed under this Part.

Constitution of Court

56.8—(1) In any matter involving the liberty of the subject and in any criminal cause or matter an application for judicial review for which leave has been granted must be made to a full Court.
(2) Any other application may be heard by a single judge in open Court unless the Court directs that it be heard—
(a) by a judge in chambers; or
(b) by a full Court.

How to make an application for administrative order

56.9—(1) An application for an administrative order must be made by a fixed date claim in form 2 identifying whether the application is for—
(a) judicial review;
(b) relief under the Constitution;
(c) a declaration; or
(d) some other administrative order (naming it)
and must identify the nature of any relief sought.
(2) The claimant must file with the claim form evidence on affidavit.
(3) The affidavit must state—
(a) the name, address and description of the claimant and the Defendant;
(b) the nature of the relief sought identifying—
(i) any interim relief sought; and
(ii) whether the claimant seeks damages, restitution, recovery of any sum due or alleged to be due or an order for the return of property, setting out the facts on which such claim is based and, where practicable, specifying the amount of any money claimed;
(c) in the case of a claim under the Constitution, setting out the provision of the Constitution which the claimant alleges has been, is being or is likely to be breached;
(d) the grounds on which such relief is sought;
(e) the facts on which the claim is based;
(f) the claimant's address for service; and
(g) giving the names and addresses of all Defendants to the claim.
(4) The general rule is that the affidavit must be made by the claimant or where the claimant is not an individual by an appropriate officer of the body making the claim.
(5) Where the claimant is unable to make the affidavit it may be made by some other person on the claimant's behalf but must state why the claimant is unable to make the affidavit.
(6) On issuing the claim form the registry must fix a date for a first hearing which must be endorsed on the claim form.
(7) The general rule is that the first hearing must take place no later than 4 weeks after the date of issue of the claim.
(8) However, any party may apply to a judge in chambers for that date to be brought forward or for an early date to be fixed for the hearing of the application for an administrative order.

(9) The application may be without notice but must be supported by evidence on affidavit.

Joinder claims for other relief

56.10—(1) The general rule is that, where not prohibited by substantive law, an Applicant may include in an application for an administrative order a claim for any other relief or remedy that—

(a) arises out of; or
(b) is related or connected to,

the subject matter of an application for an administrative order. In particular the Court may award—

(a) damages;
(b) restitution; or
(c) an order for return of property,

to the claimant on a claim for Judicial Review or for relief under the Constitution if—

(i) the claimant has included in the claim form a claim for any such remedy arising out of any matter to which the claim for an administrative order relates; or
(ii) the facts set out in the claimant's affidavit or statement of case justify the granting of such remedy or relief; and
(iii) the Court is satisfied that, at the time when the application was made the claimant could have issued a claim for such remedy.

(2) The Court may however at any stage—

(a) direct that any claim for other relief be dealt with separately from the claim for an administrative order; or
(b) direct that the whole application be dealt with as a claim and give appropriate directions under Parts 26 and 27; and
(c) in either case, make any order it considers just as to costs that have been wasted because of the unreasonable use of the procedure under this Part.

Service of claim form for administrative order

56.11—(1) The claim form and the affidavit in support must be served on all persons directly affected not less than 14 days before the date fixed for the first hearing.

(2) Where the application—

(a) relates to any proceedings in or before a Court; and
(b) has the object either—
  (i) to compel the Court or an officer of the Court to do any act relating to; or
  (ii) to quash those proceedings,

the claim form and affidavit in support must be served on the clerk or registrar of the Court and on the Judge if any objection is taken to the conduct of the Judge.

(3) A claim form relating to an application for relief under the Constitution must be served on the Attorney General.

(4) Where leave has been given to make a claim for judicial review the claimant must also serve a copy of—

(a) the application for leave;
(b) the affidavit in support; and
(c) the order giving leave.

(5) The claimant must file at the registry not less than 7 days before the date fixed for the first hearing an affidavit which—

(a) gives the name and addresses of all Defendants who have been served with the claim;
(b) states the date and place of service on each such Defendant;

(c) where applicable, states when the claim form was served on the Attorney General; and
(d) if any Defendant has not been served, states that fact and the reason for it.
(6) Where the Judge considers that any person who should have been served has not been served, the Judge may adjourn the first hearing to a fixed date and give directions for service. (Part 5 deals generally with the service of claims.)

Evidence in answer

56.12 Any evidence filed in answer to a claim for an administrative order must be by affidavit but the provisions of Part 10 (defence) apply to such affidavit.

First hearing

56.13—(1) At the first hearing the Judge must give any directions that may be required to ensure the expeditious and just trial of the claim and the provisions of Parts 25 to 27 of these Rules apply.
(2) In particular the Judge may—
(a) make orders for—
(i) witness statements or affidavits to be served;
(ii) cross-examination of witnesses;
(iii) disclosure of documents; and
(iv) service of skeleton arguments;
(b) allow the claimant to—
(i) amend any claim for an administrative order;
(ii) substitute another form of application for that originally made; or
(iii) add or substitute a claim for relief other than an administrative order;
(c) allow any person or body appearing to have sufficient interest in the subject matter of the claim to be heard whether or not served with the claim form;
(d) direct whether any person or body having such interest—
(i) is to make submissions by way of written brief; and
(ii) may make oral submissions at the hearing; and
(e) direct that claims by one or more persons or bodies or against one or more persons in respect of the same office made on the same grounds be consolidated or heard together.

Procedural Applications

56.14—Wherever practicable any procedural application during a claim for an administrative order must be made to the Judge who dealt with the first hearing unless that judge orders otherwise.

Hearing of application for administrative order

56.15—(1) At the hearing of the application the Court may allow any person who or body which appears to have a sufficient interest in the subject matter of the claim to make submissions whether or not served with the claim form.
(2) Such a person or body must make submissions by way of a written brief unless the Court orders otherwise.
(3) The Court may grant any relief that appears to be justified by the facts proved before the Court whether or not such relief should have been sought by an application for an administrative order.
(4) The Court may, however, make such orders as to costs as appear to the Court to be just including a wasted costs order.
(5) The general rule is that no order for costs may be made against an Applicant for an administrative order unless the Court considers that the Applicant has acted unreasonably in making the application or in the conduct of the application.

(Part 64 deals with the Court's general discretion as to the award of costs, rules 64.13 and 64.14 deal with wasted costs orders.)

Special provisions relating to orders for judicial review

56.16—(1) Where the claimant seeks an order or writ of certiorari to remove any proceedings for the purpose of quashing them, the claimant may not question the validity of any order, warrant, commitment, conviction or record unless—

(a) before the trial the claimant has lodged with the registry a copy of the order, etc., verified by affidavit; or

(b) can account for the failure to do so to the satisfaction of the Court.

(2) Where the claim is for an order or writ of certiorari, the Court may if satisfied that there are reasons for quashing the decision to which the claim relates—

(a) direct that the proceedings be quashed on their removal to the Court; and

(b) may in addition remit the matter to the Court, tribunal or authority concerned with a direction to reconsider it in accordance with the findings of the Court.

APPENDIX C

BARBADOS

Administrative Justice Act, No. 63 of 1980

ENACTED by the Parliament of Barbados as follows:

Citation

1.—This Act may be cited as the *Administrative Justice Act, 1980*.

Interpretation

2.—In this Act,

"act" includes any decision, determination, advice or recommendation made under a power or duty conferred or imposed by the Constitution or by any enactment;

"administrative act or omission" means an act or omission of a Minister, public official, tribunal, board, committee or other authority of the Government of Barbados exercising, purporting to exercise or failing to exercise any power or duty conferred or imposed by the Constitution or by any enactment;

"Court" has the same meaning as in the *Interpretation Act*.

Part 1
Judicial Review

3.—(1) An application to the Court for relief against an administrative act or omission may be made by way of an application for judicial review in accordance with this Act and with rules of Court.

(2) Where the Court is of opinion that a person or body against whom an application for judicial review is made is not an authority of the Government of Barbados, the Court may allow the proceedings to continue, with any necessary amendment, as proceedings not governed by this Act and not seeking any remedy by way of certiorari, prohibition or mandamus.

4.—The grounds upon which the Court may grant relief by way of the remedies mentioned in this Act include the following:

(a) that an administrative act or omission was in any way unauthorized or contrary to law;
(b) excess of jurisdiction
(c) failure to satisfy or observe conditions or procedures required by law;
(d) breach of the principles of natural justice;
(e) unreasonable or irregular or improper exercise of discretion;
(f) abuse of power;
(g) fraud, bad faith, improper purposes or irrelevant considerations;
(h) acting on instructions from an unauthorized person;
(i) conflict with the policy of an Act of Parliament;
(j) error of law, whether or not apparent on the face of the record;
(k) absence of evidence on which a finding or assumption of fact could reasonably be based; and
(l) breach of or omission to perform a duty.

5.—(1) The remedies that the Court may grant by way of relief on an application for judicial review are

(a) certiorari, for quashing unlawful acts;
(b) prohibition, for prohibiting unlawful acts;
(c) mandamus, for requiring performance of a public duty, including a duty to make a decision or determination or to hear and determine any case.

(2) The Court may, having regard to the scope of the remedies mentioned in subsection (1), grant in addition or alternatively
(a) a declaratory judgment;
(b) an injunction;
(c) restitution or damages in money; or
(d) an order for the return of property real or personal.
(3) Any of the remedies mentioned in subsections (1) and (2) may be applied for together or in the alternative in an application for judicial review; and the Court may grant one or more of them as law and justice may require, and whether applied for in the original application or not.
6.—The Court may on an application for judicial review grant relief in accordance with this Act
(a) to a person whose interests are adversely affected by an administrative act or omission;
(b) to any other person if the Court is satisfied that that person's application is justifiable in the public interest in the circumstances of the case.
7.—(1) An interlocutory application may be made in any application for judicial review, and the Court or Judge may make any interlocutory order, including an order for discovery of documents, for interrogatories and for cross-examination, and may grant any interim relief that the Court or Judge thinks fit.
(2) The Court or Judge may at any stage direct that the proceedings to which the application relates shall be stayed until further order.
8.—The Court may if it thinks fit, refuse to grant any relief under this Act if it considers that there has been undue delay in making the application for judicial review, and that the grant of the relief sought would cause substantial hardship to, or would substantially prejudice the rights of, any person, or would be detrimental to good administration.
9.—Where the Court quashes an administrative act to which the application relates, it may in addition remit the matter to the Court, tribunal or other authority concerned with a direction to reconsider the matter and to determine it in accordance with the Court's order.
10.—(1) Where a person brings proceedings alleging that any person is not entitled to act in a public office, the Court may, if satisfied that the proceedings are justified, grant an injunction restraining that person from acting in the public office, and the Court may, if it thinks fit, declare the office to be vacant.
(2) Informations in the nature of *quo warranto* are hereby abolished.
11.—Nothing in this Act affects
(a) the law relating to habeas corpus;
(b) the right of the Attorney-General to bring proceedings under this Act or otherwise, either of his own motion or at the relation of any person.
12.—The Judicial Advisory Council may make rules generally for the purposes of this Part.

Part 2
Administrative Procedures

13.—(1) It is the duty of any person or body making a decision to which this section applies, if requested in accordance with section 14 by any person adversely affected thereby, to supply to that person a statement of the reasons for the decision.
(2) This section applies to any decision that is required by law (including any enactment) or by contract to be made in accordance with the principles of natural justice or in a fair manner with the exception of

(a) any decision for which by express provision of any enactment reasons are not to be required;
(b) any such decision as is specified in the First Schedule.

14.—(1) A request for reasons under section 13 must be made on or before the date of giving of notification of the decision or within 14 days after that date.
(2) A request must be made in writing, except that where an oral hearing is held, the request may be made orally before the conclusion of the oral proceedings.
(3) In the case of postal communications, a request for reasons shall be deemed to be made at the time when it is posted and a notification of a decision at the time when it reaches the addressee.

15.—A statement of reasons under section 13
(a) must be in writing, except where the person requesting it agrees that it may be made orally;
(b) must be supplied within a reasonable time;
(c) shall be deemed to be part of the decision and to be incorporated in the record.

16.—(1) The law relating to natural justice applies
(a) to any person or body refusing, modifying, or revoking any license, permission, qualification or authority or imposing any penalty under powers conferred by any enactment;
(b) to any person or body listed in the Second Schedule and making a decision of the kind there specified.
(2) This section does not restrict the application of the law relating to natural justice in any other case.

17.—The Governor-General may by order subject to negative resolution add any item to the First Schedule or the Second Schedule or remove any item therefrom.

Part 3
Commencement

18.—This Act comes into force on a day to be fixed by proclamation.

First Schedule

(Section 13(2))

(a) Any decision other than a decision relating to a disciplinary matter made by
   (i) the Judicial and Legal Service Commission;
   (ii) the Public Service Commission;
   (iii) the Police Service Commission;
   (iv) the Statutory Boards Service Commission;
   (v) the Defence Board or other authority under the *Defence Act, 1979*.
(b) Any decision of the Minister or of a Government Official under the *Immigration Act*.
(c) Any decision relating to an order made under the *Expulsion of Undesirables Act*.

Second Schedule

(Section 16(1)(b))

Person or body	Specified decision
The Judicial and Legal Service Commission The Public Service Commission The Police Service Commission	A decision against a member of the service in question in a disciplinary matter.
The Statutory Boards Service Commission	
The Minister responsible for town and Country Planning	A decision to approve a development plan under section 9 of the *Town and Country Planning Act;* A decision given upon a review under section 19 of that Act.

The Judicial Review (Application) Rules,

([1983] S.I. 1983 No, 99)

The Administrative Justice Act 1980 (No. 63 of 1980)

The Judicial Advisory Council in exercise of the powers conferred on it by section 12 of the *Administrative Justice Act, 1980* makes the following rules:

1.—These rules may be cited as the *Judicial Review (Applications) Rules, 1983.*

2.—(1) An application for judicial review must be made by originating motion to the High Court, except in vacation when it may be by originating summons to a judge in chambers.

(2) An application under paragraph (1) must be supported

(a) by a statement, setting out the name and description of the Applicant, the relief sought and the grounds on which it is sought, and

(b) by affidavit, to be filed before the application is made, verifying the facts relied on.

(3) The Applicant must give notice of the application to the Attorney General not later than the day before the application is made, and must at the same time furnish the Attorney-General with copies of the statement and every affidavit in support.

3.—(1) The notice of motion or summons must be served on all persons directly affected.

(2) There must be at least 14 days between the service of the notice of motion or summons and the day named therein for the hearing.

(3) An affidavit giving the names and addresses of, and the places and dates of service on, all persons who have been served with the notice of motion or summons must be filed before the motion or summons is entered for hearing and, if any person who ought to be served under this rule has not been served, the affidavit must state that fact and the reasons for it; and the affidavit must be before the Court on the hearing of the motion or summons.

(4) Where on the hearing of the motion or summons, the Court is of opinion that any person who ought, whether under this rule or otherwise, to have been served has not been served, the Court may adjourn the hearing on such terms (if any) as it may direct in order that the notice or summons may be served on that person.

4.—(1) Copies of the statement in support of an application under Rule 2 must be served with the notice of motion or summons and, subject to paragraph (2), no grounds shall be relied upon on any relief sought at the hearing except the grounds and the relief set out in the statement.

(2) The Court may on the hearing of the motion or summons allow the Applicant to amend his statement, whether by specifying different or additional grounds or relief or otherwise, on such terms, if any, as it thinks fit, and may allow further affidavits to be used if they deal with new matters arising out of an affidavit of any other party to the application.

(3) Where the Applicant intends to ask to be allowed to amend his statement or to use further affidavits, he shall give notice of his intention and of any proposed amendments to every other party.

(4) Each party to the application must supply to every other party on demand and on payment of the proper charges copies of every affidavit which he proposes to use at the hearing, including, in the case of the Applicant, the affidavit in support of the application under Rule 2.

5.—(1) On the hearing of any motion or summons under Rule 2, any person who desires to be heard in opposition to the motion or summons, and appears to the Court to be a proper person to be heard, shall be heard, notwithstanding that he has not been served with notice of the motion or the summons.

(2) Where the relief sought is or includes an order of certiorari to remove any proceedings for the purpose of quashing them, the Applicant may not question the validity of any administrative act or omission unless before the hearing of the motion or summons he has furnished the Attorney General with a copy thereof verified by affidavit or he accounts for his failure to do so to the satisfaction of the Court hearing the motion or summons.

(3) Where an order of certiorari is made in any case referred to in paragraph (2), the order shall, subject to the provision of the Act, direct that the proceedings shall be quashed forthwith on their removal into the High Court.

Made by the Judicial Advisory Council this fourteenth day of June, 1983.

INDEX